WHO OWNS THE MEDIA?

Concentration of Ownership in the Mass Communications Industry

Second edition, completely revised and expanded

by
Benjamin M. Compaine
Christopher H. Sterling
Thomas Guback
J. Kendrick Noble, Jr.

Knowledge Industry Publications, Inc.
White Plains, NY and London

Communications Library

Who Owns the Media?
Second edition

Library of Congress Cataloging in Publication Data

Main entry under title:

Who owns the media?

    (Communications library)
    Rev. ed. of: Who owns the media? / Benjamin M.
Compaine. c1979.
    Bibliography: p.
    Includes index.
    Contents: Introduction ; Newspapers / by
Benjamin M. Compaine -- Book publishing / by
J. Kendrick Noble, Jr. -- Magazines / by
Benjamin M. Compaine -- [etc.]
    1. Mass media--Economic aspects--United States.
2. Mass media--Political aspects--United States.
I. Compaine, Benjamin M. Who owns the media? II. Series.
P96.E252U68   1982   380.3'0973   82-13039
ISBN 0-86729-007-2

Printed in the United States of America

Table of Contents

For two of my favorites,
sister Suzanne and nephew Lawrence

List of
Tables, Figures and Appendixes

Tables

vii

Figures

Appendixes

Preface to the Second Edition

An Editorial

In the three years since the first edition of *Who Owns the Media?* was published, the media territory has changed substantially. The cable industry, then budding, has blossomed, fed in part from and stimulating in part pay cable programming. The newspaper industry, long turned inward, was awakened by threats not only from cable but from a heretofore unexpected potential competitor, AT&T. Television broadcasters found themselves fighting political battles on several fronts: with cable operators over copyright and exclusivity; with other potential broadcasters using microwave or earth satellites, or low-power signals; and with video cassette, disc and game suppliers, who are providing alternatives for leisure-time use of the home television set. The motion picture studios, meanwhile, continue to find public taste unpredictable and steady profitability elusive. They have undergone further consolidation and changes in ownership.

Between 1979 and 1982, the nature of the discussion on media ownership has changed somewhat. In 1978, mergers and acquisitions seemed to have reached a peak of activity. Newspaper chains grew rapidly in the 1970s and many cities lost their rival newspapers. Several members of Congress were calling for preventive action and the Federal Trade Commission (FTC) held a highly visible symposium on the subject at the end of 1978. But the report issued by the FTC indicated that, when the facts were examined, there really was not much cause for action, at least not on economic or traditional antitrust grounds. Meanwhile, by the early 1980s, attention in Congress focused on efforts to rewrite the Communications Act of 1934, particularly that portion addressing the telecommunications business in general and AT&T specifically. The focus was on new technology for communication and the jargon included terms like viewdata, teletext, online electronic data bases, interactive cable, pay-per-view, DBS, MDS, LPTV, optical discs, VCRs, among others.

Indeed, the pace of technological development at times seemed to obscure the political, economic and sociocultural forces that coexist with technology. As we seem to have to continuously relearn, technology by itself does not produce change. It acts as one element, often not even the most important one.

Thus, the second edition of this book involved more than just updating the tables with the latest numbers. It had to be and was substantially rewritten and expanded to reflect these and other changes. In the process, my co-authors and I have responded to some of the gaps we discovered in the first edition. For example, a chapter has been added that identifies the companies, individuals and financial institutions who actually own the media.

Like the first edition, however, this volume does not directly address the question of *quality* of the content produced by media institutions. Nonetheless, the implied assumption is that quality of content is ultimately what elevates the subject of media ownership from an academic exercise to a lively issue, i.e., something over which there is conflict by virtue of at least two opposing points of view. Quality of media content is quite subjective; empirical evidence is difficult to gather and, if gathered, the standard of measurement may well become an additional subject of disagreement. What, for example, *should be* the content of the local 6 o'clock television news? And what is the "best" way of presenting it? Given such a morass, we have produced a work that substitutes measures of quantity as a rough approximation of quality. Presumably, if enough content providers (leaving aside the question of just what constitutes "enough") have access to sufficient distribution conduits, then information users will be able to find the level of quality they need or want.

I have been gratified by the generally favorable reception of the first edition. However, among those most negative about the first edition are those who are also critical of the existing trends and structure of the media industry, and within this group, I have detected a set of common reactions.

The most salient observation is that there is a self-appointed media elite in the United States that believes it knows what the "public" should and should not be given via the media. Ironically, this elite, which includes some journalism professors, professional media critics and some of the media "stars," would generally consider themselves politically liberal. They are the most vocal each time a newspaper folds or a media conglomerate makes a new acquisition. They would likely characterize themselves as being for "the people" and against the media barons. And yet, in the course of my experience, they seem least willing to accept the decision by "the people" in their choice of media content. These critics decry the low cultural level of so much of our television programming, for example, yet ignore that time and time again the mass public eschews the "quality" offerings of "Masterpiece Theatre" or the "McNeil-Lehrer Report" for "Dukes of Hazzard."

When pressed, some of these critics will say that the media should set a higher cultural tone and, presumably, the flock will eventually get used to it. They ignore both historical and contemporary evidence. Historically, the masses have never been highbrow. This goes back to the earliest stages of mass literacy (see, for example, Richard D. Altick, *The English Common Reader,* University of Chicago Press, 1957). As for the present, we need only look to Europe, where most broadcasting is government controlled. There, culture and serious talk shows are often dominant, and the citizenry has eagerly tuned to offshore radio stations that provide more popular programming and, more recently, has been turning to prerecorded video cassettes in greater numbers than in the U.S.—much to the consternation of government programmers. The government broadcasting authorities in Europe are also concerned about direct broadcast satellite programming, because they know, when people are free to choose, they will turn to pure entertainment programming.

A second and related observation is the obsession these critics have with television. One line of argument I hear is that television news only includes middle-of-the-road opinion. They claim that radical views, advocating structural change in the "system," rarely get exposure. While television is certainly a major social institution, it is only one among many. We know that advertising on television does not guarantee the success of a product and certainly does not insure the acceptance of an idea or position—ask any president in recent history. While television news may help set the public agenda, it does so within the context of numerous other forces. Moreover, other media, such as books, newsletters and magazines have always been the vanguard in bringing forth new ideas or trends, with television serving a different function of popularizing those cultural, social or political trends that catch on as the result of the other channels.

A corollary of the previous two points is the impression conveyed by a small subset of the media elite (though they would undoubtedly angrily deny this) that "the people" cannot separate the propaganda of advertisers or establishment programmers from something that might be called "the truth"; that the unseen audience can be led astray by those who control content of the media, and therefore they should be protected from advertisers. This group is most critical of the basic profit-motivated structure of the media industry. They do not have any ready answers or alternatives, however. And by implication they are saying that while *they* can determine what is good and bad in advertising messages, the general public cannot.

Finally, in criticizing today's media conglomerate owners for being unconcerned with quality, the media elitists seem to hold up some other era as the model of what the media should be. They may cite the existence of more than 2000 daily newspapers and the small number owned by chains at the turn of the century. They hark back to when multi-newspaper towns were commonplace. And they point to the sorry state of a particular chain paper in one town or another as evidence of how bland the chains have made the press. From these observations I have culled "The Golden Days Syndrome" and "*The New York Times* Syndrome."

Those to whom I ascribe "The Golden Days Syndrome" seem to feel that newspapers (and by extension, the media, since newspapers were at that time the only true mass medium) were better back in 1900 than today. This, despite the fact that they were frequently only eight or 12 pages, including advertising. And most newspapers were admittedly one-sided, being owned by or controlled by a labor union, political party or other special interest entity. Unless individuals purchased several papers (in a far less prosperous era than today), published by opposing groups, readers would have had a biased view of the world.

The second syndrome afflicts those who hold up *The New York Times* as the standard against which all newspapers seem to be measured. The fact is, the newspapers in Iowa City and Laredo, Texas were never great papers by any standard. Thus, if one complains they are not very good under chain ownership and without local competition, the worst we could say is they have not improved.

Perhaps we could argue that newspapers could be better (however that should be defined). But it would be hard to substantiate that the media were "better" in the good old days than they are today. Given that the newshole in today's newspaper is larger than in the competitive heyday (thanks to more advertising) and that journalistic standards result in striving for relatively objective news coverage, it may be argued that we are better off than ever before.

In all candor, I personally agree with some of the criticisms of the media elitists. "Happy talk" television news and "Laverne and Shirley" are not what I want. But I do not intend to impose my sense of what is best on a marketplace that evidently does not agree in vast numbers. Moreover, I am satisfied with my options: I have a choice of newspapers, including those from out of town. I have plenty of magazines. I have an all-news radio station. And, when I'm in the mood for it, there are the friendly personalities with all I ever wanted to know about the weather on the 6 o'clock news. And I am optimistic that alternatives will only get better, no matter where one lives, when cable or other broadband carriers expand, and as the number of electronic data bases grows larger and less expensive.

In the first edition, I tried not to reveal my biases. And I must have been successful, as some critics perceived the book as being a defense of media concentration while others saw it as an attack on the media conglomerates. This time around, I may have exposed more of my prejudices, though they have been formed in large measure by my evaluation of the data in the first edition. But just as we expect good journalists not to allow their personal opinions to affect their reporting, so I hope readers will find the sections of the book for which I was directly responsible to be evenhanded in their treatment of the issues. My coauthors in this venture—all of whom wrote for the previous edition—should not be necessarily associated with the opinions expressed either in this preface or in the conclusion of the book. Each chapter represents the work and viewpoint of the identified author.

Acknowledgements

I am grateful to my associates for their efforts on this volume. What looked like an easy update turned into an extensive rewrite for everyone. Working with experts such as Chris Sterling, Tom Guback and Ken Noble is a pleasure. I also wish to express my gratitude to the editors at Knowledge Industry Publications, Inc.—one of the many small-sized publishers that bring special interest books such as this to the marketplace. This group includes editor in chief Efrem Sigel, senior editor Ellen Lazer and associate editor Fran Epstein, who in one way or another all helped to shape and sharpen (and produce) this edition. I also appreciate the assistance of Robert Maginn, Jr. in updating much of the statistical data in this revision. Finally, thanks to the dozens of individuals and organizations who cooperated in providing data, answering questions, and contributing criticism and comment. Needless to say, however, only the authors can be held accountable for any errors, and I in particular for the integrity of the entire project.

Benjamin M. Compaine

Cambridge, MA
April 14, 1982

The profit system, while it insures the predominant conservative coloration of our press, also guarantees that there will always be a certain amount of dissidence. The American press has never been monolithic, like that of an authoritarian state. One reason is that there is always money to be made in journalism by standing up for the underdog. . . . His wife buys girdles and baking powder and Literary Guild selections, and the advertiser has to reach her.

—A.J. Liebling, *The Wayward Pressman,* 1947

1

Introduction

by Benjamin M. Compaine

Question: Should the owners of companies that create, store and transmit information be judged by a different standard than that applied by society to owners of companies producing coffee, steel, cigarettes, orange juice, or automobiles? Why or why not? The discussion and chapters that follow represent an attempt to answer this and other questions.

MEDIA FREEDOM

The mass communications industry is unique in the American private enterprise system because it deals in the particularly sensitive commodities of ideas, information, thought and opinion. Especially since the development of the broadcast media, we have become aware of the power of being able to simultaneously reach millions of individuals in the United States as well as throughout the world with a message or an image. The mass media are perceived as opinion makers, image formers, culture disseminators.

At the same time, the media in the United States have a degree of autonomy that exists nowhere else in the world. Although there are other nations that have a relatively free press, the United States is unique in allowing all forms of transmission of information to be privately owned. There is no government ownership of any significant newspaper, magazine

1

or book publisher, television or radio station or network, other than some specialized publications issued by the Government Printing Office. The telephone lines and satellites may be subject to some government regulation, but they are all privately owned.

Above all, the very foundation of our governmental system, the Constitution, singled out the press for special treatment: "Congress shall make no law . . . abridging the freedom of speech, or of the press. . . ." It may be argued that this absolute prohibition was written in an era when a handful of weekly colonial papers, a few books and magazines, laboriously turned off hand presses at the rate of 200 sheets per hour, formed the universe of the press. At the start of the Revolutionary War there were only 35 weekly newspapers in the colonies, going into a total of about 40,000 homes.[1] The *Connecticut Courant* had what was described as the "amazing circulation of 8000. . . ."[2]

Yet the politicians of that era were not ignorant of the power of the press. Thomas Paine's *Common Sense* pamphlet sold 120,000 copies in its first three months, and his views spread to virtually every literate American.[3] This one publication is given much of the credit for helping to bring Patriots watching from the sidelines into the revolutionary movement. The authors of the Bill of Rights were probably well aware of the power of the press when they wrote that document.

The media have evolved into big businesses, just as other small businesses have changed and expanded with the technology of the Industrial Revolution, the enormous population growth of the nation and the complexity of dealing in a massive economy. But today, some critics are expressing concern that the modern media are becoming increasingly concentrated in the hands of a small group of corporate executives who may try to control what and how information is gathered and distributed to the populace.*

We can only infer that the concept of diversity of opinion lay behind the press freedom clause of the First Amendment. The fear at the time was that only government might have the power to limit that diversity. But today, there is concern in some quarters that the range of opinions to which the public has access is being limited by large media conglomerates. The purpose of this book is to help sort out perceptions from reality and to give a sense of perspective to the term "media concentration." The book

---

*Actually, this is not a new concern. In 1946 Morris Ernst, in *First Freedom* (Macmillan), expressed the fear of increasing concentration of news outlets. He pointed out that there were fewer newspapers then than in 1909 (1750 vs. 2600) and fewer owners in relation to total number of papers. In 1980, however, there were still 1745 daily papers, as well as about 7600 weekly newspapers, compared to about 7700 in 1946 and 13,900 in 1909.[4]

presents a wealth of empirical statistical data and research findings, so that readers can draw their own conclusions. But it also presents an analysis of each major industry segment. The interpretations made by the authors may be subject to debate, but the empirical data should be studied carefully by those who wish to support their own positions.

BLURRING BOUNDARIES OF MEDIA INDUSTRIES

The media are the structures through which much communication takes place. Starting with the printing press—and at an increased pace in the past 100 years—more of our communication has become *mass* as technology has created the machinery to promote the mass media industries. These include the older, print-based media—books, newspapers and magazines—as well as the electronic mass media—film and radio and television broadcasting.

Mass communication historically has had certain characteristics that differentiate it from other forms of communication. First, it is directed to relatively large, heterogeneous and mostly anonymous audiences. Second, the messages are transmitted publicly, usually intended to reach most members of the audience at about the same time. Finally, the content providers must operate within or through a complex, often capital-intensive industry structure.[5] Point-to-point forms of communication, such as telephone or letter mail, traditionally have had only the third of these characteristics, and therefore cannot be described as mass communication and do not rely on the mass media.

Today, these distinctions can serve only as a starting point, for the information dissemination process is rapidly changing. Computers and connected terminals in homes and offices increasingly allow users to *select* the information they wish to receive, at precisely the time they wish to use it. Computers have made it economically feasible to mail identical, "personalized" messages to millions of recipients using the postal system that at one time was reserved for point-to-point communication. The telephone can give countless users almost simultaneous access to the same computer data base. The telephone and computer are also being combined to provide "electronic mail," perhaps doing for mail what the Xerox machine did for memos. Video and audio cassette recording devices allow individuals to record broadcast programs for replay at a time of their own choosing. Other examples could be cited.

Thus, the media arena, which in an earlier era could be described as encompassing industries known as newspaper, film, books, television, etc., today must recognize less precise boundaries for the term "mass." More crucially, the traditional media industries are finding a blurring of the boundaries among themselves. For example, if a purchased prerecorded video cassette of "The Sound of Music" is played through a television set, is the relevant medium film or television? A person viewing the movie on a television screen may not even know if the conduit is a broadcast, a cable-cast, a video cassette or disc.[6]

To facilitate common understanding, this book has used the conventional media industry terms, such as newspaper or film. Nonetheless, it must be recognized that these are becoming less applicable for designating industry boundaries. This concept will be especially clear in the chapters on theatrical film and cable television, as both industries seek to supply the content for pay cable distribution.

The changing media environment that makes a precise definition of the media arena difficult also means that competition may be coming from new, less traditional players, such as telephone companies, computer firms, financial institutions and others involved in the information business. This suggests not only a broadened arena for conflict in the marketplace, but in the regulatory environment as well, as government bodies seek to identify their territory.

AN ALTERNATIVE MEDIA FRAMEWORK

Blurring media boundaries will make the conventional industry classification decreasingly relevant for both public and private policymakers. Though we continue to concern ourselves, for example, with ownership patterns in the newspaper industry, the real issue may lie in the pathways of disseminating a *package of content* that serves the functional needs of the traditional newspaper audience. This may or may not be an ink-on-newsprint product. Thus, it may be appropriate to start discussing the media using a different classification scheme. It seems inevitable that policy decisions will have to be based on a framework other than the traditional descriptions.

Content, Process and Format

When we discuss "the media," we are in fact talking about three discrete elements: information *content* itself; the *process* by which information is gathered, stored and transmitted; and the *format* in which information is displayed for the user.[7] Firms directly involved in the media business tend to be in the content business, the process business and sometimes both. The format, be it ink on paper, images on a video tube, sound from a speaker, etc. may not be the factor that defines the medium.

The media, in their various formats, provide news, entertainment and all types of information, including advice, instruction, advertisements, statistical data, etc. Content, then, is the information that is provided by the supplier and received by the user. Certain media formats tend to specialize in offering specific types of content, but most media supply some of each. Newspapers, for example, along with their hard news, provide personality profiles as features, crossword puzzles for entertainment, a list of polling places as notices. While televised programming is largely entertainment, important news and informational content exists as well.

Process refers to both the handling and transmitting of information; processing functions include gathering, creating and storing information. A newspaper reporter, for example, researches and writes an article, then stores it in computer memory for editing, hyphenation and justification by a computer geared to typesetting and layout. Process further encompasses the transmission conduits for information, such as broadcasting, coaxial cable, mail and private parcel delivery, microwave, telephone, etc.

Format, as used in this context, refers to the form in which the content is made available to the user. This may be as hard copy, such as printed words or pictures on paper. It may be an electronic/visual representation —such as that created on a video display tube—that consists of words as well as pictures. It may be a mechanical/visual representation, such as that resulting from motion picture projection or microforms. It may also be aural, such as sounds created by a vibrating speaker cone. In many cases, several formats are combined.

Traditionally, the "media" have been defined primarily by their formats. That is, a newspaper is a manufactured product consisting of ink on newsprint; a book is ink on better quality paper and bound between discernable covers. But more recently, we have been accepting process names to denote the medium: cable and video cassette, for example. Thus we have apples and oranges. Neither video cassettes nor cable are media in the same sense as newspapers, magazines or books. The former are merely alternative means of delivering content. They are still "television," though they are not broadcasting, which itself is a transmitting option. The process, therefore, should not be confused with the format in defining the medium. A "feature film" for theatrical release, for instance, finds an increasingly large source of revenue in the video display format. Whether that product is delivered to viewers in a movie theater, to the home by cassette or disc, broadcast or cable is a matter of economics and efficiency, but of itself does not usually affect the content of the movie.

Similarly, newspaper publishers may find in the near future that some of the information now delivered as part of the traditionally printed product may be more efficiently transmitted to video display tubes (or television sets) of those subscribers requesting such data from the publisher's computer (like classified ads or stock prices). The newspaper, therefore, may become a service using part print (ink on newsprint paper) and part video (via telephone lines or cable). The end product, nevertheless, is still "a newspaper," though in several formats.

This distinction between format and process is necessary if we are to understand the boundaries of the industry in which we are investigating concentration. The importance of this content/process/format concept has not been lost on planners in and around the media industry. Some newspapers are experimenting with providing news services for cable channels or interactive viewdata systems. Several broadcasters have announced plans to repackage existing news reports for video cassette or disc sales. Many reference book publishers have themselves converted their information to online data banks or have licensed others to do so. These are just a few of the many possibilities for creative uses of content/process/format to enhance markets, reduce costs, or increase profitability. It is focusing on this new "media menu" that provides the real opportunity for continued diversity of control of media content in the future.

Over the years, changing information technologies have been providing us with new formats: the printing press led to mass produced books, newspapers and magazines; the wireless led to radio and television; other discoveries brought about motion pictures, disc and tape recordings. These have expanded the variety of ways in which information—content—can be received by users. New formats and processes have greatly expanded *accessibility* to information and opportunities for those who wished to be involved in the supply of information and entertainment. Film enlarged the audience for vaudeville and theater, and television expanded it even further. Radio and television news broadcasts are essentially a presentation of the information traditionally published by newspapers and before that by personal letter or word-of-mouth. The form of presentation has changed, but not the *type* of information.

The media arena today is a product of the continuation of this process, with additional conduits and new technology, such as computers, providing an even greater array of formats and hence access to more information (such as the ability to view the moon landing as it occurred via television).

Implications for Corporate Strategy

Businesses currently engaged in media activities or those that may be interested in using their existing resources to enter the media business, as well as public policymakers, all have a vital stake in understanding the nuances of the changing nature of media boundaries. For firms, it is a matter of strategic decisions in areas for expansion or even survival as newer technology changes the basis on which their existing enterprise is built. For example, a newspaper publishing company that persists in restricting itself to printing its product in the conventional method and distributing it over traditional conduits may find both advertising and readership being eroded by competition from other firms providing similar services but utilizing a more efficient or consumer-acceptable technology, such as cable or telephone-based viewdata, broadcast teletext, or some hybrid.

In essence, what is happening in the media arena is that the previously discrete and readily identifiable segments are coming closer together into a more fluid industry, leading to dissolution of old groupings and crystallizing of new. Media participants are increasingly using the computer for information storage and retrieval. They are using telephone lines, cable and satellites for transmitting information, either to the end user (as in the case of broadcasters) or as part of the manufacturing process (as with some newspapers). All types of publishers have video display terminals (VDTs) in the editorial and/or composing rooms. Broadcasters, such as ABC, are packaging programs for other forms of distribution while publishers, such as Playboy Enterprises, are moving toward a similar end. In the middle, the common carriers, such as General Telephone and Electronics (GTE) and American Telephone and Telegraph (AT&T) are looking increasingly like information providers, either in the form of viewdata services or by providing information directly (such as the weather, stock market information, or sports calls over a special telephone number). As all manner of information-providing firms are increasingly using the same technologies, information consumers will gradually shed their traditional perceptions of the media forms as distinct and discrete entities.

Through understanding and exploiting the fluid nature of the content/process/format mix, businesses and entrepreneurs of all sizes have the opportunity to break out of their traditional molds. Information providers can reevaluate their customers not as newspaper readers or magazine subscribers, etc., but as *information consumers,* whose interest is in the unique usefulness of the *content.* These customers should prove decreasingly loyal to a particular format or process, given the greater choices and the strengths of different formats and processes to optimize the utility of a specific type of information.

Implications for Public Policy

Government policymakers are faced with a similar challenge to longstanding practices. Decisions on how to regulate direct-to-home satellite television transmission, or on whether an electronically transmitted newspaper to a home video screen should come under the existing print newspaper interpretation of the First Amendment or be treated similar to the more regulated broadcast models, will depend in part on how well regulators understand the distinctions among information creation, processing, dissemination and format.

Thus, it is perhaps nonproductive in the longer run to focus on the concentration of media ownership using conventional concepts of newspapers, television, magazines, etc. What we must be concerned with instead is encouraging diversity of conduits for information and knowledge, while insuring opportunities for individuals and small businesses to participate in providing such information. We must recognize, for example, that the three major newsweekly magazines have direct competition from all newspapers as well as local and national televised news programs and all-news radio stations. Motion picture distributors clearly compete with television producers, but also with book publishers and certain periodicals. Special interest magazines, already knocking heads in price with mass market paperback books, may increasingly find themselves covering the same topics and even competing for advertiser dollars with video discs and programs distributed by cable operators.

SIZE AND SCOPE OF THE TRADITIONAL MEDIA BUSINESS

Figure 1.1 is a basic map of the information business. On it are placed some 80 products and services. The axes of the map are Services and Products (north-south) and Content and Conduit (east-west). The products-services axis was chosen largely because companies and economists traditionally have viewed industrial activity in this manner. Displaying corporate activities along this axis helps highlight some facets of vertical integration. It also facilitates display of the fact that traditional notions of "product" and "service" may be blurring into a middle ground of "systems," whereby customers mix and match products and services in order to achieve a desired end. Progression along this axis from the product extreme to the service extreme also may be viewed as increasing customer dependence upon supplying institutions. The conduit-content axis was chosen because it helps distinguish those companies which traditionally have viewed themselves as producers of information (such as publishers), and those companies which provide means for recording information and transmitting it. Progression along this axis from the conduit extreme might best be visualized in terms of increasing "information value-added" or in McLuhanesque terms, from medium to message.

The businesses that make up the media industry occupy roughly the extreme right quadrant along the conduit-content axis and vertically span the range of both products and services. The media include the virtually pure

Figure 1.1: The "Information Business," 1982

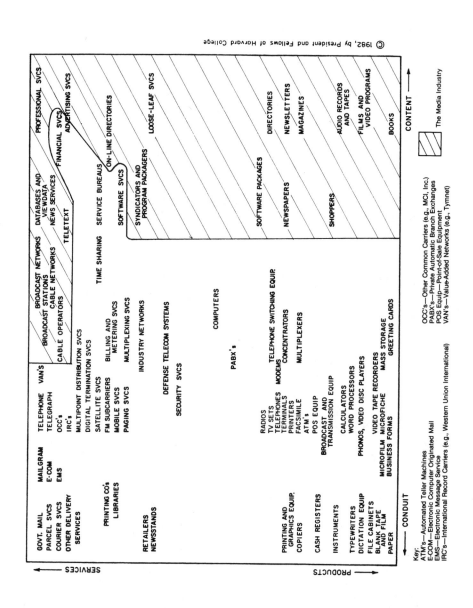

Source: Program on Information Resources Policy, Harvard University.
Used with permission.

service function of the news wire services used by publishers as well as the pure products called books or magazines. But they also stretch two-thirds of the way towards the conduit limit in the services, reflecting the broad range of transmission vehicles that are becoming available as distribution conduits. To the extent that information services are using the telephone network to transmit computer-based content, the line could be extended even further to the left. Indeed, given the substantial reliance of magazine and book publishers on the Postal Service and private delivery services, one could argue that the media extend completely along the horizontal axis as well. The demarcation criteria in 1982, however, may be based on the extent to which the conduit operator has responsibility for content. Cable and broadcast operators do make content decisions, whereas today the telephone companies and Postal Service are common carriers and thus exercise no substantial content decisions.

Compared to the telecommunications business, the entire media and entertainment business is relatively small. As indicated in Table 1.1, the mass media businesses—encompassing newspapers, broadcasting, cable, motion pictures, magazines and books together—were almost the size of the telephone industry alone: $50.6 billion in 1979. Expressed another way, all the Time Incs., CBS's, Times Mirror Cos. and Newhouses combined had revenue roughly equal to that of the American Telephone & Telegraph Co., which accounted for 85% of telephone industry revenue before its impending breakup.

REGULATORY CONFUSION AND PARADOXES

One reason for the blurring of the lines of distinction among the media results from the developing technological systems that are increasingly blind to content. For example, a digitized bit looks the same to a computer, a satellite transponder or a CRT's electron gun whether it is part of what will eventually become a *Wall Street Journal* facsimile page or of a Cable News Network transmission. Thus, it is somewhat misleading today to think in terms of markets for specific products, such as a newspaper or a television show. The more crucial distinction is among processes rather than formats.

However, we continue to base our decisions regarding regulation, market share and antitrust on the rapidly fading industry definitions. The result yields some strange outcomes. For example, a broadcaster, for many historical reasons involving technology and politics, must adhere to a "public interest" standard in judging the content of his or her programming. While broadcasters are licensed and regulated by the FCC, a newspaper has no such restrictions or obligations, other than those self-

Table 1.1: The Information Industry: Revenues and Expenditures, 1970-1979
(in billions)

Industry or Institution	Years									
	1970	1971	1972	1973	1974	1975	1976	1977	1978	1979
Communications										
Computer software and service suppliers	$ 1.6	$ 1.8	$ 2.1	$ 2.6	$ 3.2	$ 3.8	$ 4.5	$ 5.3	$ 6.3	$ 7.5
Computer systems manufacturers	b	b	12.2+	14.4+	16.6+	18.8+	21.2+	23.8+	28.0+	31.2+
Electronic components and accessories	7.3	7.3	8.8	10.8	11.3	10.1*	12.4*	15.2*	17.6*	20.3*
Mobile radio systems	1.9*	2.2*	2.4*	2.6*	2.9*	3.2*	3.5*	4.2*	5.0*	b
Satellite carriers	0.0*	0.0*	0.1*	0.1*	0.1*	0.2*	0.2*	0.2*	0.2*	0.3*
Telegraph	0.4	0.4	0.4	0.5	0.5	0.5	0.5	0.6	0.6	0.6
Telephone	18.2	20.0	22.6	25.5	28.3	31.3	35.6	40.1	45.2	50.6
Terrestrial common carriers	0.0	0.0	0.0	0.0	0.0	0.0	0.1*	0.1	0.2	0.3
Media and Entertainment										
Advertising	1.4	1.4	1.6	1.7	2.0	2.1	2.5	2.8	3.5	4.0*
•Broadcasting										
Radio	1.1	1.3	1.4	1.5	1.6	1.7	2.0	2.3	2.6	2.8*
TV	2.8	2.8	3.2	3.5	3.8	4.1	5.2	5.9	6.9	7.9*
•Book publishing	2.4	2.7	2.9	3.1	3.3	3.5	4.0	4.9	5.5*	6.0*
•Cable TV	0.3	0.3	0.4	0.5	0.6	0.9	1.0	1.2	1.5	1.5*
•News wire services	0.1+	0.1+	0.1+	0.1+	0.1+	0.1+	0.2+	0.2+	0.2+	0.2+
•Motion picture distribution and exhibition	1.2+	1.2+	1.4+	1.8	2.3	2.5	2.4	2.7	3.4*	3.6*
•Newspaper publishing	7.0	7.4	8.3	8.9	9.6	10.4	11.7	13.0	14.5*	16.1*
•Organized sports, arenas	1.1	1.2	1.2	1.2	1.4	1.4	1.6	1.7	1.8	2.1

Table 1.1: (continued)

Industry or Institution	Years									
	1970	1971	1972	1973	1974	1975	1976	1977	1978	1979
• Periodical publishing	3.2	3.2	3.5	3.9	4.1	4.4	5.0	6.1	7.3*	8.2*
Printing, book and commercial	8.8	9.1	10.0	11.0	12.0	12.9	14.9	16.5	18.4*	20.3*
Radio and TV communications equipment	9.3*	8.7*	9.1	9.7*	10.6*	11.9*	13.2*	14.5	b	b
Theaters	0.1	0.1	0.1	0.1	0.1	0.1	0.1	0.2	0.2	0.3
Postal										
Postal service	6.3	6.7	7.9	8.3	9.0	10.0	11.2	13.0	14.1	16.1
Private information delivery	0.8+	1.1+	1.3+	1.5+	1.7+	2.1+	2.3+	3.0+	3.5+	4.3+
Financial and Legal										
Banking and credit	61.1+	68.9+	77.6	101.3	136.2	132.7	144.7	b	b	b
Brokerage industries	40.6+	47.4+	55.3	61.0	64.1	69.1	80.6	b	b	b
Insurance	92.6+	103.5+	113.8	123.6	133.2	148.8	173.1	b	b	b
Legal services	8.5	9.6	10.5	12.2	13.7	14.8	16.2	b	b	b
Miscellaneous Manufacturing										
Paper and allied products	9.5	9.8	11.0	12.9	17.0	16.2	18.9	20.2	23.4*	25.6*
Photographic equipment and supplies	4.4	4.7	5.6	6.4	7.5	7.6	8.8	9.9	12.0*	13.3*
Miscellaneous Services										
Business consulting services	0.9+	1.1+	1.1	1.5	1.7	1.8	2.2	2.7*	3.2*	b
Business information services	0.8*	0.9*	1.0*	1.1*	1.1*	b	b	b	2.1*	b
Marketing research services	b	b	b	b	b	0.3+	0.4+	0.4+	0.5+	0.6+
Total Revenue	293.7	324.9	376.9	433.3	499.6	527.3	600.1	210.7	227.7	243.7

Table 1.1: (continued)

Industry or Institution	1970	1971	1972	1973	1974	1975	1976	1977	1978	1979
Government Expenditures										
Census Bureau	0.1	0.1	0.1	0.1	0.1	0.1	0.1	0.1	0.1	0.2
County agents, government	0.3	0.3	0.4	0.4	0.4	0.4	0.5	0.5	0.6	0.6*
Libraries	2.1	b	b	b	b	b	b	b	5.4*	b
National intelligence community	5.6*	5.4*	5.4*	5.7*	5.9*	6.3*	6.7*	7.4*	7.8*	8.3*
National Technical Information Service[c]	0.0	0.0	0.0	0.0	0.0	0.0	0.0	0.0	0.0	0.0
Research and development	25.9	26.6	28.8	30.6	32.8	35.3	39.0	43.0	48.3	54.3*
Schooling	70.4	76.3	83.3	89.7	98.0	111.1	121.8	131.0	140.4	151.5
Social Security Administration	1.0	1.2	1.3	1.4	1.8	2.2	2.6	2.7	3.0	3.2
Total Expenditures	$105.4	$109.9	$119.3	$127.9	$139.0	$155.4	$170.7	$184.7	$205.6	$218.1

• = Included in media industry.
* = Estimated.
+ = Lower end of estimated range.
a = Not available as of January 1981.
b = Not available.
c = Under $50 million annually.

Source: Program on Information Resources Policy, Harvard University. Copyright © 1981 President and Fellows of Harvard College. May not be reproduced without permission.

imposed by the ethics of the profession. The justification for these discrepancies in the context of the First Amendment has been the scarcity of spectrum and public ownership of the airwaves compared to lack of such conditions in print. The irony here is that most communities are served by only one newspaper while they enjoy a far greater choice in television and radio stations. Recent movements to reduce regulations on radio are in part a recognition of this anomaly.

Similar paradoxes are developing elsewhere. Cable, which is generally regulated at the municipal level, has evolved into *de facto* exclusive franchises for each area. Thus, whether there are 24 or 56 or more channels in a system, they are almost all under the complete control of the system's owners. Any non-broadcast signal provided by the cable operator does not have a fairness doctrine requirement. Cable today is thus much closer to the print model regarding content than to its seemingly closer cousin, broadcast television. Among other results, cable systems can transmit movies into the same homes and over the same receivers that could not receive such programming in the past because broadcasters would be in danger of losing their FCC-issued licenses under current regulations.

Furthermore, it is widely held that the best-selling prerecorded video cassettes have been those of pornographic movies. But beyond this, should video disc machines become mass market items, the potential exists for video publishers to provide a wide range of programming for the home or institutional television set that carries with it none of the regulation affixed to broadcast television. Those few programmers using common carrier multipoint distribution services similarly may find a freedom of content unheard of in traditional broadcasting. (It is unclear at this time whether those planning to provide satellite-to-home transmission will have any content restrictions.)

The user, of course, is oblivious to many of these distinctions. Home viewers turn a dial or push a button on their cable units and receive a variety of programming. Not aware of the legal differences between broadcast and cable, will they be confused if some political candidate tries to get equal time on a cable originated show or some special interest group finds that the programming of some religious, cultural or other cablecaster does not reflect fairness doctrine balance?

Similar confusion may reign on the "print" side. Several experiments around the country—in Los Angeles, Salt Lake City, Chicago and Washington—have used a conventional video broadcast signal to transmit textual information. There is already some debate as to who controls the vertical blanking interval, which is one conduit for sending such teletext data to users who have decoders attached to their conventional television sets. If *The Chicago Sun-Times* generates the information, should it be held to broadcast content standards? Should the FCC provide separate authorization for use of the vertical blanking intervals?

One of the battles on the print side involves the newspapers and the telecommunications industry, particularly AT&T. Among the issues that remain to be resolved is the extent to which AT&T will be able to get into the content business. This encompasses not only electronically-stored-and-transmitted news, weather, sports, consumer information, etc., but advertising that looks rather similar to Yellow Pages listings to Bell people and classified ads to the newspaper publishers.

TYPES OF OWNERSHIP PATTERNS

Ownership concentration—or lack thereof—can be split along two dimensions, each with different implications. One is horizontal integration; the other is vertical integration.

Horizontal Integration

The most typical form of horizontal integration is that of a single firm owning more than one entity in a single medium. The firm then becomes a chain owner of newspapers, magazines, cable systems, etc. This is the most frequently occurring form of media combination and has been the subject of the greatest share of scrutiny by regulators and economists. For the most part, horizontally integrated firms own properties either in geographically discrete areas or directed to different audiences. An example of the former is a firm that owns television stations in Boston, Philadelphia and Detroit. The second case would be a firm that publishes magazines for skiers, for photographers and for gourmet cooks. There are also media conglomerates, firms that are horizontally integrated in more than one medium, such as Time Inc., The New York Times Co. or Westinghouse Broadcasting Co.

A different type of horizontal integration involves what is called cross-ownership, where a firm controls more than one medium in the same market. Such would be the case of a newspaper and a television station owned by the same firm in the same city.

Vertical Integration

Most firms are vertically integrated to the degree that they bring together raw materials (or ideas), combine them into a product and service, and market them. More relevant to this discussion, vertical integration occurs when businesses representing several sequential stages of production that could be separately owned are instead directed by a single firm. An example is a publisher that owns a paper mill, has its own staff of writers and editors, performs its own typesetting, runs its own presses and even handles its own delivery to the customer.

Using the content/process/format framework, a vertically integrated media firm would likely be both the content creator and the content processor. This would encompass most daily newspapers, but fewer weekly newspapers, not many magazine publishers and almost no book publishers. Unlike daily newspapers, these others tend to contract out typesetting (although the decreasing cost of electronic typesetting equipment has caused many companies to make this an in-house function) and with very few exceptions, contract for printing. Physical delivery to newsstands, retailers or to the subscriber is by common or private carriers. Television networks have been forced to separate programming (except news) from transmission. But cable operators are rapidly integrating backwards from transmission to program creation.

Most attention in the media ownership area has focused on horizontal integration: large newspaper chains, limits on the number of broadcasting stations under a single owner, questions of whether the size of multiple system cable operators should be limited. The issue of the permissible degree of cross-ownership in a geographical area has been a long-time concern in the public policy arena. Vertical integration has been of lesser concern, but may become a central issue for debate (as will be seen in Chapter 7 on cable and pay cable).

THE ECONOMIC NATURE OF INFORMATION

Although this book incorporates the work of many economists, it is not an economist's approach to understanding the structure of the media industry.[8] The study of the media is actually an attempt at understanding the status of the flow of content—of information. It is the communication process itself that ultimately has meaning for society. Yet we have little understanding of information: What is it, how is it used, what is its value, how can—or should—it be allocated?

We frequently use the term "marketplace," as in "marketplace of ideas" to describe the ideal environment for information. But describing the information marketplace is a different order of problem than characterizing the marketplace for toothpaste, or even for newspapers. Conventional measurements do not suffice when dealing with the amorphous and inexact concept of information. For example, how does one place a monetary value on the information an airline pilot uses to guide a jet not in sight of land to a precise destination—the weather reports, the navigational aids, the on-board computer read-outs, etc., not to mention the knowledge and intuition gained by years of accumulated experience?

The term "marketplace" seems to presuppose information is indeed a commodity, like cotton, paper, or chopped sirloin steak. This may be a reasonable assumption, but it must be tested in light of other economic approaches to its nature. For example, at the other extreme, information may be viewed as a theoretical construct, having features unlike other commodities and therefore requiring unique treatment. In between there is an alternative that grants some commodity-like characteristics to information, but recognizes other distinctive features as well. For example, typical commodities are tangible, but information may not be. Most commodities lend themselves to exclusivity of possession, but information can be possessed by many individuals at the same time without anyone being deprived of it. In addition, there is frequently little or no marginal cost to the provider of information in reaching a wider audience.[9]

This alternative viewpoint is the one that is accepted for the purpose of this study. It considers information a "public good." A public good to an economist is one which has essentially no marginal cost associated with adding distribution. The best example is a television broadcast. Once the fixed costs of production have been incurred and the show is sent out over the air, there is no difference in expense to the broadcaster if one household or 21 million households tune in to the show. Thus, television (and radio) advertising is not sold at its marginal cost, since that is zero. Price always exceeds marginal cost.

The "product" of the media differs from most commodities, which are private goods. Every orange, for instance, has a cost, and each one adds weight in shipment. Selling more oranges means adding more orange trees, etc. There can be a real marginal cost—the expense of growing and shipping one more orange.

In print media, the informational content is really the public good, while the physical product—paper and ink—is a private good. In many cases, the cost of producing the first copy constitutes the bulk of total cost, just as in broadcasting the production is virtually the total cost. Costs of editorial staff, typesetting and platemaking are all necessary whether the print run will be 100 or 100,000. The incentive, therefore, for broadcasters and publishers is to increase circulation or audience for a product, since that adds little or nothing to marginal costs while justifying higher marginal revenue from advertisers in the form of higher advertising rates. The public good aspect of information is what encourages television networks and syndicated shows, as well as the desire for a firm to trade up from stations in smaller markets to larger ones. News services and print syndicates are encouraged by the same economic facts.

While it may be argued that the role of information and hence the structure of the media is ultimately a social concern, the lessons to be learned from the economists have direct relevance. For example, a presumed social goal—fostering media diversity by prohibiting certain instances of vertical integration—may reduce the flow of capital into a capital-intensive stage of the production process. This could not only be wasteful, but for a media industry (such as cable), it could result in an actual reduction in the number of programs (i.e., messages sent) and perhaps a reduction in opportunities for expression. At the very least, it could result in increased cost for the consumer, either through direct charges or indirectly through higher advertiser costs and hence prices.

GOVERNMENT INVOLVEMENT

In summarizing the interest of the Federal Trade Commission in media ownership, a senior official explained that "We're somewhat more concerned about concentration in the media [than other industries] because they are not just economic concerns but First Amendment concerns as well."[10]

The Federal Trade Commission, which until 1978 had left inquiries into media ownership mostly to the Federal Communications Commission and the Justice Department, became active in the process by focusing on this last assumption. Should a stricter standard apply to the media than to other industries "because of the media's position in American society and the importance of having many channels available for speech?"[11]

At a symposium on media ownership sponsored by the FTC in December 1978, FTC chairman Michael Pertchuck asked, "[Can] free speech be separated from the economic structure that controls the media?" Pertchuck sees competition as an alternative to regulation: "Should the government promote diversity and independence to avoid having to regulate?" In a report following the symposium, the FTC staff found no cause for the Commission to take any remedial action.

The Federal Communications Commission has long been involved in the media ownership question through its responsibility to license radio and television broadcasters. For a while it also involved itself in regulating cable and in the common or cross-media ownership of broadcasters and newspapers. Both cable and broadcasting regulation by the FCC are treated at some length in Chapters 6 and 7.

With the exception of the motion picture industry (see Chapter 5), the Justice Department has seen little cause to bring broad antitrust actions against the mass media industries. Individual firms have been affected, as in the case where Times Mirror Co. had to divest itself of the *San Ber-*

nardino (CA) *Telegram* on the grounds that it would lessen competition since that paper is located near Times Mirror's *Los Angeles Times*. Perhaps the most important Justice Department industry-wide action outside of film was the 1945 Associated Press case, which clearly placed newspapers and other media within the jurisdiction of antitrust legislation (see Chapter 2).

In 1979, the antitrust division of the Justice Department investigated the merger between newspaper giant Gannett and Combined Communications, with its extensive broadcast holdings. However, a top Justice Department official admitted:

> The antitrust laws do not flatly prohibit media conglomerates any more than they prohibit other kinds of conglomerates. Under present law, some measurable impact on competition in some market must be proven before a merger or acquisition will be held to violate the antitrust laws. Indeed, the courts have been generally reluctant to condemn conglomerate mergers where such an impact has not been shown, regardless of the social or other objections that have been asserted.[12]

ASSUMPTIONS UNDERLYING CURRENT OWNERSHIP POLICY

Implicit in the discussion of media ownership are three concepts reflecting long-standing American cultural and political traditions which have achieved virtually the status of natural law. The three are pieces of the same cloth, though each has its unique nuance. In brief, they can be summarized as follows:

1) Bigness is bad. This applies to concentration of ownership in industries other than the mass media. There is a sense, in part supported by some economists, that after reaching a certain size which brings optimal efficiencies or production, further growth of firms in an industry provides no further economic advantages to society. The key question which can rarely be answered definitively is, how can we tell when that optimal point has been reached?

2) Diversity is good. For a heterogeneous democracy to thrive, we have a deep-rooted sense that a broad spectrum of ideas and opinions must have a chance to find a public forum. To guarantee this diversity, goes the argument, we must not allow those who control the conduits to information to be controlled by a small group of gatekeepers and certainly not by government. As with the "big-

ness is bad" assumption, one question here is, "How much diversity is enough and how can this be measured?" Another piece of this truism is emerging from the unstated agenda of media critics: Must this diversity all be through the broadest of the mass media —network television? Or is there room to accept diversity through the "small media," such as limited audience magazines, newsletters, academic journals, public access cable, and other channels?

3) Localism is desirable. This implies that control over information must be geographically as well as structurally diverse. The presumption is that in a nation with many different local and state governments, we must be provided with information about our immediate political and social environment, a goal best achieved by locally based ownership, whether for television, cable or newspaper.

PUBLIC POLICY CONCERNS

Public policy particularly follows the assumption that "diversity is good." If the marketplace of ideas (ideas being broadly interpreted to include all types of content) is to succeed, we must have a sufficient number of conduits to ensure that unpopular, unorthodox and iconoclastic content has some way of entering the mass communications flow, along with mainstream content. In the media industry, this balance has historically been achieved through both competition and regulation. In the print area (at least since the advent of the steam-driven rotary press in the 1830s), enough freedom of market entry to allow diversity of ownership has been the means by which an acceptable content mix has been accomplished. In the newer electronic age, government regulation, in the form of limits on the number of broadcasting outlets and in the creation of common carriers, has dispersed ownership or guaranteed fair and equal access. In addition, several statutory and administrative requirements, such as equal time, the fairness doctrine and the prime-time access rule (see Chapter 6) have further sought to foster diversity (with ambiguous results).

Today, the technology of computers and telecommunications is adding to the options for information dissemination conduits. Extensive hearings by a subcommittee of the U.S. House of Representatives in 1981 led to the following conclusion:

The evolution of new delivery systems offering an array of new channels from a host of new program suppliers presents the historic possibility of abolishing the scarcity on which the existing regulatory scheme, and the content and behavioral rules it imposes, has been based.[13]

The applicability of this possibility, however, depends on three factors. One is the acceptance of industry boundaries other than the traditional ones. So long as the demise of a daily newspaper, for example, is treated as an isolated event, rather than as part of a restructuring of the process options for delivering content, public (and private) policy may be ill-focused. Second, public policy will have to create a competitive environment that provides opportunity for new and existing players to invest in new technologies. This means the ability to amass sufficient capital, for example, to cable the urban areas of the country or to introduce new types of information services. Finally, those most fascinated by the "power" of the mass media must recognize that not all ideas can be or will be appropriate for all media forms. That is, while expanded media outlets will cry out for content to go with them, we should not expect this to mean automatically that the unpopular or unconventional ideas will suddenly leap into prime-time television (or its future equivalent). Even if we become a nation with 54 channels of cable in our homes, there will inevitably be a handful of these that will attract the plurality of the audience at any time (just as the number of books that reach the best-seller lists represents a small proportion of the thousands of titles available).

The challenge that has faced public policymakers in the latter part of the 1970s and into the 1980s is how best to provide this competitive environment, through a combination of both regulation and realistic competition. This has been the tightrope walked by the Federal Communications Commission in its Computer Inquiry I (1971) and Computer Inquiry II (1980) rule-makings, by both the House and Senate as they unsuccessfully tried to rewrite all or part of the Communications Act of 1934 in session after session of Congress, and even by the Justice Department and the courts in antitrust suits against IBM and AT&T.

These and other events serve as lessons that neither regulation nor competition can be looked to as knee-jerk solutions to stimulating an environment of "sufficient" diversity. Under one set of circumstances, discouraging the large players from diversifying may slow down new services or force inefficient competition that results in higher prices to users. Under an alternative scenario, too few large participants may inhibit innovation, limit incentives for diversity, or create monopoly-like pricing. Thus the challenge for public policy is to approach media ownership with a position flexible enough to be applied on an *ad hoc* basis, especially as we move through a period of rapid technological and cultural change, and the accompanying realignment of economic and social needs.

OBJECTIVES OF THIS BOOK

The primary objective of this book is to bring together as much relevant data as feasible on the nature and degree of competition and ownership in the mass media business. This was not done as an academic exercise, but to provide an empirical context for the continuing debate on the structure of the traditional media segments. It will become quickly apparent, however, how artificial traditional boundaries have become. The real action—and issues—rests on the borders between the conventional industries.

A second objective, inescapable given the title of this volume, is to specifically identify the owners of media properties. This includes the corporate owners and, to the limited extent possible, many of the largest individual and institutional owners of the media corporations themselves. In addition, the book explores the extent of concentration in the media industries today and compares current levels with those of previous periods.

Caveats, Limitations and Assumptions

First caveat: This book did not set out to prove or disprove any hypotheses. Unlike much of the work in this area, it did not assume that media ownership was either too concentrated or so diverse as to not warrant further concern. At the end of the book, conclusions are presented. These, however, reflect the analyses of one individual, based on the perceived weight of the evidence and personal values assigned to their meaning. The intent of the authors has been to present the data in a manner which encourages all readers to reach their own conclusions. In the spirit of the marketplace of ideas, this book serves its purpose best if it creates the context for discussion and debate.

Second caveat and first assumption: This volume did not take on the task of questioning the underlying assumptions of the economic system of the United States, which fall roughly under the label of capitalism. It is assumed that the media and communications infrastructure will continue to operate within a system of private ownership, with an overlay of minimal government regulation. There are those critics who believe that the media industry can never be fundamentally different than at present so long as the structure incorporates the profit motive and private enterprise. The bias of this author is that, first, it is politically unlikely that there will be a radical shift in the underlying economic system and second, no one has apparently proposed a pragmatic system that would work better (in terms of access, diversity, etc.), than our current system. While alternative systems (worker cooperatives, public trusts, etc.) might result in the dominance of a different set of values in the media, they would not necessarily represent *better* values. They would merely substitute one dominant group for another.

Third caveat and second assumption: This book, therefore, does not attempt to take up a debate on what the proper role and responsibility of the media should be in American society. That has been the subject of several excellent books in itself.[14] This volume does assume media responsibility to provide reasonable access, to be generally honest and fair, and to maintain sufficient diversity, without defining standards for any of these. This assumption should not be accepted as a naiveté that believes that these qualities are constantly achieved in the real world.

First Limitation: This book has omitted consideration of the record and music publishing industries, though in some quarters they might be considered part of the media industry. This was done because they are not primary conduits for information (although we recognize that some music certainly does convey ideas).

Second Limitation: This study, as others before it, has been hampered by lack of data in certain areas, in particular financial data for privately owned firms. Not being required to release such data to the public is, naturally, one prerogative of those relatively few large firms that do not need the equity markets for capital. To the extent that privately owned firms may operate differently from those with public ownership, there may be some bias to the overall data. This limitation, however, is not viewed as critical.

*   *   *   *   *   *

In 1982 Warren Beatty won the Academy Award as best director for "Reds," an epic movie about journalist and Soviet sympathizer John Reed. Beatty, who was also producer, coauthor and the actor portraying Reed, went beyond the usual "thank you's" in his acceptance speech. He gave special tribute to the president of Paramount Pictures, which financed and distributed the movie, and to the chairman of Gulf + Western, the conglomerate that owns Paramount. Beatty said that these bulwarks of capitalism deserved credit for supporting an expensive film that sympathetically traced the beginnings of the socialist and communist parties in the United States. He seemed to be confirming A.J. Liebling's observation that introduced this chapter: that is, in a capitalist economy, those who run the media firms make their decisions not on the ideological grounds of the content *per se,* but on the basis of efficient allocation of limited resources—that is, if a property has the potential to make a profit (though it often does not), it has a good chance of finding its way onto film (or into print, onto video tape, into a data base, etc.). So long as we exist in a world of limited resources and *some* mechanism must allocate them, Beatty and Liebling seem to agree that the basic in-place economic structure can create the climate for diversity of opinion in the media.

NOTES

1. Edwin Emery and Michael Emery, *The Press in America,* 4th ed. (Englewood Cliffs, NJ: Prentice-Hall, 1978), p. 69.

2. Ibid., p. 70.

3. Ibid., p. 68.

4. *Editor & Publisher International Year Book, 1981; Historical Statistics of the United States, Colonial Times to 1970,* U.S. Department of Commerce, Bureau of the Census, Series R, 244-257.

5. Reed H. Blake and Edwin D. Haroldson, *A Taxonomy of Concepts in Communication* (New York: Hastings House, 1975), p. 34.

6. Benjamin M. Compaine, *A New Framework for the Media Arena: Content, Process and Format* (Cambridge, MA: Program on Information Resources Policy, Harvard University, 1980), p. 4.

7. Ibid., pp. 6-10.

8. For some of the better treatments on the subject by economists, see Bruce M. Owen, *Economics and Freedom of Expression* (Cambridge, MA: Ballinger Publishing Co., 1975); James N. Dertouzos, "Media Conglomerates: Chains, Groups and Cross Ownership," discussion paper prepared for the FTC Media Symposium, Washington, DC, December 14-15, 1978; James N. Rosse, "Economic Limits of Press Responsibility," *Studies in Industry Economics,* Department of Economics, Stanford University, 1975; H.E. Frech and Linda Nielsen, "Competition, Concentration and Public Policy in the Media: A Survey of Research," Working Paper in Economics #154, University of California, Santa Barbara.

9. Benjamin M. Compaine, "Shifting Boundaries in the Information Marketplace," *Journal of Communication,* Vol. 31, No. 1 (Winter 1981), pp. 132-133.

10. "FTC to Take on Media Concentration," *Advertising Age,* July 24, 1978, p. 1. Statement is from Alan K. Palmer, deputy director of the Bureau of Competition.

11. Ibid., p. 94.

12. I. William Hill, "Justice Department Probes Gannett-Combined Merger," *Editor & Publisher,* March 24, 1979, p. 11. Quotes John H. Shenefield, assistant attorney general for antitrust.

13. U.S. Congress, *Telecommunications in Transition: The Status of Competition in the Telecommunications Industry,* A Report by the Majority Staff of the Subcommittee on Telecommunications, Consumer Protection, and Finance, of the Committee on Energy and Commerce, U.S. House of Representatives, November 3, 1981, p. 21.

14. See, for example, William L. Rivers and Wilbur Schramm, *Responsibility in Mass Communications,* rev. ed. (New York: Harper & Row,

1969); Commission on the Freedom of the Press, *A Free and Responsible Press* (Chicago: University of Chicago Press, 1948); Gerald Gross, ed., *The Responsibility of the Press* (New York: Simon & Schuster, A Clarion Book, 1966).

2

Newspapers

by Benjamin M. Compaine

PROLOGUE

The newspaper industry in the early 1980s may be in the first stages of a revolution as profound as the one caused by the development of the steam driven rotary press and cheap newsprint. Or it may not be. For certain, the technology that transformed the internal methods for producing the newspaper in the 1970s, i.e., computers and video display terminals, was threatening to reach out to the world of the consumer. Systems were being put in place to create what might be called the electronic newspaper, videotext, or data base publishing. Whatever the term, implicit was the promise that the consumer would be able to get all or much of the content of the newspaper delivered via some electronic highway. Telephone lines were one route. The cable that brought in video was another. Over the air, via broadcasting, was yet a third pathway.

The traditional newspaper publishers found themselves suddenly confronted by potential competition from sources that would have seemed incomprehensible only a year or two earlier. American Telephone & Telegraph, "the phone company," seemed to be the most ominous cloud on the horizon. But all sorts of other industries were making noises about doing some of the things that newspaper publishers had always thought of as their sacred turf. Some banks, such as Citibank and Banc One Corp. (Ohio), wanted to add information services to their hoped-for electronic home banking plans. Broadcasters, such as CBS, Inc., were experimenting with text-like information services. Other types of publishers, such as Time Inc., had plans for text services that included an advertiser-financed component.

While none of these called themselves "newspaper," the traditional publishers were nonetheless worried. And with good reason. The modern newspaper is, essentially, a composite of different types of content. We call some news, some sports, some features, some display advertising, some classified advertising, etc. Studies of the uses and rewards *users* derive from the media, however, implicitly characterize the type of content of a newspaper as 1) surveillance (i.e., box scores, movie listings); 2) social connection (i.e., informed conversation at cocktail parties); 3) opinion formation; and 4) escape (i.e., entertainment).[1] Thus, users of newspapers have been buying newspapers for a multiplicity of purposes. Moreover, users have long taken this bundle of relatively unrelated types of information and fashioned their own *individualized* package. Some readers only look at sports results and certain comics. Others read just the front page. Some purchasers on any given day may buy the paper just for the movie listings or classified ads.

To the extent that other methods of delivering such parcels of content are devised, they must inevitably affect the purchasing of the ink-on-paper format we call newspapers. And, they also provide yet another option by which advertisers can reach their intended audiences.

None of this is to suggest, as some have, that the newspaper is dead. To some extent, it is true that the traditional daily paper has been dying since the 1960s. Circulation has been stagnant. Household penetration has dropped without a break since the late 1940s.[2] This might have been predicted, given the added competition of television. But the threat of electronic delivery does mean that newspaper publishers will have to consider providing users with the content already stored in their computers via electronic means. The newspaper publisher may find an opportunity—indeed, the necessity—to reduce the emphasis on the "paper" part of the label, without changing the essential nature of the information function.

This, then, is prologue to a discussion of the state of competition and ownership in the newspaper industry as it existed up to 1981. But this introduction should suggest that the balance among competitors in the newspaper segment of the mass communication industry—as in the rest of these merging fields—may be shaken by new and different types of entrants.

GENERAL CHARACTERISTICS

In 1980 the value of newspaper industry receipts was about $17.5 billion. This made newspapers by far the largest segment of the traditional mass media industry. By way of comparison, receipts for periodical publishers were $8.9 billion and for broadcasters $12 billion.

With its origins dating back to the earliest colonial days, it should not be surprising that the newspaper industry is economically mature. Table 2.1

shows a growth that has fallen short of the rate of overall growth of the economy since 1970. Compound growth since 1960 has lagged with a 7.5% annual rate of growth compared to 8.6% for the Gross National Product. Advertising revenue (Table 2.2) did keep up with general economic indicators in the 1970s as well as with the rate of increase in total advertising expenditures. But it is significant that circulation has been stagnant for years, with the daily circulation of 62.2 million in 1980 still below the peak of 63.1 million reached in 1973 (see Table 2.3).

There were 1745 daily newspapers of general circulation in 1980, a level that has remained stable since the mid-1940s. In addition, there were almost 10,000 other newspapers, including about 30 foreign-language dailies, 90 professional, business and special service dailies, and 8000 less-than-daily-frequency newspapers.[3] While this chapter concentrates on the daily newspapers of general interest, the less than daily newspapers are a vigorous part of the industry structure. They are also the most robust segment. As seen in Table 2.4, weekly newspapers have achieved significant

Table 2.1: Value of All Newspaper Shipments Compared to Gross National Product, Selected Years, 1960-1980
(Index: 1970 = 100)

Year	GNP (in billions of current dollars)	Growth Index	Year-to-Year % Increase	Value of Receipts (in billions)	Growth Index	Year-to-Year % Increase
1960	$ 506.0	52	—	$ 4.1	59	—
1965	688.1	70	36.0	5.2	74	26.8
1970	982.4	100	42.7	7.0	100	34.6
1971	1,063.4	108	8.2	7.4	106	5.7
1972	1,171.1	119	10.1	8.3	119	12.2
1973	1,306.6	133	11.6	8.9	127	7.2
1974	1,412.9	144	8.1	9.6	137	7.9
1975	1,528.8	156	8.2	10.5	150	4.2
1976	1,706.5	174	11.6	11.7	167	12.0
1977	1,889.6	192	10.7	13.1	187	12.0
1978	2,156.1	219	14.1	14.5	207	10.7
1979	2,413.9	246	12.0	16.1	230	11.0
1980	2,626.1	267	8.8	17.5	250	8.7
Compound annual % increase 1960-1980:	8.6%			7.5%		

Sources: GNP: U.S. Bureau of Economic Analysis, *Survey of Current Business*. Newspaper Shipments: U.S. Department of Commerce, *U.S. Industrial Outlook, 1981*.

Table 2.2: Newspaper Advertising Revenues Compared to Total
Advertising Expenditures and Gross National Product, Selected Years,
1945-1980
(Index: 1970 = 100)

Year	Total Advertising (in millions)	Total Advertising Index	Total Newspaper Share (in millions)	Newspaper Advertising Index	GNP Growth Index
1945	$ 2,875	15	$ 921	16	22
1950	5,710	29	2,076	36	29
1955	9,194	47	3,088	54	41
1960	11,932	61	3,703	64	52
1965	15,255	78	4,457	78	70
1970	19,600	100	5,745	100	100
1975	28,230	146	8,442	147	156
1976	33,720	175	10,022	174	174
1977	38,120	197	11,132	194	192
1978	43,970	224	12,707	221	219
1979	49,520	253	14,493	252	246
1980	54,480	278	15,541	271	267

Sources: GNP: U.S. Bureau of Economic Analysis, *Survey of Current Business.* Advertising: McCann-Erickson Advertising Agency, Inc., New York, NY, published by *Advertising Age*, annual.

Table 2.3: Daily Newspaper Circulation in the U.S., Selected Years,
1920-1980

Year	Total Daily		Sunday	
	Number	Circulation (in thousands)	Number	Circulation (in thousands)
1920	2,042	27,791	522	17,084
1930	1,942	39,589	521	26,413
1940	1,878	41,132	525	32,371
1950	1,772	53,829	549	46,582
1960	1,763	58,882	563	47,699
1970	1,748	62,108	586	49,217
1971	1,749	62,231	540	49,665
1972	1,761	62,510	603	49,339
1973	1,774	63,147	634	51,717
1974	1,768	61,877	641	51,679
1975	1,756	60,655	639	51,096
1976	1,762	60,977	650	51,565
1977	1,759	61,712	668	52,079
1978	1,764	61,836	679	53,186
1979	1,763	62,223	720	54,380
1980	1,745	62,202	736	54,676

Source: *Editor & Publisher International Year Book*, annual editions.

circulation growth, both in average size and in aggregate numbers. Similarly, advertising volume increased at a compound annual rate of nearly 14% between 1967 and 1981 (see Table 2.5). The fastest growing segment are the "shoppers," publications that are totally advertiser supported and frequently do not even contain editorial material. As indicated in Table 2.5, the advertising volume of weeklies and shoppers has grown from 7% of the level of daily papers in 1967 to an estimated 11% in 1981.

The newspaper industry is one of the country's largest manufacturing employers. As seen in Table 2.6, newspaper employment reached an estimated 386,000 in 1973, declined for a few years as the result of labor-saving technology as well as the ensuing recession, but expanded strongly since 1977. Even so, since 1960 industry employment has increased at a much lower rate than overall civilian employment. While production workers currently account for about two-fifths of this work force, their proportion has been declining.

Table 2.4: Weekly Newspapers' Circulation Growth, Selected Years, 1960-1980

Year	Total Weekly Newspapers	Average Circulation	Total Weekly Circulation (in thousands)
1960	8,138	2,606	21,328
1965	8,003	3,260	26,088
1970	7,610	3,866	29,422
1975	7,486	4,698	35,176
1976	7,530	4,955	37,314
1977	7,466	5,075	37,893
1978	7,673	5,245	40,244
1979[1]	7,954	5,324	42,348
1980[1]	7,602	5,390	40,971
Compound growth 1960-1980:			2.2%
1970-1980:			3.4

[1] Preliminary figures.
Source: Calculations based on data supplied by the National Newspaper Association.

Profitability

Interest in starting, buying and owning newspapers is a positive indicator of the financial health of the industry. The rapid rate with which newspapers have been bought at increasingly higher multiples of dollars

Table 2.5: Weeklies' and Shoppers' Ad Revenue Growth, 1967, 1972, 1977 and 1981
(in millions)

Year	Weeklies' Ad Revenue	Shoppers' Ad Revenue	Total	% Daily Newspaper Local Ad Volume
1967	$ 243.2	$ 26.4	$ 269.6	7%
1972	386.5	73.7	460.2	8
1977	734.5	154.6	889.1	9
1981[1]	1,338.8	307.7	1,646.5	11
Compound growth				
1967-1981:	13.1%	19.2%	13.9%	
1967-1977:	11.7	19.3	12.7	
1972-1981:	15.0	17.2	15.4	

[1] Estimate.
Sources: National Directory of Weekly Newspapers, 1971, 1981; Newspaper Advertising Bureau; McCann-Erickson. Compiled by Goldman Sachs & Co.

per reader or earnings is a sign of a prosperous industry. Table 2.7 lists the revenues and profits for publicly held companies that derive a substantial portion of their revenue from newspaper operations. Net profit margins ranged from about 15.5% for Capital Cities Communications (which has a substantial portion of revenue from broadcasting) to 5.2% for The Washington Post. Even so, the median percentage return on sales for this group was 8.5% in 1980, nearly twice the median margin for the *Fortune 500* industrial companies. This was down from the 9.6% median of this group in 1978.

Table 2.8 compares this group of newspaper firms with the median net profit margins for selected groups from the *Fortune* list for 1980. The newspapers equaled or outperformed most industry categories.

Consolidation

By oligopolistic standards, the newspaper industry is still relatively diversely held—at least this was true in 1977. Whereas the eight largest firms in the newspaper industry accounted for 31% of total dollar shipments in 1977, the eight largest aircraft manufacturers controlled 81%, radio and television set manufacturers, 65%, paper mills, 42%, bread and cake bakers, 40%. Between 1947 and 1977, concentration of ownership of newspapers by this measure increased by 5%, while concentration for the

**Table 2.6: Newspaper Employment Compared to Total U.S. Civilian
Employment, Selected Years, 1946-1980
(Index: 1960 = 100)**

Year	Newspaper Employment (in thousands)	Growth Index	Total U.S. Civilian Employment (in thousands)	Growth Index
1946	248	76	57,039	86
1960	325	100	65,778	100
1965	345	106	71,088	108
1970	373	115	78,627	120
1971	370	114	79,120	120
1972	380	117	81,702	124
1973	386	119	84,409	128
1974	385	118	85,936	131
1975	377	116	84,786	129
1976	384	118	87,485	133
1977	396	122	90,546	138
1978	406	125	94,373	144
1979	421	130	96,945	147
1980	432	133	97,270	148

Source: U.S. Bureau of Labor Statistics, *Employment and Earnings*, monthly.

**Table 2.7: Revenue and Profit for Publicly Owned Newspaper-Owning
Firms, 1980**

Firm	1980 Revenue (in thousands)	Net Profit (in thousands)	% Return on Sales
Affiliated	$ 206,464	$ 12,852	6.2%
Capital Cities	472,108	73,213	15.5
Dow Jones	530,700	58,883	11.1
Gannett	1,214,983	151,985	12.5
Harte-Hanks	303,664	22,697	7.5
Knight-Ridder	1,098,537	92,858	8.4
Lee	136,958	20,050	14.6
Media General	332,460	28,293	8.5
Multimedia	163,563	21,618	13.2
New York Times	733,237	40,609	5.5
Thomson[1]	522,160	68,153	13.1
Times Mirror[2]	1,857,349	139,217	7.5
Washington Post	659,535	34,335	5.2
Median Return on Sales			8.5%
Fortune 500 Median			4.8%

[1] In Canadian dollars (exchange rate used was $.82 per U.S. dollar, July 24,1981).

[2] Does not include $11.5 million of "other income."

Sources: Company financial statements; Fortune 500 median calculated from information in *Fortune*, May 4, 1981.

Table 2.8: Median Return on Sales, Selected *Fortune 500* Industries, Plus Newspapers, 1980

Industry	Median Profit Margin
Mining, crude oil production	9.2%
Pharmaceuticals	9.1
Newspapers	8.5
Tobacco	7.9
Broadcasting; motion picture production and distribution	6.5
Printing and publishing	6.2
Office equipment (incl. computers)	6.0
Paper, fiber, wood products	5.0
Apparel	3.6
Food	3.0
Motor vehicles	2.6
All industries	4.8%

Sources: Compiled from *Fortune*, May 4, 1981; newspapers from Table 2.7.

four largest firms actually decreased. Table 2.9 indicates that newspaper publishing was less concentrated than its allied publishing industries.

COMPETITION AND GROUP OWNERSHIP

This section looks at the effects the lack of competition may have in one-newspaper cities and what the roles of various group owners may be. A "group" is generally defined as the ownership of two or more daily newspapers in different cities by a single firm or individual. Newspaper competition refers to separate ownership of two or more general interest daily newspapers in the same city. It will be seen, however, that "competition" may also be given a broader definition.

Background

In the heyday of multi-newspaper cities and many independent owners, newspapers were thin—even big city papers were often only eight pages in 1900.[4] Type was still hand-set until the Linotype came into widespread use at about the same time. Many daily newspapers were designed to appeal to a select group, and there was a newspaper that expressed the political views of seemingly every faction that sprang up. Newspapers did not really compete for the same audiences. Bennett wrote in his first issue of the *Herald* in 1835:

There are in this city at least 150,000 persons who glance over one

Table 2.9: Share of Total Dollar Shipments by Largest Firms in Publishing Industries, Selected Years, 1947-1977

Year	Newspapers	Periodicals	Book Publishing
1947			
4 largest companies	21%	34%	18%
8 largest	26	43	29
50 largest	N.A.	N.A.	N.A.
1958			
4 largest companies	17	31	16
8 largest	24	41	29
50 largest	51	69	69
1967			
4 largest companies	16	24	20
8 largest	25	37	32
50 largest	56	72	77
1972			
4 largest companies	17	26	19
8 largest	28	38	31
50 largest	60	69	77
1977			
4 largest companies	19	22	17
8 largest	31	35	30
50 largest	62	67	74

N.A.: Not available.
Source: U.S. Bureau of Census, Census of Manufactures, *Concentration Ratios in Manufacturing.*

or more newspapers every day and only 42,000 daily sheets are issued to supply them. We have plenty of room, therefore, without jostling neighbors, rivals, or friends, to pick up at least 20,000 or 30,000 for the *Herald,* and leave something for those who come after us.[5]

Today, a newspaper in a multi-newspaper territory can grow primarily only by taking a subscriber from another newspaper. In the 1880s, the cost of newer, faster presses and Linotypes, and the demands of the new advertisers for circulation, brought about economies of scale which demanded a newspaper sold at a low price to a mass audience. The cost of entry increased as well. Increased specialization required by the technology of 1900 reduced the extent to which newspapers could depend on job printing during off hours as a means of subsidizing competing newspapers.[6]

Improved transportation made it possible for a single paper to distribute to a larger territory, and the telephone and telegraph also aided the same papers in covering the further away suburbs. Advertisers could also depend on customers patronizing their stores from a broader area and could therefore make use of the broadened circulation. Other trends during the beginning of the twentieth century include:[7]

1) A decline in the political partnership which had demanded that each group have a newspaper representing its view resulted in a need for fewer newspapers.

2) Advertisers found it cheaper to buy space in one general circulation newspaper than in several with overlapping circulation.

3) The Associated Press' rules for new memberships, providing exclusive territorial franchises, made acquisition of a newspaper with membership the easiest way for a nonmember in the same market to join.

Radio, then television, made inroads into newspaper functions. Perhaps the most significant factor is that despite increasing competition from newer media, newspapers have remained an important mass medium.

That interest in the printed format of the newspaper remains firm is illustrated by the makeup of those companies who purchased a newspaper in 1980: of the 52 transactions involving dailies, in 48 cases the buyer owned at least two other newspapers. These purchases continued the trend toward group ownership of newspapers and away from the independent, locally owned paper.[8] In 1923, for example, there were 31 newspaper groups that owned a total of 153 newspapers—or about 7% of all dailies. By 1954 the number of chains had tripled to 95. By 1978, 167 groups published an aggregate of 1098 newspapers, accounting for 62% of the total number of dailies. In 1980, there had been a drop in the number of groups, to 154, reflecting some consolidation of small groups into larger ones.

As newspaper groups have grown, competition among newspapers within cities has diminished. Table 2.10 follows the steady decline in the number of cities with competing papers. In 1923, 502 cities had two or more directly competing newspapers. By 1981, only 30 cities, or 2% of all cities, had head to head newspaper competition. Yet, the fact that more cities had their own daily paper in 1981 than in previous decades indicates that the publishers are following the population to the suburbs. In effect, newspapers are being *decentralized*.

Table 2.11 identifies the cities with competitive newspapers. In addition to the 30 cities that have newspapers under separate ownership, another 23 cities have newspapers that operate under the agency shop provision of the

Table 2.10: Number of Cities with Daily Newspapers and Number of Cities with Competing Daily Newspapers, Selected Years, 1923-1981

Year	Number of Cities with Daily Papers	Cities with Two or More Dailies[1]	% of Total Cities with Two or More Dailies
1923	1,297	502	38.7%
1933	1,426	243	17.0
1943	1,416	137	9.7
1953	1,453	91	6.3
1963	1,476	51	3.5
1973	1,519	37	2.4
1978	1,536	35	2.3
1981[2]	1,534	30	2.0

[1] Under separate ownership.

[2] Current to November 1981.

Sources: 1923-1973: James Rosse, Bruce M. Owen, and James Dertouzos, "Trends in the Daily Newspaper Industry, 1923-1973," Studies in Industry Economics, No. 57, Dept. of Economics, Stanford University, p. 30, Table 9. 1978 and 1981: compiled from 1978 and 1981 *Editor & Publisher International Year Book*, 1981, 1979.

Newspaper Preservation Act (see pp. 67-69). In these cities, a single firm handles all business and production for the two papers. Separate firms own and manage the papers themselves, presumably guaranteeing editorial independence.

Thus, there are actually two related trends in the area of newspaper ownership: 1) the apparently increased concentration of ownership, and 2) the decrease in intracity newspaper competition.

CONCENTRATION OF OWNERSHIP

Concentration of ownership is not a recent trend in the United States newspaper business. According to Table 2.12, the largest 25% of newspaper firms actually accounted for a lower percentage of daily circulation in 1978 than in 1923. A similar breakdown of the largest 10% and 1% of firms shows a parallel decline.[9]

Moreover, in comparison to other developed countries, concentration of ownership in the United States is relatively diverse. Nixon and Hahn found that the 20 largest newspaper firms controlled 43% of circulation in this country. Next closest was Spain, with 54.9%. Canada had 88.5% in this top group and Ireland 100%.*[10]

---

*With the exception of Canada, however, these countries have a national press, where the largest papers compete head to head.

Table 2.11: Cities with Competing Newspapers, 1981

Competitive Newspaper Cities	Agency Shop Cities
Anchorage, Alaska	Birmingham, Alabama
Little Rock, Arkansas	Tucson, Arizona
Los Angeles, California	San Francisco, California
Sacramento, California	Miami, Florida
Colorado Springs, Colorado	Honolulu, Hawaii
Denver, Colorado	Fort Wayne, Indiana
Manchester, Connecticut	Evansville, Indiana
Chicago, Illinois	Shreveport, Louisiana
Slidell, Louisiana	St. Louis, Missouri
Baltimore, Maryland	Lincoln, Nebraska
Boston, Massachusetts	Albuquerque, New Mexico
Detroit, Michigan	Cincinnati, Ohio
Columbia, Missouri	Columbus, Ohio
Fulton, Missouri	Tulsa, Oklahoma
Las Vegas, Nevada	Pittsburgh, Pennsylvania
Trenton, New Jersey	Chattanooga, Tennessee
Buffalo, New York	Knoxville, Tennessee
New York, New York	Nashville, Tennessee
Cleveland, Ohio	El Paso, Texas
Philadelphia, Pennsylvania[1]	Salt Lake City, Utah
Scranton, Pennsylvania	Charleston, West Virginia
York, Pennsylvania	Madison, Wisconsin
Cookeville, Tennessee	Spokane, Washington
Austin, Texas	
Dallas, Texas	
Houston, Texas	
San Antonio, Texas	
Seattle, Washington[2]	
Green Bay, Wisconsin	

[1] The *Philadelphia Bulletin* closed down in January 1982, making Philadelphia a non-competitive city.

[2] Application for agency shop pending before Justice Department, November 1981.
Source: *Editor & Publisher International Year Book*, 1981, plus additional reports.

The desire to own groups of newspapers—for whatever reasons—has long been compelling. E.W. Scripps started his chain in the 1880s. By 1900, there were eight major chains, including Scripps-McCrae, Booth, Hearst, Pulitzer and the Ochs papers. In 1908, Frank Munsey's assessment of the newspaper glut was:

There is no business that cries so loud for organization and combination as that of newspaper publishing. The waste under

Table 2.12: Percentage of Total Daily Circulation Accounted for by Smallest 25% and Largest 25%, 10% and 1% of Newspaper Firms, Selected Years, 1923-1978

Year	Smallest 25%	Largest 25%	Largest 10%	Largest 1%
1923	2.2%	82.5%	64.9%	22.6%
1933	2.2	84.2	67.4	23.2
1943	2.2	84.3	66.6	22.4
1953	2.3	83.6	66.6	21.0
1963	2.4	83.0	65.7	22.1
1973	2.8	80.4	66.3	20.6
1978	3.0	78.9	61.3	19.8

Source: Rosse, et al., "Trends in the Daily Newspaper Industry 1923-1973," p. 28. 1978 data added by author.

Table 2.13: Number of Newspaper Groups and Dailies They Control, Selected Years, 1910-1980

Year	No. of Groups	No. of Dailies	Average Size of Group (number of papers)	% of Total Dailies Group-Owned	% of Daily Circulation of Group-Owned Dailies
1910	13	62	4.7	—	—
1923	31	153	4.9	7.5%	—
1930	55	311	5.6	16.0	43.4%
1933	63	361	5.7	18.9	—
1935	59	329	5.6	16.9	—
1940	60	319	5.3	17.0	—
1945	76	368	4.8	21.0	42.0
1953[1]	95	485	5.1	27.0	45.3
1960	109	552	5.1	31.3	46.1
1966	156	794	5.1	46.7	57.0
1970	157	879	5.6	50.3	63.0
1977	167	1,047	6.3	59.4	71.4
1978	167	1,095	6.5	62.5	72.2
1980	154	1,139	7.4	65.3	72.9

[1] Before 1954, number of dailies may be overstated because morning and evening editions of some papers were counted as separate papers.

Sources: 1910-1970: "Number of Dailies in Groups Increased by 11% in 3 Years," *Editor & Publisher*, Feb. 23, 1974, p. 9.

1977: "167 Groups Own 1,047 Dailies: 71% of Total Circulation," *Editor & Publisher*, July 9, 1977, p. 10.

1978: "Half of Daily Circulation in 20 Newspaper Groups," *Editor & Publisher*, Sept. 16, 1978, p. 21. Current to Sept. 1, 1978.

1981: Calculated from *Editor & Publisher International Year Book*, pp. I-357-I-363.

existing conditions is frightful and the results miserably less than they could be made.[11]

Although the data in Table 2.13 clearly show a steady increase in the number of group owners and the number of dailies they control, no chain in 1980 held the potential impact in total circulation as did Hearst at its circulation peak in 1946. In that year, its newspapers had a combined circulation of 5.3 million, or 10.4% of total daily circulation. In 1980, the largest chain, Gannett Co., had a circulation of only 3.6 million, accounting for 5.7% of all daily circulation. The group of selected chains in Table 2.14 accounted for 20.4% of daily circulation in 1946 and 20.9% 34 years later.

Much of the activity of these groups over the years has involved swapping properties. As some chains have grown, others have shrunk or disappeared. The Hearst chain has either bought or established 42 dailies, merging some, selling others, suspending several. In 1940 there were 17 Hearst papers, leading all chains in combined circulation.[12] By 1980, there were only 13 Hearst newspapers, eighth in total circulation. At one time, Frank Munsey had six newspapers in New York, Washington, Baltimore and Philadelphia. They were all merged, sold or suspended.[13] The trend in groups since the end of World War II has been upward.

The term "group" as popularly defined is somewhat misleading. The tabulation in Table 2.15 shows that more than half of the so-called chains consist of four or fewer newspapers—and usually small ones at that. At the other extreme, there are 26 firms that own 10 or more newspapers. Among them they own 629 newspapers, or an average of about 24 newspapers each. The median number of papers owned by the total of 154 groups is 9, compared to an average of 7.4.

Table 2.14: Newspaper Circulation by Selected Group Owners, 1946, 1966, 1978 and 1980

Group	1946	1966	1978	1980
Gannett	1.2%	1.9%	5.5%	5.7%
Knight-Ridder	3.4	4.0	6.1	5.6
Hearst	10.4	4.4	3.0	2.1
Scripps-Howard	4.4	4.8	3.3	2.4
Newhouse	1.0	5.0	5.3	5.1
Total	20.4%	20.1%	23.2%	20.9%

Sources: *Editor & Publisher International Year Book*, 1947, 1967; A.B.C. audited circulation, Sept. 30, 1978; John Morton Newspaper Research, as reported by The American Newspaper Publishers Association, "Facts About Newspapers, 1981."

Table 2.15: Distribution by Number of Newspapers in Groups, 1980

Number of Newspapers Under Common Ownership	Number of Groups	Number of Newspapers in Category	Cumulative % of All Group-owned Newspapers
2	40	80	7.0%
3	28	84	14.4
4	19	76	21.1
5	14	70	27.2
6	9	54	32.0
7	6	42	35.6
8	6	48	40.0
9	6	56	44.8
10	3	30	47.4
11–15	4	52	52.0
16–20	8	142	64.4
21–25	3	64	68.3
26 +	8	341	100.0%
Total	154	1,139	

Average size: 7.4

Median size: 9

Source: Calculated from *Editor & Publisher International Year Book,* 1981.

Rank by Circulation

The ten largest groups, ranked by circulation in Table 2.16, accounted for just under 37% of all daily circulation in 1980. This was down from the 39% the ten held in 1978, but still above the 32% of circulation such a ranking accounted for in 1971. Gannett Co. has a slight edge over Knight-Ridder for the distinction as the group with the largest circulation. But its papers are much smaller, with an average circulation of about 44,000 compared to 103,000 for Knight-Ridder. Newhouse is the largest of the privately owned companies. Tribune Co., publisher of both the *New York Daily News* and the *Chicago Tribune,* has the largest average size per daily, 357,000.

Rank by Number of Daily Papers

Gannett Co. is also the largest as measured by number of papers owned, with 81 newspapers in 1980.* Thomson Newspapers, Ltd., a Canadian

---

*By the end of 1981 this had grown to 85 dailies, including the Spanish-language *El Diario,* which is not counted in a tabulation of general interest dailies. Gannett had also issued a prototype of a national daily scheduled for a start-up in 1982, using satellite transmission of facsimile pages to printing plants around the U.S.

Table 2.16: Ten Largest Newspaper Publishing Firms by Circulation, 1980[1]

Rank	Firm	Daily Circulation[2] (in thousands)	Number of Daily Newspapers
1.	Gannett Co., Inc.	3,563	81
2.	Knight-Ridder Newspapers[3]	3,493	33
3.	Newhouse	3,167	28
4.	Tribune Co.	2,854	8
5.	Dow Jones & Co., Inc.	2,339	21
6.	Times Mirror Co.	2,316	8
7.	E.W. Scripps Co.	1,515	15
8.	Hearst	1,321	13
9.	Cox Enterprises, Inc.[3]	1,195	19
10.	The New York Times Co.	1,108	12
	Total	22,871	238
	% of total daily circulation	36.8%	
	% of all daily newspapers		13.6%

[1] These are followed by Thomson Newspaper (U.S.), Cowles Newspapers, Capital Cities Communications, Inc. and News America Publishing, Inc.

[2] Includes papers owned December 31, 1980.

[3] Does not include two papers in which Knight-Ridder has 49.5% voting stock; and two papers in which Cox has 47% ownership.

Source: Audit Bureau of Circulation, six months ending Sept. 30, 1981.

firm that is in turn part of the Thomson Organisation conglomerate, was the second largest, with 67 newspapers, virtually all in small towns.

The 15 largest firms are listed in Table 2.17. In sum, they account for 10% of the total number of chains and own 27% of the total number of daily newspapers.

Effects of Concentration

There is a difference of opinion between those who would agree with Munsey that concentration of ownership may improve newspapers, and those who believe that chain ownership results in fewer editorial "voices," hence more homogeneous newspapers and a general reduction in quality. This viewpoint was expressed by Villard, who wrote:

> It cannot be maintained that the chain development is a healthy one from the point of view of the general public. Any tendency which makes toward restriction, standardization, or concentrating of editorial power in one hand is to be watched with concern.[14]

Table 2.17: Largest Newspaper Groups, by Number of Daily Newspapers in Group, 1980

Rank	Firm	Number of Daily Newspapers
1.	Gannett Co., Inc.	81
2.	Thomson	67
3.	Donrey Media	39
4.	Knight-Ridder	33
4.	Walls Newspapers[1]	33
6.	Freedom Newspapers	31
7.	Harte-Hanks Communications	29
8.	Newhouse	28
9.	Dow Jones	21
9.	Scripps League Newspapers	21
11.	Worrell Newspapers	20
12.	Stauffers Communications	19
12.	Cox Enterprises	19
14.	Lee Enterprises	18
	Total	459
	% of total newspapers	26.3%

[1] Includes 27 Walls Newspapers plus six owned by Jefferson-Pilot, of which Mr. Walls is a stockholder and chairman of the board.
Sources: *Editor & Publisher International Year Book*, 1981, plus newspaper, trade journal and corporate reports of acquisitions and sales.

The conflict may be made more real by reviewing an exchange of opinions in the *Columbia Journalism Review,* involving the purchase of the *Honolulu Star-Bulletin* by Gannett. An evaluation of the changes made at that paper after Gannett came in noted that two reporters, including the Washington correspondent, were fired; 12 columns, such as the surfing column and a "Nautical Notes" feature, were eliminated, as were two comic strips; the Copley News Service was canceled; a final edition was canceled, moving up the final deadline 75 minutes; 30 printers lost their regular positions and were put on a "daily basis"; three engravers were laid off and overtime was eliminated.[15] Gannett brought in a new publisher who told reporters that the cuts were needed for economic reasons and that the Honolulu paper was fourth from the bottom in year-to-year revenue improvement in the Gannett chain.[16]

In a response to this criticism, the managing editor of the *Huntington* (WV) *Advertiser* (which became a Gannett paper as part of the 1971 deal with Honolulu) wrote that the same type of things happened when the *Star-Bulletin,* an independent paper, bought the *Advertiser*. But he claims that when Gannett took over, virtually every member of the news staff got a raise, lingering union problems were settled with three years back pay, and the dingy newsroom was renovated; reporters were given a voice in policy-making and choosing their own editor; there was greater editorial freedom for columnists and reporters, and ad salesmen were given commissions as well as salary. The Huntington papers were encouraged to do investigative reporting, even to the extent of damaging previously "untouchable" community leaders. The editor wrote that the paper is opening up communication channels with the community and providing more leadership.[17]

Whether or not group ownership improves or degrades a newspaper depends on the criteria that are established for making such judgments, the state of the newspaper when the new owner arrives and, more importantly, which chain is doing the buying. Many will agree that the Knight-Ridder organization has dramatically improved the editorial quality of the *Philadelphia Inquirer* and *Daily News* since purchasing them from independent owner Walter Annenberg. Gannett, as just seen, has a more mixed reputation, but generally gets high marks for the quality of its business and editorial personnel.[18] The first priority of the Ottaway newspapers is "to improve news content, editorial quality and public service—to reach high standards of excellence. . . ."[19]

On the other hand, the newspapers owned by the Thomson group are frequently criticized. Its late founder, Lord Thomson, once compared newspapers (and television stations) to a license to print money. His creed was to get the most work for the least pay.[20] There is one Thomson paper that is reportedly earning a 45% pretax profit. "You can't make money like that and still turn out a good paper," warns a West Coast publisher.[21]

To be sure, single newspaper ownership is no guarantee of integrity or quality. Annenberg, when he owned the *Inquirer*, and William Loeb, the late publisher of the *Manchester Union Leader*, are examples of controversial owners of single papers. Peter Nichols, referring to Loeb's use of his newspaper to further his personal causes, wrote of the publisher's "florid, virulent style" in attacking those he opposes in his papers.[22]

Summing up the argument for group ownership, John C. Quinn, senior vice president for news for Gannett, notes that while each local newspaper can be tailored to the needs of the local market, it is also part of an organization large enough to have its own national news organization —such as the Gannett News Service, which includes a large Washington, DC bureau. Quinn also points out that of the 35 Gannett newspaper editorial boards that endorsed a presidential candidate in the 1976 election, 22 favored Ford and 13 Carter, implying the local autonomy of each newspaper.[23]

Addressing an International Press Institute conference in 1972, Quinn explained:

Newspaper concentration may multiply the anxiety over evil; it also increases the capacity for good. And a publisher's instinct for good or evil is not determined by the number of newspapers he owns. A group can attract top professional talent, offering training under a variety of editors, advancement through a variety of opportunitites. . . . It can invest in research and development and nuts and bolts experience necessary to translate the theories of new technology into the practical production of better newspapers.

Concentrated ownership can provide great resources; only independent, local judgment can use the resources to produce a responsible and responsive local newspaper. That measure cannot be inflated by competition nor can it be diluted by monopoly.[24]

What Quinn says is not in error. Nor, however, does it prove his case, for it echos a standard argument to support concentration of business in general. The real argument hangs on the goodwill of the people in control. And whereas under individual or small group ownership a "bad" publisher has a limited capacity for poor service, a chain that is prone to milking its properties or throwing around its influence can infect numerous localities with poor or destructive journalism.

The potential danger of group ownership lies in the concentration of financial, political and social power in relatively few people.

The four largest chains—Knight-Ridder, Newhouse, Tribune Co. and Gannett—have 21% of daily circulation among them. Of these, the Newhouse chain probably has the weakest reputation for editorial commitment. They "chop budgets and staff, hold investment to a minimum, and wring the paper dry of profits," reported one analyst.[25]

Relatively little empirical research has been done on the effects of chain ownership alone. One study, however, did find evidence that, contrary to the assertions of editorial independence on the part of chain owners, "chain papers were more likely to support the favored candidate of the press in every election."[26] More crucial, however, was the finding that in endorsing presidential candidates in the elections of 1960 through 1972, inclusive, non-chain papers were *less likely* to endorse *any* presidential candidate and that the "vast majority of chains exhibited homogeneous endorsement patterns," that is 85% or more of the papers endorsed the same candidate.[27] The study did add, however, that chains spread out over several regions were "consistently less homogeneous in each of the elections,"[28] indicating that the small, personally managed regional chains tend toward tighter editorial control than the more visible national groups.

Some examples of chain owners exerting their unified influence on editorial policy included William Randolph Hearst Jr.'s demand that his papers support the Johnson-Humphrey ticket in 1964 (though he let each paper make its own decision in 1968 and they split 8-5 in favor of Nixon-Agnew). In 1972, James M. Cox required his nine newspapers, including the *Atlanta Journal* and *Constitution,* to endorse the Nixon ticket.[29]

In a somewhat broader study of both competition and concentration of ownership, it was found that in the aggregate "there was no evidence that consumers received any benefits from concentration of ownership through chain acquisition of a daily newspaper," at least of those papers which went from independent to chain during the course of the study.[30]

In 1978, a study that set out to test the degree of direct, centralized control of news among group-owned papers found no such characteristics.[31] Thus, one fear expressed by critics of chain ownership, that "what the public reads is directed from afar by autocratic owners"[32] was found to have no trace of validity. However, the study did turn up a distinct pattern of editorial behavior that did differentiate group-owned from comparable independent newspapers. It found that in national, international, state and local news, the independent newspapers consistently had more stories, longer articles and a greater number of staff-written pieces than in the group-owned papers. The independent papers also had more news. These trends held true for the papers owned by such prestige publishers as The New York Times Co. and Dow Jones Co. At the same time, the study did show that both group and independent papers had about the same proportion of national and international stories from the news services, such as the Associated Press. However, the study did not attempt to measure quality of the editorial material.

Why the Chains Keep Buying

There are several reasons why independent newspapers are selling out and chain owners are interested in buying more.

Profit

Newspapers can be a profitable investment. The median profit for the publicly held newspaper groups in 1980 was about twice that of the largest publicly owned manufacturing businesses.

Scarce Commodity

Newspaper properties are attractive because they are a scarce commodity. With a finite market of good, potentially profitable properties, competition to buy them is strong. "Brokers keep calling me on the phone and asking, 'Well, are you ready?' " reported the publisher of the *Washington* (PA) *Observer Reporter*.[33] The alternative of starting a new paper of any size is not attractive. There just are not that many areas that can support a paper that do not already have one. In the 1960s Cowles Communications spent three years trying to establish the *Suffolk Sun* in competition with *Newsday* on Long Island and eventually gave up.

Professional Management

As profitable as newspapers can be, under the professional management of chains they can be even more so. The objective of a family-owned business is often different from one that is publicly owned or professionally managed. Minimizing taxes and maximizing cash, rather than earnings per share or return on investment, may be the objective of private owners.[34] When the new technology began paying handsome returns in labor savings, groups were encouraged to pay high multiples on a family-owned newspaper, expecting to increase profits very rapidly through production savings and other cost controls.

As a case in point, a newspaper broker tells of a deal in which a South Carolina newspaper changed hands for 60 times its earnings, but the new owner doubled earnings in the first year and after two years had increased profit to the point where he had paid an effective 20 times earnings for the property.[35] Robert Marbut, president of Harte-Hanks Communications, says he would pay "100 times earnings for a newspaper which wasn't making any money," if he thought it had the potential, under new management, to become a profit-maker.

Earnings can also be increased by bringing in professional managers and using the sophisticated business and financial services many of the chains make available. The Gannett group has a marketing team which is sent to any local paper in the chain to provide in-house consulting to find ways to boost circulation and advertising. One analyst explained why this makes a difference:

> I think the motivation of the earlier newspaper groups was essentially to be important people in the cities in which their operations were located. This orientation made them somewhat reluctant to be aggressive in pricing, advertising and circulation rates. The new managers have no such relationships.[36]

The synergy of group management can be illustrated in the unique nature of Gannett's Westchester-Rockland Newspaper group. A plant in

White Plains, NY prints nine of the dailies in the group, including three zoned editions of one of the papers. The papers, primarily afternoon editions, range in circulation from 5,000 to 50,000. The papers have some separate editorial staff, but share a common building and production equipment and can afford technology that would be prohibitive to any one of the papers alone. Moreover, certain common features and advertising inserts are combined with local news and advertising, enabling each paper to be something more than it might be otherwise. It has what might be termed a "critical mass" needed for certain newspaper economies.

Cash

Newspaper chains tend to generate large amounts of cash, not only from profits but from depreciation and amortization of goodwill. They also carry low debt in relation to invested capital and compared to other businesses. Harte-Hanks, which had a net profit of $22.7 million in 1980, generated an additional $13 million in cash through depreciation and amortization.[37] In addition, tax laws allow firms to accumulate undistributed profits to buy other communications properties, and as such are exempt from tax provisions on excess accumulated profits. This encourages further acquisition.

On the other hand, there exists little convincing evidence that being part of a group provides any advantage in gaining advertising. Most newspaper advertising is derived from local sources and the small amount of national advertising comes mostly through advertising agencies.[38] Similarly, few chains provide economies in purchasing supplies, and even labor negotiations tend to take place at the local level.

Table 2.18 lists some acquisitions and, where available, the price paid.

Strategies for Growth in Chains

Over the years, newspaper firms have followed diverse strategies for growth. They all recognize to varying degrees, however, that sizable gains can come about only through acquisition. This is due to the mature nature of the newspaper industry. Internal profit growth from circulation and advertising gains is slow. The savings from the electronic production technology of the 1970s was a welcome, but one-shot phenomenon. Other than a common recognition of the need for some sort of outside growth, chains have evolved several distinct approaches.

Figure 2.1 uses the information industry map to illustrate the range of acquisition strategies. Besides acquiring other newspapers, some publishers, such as Dow Jones Co., The Washington Post Co., Times Mir-

Figure 2.1: Newspaper Diversification

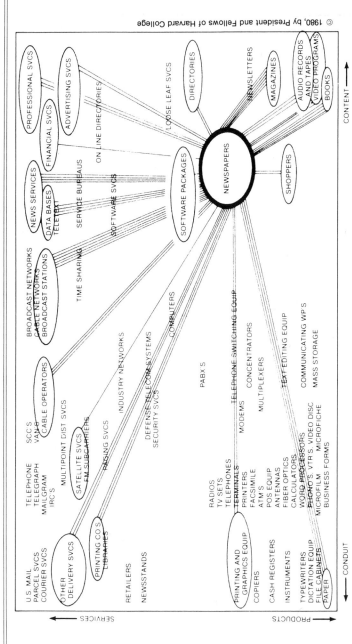

Each line indicates entry into a particular field by one of the seven newspaper publishers: Dow Jones & Co., Gannett Co., Harte-Hanks Communications, Lee Enterprises, New York Times Co., The Times Mirror Co. and The Washington Post Co.

Source: John F. McLaughlin and Anne E. Birinyi, *Mapping the Information Business* (Cambridge, MA: Program on Information Resources Policy, Harvard University, 1980), p. 33. Reprinted with permission.

Table 2.18: A Sampling of Mergers and Acquisitions in the Daily
Newspaper Industry

Purchaser	Property Purchased	Year	Price
Harte-Hanks	Wichita Falls (TX) Record-News & Times (52,000 daily)	1976	$15 million (for remaining 72% share)
Knight	Ridder Newspapers (17 daily)	1973	$174 million
Knight-Ridder	Fort Wayne (IN) News Sentinel (73,000 daily)	1980	$36 million
Capital Cities	Kansas City (MO) Star & Times (626,000 combined daily, 396,000 Sunday)	1977	$125 million
	Wilkes-Barre (PA) Times Leader (70,000 daily)	1978	$9 million
Lee Newspapers	Kansas City (KS) Kansan* (25,000 daily, 26,000 Sunday)	1976	$2 million
	Bismarck (ND) Tribune (25,500 daily)	1978	$4.8 million for 53% interest
	Lindsay-Schaub Newspapers (130,000 combined circulation) Decatur (IL) Herald & Review Carbondale (IL) Southern Illinoisian Midland (MI) Daily News* Edwardsville (IL) Intelligencer* Huron Daily Tribune (Bad Axe, MI)*	1979	$60.4 million
Donrey Media Group	Cleburne (TX) Times-Review (9000 daily, Sunday)	1976	N.A.
	Borger (TX) News-Herald (7500 daily)	1978	N.A.
	Vallejo (CA) Times Herald (30,000 daily, Sunday)	1976	N.A.
	Oskaloosa (IA) Herald	1980	N.A.
Newhouse	Booth Newspapers	1976	$300 million
Gannett	The New Mexican (Santa Fe, NM) (18,000 daily, 21,000 Sunday)	1976	300,000 shares of stock
	Valley News Dispatch (PA) (44,000 daily)	1976	$9.3 million
	Shreveport (LA) Times (146,000 daily) Monroe (LA) News-Star World (50,000 daily) + broadcast affiliates	1976	$62 million
	Speidel Newspapers	1976/1977	$170 million
	Combined Communications*	1978/1979	approximately $320 million in stock

Table 2.18 (continued)

Purchaser	Property Purchased	Year	Price
	Wilmington (DE) *News* and *Journal* (140,000 daily)	1978	$60 million
	El Diario (NY) (61,000 daily)	1981	$9 million
	Nashville Tennessean (130,000 daily)	1979	$50 million
Combined Communications (acquired by Gannett in 1979)	*Cincinnati Enquirer* (190,000 daily, 290,000 Sunday)	1975	$55 million
	Oakland (CA) *Tribune* (176,000 daily, 290,000 Sunday)	1977	$13.9 million (plus $2.8 million for Tribune Bldg.)
Rupert Murdoch	*San Antonio* (TX) *Express-News* (149,000 combined daily, 130,000 Sunday)	1974	$18 million
	New York Post (489,000 daily)	1976	$27-$30 million
Dow Jones (Ottaway Group)	*Joplin* (MO) *Globe* (40,000 daily)	1976	$12.2 million
	Essex Newspapers *Beverly* (MA) *Times* *Gloucester* (MA) *Times* (12,000 daily) *Newburyport* (MA) *News* (9,000 daily) *Peabody* (MA) *Times* (4,000 daily)	1978	$10 million
New York Times Co.	*Houma* (LA) *Daily Courier* (19,000 daily)	1980	$33 million including weekly paper and WHNT-TV, Huntsville, Alabama
	Thibodaus (LA) *Comet* (12,000 daily)	1980	
Hearst	*Midland* (TX) *Reporter-Telegram* (20,000 daily)	1978	N.A.
	Plainview (TX) *Herald* (9000 daily)	1978	N.A.
Times Mirror	*Hartford* (CT) *Courant* *Denver* (CO) *Post* (267,000 daily)	1979 1980	$105.6 million $85 million (present value)

* Sold in 1980.

Sources: *Editor & Publisher*, compilation of papers and acquisitions, January 3, 1981, January 6, 1979, January 1, 1978, December 27, 1975, December 28, 1974, plus publicly-owned company annual reports and press releases.

ror Co. and The New York Times Co. have made sizable investments in newsprint manufacturing. Almost all newspaper publishers have broadcasting properties, with the notable exception of Dow Jones Co., which made a policy of avoiding a business that required considerable government regulation. Gannett, however, concentrated very much on newspaper properties until it merged with Combined Communications in 1979. That deal brought with it a full stable of broadcasting properties. Knight-Ridder has a major broadcasting division, as do The Washington Post Co., Harte-Hanks Communications, E.W. Scripps and Cox.

A few newspaper publishers have made incursions into the allied print forms of magazine or book publishing. Times Mirror Co. has a small division that owns magazines such as *Popular Science, Outdoor Life* and *The Sporting News*. The New York Times Co. publishes *Family Circle, Tennis* and *Golf Digest*. Newhouse and Hearst both have major magazine divisions. Some newspaper publishers have been successful in book publishing, although The New York Times Co. tried and failed to establish a major trade operation. Hearst's Avon Books is a major mass market paperback publisher and Times Mirror Co. has a sizable book publishing component. Dow Jones owns Richard D. Irwin, a textbook publisher. Newhouse purchased Random House from RCA in 1980 for about $65 million.

The importance of such operations in relation to total company revenues varies considerably for the major newspaper publishers. As seen in Table 2.19, Dow Jones derived 93% of its revenue in 1980 from newspaper publishing (up from 91% in 1978). But Gannett decreased its reliance on newspaper revenue from 97% in 1978 to 77% by 1980. The Washington Post Co., on the other hand, depends on its newspapers for under half its revenue, as do Media General and Harte-Hanks. Capital Cities Communications, which has a nearly full complement of allowable broadcast properties, expanded more into print between 1978 and 1980, moving from 42% in 1978 to 65% of total revenue coming from newspaper properties in 1980.

Acquisition of Cable Systems

Newspaper firms had to make a major strategic investment decision in the late 1970s and early 1980s, i.e., whether and to what extent to expand into cable system operations. The Times Mirror Co., among those firms that are predominantly newspaper publishers, has the greatest stake in cable. Many publishers did start to buy into cable, though often as much from fear (of a potential competitor) than from a sense of new opportunity. In 1980 The New York Times Co. spent about $90 million to buy a small group of systems in New Jersey. The Tribune Co. and Harte-Hanks

Table 2.19: Interests of Major Newspaper Firms and Revenues from Various Sources, 1980

Rank (by Revenues)	Firm	Revenues (in millions)	% from News-papers	% from Broadcast & Cable	% from Other Media	% from Other Sources	Number of Daily Papers
1.	Times Mirror	$ 1,868.9	47%	8%	26%	19%	8
2.	Newhouse[1]	1,300.0	75	10	15	0	28
3.	Tribune Co.	1,230.0	67	23	0	10	8
4.	Gannett	1,215.0	77	10	10	3	81
5.	Hearst[1]	1,000.0	60	10	20	10	11
6.	Cox[1,2]	800.0	61	39	0	0	19
7.	New York Times	733.2	70	2	28	0	12
8.	Washington Post	659.5	47	41	12	0	12
9.	E.W. Scripps[1,3]	642.0	83	12	5	0	3
10.	Dow Jones Co.	530.7	93	0	7	0	15
11.	Capital Cities	472.1	65	35	0	0	2
12.	Media General	332.4	44	7	0	49	9
13.	Harte-Hanks	303.7	47	20	15	18	6
14.	Evening News Assn.	235.0	72	21	0	7	29
15.	Lee Enterprises	137.0	73	26	0	1	18

[1] Estimate. Includes only Hearst's media-related operations.

[2] Includes Cox Broadcasting, a publicly owned firm in which Cox family has 39% of common shares. 1980 revenue was $309 million.

[3] Includes Scripps-Howard Broadcasting, a separate publicly owned company in which E.W. Scripps has 74% of common shares. 1980 revenue was $77 million.

Sources: Corporate reports and, where noted, estimates.

each have relatively small multiple system operations. Newhouse paid an estimated $120 million to purchase Vision Cable Communication with its 150,000 subscribers in 1981. Altogether, Newhouse had about 500,000 subscribers, having made a policy decision to dispose of its broadcast television holdings in 1980 in favor of the rapidly expanding cable business. Dow Jones was one of the few firms to bid for a franchise to build. It won the right to wire Princeton, NJ, near its headquarters for electronic publishing and technology development. Its intention was to make the system a showcase for its technology. In late 1981 Dow Jones also purchased a 25% interest in Continental Cablevision, the 13th largest cable group. Dow Jones stated at the time that this was purely an investment and that it had no interest in purchasing a majority share. As Continental is a privately held firm, Dow Jones would have to negotiate a deal to purchase more stock.

The Dow Jones investment came after its failure to purchase UA-Columbia Cablevision, Inc. in a joint venture with Knight-Ridder. The two publishers had an agreement in principle to buy the stock in a transaction that would have cost them $247.5 million. UA-Columbia was the 11th largest cable company at the time. However, the acquisition was opposed by United Artists Theatre Circuit, Inc., a nationwide chain of movie theatres, which held 28% of the UA-Columbia stock. (The cable company was shortly thereafter sold to Rogers Cable Systems, the largest cable company in Canada.) Table 2.20 summarizes some of the larger holdings in cable systems by newspaper companies.

Why Independent Papers Keep Selling

For every purchase, there must be someone willing to sell. Privately held independent newspapers are being pressured to sell for several reasons.

Weak Management

Rising costs—including the investment in new technology, wages, newsprint and presses—call for strict controls and profit planning, which small independents cannot always get because they cannot afford the managerial types who can provide them. "The groups are corralling the bright young people and giving them publisher titles," explains one independent publisher.[39] Groups, on the other hand, can have specialists who can set up control systems for each paper, without any one having to be burdened by full development costs. Likewise, the chains can have production specialists to help in evaluating technology.

Table 2.20: Interests of Selected Major Newspaper Companies in Cable

Publisher	Cable Operations	Subscribers[1]
Cox	Cox Cable	1,056,863
Times Mirror Co.	Times Mirror Cable Television	625,000
Newhouse	New Channels Group, Vision Cable, Metrovision	500,000
Capital Cities Comm.	Cablecom General, Omnicon of Illinois, Omnicon of Michigan, Coastal Bend Cablevision, Satellite Cablevision	254,000
Landmark Communications	TeleCable Corp.	246,000
Tribune Co.	Tribune Co. Cable	85,000
The New York Times Co.	Audubon Electronics Inc.	70,000

[1] As of April 30, 1981, except Cox (Oct. 31, 1981).
Sources: *The New York Times*, June 25, 1981, p. D-1; *Broadcasting*, November 30, 1981, p. 37.

Family Squabbles

Some family managements are unprepared to deal with the realities of the "bottom line." Even at the relatively large *Oakland* (CA) *Tribune,* family problems led that paper to sell to Combined Communications in 1977. Both the father and grandfather of the publisher were former U.S. senators and "were interested in politics." With the paper to use as a power base, "business was secondary." Some family members involved in management in 1976 complained that the paper was being run "more for 'civic pride' than profit."[40] "The idea of a family-owned newspaper in the future is not probable," concludes the publisher of the family-owned *Louisville* (KY) *Courier-Journal.*[41]

In some cases, family members are just not interested in continuing the tradition. The family that owns the *Salisbury* (NC) *Post Independent* is in such a situation. The current publisher has no children. A brother has two older daughters, one of whom wants to live in the North Carolina mountains and raise a family. Another daughter finds a small (24,000 circulation) daily "boring." She would rather work for a paper like *The New York Times* or *Washington Post.*[42]

Inheritance Taxes

Another factor is the estate difficulty. A valuable newspaper property which is privately held is a taxable asset in the estate when the principal(s) die. The estate must pay the tax on the value of the property. If the estate is not well endowed with cash or other marketable securities to sell, the heirs may be forced to sell the newspaper to pay the taxes on it. The 1976 Tax Reform Act, which changed the method of determining the valuation of an asset in an estate, may have been an added factor in some 1976 sales. There was some speculation that Dorothy Schiff's sudden decision to sell the *New York Post* to Rupert Murdoch (for a reported $27 million) was because of the new law which might have put her heirs "in a less favorable inheritance-tax position."[43]

The owners of the *Salisbury Post Independent* are worried about their ability to pay inheritance tax on the 35% share owned by the firm's chairman. If the Internal Revenue Service figured tax on the 24,000-circulation daily's 1981 market value of about $20 million (instead of the asset value of about $3 million), "we wouldn't have the money to pay the taxes and we'd be out of business."[44] That is, the family members would likely have to sell to one of the many chains that has been courting them.

Tax Rates

Another aspect of the tax structure encourages selling. Income tax rates are as high as 70%, while tax on capital gains is less than half of that. By selling the newspaper in a cash transaction, the seller pays only the lower capital gains tax. If the exchange is for stock in the purchasing firm, then the swap is tax free, until the seller decides to sell the purchasing firm's stock. Moreover, in this case, the seller may then control a substantial block of the buyer's stock. The Booth chain, for example, though already publicly owned and a group owner itself, was still controlled by the Booth family. It was made vulnerable to an outside takeover when it exchanged 17% of its stock with Whitcom Investment Co. to purchase *Parade,* the national Sunday supplement magazine. When Whitcom offered this block of stock for sale several years later, Newhouse interests purchased it, giving Newhouse a wedge from which he finally bought total control of Booth in the largest newspaper cash deal up to that time.[45]

High Offering Prices

Perhaps most important most often, independent and small chain publishers are simply being overwhelmed with offers and money. Robert B.

Whittington, a vice president of the former Speidel chain, recalls feeling "like a virgin at a stag party" when hordes of publishers came wooing.[46] The *Valley News Dispatch* in Western Pennsylvania was sold to Gannett for $9.3 million, or $221 per subscriber. Gannett also bought the *Shreveport* (LA) *Times* (circ. 80,000), along with two smaller papers in Monroe, LA (combined circ. 51,000) for $61 million. When Newhouse bought Booth in 1976, the $47 per share offering price compared to a $23 a share the stock was selling for a year earlier and about $30 a share around a week before the Newhouse offer.

Such sums merely harden the attitude of some of the independent owners remaining. They are so tired of being courted that some have stopped attending publishers' conventions. One such publisher of several small papers deplores the concentration of ownership in a nationwide chain. According to the same *Business Week* article featuring Robert Whittington's comment, William Block, whose family controls the *Pittsburgh Post-Gazette,* feels that "some chain papers tend to be more cautious about controversy. You tend to play it safe when you don't own the paper yourself."

A working paper published by two Rand Corp. economists concluded that, under certain assumptions, by far the most compelling explanation for newspaper chains was the tax laws. Although they expected the Economic Recovery Act of 1981 to diminish these incentives, they recommended that tax laws be changed to further discourage such mergers.[47]

DECLINING COMPETITION AND THE "MONOPOLY" NEWSPAPER

Of more concern to some observers than the growth of chains *per se* is the decline of newspaper competition within individual markets. While 502 cities had two or more competing newspapers in 1923, including 100 cities with three or more papers, by 1980 that figure had decreased to 30 cities. And only two cities, New York and Philadelphia, had as many as three competing ownerships.

The 2% of U.S. cities, however, that had fully competing newspaper firms accounted for 22.8% of all daily newspapers sold. This was still a significant decline from 1923, when 88.8% of newspapers were sold in cities with multiple competing newspapers.

It should not be surprising that larger cities are more likely to be able to support competing newspaper firms. Even at the peak of newspaper competition, many smaller towns had only a single newspaper. Table 2.21 confirms that the circulations of competing papers are many times the size of those of monopoly newspapers.

Table 2.21: Mean Circulation of Competing and Non-Competing Newspapers, Selected Years, 1923-1980

Year	Mean Circulation of Papers with no Direct Competition	Mean Circulation of Papers with Competition
1923	4,308	22,869
1933	8,077	48,123
1943	12,334	89,079
1953	18,278	134,977
1963	23,779	203,638
1973	28,033	235,313
1978	23,330	215,524
1980	27,548	248,347

Sources: 1923-1978: James N. Rosse and James N. Dertouzos, "Economic Issues in Mass Communication Industries," paper submitted to Federal Trade Commission, Dec. 14-15, 1978, p. 57.
1980: Calcuated from circulation figures in *Editor & Publisher International Year Book, 1981*.

The issue in declining competition is whether it reduces the quality of the editorial product, lessens the diversity of opinions available to the reader, and results in a monopoly price structure for the advertisers and subscribers.

Effects on Economic Structure

An economic description of the newspaper industry is one that conforms to an economic pattern of imperfect competition: stabilization of prices for both advertising and circulation; price discrimination in charging different groups of advertisers or subscribers differing rates at the same time; and non-price competition.[48]

Economic analyses by Bruce Owen, James Rosse and Gerald Grotta have all made use of Chamberlin's concept of monopolistic competition to explain what Rosse calls the "isolate" structure of the newspaper industry.[49] Rosse prefers the term "isolate" because:

[A] typical member of the industry, alone in his city market, is isolated in the sense that cross-elasticities of demands for his products with respect to prices charged by other newspaper firms or by competing media are certainly finite and generally quite small.[50]

Thus, an isolated form is distinguished from a true monopoly in that not all demand cross-elasticities are zero. Rosse proceeds to document that economies of scale do indeed exist in newspaper publishing, helping to explain this isolate character. In essence he largely substantiates what is felt intuitively, that the cost of producing 100,000 copies of a newspaper is not 10 times that of producing 10,000 copies. Nor is the cost for one firm to produce and sell 100,000 copies of a newspaper each day twice that of two firms each publishing competing papers selling 50,000 each.

There are several areas where publishers of newspapers can effect economies of scale. Perhaps most significant is the "first copy" cost. There is a sizable fixed cost in editorial, typesetting, plate-making and other make-ready to produce the first issue off the press. Rosse indicates that for a small circulation daily, the first copy cost may be 40% of total revenue.[51] Clearly, the greater the number of newspapers which can then be printed (and sold), the lower the average cost per copy. Second, the cost of publishing additional pages declines as the number of pages increases at any constant level of circulation. This is true in part because the cost of running the press does not increase proportionally to the number of pages printed at the same time. Finally, the expense of distributing one newspaper in a given locale to a group of subscribers is less than several firms each covering that territory for the same number of total subscribers.

Advertisers also have an interest in the number of newspapers in their communities. Publishers derive 20% to 30% of revenue from circulation, which may not even cover the cost of the newsprint and ink used to print the paper. The bulk of newspaper revenue comes from advertisers, whose interest is in reaching an audience they believe consists of many potential customers. Publishers know that they can justify a higher charge to advertisers as their circulation increases. But because of the economies of scale just discussed, a single newspaper in a given location can typically offer an advertiser a lower rate than could competing papers reaching the same total market. This is recognized in part in the combination rates offered by a single publisher of morning and evening newspapers in a city. For example, in 1980 the Atlanta *Journal* and *Constitution,* under the same ownership, each had an open line rate of $2.34. But for an ad run in both papers, the advertiser paid $3.40.

This declining long-run average cost curve, however, is balanced by other factors that produce a practical limit on the extent to which a newspaper can expand. First, a large metropolitan daily faces rising transportation cost and other distribution expense, which may actually increase as circulation extends over a wider geographical area. This can be overcome somewhat, but at a cost in fixed plant, through suburban printing locations. The more limiting factor, preventing unlimited national expansion, is the highly localized demand of newspaper content. As the newspaper spreads out, it must become less complete in covering the local news of various communities and serving the need of local advertisers who are more concerned with agate line rates than overall milline rate.* It is this need to specialize in providing services for a geographically segmented audience and advertiser which ultimately offsets the economy of scale effects and determines the geographical extent of local newspaper monopoly.

"Umbrella Hypothesis"

What has resulted, then, is not *intra*city newspaper competition, but *inter*city competition, as developed by Rosse's "umbrella hypothesis."[52]

The model recognizes that while few cities have more than one daily newspaper, these newspapers nevertheless compete with other newspapers. That is, most regions of the country have a metropolitan newspaper whose circulation extends well beyond the central city, perhaps for hundreds of miles. The circulation falls off as the distance increases, but within this circulation area are "satellite cities," each with its own daily circulation that goes beyond its borders. Dailies in these level two cities may have circulation in smaller communities, which may in turn have their own local dailies. Even within the smaller community, there may be weekly newspapers, "shoppers" and other specialized media.

Figure 2.2 illustrates how each level throws an "umbrella" over the lower levels. Level one papers draw advertising from national and regional advertisers, as well as local in-city stores. They are also the most subject to competition from broadcast media, since they compete for the major national and international news as well as the advertising revenue. Newspapers at the second and third levels compete with each other only in the fringes of their natural markets, but they must compete with the papers above them and below them.

The second and third level newspapers are the ones that exist because of the needs of local readers and advertisers, which cannot be adequately fulfilled by the metropolitan daily. Even zoned editions of the big city papers cannot provide the complete coverage of local governments, school boards and sports teams, or the Main Street shopkeepers in the surrounding towns.

Moreover, it is metropolitan newspapers in particular that compete more than the smaller papers with the broadcast media. Local suburban newspapers, meanwhile, proliferate and absorb fringe area circulation. Thus, although newspapers may not have the head-to-head rivalries in the

---

*The agate line rate is the basis for the actual cost of advertising per line. The milline rate is a calculation used to compare the cost of advertising in newspapers of different circulation. It is the hypothetical cost of one line per million subscribers and is used similarly to the cost per thousand in magazines or broadcast advertising cost comparisons.

Figure 2.2: Rosse's "Umbrella" Model of Newspaper Competition

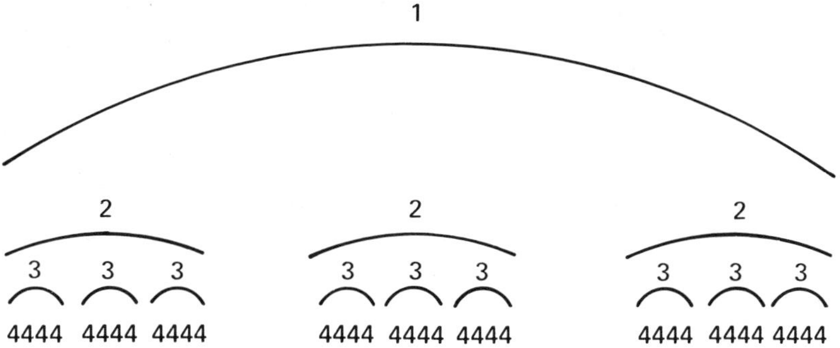

Key:
Level 1 — Newspaper in large metropolitan center
Level 2 — Newspapers in satellite cities
Level 3 — Local dailies
Level 4 — Weeklies and other specialized media

Source: James N. Rosse, "The Evolution of One Newspaper Cities," discussion paper
for the FTC Symposium on Media Concentration, pp. 50-52.

central cities as they did 75 years ago, they face more economic competition than the term "local monopoly" implies.

Clearly, the owner of a newspaper in the isolated market may still reap economic benefits, especially at the secondary and tertiary levels, where electronic media have less impact. In considering properties for acquisition, owners find that the choicest properties are the ones that have the immediate market to themselves, although Times Mirror Co.'s Otis Chandler may be overstating the case when he says these markets "give you a franchise to do what you want with profitability. You can engineer your profits. You can control expenses and generate revenues almost arbitrarily."[53]

Grotta, who agrees with Rosse's contention of economies of scale, proceeds to ask if the larger forms that result from this natural tendency toward combination and merger are "more efficient in practice,"[54] especially given the economic reality that "imperfect competition may result in wastage of resources, too high price, and yet no profits for the imperfect competitors."[55] "Have consumers of the industry's products [the advertising space for the advertiser and copies of the newspaper for the reader] received any of the potential benefit . . .?"[56]

Grotta found that "consumers receive no benefits from the assumed economies of scale" and that "consumers pay higher prices under monopoly with no compensating increase in quality or quantity of product."[57] John Langdon, however, found some conflicting evidence, at least concerning advertisers. Though concluding that "concentration of daily newspaper circulation in the hands of a single newspaper does appear to raise the general [national] and classified advertising rates to some extent," he tempers this by citing the lack of statistical results for retail advertising levels,[58] the area in which the consequences of monopoly power in a market could be expected to be the greatest.

He further stated that milline rates for advertisers may actually decrease following a merger in a market, because of the "dominance of circulation over concentration"; that is, any increase in agate line rates is more than offset by the proportionately greater increase in circulation of the combined daily. This comes from the previously discussed economies of scale: the cost associated wtih publishing one newspaper with a given circulation is lower than those of two newspapers each with a portion of that circulation. The advertiser also avoids having to pay for duplicate readership of the competing papers.

Langdon's study did find that wage rates for newspaper employees tend to be lower in non-competitive situations.[59]

Cross-Media Ownership

The effects of noncompetitive newspapers in a particular market may be mitigated by the existence of competing media, i.e., television, radio and magazines. What is potentially more insidious for readers and advertisers would be the situation where more than one medium in a locality is under the same ownership. This is reflected in concern about cross-media ownership.

Guido H. Stempel studied the effects of a complete media monopoly in one small city—Zanesville, Ohio.[60] There, the city's only newspaper, radio station and television station were under the same ownership. Comparing Zanesville's residents with those who lived in similar cities with greater media diversity, Stempel found that:

1) Zanesville residents used the news media less and were less well informed than residents in comparison cities.

2) Zanesville residents got less news than residents in two comparison cities with competitive media.

3) Despite this, Zanesville residents used less nonlocal media than those they were compared with.

4) Nonetheless, public acceptance of the media was high.

Other studies yield conflicting findings on the effects of newspaper/broadcast affiliations. One found that media with concentrated ownership covered the news in greater depth because it had more resources. But another concluded that television stations owned by newspapers carried less locally originated programming. Although J.A. Anderson found that newspaper-owned television stations departed more frequently from the norms of objectivity, he saw no other differences in the news sources and practices of television stations owned by newspapers.[61] A researcher calculated that newspaper-television cross-ownership increased story overlap between the co-owned media 16.7% compared to similar independently owned media. This additional homogenizing effect was judged to be potentially harmful to the public.[62] The same study cited a Federal Communications Commission staff report that newspaper-owned television stations provided more local news, nonentertainment and entertainment programming than other television stations.[63]

Overall, at best there are some marginal benefits resulting from newspaper-television cross-ownership. However, no responsible research has made a convincing case for overall societal advantages resulting from having a television and newspaper under the same ownership in a single market. The argument for a negative impact remains strongest in the smallest markets, where there are fewer other broadcast stations and other city newspapers available.

Although the effects may be in dispute, as a result of both FCC regulation and the general growth in the number of available broadcasting outlets, the number of distinct "voices," i.e., separately owned newspapers, AM, FM and television outlets, actually increased between 1950 and 1970 by 25%, with overall press control in the top 100 markets having peaked in 1940. Also in 1940, 23% of the broadcast voices were owned by newspapers in the same market. By 1950, the percentage had dropped to 3%.[64]

As seen in Table 6.3 (Chapter 6), newspapers owned about 7.5% of all radio stations in 1979, compared to 9.7% in 1970 and 26.4% in 1950. (This includes those located in cities other than the city in which the publisher owns newspapers). Under current FCC rulings, newspapers are prohibited from constructing or purchasing any broadcast facilities that would over-lap their newspaper market.[65] Moreover, in 1977, a U.S. Court of Appeals overturned an FCC ruling and ordered that even existing newspaper-broadcast combinations must be forced to split up. This would affect over 230 such combinations.[66]

Although Christopher Sterling warned that the trend of decreasing con-centration may have reached its peak, he concluded:

> There appears to be a multiplicity of voices to be heard and read providing news and entertainment daily. When one adds in other media originating within most of these SMSA's [Standard Metro-politan Statistical Areas], plus the many information and enter-tainment sources received but not originating in each market, the variety of voices and points of view is almost numberless.[67]

Effects on the Editorial Product

The most commonly expressed fear is that freedom of the press is en-dangered by less competition, hence less diversity of opinion. In fact, most studies have found that readers perceive little difference between com-peting and "isolate" newspapers, and researchers have found little to substantiate the view that lack of logical competition itself produces in-ferior journalism.

Two researchers in 1956 found few significant differences in content be-tween competitive and noncompetitive newspapers.[68] The one significant difference was in reporting news of accidents and disasters, in which case competing papers carried more such news. Another study found that nine types of news coverage were perceived by readers to be better after mergers than before. Overall, reader attitudes in Atlanta, Louisville, Minneapolis and Des Moines were slightly more favorable after merger eliminated head-on competition.[69]

Further research has found that competing dailies do not guarantee the "market place" of ideas which is the oft-cited rationale behind the need for competing newspapers. In examining pairs of competing papers in small cities, an investigator found only one pair that showed any tendency to compete by "issue," and there the competition was along partisan lines.[70]

Another study further substantiated the body of research unable to find significant differences in competing and noncompeting newspapers.[71] It studied the content and reader perception during a period of head-on even-ing competition in Bloomington, IN, and contrasted this with a time when one of the papers was about to fold (moderate competition) and a period five months after one of the competing dailies closed down. The hypothesis was that under conditions of intense competition, a daily newspaper would devote more of its non-advertising space to local content and sensational and human interest news and features than under conditions of noncompetition. Another hypothesis was that readers would perceive no difference in the quality of the two competing papers nor notice any difference in the amount of local news in the remaining noncompetitive paper.

In fact, the findings substantiated neither of the hypotheses. Local news content *did not* decline when competition ended, nor did the proportion of "immediate reward" items—sports, crime, accidents, etc. And, consistent with previous studies, the results confirmed that readers found no perceived difference in the surviving newspaper. Readers of the two papers were aware, however, of quantity differences in immediate reward items in the two papers. These findings support previous conclusions in similar studies of competing and noncompeting newspapers.

Another study, looking only at differences in pairs of competing newspapers, found that, in fact, there are relatively few substantial variations, although "leading" newspapers in each pair did have some common characteristics.[72] In comparing 46 newspapers in 23 markets, eliminating operations with joint operating agreements and match-ups where one paper had circulation more than twice its rival, the researchers found:

1) The amount of content in each of 20 editorial categories was almost the same.

2) Leading newspapers have a larger advertising hole.

3) Leaders used more news services.

4) The leader was more likely to be the newer paper.

5) In format, the trailing paper had larger pictures and fewer stories on page one.

Overall, the authors found "few content and relatively few consistent format differences." This dearth of difference among competing and within noncompeting newspapers may have several explanations. It could indicate that the constraints of having to sell to a mass market dictate certain formulas that editors have honed over the years. Moreover, since editors often work their way up, moving from paper to paper, they share a common training ground that they all generally follow when they run a newspaper. There may also be an element of media responsibility that editors feel, particularly when they know they are the only newspaper in town. Publishers also may be particularly sensitive to accusations of abusing "monopoly" power, but they may have learned as well that they must meet certain minimum standards to gain subscribers and the advertisers who want a decent circulation and rate. Certainly, it may be a combination of several or all of these or other factors. Perhaps it takes more than even two newspapers competing directly to provide the niche for a paper that can be more specialized, controversial or otherwise significantly different.

A study that looked specifically at the role of newspapers and television in informing the public on political issues yielded carefully qualified "circumstantial evidence that competition and diversity are important social indicators of resources for political education. . . ."[73] The authors suggest that television is not as effective as newspapers in conveying a political candidate's policy positions and that therefore the decline in the number of newspapers, especially competing newspapers in the same city, is cause for some concern.

Hicks and Featherstone added an important new aspect by studying the amount of content duplication in morning and evening papers in the same city under common ownership.[74] In the literature, the two papers would be considered to be a single "media voice," since it is hypothesized that the single owner would dictate content and editorial policy for both papers. The researchers compared the content of the two Newhouse-owned papers in New Orleans with that of another morning-evening combination owned by a small local chain in Baton Rouge and that of two newspapers in Shreveport, one of which is independently owned and the other owned by the Gannett chain. These last two published under a joint operating agreement, however.

The study found that there was no significant difference in the non-advertising space (newshole) of the six papers, all clustering around the national average of 34% to 35%. The range was from 31% to 38%, with the independent Shreveport paper having the highest newshole, the evening Baton Rouge paper the smallest.

Perhaps more surprisingly, the study found remarkably little duplication in either news or editorial content among the papers in each city. In no case was there *any* duplication of editorials, columns, cartoons and letters. In hard news and local items, the Baton Rouge combination did have some statistically significant overlap, due in part to joint coverage of state capital news, but the Newhouse papers in New Orleans and the separate Shreveport papers had miniscule duplication. Noted the publisher of the New Orleans papers: "[The reporters on each paper] fight tooth and nail for stories; it is just as competitive as it would be with separate ownerships."

The report concludes that the concept of "media voice" might be modified, since in all three cities in their study readers did get two distinct newspapers "in terms of appearance, and no duplicated news. . . ."

ANTITRUST AND LEGISLATIVE ACTIVITIES

As part of the only industry specifically mentioned for protection in the Constitution, the newspaper has been largely, although not completely, immune from judicial and legislative tampering. One important case that did affirm the government's ultimate right to insure freedom of expression was the *Associated Press* case.[75] The AP, a cooperative financed by member newspapers to provide news accounts to all, had a policy of restricting competition by making it extremely expensive to buy a new membership in a city where there were already newspaper members. The government sued the Associated Press on antitrust grounds, and the AP's defense was the First Amendment, as well as the theory that newspapers were not covered by the Sherman Act since they were not engaged in interstate commerce. More important than the substantive ruling against the AP's restrictive practice, the Supreme Court's ruling clearly placed newspapers within the jurisdiction of antitrust legislation. It is surely in the government's power to *preserve* the free dissemination provided for in the First Amendment:

> Freedom to publish is guaranteed by the Constitution, but freedom to combine to keep others from publishing is not. Freedom of the press from governmental interference under the First Amendment does not sanction repression of that freedom by private interests.[76]

Newspaper Preservation Act

With the rights of the government firmly established, the Justice Department brought an action against the two newspapers in Tucson, AZ, which had formed a joint operating company to handle advertising, business and production matters, leaving editorial staffs and policy in the hands of the separate owners of the two papers. Forty-two other newspapers in 21 cities had similar joint operating agreements. Using *Tucson* as a test case, the government charged the two papers with price fixing, profit pooling and market allocation. In 1969, the Supreme Court upheld a summary judgment supporting the government's charge.[77] This ruling brought action on a bill which had been introduced in Congress in 1967 to protect such arrangements. So the Newspaper Preservation Act was passed in 1970, in effect exempting the 22 joint agreements from antitrust prosecution. The

Act does, however, limit the right of future agreements, which must be approved by the Justice Department on a case-by-case basis. There are also sanctions for abuse of the legalized combination to prevent further competition in the market, but these have not been applied.

The concept of joint operating agreements has had its supporters and critics, with segments of the newspaper industry itself of divided opinion. The proponents of the legislation argued that two separate editorial voices were a better alternative than the single voice that would exist if an otherwise marginal paper were forced out of business or taken over entirely by the stronger paper. The opposing view was voiced not only by many small, independent dailies but by *The New York Times* and the Newspaper Guild as well. It was their contention that daily and weekly papers in the prosperous suburbs were in effect substituting for the failing metropolitan newspapers. The joint operating agreements could therefore lessen competition within the city and at the same time promote an unfair advantage over existing or potential rivals.

Critics of the Newspaper Preservation Act cite in particular the loose interpretation of the Act by the Justice Department in those cases where it has approved new joint agreements since 1970, such as the 1979 decision affecting the *Cincinnati Post* and *Enquirer*. First, they note the ability of chain-owned papers to do "creative accounting" to make contributions to corporate overhead or to purchase services from corporate headquarters at rates that help make the paper look less profitable. A money-losing newspaper could have some benefit for a chain in the form of tax write-offs to balance profits from other properties.[78]

Second, while the law supposedly mandates that joint agreements should be approved only as a last resort, when no other buyer for the paper can be found, this has not been rigorously pursued. For example, in hearings over the Cincinnati agreement, it came out that Larry Flynt, publisher of *Hustler* magazine, made a serious offer for the *Post*. Nonetheless, E.W. Scripps Co., owner of the *Post* and petitioner for the joint agreement, rejected the offer. They did this, they said, because of Flynt's presumably tainted reputation.[79] In Seattle, WA, where the Justice Department was holding hearings in late 1981 on the combination of Hearst's *Post-Intelligencer* with the Knight-Ridder affiliated *Times,* News American Corp.'s Rupert Murdoch made an offer to buy the "failing" paper from Hearst. It too was scorned.

In fact, the Supreme Court has upheld a lower court ruling that the Newspaper Preservation Act does not necessarily ban joint operating agreements between two financially healthy newspapers.[80]

What can be said for the Newspaper Preservation Act is that it has indeed kept alive some semblance of metropolitan newspaper competition in those cases where it has been applied. But in no instances has the weaker paper in the agreement been able to break out of its number two position. In only one case (Anchorage, AK) has a joint operating agreement been dissolved in favor of conventional competition. But that was not because the weaker paper in the agreement suddenly felt economically rejuvenated. It was actually due to charges over "monopoly, mismanagement and breach of contracts" brought by the *Anchorage Daily News.*[81]

In effect, the joint operating agreement preserves the *status quo.* To that extent, it may be viewed as at best only a bandaid for diversity in daily newspapers.

Combination Advertising Rates

Another issue, involving the *New Orleans Times-Picayune,* concerned the legality of a morning-evening combined advertising rate offered by the owner of the two papers. Do not such rates, which may actually be cheaper in combination than for a single paper, invoke price discrimination to the disadvantage of a competitor of one of the combination's papers? The Supreme Court ruled the practice legal, thus making it that much more difficult for a single newspaper to compete with a morning-evening edition operation offering low combination rates.[82] Advertisers would tend to go into the morning-evening combination at a rate much lower than using a morning and evening from competitive firms.

Another antitrust suit involving a similar issue was filed in early 1977 by the owner of the *Sacramento Union* against McClatchy Newspapers, owner of the *Sacramento Bee, Fresno Bee* and *Modesto Bee* (all California) as well as several radio and TV stations. The suit contended that McClatchy Newspapers was illegally monopolizing the market by offering joint ad buys between the broadcast stations or discounts for advertisements in all three newspapers.[83]

Geographical Limitations

Newspaper groups do have to show some sensitivity to antitrust laws, however. So far, the Justice Department has shown little activity concerning concentration of ownership, even as Gannett hits the 85-newspaper mark. For the most part, the chains have been careful not to buy papers that have overlapping distribution and thereby lay themselves open to charges of controlling all papers under the "umbrella."

For example, although Gannett's Westchester-Rockland Newspapers provide the basic local papers for a large contiguous area in suburban New York City, they all compete under the dominating influence of the large metropolitan papers which are widely available in their territory.

On the other hand, Times Mirror was forced to sell its *San Bernardino (CA) Sun* and *Telegram* in 1970 because of an antitrust ruling based on the predominance of the *Los Angeles Times* in Southern California and the lessening of competition that would result if the relatively nearby San Bernardino papers were brought under the same ownership. The point that geographical proximity, not overall size of the chain, is the key to control, is underlined by the ready acquisition of the San Bernardino papers by Gannett.

Advantages of Bigness

One classic argument of those most critical of industrial bigness is that a national chain can afford to sustain a loss at some of its operating units in a battle with local competitors, while those in areas without competition can reap scarcity rents.

This argument has limited application in the case of newspaper chains. First, chains tend to buy papers that have no direct local competition. Second, in those cities where chains are in head-to-head competition with independent owners, they have not fared particularly well. This includes Hearst papers in Boston, Baltimore or Seattle, or Scripps-Howard papers in Cleveland and Cincinnati.

The Gannett Case in Salem

On the other hand, the fine line between fair competition and predatory practices is not always easy to discern. A case that may illustrate the potential economic influence of a large chain involves Gannett Co., Inc. and its Salem (OR) dailies, the *Oregon Statesman* and *Salem Capital Journal* (the two were merged in 1981). Shortly after acquiring the two papers in 1974, Gannett raised advertising rates substantially and changed some policies that displeased local advertisers. Several of the largest, including national retailer K-Mart, encouraged Community Publications, Inc. to establish a free "shopper" paper with their assurance of advertising support.[84] Thus was the *Community Press* born.

Community Publications was part of Early California Industries, itself a food and chemical conglomerate headquartered in Los Angeles. According to private Gannett documents, the new shopper was taken as a serious threat to the established dailies. Salem has no television stations of its own and only a few radio stations. Its population, including suburbs, is about 100,000.

That Gannett reacted with competitive aggressiveness is not by itself unethical or illegal. But the steps that the local Gannett papers took were at the very least made easier by the fact that a large parent corporation could help finance the battle against a much smaller competitor. One Gannett memo described "Operation Demolition," the project for getting back the business lost to the shopper. Salesmen were paid bonuses for each account they could persuade to stop advertising in the shopper. Advertisers were offered significant rebates and trips to Lake Tahoe to abandon the shopper, and Gannett reportedly threatened to stop doing business with suppliers that advertised in the competition. Some advertisers were told that their accounts would not be accepted in the Gannett papers in the future if they did not stop advertising in the shopper.

The *Community Press* eventually lost most of its clients and went out of business in September 1978, two-and-a-half years from its start-up. It filed an antitrust suit against Gannett, alleging that Gannett had "systematically set out to destroy" the weekly through "extremely callous" disregard of law.[85] Community Publications accepted an out-of-court settlement in late 1981 for about $2 million. Nonetheless, the U.S. Justice Department began its own investigation into possible illegalities under the antitrust laws. And the former owner of a shopper published for eight months in competition with Gannett's *Idaho Statesman* in Boise also filed a suit in 1981, alleging antitrust behavior similar to that in Salem.[86]

Neither suits nor preliminary investigations by the Justice Department are substantiation of wrongdoing. Clearly, big companies have more resources for meeting competition than smaller companies, in any industry. It is the mixture of such "hard ball" practices with the sweet ideals of the First Amendment that Gannett in particular has associated itself with that makes these cases especially ironic, particularly from the perspective of those critical of newspaper groups in the first place.

FTC Hearings and Findings

In general, however, such events appear to be sufficiently covered by existing antitrust laws. Neither Congress nor the appropriate executive bodies have found a need to pursue wide-ranging structural changes in the newspaper industry. The Federal Trade Commission held a two-day public symposium in 1978 on concentration of ownership within all mass media. In 1980, a report issued by the FTC staff concluded that there is "relatively little the Commission can do" about the increasing number of one-newspaper towns since economies of scale are the primary reason they exist.[87] The FTC further stated that it is difficult to challenge newspaper chains on antitrust grounds because their papers usually operate in separate geographical markets.

ACTIVITY AT THE STATE AND LOCAL LEVEL

Although the federal government is usually the focus of activity in areas of media concentration, some of the action may be swinging to the state and even local level. Some states, such as Massachusetts and Connecticut, have statutes or regulations prohibiting newspaper and cable cross-ownership. In Connecticut, the State Division of Public Utility ruled that Times Mirror Co. must divest itself of either the *Hartford Courant* or two cable franchises in the Hartford area. The order was upheld by the state courts, but Times Mirror appealed in 1981 to the federal courts.[88] The public utility commissioners had ruled that the public interest was hurt by having a common owner for the two types of media.

A Massachusetts statute flatly prohibits a newspaper publisher from owning a cable system in its circulation area. This was being challenged in the state court by a weekly newspaper in Boston that was eliminated from consideration for Boston's cable franchise. It also appeared to pose a problem for Dow Jones. The publisher agreed to purchase a 25% interest in Continental Cablevision, Inc. Continental, however, had cable franchises in areas that overlapped with papers owned by Dow Jones' Ottaway Newspaper subsidiary. The state's first statement said that even a minority ownership in the cable company would not be in accordance with the stipulation of the law.

In other areas that have no state laws affecting newspaper-cable cross-ownership, there is the possibility that individual municipalities will consider the connection between the cable franchise applicant and the local newspaper in making its award for the local franchise. The Federal Communications Commission itself has no jurisdiction in the matter.

THE CANADIAN EXPERIENCE

Concentration of ownership among the 120 daily newspapers in Canada is far greater than in the United States. Two groups, Southam, with 14 dailies, and Thomson, with 40 (in addition to its U.S. holdings), own 45% of the newspapers. In total, the 10 newspaper groups control 77% of the daily newspapers, up from 58% in 1971. Of these, three groups with a total of eight papers, are French language.

Concern about concentration was heightened in 1980. Southam closed its *Winnipeg Tribune,* leaving Thomson's *Free Press* as the only daily in that city. Simultaneously, Thomson shut down the *Ottawa Journal,* giving free reign to the Southam paper, the *Citizen.* At about the same time, Thomson consolidated its two newspapers in Victoria into one.[89]

In 1981 the report of a government-appointed commission set up to investigate competition in the newspaper industry proposed:

- forcing the largest newspaper groups to make significant divestments and to limit future growth by acquisition;

- banning national newspapers that are printed at multiple sites around the country, from common ownership by a firm that published any other newspapers. Thomson has been printing and distributing its *Toronto Globe and Mail* throughout Canada;

- banning common ownership between a daily newspaper and a broadcasting outlet in the same community. Southam owned 30% of Selkirk Communications Ltd., a major broadcasting company;

- restricting "extreme concentration" of ownership within a geographical region. Irving Newspapers owns the major dailies in the New Brunswick province;

- banning the purchase of a newspaper by any enterprise that had other business interests greater in value than the newspaper.[90]

Southam and Thomson were also charged by the federal government with violating Canada's competition laws.

NEWSPAPERS AND THE TELEPHONE INDUSTRY

In mid-1980, the U.S. newspaper industry suddenly found itself facing potential competition from a quite unexpected source: the telephone industry and, in particular, the American Telephone & Telegraph Co. This threat came about as the result of economic, technological and political forces.

There was a certain irony in this: the newspaper industry has been portrayed as being powerful and increasingly concentrated. We have already seen the tendency toward "isolate" newspapers—less delicately described as local newspaper monopolies. Yet the newspaper industry, including non-daily papers, had total revenue in 1980 of $17.5 billion. This was substantially dwarfed by the revenue of AT&T alone: $50.1 billion. AT&T, of course, has been a regulated monopoly. The economic efficiency of having a single telephone company in any locality was compensated for by strict state and federal regulation on the prices the telephone companies could charge for its services. Moreover, unlike newspapers, the telephone industry has traditionally been confined to common carriage. While access to the press may be guaranteed only to those who own one, *anyone* has access to the telephone system.

Technology, however, has been blurring some of the heretofore neat traditional boundaries. The common carrier telephone industry had been a carrier of the content provided by the users: it originated no content itself. And, like the Postal Service, it was basically oblivious to what the content was. But the increasing addition of computers to the telephone network began playing havoc with the normal boundary between what was basic carriage and what was content. "Enhanced" services that involve some computer manipulation of the content were at the heart of the involved proceedings before the Federal Communications Commission, which became known as Computer Inquiry I and Computer Inquiry II.[91] Actual or proposed services, such as call forwarding and packet switching were looked on by regulators as some hybrid between pure transmission and pure content.

Providing "Enhanced" Services

In 1956, a consent decree signed by AT&T to end a Justice Department antitrust suit limited AT&T, the telephone company with 81% of all telephones and 76% of daily calls, to providing enhanced services so long as they were "incidental" to basic transmission. Thus, AT&T was able to publish its telephone directories, even though they were not strictly part of its carriage. By 1980, AT&T had revenue of about $2.5 billion from the Yellow Page directories. Certain public service features, such as providing National Weather Service recorded announcements and a recorded time announcement, had been expanded in many cities to include AT&T's own weather recording, as well as stock and sports results and a multiplicity of Dial-a-Joke, Bedtime Story, Prayer and similar "content" messages. In each case, a call to these services involved a direct charge of about 10 cents to local customers. The messages themselves are usually provided by outside parties who get a royalty of about one-third the revenue. The telephone company keeps the rest. In 1979 the Manhattan area generated about 271 million such content calls to New York Telephone, yielding revenues of about $16 million.[92]

Such activities did not seem to bother either the FCC or the newspaper industry at first. Perhaps an early signal of the coming storm occurred in Albany, New York in late 1979. AT&T's New York subsidiary performed an experiment that gave a few customers direct access to the directory assistance computer by providing those households with computer terminals with keyboards. To get the telephone number of a friend, or the local Ford dealer, the customer could bypass an operator or the outdated print directory for online access to the telephone company's computer.

Meanwhile, the U.S. Congress had been wrestling with the ingredients for a communications law to replace the Communications Act of 1934. Time and technology were showing their age on that governing statement of policy. During the 1970s, both houses of Congress held hearings on a Communications Act rewrite bill. In 1980 the Senate showed interest in a bill that would have allowed AT&T to offer certain kinds of information retrieval services. Among the potential services was an "electronic Yellow Pages." To the newspaper industry, this was like a red cape waved in front of a bull. In the context of the Albany experiment and a more ambitious one proposed in Texas[93] (since abandoned), the large newspapers saw their profitable classified advertising business being challenged by an "800 pound gorilla."

Ma Bell, said newspaper people, had the resources to overwhelm the comparatively puny newspapers. Indeed, the heretofore somnambulent newspaper industry was shaken rudely awake by the gorilla's footsteps.

The self-interest of the newspaper industry and its chief lobby, the American Newspaper Publishers Association (ANPA), came to the fore in the public policy arena. *The New York Times* candidly editorialized that "newspapers have direct interest in the growing debate about the future of American communications."[94] The same *Times* editorial succinctly spelled out the industry's fear:

> Instead of a dry, once-a-year Yellow-Pages listing of "Mike's Grocery," Ma Bell wants one day to offer minute-by-minute specials on apples and lamb chops at the supermarket. Along with the time of day, it could announce the hours remaining for a white sale on sheets and blankets. . . . And with the ball scores could come accounts of the action, and a pitch for souvenirs and tickets.

For its part, AT&T disavowed any interest in being in the news business. It was already in a venture with publisher Knight-Ridder as the supplier of the equipment and transmission facilities being used in a viewdata trial, with Knight-Ridder being responsible for all content. A similar arrangement was announced with CBS, Inc. in 1981. From AT&T's standpoint, an electronic Yellow Pages should be viewed as being no different from a print Yellow Pages. "If we don't get into it, others are going to," was one Bell System representative's response, adding that any attempt to block the phone company from converting to an electronic format would be "unfair."[95]

The deeper issue, as seen from the newspaper industry viewpoint, is whether the phone industry—and AT&T specifically—should be permitted to use its revenue, profits and assets, generated as a regulated monopoly, to then compete with much smaller businesses. In a statement to Rep. Timothy Wirth, chairman of the Subcommittee on Telecommunications, Consumer Protection and Finance, the House of Representatives body that held hearings in preparation for drafting rewrite legislation in 1981, the Southern Newspaper Publishers Association said:

> If permitted to provide competing services on a vertically inte-grated basis, a telephone company would have a significant, un-fair advantage in packaging its own information service in com-bination with its transmission function. . . .
> A structural restriction prohibiting telephone company owner-ship of the information traveling over its own facilities will pro-mote the First Amendment goal of assuring the widest possible dissemination of information from diverse services. . . .[96]

The Federal Communications Commission in its "Computer II" deci-sion proposed deregulating AT&T in areas that are relatively competitive, such as customer premises equipment and long distance phone service. AT&T would have to participate in these areas through an unregulated subsidiary that is fully separated from its regulated common carrier business.

Much of the steam of ANPA's position was blown away, however, by the settlement reached between AT&T and the U.S. Justice Department in January 1982. This was the result of a seven-year antitrust suit brought by the government against AT&T which was in its final stages of trial. In the settlement, AT&T agreed to divest itself of its 22 local operating com-panies. These accounted for about 70% of AT&T's assets, but less than 60% of its revenues. AT&T would therefore keep its Long Lines depart-ment, as well as Western Electric Co., its manufacturing arm, and Bell Laboratories. The settlement thus separated the local delivery lines from the long distance facilities and services. This apparently freed AT&T to engage in the information providing business without conflict, while pro-hibiting the newly separated local exchange companies from offering these services.

The newspaper industry did not jump to support the settlement. In-stead, it turned its attention to the potential conflict in AT&T's ownership of an intercity telephone network which could also carry AT&T's own in-formation service. ANPA issued a statement that said, in part:

> Until a showing is made that adequate alternative facilities are

available to publishers who must rely on the interexchange network to reach the public, the courts and Congress should examine the advisability of deferring AT&T's authority to provide information over its monopoly facilities.[97]

On the other hand, the settlement did make it clear that the local operating telephone companies, the ones that actually owned the wires that went into the customer's house or business, would continue to be tariffed as common carriers by the state regulatory agencies. It also meant that any newspaper publisher would have access to the local network under the exact conditions available to AT&T and anyone else. In addition, the settlement gave the local telephone companies the flexibility to offer billing and metering services. That means that if a newspaper publisher set up an electronic information service offered via telephone lines, it could have the telephone company take care of measuring how long each user was on the line. Then, the monthly telephone bill might also include a charge for the publisher's information service, saving the publisher the sizable cost of having to bill each customer separately.

Although the actual details and ramifications of the antitrust suit settlement, Computer Inquiry II and other legislation from Congress will take years to sort themselves out, print publishers will likely find themselves with potential benefits and threats as a result. They can expect additional, not fewer, sources of competition for advertisers and audiences.

DISCUSSION

The issue of concentration of newspaper ownership and the proliferation of one-newspaper-firm cities tends to raise great passions among interested parties. It is easy to find examples on an individual case basis for some abuses these trends may create. On the other hand, stepping back from specific examples yields a more objective evaluation based on the full spectrum of evidence.

First, it should be clear that no newspaper or chain dominates the nation's news dissemination. Even the largest group accounts for less circulation than did the largest group in 1946. The control over total circulation by even the largest chains has changed little over the past 30 years. The three television networks, through their newscasts, would appear to have a far greater impact on control of news flow than any combination of newspaper chains.

Second, economists recognize that there are some benefits to being part of a chain-owned newspaper. But, in addition to economic benefits, such papers have the opportunity to reduce their dependence on the wire services by being able to use news from the chain's own bureaus. A legitimate question, however, is how large a group has to be to maximize these advantages. If that could be determined, then it could be argued that further acquisitions by the chain yield no further social benefits.

The tendency toward one-newspaper-firm cities is largely economic and is due in large measure to the reluctance of advertisers, from whom newspapers derive the bulk of their revenue, to support competing newspapers when a single firm can provide the audience coverage they need more economically and hence at lower total advertising rates. A newspaper has never gone out of business for lack of editorial material. It needs readers so it can get advertisers. The sizable first copy cost and the expense of distribution over a given territory tend to favor consolidation of newspapers in all but the larger cities.

Moreover, there is little empirical evidence that either chain-owned newspapers or newspapers in single-firm cities as a group provide poorer service to readers or advertisers than independent or competing newspapers. Some newspapers—chain or independent—take advantage of their local monopoly status. But examples also exist which demonstrate how a chain owner improves a newly acquired paper. Indeed, in the Rand study that found that horizontal newspaper combinations produced few substantial economic or managerial advantages, the researchers concluded that "the absence of evidence that group newspapers, on the average, operate in a manner which is measurably different from independents can be given a positive interpretation."[98]

Certainly the chain owner has the potential to dictate editorial policy. Some do in the endorsement of political candidates (although the question of how much real impact such editorials have is still unresolved) or in ordering certain articles to be printed. Other owners, however, use the same power to demand higher editorial standards. In the end, newspapers are a local product and must fulfill the needs of a community. Most chain owners appear to recognize this and give individual editors and publishers maximum latitude. Furthermore, even one-newspaper communities appear to face intercity competition, as well as weekly and "shopper" newspaper rivals.

Perhaps an issue that has been seldom addressed and that should be a topic for further investigation is the role of the national news services and syndicators. A far more homogenizing effect on newspaper content than chain ownership may well be the standardization of national and international news through the Associated Press and United Press International, with The New York Times News Service a less frequently subscribed to supplement. Clearly the large expense in providing such around-the-world coverage explains the need for a small number of such services. Therefore, the question is, would even three or four newspapers in a single city be providing readers with anything more in national and international news than what is currently coming over the wires?

The Future

While the fundamental structure of the newspaper industry seems to be fairly stable (given the context of the basic economic structure of American industry), other forces outside the control of the newspaper publishers themselves may make moot all that has been accepted heretofore.

The previously described newspaper-telephone industry conflict may be a sign of the more overriding issues of the 1980s and beyond. The newspaper industry, like its broadcasting and other print brethren, will find it increasingly difficult to separate its own turf from those of others who used to play in separate arenas. For example, while the newspaper industry may be able to withstand competition from Ma Bell, it may find less of a pretext for legislative remedies should IBM or another computer giant wish to use its technological and marketing know-how to enter the business of delivery of consumer-oriented information to the home.

At the opening of this chapter, it was suggested that a newspaper is, when analyzed beyond its typical news, features and advertising components, a bundle of discrete content products. It is timely news and less timely analysis. It is a community bulletin board. It is entertainment. Readership studies find that some readers purchase a local newspaper because of a particular comic strip. The crossword puzzle alone may make the 20-cent price worthwhile for some. Supermarket advertisements and other display ads are another feature of the newspaper package. Infrequent newspaper users may purchase the local daily to check out the classified ads only when they are in the market for a used car or new house.

The newspaper is a different product to each user. Put in a single package, it attracts readers for many different reasons. Each user of the newspaper in effect creates his or her own content package by choosing what to read from the sizable data base that comes delivered each day. In fact, we can readily describe a newspaper using many of the same terms applied to the "new" electronic information retrieval technologies. The daily newspaper of today is an information product that:

- contains as many as 30 million bits of information;
- handles both text and graphics;
- is randomly accessible;
- is online 24 hours a day;
- is updated at least once each day;

- weighs less than three pounds and is completely portable;
- costs 25 cents or less per hour of use;
- is easy to use, i.e., "user friendly."

It is a formidable package. But parts of it can be broken off and sold by someone, to some segment of the population, at what may be a profitable price. Thus springs the concern by the newspapers that an electronic, frequently updated Yellow Pages would begin to look an awful lot like classified advertising. Banks, interested in bringing cost-saving financial services into the home via computer terminal, may find that offering a package of information products—such as movie listings, restaurant guides, sports scores, etc.—may be needed to attract customers. Real estate brokers may want to offer their own electronic listing service to customers via video terminals. Computer timesharing companies, such as CompuServe (now a subsidiary of tax specialists H & R Block), are already acting as brokers for information providers. At some point they may wish to add their own content.

The list could go on. The newspaper industry, for a time consumed by the threat from the AT&T, has now started to see possible threats from the growing and unregulated cable business. With the newer cable systems having 50 or more channels into homes under their control, newspapers have begun to see that they have no right of access should the cable franchisee in their territory refuse to lease them a channel. The cable company could provide its own text and advertising service to customers—a new threat for both newspaper advertisers and for consumer time. Ironically, newspapers have largely been excluded from owning cable franchises in the territory where they also own the newspaper.

While no one of their potential competitors is likely to mortally wound the locally based newspapers, together they may ultimately weaken the financial viability of the ink-on-newsprint newspaper. Publishers can respond by starting to offer some of their information electronically, via telephone connection between a user's terminal and their own computers. For this, an alliance with a strong telephone network is essential.

Such threats to the newspapers, however, may also be looked at quite positively from the standpoint of diversity. The one-daily-newspaper city is already more competitive than is immediately obvious. Local television and radio provide some partially overlapping functions. Shopper and weekly newspapers provide competition—the seriousness with which Gannett took on the local shopper in Salem, Oregon should be evidence of that. But the ability of anyone with access to the common carrier telephone system to provide an electronic information service—at a far lower entry cost than starting up a traditional newspaper—opens the door to a new form of competitor. The services that may be offered by or through cable are another source of competition.

Thus, we should not be surprised to see even fewer multi-newspaper towns. And, while the familiar newspaper may continue to be around, providing the major form of local information in a community, its competitive position must be analyzed in the context of the other media, both those which are already in existence and those which will likely become more prevalent in this decade.

NOTES

1. Christine D. Urban, *Factors Influencing Media Consumption: A Survey of the Literature* (Cambridge, MA: Harvard University, Program on Information Resources Policy, 1981), pp. 62-65.

2. Benjamin M. Compaine, *The Newspaper Industry in the 1980s: An Assessment of Economics and Technology* (White Plains, NY: Knowledge Industry Publications, Inc., 1980), p. 29.

3. *Ayer Directory of Publications, 1981* (Bala Cynwyd, PA, 1981), p. vii.

4. Bruce M. Owen, *Economics and Freedom of Expression* (Cambridge, MA: Ballinger Publishing Co., 1975), p. 47.

5. Quoted by John Tebbel, *The Compact History of the American Newspaper* (New York: Hawthorne Books, Inc., 1963), p. 97.

6. Owen, p. 48.

7. Frank Luther Mott, *American Journalism* (3d ed.; New York: Macmillan, 1962), p. 635.

8. *Editor & Publisher*, January 3, 1981.

9. James N. Rosse, Bruce M. Owen and James Dertouzos, *Trends in the Daily Newspaper Industry 1923-1973,* Studies in Industry Economics, No. 57 (Stanford, CA: Department of Economics, Stanford University, 1975), p. 28.

10. Raymond B. Nixon and Tae-Youl Hahn, "Concentration of Press Ownership: Comparison of 32 Countries," *Journalism Quarterly* 38:13, Spring 1971.

11. Tebbel, p. 242.

12. Willard G. Bleyer, *Main Currents in the History of American Journalism* (Boston: Houghton-Mifflin, 1927), p. 413.

13. Tebbel, pp. 219-220.

14. Oswald Garrison Villard, "The Chain Daily," *The Nation,* CXXX, 1930, pp. 595-597, cited by Gerald L. Grotta, "Changes in the Ownership

of Daily Newspaper and Selected Performance Characteristics, 1950-1968: An Investigation of Some Economic Implications of Concentration of Ownership" (unpublished doctor's dissertation, Southern Illinois University, 1970), p. 5.

15. Denby Fawcett, "What Happens When a Chain Owner Arrives," *Columbia Journalism Review,* November/December, 1972, pp. 29-30.

16. Ibid.

17. Letter to Editor from C. Donald Hatfield, *Columbia Journalism Review,* January/February, 1973, pp. 65-66.

18. Robert L. Bishop, "The Rush to Chain Ownership," *Columbia Journalism Review,* November/December, 1972, pp. 14-15.

19. Statement by James H. Ottaway Jr., in an address ("Circulation Growth of Ottaway Newspapers") to the Dirks Forum, New York, May 4, 1976.

20. Bishop, pp. 14-15.

21. "The Big Money Hunts for Independent Newspapers," *Business Week,* February 21, 1977, p. 59.

22. Peter Nichols, "Check it with Bill," rev. of Eric Veblen, *The Manchester Union Leader in New Hampshire Elections* (University Press of New England), *Columbia Journalism Review,* November/December, 1975, p. 53.

23. Address to Conference on the Outlook for the Media, New York, November 30, 1976.

24. Bishop, p. 21.

25. "The Big Money," p. 59.

26. Daniel Wackman, et al., "Chain Newspaper Autonomy as Reflected in Presidential Campaign Endorsements," *Journalism Quarterly* 52:417, Autumn 1975. In this study, a chain or group is defined as "three or more dailies in different cities under the same principal ownership or control," p. 413.

27. Ibid., p. 419.

28. Ibid.

29. Ibid., p. 413.

30. Grotta, p. 79.

31. Kristine Keller, "Quality of News in Group-Owned and Independent Papers: Independent Papers Have More," unpublished paper (Berkeley, CA: University of California, School of Journalism, 1978), p. 6.

32. Charles Seib, quote in *The Washington Post,* July 29, 1977, as cited by Keller.

33. "The Big Money," p. 58.

34. Robert E. Dallos, "Bidding Sends Prices Higher in Newspaper Acquisition Binge," *Los Angeles Times,* January 9, 1977, Sec. VI, p. 2. He is

referring to a statement made by Allen H. Neuharth, president of Gannett.

35. "The Big Money," p. 59.

36. Dallos, p. 5.

37. Company annual reports, 1980. It should be noted that firms may also make acquisitions by exchanging shares of stock.

38. James N. Dertouzos, "Media Conglomerates: Chains, Groups and Cross Ownership," discussion paper prepared for FTC Media Symposium, December 14-15, 1978, p. 11.

39. "Family Paper Faces Problems to Survive as an Independent," *Editor & Publisher,* April 28, 1973, p. 11. Quote is from Robert S. Withers, Publisher, *Rochester* (Minn.) *Post-Bulletin.*

40. "A Bitter Family Squabble Put Oakland's *Tribune* on the Block," *Business Week,* February 21, 1977, p. 60.

41. "The Big Money," p. 58.

42. Daniel Machalba, "North Carolina Paper Strives to Ward Off Bids by Press Empires," *The Wall Street Journal,* August 19, 1981, p. 18.

43. "Dolly's Last Surprise," *Newsweek,* November 29, 1976, p. 84.

44. Machalba, p. 18.

45. "Booth Aims to Thwart a Newhouse Takeover," *Business Week,* March 22, 1976, p. 48. "Newhouse Buys Majority of Outstanding Booth Stock," *Editor & Publisher,* November 13, 1976, p. 14.

46. "The Big Money," p. 62.

47. James N. Dertouzos and Kenneth E. Thorpe, "Newspaper Groups: Economies of Scale, Tax Laws and Merger Incentives." (Santa Monica, CA: Rand Corp., 1982) pp. 4-8.

48. Royal H. Ray, "Competition in the Newspaper Industry," *Journal of Marketing* 15:444, April, 1951.

49. Rosse, Owen and Dertouzos, "Trends in the Daily Newspaper Industry," p. 2.

50. Ibid.

51. James N. Rosse, "The Evolution of One Newspaper Cities," discussion paper for the Federal Trade Commission Symposium on Media Concentration; Washington, DC, December 14-15, 1979, p. 16.

52. Ibid., pp. 50-52. See also James N. Rosse, *Economic Limits of Press Responsibility,* Studies in Industry Economics, No. 56 (Stanford, CA: Department of Economics, Stanford University, 1975).

53. "The Big Money," p. 59.

54. Grotta, p. 19.

55. Paul A. Samuelson, *Economics* (6th ed., New York: McGraw-Hill, 1964), p. 498.

56. Grotta, p. 74.

57. Ibid., pp. 77-79.

58. John Henry Langdon, "An Intra Industry Approach to Measuring the Effects of Competition: The Newspaper Industry" (unpublished doctor's dissertation, Cornell University, 1969), p. 159.

59. Ibid., Chapter II.

60. Guido H. Stempel III, "Effects on Performance of a Cross-Media Monopoly," *Journalism Monographs,* No. 29 (June 1973), pp. 10-28.

61. George Litwin and W.H. Wroth, "The Effects of Common Ownership of Media Content and Influence" (Washington, DC: National Association of Broadcasters, July, 1969); H.J. Levin, *The Policy on Joint Ownership of Newspapers and Television Stations* (New York: Center for Policy Research, 1971); J.A. Anderson, "The Alliance of Broadcast Stations and Newspapers: The Problem of Information Control," *Journal of Broadcasting* 16; all cited by W. Phillips Davison and Frederick T.C. Yu, *Mass Communications Research: Major Issues and Future Directions* (New York: Praeger Publishers, 1974), p. 48.

62. William T. Gormley, *The Effects of Newspaper-Television Cross-Ownership on News Homogeneity* (Chapel Hill, NC: Institute for Research in Social Science, The University of North Carolina, 1976), p. 211.

63. Federal Communications Commission, "Second Report and Order in Docket 18110" (January 28, 1975), as cited in Gormley, *The Effects of Newspaper-Television Cross-Ownership . . .,* p. 215.

64. Christopher Sterling, "Trends in Daily Newspaper and Broadcasting Ownership, 1922-1970," *Journalism Quarterly* 52:247-256, Summer 1975.

65. Sterling, p. 247. See also U.S., Federal Communication Commission, *Second Report and Order, Docket No. 18110* ("Multiple Ownership of Standard, FM and Television Broadcast Stations," FCC 74-104, Mimeo 29942) January 29, 1975.

66. "Joint Ownership of Media Barred by Appeals Court," *The Wall Street Journal,* March 2, 1977, p. 4. Perhaps anticipating the ruling, Multimedia, Inc. and McClatchy Newspapers announced on March 4 that they would swap stations that were affected by the ruling. Others, including Newhouse, made adjustments in their broadcasting or newspaper holdings.

67. Sterling, p. 320.

68. Raymond B. Nixon and Robert L. Jones, "The Content of Non-Competitive vs. Competitive Newspapers," *Journalism Quarterly* 33:299-314, Summer 1956.

69. Raymond B. Nixon, "Changes in Reader Attitudes Toward Daily Newspapers," *Journalism Quarterly* 31: 421-433, Fall 1954.

70. Gerald H. Borstell, "Ownership, Competition and Comment in 20 Small Dailies," *Journalism Quarterly* 33:220-222, Spring 1956.

71. John C. Schweitzer and Elaine Goldman, "Does Newspaper Competition Make A Difference to Readers?" *Journalism Quarterly* 52:706-710, Winter 1975. Galen Rarick and Barrie Hartman, "The Effects of Competition on One Daily Newspaper's Content," *Journalism Quarterly* 43:459-463, Fall 1966.

72. David H. Weaver and L.E. Mullins, "Content and Format Characteristics of Competing Daily Newspapers," *Journalism Quarterly* 52:257-264, Summer 1975.

73. Peter Clarke and Eric Fredin, "Newspapers, Television and Political Reasoning," *Public Opinion Quarterly*, 42:143-160, p. 157.

74. Ronald G. Hicks and James S. Featherstone, "Duplication of Newspaper Content in Contrasting Ownership Situations," *Journalism Quarterly* 55:549-554, Autumn 1978.

75. *Associated Press* v. *United States,* 326 U.S. 1 (1945).

76. Ibid., at 20.

77. *Citizen Publishing Co.* v. *United States* 394 U.S. 131 (1969).

78. Celeste Huenergard, "Scripps Hoping for Quick Decision in Cincinnati Case," *Editor & Publisher,* February 6, 1979, p. 19. See also Michael Parks, "A Merger Plan Under Fire," *Advertising Age,* June 1, 1981, pp. S12-13.

79. Celeste Huenergard, "Cincinnati Post Called 'Unsaleable' at Hearing," *Editor & Publisher,* September 23, 1978.

80. *Newspaper Guild* v. *Edward H. Levi, Attorney General,* U.S. Court of Appeals (D.C. Circuit) 539 F.2d 755, July 1, 1976.

81. Mike Doogan, "Anchorage Daily News Files Suit to Break Joint Operating Accord with Rival Paper," *The Wall Street Journal,* February 14, 1977, p. 19.

82. *Times-Picayune Publishing Co.* v. *United States* 345 U.S. 367 (1953).

83. "Monopoly Claimed in U.S. Suit," *Editor & Publisher,* January 22, 1977, p. 40.

84. Cassandra Tate, "Gannett in Salem: Protecting the Franchise," *Columbia Journalism Review,* July/August, 1981, p. 52.

85. Joseph M. Winski and Richard L. Gordon, "Gov't. Eyes Gannett," *Advertising Age,* October 19, 1981, p. 1.

86. Ibid., p. 113.

87. "Why FTC is Stepping Away from Media Probes," *Advertising Age,* January 28, 1980, p. 14.

88. "Times Mirror Co. Loses Bid to Alter Divestiture Ruling," *The Wall Street Journal,* April 9, 1980.

89. Tony Thompson, "Canadian Feds Investigating Thomson, Southam After Deal," *Advertising Age,* September 15, 1980, p. 76.

90. "Canadian Panel Urges Action to Restrict Concentration of Newspaper Ownership," *The Wall Street Journal,* August 19, 1981, p. 19.

91. *Interdependence of Computer and Communication Services and Facilities,* (Computer I), Final Decision, 28 F.C.C.2d 11 (1966); *Second Computer Inquiry* (Computer II), Final Decision, 77 F.C.C.2d 384 (1980).

92. John C. LeGates, *Changes in the Information Industries—Their Strategic Implications* (Cambridge, MA: Harvard University, Program on Information Resources Policy, 1981), p. 2.

93. Jonathan Friendly, "Publishers Seek to Block Utility in Electronic Ad Test for Homes," *The New York Times,* December 4, 1980, p. D-21.

94. "Yellow Pages and a Fearful Press," *The New York Times,* May 14, 1981.

95. "Newspapers Protest New Phone Company Plan," *Boston Globe,* January 11, 1981, p. 24.

96. Statement of Roland Weeks, president, Southern Newspaper Publishers Association. Excerpts in "SNPA Goes 'On Record' for Diversity Principle," *Editor & Publisher,* October 24, 1981, p. 34.

97. Statement issued by the Board of Directors of the American Newspaper Publishers Association, January 25, 1982.

98. Dertouzos and Thorpe, p. 6.

Appendix 2.1

Newspapers Owned by Largest Groups, 1981

Cox Enterprises, Inc.

Atlanta Journal and Constitution (GA)
Austin American-Statesman (TX)
Dayton News and *Journal-Herald (OH)*
*Daytona Beach Journal and *News (FL)*
Grand Junction Sentinel (CO)
Longview News and *Journal (TX)*
Lufkin News (TX)
Mesa Tribune (AZ)
Miami News (FL)
Palm Beach News and *Times (FL)*
Port Arthur News (TX)
Springfield Sun and *News (OH)*
Tempe News (AZ)
Waco Tribune-Herald (TX)
West Palm Beach Post (FL)

*47% ownership

Capital Cities Communications, Inc.

General Interest Daily
  Newspapers:
Albany Democrat-Herald (OR)
Ashland Daily Times (OR)
Belleville News-Democrat (IL)
Fort Worth Star-Telegram (TX)
Kansas City Star and *Times (MO)*
Oakland Press (Pontiac, MI)
Wilkes-Barre Times Leader (PA)

Special Interest Daily
  Newspapers:
American Metal Market
Daily News Record
Women's Wear Daily

Dow Jones & Co., Inc.

The Wall Street Journal

Ottoway Newspapers:
Beverly Times (MA)
Cape Cod Times (MA)
Danbury News-Times (CT)
Gloucester Times (MA)
Joplin Globe (MO)
Mankato Free Press (MN)
Medford Mail Tribune (OR)
Middletown Times Herald Record (NY)
New Bedford Standard-Times (MA)
Newburyport News (MA)
Oneonta Star (NY)
Owatonna Peoples Press (MN)
Peabody Times (MA)
Port Jervis Union-Gazette (NY)
Plattsburgh Press-Republican (NY)
Sharon Herald (PA)
Stroudsburg Pocono Record (PA)
Sunbury Daily Item (PA)
Traverse City Record-Eagle (MI)

Evening News Association:
Detroit News (MI)
Indio Daily News (CA)
Millville Daily (NJ)
Vineland Times-Journal (NJ)

Gannett Co., Inc.

Daily Newspapers:
*Agava Pacific Daily News
   (Guam)*
*Battle Creek, Enquirer and News
   (MI)*
The Bellingham Herald (WA)
Binghamton, The Sun-Bulletin
   and *Evening Press (NY)*
Boise, The Idaho Statesman (ID)
*Bridgewater, The Courier-News
   (NJ)*
The Burlington Free Press (VT)
Camden Courier-Post (NJ)
*Chambersburg, Public Opinion
   (PA)*
Chillicothe Gazette (OH)
Cincinnati Enquirer (OH)
Cocoa, Today (FL)
The Coffeyville Journal (KS)
*Danville, The Commercial-News
   (IL)*
Eastbay Today (CA)
Elmira Star-Gazette (NY)
The El Paso Times (TX)
Fort Collins Coloradoan (CO)
Fort Myers News-Press (FL)
*Fremont, The News-Messenger
   (OH)*
Fremont Tribune (NE)
Green Bay Press-Gazette (WI)
Honolulu Star-Bulletin (HI)
Huntington, The Herald-Dispatch
   and *Advertiser (WV)*
Iowa City Press-Citizen (IA)
The Ithaca Journal (NY)
*Lafayette, Journal and Courier
   (IN)*
Lansdale, The Reporter (PA)

Lansing, The State Journal (MI)
Little Falls Daily Transcript (MN)
The Marietta Times (OH)
*Marin County Independent
   Journal (CA)*
Marion, Chronicle-Tribune (IN)
Monroe Morning World and
   News-Star (LA)
*Muskogee Daily Phoenix and
   Times-Democrat (OK)*
Nashville, The Tennessean (TN)
*New Kensington-Tarentum,
   Valley News Dispatch (PA)*
Niagara Falls Gazette (NY)
Oakland Tribune (CA)
*Olympia, The Daily Olympian
   (WA)*
The Pensacola Journal and *News
   (FL)*
Port Clinton, News-Herald (OH)
*Port Huron, The Times Herald
   (MI)*
Poughkeepsie Journal (NY)
Reno, Nevada State Journal and
   Evening Gazette (NV)
*Richmond, The Palladium-Item
   (IN)*
*Rochester Democrat and
   Chronicle* and *The Times-
   Union (NY)*
Rockford, Morning Star (IL)
The St. Cloud Daily Times (MN)
*St. Thomas, The Daily News
   (Virgin Islands)*
Salem, Statesman-Journal (OR)
Salinas Californian (CA)
San Bernardino, The Sun (CA)
*Santa Fe, The New Mexican
   (NM)*
*Saratoga Springs, The Saratogian
   (NY)*
The Shreveport Times (LA)
Sioux Falls Argus-Leader (SD)
*Springfield Daily News Leader
   and Press (MO)*
Stockton Record (CA)

Sturgis Journal (MI)
Tucson Citizen (AZ)
Utica, The Daily Press and *The Observer-Dispatch (NY)*
Visalia Times-Delta (CA)
Wausau Daily Herald (WI)
Wilmington, The Morning News and *Evening Journal (DE)*

Westchester Rockland Newspapers (NY):
Mamaroneck, The Daily Times
Mount Vernon, The Daily Argus
New Rochelle, The Standard-Star
Nyack-Rockland, The Journal-News
Ossining, The Citizen Register
Port Chester, The Daily Item
Tarrytown, The Daily News
Westchester County, TODAY
White Plains, The Reporter Dispatch
Yonkers, The Herald Statesman

Weekly Newspapers:
Bronxville Review Press-Reporter (NY)
Cherry Hill, Suburban Newspaper Group (NJ—10 weeklies)
Melbourne Times (FL)
New Kensington, Butler County News, North Hills News Record (PA—Semi-weekly)
New Kensington, The Herald (PA)
Pierz, Royalton, Royalton Banner and Pierz Journal (MN)
Saratoga Springs, Commercial News (NY)
Titusville Star-Advocate (FL)
Westport Fairpress (CT)

Harte-Hanks Communications, Inc.

Abilene Reporter-News (TX)

Anderson Independent and *Mail (SC)*
Big Spring Herald (TX)
Bryan Eagle (TX)
Corpus Christi Caller and *Times (TX)*
Corsicana Sun (TX)
Del Rio News-Herald (TX)
Denison Herald (TX)
Framingham, South Middlesex Daily News (MA)
Greenville Herald-Banner (TX)
Hamilton Journal-News (OH)
Huntsville Item (TX)
Malvern Daily Record (AR)
Marshall News-Messenger (TX)
Paris News (TX)
Russellville Courier-Democrat (AR)
San Angelo Standard and *Times (TX)*
Searcy Daily Citizen (AR)
Stuttgart Daily Leader (AR)
Wichita Falls Record-News and *Times (TX)*
Woodbury Times (NJ)
Yakima Herald-Republic (WA)
Ypsilanti Press (MI)

Other Papers:
68 non-daily papers

Hearst Corporation

Albany Times-Union and *Knickerbocker News (NY)*
Bad Axe Huron Daily Tribune (MI)
Baltimore News American (MD)
Boston Herald American (MA)
Edwardsville Intelligencer (IL)
Los Angeles Herald-Examiner (CA)
Midland Daily News (MI)
Midland Reporter-Telegram (TX)
Plainview Herald (TX)

San Antonio Light (TX)
San Francisco Examiner (CA)
Seattle Post Intelligencer (WA)

Knight-Ridder Newspapers, Inc.

Daily Newspapers:
Aberdeen American News (SD)
Akron Beacon Journal (OH)
Boca Raton News (FL)
Boulder Daily Camera (CO)
Bradenton Herald (FL)
Charlotte Observer and *News (NC)*
Columbus Ledger and *Enquirer (OH)*
Detroit Free Press (MI)
Duluth News-Tribune and *Herald (MN)*
Fort Wayne News-Sentinel (IN)
Gary Post-Tribune (IN)
Grand Forks Herald (ND)
Journal of Commerce (NY)
Lexington Herald and *Leader (NC)*
Long Beach Independent and *Press-Telegram (CA)*
Macon Telegraph and *News (CA)*
Miami Herald (FL)
Pasadena Star-News (CA)
Philadelphia Inquirer and *Daily News (PA)*
St. Paul Pioneer Press and *Dispatch (MN)*
San Jose Mercury and *News (CA)*
Seattle Times (WA)
Tallahassee Democrat (FL)
Walla Walla Union-Bulletin (WA)
Wichita Eagle and *Beacon (KS)*

Less Than Daily Newspapers:
Anaheim Independent (CA)
Arcadia Tribune (CA)
The Broward Times (FL)
The Buena Park News (CA)
Duartean (Duarte, CA)

The Florida Keys Keynoter (FL)
The Huntington Beach Independent (CA)
The La Mirada Lamplighter (CA)
Monrovia News-Post (CA)
The Orange County Evening News (CA)
Temple City Times (CA)
The Union-Recorder (Milledgeville, GA)

*Knight-Ridder owns 49.5% of the voting stock and 65% of the nonvoting stock.

Lee Enterprises, Inc.

Billings Gazette (MT)
Bismarck Tribune (ND)
Butte Standard (MT)
Carbondale, The Southern Illinoisan (IL)
Corvallis Gazette-Times (OR)
Davenport Quad City Times-Democrat (IA)
Decatur Herald and *Review (IL)*
Edwardsville, The Intelligencer (IL)
Helena Independent Record (MT)
Kansas City Kansan (KS)
Kewanee Star-Courier (IL)
LaCrosse Tribune (WI)
Lincoln Star (NE)
Madison State-Journal (WI)
Mason City Globe-Gazette (IA)
Midland Daily News (MI)
Missoula Missoulian (MT)
Muscatine Journal (IA)
Ottumwa Courier (IA)
Racine Journal-Times (WI)
Winoma Daily News (MN)

*49% ownership

Media General, Inc.

Richmond Times-Dispatch and *News Leader (VA)*

Tampa Tribune and *Times (FL)*
Winston-Salem Journal and
  Sentinel (NC)

Newhouse Newspapers

Birmingham News (AL)
Cleveland Plain Dealer (OH)
Harrisburg Patriot and News
  (PA)
Huntsville News and Times (AL)
Jersey City, Jersey Journal (NJ)
Mobile Register and *Press (AL)*
Newark Star-Ledger (NJ)
New Orleans Times-Picayune and
  States-Item (LA)
Pascagoula Press and *Chronicle*
  (MS)
Portland Oregonian and *Oregon*
  Journal (OR)
Staten Island Advance (NY)
St. Louis Globe-Democrat (MO)
Springfield Union and *News*
  (MA)
Syracuse Post-Standard and
  Herald-Journal (NY)

Booth Newspapers (Michigan)
Ann Arbor News
Bay City Times
Flint Journal
Grand Rapids Press
Jackson Citizen Patriot
Kalamazoo Gazette
Muskegon Chronicle
Saginaw News

The New York Times Co.

Gainesville Sun (FL)
Henderson Times-News (NC)
Houma Daily Courier (LA)
Lake City Reporter (FL)
Lakeland Ledger (FL)
Leesburg Daily Commercial (FL)
Lexington Dispatch (NC)

The New York Times (NY)
Ocala Star-Banner (FL)
Palatka Daily News (FL)
Thibodaus Comet (LA)
Wilmington Star-News (NC)

Seven weekly papers

E.W. Scripps Co.
(Scripps-Howard Newspapers)

Albuquerque Tribune (NM)
Birmingham Post-Herald (AL)
Cincinnati Post (OH)
Columbus Citizen-Journal (OH)
Covington Kentucky Post
  (separate edition of *Cincinnati*
  Post) (KY)
Denver Rocky Mountain News
  (CO)
El Paso Herald -Post (TX)
Evansville Press (IL)
Fullerton News Tribune (CA)
Hollywood Sun-Tattler (FL)
Knoxville News-Sentinel (TN)
Memphis Press Scimitar and
  Commercial Appeal (TN)
Pittsburgh Press (PA)
San Juan Star (PR)
Stuart News (FL)

Thomson Newspapers Limited

Ada Daily News (OK)
Adrian Daily Telegram (MI)
Albert Lea Evening Tribune (MN)
Ansonia Evening Sentinel (CT)
Atchison Daily Globe (KS)
Austin Daily Herald (MN)
Barstow Desert Dispatch (CA)
Canton Repository (OH)
Cape Girardeau Southeast
  Missourian (MO)
Carthage Press (MO)
Connellsville Daily Courier (PA)
Cordele Dispatch (GA)

Coshocton Tribune (OH)
Council Bluffs Nonpareil (IA)
Dalton Daily Citizen-News (CA)
Dothan Eagle (AL)
Douglas Dispatch (AZ)
East Liverpool Evening Review
(OH)
Escanaba Daily Press (MI)
Eureka, The Times-Standard
(CA)
Fairmont Times-West Virginian
(WV)
Fayetteville Northwest Arkansas
Times (AR)
Fitchburg Sentinel and Enterprise
(MA)
Fond du Lac Reporter (WI)
Greenville Daily Advocate (OH)
Greenville Record-Argus (PA)
Hanover Evening Sun (PA)
Herkimer Evening Telegram (NY)
Iron Mountain News (MI)
Key West Citizen (FL)
Kittanning Leader-Times (PA)
Lafayette Daily Advertizer (LA)
Lancaster Antelope Valley Ledger
Gazette (CA)
Lancaster Eagle-Gazette (OH)
Laurel Leader-Call (MS)
Leavenworth Times (KS)
Lock Haven Express (PA)
Manitowoc Herald-Times-
Reporter (WI)
Marianna, Jackson County
Floridan (FL)
Marion Star (OH)
Marquette Mining Journal (MI)
Meadville Tribune (PA)
The Middletown Journal (OH)
Mitchell Daily Republic (SD)
Monessen Valley Independent
(PA)
Mount Vernon Register-News (IL)
New Albany, The Tribune (IN)
Newark Advocate (OH)

Newburgh Evening News (NY)
Oelwein Daily Register (IA)
Opelika-Auburn News (AL)
Orange Park Daily Clay Today
(FL)
Oswego Palladium-Times (NY)
Oxnard, The Press-Courier (CA)
Petersburg Progress-Index (VA)
Piqua Daily Call (OH)
Portsmouth Herald (NH)
Portsmouth Times (OH)
Punta Gorda, The Herald-News
(FL)
Rocky Mount Evening Telegram
(NC)
The Salem News (OH)
Salisbury Daily Times (MD)
Steubenville Herald-Star (OH)
Taunton Daily Gazette (MA)
Valdosta Daily Times (GA)
Weirton Daily Times (WV)
West Covina San Gabriel Valley
Daily Tribune (CA)
Xenia Daily Gazette (OH)
Yreka Siskiyon Daily News (CA)
Zanesville Times Recorder (OH)

Times Mirror Co.

Dallas Times Herald (TX)
Denver Post (CO)
The Greenwich Times (CT)
Hartford Courant (CT)
The Los Angeles Times (CA)
Newsday (Long Island, NY)
Orange Coast Daily Pilot (CA)
Stamford Advocate (CT)

Tribune Co.

Chicago Tribune (IL)
Escondida Times-Advocate (CA)
Fort Lauderdale News (FL)
Kissimmee Osceola Sun (FL)

New York News (NY)
Orlando Sentinel-Star (FL)
Palo Alto-Redwood City Times-
   Tribune (CA)
Pompano Beach Sun-Sentinel
   (FL)
Redwood City Tribune (CA)
Van Nuys Valley News (CA)

The Washington Post Co.

Everett Herald (WA)
Trenton Times (NJ)
   (sold October 1981)
Washington Post (DC)

3

Book Publishing

by J. Kendrick Noble, Jr.

Any analysis of the book publishing industry is limited by the lack of useful, truly comparable statistics. Only since 1971 have industry data been made available by a single source, the Association of American Publishers, and even the work of that organization is affected by both questions of definitions and by partial reporting in certain categories. Only since 1977 have organized, consistent efforts been made to develop these statistics into useful industry forecasts by the not-for-profit Book Industry Study Group. Thus, more research is really needed to draw valid conclusions about almost any aspect of the overall book industry.

Yet the book publishing industry is one of our country's oldest businesses. Over the years, many of the industry's principal figures have been prolific writers, often concerned with developments in their field. Thus, there is a wealth of opinion, recorded experience and incomplete data to draw upon, although the inferences from these may vary with the analyst.

BRIEF HISTORY[1]

The very nature of the book publishing industry has changed over the years, partly due to technology, but mostly the result of the copyright.

The first book publishers were primarily printers, at least in the United States. Presses required government sanction and did much of their work for the authorities, both secular and religious. Accordingly, they were considered to be primarily manufacturers, as they continue to be categorized to this day by the Department of Commerce.

Most books in the colonies were of English origin; the publisher-printers chiefly engaged in the routine printing of documents for the church, the state and business. Lacking the economic incentive of the copyright, the author of the day wrote primarily for religious or patriotic reasons, with the blessings of the authorities. It is generally agreed that the first

American press was established in Cambridge, Massachusetts, in 1638. The first item it printed was the *Freeman's Oath*, a government document, and its first best-selling book was *The Whole Booke of Psalmes* (1640).

British books appear to have been reprinted as well as imported. Some printers engaged in bookselling while some booksellers engaged in printing, apparently with few if any royalty payments to the original English authors.

During the early part of the 18th century, as the colonists became more concerned with information about the communities in which they lived, weekly newspapers and almanacs appeared and flourished.

Perhaps best illustrative of the industry's evolution was *The New England Primer,* the first widely used, American-printed textbook. Education was then largely conducted by religious groups with the sanction of government. The book was written by a Boston printer, Benjamin Harris, and was first advertised for sale in 1691. It was mostly a compilation from contemporary English primers, with which Harris was familiar since he also imported English books and ran a bookshop. Over the next hundred years, it may have sold more than 3 million copies and certainly sold more than one million. The uncertainty as to its actual success is partly due to the fact that it was widely pirated by other printers and sold under different names. Ben Franklin called his version *The Columbian Primer* and sold 37,100 copies between 1749 and 1756. As late as the period from 1837 to 1849, about 100,000 copies of *The New England Primer* were sold.

The lesson of such blatant reprinting of the words of others was quickly recognized: if many publishers exist, capable of freely publishing anything, new authors may be discouraged from creating works and demonstrably successful works will tend to be pirated and reprinted at the expense of newer works for long periods of time.

Copyright Laws and the Colonies

The first English copyright law, "8 Anne, c.9," was passed in 1709 and led to what has been called the "golden age of publishing" in England. By creating a right to an intellectual property, it led to the separation of publishing functions from printing functions. Many of the new publishers, in fact, were booksellers rather than printers. They sought out authors in response to their perceptions of what would sell, usually bought manuscripts outright, arranged for their production, and sold the results.

In the American colonies, the comparatively lax state of the law and the high costs of transporting books appear to have encouraged American printers to reprint English books until nationalism surfaced during the American Revolution. Thomas Paine's *Common Sense* sold 100,000 copies following its publication in early 1776.

The U.S. Constitution is unique in its special provisions to ensure a thriving publishing industry. The key elements are not only the First Amendment but also Section 8, Subsection (8) of Article I, which gives Congress the power:

> To promote the progress of science and useful arts, by securing for limited times to authors and inventors the exclusive right to their respective writings and discoveries.

These two provisions not only permit free speech but provide the economic incentive for its expression. We should not lightly dismiss the fact that the Constitution, for all its skeletal format, had incorporated into it the explicit power to enact a federal copyright law. Together with the First Amendment, this expression of national intent may prove to be of great significance in preserving the traditional publishing industry in the nascent technological information age.

Noah Webster, one of this country's most successful author-publishers, was instrumental in obtaining the copyright clause. During 1781 and 1782 Webster wrote *The First Part of a Grammatical Institute of the English Language,* ultimately known as the *Old Blue-Back Speller.* Using American pronunciations and spellings as distinct from the English ones commonly employed in textbooks of the time, the book was an instrument of nationalism. Familiar with English copyright law, Webster sought similar protection for his book from Connecticut, financed the first printing, and then both sold it and lobbied for protection in other states and even before the Constitutional Convention in Philadelphia. Because of transportation difficulties, he granted reprint rights widely and, by 1783, the book was selling at the rate of 500 copies a week. By 1818, five million had been sold, and at Webster's death in 1843, it was selling a million copies a year to a nation of twenty million. As late as 1880, D. Appleton and Co., which had in 1840 acquired publishing rights to the book, reported, "We sell a million copies a year, and we have been selling it at that rate for forty years."

Factors in Formation of the Book Industry

Distribution costs, always a principal problem of the book publishing industry, played a role in the fragmentation, dispersion and lack of creativity of the earliest publishers. They also seem to have been significant in the establishment of the early publishing centers in Boston, New York and Philadelphia, from which Yankee peddlers collected their wares to be sold in their travels into the hinterlands.

Thus, with a sense of national identity and interests to inspire American writers, with copyright protection to provide economic incentives for both authors and publishers, and with the formation of printing centers and distribution channels, the modern American book publishing industry began to form in the late 18th and early 19th centuries. Indeed, a number of present-day publishers trace their origins to that period.

The early years of the 19th century were marked by improvements in transportation and production techniques. Movable type was replaced by steel engravings in 1814 and by photoengravings late in the century. In 1830, the first automatic, flat-bed power press was introduced. This was followed by the self-feeding rotary ("web") press after the Civil War. Publishers, as such, had seldom owned their own presses and had been quite willing to shift to newer, more economic production methods. This helped stimulate the evolution of the printing industry which, in turn, encouraged more publishers to dispose of their own presses.

Wars seem to stimulate book sales, perhaps because of the increased need for explanations of events, limitations on other pursuits, and the recreational needs of the military. As World War II was later to entrench today's mass market paperbacks through the distribution of them to soldiers, so the Civil War spawned the "dime novel" of the late 1800s which, with rising education levels, seemed to stimulate the reading of original works in conventional hardbound formats.

Early Attempts at Concentration

The late 19th century was a period of rapid industrial growth, of the formation of many of today's larger book publishers, of cutthroat competition, and of the development of would-be monopolies, or "trusts." While consolidation helped companies such as U.S. Steel and the Standard Oil Co. to survive and flourish, it did not do the same for book publishers.

In 1889, publisher James W. Lovell attempted to form such a trust in book publishing, at a time when distribution facilities seemed glutted, returns to publishers of unsold books were very high and profits were minimal. His United States Book Co. purchased the printing plates and inventories of about 21 publishers who either agreed to join the organization or to leave the field. Although his organization was probably the largest publisher in the United States by 1890, eight large reprinters had remained independent and, after 1891, many other regular publishers began to publish low-priced paperback editions of their own works. Lovell soon went bankrupt, and was removed by his directors in 1893. Similarly unsuccessful consolidation efforts were made in the textbook market.

In 1890, the leading textbook publishers joined to form the American Book Co. This move started with the merger of Ivison, Blakeman & Co. of New York with Van Antwerp, Bragg & Co. of Cincinnati, two of the five largest such companies, which then bought the textbook operations of two others among the big five. This "Syndicate of Four" took over the list of the fifth largest publisher, and a few years later, bought the textbook businesses of ten other companies, eventually absorbing about 30. By the mid-1890s, American Book Co. controlled an estimated 93% of the nation's textbook sales. The largest non-joiner was the then sixth-ranking firm, Ginn and Co.

Although it did survive, to be acquired by Litton Industries in 1967, the American Book Co. seems to have been a failure as an attempt to monopolize the textbook segment of book publishing through the consolidation of the major companies already dominating that segment. As with the United States Book Co. earlier, the emphasis in the merger was on assets rather than on people, on plates and inventories rather than on authors and editors. In both cases, a few independent companies survived the initial consolidation, and other companies with prior experience in the field were permitted to reenter it after an initial waiting period. And in both cases, new competitors joined in almost immediately after the trusts absorbed some of the former leading publishers of the textbook segment. In each case, the market appeared eager to support the proliferation of new suppliers. Although there are no annual data to study, and the textbook segment dominated by the United States Book Co. disappeared with its leader, we do know that Ginn and Co. went on to become one of the largest schoolbook publishers while the American Book Co.'s market share fell from 90% or more of industry sector sales in the 1890s to about 6.4% of textbook sales in the school field and perhaps 3.6% of all school and college textbook sales by 1966, despite further acquisitions.

In book publishing, therefore, history seems to suggest that it is difficult to create a monopoly with staying power, at least if the emphasis is placed on the consolidation of assets rather than on people.

TITLE OUTPUT AS A MEASURE OF INDUSTRY VITALITY

Lacking industry revenue data, it seems reasonable to examine the number of new titles produced annually as an indicator of the vitality of the book publishing industry. Table 3.1 shows that the industry grew explosively from 1880 to 1910, underwent a decline from 1910 to about 1945, and then experienced a new surge through the 1970s.

The statistics of new titles, however, may be more than measures of industry health. For one thing, they may also be viewed as indicative of the industry's contribution to the spread of new ideas and information in our society. But they can also be interpreted as signs of industry problems. For example, the surge in the late 19th century and the post-World War II expansion both coincided with the rapid growth of low-priced reprint industries, that of the dime novel in the 19th century and of the mass market

Table 3.1: Average Output of New Book Titles, by Five-Year Intervals, 1881-1980

Years	Number of New Titles[1]
1881-1885	3,612
1886-1890	4,463
1891-1895	4,923
1896-1900	6,439
1901-1905	8,048
1906-1910	10,077
1911-1915	11,200
1916-1920	9,352
1921-1925	8,883
1926-1930	10,129
1931-1935	8,880
1936-1940	10,877
1941-1945	8,496
1946-1950	9,746
1951-1955	11,927
1956-1960	13,806
1961-1965	24,559
1966-1970	30,970
1971-1975	39,183
1976-1980	35,651[2]

Compounded Annual Grcwth, 1881-1910:	+ 3.5%
1911-1945:	− 0.8%
1946-1980:	+ 5.2%

[1] Figures represent average number of new titles and editions per year.

[2] 1976-1980 data adapted from a new tabulation format which actually yields an average of 42,651. Recalculated figure represents estimate consistent with tabulation method used in prior years.

Source: Paine Webber Mitchell Hutchins, Inc. calculations, based on *Publishers Weekly* data.

paperback in the 20th century. Also, it may not be coincidental that the 1890s and the 1960s were both periods of heightened merger activity. In any event, they certainly suggest increased competition in the world of ideas from 1880 to 1910 and since 1945. This is important in view of the industry's privileged constitutional status which seems to have been intended to produce just that result.

During the early 20th century, despite the essential flatness of industry title output, most of today's major book companies either were formed or grew in relative size. At the time some critics held that bankers had become inordinately involved in the industry and that too much emphasis was being placed on profits at the expense of the idealistic publishing presumed to have prevailed in past decades. Price-cutting by large stores with book departments led to the formation of the American Publishers Association and the American Booksellers Association, both in 1900, to attempt to maintain retail prices. Members refused to sell to discounters, most notable of which was R.H. Macy and Co. The dispute went all the way to the Supreme Court, where Macy won in 1913, leading to the dissolution of the publishers' trade association. To this day the emphasis placed by large retailers on the "big book" sold at a discount continues to be a problem for publishers.

THE CHENEY STUDY

In 1931, during the depths of the Depression, the National Association of Book Publishers (formed in 1920) sponsored the publication of O.H. Cheney's *Economic Survey of the Book Industry 1930-1931.*[2] It was the first such study and remained the only one until recent years.[3]

The *Census of Book Manufactures* that year estimated industry revenues at $146 million, down from $199 million in 1929, with approximately 154 million books produced, down from 235 million in 1929. It was estimated that 217 publishers produced five or more titles in 1930. Cheney found the industry's statistics "practically nonexistent." But he did come to some conclusions as to the state of the industry fifty years ago.

In examining publishers who had produced more than five titles apiece from 1925 through 1930, Cheney found a very gradual increase in titles per house with some indication that larger houses rarely published more than 200 titles per year, excluding reprints. During the period from 1925 to 1930, the number of publishers in the group surveyed grew from 172 to 217; Cheney estimated that, in each year, about 10% of the publishers (perhaps 17 to 22) accounted for 48% to 50% of the titles published, while 17% to 22% of the companies (29 to 48) issued 50 titles or more. Each year, he reported, the 10 leading publishers accounted for 33% to 37% of the total output of these publishers. Overall, they accounted for 85% of the output of all publishers each year. Table 3.2 compares the estimated industry concentration in the 1925-1930 period, based on title output, with more recent data based on the values of shipments. If comparable, these estimates suggest almost no change in the industry's concentration ratios over a 50-year period.

Cheney observed that "mergers are the common remedy suggested for the troubles of the industry by lunch-table economics," but concluded that:

There is no magic panacea in mergers to cure the economic ills of any industry and less magic in the case of the publishing industry than in almost any other . . . For every house which would be "eliminated" through merger, several new ones could—and would—easily spring up, because the capital need is so small and the "publishing urge" so great. The rate of increase in the number of houses by fission seems always to be at least equal to the rate of decrease by fusion.

Cheney's conclusion came following the steady growth in the number of publishers despite the frequent mergers in the 1925-1930 period. Indeed, while the industry was hurt by the Great Depression, few publishers went out of business and a number of new firms were started.

Table 3.2: Concentration Ratios for the Overall Book Industry

Year(s)	Number of Companies	Value of Shipments (in millions)	Largest Companies				
			4	8	10	20	50
			Percent of Shipments Accounted For:				
1925-1930[1]	N.A.	N.A.	20	30	35	49	73
1954	804	$ 665.4	18	28	—	47	N.A.
1958	883	1,010.7	16	26	—	45	65
1963	936	1,547.8	18	29	—	52	73
1967	963	2,255.3	16	27	—	52	75
1972	1,120	2,915.4	16	27	—	52	75
1977	1,652	4,793.9	17	30	—	57	74

N.A.: Not available.

[1] Estimates for 1925-1930 based on proportion of titles accounted for at each level.
Sources: O.H. Cheney, *Economic Survey of the Book Industry 1930-1931*; U.S. Bureau of the Census; Paine Webber Mitchell Hutchins, Inc. estimates and calculations.

ACQUISITION DEVELOPMENTS

In the aftermath of World War II, the industry began to experience rapid growth, particularly in textbook sales. Even so, leaders in the industry experienced many of the problems being cited today. In 1949, Charles F. Bound concluded a study of the industry based largely on interviews containing some familiar comments:[4]

- The good publisher today knows that no fortune is to be made in the business.

- Despite nearly record sales, the book industry is facing a crisis. Greatly increased costs for material and labor since the end of the war have virtually wiped out profit margins for publication of original trade books . . . The question quite naturally arises if the solution is not to be found in increased retail prices. The answer, unfortunately, seems to be no. Prices have already been advanced as far as the publisher dares raise them.

- The great problem facing the industry is not monopoly, it is failure to cooperate.

- Distribution of trade books is chaotic and one of the greatest problems and headaches facing the entire industry.

These same statements could be made today. The industry's problems and concerns, as well as misperceptions of its strengths, seem to be as long-lived as the industry itself.

In retrospect, it can be seen that Bound was writing just as book publishing was beginning to experience one of its most profitable periods of growth. The surge was led by the textbook publishers, and many other publishers soon sought to expand through acquisitions of the textbook producers while, in turn, seeking public capital to grow faster. On October 17, 1960, Bennett Cerf, the president of Random House, which had just offered its stock to the public, spoke to the New York Society of Security Analysts and stated in part:

> It is my belief that within the next few years, some five or six great publishing combines will dominate the publishing scene, much the way that a handful of companies today dominate steel, automobiles and other truly big industries. We intend that Random House will be one of these larger companies. . . .

That was also the period in which the economist Fritz Machlup published his seminal study, *The Production and Distribution of Knowledge in the United States,*[5] coining the term "knowledge industry" and embracing within it such sectors as education, the media, computers, finance and the telephone.

The Congenerics Come of Age

Lyle Spencer, the late founder/president of Science Research Associates, once said, "There's nothing worse in publishing than being right too soon."[6] A great many electronics companies made that mistake in the mid-1960s. Despite the mergers of publishers with publishers over the years, perhaps the industry's greatest wave of consolidation in this century was of electronics companies and educational publishers in that period, anticipating that the rapid growth of both computer capabilities and of federal educational funding presaged the acceptance of computer-based instruction in the schools. These companies believed that they would provide the hardware, the capital and the management skills; publishers would provide the software, the marketing skills and the acceptance of educators. These have been inappropriately called conglomerate mergers. More accurately, they were—borrowing a term coined by Macmillan's former chairman, Raymond Hagel—the formation of "congenerics": companies with perceived interrelationships that better met the needs of common markets. The entrants included CBS, General Electric, General Telephone, IBM, ITT, Litton, RCA, Raytheon, Singer, Westinghouse, Xerox and many others, through internal and joint development or through acquisitions. When these weddings proved unproductive and both enrollments and school funds declined, some of the marriages broke up (e.g., RCA's ownership of Random House and Litton Industries' of American Book Co.) and others evidently approached the brink of dissolution.

Then a second wave of congeneric mergers appeared, establishing companies involved in a broad range of media. Examples of acquirers included Billboard Communications, Corinthian Broadcasting, Esquire, Filmways, Gulf + Western, MCA, The New York Times Co., Time Inc., Times Mirror Co., Warner Communications, a number of traditional book publishers and others. Yet a third, more recent, acquisition wave has involved European publishers seeking expansion into worldwide markets as well as greater political stability in which to operate. Acquirers of this type have included Germany's Bertelsmann; Britain's William Collins, Howard & Wyndham, Longman, Penguin, Morgan-Grampian, Pitman and Thomson Organisation; and the Netherlands' VNU and Elsevier.

Whether because of, or despite, the mergers of the 1960s and 1970s, the book publishing industry does not appear to have significantly altered with respect to long-standing characteristic trends. These trends include:

- a fairly consistent allocation of the nation's personal consumption expenditures for book purchases;

- a varying allocation of government expenditures for book purchases, dependent upon such factors as classroom enrollment;

- a steady growth rate for numbers of new titles produced and all titles in print that exceeds the rate of growth of the population;

- a steady growth in the number of firms entering and comprising the book publishing industry; and

- maintenance of a relatively consistent market share by each of the largest industry segments as well as by categories within each segment.

These observations will generally be substantiated in what follows.

Number of Book Publishing Companies

Taking as an arbitrary base period the depths of the Great Depression, for example, the number of book publishing establishments appears to have been growing at a rate of about 2.6% per year. Estimates vary of the number of companies engaged in book publishing, so that the data in Table 3.3 and the following tables should be taken as indicative rather than definitive. Still, they are enlightening.

Table 3.3 provides net figures: ongoing companies plus new formations less dissolutions. To get some idea of the rates of formation and dissolution of book publishers, Table 3.4 tabulates the number of new publishers, including nonprofit organizations, formed each year between 1968 and 1977 that published at least three books in both 1977 and 1980, and listed themselves in a standard industry guide, *Literary Market Place*, both in 1978 and 1981. The selection is unbalanced: in 1977-1978, the economy was relatively strong; in 1980-1981, it was weak. Table 3.4 indicates that of

Table 3.3: Number of Book Publishing Companies and Establishments,[1] Selected Years, 1933-1977

Year	Establishments	Companies
1933	410	N.A.
1935	505	N.A.
1939	706	N.A.
1947	648	635
1954	815	804
1958	903	883
1963	993	936
1967	1,024	963
1972	1,205	1,120
1977	1,745	1,652

[1] An establishment is a single physical plant site or factory. It is not necessarily identical with a company, which may consist of more than one establishment.
Sources: U.S. Census of Manufactures; Paine Webber Mitchell Hutchins, Inc.

38 new firms started in 1968, four became inactive by 1978. Over the ten-year period, 1968-1977, of 445 publishing entities known to have formed, 31 became inactive in 1977-1978 and 414 were still active in 1978. Likewise, of 547 entities known to have formed over the eleven-year period from 1970 through 1980, 62 became inactive in 1980-1981 and 485 were still active that year.

In combination, Tables 3.3 and 3.4 suggest to this author that perhaps 200 to 300 publishing enterprises may now be forming each year, of which about half will become inactive in eight to ten years and 88% -93% inactive in thirty years, a period which would seem to approximate their 'founders' working lifetimes.

Table 3.4: Formations and Survival Rates of Book Publishers, 1968-1980

Year	Number Formed[1]	Active in 1978	Number that Ceased Operations in 1977-1978	Number Formed[2]	Active in 1981	Number that Ceased Operations in 1980-1981
1968	38	34	4	N.E.	N.E.	N.E.
1969	67	64	3	N.E.	N.E.	N.E.
1970	48	40	8	54	50	4
1971	53	50	3	60	53	7
1972	54	51	3	60	55	5
1973	38	35	3	49	43	6
1974	39	37	2	54	49	5
1975	49	46	3	67	57	10
1976	25	23	2	57	48	9
1977	34[3]	34	0	50	45	5
1978	N.A.	N.A.	N.A.	35	33	2
1979	N.A.	N.A.	N.A.	28	22	6
1980	N.A.	N.A.	N.A.	33[3]	30	3
Annual Average	45	42	3	50	44	6

[1] Formed in year indicated and published at least three titles in 1977.

[2] Formed in year indicated and published at least three titles in 1980.

[3] Includes organizations listed for the first time without founding dates.

Note: Discrepancies in numbers for companies formed in a given year reflect the use of different sources. *Literary Market Place* often does not list new companies until they are established, thus diminishing the numbers of companies reported founded in more recent years. Older organizations may be dropped for reasons other than dissolution, or may still be listed after being acquired if they remain reasonably intact as corporate entities.

N.A.: Not applicable.

N.E.: No estimate.

Sources: *Literary Market Place*, 1977, 1978, 1980, 1981 editions; Paine Webber Mitchell Hutchins, Inc.

THE ROLES OF BOOK PUBLISHERS

Publishers, although treated in government reports as manufacturers, are really service companies. They assess the information needs of society, locate sources of that information (authors), process it into forms suitable for the market (editing), arrange for its production (printing and binding) and market it (selling and distribution). In particular, book publishers are involved with information of more than transient value, which may be unique in its content, and which is intended for the use of individual members of relatively large groups who wish easily accessible, relatively inexpensive, highly portable and readily understood information in a durable, equipment-independent format.

For certain applications, these and other characteristics such as tradition, market acceptance and established distribution channels, make it unlikely that the book will be replaced. It is difficult, for example, to conceive of the great religious works—the Bible, the Torah or the Koran—in other than their traditional formats. For certain kinds of books, such as directories, legal citations, dictionaries and encyclopedias, which are large and expensive compilations from which only specific items are usually desired, the print format seems vulnerable to encroachment from electronic formats. However, book publishers can adopt—and some already have adopted—nonbook formats.

As to society's needs, the book publishing industry continues to offer a reasonable opportunity for those with ideas to communicate. It is difficult to assess just what is "reasonable," but the term suggests ease of entry for new publishers, the existence of many publishers with differing views, and a rate of growth in titles published in excess of population growth so long as the proportion of literate citizens continues to rise. In fact, new book titles produced do show a steady, long-term growth rate greater than that of the population, as can be seen in Table 3.5.* Table 3.6 shows that book industry dollar sales have generally grown faster than the Gross National Product. The trends displayed in these and prior tables seem to indicate that the book publishing industry has met, and continues to meet, the criterion of providing "reasonable opportunity."

Market Segments

Book publishing, with its tens of thousands of new titles each year and hundreds of thousands of older titles kept in print, is the most specialized

---

*For this and subsequent tables in this chapter, growth rates (even where not actually tabulated) have been calculated using the least square growth rate method.

Table 3.5: New Titles Produced Compared to Population Growth, Selected
Years, 1934-1980

Year	New Titles	All Books in Print	Population Aged 5-64 (in millions)	New Titles/ 1000 Population	Books in Print/ 1000 Population
1934	6,788	—	108.8	62.4	N.A.
1940	9,515	—	112.5	84.6	N.A.
1945	5,386	—	116.5	46.3	N.A.
1950	8,634	—	123.0	70.2	N.A.
1955	10,226	—	132.3	77.3	N.A.
1960	12,069	—	143.7	84.0	N.A.
1965	20,234	—	156.0	129.7	N.A.
1970	24,288	—	167.5	145.0	N.A.
1975	30,004	429,000	177.2	169.3	2,421.0
1976	26,983	450,000	179.1	150.6	2,511.9
1977	27,423	478,000	180.8	151.7	2,643.6
1978	31,802	498,000	182.4	174.4	2,730.6
1979	36,112	520,000	183.8	198.0	2,851.2
1980	34,030	538,000	185.7	183.3	2,897.9

N.A.: Not available.
Sources: Bureau of the Census; *Publishers Weekly*; Paine Webber Mitchell Hutchins,
Inc.

of present-day media industries. Wherever a need for information exists in
our society, it is likely that one or more books have been, or will be,
created to serve that need. The output of the industry may be categorized
in two ways. Table 3.7 breaks down sales by type of book or by market,
while Table 3.8 tabulates sales by channel of distribution. The latter indicates that more books are sold directly to the consumer—as by direct mail
or retail sales—than by any other method. El-hi schools buy textbooks
primarily, while college stores sell textbooks as well as some trade books.

Table 3.7 shows book sales by industry category since 1971. It indicates
that professional book sales constituted the largest single category in 1980
(14.2%), followed by adult trade books (13.8%), college textbooks
(13.5%) and elementary and high school (el-hi) textbooks (13.4%). As
recently as 1977, el-hi textbooks ranked first with a 15.3% share, followed
by adult trade books with 13.3%. Of the major categories, mass market
paperback books showed the greatest growth rate over the period, 14.8%,
followed by religious books, with 14.7%, and adult trade books with
14.0%. The above-average growth of trade books in part reflects numerous new industry entrants within the past decade.

Table 3.6: Book Sales and Book Industry Sales Related to GNP, Selected Years, 1933-1980

Year	Gross National Product (in billions)	Book Industry Sales		Book Sales by All Industries	
		Book Sales (in millions)	% of GNP	Book Sales (in millions)	% of GNP
1933	$ 55.8	$ 81.7	0.146%	—	—
1935	72.2	113.0	0.157	—	—
1940	100.0	193.9	0.154	—	—
1945	212.4	293.4	0.138	—	—
1950	286.5	619.4	0.216	—	—
1955	400.0	732.8	0.183	—	—
1960	506.5	1,303.2	0.257	$1,282[1]	0.252%
1961	524.6	1,382.3	0.263	1,365[1]	0.260
1962	565.0	1,527.8	0.270	1,502.8	0.266
1963	596.7	1,534.6	0.257	1,547.8	0.259
1964	637.7	1,728.6	0.271	1,729.6	0.271
1965	691.1	1,767.1	0.256	1,817.6	0.263
1966	756.0	1,996.3	0.264	2,081.3	0.275
1967	799.6	2,134.8	0.267	2,255.3	0.282
1968	873.4	2,099.4	0.240	2,338.9	0.268
1969	944.0	2,417.2	0.256	2,521.8	0.267
1970	992.7	2,434.2	0.245	2,677.0	0.270
1971	1,077.6	2,739.3	0.254	2,814.1	0.261
1972	1,185.9	2,856.8	0.241	2,915.4	0.246
1973	1,326.4	3,142.9	0.237	3,160.2	0.238
1974	1,434.2	3,348.8	0.233	3,407.7	0.238
1975	1,549.2	3,536.5	0.228	3,789.3	0.245
1976	1,718.0	3,967.5	0.231	4,179.7	0.243
1977	1,918.0	4,793.9	0.250	5,007.7	0.261
1978	2,156.1	5,398.2	0.250	5,640.6	0.262
1979	2,413.9	N.A.	—	5,711.3[2]	0.237
1980	2,730.6	N.A.	—	—	—

[1] Rounded.

[2] Preliminary.

N.A.: Not available.

Sources: *Publishers Weekly*; U.S. Bureau of the Census; Paine Webber Mitchell Hutchins, Inc. Book sales by all industries include books published by firms not classified as book publishers. Census Department figures for book industry sales are 8% to 14% lower than industry sales calculated by the Association of American Publishers since 1963.

Table 3.7: Book Publishing Market Sizes, Shares and Growth Rates, Selected Years, 1971-1980

Category	1971	1972	1977	1978	1979	1980	Percent Share of Total, 1980	Growth Rate 1971-1980
GNP (in billions)	$1,077.6	$1,185.9	$1,918.0	$2,156.1	$2,413.9	$2,626.1	—	10.4%
Personal Consumption Expenditures (in billions)	672.2	737.1	1,205.5	1,348.7	1,510.9	1,672.7	—	10.7
All Books (in millions)	2,917.8	3,017.8	5,142.2	5,792.5	6,332.2	7,039.4	100.0%	10.9
Textbooks	877.7	872.9	1,405.6	1,569.9	1,755.6	1,893.0	26.9	9.4
El-hi	498.6	497.6	755.9	833.4	930.1	940.3	13.4	8.0
College	379.1	375.3	649.7	736.5	825.6	952.7	13.5	11.6
Technical, Scientific, Professional	353.0	381.0	698.2	804.6	885.1	999.1	14.2	12.8
Tech./sci.	122.3	131.8	249.3	277.5	301.1	334.8	4.8	12.5
Bus./prof.	178.3	192.2	286.3	333.3	370.0	424.4	6.0	9.9
Medical	52.4	57.0	162.6	193.8	214.0	239.9	3.4	20.6
Religious	108.5	117.5	250.6	275.6	295.4	351.4	5.0	14.7
Bibles, hymnals, etc.	54.4	61.6	116.3	134.6	138.9	168.3	2.4	13.2
Other	54.1	55.9	134.3	141.0	156.5	183.1	2.6	16.1

Table 3.7: (continued)

Category	1971	1972	1977	1978	1979	1980	Percent Share of Total, 1980	Growth Rate 1971-1980
General Trade[1]	1,075.6	1,134.2	2,178.0	2,484.0	2,676.9	3,029.8	43.0%	12.9%
Book clubs	229.5	240.5	406.7	463.2	501.7	538.3	7.6	10.9
Mail order	194.6	198.9	396.4	440.4	485.8	566.9	8.1	13.5
Trade	422.7	442.0	832.4	971.4	1,016.1	1,185.4	16.8	12.6
Adult	311.6	331.1	670.2	788.0	831.1	974.6	13.8	14.0
Hardbound	242.0	251.5	501.3	586.0	608.3	695.9	9.9	13.2
Paperbound	69.6	79.6	168.9	202.0	222.8	278.7	4.0	16.4
Juvenile	111.1	110.9	162.2	183.4	185.0	210.8	3.0	7.7
Hardbound	108.9	106.5	136.1	145.2	151.5	168.5	2.4	5.2
Paperbound	2.2	4.4	26.1	38.2	33.5	42.3	0.6	34.6
Mass Market Paperbacks	228.8	252.8	542.5	609.0	673.3	739.2	10.5	14.8
Rack size	226.7	250.0	487.7	544.3	603.2	653.3	9.3	13.2
Non-rack	2.1	2.8	54.8	64.7	70.1	85.9	1.2	54.7
General Reference	301.0	278.9	294.4	341.2	383.5	384.7	5.5	3.8
Standardized Tests	25.3	26.5	44.6	51.9	61.6	67.2	1.0	11.9
University Press	39.3	41.4	56.1	62.2	68.0	80.7	1.1	7.9
Not Specified	152.0	165.4	214.7	203.1	206.0	233.5	3.3	3.9

[1] General trade totals include book clubs, mail order, trade (both adult and juvenile) and paperbacks.

Note: AAP calculations include non-rack-sized paperback books with adult trade books. They have been included here in the mass market paperback category, which is consistent with past AAP reports.

Sources: Association of American Publishers; Paine Webber Mitchell Hutchins, Inc.

Table 3.8: Book Industry Sales by Distribution Channel, 1972-1979
(in millions)

Distribution Channel	1972	1973	1974	1975	1976	1977	1978	1979	Percent Share of Total Market, 1979	Growth Rate 1972-1979
General retail	$ 466.4	$ 560.2	$ 650.2	$ 783.0	$ 907.1	$1072.1	$1251.3	$1411.1	23.3%	17.3%
College stores	409.9	438.3	507.7	583.5	649.6	735.1	840.0	866.8	14.3	9.8
Libraries/ institutions	284.8	285.1	285.4	321.9	354.2	397.2	459.5	496.0	8.2	9.1
Schools	610.5	664.6	735.5	795.7	802.3	903.5	999.0	1116.9	18.4	8.6
Direct	802.9	859.6	994.7	1016.9	1202.5	1305.5	1488.4	1659.5	27.4	11.1
Other	30.5	39.5	39.4	51.9	40.4	45.4	52.2	52.1	0.9	6.5
All domestic	2605.0	2847.3	3212.7	3554.9	3955.9	4458.8	5089.6	5602.3	92.4	11.8
Export	220.2	220.2	282.6	324.8	365.6	424.1	447.7	462.3	7.6	12.9
Total	$2825.9	$3067.5	$3495.3	$3879.7	$4321.5	$4882.9	$5537.5	$6064.6	100.0%	11.9%

Note: Discrepancies in totals are due to rounding.
Sources: Book Industry Study Group; Paine Webber Mitchell Hutchins, Inc. estimates (for 1973 and 1974) and calculations.

Operating Margins

The Association of American Publishers supplies net income from operations for those publishers that report such information. The data in Table 3.9, which show college textbook publishers to have had the highest operating margins in 1980, are based on AAP compilations, but have been modified in an attempt to adjust for the differing numbers of companies that have reported from year to year. The margins must be considered as estimates since the working assumptions in this adjustment were that the larger publishers were most likely to report and that margins tended to vary with market shares, neither of which is necessarily true. Certain large publishers are known not to have reported to the AAP from time to time and, in some industry sectors, a majority of industry participants do not report. Thus, a better assumption is that the data reflect the results of the membership of the AAP and are not necessarily indicative of the industry segments of which they are samples.

The trendline estimates in Table 3.9 are the statistical expectation of the operating margin based on normalizing operating margins over the industry segment for the 1971-1980 period. They are based on models derived from sample reports by companies of known different sizes. For some

Table 3.9: Samples of Publishers by Sector, Ranked by Estimated Operating Margins, 1980[1]

Sector	Operating Margin	Rank	Trendline[2]	Rank
College textbooks	20.4%	1	16.3%	3
El-hi textbooks	19.0	2	17.4	2
Juvenile trade books	16.9	3	10.5	6
Business & other professional	14.2	4	0.9	8
Medical books	13.2	5	N.E.	—
Mail order publications	13.1	6	-2.2	10
Professional books (total)	12.4	7	10.6	5
Book clubs	11.0	8	12.4	4
Technical & scientific books	9.4	9	18.6	1
Trade books (total)	8.2	10	0.9	9
Adult hardbound trade	5.6	11	4.2	7
Adult paperbound trade books	3.8	12	N.E.	—
Religious trade books	2.4	13	N.E.	—
Mass market paperbacks	1.4	14	-5.6	11

N.E.: Not estimated.

[1] Operating margins are pretax.

[2] See text for explanation.

Sources: Paine Webber Mitchell Hutchins, Inc. calculations based on Association of American Publishers statistical reports.

categories, the Association of American Publishers has, in some or all years, provided breakdowns of operating margins by size of publisher for samples reporting to it. Again, for many categories the samples are small and may well be unrepresentative of the universe of book publishers. Table 3.10 has attempted to calculate margins for those companies which comprise the top, middle and bottom thirds of industry participants, divided into equal numbers of companies, using the assumptions described above: that the larger companies tend to be more likely to report their earnings to AAP in all categories.

The first set of margin estimates for each group in Table 3.10 are estimated actual results in 1980. The second set, which are in agreement with the trendline sector estimates of Table 3.9, are "normalized" estimates based on data for the decade from 1971 through 1980.

While differences exist among the various estimates of operating margins by industry sector and by size of company, certain patterns do stand out. One is that larger companies in each sector, those with larger market shares, tend to show the highest margins. This phenomenon can be seen throughout American industry. A second pattern may be less easy to discern from the data: high margins are dependent on high product differentiation. For example, estimated profits of mass market paperback publishers in 1980 are low or nonexistent, for while this sector has relatively few participants, it has few differences in the product line from publisher to publisher. The adult hardbound and religious trade sectors also show relatively low margins. But in contrast with mass market paperbacks, these sectors have enormous numbers of participants whose ranks are steadily growing. At the other end of the profit spectrum, in the textbook and professional categories—where books are often highly specified

Table 3.10: Estimated Operating Margins for Different Size Publishers, by Selected Industry Sector, 1980

Sector	Smallest Third	Middle-Sized Third	Largest Third
Trade books (total)	8.8%	8.8%	8.7%
Trendline	1.6	9.8	8.5
Professional books (total)	12.8	11.3	13.0
Trendline	9.6	10.2	12.0
El-hi textbooks	11.7	15.6	24.9
Trendline	13.2	14.4	23.8
College textbooks	9.4	14.2	25.4
Trendline	1.9	17.1	25.4

Sources: Paine Webber Mitchell Hutchins, Inc. estimates based on Association of American Publishers statistical reports.

for their uses—profit margins are above average. The high margins of juveniles are likewise associated with product differentiation; some successful books can be sold for generations and have no substitutable equivalents: e.g., *Winnie-the-Pooh.*

The comparative operating margins by size shown in Table 3.10 can be contrasted with data for the overall industry by referring to corporate income tax returns compiled by the Internal Revenue Service. Unfortunately, these data are not available until several years after their submission, but even so they are of interest. Table 3.11 presents such an analysis. Returns are arrayed by asset size (not adjusted for inflation and the growth of the economy). Pretax income margins (Mar) consist of net income, less

Table 3.11: Estimated Pretax Margins and After-tax Return on Equity, Selected Years, 1963-1974

Company Assets (in thousands)		Fiscal Year Ending June 30						
		1963	1965	1967	1969	1971	1973	1974
Total	Mar	9.29%	10.26%	9.47%	5.89%	6.79%	6.59%	8.98%
	ROE	8.71	13.86	10.00	5.58	7.22	N.A.	N.A.
$0-$100	Mar	(3.42)	4.88	(6.35)	5.89	(4.69)	0.69	2.97
	ROE	N.A.	11.22	13.61	5.58	N.A.	N.E.	N.E.
$100-$500	Mar	3.53	4.54	4.41	(1.69)	0.91	4.44	3.44
	ROE	5.85	9.84	9.90	N.A.	0.85	N.E.	N.E.
$500-$1000	Mar	6.56	6.30	1.97	1.09	0.36	7.84	(0.42)
	ROE	9.83	11.22	N.A.	N.A.	N.A.	N.E.	N.E.
$1000-$5000	Mar	10.85	10.44	10.92	7.83	0.44	4.76	8.15
	ROE	13.46	15.90	12.46	N.A.	N.A.	N.E.	N.E.
$5000-$10,000	Mar	8.33	11.55	10.91	3.18	7.40	2.47	9.99
	ROE	9.96	13.38	10.34	2.22	9.15	N.E.	N.E.
$10,000-$25,000	Mar	10.68	11.60	7.88	7.70	3.69	3.74	2.93
	ROE	9.20	13.41	7.15	7.21	3.15	N.E.	N.E.
$25,000-$50,000	Mar	14.23	12.78	10.85	7.72	5.48	8.42	10.82
	ROE	11.97	12.64	9.29	7.24	4.47	N.E.	N.E.
$50,000-$100,000	Mar	4.86	12.04	13.69	7.20	11.41	8.26	15.23
	ROE	5.56	17.36	11.82	6.70	10.01	N.E.	N.E.
$100,000-$250,000	Mar	2.88	8.71	8.86	15.21	10.85	10.03	15.56
	ROE	3.80	14.36	8.28	11.24	12.26	N.E.	N.E.
$250,000 +	Mar	N.A.	N.A.	14.25	4.99	8.07	6.41	6.52
	ROE	N.A.	N.A.	16.43	5.06	7.64	N.E.	N.E.

Mar: Pretax margin.
ROE: After-tax return on equity.
N.A.: Not available.
N.E.: Not estimated.
Negative returns on sales are given in parentheses.
Sources: Paine Webber Mitchell Hutchins, Inc. based on Internal Revenue Service data.

deficits, divided by reported business receipts. Return on equity (ROE) figures are obtained by dividing aftertax net income, less deficits, by year-end net capital stock, surplus and retained earnings.

Based on samples reported by the AAP, estimated industry margins increased in 1975 (when price controls were lifted), rose strongly in 1976, eased in 1977, went up sharply in 1978, and eased in 1979 and 1980, and perhaps in 1981. Overall, margins were probably higher in 1981 than in 1974, and perhaps exceeded the peak margins of the 1965-1967 period in 1976-1979.

Measures of Productivity

During the 1970s, both the number of books printed and the number of employees in the book publishing industry grew about 3% per year, as shown in Table 3.12. As the numbers of publishers, new titles and books in print also grew, these figures do not clearly illustrate productivity trends in the industry. However, it would appear that the average new title is selling fewer copies, that the average new firm is producing fewer new titles (i.e.,

Table 3.12: Book Publishing Employees, Books Produced, New Titles and Establishments, Selected Years, 1972-1980

	1972	1974	1976	1977	1978	1979	1980
Books Produced (in millions)	1,436.6	1,529.8	1,551.9	1,646.6	1,728.0	1,755.0	1,804.6
Employees (in thousands)	57.1	54.4	58.2	59.5	63.5	70.7	72.7
New Titles							
(Old series)[1]	26,868	30,575	26,983	27,423	—	—	—
(New series)[1]	—	—	32,352	33,292	31,802	36,112	34,030
Titles in Print	N.A.	418,000	450,000	478,000	498,000	520,000	538,000
Total Number of Publishers							
Books in Print	6,113	—	—	7,279	—	—	—
LMP	959	—	—	1,234	—	—	—
Census Bureau Establishments	1,205	—	—	1,745	—	—	—
Companies	1,124	—	—	1,652	—	—	—

[1] AAP changed its methods for tabulation of new titles in 1976. The new series covers 18 months.

N.A.: Not available.

Sources: Bureau of the Census; Book Industry Study Group; *Publishers Weekly; Books in Print; Literary Market Place (LMP);* Paine Webber Mitchell Hutchins, Inc. estimates.

that the company is of smaller size) and has fewer employees, and that the industry's productivity is being achieved both in terms of titles per employee and units per employee. In short, the industry's output is becoming more specialized.

Table 3.12 does not necessarily imply that the industry is becoming less efficient. The longer-term consistency in margins (and probably in return on equity as well) argues otherwise. What the data do suggest is that the efficiency of book publishing is not measured merely in units produced, but in the value of the information produced relative to the expenses associated with its production. More specialized information being produced for smaller audiences might logically be expected to be more valuable per unit produced; productivity in this industry is indeed measured in part by the number of titles produced per worker and not by the number of units per worker alone. Hence, any trend toward above-average inflation in book prices may be justified as demonstrated in the marketplace by industry margins. Furthermore, this implies that small, highly specialized publishers with short production runs of very expensive titles can be as profitable as very large ones with long production runs of inexpensive titles. Table 3.10 illustrates this point.

INDICATORS OF CONCENTRATION

In 1979, American Express made a bold cash bid for McGraw-Hill which, if accepted, would have been the largest acquisition ever of a company long identified chiefly as a book publisher. That same year, both Mattel and American Broadcasting Cos. bid for Macmillan and the latter did acquire The Chilton Co., a publisher of books and trade magazines. Other publishing companies are frequently identified as real or possible acquisition targets. Thus, it has appeared that a great merger wave and resulting concentration is taking place. Closer study, however, suggests that recent developments are not inconsistent with long-term concentration trends in the industry and thus do not seem likely to lead to a significant alteration in the industry's degree of concentration.

Table 3.13 presents a comparative history of recent merger activity. This table suggests that known mergers, usually of larger-size companies, tend to take place in the book publishing industry at perhaps 3.6 times the rate of mergers in all manufacturing industries; that, with respect to all mergers, the number in the publishing and printing industries overall is a reasonably consistent 2.5%; and that the average rate of book publishing mergers from 1976 through 1980 (1.16%) was below the average rate of the prior thirteen years (1.96%). Table 3.13 and Table 3.4 viewed together indicate that the rate of acquisition has been a small fraction of the rate of formation of new companies (perhaps 13%-14% in the 1972-1977 period,

Table 3.13: Estimated Mergers and Merger Rates, 1963-1980

Year	Manufacturing[1]			All Mergers			Book Publishing		
	Number of Mergers	Number of Companies (in thousands)	Rate	Total	Print/Publishing Mergers	Print/Publ. Share	Number of Mergers	Number of Companies	Rate
1963	861	196.7	0.44%	1,361	—	—	10	936	1.07%
1964	854	199.5	0.43	1,950	—	—	8	943	0.85
1965	1,008	199.2	0.51	2,125	—	—	23	949	2.42
1966	995	202.4	0.49	2,377	—	—	25	956	2.62
1967	1,496	211.4	0.71	2,975	—	—	29	963	3.01
1968	2,407	204.7	1.18	4,462	—	—	47	993	4.73
1969	2,307	216.1	1.07	6,107	172	2.82%	44	1,024	4.30
1970	1,351	212.3	0.64	5,152	117	2.27	13	1,057	1.22
1971	1,011	213.6	0.47	4,608	106	2.30	11	1,090	1.01
1972	911	217.4	0.42	4,801	91	1.90	9	1,124	0.80
1973	874	222.1	0.39	4,040	91	2.25	6	1,214	0.49
1974	602	217.3	0.26	2,861	66	2.30	24	1,311	1.83
1975	439	221.4	0.20	2,297	47	2.05	16	1,416	1.13
1976	559	217.9	0.26	2,276	58	2.55	17	1,530	1.11
1977	590	N.A.	—	2,224	57	2.56	28	1,652	1.69
1978	607	N.A.	—	2,106	65	3.09	14	1,784[2]	0.78
1979	658	N.A.	—	2,128	58	2.73	20	1,927[2]	1.04
1980	725	N.A.	—	1,889	57	3.02	25	2,081[2]	1.20

[1] Includes mining.

[2] Estimate.

N.A.: Not available.

Sources: Federal Trade Commission and Internal Revenue Service for manufacturing (and mining); W.T. Grimm & Co. for all mergers. *Publishers Weekly, U.S. Census of Manufactures* and *Annual Survey of Manufactures* for book publishing industry; Paine Webber Mitchell Hutchins Inc., estimates and calculations.

for example), so that the industry continues to grow, as previously demonstrated; that cycles in publishing mergers appear to parallel cycles in other industries and are, therefore, apparently tied to broad economic factors affecting all industry; and, finally, that the greatest period of recent book publishing merger activity was that from 1965 through 1969.

Table 3.13 does not establish that there is no concentration taking place in the book publishing industry, but merely that there is little indication that any trends toward concentration are being significantly altered by recent merger activity. Historically, the industry has always been characterized by mergers and acquisitions, and virtually all current publishers of any size have made one or more such transactions in achieving their present dimensions.

Rationales for Mergers and Acquisitions in Book Publishing

Every book title is a unique information product with a unique niche to fill in society's information requirements. Most publishers have started with single titles, or with very few, and have rather quickly filled their target niches. Once that took place, their unit growth became modest or even negative while their cash flow continued to be high. This cash flow provided the resources to create new information products or to acquire them in the form of "lists" (rights to, and inventories of, other companies' books), or companies (with their specialized editorial staffs, which seems to have been the most successful approach). The continuing sales of "backlist" books—those few titles that have proven long-range appeal— have historically distinguished the unprofitable start-up publishing operation from the successful, profitable older company and seem to have represented the greatest economic difference between the two. Thus, financially, existing publishers with established backlists have always been attractive investments to other publishers, in contrast to the uncertain investments required to publish new and unproven titles.

The industry has been characterized by a relatively large number of new company formations each year. This is because: 1) it is still possible for many individuals or small groups to enter most sectors of book publishing with relatively limited funds; 2) publishing is involved with the world of ideas; and 3) many people have ideas that they consider worth publishing. (Such factors are substantiated by the data in Tables 3.3, 3.4, 3.12 and 3.13.) These new entrants, once established, but often handicapped by a dearth of new capital or new ideas, have been those most frequently targeted for acquisition in the past. As in the cases of the United States Book Co. and the American Book Co. the acquisition of lists or other assets has tended to provide only temporary success in the book publishing industry. Most successful acquirers have retained at least the key editorial staffs and often the entire organizations of the acquired publishers, because the key to successful publishing is having the right people, and their ideas. The economies of scale achieved through mergers are most obvious in selling and distribution, are somewhat less evident in manufacturing and administration, and may be nonexistent in editorial functions.

In fact, for some time many successful publishers have gone so far as to create new publishing subsidiaries from their own personnel, to hold on to key editors, salesmen or specialty markets. Examples include Prentice-Hall's formation of Goodyear (later sold to SFN Cos., Inc.) and Reston Publishing, and Richard D. Irwin's establishment of Dorsey Press, Learning Systems Co. and Business Publications, Inc. There seem to be limits, either in the markets or in the successful management of creative publishing people, to the growth and profitability of tightly integrated publishing enterprises.

Thus, perhaps among all industries, publishing seems least likely to develop into a single, monolithic source of coherent opinion and information unless the industry's role is usurped or closely controlled by an even larger institution such as government.

Concentration Among Suppliers, Vendors and Customers

While, in general, the concentration of the overall book publishing industry does not appear to be changing significantly, its members could be affected by concentration trends in related industries: among its suppliers, such as book printers; its channels of distribution, such as book retailers; or its customers, such as schools and school districts (whose numbers have been steadily declining). Table 3.14 compares the first two of these sectors with book publishing.

Concentration in book publishing has declined from its peak in the 1960s. Some modest concentration does seem to be underway in book printing, but it does not presently pose a problem for book publishers because it is in part due to, and is being accompanied by, the growing use by large printers of technology designed to handle short-run books more efficiently. Thus, for some time, publishers of all sizes may be able to continue to reduce manufacturing costs for their products relative to revenues, which has already been a long-range trend.

Although not apparent in the concentration ratios for retailing in general, there has been a recent tendency for such rapidly growing retail bookstore chains as Waldenbooks and B. Dalton to account for larger shares of retail book sales. Indeed, as suggested by Table 3.7, these chains, by making books more widely available to American consumers, may be increasing book publishers' overall sales; at the least, retail sales, including

Table 3.14: Comparative Concentration Among Book Publishers, Book Printers and Retailers, Selected Years, 1947-1977

| Year | Percent of Value of Shipments Accounted For by: | | | | | | | | | | | |
| | 4 Largest | | | 8 Largest | | | 20 Largest | | | 50 Largest | | |
	Pubs.	Prtrs.	Rets.	Pubs.	Prtrs.	Rets.	Pubs.	Prtrs.	Rets.	Pubs.	Prtrs.	Rets.
1947	18%	N.A.	N.A.	29%	N.A.	N.A.	48%	N.A.	N.A.	N.A.	N.A.	N.A.
1954	21	N.A.	N.A.	32	N.A.	N.A.	51	N.A.	N.A.	N.A.	N.A.	N.A.
1958	16	24%	10%	29	34%	13%	48	51%	16%	69%	68%	19%
1963	20	19	7	33	30	9	56	48	16	76	66	21
1967	20	21	7	32	30	10	57	48	17	77	64	21
1972	19	24	11	31	36	15	56	53	20	77	68	24
1977	17	25	9[1]	30	35	13[1]	57	49	21[1]	74	64	25[1]

N.A.: Not available.

[1] Statistical projection.

Sources: Bureau of the Census, *Concentration Ratios in Manufacturing* and *Retail Trade, Publishers Weekly,* Paine Webber Mitchell Hutchins, Inc.

direct sales, grew faster during the 1970s than in any other decade. On the other hand, this phenomenon does seem to pose potential problems for the book publishing industry. The emphasis some chains tend to place on heavily promoted "big books" may make it harder for smaller companies to bring their wares to readers' attention, both directly—because obtaining retail displays of their more specialized books becomes more difficult—and indirectly—because the positions of traditional bookstores are placed in jeopardy by the growth of the chains. However, similar concerns have been expressed by industry observers since at least the early 1920s, when large department stores were accused of the same practices and potential effects on the industry, with little apparent harm actually resulting. Indeed, O.H. Cheney had lamented the lack of bookstores outside the major East and West Coast population centers. For all their alleged potential ill effects, the large book retailing chains have brought a reasonable selection of books to parts of the country that previously had virtually no retail access.

Concentration by Industry Segment

Concentration ratios for the book publishing industry segments charted in Table 3.15 suggest no significant changes in the market shares held by the four largest publishing companies overall, or by the leading companies in many segments. That may, however, reflect trends in constituent markets. For example, the el-hi textbook market was larger than the college textbook market but growing at a slower pace; the mass market paperback market was smaller than the trade market but growing faster (Table 3.8); and the Bureau of the Census redefined the reference book market to include dictionaries and the like, as well as the subscription reference (encyclopedia) group which had originally comprised "reference books" and which had also long been dominated by four companies. Thus, the growth rates of the various company groups in Table 3.15 are, in part, misleading because of the definitions used and because of the highly specialized structure of the industry.

POSSIBLE FUTURE TRENDS IN CONCENTRATION

In combination, the data supplied in Table 3.15 and the irregular samples of the Association of American Publishers' statistical reports suggest that during the decade of the 1970s, while the total number of publishers rose, there may have been a slight decline in the numbers of publishers in the adult trade paperback, medical, business and professional, technical/scientific, book club, mail order, schoolbook and college textbook fields. However, due to the methodology used, these results may simply reflect the fact that relatively fewer and larger participants reported figures to the AAP in recent years. By the same token, the numbers of adult hardbound trade, religious, reference and professional book publishers almost certainly rose during the period. No significant trends were evident in the numbers of juvenile and mass market paperback publishers.

An indication of likely further consolidation through dissolution or merger may be found in the margins of the various groups (see Tables 3.9 and 3.10). Based on sketchy data, margins apparently fell (or remained low) during the 1970s in such fields as mass market paperbacks, some mail order sectors, and certain, small business, trade, religious and even college textbook publishing operations. In 1979 and 1980 margins seem to have improved for both book clubs and medium-sized trade and schoolbook publishers. Accordingly, other trends affecting these segments may not persist.

The mass market paperback industry continues to be the book publishing segment with the worst profit trend. Indeed, the smaller participants in that area may have incurred continuing losses throughout the 1970s. It is therefore not surprising that none of these companies is publicly held, nor that numerous mergers involving such operations have been proposed and executed in recent years.

The problems affecting mass market paperback publishers seem to have been of three principal types: 1) distribution—excessive returns of unsold books from retail outlets; 2) expenses—particularly increasing royalty payments for bestsellers, so as to obtain shelf space for other, less popular publications along with the expectation that the "blockbusters" will make up in volume what they lack in margins; and 3) pricing—an inability to price their products so as to adequately cover the first two expenses. In an age of specialization, of segmented markets and targeted products, mass market paperbacks, as their name suggests, need to change and become aimed at more specifically defined groups of readers. That such change is possible has been demonstrated by such publishers as Harlequin, which created a new genre of women's romantic fiction using a stable of authors at relatively low royalty expense. This publisher also developed new methods of marketing, such as direct mail, thereby reducing returns. With the two deadliest expense elements under control, Harlequin was able to achieve above average profit margins while underpricing its standard paperbacks. Although some other paperback publishers have since emulated Harlequin in detail, more mass market publishers may have to adopt equally innovative strategies to survive.

Pressures on Other Book Publishing Categories

During the first half of the 1980s, it seems likely that federal cutbacks

Table 3.15: Market Shares by Numbers of Companies and Book Types

Type of Book	1958	1963	1967	1972	1977	Growth Rate
	(dollars in billions)					
All Book Publishing:						
Total shipments	$1,010.7	$1,547.8	$2,255.3	$2,915.4	$5,007.9	8.5%
Top 4 companies	16%	18%	16%	16%	16%	8.2
Top 8 companies	26	29	27	27	29	8.9
Top 20 companies	45	52	52	52	54	9.3
Top 50 companies	65	73	75	75	73	9.1
Textbooks:						
Total shipments	$ 281.7	$ 471.1	$ 733.6	$ 809.6	$1,408.7	8.3%
Top 4 companies	33%	32%	29%	33%	35%	8.7
Top 8 companies	50	54	50	54	57	8.9
Top 20 companies	76	81	79	80	80	8.5
Top 50 companies	93	94	94	95	95	8.4
Technical, Scientific, Professional Books:						
Total shipments	$ 116.0	$ 156.3	$ 240.2	$ 403.0	$ 684.1	10.0%
Top 4 companies	27%	32%	38%	39%	40%	12.3
Top 8 companies	43	49	54	57	55	10.5
Top 20 companies	71	68	74	76	75	10.5
Top 50 companies	91	87	91	92	89	10.1
Religious Books:						
Total shipments	$ 58.6	$ 81.1	$ 110.4	$ 131.2	$ 236.3	7.2%
Top 4 companies	30%	22%	27%	36%	26%	7.6
Top 8 companies	45	37	46	51	42	7.6
Top 20 companies	70	65	74	76	68	7.4
Top 50 companies	90	89	96	97	91	7.4

Table 3.15: (continued)

Type of Book	1958	1963	1967	1972	1977	Growth Rate
			(dollars in billions)			
Trade Books:						
Total shipments	$ 274.7	$ 458.2	$ 657.7	$1,006.7	$1,895.6	10.4%
Top 4 companies	39%	30%	28%	29%	31%	9.3
Top 8 companies	53	46	46	47	48	10.0
Top 20 companies	72	59	70	74	76	11.2
Top 50 companies	90	89	91	92	92	10.6
General Reference Books:[1]						
Total shipments	$ 163.6	$ 207.3	216.3	$ 235.3	$ 305.4	2.7%
Top 4 companies	—	87%	81%	71%	62%	0.2
Top 8 companies	—	96	91	82	74	0.8
Top 20 companies	—	100	N.A.	94	92	2.1
Top 50 companies	—	—	100	99+	98	2.6
Other:						
Total shipments	$ 96.0	$ 154.8	$ 200.1	$ 174.1	$ 159.5	2.4%
Top 4 companies	—	37%	48%	—	51%	4.4
Top 8 companies	—	48	61	—	67	4.6
Top 20 companies	—	68	78	—	88	4.2
Top 50 companies	—	85	92	—	98	3.4
Not Specified:						
Total shipments	$ 20.2	$ 18.9	97.0	$ 155.5	$ 318.1	17.4%

[1] Encyclopedias and, from 1972, includes dictionaries, etc.
Sources: William S. Lofquist, Department of Commerce; Paine Webber Mitchell Hutchins, Inc. calculations.

may at least potentially impair sales of books to the institutional markets: schools and libraries in particular. Moreover, the growing importance of new technologies for the delivery of entertainment and information raises questions about the book as a competing delivery system. The unique characteristics of the book make it improbable that we will witness its demise in the foreseeable future, perhaps not for centuries. However, the effects of these twin changes—economic and technological—will certainly be felt, probably in terms of the ways books are focused, marketed and used, and possibly in terms of change in the structures of segments of the book industry.

During the 1970s, new economic patterns became evident in two industry segments under stress. The mass market paperback industry, as we have shown, suffered because its products lacked differentiation in an increasingly segmented information market environment. The effects of technology on the industry as a whole could produce similar stresses, forcing it to differentiate its products from those most likely to be replicated or replaced by nonprint formats. At the same time, the growth of new competition for readers' time and interest is likely to further encourage all media to become increasingly specialized and to witness the least specialized becoming the most vulnerable.

The mass market paperback industry, by definition, seems likely to continue to be troubled. Unless it is able to differentiate its wares, this sector is likely to become even more concentrated through the dissolution of smaller companies or through their forced sale to larger companies who can achieve some economies of scale. If publishers have, or can develop, highly differentiated products, however, they may able to capitalize on the new media. For one, they can adapt their wares to new video or electronic formats at lower cost than could be achieved by start-up ventures with no print markets. Second, by using the increasingly segmented audences watching special interest cable programming, publishers themselves can "narrowcast" their books to reach the appropriate readers more effectively than was ever before achieved by direct mail. It also seems probable that print products that enlarge upon, or extend, popular video products will benefit in the future as they have in the past. *Scoring Big at Pac-Man,* for example, was listed as one of the mass market bestsellers in an April 1982 edition of *The New York Times.* And, of course, movies and television have long aided the sales of related books.

For the el-hi industry in the 1970s demographics were unfavorable and there was some paring of expenditures, particularly toward the end of the decade. Both large and small publishers within this segment retained, or even improved, margins for most years while middle-sized publishers' margins came under pressure, resulting in a "U-shaped" profit margin picture. If the cutbacks in governmental expenditures do severely impact the book publishing industry, this pattern of the medium-sized firms being most seriously affected—a pattern evident in other mature industries—may reappear in book publishing segments. In the el-hi industry, the U-shaped pattern of margins seemed to reflect retrenchment by the larger publishers, who concentrated on major subordinate markets such as textbooks in reading, reducing competition in the smaller subordinate markets in which small publishers thrived, but increasing competition in the key markets in which the middle-sized publishers typically held positions significant to their profits.

In textbook publishing, book lists are differentiated in part by the provision of services, such as consulting to customers. Medium-sized publishers typically found it difficult to provide comparable packages. If government cutbacks do significantly affect books, el-hi books seem logical victims. Other potentially vulnerable categories include college texts, juvenile, adult hardbound trade, professional and university press books. The appropriate strategies for the affected middle-sized companies in these sectors seem to be: 1) to specialize in smaller markets or 2) to acquire other companies to achieve large enough market shares to compete with the leaders. Of course, heavy developmental expenditures to achieve large size through internal expansion is yet another strategy, but it is difficult and slow to accomplish. Accordingly, government cutbacks might reduce the number of middle-sized companies by encouraging their merger or dissolution, or might lead them to acquire small companies with profitable niches. Conceivably, however, they might also lead to the establishment of more small specialist companies.

The Impact of Federal Fund Cutbacks

Federal or other government expenditure cuts will not necessarily lead to reduced purchases of books, including textbooks. The introduction of large-scale federal funding programs in the 1960s appeared to lead to only one year of above-average el-hi and college textbook sales, and then to approximately five years of relatively weak sales in both categories—exactly the opposite of what had been anticipated. The new federal programs often specified the purchase of books, were legally supposed to augment previous expenditures rather than to replace them, and often provided for new, book-intensive purchase categories such as classroom libraries. Accordingly, the poor actual sales experience has been blamed on such other factors as federal fund cutbacks (from levels that had been expected), the growth of the used-book business at the college level, and teacher militancy at the el-hi level (in the belief that teachers' salaries were claiming larger shares of educational expenditures).

There is little evidence, however, of any of these factors having a major impact in the real world. One hypothesis, therefore, that explains the minimal impact of federal funds on book sales, is twofold. First, local funds were replaced by, rather than supplemented by, federal funds. Second, at least initially, those funds also paid for the massive introduction of audiovisual hardware so that audiovisual software (films, records, tapes and the like) subsequently competed as never before for instructional dollars that previously would have gone for textbooks. The evidence for this appears in the enormous growth in the A/V sector between 1965 and 1967 (and from 1966 to 1970, the years in which textbook sales weakened), the slowed growth of the audiovisual sector later in the 1970s when textbook sales stabilized, and the tendency before and since in el-hi schools to regard audiovisuals as supplementary rather than basal materials. In an economic sense, "supplementary" has a meaning equivalent to "discretionary" in the schools. Thus, once schools have adjusted to the overall impact of reduced federal and local expenditures, textbooks may well claim larger shares of reduced overall expenditures and conceivably larger absolute amounts as well.

LEADING PUBLISHERS*

Concentration among the largest book publishers in the U.S. decreased between 1978 and 1980. The 13 leading publishers, identified in Table 3.16, accounted for about 57% of all industry book sales in 1980, down from close to 59% two years earlier. Time Inc. is the largest book publisher in the U.S. Its sales growth between 1978 and 1980 was far greater than that of any of the other leading publishers identified in Table 3.16. Moreover, Time's growth was virtually all generated internally, without the benefit of acquisitions. The largest portion of Time Inc.'s book revenue comes from its Time-Life Books division, which markets its book series via mail order. Time Inc. also includes revenue from Book-of-the-Month Club (BOMC), acquired in 1977. BOMC does not actually publish its own books, but distributes the books published by others. However, even without BOMC revenues, Time's revenues exceed those of the second largest publisher, McGraw-Hill, Inc. Time also owns trade and textbook publisher Little, Brown.

McGraw-Hill, Inc.'s book division includes text, trade and professional books. Increased revenues of 16.4% over two years lifted it from third to second largest publisher. Reader's Digest, like Time Inc., sells most of its books via direct mail. Its line includes the condensed book series, as well as numerous one-shop books on home repairs, home legal reference manuals

---

*This section added by Benjamin M. Compaine.

Table 3.16: Leading Book Publishers, by Revenue, 1978 and 1980
(in millions)

Rank, by 1980 Sales	Company	1978	1980	% Increase 1978-1980
1	Time Inc.	$ 360.9	$ 498.0	38.0%
2	McGraw-Hill, Inc.	305.3	355.3	16.4
3	Reader's Digest Assoc.[1]	306.0	340.0	11.1
4	CBS, Inc.[1]	292.0	320.0	9.6
5	Doubleday & Co., Inc.[1,2]	285.0	316.0	10.9
6	Grolier, Inc.	242.8	312.7	28.8
7	Harcourt Brace Jovanovich	248.0	294.7	18.8
8	Encyclopaedia Britannica[1]	250.0	280.0	12.0
9	Scott & Fetzer Co., Inc.[3]	273.0	279.2	2.3
10	SFN Cos., Inc.[2]	225.2	270.8	20.2
11	Times Mirror Co., Inc.	214.2	263.6	23.1
12	Macmillan, Inc.	207.9	240.0	15.4
13	Prentice-Hall, Inc.	189.0	231.6	22.5
	Total, 13 leading companies	$3399.3	$4001.9	17.7%
	Total industry	5792.5	7039.4	21.5%
	% of industry accounted for by 13 leading companies	58.7%	56.9%	

[1] Estimate.

[2] Fiscal year ends April 30.

[3] Fiscal year ends Nov. 30.

Source: *BP Report*, July 20, 1981, Knowledge Industry Publications, Inc.

and the like. CBS Inc.'s book publishing is mostly text and professional. Imprints include Holt, Rinehart and Winston, which publishes some trade as well as textbooks; W.B. Saunders Co., a medical book publisher; Praeger, which issues professional books, and BFA Education Media, which publishes textbooks and supplementary materials.

Doubleday & Co., the fifth largest publisher, with 1980 revenue of about $316 million, is best known for the trade books published under the corporate imprint. It also runs the largest book club, the Literary Guild, and a brace of other specialized book clubs. Doubleday owns Dell, the mass market paperback publisher, as well as Delacorte and Dial Press. Grolier, Inc. has apparently rebounded from its setbacks in the mid-1970s. The encyclopedia and mail order book publisher was close to bankruptcy, but its sales in recent years have been strong.

Although most of the publishers listed in Table 3.16 have made acquisitions over the years, none made any substantial purchase between 1978 and mid-1982. The increases in sales calculated in the table, therefore, reflect true internal growth, generated by higher prices or increased number of units sold. Appendix 3-1 identifies the imprints of the firms charted in Table 3.16.

Leading Trade Publishers

Trade books, the fiction and nonfiction titles that are addressed to the general consumer, are the most visible segment of the book publishing industry because they enjoy wide distribution through bookstores across the country and their authors appear on the various radio and television talk shows. Though perhaps the most glamorous segment of the business, trade publishing is not the largest. Most publishers lose money on hardcover trade books. Profit, to the extent that any exists, is made by selling rights to a paperback publisher.

For many years, Random House has been the largest trade hardcover publisher. As seen in Table 3.17, Random House had 1980 sales of about $95 million. The company was sold by RCA to the Newhouse family interests in 1980. Simon & Schuster, in recent years part of the Gulf + Western conglomerate, almost doubled its sales between 1978 and 1980, in the process moving up from fourth rank to become the second largest trade publisher, with about $80 million in 1980 revenue. Harper & Row, the third largest publisher, completed its acquisition of Lippincott in 1978; the Minneapolis Star & Tribune Co. sold its 40% interest in Harper & Row in 1981.

All figures in Table 3.17 are estimates. Publishing companies do not report separately from other book publishing revenue the portion derived from various sectors. Of course those firms that are privately held report no revenues or profits. The largest hardcover trade publishers accounted for about 71% of sector revenue in 1980, compared to 67% in 1978.

Leading Mass Market Paperback Publishers

Mass market paperback publishing is one of the most concentrated segments of the book publishing industry. This is in large measure due to the substantial capital requirement and difficulty in obtaining national distribution to the 100,000 outlets serviced by magazine and book wholesalers. The very term "mass market" implies considerable investment in printing, even if the distribution were available. By definition, a publisher cannot be a short-run, special interest participant in mass market paperbacks. Yet despite the concentration, the economics of this segment have resulted in generally low profit margins for even the leading firms.

In 1980, Bantam maintained its long time position as the largest mass

Table 3.17: Leading Hardcover Trade Publishers, by Revenue, 1978 and 1980
(in millions)

1980 Rank	Company	Parent Company	1978 Sales	1980 Sales	% Increase 1978-1980
1	Random House	Newhouse Publications	$ 80.0	$ 95.0	18.8%
2	Simon & Schuster	Gulf + Western	40.5[1]	80.0[1]	97.5
3	Harper & Row	Harper & Row, Publishers, Inc.	61.8	68.8	11.3
4	Doubleday Publishing	Doubleday & Co., Inc.	50.0	64.0	28.0
5	Crown/Outlet	Crown	40.0	50.0	25.0
6a	Little, Brown	Time Inc.	22.0	26.0	18.2
6b	Putnam Publishing Group	MCA, Inc.	22.0	26.0	18.2
7	Macmillan	Macmillan, Inc.	20.0	24.2	21.0
8	William Morrow	Hearst Corp.[2]	18.5	23.0	24.3
9	Houghton Mifflin	Houghton Mifflin Co.	17.1	19.3	12.9
10	Grosset & Dunlap	Filmways, Inc.	17.0-18.0	17.0-18.0	–
	Total, 11 leading hardcover trade publishers		$389.4	$493.8	26.8%
	Total adult trade hardcover		586.0	695.9	18.8%
	% accounted for by 11 leading publishers		66.5%	71.0%	

[1] Fiscal year ends July 31.

[2] Hearst Corp. acquired William Morrow in February 1981. Up to that time it was owned by SFN Cos., Inc.

Source: *BP Report*, August 31, 1981, Knowledge Industry Publications, Inc.

market publisher, with total revenue of about $101 million, or a 15% share of the total market (down from an 18% share in 1977). Bantam is owned by German publisher, Bertelsmann. The eight largest paperback publishers listed in Table 3.18 accounted for almost 75% of sales in the U.S., and the 13 largest firms accounted for 89% of sales in 1980.

Leading Textbook Publishers

Tables 3.19 and 3.20 provide the rankings of the leading college and el-hi textbook publishers, respectively. McGraw-Hill has been among the fastest growing college text publishers since 1975, experiencing a 65.8% increase in sales between 1975 and 1979. Prentice-Hall, however, remains the leading publisher, with 1979 sales of $105 million. Wadsworth Publishing Co. made the largest percentage gain, with sales up 77% in the 1975-1979 period. Overall, concentration among the 11 largest college publishers decreased substantially during the five years.

Among publishers of elementary and high school textbooks, SFN Cos. (formerly Scott, Foresman), remains the leader. Houghton Mifflin was the fastest growing among those who relied on internal growth. Two acquisitions included Esquire's purchase of Allyn & Bacon and D.C. Heath's addition of American Book Co. (acquired from Litton Educational Publishing).

DISCUSSION

In considering ways in which today's book publishing industry might change, and how it might evolve into new forms, including more concentrated ones, it is helpful to recall those historical factors which shaped the industry's intrinsic characteristics. Whereas publishers frequently began as printers (manufacturers) or booksellers (retailers), the industry changed with the advent of the copyright and national markets. As a result, few book publishers now do their own printing. The desirability of using printing facilities closer to markets and of being able to choose among a variety of competing technologies and suppliers has tended to separate this function from book publishing. Moreover, except for possible bookstores at their own company facilities, few book publishers presently operate such stores. Those that do, such as Doubleday, carry the wares of a large number of competitors and not merely their own. Today, in fact, even the traditional editorial functions of publishers are often separated to some degree. El-hi books, which were traditionally prepared in-house, are now sometimes prepared by independent, specialist firms. In addition, a number of affiliated and/or separate editor/author groups now serve the

Table 3.18: Leading Mass Market Publishers, by Revenue, 1978 and 1980
(in millions)

1980 Rank	Company	Parent Company	1978 Sales	1980 Sales	% Increase 1978-1980
1	Bantam[1]	Bertelsmann	$ 93.0	$101.0[2]	8.6
2	Harlequin (U.S. sales)	Harlequin Enterprises	45.0-50.0	75.0-80.0[4]	63.2
3	New American Library[1]	Times Mirror Co., Inc.	60.0	67.0-68.0	12.5
4	Dell[1]	Doubleday & Co., Inc.	60.0	65.0-68.0[4]	10.8
5	Pocket Books	Simon & Schuster/Gulf + Western	40.0-43.0	63.0[3]	51.8
6	Fawcett (including Crest, Gold Medal and Popular Library)	CBS, Inc.	59.0-60.0	60.0-61.0	1.7
7	Avon[1]	Hearst Corporation	50.0-52.0	56.0	9.8
8	Ballantine[1]	Random House/Newhouse	46.0-47.0	53.0	14.0
9	Berkley/Jove[5]	MCA, Inc.	28.0-29.0	37.0	29.8
10	Warner[1]	Warner Communications	24.0	34.0[4]	41.7
11	Ace	Filmways, Inc.	15.0	17.0-19.0	20.0
12	Playboy	Playboy Enterprises	6.0	12.0	100.0
13	Pinnacle	Michigan General	8.7	11.2	28.7
	Total, 13 leading mass market publishers		$541.2	$657.2	21.4%
	Total mass market		609.0	739.2	21.4%
	% accounted for by 13 leading publishers		88.9%	88.9%	

[1] These publishers have substantial sales in trade paperbacks and related items such as calendars, puzzle books, etc. Avon's are in the $12 to $14 million range; Ballantine's are between $13 and $15 million; Warner's are in the $6 to $7 million range; and NAL's are in the $5 million area.

[2] Bantam has substantial sales outside the U.S. through its Transworld subsidiary, Corgi. Overall 1979 company sales were $108 million of which $15 million were attributed to Corgi; overall 1980 company sales were $117 million of which $16 million were attributed to Corgi.

[3] Fiscal year ends July 31.

[4] Estimate.

[5] Berkley/Jove reported combined results for the first time in 1979. In 1980 Berkley's sales are estimated at $22 million vs. $15 million for Jove.

Source: BP Report, September 14, 1981, Knowledge Industry Publications, Inc.

Table 3.19: Leading College Textbook Publishers, by Revenue,
1975 and 1979
(in millions)

1979 Rank	Company	1975 Sales	1979 Sales	% Increase 1975-1979
1	Prentice-Hall	$ 81.5	$105.0	28.8%
2	McGraw-Hill	55.0	91.2	65.8
3	CBS Publishing	41.8	52.0	24.4
4	SFN Cos.	35.5	49.1	38.3
5	Macmillan	28.0	41.0	46.4
6	Harcourt Brace Jovanovich	32.0	40.0	25.0
6	John Wiley & Sons	30.0	40.0	33.3
8	Addison-Wesley	22.0	34.8	52.2
9	Richard D. Irwin	24.7	33.5	35.6
10	Harper & Row	22.2	32.2	45.0
11	Wadsworth Publishing Co.	17.5	31.0	77.1
	Total, 11 leading companies	$390.2	$549.8	40.9%
	Total college texts	530.6	825.6	
	% accounted for by 11 leading publishers	73.5%	66.6%	

Source: *The College Market, 1981-86*, Knowledge Industry Publications, Inc.

industry, particularly in the preparation of textbooks and trade books.

It has thus become increasingly true that the publisher operates as a contractor. It assembles the people, facilities and resources to best serve a particular market information requirement, maintaining in the course of time only those individuals, facilities and functions that are particularly scarce, profitable or continually required. (There are always apparent exceptions to any rule. Typesetting, the transformation of manuscripts into print symbols, relegated to printers decades ago, is reappearing in publishers' offices as the cost of sophisticated word processing and electronic typesetting equipment has decreased substantially while ease of use has been enhanced.)

Even so, the industry has always been characterized by acquisitions. In the 19th century these seem to have consisted primarily of "lists" of titles, and often of the individual letterpress plates from which they were printed, in fields identical to those being served by the acquirer. At the turn of the century, the emphasis gradually shifted to the acquisitions of companies— both books and the people who had published them in identical fields— and then, as the differences among sectors became less distinct, to the acquisition of publishers in complementary fields. For the past 20 years, with the blurring of distinctions among different media sectors, acquisitions both *of* book publishers and *by* them have tended to be across the media spectrum.

Table 3.20: Leading El-Hi Publishers, by Revenue, 1976 and 1980[1]
(in millions)

1980 Rank	Company	1976 Revenues	1980 Revenues	% Increase 1976-1980
1	SFN Cos.	$129.0	$ 177.9	37.9%
2	Harcourt Brace Jovanovich	115.0	155.0	34.8
3	Houghton Mifflin	72.0	125.8	74.7
4	Scholastic	80.0	110.0	37.5
5	McGraw-Hill	59.0	92.6	56.9
6	Xerox (Ginn, XEP)	85.0	90.0	5.9
7	CBS (Holt, BFA, Winston Press)	72.0	80.0	11.1
8	Macmillan	55.0	65.0	18.2
9	Esquire (incl. Allyn & Bacon)	25.0	55.0-60.0	130.0
10	Heath (incl. American Book Co.)[2]	21.0	50.0-52.0	142.9
	Total	$713.0	$1004.8	40.9%
	Total, el-hi segment	N.A.	N.A.	
	% accounted for by 10 leading publishers	N.A.	N.A.	

[1] Revenue figures include test, school supply and audiovisual materials sold by these publishers to el-hi market. Thus, figures overstate textbook sales and are not comparable to AAP figures for el-hi text sales.

[2] Includes sales of American Book Co. for 1980. 1976 figure is for D.C. Heath only.

N.A.: Not available.

Sources: *Educational Marketer*, September 21, 1981, Knowledge Industry Publications, Inc.; *The El-Hi Market 1982-87* (White Plains, NY: Knowledge Industry Publications, Inc., 1982).

There are many reasons why the larger book publishers (and many small ones) have greatly broadened the bounds within which they operate. Among them are: governmental limitations on acquisitions in segments in which one's position is already large or in which there are related restrictions, such as distribution channels; the rapid proliferation of new methods of conveying information, formerly considered the exclusive province of a well-defined book format; the continuing breakdown of distinctions among existing media (e.g., "instant books" prepared from film scripts, and online computer data bases, such as LEXIS, used in lieu of law books); the growing interrelationships of the media in appearance (e.g., the use of four-color illustrations), distribution, content, markets and the like; the explosion in the use of copying devices, undermining some categories of book sales and the values of the copyrights on which the industry is based; the proliferation of new technologies both within the industry and in the markets it serves; the growing affluence of society and the declining costs of technology; changing popular tastes; the trend to ever greater market segmentation; and the desirability of selling expensive information to the largest possible market at the lowest incremental price per unit.

Table 3.21 presents two series of estimates of personal consumption expenditures for books, maps, sheet music, periodicals and newspapers. The older series (which included sheet music along with books and maps) indicated that the effects of television (and of radio) on the proclivity to spend a constant share of personal consumption expenditures on print media over the last fifty years had been insignificant. The new series, which reallocates music to the newspaper/periodical group, does not change this conclusion as far as books are concerned. (The significant change in the new series regarding newspapers and periodicals, however, makes these figures suspect.) As many of the new media in popular use in the early 1980s tend to strongly resemble traditional television (e.g., cable, video cassette and disc players, subscription TV, etc.), book purchases seem likely to remain steady for a long time. (It is as yet too early to assess the likely impact of online data bases and videotext, which still primarily represent potential as opposed to actual use.)

It should not be surprising, therefore, that book publishers find it difficult to adapt to change; to think of their operations as marketing information; to alter media formats nearly as readily as they alter page sizes or typefaces; to become media congenerics. They, like most of us, are used to thinking in one, two or three dimensions. They are book publishers and the book is here to stay. Yet, the larger publishers today—smaller publishers as well—would do well to think of their products, their markets and their operations in terms of a very much larger number of dimensions of information. Consider but a few:

- Type: raw or organized data; commentary; interpretation; analysis; imagery.

- Time requirement for access: instantaneous; in a day; in a year; indefinite.

- Place requirement: anywhere; in the home; in the office; while traveling.

- Most effective transfer system: text; symbols; graphics; sound; speech.

- Required durability: none; for some limited period of time; indefinite.

- Value (appropriate price): very low; low; moderate; high; very high.

- Probable use: entertainment; instruction; reference; business; guidance.

- Source: authors; institutions; transactions; instrumentation; history.

- Method of use: as is; in combination with other media; interactive.

- Acquisition method: typing; recording; photographing; computing; sampling.

- Distribution channel: mail; stores; broadcast; telephone; cable; satellite.

- Method of payment: subscription; installment sale; time charge; advertising.

As a result, some book publishers may be acquired by other types of media companies instead of expanding into other areas themselves. But publishers can be the innovators or the acquirers in appropriate circumstances.

Publishers Venturing Into Alternate Media

The starting point for any publisher considering entry into a combination is to determine the characteristics of the information resources he or she already has available which can be repackaged without additions or with such limited additions as new mailing lists, new authors or new outside distribution or production arrangements. The publisher should also attempt to determine which new packages would offer the most attractive new profit potentials, and/or insurance against the loss of current profits, with the smallest additions of people, equipment and other assets. The optimum combination is a complex of people, experience, products and management that can be of mutual benefit with the least duplication and waste.

Because each type of historically different media producer has developed in an environment in which the respective media were considered unique—each with its own markets, channels of distribution, sources and processing techniques—in most cases a publisher exploring an alternate sector needs an established entity: an acquisition or perhaps a co-venturer. This is equally true for book publishers as for magazine and newspaper publishers, producers of film, tapes and recordings, and so on. In addition, combinations may reduce risks because of the product lines, ex-

Table 3.21: Personal Consumption Expenditures for Printed Materials, Selected Years, 1934-1980

		Personal Consumption Expenditures					
		Books & Maps		**Newspapers & Periodicals**		**Total Print**	
Year	Total (in billions)	Old Series	New Series	Old Series	New Series	Old Series	New Series
1934	$ 51.3	0.321%	—	0.859%	—	1.180%	—
1940	71.0	0.330	—	0.830	—	1.159	—
1945	119.5	0.436	—	0.808	—	1.243	—
1950	192.0	0.351	—	0.779	—	1.130	—
1955	253.7	0.342	—	0.737	—	1.079	—
1960	324.9	0.351	—	0.666	—	1.017	—
1970	621.7	0.381	—	0.630	—	1.011	—
1971	672.2	0.368	—	0.635	—	1.003	—
1972	737.1	0.345	0.396%	0.639	0.632%	0.984	1.028%
1973	812.0	0.342	0.381	0.733	0.616	1.064	0.997
1974	888.1	0.341	0.372	0.792	0.606	1.133	0.978
1975	976.4	0.368	0.387	0.766	0.578	1.139	0.964
1976	1084.3	0.339	0.357	0.747	0.558	1.086	0.915
1977	1205.5	0.365	0.380	0.749	0.551	1.114	0.932
1978	1348.7	N.A.	0.408	—	0.552	—	0.959
1979	1510.9	N.A.	0.409	—	0.538	—	0.947
1980	1672.8	N.A.	0.416	—	0.527	—	0.944

N.A.: Not applicable.
Note: Discrepancies in totals are due to rounding.
Source: U.S. Department of Commerce; Paine Webber Mitchell Hutchins, Inc. calculations.

perience and relationships they are able to contribute.

There are literally thousands of publishers of printed information products and additional thousands of producers of information and entertainment in other media formats. All face similar uncertainties at present. Moreover, most were created by the entrepreneurs who now head them, many nearing the ends of their careers and without successors ready to take up the reins. Thus, many such companies have limited alternatives to mergers.

Finally, many of the new media are considerably more capital-intensive than were their predecessors. Although the declining costs of technology will foster the rapid growth of small, specialized suppliers of content, distribution itself will, for the foreseeable future, require large organizations with extensive capital.

It therefore seems logical to anticipate the continuing growth of a large number of information congenerics, including ones engaged in book publishing. The formation of several such organizations, indeed, seems preferable, from society's perspective, to the alternative of a single large entity —government or perhaps a telecommunications giant—stepping into the breach by default as has occurred in other countries. This trend toward congenerics should ensure the continuation of the tradition fostered by our Constitution, that government be balanced by a citizenry well-informed by numerous sources of information independent of government and, for that matter, independent of any single organization or establishment.

NOTES

1. All historical data and quotations on pages 95 to 99 come from *Textbooks in Education* (New York: American Textbook Publishers Institute, 1979).

2. O.H. Cheney, *Economic Survey of the Book Industry, 1930-31* (New York: R.R. Bowker Co., 1931). All references to Cheney and quotes from his material come from this source.

3. For a more recent study of the general book industry, see Benjamin M. Compaine, *The Book Industry in Transition: An Economic Study of Book Distribution and Marketing* (White Plains, NY: Knowledge Industry Publications, Inc., 1978).

4. Charles F. Bound, *A Banker Looks at Book Publishing* (New York: R.R. Bowker Co., 1950).

5. Fritz Machlup et al. (Princeton University Press, 1972).

6. Personal conversation with the author.

Appendix 3.1

Imprints and Publishing Subsidiaries of Leading U.S. Book Publishers

Parent Company	Imprints
CBS Inc.	Dryden Holt, Rinehart & Winston Popular Library Praeger Special Studies W.B. Saunders Co.
Doubleday	Delacorte Press Dell Dial Press Doubleday J.G. Ferguson Laidlaw Brothers Literary Guild and other clubs
Encyclopaedia Britannica	G.&C. Merriam Co.
Grolier	Franklin Watts Grolier Scarecrow Press
Harcourt Brace Jovanovich	Academic Press Harcourt Brace Jovanovich
Harper & Row	Basic Books T.Y. Crowell Harper & Row A.J. Holman J.B. Lippincott
Hearst	Avon William Morrow
Macmillan	Berlitz Publications Collier Crowell-Collier The Free Press Glencoe Publishing Macmillan

Parent Company	Imprints
McGraw-Hill	Gregg
	McGraw-Hill
	Schaum/Paperback
	Shepard's Citations
	Webster
Newhouse	Ballantine
	Fawcett Books: Crest, Gold Medal, Premier, Columbine, Coventry, Juniper
	Alfred A. Knopf
	Random House
Prentice-Hall	Appleton-Century-Crofts
	Prentice-Hall
	Reston Publishing
	Spectrum Books
SFN Cos.	Fleming H. Revell
	Scott Foresman
	Silver Burdette
	South-Western Publishing
	University Park Press
Time Inc.	Book-of-the-Month Club and other clubs
	Little, Brown
	Time-Life Books
Times Mirror	Harry N. Abrams
	Matthew Bender
	C.V. Mosby
	New American Library
	Southwestern
	Year Book Medical Publishers

4

Magazines

by Benjamin M. Compaine

As a modern publishing form, the magazine is barely a hundred years old. By the early 1980s the magazine industry had substantially completed a fundamental change. For much of their life, magazines served as the mass medium in American society. Now that other media, principally television, serve that purpose, magazine publishers are justifying their existence by serving either portions of the entire literate audience, or small groups of readers with intense interest in a particular subject. This change does not mean, as has been reported, that the mass circulation, general interest magazine is dead. It does mean that an increasing proportion of magazines published—and probably of total magazine circulation—will be accounted for by special interest or limited audience publications.

The terms *magazine* and *periodical* are used interchangeably in this section. Moreover, a magazine is defined as a publication that appears—or at least is intended to appear—on a regular basis with a minimum frequency of four times annually under a common title. This definition excludes from discussion many of the annual publications that are listed by magazine publishers in *Standard Rate & Data Service*'s consumer magazine and business magazine directories. Publications issued less frequently than quarterly are not counted in determining size of publishing groups.

EVOLUTION OF MAGAZINES

Magazines evolved because of two unique characteristics that differentiated them from newspapers. First, since they did not have to carry up-to-the-minute news, they could rely on more leisurely delivery systems than newspapers, especially to spread-out rural areas. More importantly, in an age before television and radio, they were able to offer an advertiser national coverage. As Americans spent increasing amounts of money on raising their material standard of living, magazines benefited from the expanding market for the goods and services advertisers offered.

Throughout the 20th century, the magazine responded to the dynamics of several factors:

1) more people with more money for discretionary spending;
2) the spread of popular education;
3) the increase in the amount of leisure time.

The magazine has always faced competition in taking advantage of these changes. In the early years of the century, newspapers were the primary competition and, to a lesser extent, books. Soon movies became an important form of entertainment. In the twenties, radio swept the nation, unmatched in speed of penetration until television came along beginning in the late 1940s. And inexpensive paperback books, getting under way just before World War II, have become a major form of mass media in the past two decades.

Under this barrage of competition, magazines nonetheless continued to expand, for in many ways each new medium helped the older ones. As book publishers have learned that a successful movie spurs rather than harms book sales, so magazine publishers have been able to take advantage of television. Popularity of televised spectator sports has stimulated sales of sports magazines, and fast-breaking news on TV has created opportunities for deeper analysis and perspective in the news weeklies (since 1946 the combined circulation of the news weeklies has about quadrupled).

MAGAZINES BECOME MORE SPECIALIZED

Perhaps the most significant reason for the magazine's survival has been its ability to adapt to a changing role in society. It is no longer needed as a national advertising tool for mass-oriented products. Television can supply far-flung regions with the same advertisement seen in New York at the same time. Nor is it needed purely for entertainment, as television and the movies satisfy those needs. Magazines have changed—out of necessity as much as through foresight—into a medium for serving discrete interests within the mass population. Whereas most magazines used to be published for a mass readership, today even most of the so-called mass consumer magazines have narrowed their audiences down to definable proportions.

This specialization covers not just consumer magazines but the diverse information needs of business and the professions through a steadily increasing number of trade magazines, both paid and controlled (sent free to an eligible population) circulation. As with consumer magazines, business magazines serve the need of advertisers who wish to reach a well-defined audience for their product or service.

Number of Magazines Increasing

One indication of this specialization is that the number of magazines has been growing, even though total magazine circulation is fairly level. In 1950 there were 6960 periodicals in the *Ayer Directory*.[1] By 1981 the number had increased by 47%, although with deaths and births, the actual number of different titles is no doubt much greater. Most of these new magazines have been small circulation, specialized publications serving alumni groups, industry associations, clubs, professional societies and the numerous consumer interests that have emerged. But growth in total circulation has been less, since it takes many 25,000 and 150,000 circulation magazines to replace the mass circulation versions of *Life, Saturday Evening Post, Look* and *Colliers.* (Although the first two have reappeared, they are both structured to survive on less circulation than the six or eight million of their predecessors.)

Publishers have always been quick in sensing new interests within the public and then establishing new publications to cater to them. When the movies made Hollywood the center of attention for those curious about the private lives of the stars, *Photoplay* appeared and grew into a fat fan magazine. In 1934, with model railroad hobbyists numbering in the hundreds, an entrepreneur put out *Model Railroader,* a magazine whose circulation is now near 175,000. And when, in 1951, the aqualung made underwater adventure available to skilled swimmers, an enthusiast launched *Skin Diver,* now selling 166,000 copies a month.

Whole categories have sprung up to meet new interests and imitators join the successful innovators. By 1981 there were magazines for gamblers, private pilots, brides-to-be, horse breeders, home decorators and fixer-uppers, antique collectors, followers of politics, sports, news, hair styles and psychology. Business periodicals exist for food engineers, automotive mechanics, consumer electronics, retailers, computer programmers, and even for magazine publishers.

The Fragmenting Society[2]

To elaborate on the earlier list of factors that have contributed to the general climate of magazine readership, it is necessary to comment on those causes that have forced the magazine industry, more than the other media, to diversify:

- Job specialization. A more complex society creates a need for specialized subgroups of managers, engineers, researchers, financiers. To meet the needs of these subgroups, many of which don't understand the language of the other, there are special publications tailored to their needs—the business and professional press.

- The assertion of new freedoms and tastes. American society is becoming more permissive, resulting in magazines that have responded to different groups asserting their potential of becoming new markets. This includes the "new" women's magazines like *Ms.*, the city magazines like *Philadelphia,* or the sex magazines beginning with *Playboy* to the more explicit *Hustler.* Youth is served as *Rolling Stone* moves beyond rock music to youth culture, while blacks are finding a continually widening range of magazines directed at them.

- Spread of education. In the past two decades, higher education has become mass education in the U.S. Half of all high school graduates now go on to further education. In 1960, only 16.5% of the 25 years old and over population had at least some college. This had increased to 31.1% by 1979. The result has been the creation of a vast college-educated, literate audience with a multiplicity of personal and intellectual interests.

- A consumer haven. With a market as vast and wealthy as that of the U.S., almost any well-presented idea can create a highly lucrative, if limited, submarket for itself.

- Increased opportunities to pursue interests. More than just leisure time, Americans have the discretionary income to embrace a wide variety of pursuits, from bowling to camping, furniture building to wine-making. People with similar interests join together, identifying with one another. Advertisers have adapted to new consumer trends by seeking out publications that will reach like groups of consumers. Among other things, they've learned that an individual will not react to a liquor ad found in *TV Guide* as he would to one in *Gourmet.*

ROLE OF MAGAZINES

Throughout their history—and because of it—magazines have made substantial contributions to society and popular culture.

First, by their very diversity, they have provided the populace with an inexpensive and open marketplace for an exchange of ideas, opinions and information, as well as a forum for debate. Among the more than 10,000 periodicals in existence, there are magazines devoted to subjects from Ukranian culture to the problems of retirement. This diversity has come at something of a price to the publisher: the high level of failure among the seemingly secure and established publications as well as the new ones. It has been calculated that of the 40 magazines with a circulation of over one million in 1951, fully 30% were no longer publishing by 1974.

Second, magazines play a role in the public enlightenment. Magazines have often taken the initiative in delving into national issues and problems, going back at least to the muckraking days of Ida Tarbell and Lincoln Steffens at *McClure's*. They have dealt with such concerns as the problems of black equality, poverty in the midst of affluence, the decay of the cities, the administration of justice, the war in Vietnam, the corruption of politicians. In many cases, these issues were first brought up by the small, limited audience magazines and were then picked up for mass attention by the big magazines, sometimes years later. Consumer education has been a major topic for the *Journal of Home Economics* since the 1930s; the *New Republic* headlined "Consumers United!" back in November 1933.

Third, the magazine has long been the communicator and sometimes initiator of popular culture. The comic book heroes are an obvious example. But magazines also help create fads, in language as well as form. Often a scholarly journal will use certain words, such as "rubric." These words are picked up by the small circulation, high-brow periodicals like *New York Review of Books,* then make their way to an *Esquire,* and finally are adopted for ultimate diffusion by *Time* or *Newsweek*. Skipping the intermediate steps, *Time* picked up a Susan Sontag essay in *Partisan Review* about something she called "camp." Within weeks after *Time*'s article the term was cropping up in the other mass media.

Fourth, magazines have provided a wide range of diversion—from sexual escapism to informative pieces on the space program.

Finally, they are instructors that help with daily living: they tell how to prepare food better, or to cope with the rigors of living in New York, how to order wine, how to build a radio receiver, or where to go for a quiet vacation. *Better Homes & Gardens* once estimated that 2.2 million readers clip something for future reference from an average issue. *Hot Rod* has been found to be very popular in school libraries and is ordered in bulk by teachers who have found that issues hold great appeal for slow readers.

DEVELOPMENT OF THE INDUSTRY

The American magazine dates back to February 1741, when Andrew Bradford brought out *American Magazine, or a Monthly View of the*

Political State of the British Colonies. His first issue beat Benjamin Franklin's *General Magazine* by three days.[3]

For the next 150 years, magazines existed on a small scale and with limited life—Bradford's effort died in three months, Franklin's lasted only twice as long. Most magazines were for a small set of the educated and had limited circulations, 2000 to 3000 being good-sized. The modern magazine can find its origins in two events of the late 19th century. In 1879 Congress decided to provide low-cost mailing privileges for periodicals. This helped fuel the boom in publishing, already being fed by the growth in secondary education, as the number of magazines leaped from 700 in 1865 to 3300 in 1885. Still, a large circulation was 100,000. Then, in October 1893, Frank A. Munsey announced a reduction in his *Munsey's Magazine* subscription price from $3 to $1 per year and his single-copy price from 25 cents to a dime. Munsey was putting into practice what was then just an emerging concept, that by selling his magazine for less than its cost of production, he could achieve a large circulation. His profits would come from the large volume of advertising a hefty circulation would attract. For the first time, publishers such as Cyrus Curtis, Edward Bok, S. S. McClure and others began to provide magazines for the masses, filling the gap between the "class" books such as *Harper's* and *Scribner's* and inexpensive pulp readers like the *People's Literary Companion.*

Munsey's idea worked. Circulation of his first 10-cent issue was 40,000. By April 1895 it was up to 500,000. At the beginning of the 20th century, the characteristics of the modern magazine had begun to emerge.

- Magazines had become low in price, typically 10 cents, sometimes five cents.

- As a result of this low price, mass production and mass distribution, they had achieved previously undreamed of circulations. By 1900 the *Ladies' Home Journal* was near one million.

- The role of advertising became paramount. Publishers needed it to make their low circulation prices work, while advertisers were attracted to magazines for the first time as a means of reaching a national market.

- In attempting to serve wider audiences, magazine content was reaching out to appeal to new and diverse interests.

By the early years of the 20th century, the magazine industry was dominated by giant publishers. In 1918, Curtis Publishing Co.'s three big magazines, *Saturday Evening Post, Ladies' Home Journal* and *Country Gentleman,* accounted for 43% of all national advertising dollars spent in consumer and farm publications. In 1920 the five leading magazines in advertising revenues, grossed $41.9 million, or 56% of the total. By 1980 such dominance had waned somewhat. Time Inc., the largest publisher in advertising revenue, accounted for 16.3% of the total, while the five leading magazines (*TV Guide, Time, Newsweek, Parade* and *Sports Illustrated*) together brought in about 28% of all magazine ad revenue, down from about 31% in 1973.[4]

If any single characteristic dominates the history of the magazine it is its constant state of flux. Since 1900 thousands of publications have come and gone. In 1930, 25 consumer and farm magazines had circulations in excess of one million. Thirty years later, 15 were out of business. Yet others keep trying. Many of today's top magazines did not even exist 30 years ago: *Sports Illustrated, TV Guide, Playboy,* to name a few. Others are creations of the 1970s: *Ms., Self, Omni, People.*

COMPETITIVE NATURE OF MAGAZINE BUSINESS

Magazine publishing has been a vigorous, highly competitive business primarily because of its economic structure. It has traditionally been an easy field to enter. With a month or two credit from a printer, one or two people can put out a first issue with almost no capital. Multimillion-dollar full-blown national distribution explosions from a Time Inc. notwithstanding, magazine publishing is still possible for low rollers. Hugh Hefner reportedly assembled the first issue of *Playboy,* appropriately enough, from his bedroom, while *Rolling Stone* began in a loft.

Besides its dynamic nature, a second pervasive feature of the industry is the central role of the entrepreneur: the individual with a concept. Time and again the history of periodical publishing proves the role of the idea to be paramount. Money and initial execution are secondary. Hadden and Luce initiated the news summary magazine concept and got an edge that *Newsweek* is still trying to overcome. DeWitt Wallace didn't do a mammoth marketing study before launching *Reader's Digest,* he just "felt" that it could sell and used his intuition to guide him. Publishing histories are dominated by the names of men, rarely organizations. It was Edward Bok who made the *Ladies' Home Journal* the largest circulation magazine in the world for a time and Cyrus Curtis who made the *Saturday Evening Post* into the most successful weekly of its time. Curtis could somehow sense a market for a new publication: business associates and advertising people had advised him against starting the *Journal* and later the *Post.*

Theodore Peterson, author of *Magazines in the Twentieth Century,* divides publishers into two rough groups: the missionaries and the merchants. Their behavior is often similar, but their motivation differs. Those in the former group are publishers devoted to their cause, some "secular gospel." *Reader's Digest*'s Wallace preached optimism; Luce believed in the efficacy of photographs as vehicles for information and education; Harold Ross of the *New Yorker* strived for perfection; and Bernarr Macfadden of *True Story* and *True Romances* used his publications to either directly promote his cause of bringing "health and joy through exercise, diet and the simple life" or to amass profits to further such ends through his foundation.

The merchants are not particularly champions of some cause. They regard magazine publishing strictly as a business enterprise to be operated for little else than profit. Nonetheless, in pursuit of this, they often put out superior publications, such as S. S. McClure's *McClure's Magazine* in its muckraking days. Condé Nast saw a niche for fashion publications catering to luxury-loving readers who would be attracted by slick, elegant publications, and the result was *Vogue, Glamour* and *Mademoiselle*. Wilford Fawcett and George T. Delacorte Jr. found profits in magazines edited for a lower level of sophistication. Fawcett's *Captain Billy's Whiz Bang* was followed by his copy of the confession magazines, then *Mechanix Illustrated*, working on the formula made successful by *Popular Mechanics*. *Men* copied *Esquire, Spot* followed *Life* and not even Superman was immune from an imitation in Captain Marvel. A more recent merchant is Bob Guccione, whose *Penthouse* is the first serious threat to *Playboy*.

Magazine history is littered with a sense of *déjà vu*. Time Inc.'s *People* was preceded by Newsweek's *People Today,* introduced in 1950 as a 10-cent magazine "to portray . . . in words and pictures people in all their facets—at work, asleep, or very much alive." In 1900 outdoorsmen could subscribe to *Shooting and Fishing* and *American Golf*; today they can choose from *Field & Stream, Golf* and *Golf Digest,* among others. Today publishers are complaining about the hardships being imposed by the increase in second-class postage rates. Rate hearing in 1949 and 1962 produced the same complaints, but the resulting increases came and there has been little change in the string of new magazines started, nor can any publications trace their demise to the postal burden alone.

The industry is highly fragmented, so much so that no one company or group of companies dominates it. While *TV Guide* accounts for 4.2% of the combined per issue sales for 953 consumer magazines, the great diversity of magazine editorial matter, combined with the considerable segmentation of interests within the population, insures the existence of a large number of differentiated publications.

The great diversity of publishers and publications has its counterpart in a paucity of detailed information about the industry. Publishers are extremely close-mouthed about the economics of their operations; only a small minority report to the Publishers Information Bureau, an industry clearinghouse for advertising and circulation data. Most small publishing houses and many of the largest are privately owned and therefore need not release any of the details of their operation. Even many publicly owned firms, such as Times Mirror Co. and CBS, lump operating figures of various enterprises together, making an analysis of magazine finances difficult.

SIZE OF THE INDUSTRY

The periodical publishing industry is a relatively small segment of the total industrial milieu and accounts for 25% of shipments of the print media industry. Value of shipments in 1980 was an estimated $8.9 billion, up 319% since 1960 and an increase of 180% from 1970. During the same periods, the overall economy, as measured by current dollar GNP, showed increases of 419% and 167%, respectively. Thus, as seen in Table 4.1, the relatively sluggish growth of magazines of the 1960s has given way to a decade of near-average expansion. Industry employment in 1980 reached 82,100,[5] 20% of the number of employees in the newspaper industry, although periodicals had shipments equal to 51% of newspapers.

Table 4.1: Value of Periodical Shipments Compared to Gross National Product, Selected Years, 1960-1980

Year	GNP (in billions)	Industry Value of Shipments (in millions)
1960	$ 506.0	$2,133
1965	688.1	2,626
1970	982.4	3,195
1975	1,528.8	4,380
1978	2,106.6	6,612
1979	2,413.9	8,052[1]
1980	2,626.1	8,937[1]
% Increase		
1960-1980:	419.0%	319.0%
1970-1980:	167.3%	179.7%

[1] Estimate.

Sources: U.S. Bureau of the Census, as published in the *U.S. Industrial Outlook, 1981* and previous editions. GNP: U.S. Bureau of Economic Analysis.

Circulation

There are no current complete tabulations of magazine circulation, in part owing to the large number of magazines and the fact that many do not belong to an auditing agency. In 1975, when the Magazine Publishers Association (MPA) last tabulated total annual copies of all general and farm magazines, annual sales had reached 5.7 billion copies, an increase of 34% from 1960. The average circulation per issue was 334,000, compared to 250,034 in 1960.

In 1980, 953 consumer magazines that reported their circulation sold an aggregate of 425.7 million copies per issue, substantially above the rate of 10 years earlier, but lower than in 1975. But of more interest is the calculation, seen in Table 4.2, that circulation per adult was also greater than in any of the years other than 1975. Average circulation per issue, at 447,000, was also well above the level of the late 1960s and early 1970s. However, there does appear to be the beginning of a trend in the end of the 1970s towards a slowing in circulation growth relative to the population.

In recent years magazine publishers have been concentrating more on "quality" circulation rather than numbers. Rapidly increasing postal costs —second-class rates alone were up 487% between 1971 and 1980—as well as significant increases in paper costs have forced publishers to look to the consumer to carry a greater share of the expense. Some publications have built their distribution around greater emphasis on newsstand sales as a result: *Playboy* has long concentrated in this area, while some women's magazines—CBS' *Woman's Day* and The New York Times Co.'s *Family Circle*—are virtually all single-copy sales. Time Inc. has sold its new and successful *People* through newsstands and supermarkets, offering subscriptions only through offers in the magazine itself and then only at a price relatively close to the single-copy price.

It should be no surprise, therefore, that magazine prices have advanced substantially faster than consumer prices in general during the 1970s. The average subscription cost of general interest magazines in 1970 was reported to be $8.47. This was up 135% to $19.87 by 1980. During this period, consumer prices rose 111%. All periodicals, including academic journals and technical, professional and business periodicals, advanced even more, 232%, from $10.41 to $34.54.[6] Single-copy prices have risen commensurately.

Number of Magazines

The number of periodicals increased more than 52% between 1950 and 1981, with 10,873 periodicals of all types publishing in 1981. This was a

Table 4.2: Consumer Magazine Circulation in the United States, Selected Years, 1954-1980

Year	Number of Magazines	Aggregate Circulation Per Issue (in millions)	Average Circulation Per Issue (in thousands)	Circulation Per Adult
1954	575	254.5	443	2.36
1960	545	245.0	450	1.98
1965	768	291.9	380	2.18
1970	1009	307.0	304	2.11
1975	924	444.4	481	3.03
1978	1089	464.3[1]	488[1]	2.80
1979	1062	440.4[1]	480[1]	2.65
1980	1124	425.7[1]	447[1]	2.57
Percent Increase (Decrease)				
1960-1965:	40.9%	19.1%	(15.6)%	10.1%
1965-1970:	31.4	5.2	(20.0)	(3.2)
1970-1975:	(8.4)	44.8	58.2	43.6
1975-1980:	21.6	(4.2)	(7.1)	(15.2)
1954-1980:	95.5	67.3	.9	8.9

[1] Omits magazines counted in total that do not report circulation.

Sources: Number and aggregate circulation from Audit Bureau of Circulation (ABC). ABC derives these figures by adding to its own 400-plus members other consumer titles listed in Standard Rate & Data Services' *Consumer and Farm Publications Rates and Data*. This includes publications of less than quarterly frequency. Circulation per adult calculated from adults 16 years and older, July 1, 1979, from U.S. Bureau of the Census, *U.S. Census of Population: 1960 and 1970* Vol. 1 and *Current Population Reports*, series P-25, No. 870 for 1980.

record number of magazines published. Among the most common frequencies of publication listed in Table 4.3, the quarterly schedule showed the greatest increase in popularity, with 880 more titles—146%—in 1981 than in 1950. Monthly publication remains the most common interval, with 40% of the periodicals appearing at that rate. Bimonthly publication also showed a strong preference, with much of the growth coming in the 1950-1960 period. The popularity of the less frequent bimonthly and quarterly schedules may reflect the many scholarly journals born in the boom years of higher education as well as the specialization of consumer and business periodicals.

Advertising

Magazine advertising revenue, although strong in recent years, suffered major inroads in its share of total advertising dollars with the development of television. Consumer magazines accounted for about 13% of all advertising expenditures in 1945. That fell to as low as 5.2% in 1975, before rebounding to 5.9% in 1977, the level it maintained in 1980. Business magazines accounted for an additional 3.1% of advertising in 1980.

In 1980, about $3.2 billion was spent by advertisers in consumer magazines, more than twice the level of only five years earlier (an increase well in excess of the inflation rate). Business publications did not perform quite as strongly, with an 84% increase. Together, however, they outperformed overall advertising growth, which was up 94% between 1975 and 1980. Table 4.4 traces advertising expenditure trends in magazines since 1935 and shows that periodicals regained market share after a long 30-year slide that ended in 1975.

A tabulation of advertising revenue and pages in those general magazines that reported to the Publishers Information Bureau arm of the MPA shows that magazine revenue gains between 1970 and 1980 performed close to the overall economy, although since 1950 magazines have lost considerable ground to GNP. Moreover, Table 4.5 shows revenue has advanced at almost three times the rate of advertising pages from 1970 to 1980. Even more dramatically, since 1950 the 70% growth in annual advertising pages spawned a 617% hike in advertising revenue. This has been the result of a rapid escalation in average per page cost for magazines, from $5886 for this group in 1950 to $24,812 in 1980.

Table 4.3: Number of Periodicals, by Frequency, 1950, 1960, 1970 and 1981

Frequency	1950	1960	1970	1981	Percent Increase 1950-1981
Weekly	1,443	1,580	1,856	1,921	33.1%
Semimonthly[1]	416	527	589	667	60.3
Monthly	3,694	4,113	4,314	4,199	13.7
Bimonthly	436	743	957	1,193	173.6
Quarterly	604	895	1,108	1,484	145.7
Other	367	564	749	1,409	283.9
Total	6,960	8,422	9,573	10,873	56.2

[1] Includes bi-weeklies (every other week).

Source: *Ayer Directory of Publications*, annual (Bala Cynwyd, PA: Ayer Press). Some portion of the increase over the years may be due to better reporting on the part of the *Ayer Directory*. Figures refer to year of completion of Directory, usually that of preceding year shown.

(However, magazine ad rates have gone up less than any other mass medium since 1967 on an absolute dollar basis and only radio advertising has increased less on a cost per thousand basis.[7])

Table 4.4: Advertising Expenditures in Magazines, Selected Years, 1935-1980

Year	Total (in millions)	Magazines (in millions)	Business Publications (in millions)	Percent of All Advertising Expenditures
1935	$ 187	$ 136	$ 51	11.1%
1945	569	365	204	19.8
1950	766	. 515	251	13.4
1955	1,175	729	446	12.8
1960	1,550	941	609	13.0
1965	1,870	1,199	671	12.3
1970	2,063	1,323	740	10.5
1975	2,458	1,539	919	8.7
1978	3,997	2,597	1,400	9.7
1979	4,507	2,932	1,575	9.1
1980	4,920	3,225	1,695	9.0

Sources: 1935-1970: *Historical Statistics of the U.S.: Colonial Times to 1970.*
1975-1980: *Advertising Age*, compiled by McCann-Erickson, New York.

INDUSTRY STRUCTURE

There were 2860 periodical publishing companies in 1977, according to the 1977 Census of Manufactures. The periodicals they publish can be roughly divided into three catgories: consumer, farm and business. By far the largest segment is the general consumer magazines, accounting for almost 60% of magazine revenue. Farm publications make up only 15% of the market, with business, trade, organization and professional magazines accounting for the remainder.[8]

Revenue Structure

Traditionally, magazines derived the bulk of their revenue from advertising. Although advertising is still the primary component of revenues, circulation income has been providing an increasing share in recent years, especially for consumer magazines. Most business magazines are still supported almost exclusively by advertisers, since they tend to be sent free to their audience.

Table 4.5: General Magazine Advertising Revenue and Pages Compared with GNP, Selected Years, 1929-1980

Year	Number of Magazines	Adv. Revenue (in millions)	Adv. Pages	Average Rev./Page	GNP (in billions)
1929	61	$ 185.7	N.A.	—	$ 103.4
1933	106	92.6	N.A.	—	55.8
1945	97	286.7	N.A.	—	212.3
1950	85	396.7	67,392	$ 5,886	286.2
1960	79	380.0	74,861	11,087	506.0
1965	91	1,055.3	80,147	13,167	688.1
1970	89	1,168.7	76,924	15,193	982.4
1971	91	1,235.2	77,008	16,040	982.4
1972	83	1,297.7	82,007	15,824	1,063.4
1973	85	1,309.2	85,665	15,283	1,171.1
1974	93	1,366.3	86,305	15,831	1,306.6
1975	94	1,336.3	80,735	16,552	1,412.9
1976	93	1,622.0	93,253	17,394	1,528.8
1977	96	1,965.4	103,307	19,025	1,889.6
1978	102	2,374.2	115,266	20,597	2,106.6
1979	102	2,671.1	119,832	22,290	2,413.9
1980	102	2,846.1	114,705	24,812	2,626.1
% Increase					
1950-1980:	20%	617%	70%	322%	818%
1960-1980:	29	649	53	124	419
1970-1980:	15	144	49	63	167

N.A.: Not available.
Sources: Advertising: Publishers Information Bureau (does not include Sunday supplements). GNP: U.S. Bureau of Economic Analysis.

In the late 1960s advertising accounted for 60% of total receipts for general consumer magazines. But by 1978 it accounted for only 48% of revenue,[9] as publishers pushed up subscription and newsstand prices and accepted lower circulation and slower growth rather than offer the discount subscriptions of the past. While farm publication advertising revenue has held steady at about 80% of the total, even business publications have experienced an increase in circulation revenue, dropping the advertising proportion from 78% in 1967 to 65% in 1978.[10] [This may be somewhat misleading when viewed as an average, in that business publications tend to be either mostly free or mostly paid. The change may be the product of both: 1) paid-for business magazines sharing a trend similar to consumer magazines while the controlled circulation publications continue being 100% advertiser supported; and 2) paid-for business magazines simply increasing in number.]

Production and Distribution Structure

The magazine business is a relatively easy one to enter as measured by capital needs because it is an almost pure "content" business. In terms of the information business map in Chapter 1, magazine publishing itself involves almost exclusively the services of the upper righthand corner of the map. Few magazines, for example, have done their own typesetting (although the decreasing cost of phototypesetting technology has made this economically attractive to increasingly smaller publishers). Meredith Corp. is the only major publisher that prints its own publications. Almost all, from Time Inc. on down, contract out their printing to commercial printers. Finally, magazine publishers rely on third parties for delivery of their final product. Most publishers depend on the U.S. Postal Service to provide delivery—that being the only delivery service, including telephone and broadcasting—that has penetration to 100% of all households and institutions in the country.

CONCENTRATION

Besides the considerable number and diversity of magazines, the periodical publishing industry shows relatively less concentration of ownership than large industries overall and a nearly steady decline in concentration between 1947 and 1977 (see Table 4.6). Compared to newspaper and book publishing, periodical publishing is marginally more concentrated, but the trend through 1977 was toward a slight lessening in concentration for periodicals, while newspapers in particular showed a slight increase. (See Chapters 2 and 3.)

Table 4.6 also indicates that the number of periodical publishing companies had reached an all-time high in 1977, with 2860 identified publishing firms, an increase of 17% since the previous census.

Many of the largest circulation magazines are independent—that is, published by firms that publish few other magazines. Of the leading magazine publishers in terms of revenue, three (Reader's Digest, Triangle and the Washington Post Co.*) have only two titles.

There are about 315 multiple title publishers of consumer, farm and business periodicals identified by Standard Rate & Data Service (SR&DS) in mid-1981. (SR&DS itself does not provide the tally.) There is some double counting, in that some groups, such as Ziff-Davis and Harcourt Brace Jovanovich, are included in both business and consumer/farm sectors. On

---

*Having sold *Inside Sports* in 1982, *Newsweek* became the firm's only magazine.

Table 4.6: Concentration in the Periodical Publishing Industry, Selected Years, 1947-1977

	1947	1958	1963	1967	1972	1977	Median for Large Industrial Firms, 1977[1]
Number of companies	2106	2246	2562	2430	2451	2860	—
Value of shipments (in billions)	$1.1	$1.7	$2.3	$3.1	$3.5	$6.1	—
Percentage accounted for by:							
4 largest	34%	31%	28%	24%	26%	22%	36%
8 largest	43	41	42	37	38	35	52
20 largest	50	55	59	56	54	52	76
50 largest	N.A.	69	73	72	69	67	90

N.A.: Not available.

[1] By 2-digit SIC groups.

Source: U.S. Bureau of the Census, *Census of Manufactures, 1977*, Table 7.

the other hand, SR&DS lists only those publishers that accept advertising for their magazines. The listing is also incomplete, since Triangle (*TV Guide* and *Seventeen*) is not included and other publishers may be omitted as well. Furthermore, many publications, such as academic journals, are not listed in any SR&DS publications, yet many of these journals do accept advertising and are published by groups. (John Wiley and Elsevier are among the many book publishers with a stable of journals. Pergamon Press alone published 226 journals in 1978.[11])

For all these reasons, it is difficult to accurately measure the quantity of magazines that are published as part of multi-title firms. It can be calculated that identifiable business and consumer/farm magazine groups published 1429 titles of quarterly or greater annual frequency in 1980, which accounts for 13.1% of the 10,873 periodicals identified by the *'81 Ayer Directory*. This compares to 13.5% of titles published by such groups in 1978.

Group-Owned vs. Non-Group-Owned Magazines

As might be reasonably expected, there are some overall differences between magazines published as part of a group and those that are independent. Table 4.7 summarizes selected characteristics of the two types of ownership. The average circulation of non-group-owned consumer periodicals is about one-third that of group-owned titles. As an independent magazine becomes larger, more visible and presumably gains greater revenue and profit potential, it often becomes a more promising prospect either for purchase by a group publisher or for gaining the financial wherewithal to start or purchase additional publications itself, either way eventually becoming part of a group.

The subscription price of both types of magazines is quite similar, reflecting in part the common competition they face for the consumer's magazine budget and price expectations. They also must factor in the same postal rates. Single-copy sales tend to be insignificant for most small magazines and therefore were not calculated here.

On the other hand, basic cost per thousand (cpm) advertising rates are substantially higher for the sample of independent magazines, again a likely outcome of the tendency of this group to include a greater proportion of small, highly selective special interest magazines with their commensurately higher cpm than general interest periodicals.[12]

Among business periodicals, which tend to have small circulations because they are almost all limited audience, special interest publications, there is virtually no substantial difference in average circulation between the group and non-group publishers. The sample of non-group publishers, however, has an only slightly higher percentage of paid subscribers, again not likely to be statistically significant.

Table 4.7: Selected Characteristics of Group-Owned and Independently Published Magazines, 1980

Type of Publication	Group-Owned	Non-Group-Owned
Consumer		
Average circulation (mean)	669,173	249,567
Subscription cost	$13.05	$13.25
Cost per thousand (CPM)		
one-time black and white ad	$14.56	$25.67
Business		
Average circulation	35,439	41,065
% paid	30%	33%

Sources: Non-group figures from sample of magazines listed in SR&DS, May and June, 1981. Group-owned from tabulation of actual circulation and subscription prices of all such magazines listed in SR&DS, May and June, 1981. CPM for groups taken from sample of group-owned magazines.

Largest Magazines

Table 4.8 lists the 50 leading A.B.C. magazines in 1980 by circulation per issue. *TV Guide* passed long-time leader *Reader's Digest* in the early 1970s. The gap narrowed in 1980, as *TV Guide*'s circulation declined more than did *Reader's Digest*'s. The 17.9 million for *Reader's Digest,* however, represents domestic circulation only, with another 12 million in 14 languages sold abroad. The top 10 magazines alone account for 22% of the total aggregate per-issue circulation of the magazines counted in Table 4.2.

Of the top 10, seven have long been among the leaders. The demise of the old *Life, Look* and the *Saturday Evening Post,* long in the top ranks, opened the way for *National Geographic, Modern Maturity* and *Good Housekeeping,* the junior members of the top 10.

Although 72% of the leading circulation magazines are part of magazine publishing groups, ironically the four largest are nominally independent. *TV Guide* is controlled by Walter Annenberg's Triangle Publications, which also owns 36th ranked *Seventeen. Reader's Digest* is part of a $1 billion firm that derives a substantial portion of its income from books and other audiovisual media materials, but the company publishes only one other small magazine, *Families,* started in 1981. *National Geographic* is published by the society and subscribers are technically "members." Even

Meredith Corp., publisher of *Better Homes & Gardens,* publishes only one other magazine of more than quarterly frequency (*Metropolitan Home*).

Of the remaining top 50, Hearst runs three with 9.8 million circulation, Time Inc. has four with 10.5 million circulation (most of which are weeklies, while Hearst's are monthlies), CBS three with 11.3 million per issue and Charter Co. two with almost 10 million circulation. Times Mirror, Condé Nast (Newhouse) and Triangle are other organizations with more than one periodical in the list.

Leading Publishers*

By Revenue

With its three profitable weekly magazines, a bi-weekly and now three monthly magazines, Time Inc. is by far the largest magazine publisher in the United States. Table 4.9 identifies the largest publishers by revenue derived from periodical publication. Triangle Publications, Inc. had an estimated $494 million in revenue, mostly from *TV Guide.* Hearst Corp., publisher of *Good Housekeeping* and *Cosmopolitan,* among others, was a distant third. Revenue for CBS Inc., Newhouse and The New York Times Co. were enhanced by advertising revenue from the Sunday newspaper magazines they publish, *Parade, Family Weekly* and *The New York Times Magazine,* respectively. McGraw-Hill is the only predominantly business periodical publisher in the group.

By Number of Magazines

At the end of 1980 there were 100 identifiable firms publishing more than one consumer or farm magazine. Among them they published 371 periodicals. With little overlap in membership, 215 firms published two or more domestic business publications, accounting for 1066 titles. The average size of the business magazine group was almost five titles per company, while consumer publishers owned an average of 3.7 periodicals each. The most significant difference in the two categories is in average circulation per magazine. As seen already in Table 4.7, the typical group-owned business magazine had a 1980 circulation of 35,000, about 30% paid, the remainder free. The consumer magazines owned by chains averaged a paid circulation of 669,000.

---

*In Tables 4.9 through 4.13 publishers are identified by parent company, with relevant publishing subsidiaries in parentheses.

Table 4.8: 50 Largest Circulation A.B.C.-Audited Consumer and Farm Magazines and Their Owners, 1980[1]

Rank (by circulation)	Magazine	Publisher	Circulation
1.	TV Guide	Triangle Publications, Inc.	17,981,657
2.	Reader's Digest	Reader's Digest Association, Inc.	17,898,681
3.	National Geographic	National Geographic Society	10,711,886
4.	Better Homes & Gardens	Meredith Corp.	8,052,693
5.	Woman's Day	CBS, Inc.	7,748,069
6.	Family Circle	New York Times Company	7,529,734
7.	Modern Maturity	The American Association of Retired Persons	6,748,925
8.	McCall's	McCall Publishing Company	6,218,169
9.	Ladies' Home Journal	Charter Company	5,601,449
10.	Good Housekeeping	Hearst Corporation	5,290,833
11.	National Enquirer	National Enquirer, Inc.	5,051,496
12.	Playboy	Playboy Enterprises, Inc.	5,011,099
13.	Time	Time Inc.	4,358,911
14.	Redbook	Charter Company	4,353,745
15.	Penthouse	Penthouse International, Ltd.	4,330,949
16.	The Star	World News Corporation	3,508,558
17.	Newsweek	Washington Post Company	2,964,279
18.	Cosmopolitan	Hearst Corporation	2,837,325
19.	American Legion	The American Legion	2,599,187
20.	People	Time Inc.	2,499,573
21.	Prevention	Rodale Press, Inc.	2,429,439
22.	Sports Illustrated	Time Inc.	2,265,760
23.	U.S. News & World Report	U.S. News & World Report, Inc.	2,055,993
24.	Field & Stream	CBS, Inc.	2,021,599
25.	Glamour	Condé Nast (Newhouse)	1,935,636
26.	Popular Science	Times Mirror Company	1,933,262
27.	Smithsonian	Smithsonian Institution National Associates	1,904,515
28.	V.F.W. Magazine	Veterans of Foreign Wars of the United States, Inc.	1,844,891
29.	Globe	Midnight Publishing Corporation	1,802,988
30.	Southern Living	Progressive Farmer	1,783,152
31.	Outdoor Life	Times Mirror Company	1,733,692
32.	Popular Mechanics	Hearst Corporation	1,677,303
33.	Elks Magazine	Benevolent and Protective Order of Elks of the U.S.	1,651,862
34.	Today's Education	National Education Association of the U.S.	1,651,783
35.	Mechanix Illustrated	CBS, Inc.	1,626,182
36.	Seventeen	Triangle Publications, Inc.	1,552,884
37.	Parents (Gruner & Jahr)	Parents' Magazine Enterprises, Inc.	1,515,707
38.	Workbasket	Modern Handicrafts Publications	1,472,139
39.	Boy's Life	Boy Scouts of America	1,462,745

Table 4.8: (continued)

Rank (by cir- culation)	Magazine	Publisher	Circulation
40.	*True Story*	Macfadden Group, Inc.	1,432,900
41.	*Hustler*	Flynt Publications	1,420,678
42.	*Sunset*	Lane Publishing Company	1,417,304
43.	*Changing Times*	The Kiplinger Washington Editors, Inc.	1,407,690
44.	*Life*	Time Inc.	1,338,026
45.	*Organic Gardening*	Rodale Press, Inc.	1,335,699
46.	*Ebony*	Johnson Publishing Company	1,287,670
47.	*Nation's Business*	Chamber of Commerce of the U.S.	1,265,555
48.	*New Woman*	New Woman, Inc.	1,251,595
49.	*Sport*	Southwest Media, Inc.	1,222,718
50.	*Farm Journal*	Farm Journal, Inc.	1,221,387
	Total — 50 Magazines		180,219,972

[1] Non-Group publishers are underlined. Does *not* include magazines published as supplements to weekend newspapers, such as *Parade* (Newhouse) and *Family Weekly* (CBS).
Source: Magazine Publishers Association, A.B.C. Circulation second six months 1980.

Tables 4.10 and 4.11 identify the largest publishers in the consumer and business areas, respectively, by number of magazines. Broadcasting giant American Broadcasting Companies has moved determinedly into the magazine business in recent years, having purchased *Los Angeles* magazine, several special interest periodicals, two groups of farm publications and controlling interest in business magazine and book publisher Chilton. Hearst is one of the oldest groups with many long-running titles. *Cosmopolitan* was founded in 1836, *Harper's Bazaar* in 1867. Hearst made a major acquisition in 1980 when it purchased the business periodicals of United Technical Publications, Inc. from Cox Broadcasting Co. for about $261 million.

There is great diversity among the magazines published by these groups. Harcourt Brace Jovanovich, best known as a book publisher, owns farm and business publications; the average combined circulation of one issue of its 53 magazines is only 1.2 million. On the other hand, CBS has a stable of mass circulation and special interest magazines, with an average total circulation per issue of each publication of 13.6 million. Scholastic magazines are sold almost exclusively through subscriptions in school while CBS and Newhouse publish magazines distributed as part of weekend newspaper packages. The publishers in Table 4.10 account for 11% of

Table 4.9:   Largest Magazine Publishers in the U.S., by Revenue, 1980

Rank (by revenue)	Publisher	Revenue from Magazine Publishing[1] (in millions)	Number of Domestic Magazines
1.	Time Inc.	$ 747	7
2.	Triangle Publications	494	2
3.	Hearst Corp.	324	21
4.	CBS Inc.	305	10
5.	Washington Post Company[2]	241	2
6.	McGraw-Hill, Inc.	230	28
7.	Reader's Digest Association, Inc.	214	2
8.	Newhouse (Condé Nast)	195	7
9.	New York Times Co.	192	4
10.	Charter Co.	182	3[3]
11.	Meredith Corp.	167	8
12.	Playboy Enterprises, Inc.	162	3[4]

[1] All revenues are estimated, except for Time Inc. and Playboy Enterprises, Inc.

[2] Includes *Inside Sports*, sold in 1982.

[3] Includes *Sport*, sold in 1981 to Southwest Media Corp.

[4] Includes *Oui*, sold in 1981 to Goshen Litho, Inc.

Sources: Figures for Time Inc. and Playboy Enterprises, Inc., as reported in 10-K and annual reports. Figures for other companies derived from corporate reports or calculated from estimated subscription and advertising revenue. In all cases, estimates reflect net revenue, after discounts, etc.

the consumer and farm groups and 33% of the number of titles published by these groups.

The magazines in each group are included in Appendix 4.1. The breadth of magazine coverage is evident by examining the titles for each group.

Harcourt Brace Jovanovich is the leading business periodical publisher in number of titles with 53, well ahead of McGraw-Hill. The total circulation of the HBJ publications, however, is substantially below that of McGraw-Hill. The publishers of business periodicals tend to be less well known than their consumer magazine counterparts. Business publications are a decidedly less glamorous side of the business for most journalists. There is little crossing-over between firms on the consumer and business publications list.

By Magazine Circulation

The most common method for calculating total circulation for all magazines or for any group is to sum up the average circulation for one

Table 4.10: Largest Consumer and Farm Magazine Publishers, by Number of Magazines in Group, 1980

Rank (by number of magazines)	Publisher	Number of Magazines in Group	Total Annual Circulation (in thousands)	Total Average Circulation (in thousands)
1.	Ziff-Davis Publishing Co.	17	68,867	6,268
2.	Webb Co.	15	71,462	9,283
3.	Hearst Corp.	14	149,043	12,938
4.	Petersen Publishing Co.	13	60,503	5,042
5.	American Broadcasting Cos., Inc.	11	28,039	2,047
6.	CBS Inc.	10	186,215	13,569
7.	Charlton Publications Inc.	9	27,646	4,087
7.	Scholastic Magazines, Inc.	9	76,552	6,104
9.	The Laufer Co.	8	14,580	1,215
9.	Meredith Corp.	8	128,829	12,002
9.	Macfadden Group, Inc.	8	59,021	3,611
	Total	122	870,757	76,116

Total consumer groups: 100
Total titles for groups: 371

Source: Compiled from Standard Rate & Data Service, *Consumer Magazine* and *Farm Publication Rates and Data*, May 27, 1981.

issue of each magazine. By this reckoning, which is the basis for the MPA's computations in Table 4.2, Triangle Publications, with *TV Guide* and *Seventeen,* would be the largest, followed by Reader's Digest, CBS Inc., Time Inc., Charter Co. and Hearst Corp. However, since both revenue and the impact of a magazine are based on how many copies it sells annually, it is more useful to factor in frequency per issue, so that a weekly publication, for example, carries 4.3 times the weight of a monthly of the same circulation per issue.

Table 4.12 has ranked the consumer magazine publishers by total copies circulated in 1980. Triangle, by this accounting, is still the largest magazine publisher. But Time Inc., with its stable of weeklies, achieves the second largest position, at more than twice the size of third-ranked New York Times Co. Reader's Digest Association, Inc. is the fourth largest and CBS Inc. is number five in circulation. In all cases, foreign editions have not been included.

For purposes of comparison, the table also calculates circulation on a straight per-issue basis. These 18 magazine publishers produced 130 titles, or 14% of the magazines in Table 4.2 for which circulation was also tabulated. Their combined circulation per issue of 169 million represents 40% of all consumer magazines charted in Table 4.2.

Table 4.11: Largest Business Magazine Publishers, by Number of Magazines in Group, 1980

Rank (by number of magazines)	Publisher	Number of Business Periodicals
1.	Harcourt Brace Jovanovich Publications, Inc.	53
2.	McGraw-Hill, Inc.	28
3.	American Broadcasting Cos.	26
4.	Penton/IPC	25
4.	Reed Holdings, Inc.	25
6.	Williams & Wilkins Co.	21
7.	Capital Cities Communications (Fairchild Pub.)	19
7.	Dun & Bradstreet, Inc. (Technical Pub. Co.)	19
9.	Harper & Row Publishers (with Lippincott)	17
10.	Communications Channels, Inc.	14
	Total	247

Total business groups: 215
Total titles: 1066

Source: Tabulated from Standard Rate & Data Service, *Business Publication Rates and Data*, June 24, 1981. Table includes only those periodicals that solicit advertising through SR&DS listing. Thus, journal publishers such as John Wiley are not covered.

The largest business publications groups are shown in Table 4.13. The calculation is based on a strict sum of the circulation of one issue of each title. Only McGraw-Hill has a significant number of weeklies with sizable circulation (although the largest, *Business Week,* is sometimes considered a consumer publication). Reed Holdings, Inc. is essentially the Cahners Publishing Co.'s list. While there are far more business magazine groups than consumer/farm publishing groups (215 compared to 100), and the number of titles per group is greater, the circulation per group is dramatically lower. Business publications, by their very nature, tend to be highly specialized (*Southern Pulp & Paper Manufacturer* and *Kitchen Business* are typical titles) and thus their possible audience is strictly limited. That, of course, is their attraction to advertisers—the very selective market they deliver.

The total circulation of these largest business publication groups, 13.6 million, represents 38% of the 36.2 million per issue circulation of the 1021 magazines published by groups,* the same proportion as in 1978. These groups also account for 21% of the magazines, though they are only 5% of the total number of groups.

*Of the 1066 business publication titles noted in Table 4.11, 1021 have reported 1980 circulation.

Table 4.12: Largest Consumer and Farm Magazine Publishers, by Total
Annual Circulation, 1980

Rank (by total circulation)	Publisher	Total Annual Circulation[1] (in thousands)	Total Combined Circulation per Issue (in thousands)	Number of Magazines Published[2]
1.	Triangle Publications, Inc.	964,739	19,759	2
2.	Time Inc.	538,085	12,464	7
3.	New York Times Co.	221,130	10,510	4
4.	Reader's Digest Assn. Inc.	220,329	18,361	2
5.	CBS Inc.	186,215	13,569	10
6.	Washington Post Co.	164,795	3,592	2
7.	Hearst Corp.	149,031	12,938	14
8.	Meredith Corp.	128,829	12,003	8
9.	Charter Co.	122,255	10,188	2
10.	Newhouse (Condé Nast)	83,072	7,089	7
11.	McCall's Publishing	80,703	6,725	2
12.	Scholastic Magazines, Inc.	76,552	6,104	9
13.	Playboy Enterprises, Inc.	74,545	6,572	2
14.	Webb Co.	71,462	9,283	15
15.	Ziff-Davis Publishing Co.	68,867	6,287	17
16.	Petersen Publishing Co.	60,503	5,042	13
17.	Times Mirror Co.	59,633	5,501	6
18.	Macfadden Group, Inc.	59,023	3,611	8
	Total	3,329,768	169,598	130

[1] Average circulation per issue x frequency.

[2] As of October 1981.

Source: Tabulated from Standard Rate & Data Service, *Consumer Magazine and Farm Publication Rates and Data*, May 27, 1981.

Relative Group Size

Most group publishers are relatively small in aggregate circulation. Of the 91 consumer groups (farm publication groups were not included), Table 4.14 tabulates that 33, or 36%, have aggregate circulation for all their magazines of under 300,000. At the other extreme, only eight group owners have total per issue circulation in excess of 10 million.

Among business magazine publishers, two-fifths of the groups have only two periodicals, while over three-fourths own five or fewer publications. As seen in Table 4.15, more than a third of these groups have aggregate circulation of under 50,000, and 91% send out fewer than 500,000 per issue of all titles. This again confirms the specialized and extremely diverse nature of the business periodicals end of the industry.

Table 4.13: Largest Business Publications Groups, by Total Circulation, 1980

Rank (by total circulation)	Publisher	Total Circulation (in thousands)	Number of Titles in Group
1.	Penton/IPC	2,886	25
2.	McGraw-Hill, Inc.	2,486	28
3.	American Broadcasting Cos. (Chilton, Hitchcock, etc.)	1,627	26
4.	Reed Holdings, Inc. (Cahners Pub.)	1,407	25
5.	Dun & Bradstreet, Inc. (Technical Publishing Co.)	1,248	19
6.	Harcourt Brace Jovanovich	1,164	53
7.	American Medical Association	781	11
8.	Medical Economics Co.	743	7
9.	Capital Cities Communications, Inc. (Fairchild Publications, Inc.)	698	19
10.	Irving-Cloud Publishing Co.	543	8
	Total	13,583	221
	Total for all business groups[1]	36,183	1,021

[1] Includes only those magazines reporting 1980 circulation.

Source: Tabulated from Standard Rate & Data Service, *Business Publication Rates & Data*, June 24, 1981.

Table 4.14: Circulation Size of Consumer Magazine Groups, 1980[1]

Total per Issue Circulation	Number	Percent	Cumulative Percent
Under 300,000	33	36%	36%
300,000 to 999,999	20	22	58
1 million to 3 million	14	15	73
3 million to 10 million	11	12	85
Over 10 million	8	9	94
Not reported or unpaid	5	6	100
	91	100%	

[1]Does not include farm magazine groups.

Source: Calculated from circulation reported in Standard Rate & Data Service, *Consumer and Farm Magazines*, May 27, 1981.

Table 4.15: Circulation Size of Business Magazine Groups, 1980

Total per Issue Circulation	Number	Percent	Cumulative Percent
Under 50,000	87	40%	40%
50,000 to 99,999	39	18	58
100,000 to 199,999	36	17	76
200,000 to 499,999	34	16	91
500,000 to 1 million	7	3	94
Over 1 million	6	3	97
Not reported	6	3	100
	215	100%	

Source: Calculated from circulation reported in *Standard Rate & Data Service Business Publications Data*, June 24, 1981.

TRENDS IN NEW PUBLICATIONS

In 1973 about 127 new consumer magazines were announced or made their first appearance. Some of them were major, well financed operations, such as George Hirsch's *New Times* or Bob Guccione's *Viva*. Others were obscure and of uncertain origins, like *New Awareness* and *Alaska Geographic*. Of these four, by 1981, not one was still a going concern.

Premature Obituaries

Five times in this century the doubters have written off the magazine's future.

1) After World War I, when the automobile became established as a legitimate business and pleasure vehicle for the masses, observers felt that people would no longer have time to read magazines.

2) In the mid-twenties, the radio was the source of dire predictions—who needs to read when you can just listen to the box?

3) Still later in that decade, the addition of "talkies" to the movie world added more cause for doom.

4) Then, of course, came television after World War II, the medium that did knock the others for a loop and which, more than any single factor, has changed the nature of the other media.

5) Finally, in the late 1960s and early 1970s, the demise of such icons as the *Saturday Evening Post, Look,* then *Life,* convinced many that magazines had finally had it.

But they have not gone away. True, evidence points to a different role for the magazine, but its survival seems assured.

Turnover, New Titles and Interests

In 1979, 211 new magazine start-ups were announced, following 235 launchings in 1977 and 254 in 1975.[13] Most were consumer magazines:

	1975	1977	1979
Total new magazines	254	235	211
Consumer	N.A.	157	107
Business	N.A.	78	104

As is frequently the case, many do not last long, often but not always because they are undercapitalized. Among the major launchings of 1973, *New Times* entered the world having to turn away venture capital. It was sold in 1978 to entertainment conglomerate MCA Inc., which nonetheless let it fold before the year was over. Its place in the magazine lineup was taken by *The Runner,* from the same firm.

Also in 1973 *Penthouse,* flush with success, added a woman's magazine, *Viva.* That too was allowed to expire in 1978, as the company also brought out a replacement, *Omni.* McCall's gave *Your Place* a big build up, being its first new publication in 102 years. Introduced in February 1978, it too quit publishing before it celebrated its first birthday. McCall's, however, had a replacement waiting with *Working Mother.*

Harcourt Brace Jovanovich, which spent $4 million on *Human Nature,* a slick consumer magazine started in November 1977, folded the magazine in 1979.

Clearly magazine publishing is high risk, yet it brings a constant stream of hopefuls into the marketplace each year. Among start-ups announced in recent years were *Kosher Home, Skateboard World, Ohio, Violent World, California Arts* and *Death Education.*

Publishers are quick to respond to new interests, industries and trends. The increased penetration of cable television and other home video devices, such as the video cassette recorder, has apparently created a market of readers for such magazines as *Video Review* and *Videography.* Triangle tried to reach this audience with *Panorama,* presumably a magazine for videophiles who did not want the more mundane features of

TV Guide. The magazine folded in under 18 months.

More successful, apparently, has been the proliferation of magazines serving the expanding personal computer market. Some, such as *Computerworld* and *Datamation,* were covering the computer industry for some time. But others, such as *Byte, Interface Age* and *Mini-Micro Systems* have been started or repositioned to reflect the broadening base of personal computer users. Moreover, the publishers of these magazines cover the range from McGraw-Hill and Technical Publishing Co. to shoe-string entrepreneurs. Time Inc. was reported to be planning a cable television magazine itself. The interest in energy produced a consumer publication called *Energy Age* and a general fascination with high technology has resulted in a flurry of offerings such as *High Technology,* also for the consumer market.

This profusion of new titles, added to the constantly changing titles over the years, has been the reason that magazines as an industry have been able to survive as well as they have. As leisure time for most Americans has increased, they have discovered a great assortment of hobbies, cults and pursuits. Interests have become more diversified and publishers have always been quick to establish new magazines catering to them. Titles such as *Shooting and Fishing, American Golf, Bird-Lore* and *Snap-Shots* are not of today—these were the special interest publications of 1900. One can scarcely name a specialized subject that does not have its own publication. Moreover, it has already been shown that as a title in a new category becomes successful, it is copied by others.

Even television may have given a boost to some magazines. Although TV is blamed for the demise of the entertainment value of magazines, as another medium of information, television often whets the appetite of its viewers for more information. Thus, *Time*'s newsstand sales jumped 34% in the last six months of 1973, the period of great television coverage of the Watergate hearings, drastically reversing the steady decline in single-copy sales that had been occurring since 1964. The growth of *TV Guide* is of course linked closely to the penetration of television, and a publication such as *Sports Illustrated* can look to television's expanding coverage of sports as a factor in its success.

ROLE OF THE ENTREPRENEUR

Quite possibly, more than in any other industry the success or failure, the mediocrity or acclaim, of a general interest magazine can be traced to a specific individual: a Hugh Hefner, De Witt Wallace, Henry Luce, Cyrus Curtis, a Bok, Gingrich, McClure or Ross. Magazines—the best magazines— have long been closely associated with a personality. And although it doesn't have to happen, all too frequently when that individual passes from the scene, the magazine begins to fade also. It may survive, but as a different book, reflecting the personality of another.

It is this observation that has led Clay Felker, among others, to postulate the life cycle hypothesis of magazine longevity. "There appears to be an almost inexorable life-cycle of American magazines that follows the pattern of humans," wrote Felker, former editor of *Esquire* and *New York Magazine,* in the Spring 1969 issue of *The Antioch Review.* That pattern is "a clamorous youth eager to be noticed; vigorous, productive middle-age marked by an easy-to-define editorial line; and a long, slow decline, in which efforts at revival are sporadic and tragically doomed."

This hypothesis strikes a logical note because magazines are so intensely personal. A successful editorial policy is more than just the assembling of data by a committee or an analysis of a market—the fall of the *Saturday Review* under Nicholas Charney and John Veronis demonstrates that. "A key fact about magazines," notes Felker, is that unlike any other mass medium, "one man can influence every idea, every layout, every word that appears in print." Yet a basic problem that faces the successful magazine is that both the publishers and their formulas become obsolete. And a corollary of this hypothesis is that the bigger the book is, the more reluctant it is to change.

One of the significant trends in recent years has been the increased willingness of chains to undertake start-ups. Traditionally, the large firms have acquired existing publications: the survivors from the many start-ups undertaken by individuals and small publishers. The attitude of many large publishers was summed up by John Purcell, former executive vice-president of CBS. Asked why CBS did not engage in more start-ups, he noted that some were being considered but added: "Bear in mind that the equivalent of starting a new magazine the size of *Road & Track,* with all its success, is just about the same as adding another issue of *Woman's Day,* which has a lot less risk."[14]

Nonetheless, the high prices being paid for successful publications by acquisition-minded firms have made start-ups relatively more attractive. Staid Condé Nast introduced *Self* in 1978. As noted, McCall's has started two new publications recently. Hearst performed a near start-up in repositioning its old *Science Digest,* and New York Times came out with *Us* (and later sold it). Time Inc., of course, has long been the exception of the giant willing (and rich enough) to engage in start-ups on a regular basis. They have also been known to stick with an unprofitable publication for several years, while today even well-financed magazines seem to be given but a year or two in which to make it. Henry Luce kept *Sports Illustrated* alive for seven years before it made money.

Starting a New Magazine

For the most part, however, magazines are still started by independent entrepreneurs. Starting a new magazine takes a set of skills very different from those required to successfully manage ongoing magazines. The entrepreneurial type personality is often absent in large firms and compensation for the initiators of new projects is difficult to determine. Existing publicly owned businesses also tend to shy away from high risk ventures that might dilute earnings on the income statement. Thus, the strategy of established publishers seems to involve letting the independent operator take the risks and raise the financing, then buying him out when things look successful, using the corporate strengths to expand a going concern. CBS has followed this line, as have Ziff-Davis, Times Mirror and Hearst, among many.

A listing of some of the magazines started in the 1960s and 1970s (see Table 4.16) gives ample evidence that a big bankroll is not enough to ensure longevity—and a shoestring budget does not doom a good, well-executed idea. *Playboy* began life in less expensive times, but still at the bargain start-up cost of $16,000. More recently, *High Times* had a $25,000 bankroll, *Rolling Stone* all of $6500 and *Mother Earth News* only $1500. *Vegetarian Times,* a slick bimonthly with 32,000 circulation, started with what capital the founder could save from his salary as a nurse. *Jazz* began life with the modest savings accounts of four friends, plus "sweat equity," a substantial but noncash investment. All except the latter were still in operation in 1981.

On the other hand, Triangle Publications, Inc. spent millions on introducing *Good Food* in 1974 and it failed to last a year. *Panorama* did not survive much longer in 1980-1981. Harcourt Brace Jovanovich, a major book and farm magazine publisher, reportedly spent $4 million on *Human Nature* before abandoning it before its second birthday. McCall's tried *Your Place,* with plenty of publishing talent and dollars behind it, but it died in under a year. *Politicks and Other Human Interests,* an independent endeavor aimed at a limited audience, received considerable trade attention, yet had to give up the fight after running through nearly $1 million in six months.

All else being equal (which is rarely the case), a well-financed venture certainly has a better chance of survival than one struggling from issue to issue. But as one magazine entrepreneur has concluded, money's importance has unfortunately been overemphasized, at least in the start-up phase. Too fat a bankroll can erode some of the hunger and urgency that the shoestring operators experience. Paradoxically, the most logical sources of funding, the existing magazine publishing groups, are the most reluctant to invest in new magazines (Time Inc. being the long-term excep-

Table 4.16: Selected Consumer Magazine Start-Ups Since 1969, by Entrepreneurs and by Publishers

Entrepreneurial Start-Ups	Year	Entrepreneurial Start-Ups	Year
Ambiance*	1978	Intellectual Digest*	1970
American Photographer	1978	Kosher Home	1978
Astronomy	1973	L'Officiel/U.S.A.	1970
Backpacker	1973	Mariah	1976
Black Enterprise	1970	Moneysworth	1970
Book Digest	1974	Mother Earth News	1970
Byte	1974	Ms.	1972
Calendar	1976	New Dawn*	1976
Blair & Ketchum's Country Journal	1974	New Harvest	1979
Equus	1977	New Times*	1973
Essence	1970	Nuestro	1977
Firehouse	1976	On the Sound*	1972
Food & Wine	1977	Penthouse	1969
Gambler's World*	1972	Plants Alive	1972
Gallery Magazine	1971	Playgirl	1973
Games	1977	Quest	1977
Genesis	1972	Sail	1970
High Times	1979	Soap Opera Digest	1975
Horse, of Course	1971	Vital*	1977
Hustler	1974	WomanSports*	1973

Magazine Publisher Start-Ups	Year	Publisher[1]
Americana	1973	American Heritage
Apartment Life	1969	Meredith
Dirt Bike Magazine	1972	Daisy/Hi-Torque
Discover	1980	Time Inc.
Epicure*	1972	CBS
Families	1980	Reader's Digest Association, Inc.
Geo	1979	Gruner & Jahr
Good Food*	1973	Triangle
Human Nature*	1978	Harcourt Brace Jovanovich
Inside Sports	1980	Newsweek, Inc.
Look*	1979	Filipacchi
Money	1972	Time Inc.
Motorboat	1973	United Marine Publishing
New West	1974	New York Magazine
Omni	1978	Penthouse
Oui	1972	Playboy
Outside	1977	Rolling Stone
Panorama*	1980	Triangle
People	1974	Time Inc.
Petersen's Photographic Magazine	1972	Petersen Publishing
Pizzazz*	1977	Cadence
The Runner	1979	MCA

Table 4.16 (continued)

Magazine Publisher Start-Ups	Year	Publisher[1]
Self	1979	Condé Nast
Us	1977	New York Times Company
*Viva**	1973	Penthouse
*Your Place**	1978	McCall's
Working Mother	1979	McCall's
Non-Magazine Organization Start-Ups	**Year**	**Publisher**
Smithsonian	1970	Smithsonian Institution
Travel & Leisure	1970	American Express Company

*Not being published as of August 1981.

[1] For identification of ownership affiliation. The legal corporate entity may be different.

Source: Knowledge Industry Publications, Inc.

tion). A top executive of ABC's Publishing Group said that starting a new magazine is "like drilling for oil in Central Park."[15]

GROUP PUBLISHING

There is a good reason why most magazines are published by multi-magazine groups: a single book, especially one of limited audience circulation, must carry too great a burden of overhead to make economic sense. The economies of scale are not great in magazine publishing, but the natural limits to the size of the consumer and business special interest books make acquisitions and start-ups a necessity if a company wishes to keep growing. Once a periodical reaches a saturation point, ad revenue growth becomes limited to cost per thousand increases or total pages. Take *New York* magazine, for example. From a start-up circulation of 50,000 in 1968, circulation grew rapidly to 171,000 by 1969, 292,000 in 1971, 342,000 in 1973 and 391,000 in 1978. The rate of circulation growth was 35% from 1969 to 1970, 26% the next year, down to 10% in 1972 and slowed to 6% in 1973. Between 1973 and 1978, circulation grew an average of 2.7% annually. So after some heady growth, *New York* logically turned to the outside for further revenue increases, first by its acquisition of the *Village Voice* and then the *New West* start-up (since sold). Yet there are few notable economies that can result from having these three publications under the same corporate banner.

In a few areas, it's true, group publishers do gain some synergistic advantages over a one-magazine publisher:

- A publisher of well established magazines has greater leverage in getting distribution of a new book and may be able to negotiate a more favorable deal with a national distributor.

- Bulk acquisition of paper may be slightly less expensive and easier.

- Printing contracts can be negotiated en masse.

- Subscription fulfillment contracts for a small circulation book can be combined with other books for a more economical rate.

- In-house circulation staffs can be centralized.

- A good publishing group can also provide corporate research and management expertise adding to this economic leverage.

On the other hand, most magazine operations must be run as separate entities and their costs vary little from independent to group status. Editorial staffs for each book are generally strictly segregated, often because of the disparate subject matter of the books: CBS' *World Tennis* has little in common editorially with *Rudder* or *Woman's Day*. Similarly, advertising staffs are separate, although regional offices can be combined in a single facility and many groups of small magazines sell insertions on a package basis. Macfadden's Women's Group, for example, sells for all eight books in combination. Postage on subscription mailings is strictly per unit, and mailing cost for the magazines is figured separately for each title.

There are then minimal economies of scale: some small cost savings in printing, paper and production, some helpful leverage in distribution and little else. The quest for a chain then lies in the fact that magazine publishing is an industry with good margins, but on a small scale. Time Inc., for example, had an 11.7% pretax profit for publishing operations in 1981. In its heyday (1974), Playboy had earnings before taxes on its magazine of 21%. (In 1978 it was under 10%.) McGraw-Hill had a 1980 operating margin of 19.4%. The *New Yorker* magazine, the only major publicly owned firm with income almost exclusively from a single magazine, had a pretax profit of 11.4% in 1980. Although the magazine industry as a whole reports an average 3% to 6% pretax earnings, there are many profitable magazines making 15% or more before taxes, according to an official of an acquisitions-minded firm.

While starting a new magazine has a certain excitement, buying an existing one is quicker, easier and not necessarily more expensive. The key is buying at the right price. Profitable periodicals either are not for sale or are available only at a high price, while unprofitable publications are usually in bad straits for a reason.

"What you're buying is good will," noted an analyst at one of the most highly regarded special interest publication groups. This firm looks for a 30% to 50% return on its investment—and never less than 25%. It boasts of this because it does with the publication what the seller was not doing, and that is more than just cutting costs. It may mean that the magazine was underpriced or that its cpm was too low for its category. The New York Times paid $8 million for *Family Circle* and claims that the investment was paid for in two years. Ziff-Davis expected a similar payback on *Psychology Today*. Once a title saturates its market, opportunity for growth of circulation and ad revenue become tied to higher rates rather than more purchasers and ad pages. A publisher thus tends to seek another magazine.

As in any make or buy decision, there are cost tradeoffs in acquiring or starting a periodical. The first question is, "Do we want a title in this marketplace?" If yes, then the field of available publications can be scouted. The cost of available magazines must be compared to the cost of starting fresh. An important factor in the equation is the management that comes with a new publication. In developing a publication internally, a company must include the cost of the management time used in developing the new publication, an expense that would be far greater in most cases than in acquiring an existing book.

In many ways it is surprising that a giant like CBS would even bother with magazines like *Pickup, Van & 4WD* or *American Photographer,* both of which it purchased. The latter had a guaranteed circulation of only 100,000 when it started in 1978, against well-established competition. Two years later, when CBS acquired it, circulation had passed 200,000. Its advertising pages increased by 33% between 1979 and 1980, but were still only 416, compared to 1691 for *Popular Photography. Pickup, Van & 4WD,* which was even smaller in 1973, had a 265,000 circulation in 1980. Yet, since just about the same amount of time and investigation are required to purchase a magazine with a potential of 100,000 circulation as to acquire one of 500,000 circulation, the usual scenario would be for the smaller groups or independents to take over the limited audience publications, while the bigger companies used their earnings to buy magazines with more substantial cash flows. Clearly, potential for growth must be a major factor in the decision. Table 4.17 identifies some of the consumer magazines acquired by major publishers.

MAGAZINE NETWORKS FOR SPECIAL PUBLISHERS

A general interest magazine is, in molecular form, many different

Table 4.17: Selected Consumer Magazine Acquisitions by Major Publishers

American Broadcasting Companies	Macfadden Group, Inc.
Los Angeles (1977)	*Us* (1980)
Modern Photography (1976)	
High Fidelity (1976)	New York Times Company
	Family Circle (1969)
CBS	*Tennis* (1972)
American Photographer (1980)	*Golf Digest* (1969)
Sea (1973)	
Woman's Day (1977)	Petersen Publishing
Audio (1979)	*True* (1974; suspended 1976)
Family Weekly (1980)	
	Playboy
Charter Publishing Company	*Games* (1978)
Ladies' Home Journal (1977)	
Redbook (1977)	13-30 Corporation
Sport (1977; sold 1981)	*Esquire* (1979)
American Home (1977; suspended 1977)	
WomanSports (1977; suspended 1978)	Times Mirror
	Ski (1972)
Condé Nast	*Golf* (1972)
Gentlemen's Quarterly (1979)	*Popular Science* (1970)
	Outdoor Life (1970)
	Sporting News (1978)
Dow Jones	
Book Digest (1978)	Ziff-Davis
	Psychology Today (1973)
Gruner & Jahr AG	*Intellectual Digest* (1973; suspended 1974)
Parents (1978)	*Sport Diver* (1977)
Young Miss (1978)	*Backpacker* (1979)
	The Runner (1980)

Source: Knowledge Industry Publications, Inc.

specialized topics combined within one cover. Conversely, the special interest and limited audience magazines taken together reach a general audience. It is this second point that provides a unique marketing device for some special interest publishing groups. By offering advertisers in several highly specialized books a discount over single-title insertions, the network makes general advertising more attractive. For instance, it is difficult to convince a cigarette manufacturer to promote its brand in *Stereo Review*, with a possible cpm of $26.74 on a circulation of 550,000. However, by selling a package with *Boating* and *Skiing,* Ziff-Davis offers over 1.1 million circulation and a cpm of $19.27. A black and white page in *Boating, Car and Driver, Cycle, Flying* and *Skiing,* offering the equivalent of a 2.2 million circulation magazine, yields a cpm which begins to be competitive with *Playboy.*

In addition to Ziff-Davis, Petersen Publishing has its "Action Group" network; Condé Nast offers a four-book combination; and Hearst, Macfadden Sterling Women's Group, Times Mirror, CBS and many other group publishers offer comparable arrangements.

THE TREND TOWARD GROUPS

One group publishing several magazines is not an innovation. Curtis, Hearst, Time, Fawcett and Macfadden operations are among the many that have long been group publishers. The increased desirability of special interest consumer and business publications, however, makes multi-magazine houses all the more necessary for the future. When giant CBS decided to get into magazines, it did not launch or buy up mass circulation magazines but chose to accumulate a stable of smaller special interest books. With the exception of *Field and Stream,* none of them until *Woman's Day* was significant by itself, but as a group they provide substantial revenue and potentially strong profits. The New York Times Co., while purchasing *Family Circle,* has also taken over *Tennis* and *Golf Digest.* Time Inc., accustomed to circulation figures in the millions, has added *Money,* with its modest potential, to its house as well as *People* and the new *Life,* which have circulation ambitions more in keeping with Time Inc.'s tradition.

ABC got into the magazine business by acquiring *High Fidelity* and *Modern Photography,* and has expanded its presence in the industry through the purchase of additional limited audience consumer, farm and business magazines.

With the re-emergence of *Life*, the success of *People* and the staying power of *Us,* it may seem that mass circulation magazines are making a comeback. But even at two or three million circulation, these are a shadow of the eight and nine million of the old mass circulation periodicals. And these popular magazines tend to get the publicity, while the scores of small business and special interest magazines, independent and group owned, make up the bulk of the industry.

With the risk still high and the entry cost great, new mass circulation books will be a rarity in the field. Publishers will thus have to rely on good profits yielded by relatively small revenues from several publications for company or division viability.

FOREIGN PUBLISHERS IN U.S. MARKET

The strength of many foreign currencies vis-à-vis the U.S. dollar in the late 1970s was only a small part of the increased interest on the part of foreign publishers in entering the U.S. market. European publishers see the U.S. as a vast market, with a far greater potential for a title than the magazines they publish in their home bases. Although the entry of the foreigners has involved buying up some going magazines, they have also committed funds to the start-up of new publications.

Among the ventures:

- Gruner & Jahr, Germany's largest publisher (*Stern, Brigitte*), has set up a U.S. subsidiary to publish *Geo,* a slick picture magazine not unlike *National Geographic.* In April 1978, the company also purchased Parents' Magazine Enterprises, publisher of the 1.6 million circulation monthly *Parents',* as well as *Children's Digest, Humpty Dumpty* and others. Gruner & Jahr is itself 75% owned by German publishing giant Bertelsmann Gütersloh, which directly owns a majority interest in leading U.S. mass market paperback publisher Bantam Books. *Geo,* however, did not catch on with enough readers or advertisers to satisfy the publisher. Gruner & Jahr sold the magazine in 1981 to Knapp Publications (publisher of the successful *Bon Apetite* and *Architectural Digest*).

- Daniel Filipacchi tried to revive *Look,* killed by Cowles Communications in 1971. Aiming at a 1 million circulation biweekly, with primarily newsstand distribution, he fell far short of his goal and suspended publication in 1979 after about a year's effort. Filipacchi had previously acquired Popular Publications, Inc., a group that included *Argosy, Camera 35* and *Railroad.* Filipacchi's French publishing base includes *Paris-Match* (which sells nearly 800,000 weekly) and the sex-oriented *Lui.*

- Britain's Associated Newspapers Group Ltd., the owner of some 45 publications, bought a minority interest in the *Soho Weekly News* (which folded in 1982) and financed Clay Felker's brief takeover of *Esquire* in 1977. (In April 1978 Associated sold most of its interest in *Esquire* to a U.S. firm, 13-30 Corp.)

- *The Economist,* Britain's respected financial weekly, is looking for expanded circulation in the U.S. with added coverage of U.S. events and a beefed-up U.S. editorial operation. In 1981 it began printing its U.S. edition domestically.

- Harlequin Enterprises, the Canadian publisher best known for its romance novels, has started a magazine publishing empire in the U.S. Its first step in that direction was the acquisition of the Laufer Company, which publishes *Tiger Beat* and associated periodicals for teenagers as well as a series of Rona Barrett gossip magazines. Total group circulation is about 1.2 million.

- In the business publications area, Britain's Reed International group acquired the large Cahners group in the U.S.

So far the presence of the foreign publishers is rather small. Their interest in the market can only add to the competition for the acquisition of existing publications, driving their prices higher. But their willingness to start up new ventures can also add to the diversity of magazines for the consumer. And, if they follow the form of most publishers, profits will be kept in the country to add further publications.

U.S. VENTURES ABROAD

U.S. publishers have also been active in other parts of the world. Reader's Digest publishes about 39 international editions in 15 languages. (*Canadian Reader's Digest* is a separate entity.) Each is locally edited under general supervision from U.S. headquarters. These international editions have a combined circulation of about 12 million.

Hearst has long been involved in overseas publishing, directly and through the licensing of its titles to local publishers. *Mechanica Popular* is Latin America's look-alike of *Popular Mechanics*. Hearst also owns Great Britain's National Magazine Co., which publishes British versions of some Hearst titles, as well as magazines unique to its own markets.

Condé Nast is also active in international publishing, with both licensing and foreign subsidiaries. *Vogue*'s British, Italian and French editions, for example, are owned, while the Australian edition is published under license. Condé Nast, like Hearst, also publishes titles overseas that do not have U.S. counterparts.

Time and *Newsweek* both have extensive international editions that are substantially different editorially from the domestic editions. *Newsweek* has Atlantic and Pacific overseas editions with further geographic subdivisions, while *Time* has these as well as Canadian and Latin American editions. All are printed in English. *Time* has overseas sales of about 1 million copies per issue, while *Newsweek,* without a Canadian edition, has a circulation of about half that.

Family Circle publishes an Australian edition. Taking advantage of the proliferation of supermarkets (its primary sales outlet), it entered into an agreement with the Blue Chip Stamp Co. of Japan for a Japanese edition. Thus, as foreign publishers look to the U.S. as an expansion market, U.S. publishers continue to use their editorial formulas to tap an increasingly literate market throughout the world.

MAGAZINES AND NEW MEDIA

The magazine business suffered a dramatic erosion of its share of media advertising when television entered the marketplace. Magazine share dropped from 13% in 1945 to 9% by 1950 and did not bottom out until it hit 5.2% in 1975. The newspaper industry felt its major blow during the 1930s, in competition from radio. Television eroded the newspaper share from 32% in 1950 to about 29% by 1980.

Thus, magazine publishers are seeking to protect themselves from potential threats suggested by the increased penetration of cable for video programming, while concurrently taking advantage of opportunities the technology allows. For example, today's largest magazine owes its being to television—Walter Annenberg accurately foresaw the opportunity the young industry provided for a localized guide for television program schedules. Today, more than one publisher is fighting to provide cable program guides. By mid-1981, one source estimated that there were "at least ten competitors in the new market," about half of them under a year old.[16]

An earlier discussion noted the proliferation of both consumer and trade magazines targeted to hobbyists, and professional users and purchasers of computers and new video equipment. These offerings are coming from both entrepreneurs and the large group publishers. Among those following the market are McGraw-Hill (e.g., *Byte*), North American Publishing (e.g., *Videography*), Technical Publishing—a Dun & Bradstreet subsidiary—(e.g., *Datamation*), McPheters, Wolfe & Jones (*Interface Age*) and Wayne Green, Inc. (e.g., *Kilobaud Microcomputing*). The list includes the familiar corporations and the upstarts. One Dun & Bradstreet entry, *Output,* has already come and gone.

Publishers Seek to Capitalize on Content Expertise

In addition to seeking opportunities in magazine publishing, many publishers are looking for ways to use their editorial strengths and advertising base to *use* the developing media formats. Time Inc., Condé Nast, Hearst, CBS, Meredith, Playboy and McGraw-Hill are among those actively pursuing such opportunities. In many cases, these plans are being formulated as joint ventures with partners that bring other types of specialization, either in production or distribution. For example, Hearst and American Broadcasting Cos. announced a venture in 1981 to produce and supply women's programming for cable television. Hearst, on its part, was expected to provide programming ideas from its women's magazines, which include *Good Housekeeping, Harper's Bazaar,* and *Cosmopolitan.* ABC would likely provide production and cable networking expertise. The joint venture will also explore other video distribution alternatives, such as video cassettes or discs.[17]

Meredith Corp. announced formation of its own video "publishing" unit. Again, with content inspired by articles in its magazines, such as *Better Homes & Gardens,* Meredith expected to deliver programming to cable operators via satellite and also sell programs on cassette and disc. In addition, Meredith was looking forward to using interactive cable systems—when (and if) they become widespread, to develop programming and advertising that could take advantage of that capability. In the meantime, Meredith has been participating with CompuServe, Inc. (see Chapter 7), in providing supplementary editorial content from recent issues of its magazines "online" to subscribers of CompuServe's data base system.[18]

CBS, which had been providing editorial material drawn from some of its magazines on Knight-Ridder's Viewtron viewdata prototype system in Florida in 1980-1981, announced in late 1981 its own experiment of a viewdata system in a venture with AT&T for 1983. Time Inc., pursuing a different strategy, was planning to use some of its magazine and book publishing expertise to set up a national cable-based teletext system, to be sold as a pay "tier" (see description of tiers in Chapter 7). Playboy became half partner in a joint venture with some cable system operators. Its service, dubbed "Escapade," was expected to be a video version of *Playboy*'s well known editorial content. Finally, McGraw-Hill was looking at opportunities for providing some of its newsletters, such as its daily "Oilgram," to customers via computer and telephone lines. This plan was actually speeded up in part when a long strike of postal workers in Canada convinced the company to begin offering its oilgram newsletter to Canadian customers online.

DISCUSSION

Not all magazine publishers will find it easy to transfer their content expertise to a video or electronic text delivery. On the other hand, just as new alternatives have always made it less necessary to rely on the existing options, so will the availability of new technologies have a long-term impact on magazine publishing. Inevitably, some of the capital and talent that in an earlier period would have been devoted to starting a new print magazine will in the future be channeled toward the expanded opportunities for providing special interest or limited audience video content. This situation was impossible when video was limited to the broadcasting spectrum. But with the expansion of cable and video cassettes and discs, those with editorial messages—and advertisers wanting to reach the particular audiences those messages address—will find expanded potential in formats other than print.

The traditional magazine, in the meantime, seems to be in no immediate danger of being overwhelmed by electronic technologies. The magazine industry is diverse, dynamic and responsive to change. Like book publishing, it is a field with relatively low capital entry barriers, so long as the publisher is not trying to start a mass circulation consumer publication. Magazine publishing (like book publishing), utilizes outside services for virtually its entire physical production and distribution process, unlike most newspapers that tend to own their own presses and control their own delivery. Indeed, it may be argued that this guaranteed access to a distribution channel is the most important single factor in maintaining diversity and dynamism.

The fact that there are more than 10,000 different magazine titles published by thousands of firms, however, does not accurately reflect the degree of competition or concentration in the industry. Almost by definition, the objective of each magazine is to create its own monopolistic sphere by catering to a distinct audience segment. *Motorcycle Product News* does not compete with *Time* or *College and Research Libraries*. *Ski* and *Skiing* magazines do battle for the same audience, but are not in direct competition with *Prairie Farmer* or *Teen*. Magazines are perhaps the best example of monopolistic competition—many similar products, but each one perceived as being different enough from the others to create its own unique market. The distinction may be by geography (*Philadelphia, Southern Living, Wisconsin Agriculturalist*), specialized content (*Popular Photography, Insurance Marketing*), demographics (*Town & Country, Modern Romances, Seventeen*), intellectual level (*Harper's, Marvel* comics, *New Yorker*), generalized content (*People, TV Guide, Better Homes & Gardens*) or other designations.

Although it may be argued that newspapers do not compete with one another in different cities, daily newspapers all tend to provide the same function for a single mass audience each day. Although a fire in Cincinnati and a budget hearing in San Jose are reported only locally, any given paper across the country on a given day will have much the same national and international news, similar types of local stories and advertising. Magazines have no such similarities.

It is for this reason, perhaps, that group ownership of magazines is seldom raised when discussion turns to media concentration. It is not easy to support the hypothesis that the purchase by ABC of Chilton's *Hardware Age* gives that magazine an unfair advantage over other magazines. Nor should the fact that Times Mirror publishes *Popular Science* and *Outdoor Life* have any impact on the free flow of ideas through these or other magazines.

Moreover, many magazines also face competition from thousands of newsletters, such as "Old House Journal" or "Kiplinger's." While many of these cost far more than magazines and are thus directed to special business audiences, they serve as an even less expensive format than magazines in which a publisher may provide information for a distinct market. Newsletters tend to be supported 100% by circulation revenue and thus can serve many diverse audiences that are too small to support an advertising-backed publication.

The nature of the market is such that competition is restricted to a great extent by the limited audience for most publications. The first publisher to discover a market niche, either in a trade or the consumer area, has an edge in reaching those interested in that subject. Sometimes there is room for a second or third publication. In the case of fads, such as the sudden discovery of running, several magazines may hit the market at once, but the size of the market—both the limited advertising base and the potential universe of subscribers—may not economically be able to support all the entries. In this case, the better financed publication may be able to survive best and the strength of being part of a large publishing entity may be an advantage over an independent entrepreneur.

But in most cases, magazines are started to fill a niche that no one else has noticed or one which was felt to be too small to deal with. While an individual may not consider it worthwhile to run a business publication with a potential free circulation of 5000, a group that specializes in such periodicals may start or acquire at an early stage such a magazine and use its management and marketing skills to make it a profitable operation.

A recent example of an individual magazine finding and filling a void was the 1978 introduction of *American Photographer*. The dominant magazines for amateur photographers are *Popular Photography* (Ziff-Davis) and *Modern Photography* (ABC). *Petersen's Photographic* (Petersen) is a distant third. Entrepreneur Alan Bennett saw all these magazines as being editorially oriented to the technical and engineering aspects of photography and thus created a magazine that concentrated on the creative side. As a result he was able to attract a different type of subscriber, thus offering new reach to advertisers. Subsequently, he sold the magazine to CBS.

Except for the largest mass circulation magazines, publishers must also be aware of the limited resources of their advertisers. Bobit Publishing

Co.'s *School Bus Fleet* may be the only vehicle for advertisers that wish to reach that market. But the many small suppliers who advertise in the periodical would have to cut down on their space or stop advertising altogether if the publisher exercised its "monopoly" position to raise rates with abandon. At the same time, most special interest publishers have a limited universe of potential advertisers and cannot afford to lose too many.

Magazine publishing is an easy entry field and this brings into it a profusion of new products each year. The tendency is for successful publications to be purchased by multiple title publishers, or for the success of one title to provide the resources for the publisher to start or acquire additional publications and thus become a group. Despite the high mortality rate and the competition from other media, the growth in additional magazine titles shows no sign of letting up. In addition, a single magazine with even a small, but perhaps influential audience (in a specialized field), can be a very effective voice, even when published by a company that owns no other magazines. Along with books, magazines provide society with a broad range of information, education and entertainment.

NOTES

1. *Ayer Directory of Publications,* annual (Bala Cynwyd, PA: Ayer Press).

2. See Jean-Louis Servan-Schreiber, *The Power to Inform* (New York: McGraw-Hill, 1974), pp. 36-38.

3. Among the better histories of magazines are James L.C. Ford, *Magazines for Millions* (Carbondale, IL: Southern Illinois University Press, 1969); Frank Luther Mott, *A History of American Magazines,* 5 volumes (Cambridge, MA: Harvard University Press, 1968); Theodore Peterson, *Magazines in the Twentieth Century* (Urbana, IL: University of Illinois Press, 1964); and John W. Tebbel, *The American Magazine: A Compact History* (New York: Hawthorn Books, 1969).

4. Calculated from Publishers Information Bureau gross advertising revenue.

5. *U.S. Industrial Outlook, 1981,* U.S. Dept. of Commerce (Washington, DC: Government Printing Office, 1981), p. 96.

6. *Bowker Annual of Library and Book Trade Information* (New York: R.R. Bowker Co.) 1971 and 1981 editions.

7. *Advertising Age,* Sept. 26, 1977, p. 87.

8. Rose Marie Zummo, "Periodical Publishing," *U.S. Industrial Outlook,* 1981, p. 95.

9. Ibid., p. 96.

10. Ibid.

11. Dantia Quirk, *The Library Market for Publications and Systems, 1979-83* (White Plains, NY: Knowledge Industry Publications, Inc., 1978), p. 81.

12. Benjamin M. Compaine, *The Business of Consumer Magazines* (White Plains, NY: Knowledge Industry Publications, Inc., 1982).

13. *Folio,* December 1977, January 1977, and personal telephone interview, October 1981.

14. *Media Decisions,* June 1978, p. 46.

15. Compaine, pp. 108-109.

16. John Andrew, "Cable-Guide Publishers Fighting it Out; Giant TV Guide is Lurking in the Background," *The Wall Street Journal,* March 24, 1981, p. 37.

17. Maurine Christopher, "Hearst and ABC Tell Cable Plan," *Advertising Age,* February 2, 1981, p. 2.

18. Jacques Neher, "Meredith Taking its Franchise to Cable," *Advertising Age,* February 2, 1981, p. 70.

Appendix 4.1

Magazines Published by Major Groups*

American Broadcasting Companies—37 (including Chilton Co.)

Consumer:

High Fidelity (M)
Modern Photography (M)
Schwann Record & Tape Guide (M)
Los Angeles (M)

subtotal: 1,251,244 paid

Farm:

Prairie Farmer (BW)
Wallaces Farmer (BW)
Wisconsin Agriculturist (SM)
Dairy Herd Management (M)
Feedlot Management (M)
Hog Farm Management (M)
Miller Agriculturist (M)

subtotal: 675,478 paid/unpaid

Business/Trade:

Quality (M)
Assembly Engineering (M)
Industrial Finishing (M)
Infosystems (M)
Office Products Dealer (M)
Woodworking & Furniture Digest (M)
Machine Tool Blue Book (M)
Farm Store Merchandising (M)
Feedstuffs (W)
Garden Supply Retailer (M)
Tack 'N Togs Merchandising (M)

Chilton Co.:

Accent (M)
Automotive Industries (M)
Automotive Marketing (M)
Commercial Car Journal (M)

---

*Notes: Circulation for groups most current available to December 1980. Titles in group current, where changes known, to November 1981.

Key: (M) monthly; (BM) bimonthly; (SM) semimonthly; (W) weekly; (BW) biweekly; (Q) quarterly; (10x, etc.—10 times annually).

Distribution (M)
Electronic Component News (M)
Hardware Age (M)
Instruments & Control Systems (M)
Instrument & Apparatus News (M)
Iron Age (W)
Jewelers Circular—Keystone (M)
Motor/Age (M)
Product Design and
Development (M)
Review of Optometry (M)
The Specialist (BM)

subtotal: 1,627,157 unpaid/paid

Total: 3,553,879 paid/unpaid

American Chemical Society—15

Business/Trade:

Biochemistry (BW)
Chemical Reviews (BM)
Inorganic Chemistry (M)
Journal of Agriculture & Food
Chemistry (BM)
Journal of the American Chemical
Society (BW)
Journal of Chemical Information &
Information Science (Q)
Journal of Medicinal
Chemistry (M)
Journal of Organic
Chemistry (BW)
Journal of Physical
Chemistry (BW)
Macromolecules (BM)
Chemical & Engineering News (W)
Chemical Technology
(Chemtech) (M)
SciQuest (10x)
Environmental Science &
Technology (M)
Analytical Chemistry (M)

Total: 246,993 paid

Cahners Publishing Co.
—See Reed Holdings, Inc.

CBS Inc.—10

Consumer:

American Photographer (M)
Mechanix Illustrated (M)
Woman's Day (15x)
Cycle World (M)
Pickup, Van & 4WD (M)
Road & Track (M)
Field & Stream (M)
World Tennis (M)
Audio (M)
Family Weekly (W)

Total: 13,569,188 paid
(Does not include 12.4 million for
Family Weekly, a Sunday
newspaper supplement.)

Capital Cities Communications,
Inc.—19
(Fairchild Publications, Inc.)

Business/Trade:

Clinical Psychiatry News (M)
Electronic News (W)
Energy Users News (W)
Family Practice News (M)
Footwear News (SM)
Heat Treating (M)
HFD Retailing Home
Furnishings (W)
Home Fashions Textiles (10x)
Internal Medicine News &
Cardiology News (SW)
Men's Wear (BM)
Metal/Center News (M)
Metalworking News (W)
MIS Week (W)
Multichannel News (W)
OB Gyn News (SM)

Pediatric News (M)
Skin & Allergy News (M)
Sportstyle (24x)
Supermarket News (W)

Total 698,084 paid/unpaid

Charlton Publications, Inc.—9

Consumer:

Charlton Comics Group (BM)
    (16 titles)
Charlton Crossword Group (BM)
    (5 titles)
Charlton Muscle Group (BM)
    (3 titles)
Country Song Roundup (M)
Hit Parader Combination (M)
Official Karate (8x)
Real West (BM)
Rock and Soul Songs (8x)
Gung-Ho (M)

Total: 4,086,816 paid

Chartcon, Inc. (Charter Co.)—2

Consumer:

Ladies' Home Journal (M)
Redbook (M)

Total: 10,187,914 paid

Chilton
—See American Broadcasting Cos.

Communications Channels, Inc.—14

Business/Trade:

Adhesives Age (M)
Trusts and Estates (M)
Apparel South (9x)
Business Atlanta (M)

Container News (M)
Elastomerics (M)
Fence Industry (M)
Modern Paint and Coatings (M)
Southwest Real Estate News (M)
National Real Estate Investor (M)
Pension World (M)
Shopping Center World (M)
Refuse Removal Journal (M)
Southeast Real Estate News (M)

Total: 264,916 unpaid/paid

**Condé Nast Publications Inc.
(Newhouse)—8**

Consumer:

Brides (BM)
Gentleman's Quarterly (M)
Glamour (M)
House & Garden (M)
Mademoiselle (M)
Self (M)
Vogue (M)
Parade (W) (Newhouse)

Total: 7,089,397 paid
(Does not include 21,644,000 for
Parade, a Sunday newspaper
supplement.)

Dun & Bradstreet, Inc.—19

Technical Publishing Co.:

Business/Trade:

Consulting Engineer (M)
Datamation (13x)
Electric Light & Power (M)
Plant Engineering (BW)
Pollution Engineering (M)
Power Engineering (M)
Purchasing World (M)

American Journal of
Cardiology (M)
American Journal of Medicine (M)
American Journal of Surgery (M)
Cutis (M)
Dun's Review (M)
Firm Engineering (M)
Mining Equipment
International (9x)
World Construction (M)
Control Engineering (M)
Graphic Arts Monthly (M)
Highway & Heavy
Construction (M)
Industrial Research/
Development (M)

Total: 1,248,150 unpaid/paid

Fairchild Publications, Inc.
—See Capital Cities
Communications, Inc.

Harcourt Brace Jovanovich, Inc.—63

Farm:

Kansas Farmer (SM)
Michigan Farmer (SM)
Missouri Ruralist (SM)
Ohio Farmer (SM)
Pennsylvania Farmer (SM)
Nebraska Farmer (SM)
Colorado Rancher & Farmer (M)
Florida Grower & Rancher (M)
Flue Cured Tobacco Farmer (8x)
Peanut Farmer (7x)

subtotal: 578,177 paid/unpaid

Business/Trade:

Body Fashions/Intimate
Apparel (M)
Communications News (M)
Dental Industry Newsletter (M)

Dental Laboratory Review (M)
Dental Management (M)
Drug & Cosmetic Industry (M)
Electronic Technician/Dealer (M)
Fast Service (M)
Flooring (M)
Food Management (M)
Gourmet Today (BM)
Hearing Instruments (M)
Home & Auto (BW)
Hosiery & Underwear (M)
Hotel and Motel Management (M)
Housewares (21x)
Industrial Education (9x)
Kitchen Planning (6x)
LP-Gas (M)
Market Maker Body Fashions/
Intimate Apparel (10x)
Paper Sales (M)
Pets/Supplies/Marketing (M)
Professional Remodeling (M)
Quick Frozen Foods (M)
Rent All (M)
RSI (M)
Snack Food (M)
Telephone Engineer &
Management (BM)
Toy Hobbies & Crafts (M)
Toys Trade News (5x)
Geriatrics (M)
Hospital Formulary (M)
Modern Medicine (21x)
Neurology (M)
Physicians Management (M)
Energy Management Report (M)
Petroleum Engineer
International (12x)
Pipeline & Gas Journal (14x)
Blood (M)
Journal of Pediatric Surgery (BM)
Progress in Cardiovascular
Diseases (BM)
Seminars in Arthritis &
Rheumatism (Q)
Seminars in Hematology (Q)
Seminars in Nephrology (Q)

Seminars in Nuclear Medicine (Q)
Seminars in Oncology (Q)
Seminars in Perinatology (Q)
Seminars in Roentgenology (Q)
Seminars in Ultrasound (Q)
Golf Business (M)
Lawn Care Industry (M)
Pest Control (M)
Weeds Trees and Turf (M)

subtotal: 1,163,937 paid/unpaid

Total: 1,742,114

**Harper & Row Inc. (includes
J.B. Lippincott Co.)—19**

Business & Trade:

*American Journal of
  Pathology* (M)
Anesthesiology (M)
*Journal of Obstetrics, Gynecologic
  & Neonatal Nursing* (BM)
Obstetrics and Gynecology (M)
*American Journal of
  Clinical Pathology* (M)
American Surgeon (M)
Annals of Surgery (M)
Cancer (SM)
Clinical Nuclear Medicine (M)
Clinical Pediatrics (M)
Clinical Preventive Dentistry (M)
*Diseases of the Colon &
  Rectum* (8x)
Hospital Pharmacy (M)
Investigative Radiology (BM)
Laboratory Medicine (M)
NITA (BM)
Ophthalmology (M)
Spine (BM)
Transfusion (BM)

Total: 376,330 paid/unpaid

Hearst Corp.—21

Consumer:

Cosmopolitan (M)
Cosmopolitan Living (Q)
Good Housekeeping (M)
Sports Afield (M)
Connoisseur (M)
Motor Boating & Sailing (M)
Popular Mechanics (M)
Science Digest (M)
Harper's Bazaar (M)
House Beautiful (M)
*House Beautiful's Building
  Manual* (Q)
*House Beautiful's Home
  Decorating* (Q)
Town & Country (M)
Country Living (BM)

subtotal: 12,937,706 paid

Business/Trade:

American Druggist (M)
Motor (M)

United Business Publications, Inc.
(subsidiary):

Electronic Products Magazine (M)
Floorcovering Weekly (W)
Industrial Machinery News (M)
Office Products News (M)
Office World News (SM)

subtotal: 509,272

Total: 13,446,978

Irving-Cloud Publishing Co.—8

Business/Trade:

*Fleet Maintenance &
  Specifying* (M)

Hardware Merchandiser (M)
Management/Maintenance (M)
Jobber Topics (M)
Super Service Station (M)
Warehouse Distribution (10x)
Dental Lab Products (6x)
Dental Products Report (10x)

Total: 543,453 unpaid

The Laufer Co.—8

Consumer:

Tiger Beat Group (M):
Tiger Beat
Tiger Beat Star
Tiger Beat Star Super Special
Right On!
Dazzle

Rona Barrett's Hollywood
Network (M):

Rona Barrett's Hollywood
Rona Barrett's Daytimers
Country Fever

Total: 1,215,000 paid

Macfadden Group Inc.—8

Consumer:

True Story (M)
True Confessions (M)
Secrets (M)
True Romance (M)
True Experience (M)
True Love (M)
Modern Romances (M)
Us (SW)

Total: 3,610,631 paid

McGraw-Hill, Inc.—28

Business/Trade:

American Machinist (M)
Architectural Record (M)
*Aviation Week & Space
Technology* (W)
Business Week (W)
Chemical Engineering (BW)
Chemical Week (W)
Coal Age (M)
Data Communications (M)
*Electrical Construction &
Maintenance* (M)
Electrical Wholesaling (7x)
Electrical World (SM)
Electronics (BW)
*Engineering and Mining
Journal* (M)
Engineering News-Record (W)
Fleet Owner (M)
*F.W. Dodge Construction
News* (4x)
Graduating Engineer (4x)
Housing (M)
Industry Mart (9x)
Modern Plastics (M)
NC Shopowner (Q)
Physician and Sportsmedicine (M)
Postgraduate Medicine (M)
Power (M)
Textile Products and Processes (M)
Textile World (M)
33 Metal Producing (M)
International Management (M)
(English edition)

Total: 2,486,489

Meredith Corporation—8

Consumer:

Metropolitan Home (M)

Better Homes and Gardens (M)
*Better Homes and Gardens
   Building Ideas* (Q)
*Better Homes and Gardens
   Remodeling Ideas* (Q)
*Better Homes and Gardens
   Country Home and Kitchen
   Ideas* (Q)
*Better Homes and Gardens
   Decorating Ideas* (Q)
Sail (M)

subtotal: 11,204,830 paid

Farm:

Successful Farming (13x)

subtotal: 797,787 paid/unpaid

Total: 12,002,617

The New York Times Co.—4

Consumer:

*The New York Times
   Magazine* (W)
Family Circle (17x)
Golf Digest (M)
Tennis (M)

Total: 10,201,923 paid (Does not
include 1.4 million for *New York
Times Magazine,* a Sunday
newspaper supplement.)

North American Publishing Co.—11

Consumer:

Yacht Racing/Cruising (10x)

subtotal: 37,325 paid

Business/Trade:

*American Import & Export
   Bulletin* (M)
*American School & University
   Magazine* (M)
Business Forms Reporter (M)
In-Plant Reproductions (M)
Lab World (M)
Marketing Bestsellers (M)
Package Printing (M)
Printing Impressions (M)
World-Wide Printer (6x)
Zip (9x)

subtotal: 328,230 paid/unpaid

Total: 365,555

Penton/IPC—25

Business/Trade:

*Airconditioning & Refrigeration
   Business* (M)
Energy Management (6x)
Government Product News (M)
Hospitality-Lodging (M)
Hospitality-Restaurant (M)
Hydraulics & Pneumatics (M)
Material Handling Engineering (M)
Occupational Hazards (M)
Power Transmission Design (M)
Precision Metal (M)
School Product News (M)
Welding Design & Fabrication (M)
Welding Distributor (BM)
*Handling & Shipping
   Management* (M)
Modern Office Procedures (M)
*Foundry Management &
   Technology* (M)
Industry Week (SM)
Machine Design (28x)

*Management Personnel Time
    Network* (M)
New Equipment Digest (M)
Production Engineering (M)
Airtransport World (M)
*Heating/Piping/Air
    Conditioning* (M)
Materials Engineering (M)
Progressive Architecture (M)

Total: 2,885,770 unpaid/paid

Petersen Publishing Co.—13

Consumer:

Car Craft (M)
4 Wheel & Off-Road (M)
Guns & Ammo (M)
Hot Rod Magazine (M)
Hunting (M)
Lakeland Boating (M)
Motorcyclist Magazine (M)
Motor Trend (M)
*Petersen's Photographic
    Magazine* (M)
Rudder (M)
Sea & Pacific Skipper (M)
Skin Diver (M)
'Teen (M)

Total: 5,041,878 paid

Playboy Enterprises Inc.—2

Consumer:

Games (BM)
Playboy (M)

Total: 5,803,522 paid

**Reed Holdings, Inc.—25
(Cahners Publishing Co.)**

Business/Trade:

Appliance Manufacturer (M)
Brick & Clay Record (M)
*Building Design &
    Construction* (M)
Building Supply News (M)
Ceramic Industry (M)
Construction Equipment (13x)
Design News (SM)
EDN (SM)
Electronic Business (M)
*Foodservice Equipment
    Specialist* (M)
Mini-Micro Systems (M)
Modern Materials Handling (18x)
Modern Railroads/Rail Transit (M)
Package Engineering (M)
Plastic World (M)
*Professional Builder &
    Apartment Business* (M)
Purchasing Magazine (M)
Restaurants & Institutions (SM)
*Security Distributing &
    Marketing* (M)
Security World (M)
Specifying Engineer (M)
Traffic Management (M)

Milton Kiver Publications:

*Electronic Packaging
    Production* (M)
Electro-Optical Systems Design (M)
Semiconductor International (M)

Total: 1,406,817

Scholastic Magazines, Inc.—10

Consumer:

Co-ed (10x)
Forecast for Home Economics (9x)

Scholastic Coach (10x)
Scholastic Newstime (W)

Scholastic Magazines Groups (10x):
Senior Scholastic
Scholastic Voice
Scholastic Search
Scholastic Scope
Science World
Junior Scholastic

Total: 6,103,961 paid

Technical Publishing Co.
—See Dun & Bradstreet, Inc.

Time Inc.—7

Consumer:

Fortune (BW)
Life (M)
Money (M)
People (W)
Sports Illustrated (W)
Time (W)
Discover (M)

Total: 12,464,410 paid
(Does not include *Discover*.)

Times Mirror Co.—22

Consumer:

Homeowners How to (BM)
Golf Magazine (M)
Outdoor Life (M)
Popular Science (M)
Sporting News (W)
Ski (7x)

subtotal: 5,953,325 paid

Business/Trade:

C.V. Mosby Company:

American Heart Journal (M)
American Journal of Infection Control (Q)
American Journal of Obstetrics & Gynecology (SM)
American Journal of Orthodontics (M)
Clinical Pharmacology and Therapeutics (M)
EMT Journal (Q)
Heart & Lung: Journal of Critical Care (BM)
Investigative Opthalmology and Visual Science (M)
Journal of Allergy & Clinical Medicine (M)
Journal of Hand Surgery (BM)
Journal of Laboratory and Clinical Medicine (M)
Journal of Pediatrics (M)
Journal of Prosthetic Dentistry (M)
Journal of Thoracic & Cardiovascular Surgery (M)
Oral Surgery, Oral Medicine and Oral Pathology (M)
Surgery (M)

subtotal: 260,779

Total: 6,214,104

Webb Company—14

Consumer/Farm:

Beef (M)
Consumer Life (Q)
Family Handyman (10x)
Family Food Garden (9x)
Farmer (SM)

Farm Industry News (10x)
Farm Industry News/South
Farm Industry News/Midwest
Friendly Exchange (Q)
Frontier Magazine (M)
Irrigation Age (9x)
National Hog Farmer (M)
Passages (M)
Snow Goer (5x)
Snow Week (17x)
TWA Ambassador

Total: 9,282,772 unpaid/paid

Williams & Wilkins Company—21

Business/Trade:

American Journal of Physical
  Medicine (BM)
Endocrinology (M)
Gastroenterology (M)
Investigative Urology (BM)
Journal of Biological
  Chemistry (SM)
Journal of Clinical Endocrinology
  & Metabolism (M)
Journal of Histochemistry &
  Cytochemistry (M)
Journal of Immunology (M)
Journal of Investigative
  Dermatology (M)
Journal of Nervous & Mental
  Disease (M)
Journal of Pharmacology &
  Experimental Therapeutics (M)
Journal of Trauma (M)
Journal of Urology (M)
Laboratory Investigation (M)
Microbiological Reviews (Q)
Neurosurgery (BM)
Obstetrical & Gynecological
  Survey (M)

Plastic & Reconstructive
  Surgery (M)
Stain Technology (BM)
Survey of Anesthesiology (BM)
Urological Survey (BM)

Total: 121,006 paid/unpaid

Ziff-Davis Publishing Company, Inc.—22

Consumer:

Adventure Travel (BM)
Backpacker (BM)
Boating (M)
Camera Arts (BM)
Car and Driver (M)
Cycle (M)
Flying (M)
Modern Bride (BM)
Popular Electronics (M)
Popular Photography (M)
Psychology Today (M)
Skiing (7x)
Sport Diver (BM)
Stereo Review (M)
Fly Fisherman (7x)
Yachting (M)
US Air Magazine (M)

subtotal: 6,268,500 paid

Business/Trade:

Business & Commercial Aviation (M)
Meetings & Conventions (M)
Photomethods (M)
Travel Weekly (SW)
Hotel & Travel Index (Q)

subtotal: 251,823 paid/unpaid

Total: 6,520,323

5

Theatrical Film

by Thomas Guback

The long-term propensity toward concentration of ownership, endemic to the capitalistic system, is exemplified by the motion picture industry. Its history and present status show as well the recurrent waves that propel this business to market concentration and the inevitable rise of giant concerns that not only dominate the film business, but also spread to allied communications sectors and other industrial and service fields. In some respects, it is no longer sufficient to talk just about a film industry, as if it were comprised of a set of discrete companies operating exclusively in that business. Expansion and diversification have spawned entertainment conglomerates operating globally that are major sources of mass amusement for us and the rest of the world.

HISTORICAL OVERVIEW

From its beginning, the film industry has been characterized by repeated attempts at domination by a small number of firms that customarily tried either to exclude others from the business or to deprive competitors of resources. The industry developed from the monopoly position conferred upon Edison by the patent he received for a motion picture camera invented in 1889. A peephole machine, patented in 1891, was introduced to the public in the Kinetoscope parlor that opened in New York City in 1894. Although it attracted clientele because of its novelty, the Kinetoscope was limited commercially. A significant advance in scale was achieved when the film projector was introduced in 1896 by Edison. It was followed immediately by devices from other companies. These made their debuts in vaudeville houses where their short, 50-foot reels of plotless occurrences allowed films to become one of the string of acts that entertained audiences.

By the turn of the century, Edison, Biograph and Vitagraph were the three principal companies that produced films and marketed equipment.

Their pictures, sold outright to users, probably were of less financial importance than the projecting apparatus they sold, not unlike the soon-to-develop broadcasting business in which set manufacturers operated stations so as to encourage public demand for radio receivers. Although the three companies tried to control the industry by refusing to sell cameras to others, the obstacle was overcome by enthusiastic businessmen who imported cameras from Europe or found ways to obtain them in North America. Little capital was needed to produce the short films of the day, and the possibility of quick profits undoubtedly appealed to speculators. Necessarily, there was extensive patent litigation similar to periods in the telegraph and telephone industries when suits alleged broader plaintiff control of apparatus than defendants were willing to concede. In this way, litigation was used as a weapon to cripple competitors and assert spheres of monopolistic control.

Short films gradually gave way to longer productions offering development of story lines. Theaters were opened specifically to show films, thereby legitimizing the new medium and establishing a path away from the vaudeville stage that the medium began to take. The possibility for quick profit from little investment enticed entrepreneurs to enter exhibition, and probably 10,000 theaters of varying quality and comfort existed by 1910. That film already had become a commodity by this time, and had been staked out by the private sector, necessarily dictated what was being done with the medium. This was evident as amusement dominated—if not excluded—other ways in which the medium could have been employed.

To increase spectators and earnings, exhibitors realized they needed frequent program changes. This was made possible, first by exhibitors trading films among themselves, and then by the establishment of exchanges, beginning in 1902. Within a few years, well over 100 exchanges existed, institutionalizing the producer-wholesaler-retailer chain in the film industry. Indeed, by 1905, industrial and occupational specialization and differentiation already had been established.

Rise and Fall of MPPC

To control an increasingly fluid industry, the seven largest American producers, the leading importer-distributor and two French producers established the Motion Picture Patents Company (MPPC) in 1908. In addition to pooling their patents and acknowledging Edison's claim, the MPPC licensed only its members to manufacture cameras and produce pictures. Eastman Kodak, moreover, agreed to sell raw stock only to licensees of the Trust. To further control the industry, the MPPC granted licenses to 116 distributors who were to deal only with exhibitors licensed by the Patents Company. The exchanges also agreed to handle only films from MPPC members, who pledged to channel their films only through these distributors.

By restraining trade, the MPPC achieved almost complete control of the market and reaped the largest profits ever made in the industry up to that time.[1] To further tighten control, the MPPC in 1910 established its own distribution subsidiary, General Film Company, and forced other exchanges out of business. In 1915, however, federal courts dissolved General Film because it restrained commerce. Two years later, the Supreme Court, attempting to stimulate competition in the industry, held that the MPPC had monopolized the film business and that its exclusive licensing procedures were illegal. Other suits effectively killed the MPPC, and it was not until the innovation and diffusion of sound motion pictures that patents were used again to thwart competition and assert oligopolistic control.

With the power of the MPPC broken, independent companies were allowed to develop, and with them came the star system and the feature film. The foundation also was prepared for the rise of new firms that eventually dominated the industry. Whereas previous control had centered on patent supremacy, the 1920s saw a battle for theaters, because large holdings conveyed bargaining power and market strength. Vertical integration became a primary business objective. "The industry had already passed from one of many small independent companies to one controlled by a few relatively powerful organizations. . . . By 1927, the industry was launched in a period of reckless spending and extravagance which would have meant the inevitable wreck of enterprises in more settled lines. Of necessity, financial dependence on Wall Street increased enormously."[2]

The industry quickly conformed to the classic model of internationalization. World War I and its aftermath allowed America to assert its economic and political interests abroad, and the nation swung from being a debtor to an international creditor. The war had disrupted European film industries, whereas the productive capacity of American companies was burgeoning, and this in turn prompted the development of new markets in which investments could be amortized. In the decade up to 1923, the volume of America's film exportation quadrupled and by 1925 it stood at 235 million feet. During these dozen years, film exports to Europe increased five times and exports to the rest of the world 10 times, as the industry staked out markets in the Far East, Latin America and elsewhere. It was possible for American films to achieve this dominance because, in part, investments in them were recouped in the home market, which had about half the world's theaters, and thus films could be rented abroad at rates often undercutting those of foreign competitors. The maintenance of overseas markets for American films eventually became an important aspect of the industry's foreign policy and set the tone for the later exportation of television programs, part of what has been called America's "media imperialism."[3]

The 1920s and 1930s

During the 1920s, several technically different sound-on-film and sound-on-disc systems emerged, and corporations exploiting key patents asserted as much control as they could, hoping to keep competitors out of the field. Subsidiaries of the American Telephone & Telegraph Company entered into agreements with Hollywood producers for the use of sound recording equipment. Battles from the radio broadcasting industry carried over into the film business as the Radio Corporation of America innovated its sound film system, cracking the industrial control that had been created by AT&T. To enter the film field, RCA was instrumental in organizing the Radio-Keith-Orpheum Corporation in 1928, which became an instant vertically integrated major producer. Almost all the rest of the industry, however, was tied to AT&T through exclusive contracts not unlike those instituted earlier by the MPPC. RCA filed a complaint charging AT&T and its affiliates with unlawful restraint of trade, but an out-of-court settlement in 1935 conceded RCA's place in the sound film industry.

As it entered the 1930s, the industry was dominated by five vertically integrated companies that exercised control through important holdings and trade practices. Together they produced about half the total number of motion pictures, but a much larger share of the grade A features. Although they controlled or owned only about an eighth of all theaters, most were key first-run houses that gave the majors influence far beyond their numerical share. Nonetheless, the industry was not spared from the general economic crisis. In 1933, Paramount was judged bankrupt, while RKO and Universal went into receivership. The Fox Film Corporation was reorganized and emerged as Twentieth Century-Fox.

Restraints of Trade

Constant maneuvers by companies to control their markets and to avoid competition not only prompted suits by others that felt deprived of reasonable attempts to compete, but also stimulated governmental efforts to destroy restraints of trade. Antitrust cases since the late 1920s probably had made the major distributors "well aware that their system of control violated the Sherman Act,"[4] but they persisted in attempts to maintain their positions. In 1938, the Justice Department filed a complaint against the five major companies and three minor companies, accusing them of combining and conspiring to restrain trade in the production, distribution and exhibition of films, and of attempting to monopolize motion picture trade. The five majors accepted a consent decree in 1940. The government reopened the case in 1944 and demanded that the five majors divorce their exhibition circuits and that certain trade practices engaged in by them and the three other defendants be ruled illegal.

The case was fought to the Supreme Court, which in 1948 upheld a lower court's decision that, among other things, "two price-fixing conspiracies existed—a horizontal one between all the defendants [and] a vertical one between each distributor-defendant and its licensees." Block booking, the practice in which distributors would only rent entire packages of films to theaters, forcing them to accept poorer films in order to get the ones they really desired, was held to be illegal. In its place competitive bidding arose with exhibition licenses "to be offered and taken theatre by theatre and picture by picture."⁵ Exhibition circuits were divorced from the major production-distribution companies and some theater chains were dissolved. In 1948, RKO, Warner, Twentieth Century-Fox and National Theaters agreed to consent decrees, and Paramount followed the next year. In 1951, further decrees were entered with Warner, Twentieth Century-Fox and National Theaters. Loew's finally agreed to a decree in 1952.

Although the rise of television makes it difficult to determine the precise impact of the *Paramount* decision, several points are clear. Columbia, Universal, United Artists and some smaller companies were able to obtain larger shares of the market. Theater operators gained greater control over their business, especially in the selection of films, while independent producers and foreign filmmakers had better opportunities to have their films exhibited. Moreover, the majors were cut loose from large investments in theaters at precisely the moment when theatrical attendance tumbled. Enforcement of the industry's censorship system, embodied in the Production Code, became more difficult because the major studios no longer owned theaters, whereas exhibitors as well as producers were willing to expand the screen's verison of morality in order to compete with television.

Developments from 1945 Through the 1960s

In the 1950s and 1960s, the foreign market became even more important to America's major production-distribution companies and yielded about half of their theatrical revenue. Prior to World War II, it had contributed about a third of such revenue. Western Europe and Canada were particularly valuable markets, as they still are, and the American position there and elsewhere was solidified thanks to two lines of policy. Extensive coordination between the U.S. State Department and film exporters materially assisted the companies in enlarging their foreign market shares and elevated film commerce to political and diplomatic levels. In addition, the major companies in 1945 established the Motion Picture Export Association (MPEA) under whose umbrella members could eliminate competition among themselves and present a united front to governments and industries abroad. The MPEA and the State Department worked to eliminate obstacles to the circulation of U.S. films overseas. In 1961 and 1969, the American companies established two companion export associations to develop the English- and French-speaking areas of Africa into suitable markets.

The growth of television abroad provided further opportunities for the American entertainment business. In 1959 the Television Program Export Association (TPEA) was created. By 1962, members included the three commercial broadcast networks, several independent and some major producers of TV programs. Toward the end of the 1960s, however, production for television already had begun to be split between Hollywood major studios and the networks themselves, diminishing the ranks of the independents. Federal Communications Commission rules eventually obliged the networks to end their production and syndication businesses, and this left the motion picture companies as the strong contenders in the field. The TPEA finally was dissolved in 1970, but even by that time the MPEA had brought foreign television matters under its own wing, where they still remain.

Another significant development during the 1950s and 1960s was the growth of American investment in foreign filmmaking. Shooting films abroad on location, as well as financing European producers, was expanded. American companies wanted to deplete their accounts of foreign earnings that could not be repatriated due to international monetary problems. U.S. producers also took advantage of European subsidization programs designed to stimulate national film production. In the United Kingdom, local filmmaking was largely displaced by subsidiaries of American companies.

At home, the rapid expansion of television following the end of the 1948-1952 licensing freeze significantly expanded the demand for programming. The smaller Hollywood firms and the independent producers responded first by creating series especially for the new medium and by releasing theatrical films. The major studios held out until the mid-1950s, when they unleashed an avalanche of pre-1949 films. This marked the first wave of product recycling, to be followed many years later by release of theatrical features to pay television and then to video cassettes and video discs. Another dimension to the service relationship between the film industry and television was added in 1966 when made-for-TV features debuted.

Changing Industry Structure

The sale of films' TV broadcast rights indicated not only the expansion of the market for production-distribution companies, but also how they dealt with financial difficulties that were becoming acute in the late 1950s and early 1960s. In need of cash and unable to carry huge overhead expenses, companies began to dispose of various kinds of assets. This involved the dismantling of production facilities, the sale of real estate and other properties, and the termination of contracts for stars, writers, directors and other personnel. The theater chains of the majors already had been spun off because of antitrust consent decrees.

Motion picture production dropped considerably; studios did not have to churn out dozens of films because they no longer owned the circuits in which to play them. Their dominant interest became maximization of revenue from production and distribution, rather than from the ownership of theaters. Double features became a thing of the past, as did matinees in many communities. Admissions to theaters fell from about $1.7 billion in 1946 to only $.9 billion in 1962, and this paralleled a decline in the number of theaters, from about 18,600 in 1948 to fewer than 12,700 in 1962. Several production-distribution companies had deficit years and assumed the burdens of significant long-term debt. Wide-screen techniques and color were used to try to lure spectators away from television sets. Production costs skyrocketed, particularly for blockbuster films, and massive advertising and marketing campaigns became common to ensure the public's patronage. It was a case of a reduced supply trying to maintain a profitable level of consumption.

Although it is common to assess this as a bleak financial period, it is clear that industrial and banking forces outside the industry had a more sanguine outlook. It might have been for the future of these businesses. But it was definitely for the vault properties and other assets they still owned. Some companies, Paramount and United Artists, for example, became small parts of massive conglomerates, while in others outsiders fought for control and usually obtained it. A few of the companies, such as Disney and Warner, became diversified entertainment corporations themselves.

The 1970s and 1980s

Although there were annual fluctuations for individual companies and for the industry as a whole, the production-distribution sector had managed to turn itself around financially by the early 1970s. Several block-busters, especially in the last half of the decade, materially improved economic conditions for major companies. Some, finding themselves cash rich, looked for acquisitions in or out of the entertainment business, and this perpetuated the conglomerate trend. It annoyed exhibitors, though, who argued that such money should be reinvested in production to in-crease film supply. They also claimed that rental terms, demanding high shares of the box office gross, were squeezing the business out of them, and that they were not participating proportionally in the industry's suc-cesses. Advances and guarantees emerged as common terms in rental con-tracts. Blind bidding (see p. 224) became a standard complaint of first-run exhibitors who launched grass roots campaigns in the late 1970s to have that trade practice made illegal on the state level. Meanwhile, exhibitors in many communities continued to allocate (split) product among them-selves, although they have insisted that this is not an anti-competitive prac-tice. Concession sales have become an increasingly important revenue source for many theater owners, a development obvious to many theater-goers in the form of the price of their popcorn.

The expansion of pay television and the home video market (foreign as well as domestic) constitutes an exceptionally attractive revenue potential for Hollywood companies. Their owners and financiers see new opportuni-ties for recyling films and generating profit. Production of programs specif-ically for pay TV is another profitable route, and the majors look forward to claiming that market as they did commercial television three decades earlier (see chapter 7). Many first-run theater owners necessarily feel threatened by these developments, but the chief circuits continue to grow, with General Cinema approaching 1000 screens. Some are diversifying, too, perhaps as a hedge against an uncertain future. Second-run theaters, however, could see their ranks decimated by expansion of pay TV and home video, and distrib-utors' policies favoring those delivery systems. Particularly vulnerable are low grossing theaters in small towns, which might go the way of the corner grocery and the mom-and-pop soda fountain.

PREVIOUS STUDIES AND INVESTIGATIONS

The literature about film runs an extreme range from the most obscur-antist academic study of cinema theory to the parochial reportage of the trade journals. In the latter category, periodicals such as *Variety, The Hollywood Reporter, Box Office* and the *Independent Film Journal* pro-vide a chronicle of events, but without benefit of context or framework. As one would expect, their writings, although occasionally critical of some specific practice, are supportive of the industry as a whole and raise no questions about its role and function.

The bulk of non-trade writing about film deals with theoretical or aesthetic matters, and a smaller share concerns itself with historical aspects and occasionally with social significance and effects. It is curious that, although film is a multi-billion dollar business and firmly entrenched in the cultural industry sector of capitalism, relatively little has been written about its commercial structure and policies or about film's basic identity as a *commodity*.

Government Investigations and Activities

Before 1960s

Aside from the private sector, government literature is a basic source of information about industrial aspects of the film industry. In addition to material developed for litigation or other judicial proceedings, some government agencies have prepared economic studies of the industry, while numerous Congressional inquiries have highlighted one or another perennial problem.

In 1940, for example, the House Committee on Interstate and Foreign Commerce held hearings on a bill that would have ended compulsory block booking and blind buying of theatrical films.[6] Since the early 1930s, legislation had been introduced to curb these practices, and this hearing was yet another forum in which adversaries could argue their cases. The Motion Picture Producers and Distributors of America, representing the major companies and several independents, strongly opposed the bill, and some exhibitors allied themselves with that side. Other theatrical interests enthusiastically endorsed the proposed legislation, and they were joined by morality groups who believed that the end of block booking and blind buying would prevent films they considered unwholesome from reaching the screens. Such legislation was never enacted, but block booking was made illegal in the *Paramount* case, whereas blind buying still persists in about half the states.

One of the earliest comprehensive government studies was *The Motion Picture Industry—A Pattern of Control* (1941), prepared for the Temporary National Economic Committee's monograph series about concentration of economic power in America. The study explained the economic development of the film industry and, as the document's Letter of Transmittal pointed out, how the "struggle for dominance [by a few large companies] goes forward ruthlessly, with ofttimes little regard for the . . . industry's social responsibilities."[7] The monograph argued that it would be a "mistake to assume that any such cure-all as 'divorcement of exhibition

from production' or 'restoration of competition in the production field' "
would resolve the film business's problems because they "are part of the
large problem of the development and direction of American industry."[8]

In the *Paramount* decision, the Supreme Court formally outlawed certain business practices, but the Senate Select Committee on Small Business
held hearings in 1953 and 1956 on film industry trade practices,[9] charging
that the Justice Department had been reluctant to monitor the industry and
enforce the decrees. According to the Committee's 1953 report, "Spokes-
men for the Department of Justice . . . admitted tacitly that they are ill-
equipped to discharge their responsibilities under the court decrees
[because of] the heavy volume of complaints from exhibitors" and under-
staffing. The Committee recommended "a more forceful and more vigilant
policy on the part of the Antitrust Division of the Department of Justice in
assuring compliance with the decrees. . . ."[10] Three years later, the Committee took note of the declining number of independent exhibitors and
again reviewed distributor-exhibitor relations. Reluctant to recommend
any federal intervention, the Committee could only call upon "responsible
leaders on both sides [of the industry to] put a stop to the constant
fratricidal warfare which does nothing but worsen a difficult situation."[11]

1965 to Present

In 1965, the Federal Trade Commission concluded an investigation of
industry performance since the consent decrees and forwarded its report to
the Department of Justice. The FTC recommended that Justice "consider
the feasibility of instituting contempt or other appropriate action" against
Paramount Pictures and Universal for alleged violation of consent decrees
to which they had agreed in 1949 and 1950.[12] The FTC pointed out,
however, that the alleged violations apparently had ceased in 1962.
Perhaps the Department of Justice saw this as sufficient justification for
not instituting a formal complaint against the two companies.

Unemployment in the film industry was reviewed during Congressional
hearings in 1961-1962 and 1971. The first investigation included motion
pictures as one of many domestic industries affected by exports and imports.[13] Runaway production policies of American film producers were
singled out for criticism, although the blame ultimately was thrown on
foreign governments that prohibited American film companies from
exporting earnings, thereby enticing them to make pictures abroad to
spend that revenue. Film subsidization programs in foreign countries and
lower labor costs also were shown to have drawn production away from
Hollywood. It was clear, however, that American companies were following their self-interest in shifting production abroad. But the committee

found no fault with that, even though it dramatically affected domestic employment, and stemmed from their desire to exploit foreign markets. The basic premise of global expansion was tacitly accepted.

Hearings in 1971 were prompted by publicity about extraordinarily high unemployment levels among Hollywood craft and artistic personnel—the result of declining production and the years of sour financial performance of production-distribution companies.[14] The hearings also considered the proposed Domestic Film Production Incentive Act of 1971, which would have provided tax advantages for films made in America—in effect a public subsidy to private interests. Although importation of foreign-made television programs occasionally was pointed to as contributing to unemployment, testimony was diffuse, inconclusive and lacking perspective. Witnesses failed to relate film industry unemployment to the context of general unemployment and the dynamics of a private enterprise economy. There was a uniform absence of demands for basic structural changes, and consequently the meager solutions that were considered only involved at most minor tampering.

The Domestic Film Production Incentive Act was never reported out of committee, but the production sector did not need it because theatrical motion pictures and television programs became eligible for investment tax credits under the Revenue Act of 1971. Public hearings on this legislation do not disclose any presentations by the production-distribution companies or their trade association, but the industry did lobby to be assured of inclusion in the Act. Also about this time, tax laws were construed to allow so-called tax shelter arrangements for production and distribution of films, a practice that drew criticism from some quarters for its alleged abuses. In hearings on the Tax Reform Act of 1975, all sectors of the industry urged Congress not to eliminate these advantages for film investors.[15] Subsequently, tax laws were construed more rigidly, but deals are still arranged to allow benefits for high income investors.

In 1978 the Small Business Administration responded to pleas from the capitalist sector about the shortage of financing for independent film-makers and small production companies. The SBA selected six companies for a test program that was to provide government or government-guaranteed loans to privately owned enterprises investing in film production.

The position of the production-distribution companies favoring unfettered growth of pay television was presented in testimony in 1975 and 1976.[16] Other federal government hearings inquired into the role of film and the film industry as international propaganda vehicles in the Cold War and inevitably touched on the development and structure of Hollywood's overseas market.[17] The Informational Media Guaranty Program was reviewed in 1967,[18] and the U.S. film industry's global status was considered in 1977 hearings[19] that stressed the importance to this country's balance of payments of Hollywood's film exports.

The Federal Trade Commission in 1967 published a 50-year review of the Webb-Pomerene Export Trade Act. That measure permits companies presumably competitive in the domestic market to combine in order to form export cartels. One of these is the Motion Picture Export Association of America (MPEAA), to which the major film production-distribution companies belong. The FTC declared that the "kind of firms which have gained advantages from the act has not been the smaller firms in our economy, but rather those which are large in an absolute sense and which simultaneously have major positions in the markets they serve." The Commission concluded that, "More often than not those exercising the right [to form export cartels] were least in need of it."[20]

Also in 1967, the Senate Judiciary Committee's hearings on International Aspects of Antitrust paid special attention to the Webb-Pomerene Act, but the exportation of American films was not studied at all,[21] despite the motion picture industry being among the chief beneficiaries of that legislation.

In 1978, the FTC issued a staff analysis largely updating the 1967 study of the Webb-Pomerene Act. The Commission pointed out that the MPEAA "appears to be the only [export] association that helps to divide business among its members,"[22] in addition to the more customary function of setting floor or ceiling prices in foreign areas where its members do business.

The long and involved history of industry litigation and consent judgments was not touched by the House Committee on the Judiciary when it investigated in 1958 and reported in 1959 on the *Consent Decree Program of the Department of Justice.*[23] The film industry also escaped specific attention when the Senate Committee on the Judiciary examined economic concentration between 1964 and 1970.[24] The Senate Committee on Finance similarly overlooked the international operations of the production-distribution companies in its 1973 study of multinational corporations.[25] However, the House Committee on the Judiciary, in its investigation of conglomerate corporations in 1969 and 1970, and in its report published in 1971, did review Gulf + Western Industries (Paramount's parent) as well as the now defunct National General Corporation (which started from the divorced Fox theater circuit). But the study of each company touched film industry matters only incidentally.[26]

Diversification of communications companies, cross-media ownership, growth of market shares for some and corresponding reductions in competition were spotlighted repeatedly throughout the 1970s, but the issue was not examined until the FTC's 1978 *Symposium on Media Concentration.*[27] However, the motion picture industry (like the recorded music business) was not reviewed. Television and newspapers were the center of those proceedings. Similarly, the House Committee on Small Business held hearings on *Media Concentration* in 1980 but inexplicably ignored the film sector.[28] The reason for this is elusive because in production, distribution, and exhibition, small enterprises abound.

Throughout the 1970s and into 1980, a series of studies by the Senate Committee on Government Operations and the Committee on Government Affairs continued the decades-old task of inquiring into industrial concentration in America, and the roles of major banks, stockholders and other investors.[29] Although the motion picture business was not selected for specific examination, some major companies fell into view because of their ownership of broadcast stations, an area that was studied. Other film companies' parent corporations were identified for inquiry because of their size or their relation to America's largest banking and investment houses. The value of these Senate documents is that they clearly reveal how the dominant film companies are integrated into the nation's financial and economic centers.

The industry's censorship system was considered in 1960 by the House Committee on Post Office and Civil Service.[30] Hearings in 1977 by the House Committee on Small Business dealt with independent producers' charges that they were treated unfairly by the Classification and Rating Administration, which the major Hollywood production-distribution companies helped to establish. The Committee found no evidence of discrimination, but avoided studying the adequacy of the rating system and the secrecy in which rating decisions are made.[31]

Private Studies and Articles

Among nongovernmental studies of the business, one of the earliest to explain institutional matters, albeit from the industry's point of view, was *The Story of the Films* (1927) edited by Joseph Kennedy, who at the time was president of FBO Pictures Corp. and soon was to be involved with RKO. An unusual aspect of the volume was its recognition of the impact American films were having overseas, even at that time, "as silent salesmen for other products of American industry"[32]—and presumably for American ideology as well. In the late 1930s, Kennedy became ambassador to the United Kingdom where he worked on behalf of the American film industry to maintain its position in that important market.

The importance of overseas markets was stressed even earlier, at the Eighth National Foreign Trade Convention in 1921, when the vice president of the National Association of the Motion Picture Industry told the audience: "The American motion picture has so far maintained its lead that today it has to a large extent crowded its competitors off the screen; and, it is telling the story of America. . . . It is by that very means assisting in creating a desire for American goods and products." He called on bankers "to recognize in a negative of a motion picture . . . a form of bankable security not only as good, but superior to ordinary merchandise."[33]

William Seabury, in *The Public and the Motion Picture Industry* (1926) and *Motion Picture Problems—The Cinema and the League of Nations* (1929),[34] claimed that the capture of markets abroad by American film companies had a detrimental impact on the foreign development of filmmaking. The latter book demonstrated how international attempts to deal with the problem were short-circuited by American interests.

Early industry studies of the domestic industry were done by Hampton,[35] Lewis,[36] and Ricketson.[37] Raymond Moley's friendly treatise on *The Hays Office* (1945) also is important.[38]

A landmark was Huettig's *Economic Control of the Motion Picture Industry* (1944),[39] highlighting industrial organization and trade practices at the moment they were under litigation by the Department of Justice. The author declared that "concentration of control exists in the pervasive influence exercised by the five theater-owning companies (Paramount, Loew's, Warner Brothers, Twentieth Century-Fox, and RKO) over the production, distribution, and exhibition of films. The nature and extent of the influence varies in each branch of the industry, but its existence is indisputable."[40] The possibility for new competition was felt to be slight. "Only by springing forth as a fully integrated unit, equipped for production, distribution, and exhibition simultaneously, could a new company secure a substantial share of the market. The costs and risks currently attached to any such venture make it unlikely."[41]

Economic aspects of the industry occasionally have been treated in journal articles, and more rarely as chapters in collections, but only Conant has offered a book-length treatment of antitrust problems. This careful and detailed study, published in 1960, warned that monopoly power in the industry "can be offset only to the extent of continuous vigilance by the Department of Justice to insure free entry of rivals into the market."[42] Conant found that although the Paramount decrees had destroyed some restraints of trade, they did not go far enough to generate competition in all sectors of the industry.

More recently, the short report of the Washington Task Force on the Motion Picture Industry argued in 1978 that the "major producers/distributors are effectively limiting competition by maintaining tight control over the distribution of films, both by their failure to produce more films and by their failure to distribute more films produced by others." While discounting any "invidious or criminal intent" on the part of film company managers, the study's authors charged nonetheless that major companies "tacitly limit production among themselves and . . . create sufficient barriers to entry to effectively squash new competition."[43] The pro-industry critique of the report was provided by A.D. Murphy in *Variety* (July 5, 1978).

David Waterman's dissertation, *Economic Essays on the Theatrical Motion Picture Industry* (1979), was organized around postwar changes in demand for films and the impact of the *Paramount* decrees on the industry's structure and trade practices. In part, he compared economic models of alternative industry structures and concluded "that the lowest admission prices, the highest attendance, and the greatest supply of films will result from the most competitive commercial industry structure possible." Although he admitted that "Competition does not at all guarantee a healthy and responsive commercial film industry," he judged that the alternatives seem worse.[44]

The long-neglected relationship between the banking community and the film business was described by Janet Wasko in *Movies and Money: Financing the American Film Industry*.[45] In addition to a case study showing D.W. Griffith's reliance on banks, Wasko traced the last three decades of industry bank connections and demonstrated that financial institutions do not have to meddle in content because friendly corporate management is a surrogate for their influence.

Another side was dealt with by Thomas Guback in *The International Film Industry* (1969),[46] which explained the transatlantic trade in films since 1945. The author demonstrated how the major companies, allied in the Motion Picture Export Association of America, had regained and enlarged their position in Europe after World War II, not only through the export of films, but also through production abroad that took advantage of foreign subsidy programs. The study identified cultural dangers that flowed from the economic structure and foreign policy of the American majors.

Foreign Studies

Several studies written abroad also have considered, in varying degrees, the economic status of the film business in America, frequently relating it to problems in foreign countries. In *Money Behind the Screen* (1937),[47] Klingender and Legg outlined the domination of the British cinema by a handful of American companies and sketched the banking and financial interests behind them. A few years later, Bächlin also explored economic aspects of the American film industry, analyzed its oligopolistic structure, and showed its impact on the prewar film business in Europe.[48] The study built upon the concept of film as commodity in capitalist society, and although factual material is now dated, the basic premises retain their validity. Mercillon in 1953[49] examined the monopolistic structure of the American industry, and Batz[50] a decade later devoted part of his study to showing how American film companies were related to the economic and cultural crisis of European film industries. In 1972, Degand[51] drew upon new material and pointed out how the American majors, by integrating themselves with national film industries in Europe, were therefore integrated with the film and cultural policies of the European Economic Community. He argued that a European cinema could not exist as long as it was tied to American finance and distribution. Bonnell in 1978[52] examined the problems and economics of the French industry primarily from the standpoint of consumption, and his findings necessarily are relevant to understanding the consequences of American companies' operations in that country.

The Council of Europe sponsored a symposium in Lisbon in 1978 concerning *Cinema and the State* (1979). Although the objective was to evaluate the position of film industries and state support in Europe, that task necessitated reference to the role of American companies and their pictures. The meeting's report concluded that:

> One of the main obstacles to the free circulation of films stems from the dominant position of a few companies. For example, the American firms which are members of the MPEA are in a position to apply certain pressures. The cold calculations of commercial profit and the play of world economic forces are thus a constant threat to European cultural identity.[53]

The Commission of the European Communities, in cooperation with the Council of Europe, financed studies that were submitted to the 1980 Strasbourg conference on the state's role *vis-à-vis* culture industries. Among them was Nicholas Garnham's *The Economics of the U.S. Motion Picture Industry*, which concluded that the "power and prosperity of the [American] Majors is based upon control of worldwide distribution networks which give them alone the possibility to balance, on a world scale, production investment with box-office revenue."[54]

In 1978, Pochet and Pitoun surveyed the United States as a market for French films. They concluded, not unexpectedly, that although governmental restrictions were absent, the industrial structure in the American market contributed significantly to the weak circulation of French motion pictures (and those from other countries, too). They reported: "Whereas

American film production has conquered an important part of the French market, by contrast French films have not been able to obtain more than 1 percent of the American market. In television, the inequality of exchange is even more evident."[55]

Postwar studies in the United Kingdom were done by Political and Economic Planning,[56] a private research organization, in 1952 and 1958. These described the status of the British industry after decades of American supremacy and demonstrated how the American majors, by extending their control to Britain, had stunted the growth of an indigenous production industry there. Spraos in 1962[57] analyzed the erosion of the exhibition sector in the United Kingdom, and Kelly in 1966[58] again considered, in part, the operation of American subsidiaries in that country. The same year, the Monopolies Commission[59] issued its report on the supply of films in the United Kingdom and pointed to the role played by American production and distribution subsidiaries. The Association of Cinematograph, Television and Allied Technicians published a report in 1973 calling for nationalization of the film industry, from raw stock manufacture through exhibition.[60] Again, it identified the dominant position of the American majors and the influence they exerted over industry policy, trade practices and labor relations. The Prime Minister's Working Party, in its 1976 report on the *Future of the British Film Industry,* briefly mentioned that the supply of finance for British film production depended partially on the changing policies of the major American distribution companies.[61]

Elsewhere, the massive study of the German film industry by Roeber and Jacoby (1973)[62] gave some attention to the operations of American companies. They receive only passing notice from Giannelli,[63] even though Italy was (and continues to be) a major market for American films and draws considerable American production investment. Berton's examination of Canada in part described how American companies and the MPEAA operated there, particularly in the 1940s and 1950s. Canada's failure to develop a domestic feature film industry can be explained largely by American companies' control of the market, the study argued.[64]

This conclusion was seconded by Manjunath Pendakur (1979), who also showed how the policy of the Canadian Film Development Corporation had shifted to one of accommodating and attracting American investment for films made in Canada.[65] Rather than being indigenous productions, these imitated the international style favored by American distributors. Consequently, nascent Canadian feature film making was being turned into a branch plant of Hollywood.

A general assessment of governmental and nongovernmental studies of economic aspects shows the continuous proclivity in the industry for collusion, parallel action to restrain trade, anti-competitive practices, and oligopolistic control. Patterns of dominance in the American market are carried abroad by the major companies, which cannot escape blame for the inability of many foreign countries to develop indigenous film production industries. The worldwide operation of American companies necessarily has cultural and social consequences as well that are now being clarified and understood.

ROLE OF FILM

In the United States—as in other countries in which film is dominated by the private sector—the medium has grown almost entirely as a means of mass amusement, built predominantly around fictionalized portrayals. People have become accustomed to identifying film as a form of entertainment, and exposure to the medium customarily is for the purpose of diversion. As a recording medium and a vehicle for communication, film naturally can be employed in a variety of ways, and the theatrical film business is only part of a larger industry that embraces nontheatrical film uses as well, including educational and instructional films. All of us routinely see television commercials as well as news and public affairs on film. Instructional motion pictures are used commonly in the educational system and by the military; scientific work often is photographed for later reference, and films made by religious groups openly convey their norms and values.

However, the distinguishing characteristic of film in the capitalist economy is its profit-seeking objective. A large and powerful business has evolved for the purpose of manufacturing and circulating motion pictures as *commodities,* with little regard for the medium's instructive capacity, its ability to be used for social transformation and its potential for contributing to the solutions of society's problems. Indeed, as with the content of the other media, the film industry mitigates against basic structural changes in the institutions of the country, and as a consequence, it functions implicitly to maintain the existing system.

It is true, of course, that not all films are frivolous escapist fare, and that many are dreadfully serious. However, what they have in common is an identity primarily as a commodity. Their production, distribution and exhibition are prompted by the anticipation of financial returns on investments. Marketplace considerations dictate that economic interest take precedence over significance. This is embodied in the slogan "giving the public what it wants," which means, in reality, "selling profitably what the public can be enticed to buy." Sales validate what is sold, according to this system of logic, and what is offered for sale is entertainment, occasionally of the most violent kind.

Naturally, not every entertainment film is profitable. But this does not deny that the basic thrust of the industry is centered on amusement, and usually within such well-defined parameters that even culturally similar entertainment films from other English-speaking lands or western Europe hardly are distributed in the United States. Moreover, the feature-length documentary is virtually a lost art in America, with distribution and exhibition limited to the noncommercial sector of the industry.

Although films overtly entertain, they covertly teach. More than a half century ago, the previously mentioned Kennedy collection pointed out how desire abroad for American goods was created by the exportation of American films. Their propaganda value certainly was the reason why the industry and the government worked together to have them broadly distributed overseas in the years after World War II. It also was the rationale behind the Informational Media Guaranty program that allowed film companies to sell some of their soft currency earnings to the American government for dollars, just to make sure that our films would be exhibited in critical foreign areas. Inasmuch as the social and cultural role of film has always been acknowledged, it is not surprising that many countries are now beginning to rebel against the cultural invasion by American media. Nor is it surprising that American media struggle to maintain their foreign markets.

Censorship and Industry Codes

The impact of film on society, especially on supposedly impressionable young minds, has been a subject of concern for as long as films have existed. Municipal and state censorship (primarily against immorality and nudity) and pressure from religious and other groups, which usually worked through government, have plagued the business from its earliest days. Indeed, one of the chief tasks of the industry's trade associations over the years has been to defuse external censorship and to create a system of internal industry censorship. Individual freedom of speech, already shaped by the economic context, was further constrained by the collective judgement embodied in industry-wide codes. The present attack on television content by some religious groups in the name of morality is but a reincarnation of the impatient efforts by predecessors to impose their version of values on motion picture content.

Until the late 1960s, the dominant themes in the industrial censorship system were the elimination of nudity and sexual innuendo, the preservation of family life, the maintenance of rigid social, racial and gender roles, reinforcement of the crime-doesn't-pay dictum, and general support for the ideology of the American way of life. Violence, terror and brutality were treated more leniently.

Industry codes of various dates spelled out these guidelines, and the Production Code Administration enforced them, a task made all the easier because the major producers, who supported the Code, owned major first-run theater circuits. State and municipal censorship boards oversaw film content as well. Inasmuch as the Supreme Court in 1915 had declared that exhibition of films was a business, and not properly to be considered as part of the nation's press, this medium of communication was not seen as deserving the shield of the First Amendment.[66] In 1952, however, the Supreme Court found that motion pictures did warrant constitutional protection,[67] and that decision led to two decades of litigation that by and large struck down censorship laws across the country.

In the 1950s and 1960s, films produced by independent companies and others imported from abroad began to stretch the restraints of the Production Code, and some ignored them altogether. Hollywood's version of morality was becoming quicky antiquated, while competitive pressures pushed producers toward themes, language and sexual content that were not then offered on television. Consequently, the old Code was replaced in 1966 with a more liberal, streamlined version, and two years later a system of classification was introduced so that the young and the adolescent would not be admitted to films with content unsuitable for them. Previously, every film exhibited had to be potentially suitable for a child's eyes and ears, but the new system recognized that not every film had to be made on that level. In the late 1970s, the Code and Rating Administration was subtly renamed the Classification and Rating Administration (CARA), a change interpreted by some groups as the death of production content guidelines. The U.S. Catholic Conference was not alone in criticizing the classification system for rating some films PG (Parental Guidance) that should have been awarded an R (Restricted). This continues to be a problem for CARA, which has done little to provide additional information to the public as to why films receive the ratings they do. A test project or two has been run, but the system remains basically unchanged after more than a decade. Its administrators seem more intent to deflect public criticism than to respond to public need. As always, CARA's proceedings are conducted with Star Chamber secrecy, even though they have considerable social consequences.

Since the mid-1960s, Hollywood's "new freedom" has been exercised largely to provide more graphic violence, sexual portrayals, gripping terror and explicit language, but has led to little analysis or critique of social and economic problems. Indeed, no formal code ever has prohibited their treatment on the screen, yet such subjects have been constrained by the emphasis on entertainment.

MEANS OF DISTRIBUTION

The flow of films from producer to public involves three chief commercial markets that, for the most part, are analogous to those normally found in industrial organizations. The producer (manufacturer) employs a distributor (wholesaler) to handle the finished product. The distributor licenses the film to an exhibitor (retailer), who in turn deals with the public (consumer). But the film business is not quite as simple as this because theater companies occasionally finance production. Moreover, major companies, which are both producer and distributor, often finance the production of so-called independent companies, and also pick up for distribution films already completed by others.

The distribution company charges a fee for its service, often at least 35% of film rental payable by theaters, and this covers the basic overhead of the organization. In addition, a distribution company deducts from film rental payable to producers the costs of promotion and advertising directly associated with the film. If the distributor has advanced production money (or guaranteed the advance of production money), it charges for that service as well. Necessarily, this description is very general; endless complications and refinements exist in particular cases.[68]

The motion picture theater held a monopoly during the first four decades of the film industry's life. If you wanted to see a movie, you had to see it there. But since the 1940s, other ways have been innovated to distribute filmed entertainment to the public, and the theater can no longer take its audience for granted. Although major production-distribution companies initially withheld their film libraries from television exhibition, they have long since admitted that television is an important source of revenue, and have cooperated with it. Their enthusiastic encouragement of unregulated pay television has been apparent as well.

The public consumes its filmed entertainment in several ways. Traditionally, it has dealt with exhibitors as retail outlets. A spectator buys a ticket that admits him/her to a hall in which a film is shown. The transaction in this case consists of renting a portion of a theater's space to view shadows projected on a screen.

A spectator also can view a film delivered in a variety of ways to the home television set. In the case of a commercial broadcast, the transaction, rather than being based on the direct payment of money by the spectator, involves the television network or station selling to advertisers the collective attention of the thousands or millions of viewers who have been assembled to watch the film. The broadcaster pays for the film and offers it as the "free lunch" to viewers. Regardless of whether film or other content is offered, the function of the broadcaster is to gather audiences and to sell them to advertisers. This deviates from the pattern of noncommercial television in which the broadcast becomes more a public service and less a commodity involving direct exchange of money or attention. It also deviates from the pay television model, in which the household pays a flat monthly fee or is charged on a per-program basis.

In any of the above cases, however, the consumer takes part in a service transaction and no physical product changes hands. The development of the video cassette and the video disc modifies the relationship because when the recording medium is sold (as opposed to being rented), it is a product to which the buyer acquires ownership and private viewing rights. This is an extension of direct sales to consumers of 8mm and 16mm versions of (usually old) films, a very tiny market to be sure, but one which has existed for decades. The growing number of video recorders in public hands, estimated to be close to 3 million at the end of 1981, also increases the possibility of copying films directly from a television broadcast (or from another patched recorder). This is a matter of concern for companies that sell prerecorded cassettes of films and, naturally, for producers of those films.

Figure 5.1 identifies the ways in which theatrical films can be delivered to consumers. The major or mass markets are theaters and commercial television. Sub-markets include school, military, penal and other institutional outlets, commercial aircraft (and ocean liners), and the miniscule number of home movie purchasers. Home video, a developing mass market, is served by prerecorded video cassettes and discs. Distributors earn between $30 million and $40 million annually from sub-markets, plus about $20 million from airlines. Military TV stations and base theaters probably contributed about $17 million annually to distributors of theatrical films and television programs in the late 1970s. Movies on video tape or disc are likely to exceed these other markets combined by the mid-1980s.

The major markets are themselves composites of smaller ones. Theatrical exhibition can be described by the kind of theater—drive-in or hardtop—and by where a particular house stands in line, waiting its turn to rent a film. In most communities, there are first-run houses that show major films as soon as they are released, and behind them are subsequent-run houses that play majors' reissues as well as newly released films from minor producers and distributors. Very large cities normally have a few theaters that play showcase or flagship runs, before films go into broader distribution in first-run theaters. Depending upon the film, three months or so may elapse between its big-city premiere and its initial run in a small community, with a corresponding drop in rental rates and length of run.

Within theatrical exhibition, there also is a division of houses according to the type of film played. Throughout the country, there are some

Figure 5.1: Distribution Channels for Theatrical Film

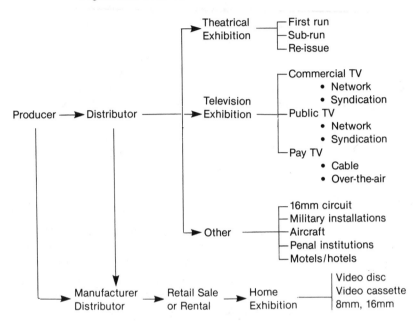

Source: Author.

theaters that show only X-rated films, and in very large cities it is common to find a few houses exhibiting only foreign pictures. In addition, there are about 500 theaters showing Spanish-language films,[69] while other houses present pictures oriented to black audiences.

On television, theatrical films are exhibited by national networks, each having about 200 affiliated stations that can broadcast a film simultaneously. Beyond that is the syndication market, consisting of individual stations to which distributors lease packages of films. Separate from the advertiser-supported medium are pay television networks, with local cable TV affiliates to which households subscribe, and over-the-air pay television stations.

General Patterns of Release

A general domestic sequential release pattern describes how a typical film flows through the primary motion picture markets. Traditionally, the film is released by the distributor to flagship and first-run theaters, and if it is a major picture, it may play simultaneously on 800 to 1000 screens. Perhaps four to five months later, it may complete its opening run in theaters in small communities. A year or more after its initial theatrical release, the film may appear on pay television. This can coincide with, or precede, its rerelease to theaters—an aggravating point that causes opposition to pay television from some exhibitors, especially neighborhood houses that depend upon reissues.

The film may have its first network telecast three years or so after its theatrical release, with a second network telecast two or more years after the first. At that point, the film is likely to be released by the distributor for syndication to individual stations. Syndication rates are based on the size of the station's market. However, large city stations can afford to pay premium prices for films just entering syndication, and it is not uncommon for smaller communities to have to wait.

Within this general release sequence fall the sub-markets. The limited audiences of military bases, airline exhibition and the college circuit normally are served before television networks. Foreign theatrical release can follow domestic release by several months or more, which gives the distributor a feel for a film's promotion campaign and drawing power, and reason to modify advertising techniques and perhaps rental rates. There are exceptions to this rule. An important one was *Superman II,* which opened abroad before its release in the North American market in 1981.

The rapidly growing home video market has had to be inserted into this sequential release pattern, and it is moving closer to the time of first theatrical release. Indeed, early in 1980, Twentieth Century-Fox announced it would issue video cassettes of certain films simultaneously with their release for theatrical exhibition. This day-and-date cassette release, according to corporate strategy, was supposed to take advantage of the already-existing multi-million dollar advertising campaigns developed for theatrical release, and would be similar to tying in the marketing of book, soundtrack album and, occasionally, toys, t-shirts, and other film-related merchandise. The directors of the National Association of Theatre Owners promptly condemned Fox's policy. Subsequently, the film company revised its general release plans and announced that the cassette version of selected pictures would not be offered to the public until 90 days after initial theatrical release. This provided some clearance for first-run exhibitors, but was still a threatening sign for second-run houses. In any case, Fox issued *Nine to Five* on cassette less than three months after it first appeared in theaters, causing new worries for exhibitors. They were hardly assuaged when Fox announced that the film would not appear on pay television until a year or so after its initial theatrical release, and that exibitors would be apprised of dates when future films would be offered on cassettes.

Exceptions

As the above indicates, distribution of films can deviate from the general model for several reasons. An exceptional box-office attraction may be rereleased for theatrical exhibition before being licensed for television because the distribution company management believes a subsequent nationwide theatrical run will generate further revenue without diminishing the price a TV network would likely bid for the film. For example, Twentieth Century-Fox initially released *Star Wars* on May 25, 1977 and rereleased it in about 1700 theaters on July 21, 1978, asking exhibitors to take the film for seven-week engagements. Its reissue produced about $35 million in rentals, and not until March 1982 was the film made available for video cassette distribution.[70] Paramount's *Grease* was beginning its fourth reissue in May 1980, after its opening two summers earlier, and managed to gross about $2.2 million during one week in over 1000 theaters in North America.[71] Disney, with its perennial reissues, expected to amass $11 million in rentals in 1980 from its third rerelease of *Lady and the Tramp*. The same year, the company anticipated $7 million for the second reissue of *Mary Poppins*.[72]

Other patterns exist for films that do poorly at the box office and demonstrate no hope for theatrical rerelease. If such is the case, a film may be pulled from distribution before additional overhead and promotional expenses are incurred. If the film has any potential at all, it may be offered to pay television shortly after the initial, and abbreviated, theatrical run is completed, but television networks may ignore it altogether because it has no ability to draw an audience. In that case, the distributor may decide to syndicate it, or simply to forget about the picture. The management of United Artists had decisions of this nature to make about *Heaven's Gate,* which opened in November 1980 and was withdrawn almost immediately from distribution. The $35 million film was re-edited to a shorter length and launched again in the spring of 1981. Norbert Auerbach, UA's president and chief executive officer, told investment analysts and brokers at the time that "we are optimistic that the revenues which will flow from worldwide theatrical release—as well as the ancillary revenues from television, cable and other special markets—will pull this chestnut out of the fire."[73]

During release and rerelease, the availability of a film can depend upon whether the distribution company considers it worth its trouble to deal with a particular theater. At the end of May 1981, *The Empire Strikes Back* was still playing a first-run engagement in a theater in Seattle, where the film celebrated its first birthday in release.[74] Meanwhile, an exhibitor in a town of 4000 souls in Colorado was complaining in the trade press that he was never given the chance to play the film before Fox took it out of general release. He claimed that the picture was to be reissued in the summer, but only to theaters that could run it for at least four weeks, which he was unable to do in his town. He wrote: "How does a theater manager tell his steady patrons, who have been waiting to see 'Empire' and who will once again be bombarded with ads for it on TV, radio and in print, that the top film of 1980 will not be shown in our town because Fox could not care less about small town theatres and their customers?"[75]

Occasionally new, longer versions of films are made especially for television by the insertion of material not included in the original theatrical release. This allows a network to show a film in two parts, hopefully with audience carry-over, and to add more commercial minutes. The television versions of *Airport '77* and *King Kong* are longer than those originally cut for theaters.

A recent trend in film financing involves the presale of television rights —that is, a network may guarantee to buy a film based on its script and stars, before the picture goes into production. This allows the producing company to take into account the special needs of material presented on television and to shoot two versions of scenes involving nudity or violence. The network gambles, hoping that the film will be a winner, and that its presale price will be a bargain compared to what the producer could demand later, after the popularity of the film is demonstrated.

Role of Theaters

The mechanics of theatrical distribution revolve around the three heavy theater-going periods of the year—summer, Christmas, Easter—and major distributors usually hold what they consider to be their best films for release at those times. The rest of the year may be the doldrums, to be filled by exhibitors with products from minor distributors or with other films offered by the majors. Most films now released by the major companies are on a blind bid basis, at least in states where this practice is still legal. Blind bidding requires the exhibitor to offer terms for a film before having seen it. Indeed, the film may not even be near completion. Pictures are put out for bid to first-run theaters six to nine months before the anticipated release date, and sometimes this is stretched to 10 or 11 months.

Some companies occasionally offer a cancellation clause that gives an exhibitor who won a blind bid the right to reject the film within 48 hours after having seen it. Often this is cosmetic because a film may not be available for screening until just shortly before its release, and an exhibitor who rejects it must try to book, at very short notice, another picture in its place. Moreover, a distributor may be obliged at the last moment to postpone release because the film has not been completed.

A distribution company that solicits bids on a film in a market may decide to reject all bids and to negotiate terms with exhibitors. Indeed, the bidding process itself may be illusory because in many markets some or all of the exhibitors may be involved in a product split. In this case, the distributor's bid solicitation letter to all the market's exhibitors is a *pro forma* ritual, inasmuch as supposedly competitive exhibitors already have agreed among themselves that all but one will refrain from seeking a license for the picture. Exhibitors not party to the split generally find it difficult to rent quality first-run films. Bidding also may be bypassed because a distributor and a particular theater are "married"—meaning that the distributor first will offer its pictures to that theater, and the theater will give preference to films from that distributor. For example, United Artists had preferred customers in many markets and did not put films up for bid until the late 1970s.

Splits and marriages exist in the gray area between what are and what are not attempts to restrain trade and competition. Since the early 1950s, the Justice Department had held that splitting, for example, was an acceptable practice. But after lengthy study of the matter, including a review of opinions from the industry, it issued a news release on April 1, 1977 declaring that splitting was illegal. Under the auspices of the National Association of Theatre Owners, a case was brought in Federal District Court in Charlottesville, Virginia, seeking a declaratory judgment on the legality of non-predatory splitting. In February 1981, the presiding judge reversed the Justice Department prohibition on splitting, which signaled a victory for exhibitors. Shortly thereafter, six major distributors were allowed by the court to intervene and to appeal the decision. Attorneys representing exhibition interests objected to this, declaring that the distribution companies were not entitled to intervene "because it is the responsibility of the Attorney General of the United States, not the distributors, to set the antitrust policy of the Department of Justice, to control the course of Government litigation, and to determine what is in the public interest."[76]

Exhibitors had not necessarily been engaging in fierce competition for product before the 1981 court decision. After a brief hiatus following the Justice Department's 1977 declaration, many exhibitors quietly resumed splitting with tacit acquiescence of distributors. Consequently, the 1981 decision is not likely to have much practical effect on what has been happening, except to legalize it. Nonetheless, throughout the late 1970s, some independent exhibitors in several markets across the country were suing competitors who allegedly were splitting product. Plaintiffs charged restraint of trade and conspiracy to deprive them of suitable first-run films.

Bid solicitation letters suggest terms that guide an exhibitor in making an offer. If a split is not operating, an exhibitor often will try to exceed these in order to keep a picture from falling into the hands of a competitor, and this becomes particularly risky when a film is blind bid. The distributor's appraisal of the exhibitor's offer is highly subjective because many variables are involved, not all of which are stated on paper.

A bidding exhibitor identifies the name, location, and capacity of the theater in which the film is to be played. The bid also sets an opening date, which normally is the release date specified by the distributor, and states whether the run is to be exclusive or one leg of a multiple release in a market. The length of run in weeks is specified and occasionally conditions are offered for a holdover. The most important part of the bid are the terms. On a major release, a distributor will request 90% of the gross admissions after deduction of an agreed figure for house overhead, versus a straight 70% of the gross, whichever is greater. In addition, a distributor can require a minimum guaranteed rental and advance payment. The percentage terms normally change every second or third week toward the exhibitor's favor, but then attendance also falls throughout the run.[77] It is entirely possible, of course, for an exhibitor to guarantee, say, $25,000 on a run and not take in that much at the box office, but the theater is still liable for the entire amount.

Blind bidding is practiced customarily only by the major distributors. Exhibitors consider it so onerous that they have persuaded legislatures in 22 states, as of mid-1981, to declare it illegal, and anti-blind bid bills are pending in other states as well. This war between theatrical and distribution interests has provoked each side to mount extensive lobbying efforts and to summon heavy artillery for duty. The major companies, through the MPAA, have managed to retain important markets such as California, Texas, Illinois and New York. But the area in which blind bidding still is legal has been eroded by exhibitors' grass roots campaigns. In a counterattack on anti-blind bid statutes, major companies have declared they will avoid location filming in states that have enacted such laws. Exhibitors have labeled this a simple attempt by producers to intimidate legislators. Substantial differences in anti-blind bid statutes approved in the several states have begun to harass distributors. The Ohio law, for example, also forbids advances and guarantees. A federal judge in 1980 upheld the constitutionality of the law when the MPAA tested it in court.

Why have exhibitors engaged in blind bidding? For one thing, there are never enough good commercial products, and in order to obtain what is available, they feel they must resort to buying films before viewing them. They also believe that the majors are in a position to spend millions on lavish promotion and advertising campaigns that stimulate business. Furthermore, major company products frequently boast name stars who have proven box office appeal. Exhibitors also think they have a better chance of acquiring a box office smash from the majors because of the majors' previous track record.

Although many films from the majors do not live up to these expectations—and blind bidding can be a way of hiding disasters—it takes only a couple of substantial hits each year for a theater (and a distributor) to do well. Minor companies usually do not offer films for blind bid because they cannot command the same prestige or expectations. In many cases contractual terms for films are negotiated instead of bid. Regardless, majors tie up theaters months in advance for lengthy runs, at peak theater-going periods, a practice that works against the exhibition of other films. One only need note that at the beginning of July 1981, just seven films released by major distributors were playing simultaneous first-run engagements on more than 8000 screens.[78]

The release of a film by a major frequently demands capital reserves to which a smaller company does not have access. While hype cannot guarantee the success of any picture, it is unusual to find smash hits that have not been heavily promoted. Part of this involves the orchestration of a release campaign with publicity and advertising for weeks and months prior to the actual opening, so that a "want-to-see" attitude is developed in the public and an audience is created. Concerning *Clash of the Titans,* Richard Kahn, senior vice president for worldwide marketing of MGM, revealed that "We had a poster advertising our film 26 months before the release of the film. What we were trying to do was to create a platform of awareness so that when the big pre-release advertising campaign was set off, there would be a cushion of receptivity."[79] The foreign market also was subjected to this barrage. The strategy of a media blitz requires the simultaneous nationwide release of the film, sometimes in over 1000 theaters. *Cannonball Run* in mid-1981 was reported to be opening in over 1600 theaters, which was probably the largest break for any first-run engagement.[80] The advertising budget was about $5 million, but that only carried the film through the opening day. Moreover, the picture had tie-in promotion from businesses such as Dr. Pepper, Budweiser and the Seven-Eleven convenience stores.

The entire film industry was reported to have spent $750 million on advertising and promotion in 1980.[81] The president of distribution for Columbia claimed at the end of the 1970s that it cost a minimum of $2 million to market a film domestically, and he estimated that the company would spend about $70 million to push about 20 releases during 1979.[82] Similarly, the chief operating officer of Twentieth Century-Fox revealed in

1980 that the typical Fox film cost $8.5 million to make and at least $6 million to sell nationally.[83]

Foreign Films

These expenditures can be contrasted with the procedures for distributing foreign films in the United States. American distribution companies share overseas markets with foreign competitors (who are frequently dominated by the majors), but the United States market is dominated by American companies. Thus, a foreign-language film, to be released in this country, must be picked up by an American distributor, and the majors rarely do that unless they have an investment in the picture. Consequently, the distribution of imported films is handled by much smaller companies, some of which specialize in this aspect of the business.

Although the United States has been a world power for years, it is still a curiously provincial nation when it comes to motion pictures. Public taste in films has been formed and cultivated for decades by the vertically integrated industry in which majors showed their films in their own theaters, and these acquired patterns of preference persist. Aside from theaters in a few major metropolitan areas and in a handful of university-oriented communities, foreign films simply are not exhibited in the commercial sector. During the year ending in September 1977, 54 imported pictures opened in New York City, the foreign film capital of America. Only a few such films earn more than $1 million in rentals nationwide. During 1977 for example, *Cousin Cousine* earned about $3.3 million and *Black and White in Color* about $1.4 million, and those were leaders.[84] In 1978, the foreign film with the most prospects, *Madame Rosa,* had less than $1.7 million in rentals, which even the reissue of *Blazing Saddles* was able to beat.[85]

One of the more successful foreign-language films was *La Cage aux Folles* (distributed by United Artists), which grossed about $10.4 million in its first year of release and returned close to $6.8 million in rentals by the end of 1980.[86] Its sequel in 1981 was reported to be doing even better business. *Tess* and *The Last Metro* also were expected to have respectable financial results, at least by foreign film standards, as was *Breaker Morant.*

In the late 1970s, a small distributor may have had to invest $100,000 to market an imported film in the United States, and a good portion of that would have been spent in New York City for advertising, promotion and prints. Some foreign films start life in America with two dozen prints, and only a few eventually have over 200 in circulation. To break even, an imported film may need a box office gross of at least $400,000. A picture's reviews and track record in New York largely determine whether it will be distributed nationally and selected by exhibitors in other markets.

Dominance of the Major Firms

A pattern of circularity that has become a closed ring persists in the film industry. The major distribution companies have roots going back more than a half century. During that time, their trade practices, structure and horizontal cooperation were successful in excluding new entrants from the field and stunting the growth of already existing competitors. Indeed, the companies that have been established in the last 30 years or so have had to hang on to ledges around the mountain of the majors. Typically this has meant specializing in some species of film and catering to a specific market that the majors have not elected to stake out. In practice, this yields G-rated films for the children's market, exploitation and sexploitation films for drive-ins, X-rated films for adult theaters, or motorcycle/trucking films and the like for some regional audiences. Even some independent production, which the *Paramount* decrees were supposed to have encouraged, depends upon the majors' financing and distribution.

The scale on which the core of the industry operates has become so substantial that entrants and challengers must arrive on the scene, not only fully grown, but also with considerable capital or ways of obtaining it. In this respect, things have changed little since Huettig found that to be the case almost 40 years ago. It is not so much that good films are extraordinarily expensive, at least by the standard of the majors. Arthur Krim, now chairman of Orion Pictures Corporation, has pointed out that when he was with United Artists, "eight of our 10 Academy Award-winning pictures were little pictures. Their average cost was only slightly over $2 million."[87] But awards do not pay bills, and films must cover not only their own production and distribution costs, but also general company expenses. For example, the extensive global distribution organization and sales force of United Artists requires about $25 million annually to operate.[88] The company has 35 distribution offices in North America and 123 overseas, of which 55 are subdistributors.

Money is not invested in production without reasonable assurances that the resulting pictures will be exhibited broadly enough, in theaters and through television, to cover expenses and yield profit, at least commensurate with risk. The larger the size of the actual (or perceived) market, the greater the investment can be. The growth of ancillary markets gives the distributor further opportunities to squeeze extra dollars out of films. It is true, of course, that the distributor must book a film into theaters, and many hundreds of them, at the right time of year. But revenue from other sources can be extremely important, too, and can reduce risk materially. The president of Columbia Pictures Industries told investment analysts and brokers in 1978 about the financial arithmetic for *Close Encounters of the Third Kind:*

> Our cash negative [cost] on this picture was about $17.5 million.
> We took in $6.75 million of outside financing, which reduced our
> negative investment to $10.8 million. Our releasing costs to cash
> breakeven were $8 million. That, again, brought our overall in-
> vestment up to $19 million. We had exhibitor guarantees of some
> $21 million, which meant *before we released the picture we were
> $2 million ahead of the game.* This was before any attribution of
> value to television, pay cable, or to merchandising rights.[89]
> (Emphasis added.)

This film is not an exception. Careful control of production and marketing
costs, combined with guaranteed theatrical playdates, pre-sales to foreign
cinemas and to television worldwide, and estimates of revenue from pay
TV, home video and other sources, mean that a motion picture can be profitable before it is released. This situation is roughly analogous to the days
of the integrated companies in which block booking of pictures in independent houses and assured playdates in company-owned theaters provided
the locked-in markets that just about guaranteed profitability.

The majors have resources accumulated and built over decades that
have carried them through bad years and bad decisions. These distributors
know they can get the bulk of their films booked—and booked widely—
because there are exhibitors who need them, and large national and
regional circuits with centralized decision-making are the guaranteed
customers with thousands of important screens. The rules of the system
dictate that an exhibitor try to book the most commercial film, and this
means that pictures with little perceived commercial value stand in line far
behind the potential blockbusters. The majors often are the ones with well-
performing commercial films, but they are well-performing sometimes
because they are booked widely and heavily promoted.

INDICATORS OF STRUCTURE AND GROWTH

A basic problem in providing a statistical profile of the film industry is
that important data often are published in less than complete form and
some figures are not available publicly at all. Companies and trade
associations in the industry dispense information when it serves their interests. The industry exercises a monopoly of knowledge and therefore is
in a position to impose selective ignorance. The federal government collects and publishes data, but that is done less to give an investigator a view
of the industry's structure and operation, and more to show how the in-

dustry fits into the general economy on the national, state and local levels. Furthermore, the privacy of private enterprise is preserved because no single-company data are published by the government, and no companies ever are identified by name.

The United States is the world's largest film market, and for more than half a century has been the world's leading exporter of filmed entertainment. Specific organizational and financial information on these points fill in the otherwise colorful and glamorous aspects of the industry that draw attention away from basic and determinative economic concerns. Companies in the industry are important because they are merchants of culture, dealing not only in theatrical films, but also television programs, and frequently recorded music, books and magazines. Their empires, often spreading beyond the media to other service and manufacturing sectors, are integrated with the nation's centers of economic power. Production and distribution companies have global influence as well.

Size

The social significance of the film industry is far greater than the revenue of its companies would indicate. Although many familiar names fall within *Fortune*'s top 1000 industrial firms (see Table 5.1), they do so mostly by virtue of their diversified, conglomerate activities. When only revenue from filmed entertainment is considered (see Table 5.2), companies appear appreciably smaller, overshadowed by hosts of corporations in all industrial sectors customarily thought of as dominating the economy. Even within the domain of the mass media, as Table 5.3 demonstrates, many broadcasting and publishing companies have far greater revenue, income and assets than their film industry counterparts. Knight-Ridder Newspapers, for example, is larger in these categories than General Cinema Corp., which owns the world's biggest theater circuit and is a major soft drink bottler. CBS Inc. has revenue greater than the combined figure for Warner Communications, Walt Disney and Twentieth Century-Fox.

The "film industry" consists of establishments in the production, distribution and exhibition sectors as well as those that provide allied services, e.g., processing and titling, casting bureaus, wardrobe and property rentals, film delivery services, bookers, etc. Within the economy at large, the film industry accounts for about 0.4% of the Gross National Product.[90] As Table 5.4 shows, for 1977 there were over 5400 establishments with payrolls in production, distribution and allied services, and close to 10,700 theatrical establishments. (A multi-screen theater complex counts as one business establishment.) Together, their receipts were estimated to be $7.9 billion in 1977. That same year, theatrical establishments accounted for

Table 5.1: Selected Companies with Interests in the Motion Picture Industry Ranked According to Revenue in *Fortune* Magazine's 1000 Largest American Industrial Firms, 1980

Rank	Company
29	Eastman Kodak Co.
57	Gulf + Western Industries Inc.
[84]	Loews Corp.
[177]	Avco Corp.
183	Warner Communications Inc.
[222]	Fuqua Industries Inc.
256	MCA Inc.
[322]	Walt Disney Productions
337	Twentieth Century-Fox Film Corp.
362	General Cinema Corp.
389	Columbia Pictures Industries Inc.
[517]	United Artists Corp.
579	Wometco Enterprises Inc.
723	Taft Broadcasting Co.
724	Filmways Inc.
[740]	United Artists Theatre Circuit Inc.
796	Technicolor Inc.
825	Metro-Goldwyn-Mayer Film Co.

Source: *Fortune*, May 4, 1981 and June 15, 1981; company annual reports for 1980.
[   ] = Rank order of a nonindustrial corporation if it had been classified as "industrial" by Fortune.

33% of film industry receipts, a decline from the 39% reported in the 1972 business census. Table 5.5 indicates that whereas slightly more than five out of 10 industry employees worked in the theatrical sector, they earned only about $2.50 out of every $10 paid as wages. More than half of all wages were paid to employees in production and allied services.

Compared to other mass media (see Table 5.6), the film industry has more establishments than newspapers and broadcasting combined, but this is due solely to the number of theaters. The film industry payroll ranks behind that of newspapers and broadcasting.

In 1978, according to data from the Department of Commerce, the public spent about $4.3 billion for admission to film theaters (not including concession sales), or about 0.3% of all personal consumption expenditures (see Table 5.7). This was more than double the sum spent to see spectator sports, but less than the amount spent for flowers, seeds and potted plants. Although paid admission to motion picture theaters was almost four times greater in 1980 than in 1930, total personal consumption expenditure in that period increased more than 22 times and expenditures for ad-

Table 5.2: Filmed Entertainment Revenue[1] of Publicly Owned Companies with Interests in the Motion Picture Industry, 1980 (in millions)

Company	Filmed Entertainment Revenue	Total Revenue	Filmed Entertainment as % of Total Revenue
MCA Inc.	$ 682.8	$ 1,297.1	52.6%
Gulf + Western Industries Inc.	676.0[2]	5,338.5	12.7
Warner Communications Inc.	668.9	2,059.4	32.5
Twentieth Century-Fox Film Corp.	653.5	865.2	75.5
Columbia Pictures Industries Inc.	599.3	691.8	86.6
United Artists Corp.	395.1[3]	424.8	93.0
General Cinema Corp.	307.8	759.4	40.5
United Artists Theatre Circuit Inc.	223.5	227.1	98.4
Metro-Goldwyn-Mayer Film Co.	181.2	181.2	100.0
Walt Disney Productions	161.4	914.5	17.6
Filmways Inc.	106.5[4]	168.6	63.2
Commonwealth Theatres Inc.	69.9	73.2	95.5
Loews Corp.	54.7[5]	4,535.1	1.2
Wometco Enterprises Inc.	48.7[6]	357.2	13.6
Cablecom-General Inc.	11.7[7]	46.8	25.0
First Artists Production Co. Ltd.	10.5	27.1	38.7
Cox Broadcasting Corp.	2.4	309.2	.8

[1] Includes revenue derived from theatrical motion pictures, material produced for television, and the operation of theaters and film processing plants. It is likely that revenue is included as well from concession sales in theaters and the licensing of trademarks and characterizations.

[2] Paramount Pictures Corp. and its subsidiaries.

[3] United Artists Corp. revenue is about 9% of total revenue for its parent company, Transamerica Corp.

[4] Entertainment and entertainment services, including recording studios.

[5] Loews Theatres Division.

[6] Motion picture theaters and tourist attractions.

[7] Video Independent Theatres Inc.

Source: Company annual reports and Form 10-K reports for 1980.

mission to all spectator amusements were more than seven times larger (see Table 5.8). In 1930, about $8 of every $10 spent on spectator amusements went for theater tickets, but by 1980 the share was slightly more than $4 out of $10. Moreover, in 1930, admission to motion pictures accounted for

Table 5.3: Selected Publicly Owned Companies with Interests in the
Motion Picture Industry or Other Mass Media, 1980
(in millions)

Company	Revenue	Net Income	Assets
Eastman Kodak Co.	$ 9,734.3	$ 1,153.6	$ 8,754.0
RCA Inc.	8,011.3	315.3	7,147.6
Gulf + Western Industries Inc.[1]	5,338.5	255.3	5,416.8
Loews Corp.	4,535.1	206.1	9,125.1
CBS Inc.	4,062.1	193.0	2,301.2
Time Inc.	2,881.8	141.2	2,370.6
American Broadcasting Cos. Inc.	2,280.4	146.3	1,410.9
Avco Corp.[2]	2,150.0	118.6	5,843.5
Warner Communications Inc.	2,059.4	137.1	1,768.8
Times Mirror Co.	1,868.9	139.2	1,734.8
Fuqua Industries Inc.[3]	1,589.5	64.6	864.2
MCA Inc.	1,297.1	125.4	1,390.6
Gannett Co. Inc.	1,215.0	152.0	1,211.7
Knight-Ridder Newspapers Inc.	1,098.5	92.9	862.4
McGraw-Hill Inc.	1,000.1	86.4	785.5
Walt Disney Productions	914.5	135.2	1,347.4
Twentieth Century-Fox Film Corp.	865.2	54.6	753.9
General Cinema Corp.	759.4	29.9	441.8
The New York Times Co.	733.2	40.6	449.5
Columbia Pictures Industries Inc.	691.8	44.9	488.5
Washington Post Co.	659.5	34.3	429.1
Dow Jones and Co.	530.7	58.9	396.6
Metromedia Inc.	453.9	54.8	544.1
United Artists Corp.[4]	424.8	20.1	481.7
Playboy Enterprises Inc.	363.2	13.1	320.5
Wometco Enterprises Inc.	357.2	20.8	337.6
Cox Broadcasting Corp.	309.2	56.4	461.3
Taft Broadcasting Co.	235.9	31.7	456.7
United Artists Theatre Circuit Inc.	227.1	6.5	168.4
Technicolor Inc.	197.9	17.7	124.5
Metro-Goldwyn-Mayer Film Co.	181.2	16.5	280.8
Filmways Inc.	168.6	1.6	242.0
Viacom International Inc.	160.1	15.7	367.9
Commonwealth Theatres Inc.	73.2	2.8	39.9
Cablecom-General Inc.	46.8	6.3	71.4
Movielab Inc.	37.5	1.8	21.0
First Artists Production Company Ltd.	27.1	.4	17.3
Inflight Services Inc.	22.0	.4	13.0

[1] Parent of Paramount Pictures Corporation.
[2] Parent of Avco-Embassy Pictures Corporation.
[3] Parent of Martin Theatre Circuit.
[4] Subsidiary of Transamerica Corporation.
Source: Company annual reports and Form 10-K reports for 1980.

Table 5.4: Indicators of Size of the Motion Picture Industry, Selected Years, 1963-1977
(receipts and payroll in millions)

	1963	1967	1972	1977
Motion picture production, distribution and allied services				
Number of establishments	3,729	4,565	8,555	10,724
Receipts	$ 1,520	$ 2,183	$ 2,920	$ 5,412
Establishments with payroll	2,829	3,375	4,704	5,473
Receipts	$ 1,510	$ 2,169	$ 2,857	$ 5,314
Payroll	$ 479	$ 699	$ 795	$ 1,377
Paid employees	48,806	64,581	64,660	88,372
Motion picture theaters				
Number of establishments	12,652	12,187	12,699	11,815
Receipts	$ 1,063	$ 1,293	$ 1,833	$ 2,606
Establishments with payroll	12,040	11,478	11,670	10,696
Receipts	$ 1,057	$ 1,283	$ 1,816	$ 2,570
Payroll	$ 250	$ 281	$ 381	$ 462
Paid employees	112,521	112,109	127,435	112,210
Total				
Number of establishments	16,381	16,752	21,254	22,539
Receipts	$ 2,583	$ 3,476	$ 4,753	$ 8,018
Establishments with payroll	14,869	14,853	16,374	16,169
Receipts	$ 2,567	$ 3,452	$ 4,673	$ 7,884
Payroll	$ 729	$ 980	$ 1,176	$ 1,839
Paid employees	161,327	176,690	192,095	200,582

Sources: U.S. Department of Commerce, Bureau of the Census: *Census of Selected Service Industries, Motion Pictures*; 1963, 1967, 1972, 1977.

about 1% of total personal consumption, while in 1980 it represented less than 0.2%. It is clear that going to the movies—even with sensational box office receipts in recent years and higher ticket prices—is not the dominant form of out-of-home entertainment it once was, and that there has been a significant reallocation of personal expenditures that has affected theatrical admissions. The future, moreover, holds very little prospect for real growth, in view of changing population demographics, the rapid spread of pay television and the rise of the home video market.

Although ticket prices have risen constantly, it was only in the 1970s that they increased rapidly enough to catch up with the general rise in consumer prices behind which they usually have lagged. The 1979 average ticket price of $2.52 was more than 7% higher than the previous year's figure (see Table 5.9). Although this was the largest price rise since a 7.4% hike in 1975, it was still below the rate of increase for all services in 1979.[91] A few 1980 sum-

Table 5.5: Motion Picture Industry Establishments, Employees, Payroll, 1977

	Establishments	Employees	Payroll (in millions)
Film production and services	4,103	70,658	$1,113.5
Film production except TV	1,465	22,750	315.9
Film and tape production for TV	1,285	29,952	503.7
Services allied to production	1,353	17,956	293.9
Film distribution and services	1,370	17,714	$ 263.1
Film exchanges	926	12,529	180.1
Film or tape distribution for TV	191	3,070	61.2
Services allied to distribution	253	2,115	21.8
Motion picture theaters	10,696	112,210	$ 461.9
Theaters, except drive-in	7,814	93,321	376.6
Drive-in theaters	2,882	18,889	85.3
Film industry total	16,169	200,582	$1,838.5

Source: U.S. Department of Commerce, Bureau of the Census, *1977 Census of Selected Service Industries, Motion Pictures.*

mer releases in major markets commanded $5.50 for an adult ticket. Some exhibitors, however, have set bargain matinee prices at $1 or $1.50, not only for reissues, but also for current releases. They point out that generous sales at the concession counters make such ticket prices worthwhile.

Globally, the United States has been a dominant cinematic power, at least in commercial terms, for more than 60 years. American companies have the only international distribution chains, and this has given them the ability to place their films in theaters around the world, while maintaining

Table 5.6: Mass Media Industries Establishments, Employees, Payroll, 1978

Industry	Establishments	Employees	Payroll (in millions)
Motion pictures	14,663	193,893	$ 2,032.6
Newspapers	7,875	380,413	4,648.3
Radio & TV broadcasting	5,969	167,544	2,529.9
Periodicals	2,606	80,856	1,252.2
Book publishing	1,448	63,223	914.9
Phonograph records	575	24,544	302.8

Source: U.S. Department of Commerce, Bureau of the Census, *County Business Patterns, 1978.*

Table 5.7: Selected Personal Consumption Expenditures, 1978[1]

	Expenditures (in millions)
Personal consumption expenditures	$ 1,350,762
Admission to film theaters	4,261
Admission to legitimate theaters, opera, etc.	1,271
Admission to spectator sports	1,841
Funeral and burial expenses	4,236
Flowers, seeds, potted plants	5,025
Cleaning, laundering, dyeing, pressing, alteration, storage, repair of garments	4,585
Books and maps	5,420
Magazines, newspapers, sheet music	9,975
Foreign travel by U.S. residents	11,576
Tobacco products	17,909
Radio and TV receivers, records, musical instruments	19,496
Physicians	31,214
Gasoline and oil	50,908

[1] Figures are subject to revision.

Source: U.S. Department of Commerce, Bureau of Economic Analysis, *Survey of Current Business*, July 1979.

a virtual monopoly of their home market. In most countries, American films take the largest share of all rentals, but in a few markets they trail the domestic industry, although they out-distance all other competitors. For the last three decades or so, American distributors have received just about half of their theatrical rentals from abroad, although this fluctuates annually depending upon the tides of box-office smashes. American films exhibited in overseas markets naturally deprive foreign producers of the chance to amortize their own films, but the sums lost to them cannot be estimated in any practical way. Table 5.10 indicates that worldwide rentals for the American majors have exceeded the $1 billion mark since 1974.

These data can be compared with others in Table 5.11 that show the division in foreign rentals between motion pictures and television. Theatrical sources provide about 75% of total rentals. The major companies— that is, members of the Motion Picture Export Association of America— generally account for about 85% to 88% of all foreign rentals, with their share of television rentals being slightly less and theatrical rentals slightly more.

The overall economic health of the film industry can be judged from Table 5.12, which demonstrates the sector's ability to operate profitably and reward private investors.

Table 5.8: Expenditures for Admissions to Film Theaters, Selected Years,
1930-1979
(in millions)

Year	Admission to Film Theaters	Admission to Spectator Amusements[1]	Personal Consumption Expenditures
1930	$ 732	$ 892	$ 69,916
1935	556	672	55,764
1940	735	904	70,979
1945	1,450	1,714	119,493
1950	1,376	1,781	191,966
1955	1,326	1,801	253,665
1960	956	1,652	324,903
1965	1,067	2,123	430,154
1966	1,119	2,310	464,793
1967	1,128	2,404	490,358
1968	1,294	2,653	535,932
1969	1,400	2,903	579,711
1970	1,429	3,141	618,796
1971	1,350	3,359	668,171
1972	1,583	3,487	733,034
1973	1,524	3,870	809,885
1974	1,909	4,621	889,603
1975	2,115	4,775	979,070
1976	2,036	5,471	1,089,867
1977	2,372	6,802	1,209,968
1978	2,643	7,373	1,350,762
1979	2,821	5,391	1,509,800
1980	2,749	6,424	1,672,766

[1] Includes motion picture theaters, legitimate theaters, opera, spectator sports and entertainments of nonprofit institutions.

Sources: U.S. Department of Commerce, Bureau of Economic Analysis, *Survey of Current Business* for various years; Bureau of Census, *Statistical Abstract of the United States*; and National Association of Theatre Owners, *Encyclopedia of Exhibition, 1981*.

Employment

Data for industry employment, compensation and wages are displayed in Table 5.13. The peak years for employment were 1946 and 1947 (253,000 full- and part-time workers in each year), but the industry has rebounded in the 1970s after two decades of decline. Table 5.14 shows that most film industry companies grouped in *Forbes*' 818 largest employers do

Table 5.9: Average Motion Picture Admission Prices, Selected Years, 1948-1980

Year	Admission Price	Admission Price Index (1967 = 100)	Consumer Price Index (1967 = 100)
1948	$ 0.36	29.5	72.1
1954	0.49	40.2	80.5
1958	0.68	55.7	86.6
1963	0.86	70.5	91.7
1967	1.22	100.0	100.0
1971	1.65	135.2	121.3
1974	1.89	154.9	147.7
1975	2.03	166.4	161.2
1976	2.13	174.6	170.5
1977	2.23	190.2	181.5
1978	2.34	191.8	195.3
1979	2.52	206.6	217.7
1980	2.69	220.5	

Sources: National Association of Theatre Owners, *Encyclopedia of Exhibition, 1980*; Motion Picture Association of America data as published in Warner Communications Inc., *Financial Fact Book 1981*. Consumer price index: U.S. Bureau of Labor Statistics, *Monthly Labor Review*.

not rank within the nation's 500 largest employers, but when they do it is because they have diversified interests beyond motion pictures.

Data presented in Table 5.6 indicated that the film industry had close to 194,000 employees in 1978, slightly more than the broadcasting industry but only about half as much as the newspaper industry. Of those employed in the motion picture industry in 1977 (Table 5.5), about 9% were in film distribution and services, 35% in production and services, and 56% in exhibition. For July 1978, the Bureau of Labor Statistics reported that the industry had 234,100 employees, of which 60% worked for theatrical establishments.[92] Overall, women accounted for 37% of all employees, but in the exhibition sector that figure was 42%.

Number of Firms

The actual number of motion picture production and distribution companies is elusive. The Bureau of the Census publishes data pertaining to establishments, but that term is not synonymous with company. An establishment is a single physical location at which business is carried out, and so a company may consist of one or a dozen establishments. Table 5.15 shows that as of 1977 there were almost 1500 establishments engaged in non-TV

Table 5.10: Estimated Rental Revenue of Major Film Companies, 1963-1980[1]
(in millions)

Year	Foreign Revenue	Domestic Revenue	Worldwide Revenue[2]
1963	$293.0	$ 239.4	$ 532.4
1964	319.9	263.2	583.1
1965	343.5	287.2	630.7
1966	361.5	319.5	680.9
1967	357.8	355.9	713.7
1968	339.0	372.3	711.3
1969	348.4	317.4	665.8
1970	360.4	381.3	741.7
1971	347.0	336.7	683.7
1972	388.6	426.4	815.1
1973	428.9	390.5	819.4
1974	494.8	545.9	1,040.7
1975	604.0	628.0	1,232.0
1976	571.0	576.6	1,147.5
1977	563.0	802.7	1,365.7
1978	829.5	1,119.9	1,949.4
1979	909.4	1,067.7	1,977.0
1980	909.4	1,182.6	2,092.0

[1] Members of Motion Picture Association of America.

[2] Discrepancies between worldwide revenue and totals of foreign and domestic revenue are due to rounding.

Source: Motion Picture Association of America data as published in *Variety*, June 25, 1975; September 1, 1976; June 14, 1978; July 2, 1980; August 12, 1981.

motion picture production and that films from them flowed through more than 900 exchanges to theaters and other points of exhibition.

There probably are several hundred active and inactive motion picture production companies in the United States. The output of operating companies consists not only of theatrical films but also nontheatrical films in religious, educational, industrial and documentary forms. Similarly, there are several hundred film distributors, but somewhat less than 200 offer pictures to the commercial theaters. One measure of distributors is the number of companies that submit feature films to the Classification and Rating Administration, but this underestimates distributors of adult films. In any case, since the mid-1970s, the numbers of companies submitting features were: 1975—191; 1976—201; 1977—174; 1978—147; 1979—127; and 1980—115. Usually, about 10% of these are identified as "production

Table 5.11: Estimated Foreign Rentals of American Film Companies,
1971-1979
(in millions)

Year	Foreign Motion Picture Rentals	Foreign Television Rentals	Total Foreign Rentals
1971	$230	$ 75	$305
1972	258	84	342
1973	275	115	390
1974	350	110	460
1975	424	106	530
1976	379	152	531
1977	375	190	565
1978	550	227	777
1979	608	281	889

Source: Motion Picture Export Association of America data as reported to the U.S. Department of Commerce and published annually in *U.S. Industrial Outlook.*

company" rather than "releasing company." More than half of them submitted only one film for rating in a given year, and about three-quarters submitted no more than two films.[93] The proportions vary from year to year, of course, but the rule is overwhelmingly accurate. So is the trend toward a declining number of distributors.

Another estimate is based upon data from the Motion Picture Association of America. Table 5.16 shows that the number of "national distributors" peaked in the early 1970s, and that there were about as many national companies in 1980 as there were at the end of the 1960s.

Annual Releases

The number of annual releases is not any easier to establish than the number of production and distribution companies. Part of the problem is due to faulty data gathering by the industry and the government, and this is complicated by definitional problems, if not by the nature of the business itself. Each year, there are hundreds of projects started that never reach the filming stage. Of those that do, an unidentifiable number are never completed. Some of the finished pictures may never be released by their producers, for one reason or another, and not all films put into distribution are selected by theater owners for exhibition. Among those that do reach screens, some will have so few playdates that it is hardly worth counting them as released features. Occasionally, made-for-TV pictures are released theatrically outside the United States, and some televi-

Table 5.12: Motion Picture Industry Corporate Profits and Dividend
Payments, 1930-1978
(in millions)

Year	Corporate Profits Pre-Tax	Post-Tax	Net Dividend Payments	Year	Corporate Profits Pre-Tax	Post-Tax	Net Dividend Payments
1930	$ 51	$ 42	$33	1955	$124	$ 61	$ 26
1931	2	(2)	26	1956	89	30	32
1932	(82)	(86)	10	1957	55	16	26
1933	(40)	(43)	5	1958	15	(19)	25
1934	2	(2)	7	1959	44	0	12
1935	13	8	6	1960	49	1	22
1936	29	19	26	1961	23	(47)	8
1937	33	23	28	1962	6	(47)	22
1938	39	28	21	1963	19	(33)	25
1939	41	30	15	1964	86	22	33
1940	51	37	18	1965	104	39	3
1941	78	52	24	1966	131	46	16
1942	155	78	26	1967	94	30	16
1943	253	104	35	1968	138	55	33
1944	246	108	33	1969	(13)	(71)	50
1945	238	99	35				
1946	304	177	61	1970	93	8	10
1947	224	134	59	1971	15	(29)	24
1948	142	71	54	1972	1	(50)	17
1949	128	69	60	1973	94	46	13
				1974	190	116	31
1950	112	60	38				
1951	101	42	55	1975	226	131	30
1952	84	33	48	1976	427	313	54
1953	80	35	33	1977	426	239	86
1954	136	71	33	1978	551	296	160

Note: Amounts in parentheses indicate deficits.
Source: U.S. Department of Commerce, Bureau of Economic Analysis, as reprinted in National Association of Theatre Owners, *Encyclopedia of Exhibition, 1979.*

sion programs have been re-edited as well for foreign release. Moreover, it is impossible to state with precision the number of foreign pictures that are released in the United States because of the extensive overseas production and financing activities of American companies, which raise questions about how a "foreign" film can be defined.

With these limitations considered, Table 5.17 shows that the annual number of features released by national distributors has been decreasing consistently since 1940, with the number of new releases in the late 1970s

Table 5.13: Employment, Compensation and Wages in the Motion Picture Industry, Selected Years, 1930-1978

Year	Employees (in thousands)	Compensation (in millions)	Wages and Salaries (in millions)
1930	160	$ 313	$ 311
1935	159	282	280
1940	192	353	339
1945	238	573	552
1950	249	688	658
1955	231	805	774
1960	187	810	772
1961	185	860	815
1962	177	841	791
1963	175	858	806
1964	176	918	863
1965	181	1,027	966
1966	187	1,127	1,040
1967	193	1,181	1,100
1968	194	1,270	1,172
1969	202	1,399	1,277
1970	201	1,386	1,274
1971	200	1,437	1,277
1972	199	1,480	1,343
1973	204	1,595	1,429
1974	203	1,763	1,575
1975	204	1,873	1,662
1976	205	2,141	1,888
1977	210	2,427	2,133
1978	213	2,787	2,445

Source: U.S. Department of Commerce, Bureau of Economic Analysis, as reprinted in National Association of Theatre Owners, *Encyclopedia of Exhibition, 1979.*

about a third the level for 1940. The number of features submitted to the Classification and Rating Administration shown in Table 5.18 demonstrates a similar trend. Although submission is not mandatory, these data are more comprehensive than those in Table 5.17 because the latter excludes pictures offered by non-national distribution companies.

Whichever measure one wants to use, one point is incontestable. The investment tax credit and various tax shelter arrangements helped through Congress by film industry pressure did not increase film production during the 1970s. Indeed, compared to the first half of that decade, the number of releases from 1975 through 1979 actually declined. (It is impossible to determine, of course, if the level of film production would have been even

Table 5.14: Selected Companies with Interests in the Motion Picture Industry Ranked According to Employees in *Forbes* Magazine's 818 Largest American Employers, 1980

Rank	Company	Number of Employees (in thousands)
21	Eastman Kodak Co.	129.5
27	Gulf + Western Industries Inc.	116.0
210	Loews Corp.	29.4
214	Transamerica Corp.	28.9
234	Avco Corp.	26.9
261	Walt Disney Productions	24.0
322	MCA Inc.	18.0
353	Fuqua Industries Inc.	15.6
[390]	General Cinema Corp.	12.8
470	Warner Communications Inc.	9.4
514	Twentieth Century-Fox Film Corp.	7.0
[530]	United Artists Theatre Circuit Inc.	6.4
[639]	Columbia Pictures Industries Inc.	3.5
[660]	Technicolor Inc.	3.2
[665]	Commonwealth Theatres Inc.	3.1
[701]	Filmways Inc.	2.5
[742]	Metro-Goldwyn-Mayer Film Co.	1.9

[ ] = Rank if classified by *Forbes*.
Sources: *Forbes*, May 11, 1981; company Form 10-K reports.

lower without the incentives.) One only can conclude for certain, particularly for investment tax credit applicable beginning in 1971 to production of filmed entertainment, that the tax incentives resulted in payment of lower corporate income taxes.

Number of Theaters

The number of motion picture theaters is a problematic statistic that has been complicated in recent years by the rise of multi-screen theater complexes, either newly constructed or resulting from the remodeling of single-screen houses. Other difficulties arise because estimates by the Motion Picture Association of America do not necessarily match those provided in recent years by the National Association of Theatre Owners, which cites "various sources" as the basis for its own figures.[94] The Bureau of the Census counts establishments, and not until the 1977 census did it report figures on screens, and then incompletely. The Department of Commerce admitted in a 1976 publication that precise figures "are lacking since chain operators are reluctant to release such information."[95] Personal queries to circuit operators across the nation routinely go unanswered. Even the *En-*

Table 5.15: **Motion Picture Production and Distribution Establishments
with Payroll, 1967, 1972, 1977**

Type of Establishment	1967	1972	1977
Film production, other than TV	909	1392	1465
Film or tape production for TV	686	1138	1285
Film exchanges	710	877	926
Film or tape distribution for TV	147	151	191

Source: U.S. Department of Commerce, Bureau of the Census; *Census of Selected
Service Industries, Motion Pictures*, 1967, 1972, 1977.

Table 5.16: **National Distributors of Motion Pictures, Selected Years,
1930-1980**

Year	Number of Distributors	Year	Number of Distributors
1930	9	1970	22
1935	10	1971	22
1940	11	1972	25
1945	11	1973	23
1950	15	1974	25
1955	12		
1960	12	1975	24
		1976	23
1965	14	1977	19
1966	16	1978	20
1967	18	1979	22
1968	19		
1969	19	1980	19

Source: Based upon data from the Motion Picture Association of America.

cyclopedia of Exhibition, published by the National Association of
Theatre Owners, conspicuously omits not only the number of screens in
various regional and national chains, but also the names of circuits. One is
forced to conclude, as did a writer for *Variety* in 1975, that for some
obscure reason most exhibitors want to keep secret the number of their
screens.[96] (Secrecy pervades other sectors of the industry as well.) Table
5.19 thus must be viewed as only an approximation. But, there is no doubt
that the number of multi-screen indoor houses has risen dramatically in the
1970s, and that the number of drive-ins has declined slightly, due to urban
sprawl and the increase of real estate values on community peripheries.
Table 5.20 reports the number of multi-screen establishments and their
receipts, as recorded by the 1977 business census.

Table 5.17: Motion Pictures Released by National Distributors, Selected Years, 1935-1980

Year	New Releases	Reissues	Total
1935	388	3	391
1940	472	3	475
1945	367	8	375
Average, 1940-1949	421	25	446
1950	425	48	473
1955	281	38	319
Average, 1950-1959	338	36	374
1960	233	15	248
1961	225	15	240
1962	213	24	237
1963	203	20	223
1964	227	15	242
1965	257	22	279
1966	231	26	257
1967	229	35	264
1968	241	17	258
1969	241	10	251
Average, 1960-1969	230	20	250
1970	267	39	306
1971	282	32	314
1972	279	39	318
1973	237	38	275
1974	238	45	283
1975	195	40	235
1976	191	30	221
1977	167	32	199
1978	171	20	191
1979	189	26	215
Average, 1970-1979	222	34	256
1980	192	42	234

Source: Motion Picture Association of America.

Table 5.18: Motion Pictures Rated by the Classification and Rating Administration, 1965-1980

Year	Total	MPAA Companies[1]
1965	191	175
1966	168	149
1967	215	206
1968	230	201
1969	325	171
1970	431	181
1971	513	177
1972	540	208
1973	584	185
1974	523	151
1975	459	123
1976	486	119
1977	378	95
1978	334	125
1979	367	138
1980	330	129

[1] Allied Artists, Avco-Embassy, Columbia, Metro-Goldwyn-Mayer, Paramount, Twentieth Century-Fox, United Artists (distributing MGM films after 1973), Universal and Warner. Beginning in 1978, Buena Vista (Disney) is included, as is Filmways in 1980. Allied Artists submitted no films for classification in 1979 and 1980.
Source: Motion Picture Association of America, Classification and Rating Administration.

Company Finances

A review of company revenue by business segment (Appendix 5.1) provides another indicator of structure and shows some of the dramatic financial changes that have taken place in the industry during the 1970s.

Except for Twentieth Century-Fox, which was merged into a private company in 1981, all the major production-distribution corporations are publicly owned and file annual reports. But several of the important exhibition circuits are not publicly owned and no financial data about them are available.

Nonetheless, problems exist even with the information that is publicly available. For one thing, company accounts—which constitute the financial history of corporations—are forever being reclassified and restated. A check through ten years of a company's annual reports usually will reveal that a revenue or income figure for an earlier year has been revised upward

Table 5.19: Motion Picture Theaters, Selected Years, 1948-1980

Year	Number of Theaters

A) Commerce Department Census

Year	Number of Theaters
1948	18,532
1954	18,491
1958	16,354
1963	12,652
1967	12,187
1972	12,699

B) Industry Estimates

Year	Indoor	Drive-In	Total
1964	9,200	3,540	12,740
1965	9,240	3,585	12,825
1966	9,290	3,640	12,930
1967	9,330	3,670	13,000
1968	9,500	3,690	13,190
1969	9,750	3,730	13,480
1970	10,000	3,750	13,750
1971	10,300	3,770	14,070
1972	10,580	3,790	14,370
1973	10,850	3,800	14,650

Year	Indoor Screens	Drive-In Screens	Total Screens
1974	11,612	3,772	15,384
1975	12,175	3,822	15,997
1976	12,996	3,833	16,829
1977	12,990	3,564	16,554
1978	13,129	3,626	16,755
1979	13,439	3,656	17,095
1980	13,918	3,454	17,372

Sources: A: U.S. Department of Commerce, *Census of Business.*
B: Motion Picture Association of America; beginning in 1977, National Association of Theatre Owners. The 1980 estimate is for August.

or downward due to new accounting board principles, as the result of changes in reporting requirements of the Securities and Exchange Commission, because of acquisitions or divestitures, or due to expanding and contracting lines of business. Publicly owned firms must report on revenues and operating profits by major business segments, i.e., those accounting for at least 10% of revenues. Nonetheless, all companies do not cut the revenue pie in the same way. One may list revenue according to the buyer (i.e., network television, syndication, theaters, etc.), another may

Table 5.20: Single and Multi-Screen Theater Establishments, 1979[1]
(receipts in millions)

Type of Establishment	Single-Screen Establishments	Multi-Screen Establishments			
		Total	2 Screens	3-4 Screens	5 or More Screens
Indoor	5,303	2,511	1,685	663	163
Receipts	$ 861.0	$1,215.5	$633.4	$402.1	$179.9
Drive-In	2,558	324	N.R.	N.R.	N.R.
Receipts	$ 303.4	$ 122.3	N.R.	N.R.	N.R.
Total	7,861	2,835	N.R.	N.R.	N.R.
Receipts	$1,164.4	$1,337.8	N.R.	N.R.	N.R.

[1] An establishment is a single physical location at which business is conducted. It is not necessarily identical with a company or enterprise, which may consist of one or more establishments. In terms of the above table, it is more convenient to think of a theatrical establishment as a site at which films are exhibited. The site may have one or more screens.
N.R.: Not reported.
Sources: U.S. Department of Commerce, Bureau of the Census, *Census of Service Industries, Motion Pictures, 1977*; additional information supplied to the author by the Bureau of the Census.

list it according to the item marketed (theatrical features, television series, made-for-TV films, etc.). Some companies combine two related business segments, such as recorded music and music publishing, while others may make no distinction in financial reports between theatrical revenue from the United States and overseas. At least up until 1980, revenue from pay television and video cassettes might be included in the theatrical category rather than under separate headings. Furthermore, Canada is considered a domestic market by most companies although it consistently has been one of the largest foreign markets as far as rental revenue is concerned. Finally, the business done by production-distribution companies, or theater circuits, may be absorbed into the accounts of a much larger parent, leaving significant holes in an industry-wide tabulation.

DEGREE OF INDUSTRY CONCENTRATION

Conditions of industrial structure necessarily intersect with ownership and markets, and in the motion picture business this becomes all the more crucial because as a medium of communication, film sets before us images and ideas that influence us and our cultures. In this respect, patterns of concentration and control in film are of more concern than, for example, machine screw manufacturing, plastics, saw mills, or laundries. The extent of centralized control affects entry and the ability of new and smaller competitors to thrive. Inasmuch as the American film industry is a global enterprise, consequences of this kind are multiplied throughout other countries.

Power is conveyed by the ownership of resources, whether they be in the form of cash, studios, films, distribution companies, theaters, etc. Power is translated into the ability to decide how those resources will be used, and by whom. In the film industry, it can mean, for example, the authority to select who will make what kinds of films, or which films will be accepted for national and global distribution, or which films will be exhibited. Concentration renders that power all the more influential and awesome. Indeed, the film business can be understood as several pyramids of concentration in which the business and cultural decisions of a few companies predominate. There remain instances, however, where small firms have achieved some measure of success supplementing limited financial resources with ingenuity, creativity and persistence.

Regardless of the ease or difficulty of entry, and the fluctuating numbers of companies in one or another part of the film industry, there is a further indicator of concentration, one that is consistently overlooked because it is taken for granted. Although market shares may shift periodically, and a merger now and then may create even larger enterprises, the industry remains fixed within the capitalist sector of the economy, which means it is owned and managed by a single class. This establishes the medium's functions. Ultimately, that is the principal measure of concentration. Identification of the specific who (or what) within that class only serves to pinpoint more precisely where the profit motive is interpreted. It does not change the nature of that motive.

Distribution and Production

The superficial aspects of concentration should be dealt with first. It is common knowledge that three periods—summer, Christmas, Easter—generate the bulk of film rentals. MGM has declared that 17 weeks provide 40% to 50% of its theatrical rentals.[97] Furthermore, the bulk of rental for most films is earned within a few months of release,[98] and amortization increasingly is helped by advances from theater owners and presale to television. Films are pushed into distribution, and after their relatively short life in theaters, are moved aside to make room for others that must be amortized. Declining production and longer theatrical runs operate in unison. When a film is booked into a first-run theater for seven or eight weeks—a few films longer, others less—the house needs only 10 or so such films a year to operate, although exhibitors would like to have blockbuster audiences every day. About a third of national admissions comes from nine major metropolitan areas, but these account for less than a quarter of promotional expenditures.[99] The territories served by film exchanges in four cities typically generate a third of all rentals.[100] In terms of indoor theaters, the 1972 census found that those going into operation between 1964 and 1972 represented less than 30% of all establishments, but that they took in 43% of all receipts.[101]

Overseas, the top five markets for American companies in 1979 yielded about 46% of all foreign rentals and the top 10 contributed just about 70%—a pattern that seems to have stabilized at that level.[102] The entire 1979 export market was worth about $909.4 million. In any recent year, there probably are about 3600 feature films made throughout the world, but American production, routinely less than 10% of that amount, occupies about half of world screen time and probably captures close to that share of the world box office. This is all the more startling because the bulk of this revenue abroad is earned by just a small number of films, as it is in the United States.

In 1978, for example, the top 10 films had gross box office receipts of $1.2 billion in the United States-Canadian market, while the total U.S. box office was estimated to be $2.7 billion.[103] The same year, some 40 films had rentals of more than $8 million each, which was also the case in 1980. Indeed, a half dozen films each year can generate perhaps a third of the American box office, and the top 10 or dozen can garner at least a half. Throughout the 1970s, the Classification and Rating Administration reviewed an average of considerably more than 400 films each year. It is clear then that at the top of the box office pyramid is a handful of films that earn half the rentals, while what is left is shared by several hundred other pictures.

But these figures really do not identify the extent of concentration in the industry. The "mega-hits," as a rule, are from the major distributors—Columbia, Paramount, Twentieth Century-Fox, United Artists (which handled films in the domestic market for Metro-Goldwyn-Mayer throughout most of the 1970s), Universal and Warner. In 1980, these companies distributed the 10 highest rental films in the North American market and received $460.7 million for them, a share that hardly fluctuates from one year to the next. Of the 33 films earning $10 million or more in rentals in North America in 1980, the above companies distributed 29 and received $775 million. Three others, distributed by Buena Vista (Disney), Filmways and Avco-Embassy, received $51 million in rentals. Taft was the only independent to be ranked among distributors of films with rentals of $10 million or more, and its sole picture in that category received $10.6 million. Of the 96 new releases to receive at least $2 million in rentals, 69 were handled by the six leading distributors, 10 others were handled by three other MPAA companies (Buena Vista, Filmways and Avco-Embassy), and 17 were handled by independent distributors. Table 5.21 summarizes the situation for 1980. Figures for previous years would be appreciably similar.

Overall, the majors distribute a small portion of films on the market and themselves constitute probably only 6% or 7% of all distribution companies. Table 5.22 shows that during the 1970s, MPAA companies accounted for between a fourth and two-fifths of all films rated by the Classification and Rating Administration. Taking into account only national distributors, Table 5.23 indicates that MPAA companies distributed almost 60% of all new releases. The addition of Buena Vista and American International (acquired by Filmways in 1979) increases the share to 70%. Inclusion of reissues would have no substantive effect on the percentages.

The share of domestic rentals accounted for by each of the major companies is identified in Table 5.24, with Universal being the clear leader in 1980, followed by Paramount and Twentieth Century-Fox. As indicated, throughout the 1970s, the majors captured between 70% and 89% of the revenue accruing to films earning more than $1 million in domestic rentals. Adding receipts for Buena Vista and American International pushes the upper limit to 95% in 1978 for the eight top distributors. During the 1970s, the top three distribution companies accounted for more than 50% of North American rentals. Inasmuch as the majors are the only companies

Table 5.21: Market Domination by Six Leading Distributors[1] of Theatrical Films, 1977 and 1980
(rentals in millions)

	1977	1980
Top 10 grossing films in North America		
Number handled	9	10
Rentals	$344.8	$460.7
Films with $10 million or more in North American rentals		
Number handled	23 of 28	29 of 33
Rentals	$622.6	$775.0
Films with $2 million or more in North American rentals	53 of 78	69 of 96

[1] Columbia, Paramount, Twentieth Century-Fox, United Artists (distributing for Metro-Goldwyn-Mayer), Universal and Warner. MPAA member companies in 1980, which included the above plus Avco Embassy, Buena Vista (Disney) and Filmways, distributed 32 of the 33 films earning rentals of $10 million or more, and 79 of the 96 films earnings rentals of $2 million or more in the United States-Canadian market.
Source: *Variety*, January 4, 1978; January 14, 1981. Reissues are excluded.

Table 5.22: Films Distributed by MPAA Companies[1] as Percent of All Films Rated by the Classification and Rating Administration, 1970-1980

Year	MPAA Films as % of All Films
1970	42.0%
1971	34.5
1972	38.5
1973	31.7
1974	28.9
1975	26.8
1976	24.5
1977	25.1
1978	37.4
1979	37.6
1980	39.1

[1] Allied Artists, Avco Embassy, Columbia, Metro-Goldwyn-Mayer, Paramount, Twentieth Century-Fox, United Artists (distributing MGM films after 1973), Universal and Warner. Beginning in 1978, Buena Vista (Disney) is included, and in 1980 Filmways. Allied Artists submitted no films for classification in 1979 and 1980.
Source: Motion Picture Association of America, Classification and Rating Administration.

with international distribution chains, they do not have to share the foreign market with minor or independent American distributors. If revenue from television programs is added to that from American theatrical films shown abroad, then between 85% and 90% of all rentals are earned by the eight leading companies.

Agreements among the major distributors have decreased the number of companies operating abroad. Paramount and Universal formed Cinema International Corporation in 1970, with each owning 49%. Since then, CIC has handled distribution of Paramount and Universal films in most foreign territories, in addition to operating theaters in Europe, South America, and South Africa. CIC also began foreign distribution of MGM films in December 1973, after MGM shut down its global organization. CIC is reported to be the world's largest distributor of films, and in fiscal 1977 accounted for a third of American films' foreign rentals. Its revenue was about $133 million in 1977 and was expected to be about $145 million in 1978.[104] In addition, CIC produced *The Sorcerer,* which was distributed in the western United States by Universal and in the east by Paramount.

Late in 1981, MCA, Paramount, United Artists and MGM established United International Pictures to distribute their theatrical films abroad. UIP absorbs the functions of CIC and folds in United Artists' extensive foreign distribution network, thus creating the largest overseas marketing operation for motion pictures.

Table 5.23: Major Company Share of New Releases Handled by National Distributors, 1970-1980

Company	1970	1971	1972	1973	1974	1975	1976	1977	1978	1979	1980	Total, 1970-1980 Number	Total, 1970-1980 Percent
Total New Releases	267	282	279	237	238	195	191	167	171	189	192	2408	100.0%
MPAA Companies:													
Allied Artists	7	8	8	1	3	7	6	4	2	—	—	46	1.9
Avco-Embassy	11	6	13	11	10	15	8	5	10	11	10	110	4.6
Columbia	28	37	27	16	21	15	15	10	14	20	15	218	9.1
Metro-Goldwyn-Mayer	21	20	22	16	[1]	[1]	[1]	[1]	[1]	—	[1]	79	3.3
Paramount	16	21	14	26	23	11	18	15	14	16	17	191	7.9
Twentieth Century-Fox	14	16	25	14	18	19	18	14	7	14	16	175	7.3
United Artists	40	26	20	18	21	21	22	14	19	23	22	246	10.2
Universal	17	16	16	19	11	10	13	17	21	15	18	173	7.2
Warner	15	17	18	22	15	19	11	14	18	19	24	192	8.0
Total	169	167	163	143	122	117	111	93	105	118	122	1430	
MPAA companies as % of total new releases	63.3%	59.2%	58.4%	60.3%	51.3%	60.0%	58.1%	55.7%	61.4%	62.4%	63.5%		59.4%
Buena Vista (Disney)	4	5	4	4	5	6	5	5	5	5	3	51	2.1
American International	25	24	28	19	18	17	17	18	13	11	9	199	8.3
MPAA companies, Buena Vista and Amer. Internat'l. as % of total new releases	74.2%	69.5%	69.9%	70.0%	60.9%	71.8%	69.6%	69.5%	71.9%	70.9%	69.8%		69.8%

[1] Distributed by United Artists.

Source: Motion Picture Association of America.

Table 5.24: Major Company Share of U.S.-Canadian Market Receipts for Films Earning Rentals of $1 Million or More, 1970-1980

Company	1970	1971	1972	1973	1974	1975	1976	1977	1978	1979	1980
Columbia	14.1%	10.2%	9.1%	7.0%	7.0%	13.1%	8.3%	11.5%	11.6%	11.0%	14.0%
Metro-Goldwyn-Mayer	3.4	9.3	6.0	4.6	[1]	[1]	[1]	[1]	[1]	[1]	[1]
Paramount	11.8	17.0	21.6	8.6	10.0	11.3	9.6	10.0	23.8	15.0	16.0
Twentieth Century-Fox	19.4	11.5	9.1	18.8	10.9	14.0	13.4	19.5	13.4	9.0	16.0
United Artists	8.7	7.4	15.0	10.7	8.5	10.7	16.2	17.8	10.3	15.0	7.0
Universal	13.1	5.2	5.0	10.0	18.6	25.1	13.0	11.5	16.8	15.0	20.0
Warner	5.3	9.3	17.6	16.4	23.2	9.1	18.0	13.7	13.2	20.0	14.0
Total	75.8%	69.9%	83.4%	76.1%	78.2%	83.3%	78.5%	84.0%	89.1%	85.0%	87.0%
Buena Vista (Disney)	9.1	8.0	5.0	6.5	7.0	6.0	6.7	5.6	4.8	4.0	4.0
American International	N.R.	N.R.	N.R.	N.R.	3.8	3.4	3.8	3.4	1.4	5.0	N.R.
Total	84.9%	77.9%	88.4%	82.6%	89.0%	92.7%	89.0%	93.0%	95.3%	94.0%	91.0%

[1] Distributed by United Artists.

N.R.: Not reported.

Sources: *Variety*, January 15, 1975; February 11, 1976; January 18, 1978; January 10, 1979; January 28, 1981.

Other American distribution companies frequently engage in joint ventures abroad. As of 1977, for example, Columbia shared about a dozen foreign offices each with Fox and Warner, and in late 1978 announced the merger of its Australian distribution facility with Fox.

Joint Ventures

In the domestic market, the major companies interlock in several ways. Since late 1973, MGM films have been distributed by United Artists, with two companies agreeing on how pictures would be handled and on what terms.[105] In 1981, MGM bought United Artists from Transamerica. On the production level, several so-called independent companies are associated with one or another of the majors for purposes of financing and distribution. But there are numerous instances of the majors coproducing films among themselves. These ventures include *Towering Inferno,* a blockbuster of the 1970s, which was jointly financed and distributed by Warner and Twentieth Century-Fox, a situation analogous to Ford and General Motors jointly manufacturing and marketing a new automobile. Columbia and Universal were teamed for *1941* and *The Electric Horseman,* and Columbia cooperated with Twentieth Century-Fox for *All That Jazz.* MGM and Warner were involved in *The Goodbye Girl, Grand Hotel* and *Bogart Slept Here.* Warner also coproduced *Meteor* with American International. United Artists worked with Allied Artists on *The Betsy,* and UA coproduced *Network* with MGM. Paramount and Disney coproduced *Popeye* and *Dragonslayer.* Universal and RKO entered into a three-year agreement in 1980 for coproduction of an undisclosed number of pictures.

In terms of properties, Warner and Columbia established The Burbank Studios in January 1972 in order to operate the studio and production facilities owned by each of them. On another level, when two companies have films on very similar subjects, they might attempt to avoid excessive duplication. This happened with Universal's *Two Minute Warning* and Paramount's *Black Sunday* (both distributed abroad by CIC). Officials of Universal and Paramount met to discuss how to minimize similarity, and Universal eventually agreed to make certain edits in its picture.[106]

Concerning trade practices, United Artists had a long-standing policy against blind bidding, but this was abandoned in 1977, allegedly because other majors prevailed upon UA management to bring the company into line with the majors' policy.[107] The majors, moreover, are members of the Motion Picture Association of America at whose meetings industry problems are considered. Such was the case when company representatives agreed to a common policy of vigorous opposition to anti-blind bidding legislation introduced in state legislatures. The majors also belong to the

Motion Picture Export Association of America and other film export organizations that allow them to operate in concert in foreign markets. There are, therefore, a variety of ways in which companies interact at home and overseas.

Growing Ancillary Channels

Of course, the theatrical motion picture is no longer the sole line of filmed entertainment. Major and independent producers provide most of the non-public affairs and non-sports programming on commercial television. Federal suits against the networks, seeking to open these markets even further, were settled by consent decrees with NBC in 1976 and with ABC and CBS in 1980.[108] A few of the majors have strong television production subsidiaries that contribute important revenue. As tables in Appendix 5-1 demonstrate, MCA derived more revenue from television than from theaters during the 1970s, and Paramount and Columbia also drew considerable revenue from licensing material to television.

Prime-time TV schedules now are chaotic compared to what they were just a decade ago. Today, one series after another becomes a casualty in the ratings war, while specials, mini-series and frequent reshuffling of program schedules are the rule. At the beginning of the 1980-1981 season, it seemed that seven companies (Columbia, Disney, MGM, Paramount, Twentieth Century-Fox, Universal and Warner) were to provide about 14 hours of *regular* prime-time programming weekly, not counting theatrical films, made-for-TV films, or specials. Independents coproducing with the majors were to supply another five-and-a-half hours. Other independents were to account for about 26 hours more of prime-time programming.[109] Compared to several previous seasons, the majors' share of regular series was down somewhat in 1980, while the independents continued the trend of slightly enlarging their portion.[110]

Major Hollywood production-distribution companies have found a growing market in pay television and video cassettes and discs whose potentials are such that the creative community in Hollywood, through their unions, have held strikes to obtain a part of it. Early in 1980, Fox management reported that pay television was paying from $750,000 to $2 million per picture, and that licensing fees for cassettes/discs were in the $50,000 to $200,000 range.[111] Later that same year, Alan Hirschfield, then Fox's chief operating officer, declared that "Hollywood is presently receiving an inordinately low 20% of the pay cable dollar . . .; the distributor middleman receives 30%, and the system owner is getting 50%. One company [Home Box Office] dominates the marketplace, controlling almost 70% of the customers for distribution of programming, and two companies control 85%.'' Future expansion for the film industry, he predicted, would be in pay TV and home video because "in constant 1980 dollars, it is . . . unlikely that theatrical revenue will grow over the next five years.''[112] Gerald Levin, head of Time Inc.'s Home Box Office, estimated in mid-1981 that by the following year the home video markets would generate $500 million in revenue for film producers and distributors, and that home video would rival theaters as a revenue source before too many years passed.[113] Meanwhile, the International Tape/Disc Association gave a gold certification to 28 film cassettes that achieved gross sales of $1 million at retail list price. All were from the major companies: Paramount (seven), Warner, MCA and Twentieth Century-Fox (five each), MGM (four), and Columbia (two).[114]

New Markets and New Trends

When all these details are sifted and fall into place, a long-term evolution that has affected profoundly the various sectors of the film industry becomes apparent. Particularly for production and distribution, the last three decades have seen the emergence of several important kinds of new markets, initially in the United States, and then abroad.

First, of course, commercial television became a buyer of theatrical features, series and TV features. Second, the rapid development of pay TV in the last half of the 1970s, and third, the innovation of video cassettes and video discs at the end of the 1970s, provided further sales opportunities. In the 1980s, therefore, several ancillary markets exist for the typical theatrical film, and these contribute measurably to reducing (if not eliminating) the financial risks associated with production.

The relationship between television and the film industry has sorted itself out. In contrast to the situation in many other countries, where the content of TV generally is produced by the broadcasting company itself, in the United States most of it is provided by outside suppliers working in close association with the networks. But the home video and pay TV markets still are relatively unsettled and fluid. Consequently, relations between suppliers and retailers are continually developing, and it is not surprising to see familiar companies vying for at least a beachhead in these markets and, if possible, the opportunity to stake out spheres of interest and control.

In the early 1970s, the networks were squeezed out of TV program production and syndication, and subsequently they lost the battle to obstruct the proliferation of pay television. For various reasons, CBS and ABC also closed down their theatrical film production subsidiaries. But the growth of video entertainment sources outside the commercial TV system, and prophesies drawn from the stabilization (and perhaps decline) in overall viewing of commercial TV, suggest that if the network companies wish to continue to enlarge their revenue base, they had better look to new markets. These, of course, are home video, pay TV and cable TV.

In May 1980, CBS created a cable unit (later upgraded to division status) that produces and acquires entertainment and informational programming for distribution via satellite to cable systems around the nation. The service was inaugurated in 1981 over systems with about 3 million subscribers. CBS also established its Video Enterprises Division in 1980 to manufacture and distribute video cassettes and discs. This division, which in addition produces or acquires program material suitable for home video, as well as for pay TV and cable TV, formed a major joint venture with Metro-Goldwyn-Mayer Film Co., and its first video cassette releases appeared late in 1980. CBS plans to use the distribution system of its Records Group as the basis for a global home video marketing network. Similarly, ABC Video Enterprises, Inc. provides software for video cassettes and discs, and it, too, initiated a cable programming service in 1981 over the Warner-Amex system. Both ABC and CBS reactivated their theatrical film production subsidiaries in 1979 and 1980, respectively. *Back Roads,* distributed theatrically by Warner, was the first CBS feature to appear. ABC, whose films are distributed to North American theaters by Twentieth Century-Fox, began production in 1981. Meanwhile, RCA and Columbia Pictures started a joint venture in 1981 to market home video products outside North America, with particular emphasis directed toward Western Europe and Australia.

As program suppliers, the networks' expansion into the home video and cable fields was ratified in mid-1981 by the FCC, which declared that its financial interest rules do not prevent network acquisition of non-broadcast rights to new programs. Consequently, the network companies are not barred from acquiring software and selling it to cable systems, or retailing it in video cassette and disc formats. This ruling, sought by the networks, was strongly opposed by the MPAA and independent companies. These interests, naturally, wanted to be the chief software suppliers, leaving the networks to provide the hardware and the international retail distribution system.

As a result of burgeoning ancillary markets not only have the major film companies slightly increased the number of pictures they distribute, but, in addition, two of the networks have reentered theatrical film production. Plans also abound for programming made specifically for pay TV, cable systems and home video.

Film Theaters

On the retail level of the industry, there are literally thousands of companies in exhibition, from mom-and-pop operations to multimillion dollar enterprises. A few of these companies, however, have such substantial holdings and revenue-generating ability that they are set apart from the rest just as is the case for some firms involved in production and distribution. Although the latter exercise their power in a national and international sphere, exhibition companies can assert their dominance on other levels. Several large chains, such as General Cinema and United Artists Theatre Circuit, have national importance. Others, such as Commonwealth and Fuqua's Martin Theatres, have significant regional holdings. Some, including Pacific Theatres, Georgia Theatre Co., and Kerasotes are major statewide groups. Chains exist as well that are important in specific cities, such as Wehrenberg in St. Louis or Cinemette in Pittsburgh. Although Wometco has holdings in the Caribbean, American exhibitors as a rule confine their business to the domestic market. This is not the case with production-distribution companies because Paramount, Fox and CIC have circuits overseas.

In the domestic market, small towns frequently constitute monopoly situations for some exhibitors, but the possibility of competition increases with the size of the community. It is not uncommon, therefore, to find three or four major national and regional chains, plus some smaller companies, in moderate-size metropolitan areas. Although all are in the exhibition business, they might not be directly competitive because of market segmentation among first-run, second-run, drive-in, ethnic and adult theaters. Consequently, apparent competition may be effectively reduced, as it also is when each of the few companies owns several theaters in the same town, and when rival firms agree to split first-run product among themselves.

Table 5.25 presents the holdings of several large theater chains, although the list is by no means all-inclusive. The location of the theaters is of considerable importance because that can generate substantially diverse revenue for different chains with the same number of screens. If one assumes 17,300 screens in the nation, then the top three chains account for about 14% and the top five almost 19%. But this understates the position of the large chains because drive-ins are included in the national figure, and the major chains consist almost exclusively of conventional theaters. Furthermore, as *Paramount* and other cases have taught, holdings amounting to a small proportion of all theaters can convey considerable market leverage. For example, at the time the Justice Department brought its case to force the five major distributors to sell their theaters, the majors wholly or partially owned only about 17% of all theaters in 1945.

The *Paramount* decision made circuit-wide booking and package leasing illegal. Although there is competition for spectators in most communities and large chains face each other regionally and nationally, the major pro-

Table 5.25: Number of Screens in Selected Theater Circuits

Company	Number of Screens	Date
Domestic		
General Cinema	916	October 31, 1980[1]
United Artists Theatre Circuit	877	February 26, 1981[2]
American Multi Cinema	610	January-February 1981[3]
Plitt Theatres	531	June 24, 1981[6]
Commonwealth Theatres	350	September 30, 1980[1]
Pacific Theatres	350[11]	January 28, 1980[4]
Fuqua Industries (Martin Theatres)	280	December 31, 1980[9]
Mann Theatres	266	June 23, 1980[4]
Kerasotes Theatres	180[11]	October 1978[5]
Cobb Theatres	160	May 1981[4]
Cinemette	160	February 22, 1978[6]
Loews Corp.	142	August 12, 1980[7]
Stewart & Everett	138	December 31, 1978[8]
Cablecom-General	122	November 30, 1980[2]
Gulf States	120	December 31, 1978[8]
Foreign		
Twentieth Century-Fox		
Hoyts Theatres Ltd. (Australia)	76	December 27, 1980[1]
Amalgamated Theatres Ltd. (New Zealand)	28	December 27, 1980[1]
Gulf + Western Industries		
Famous Players Ltd. (Canada)	387	July 31, 1980[9]
Various screens in France	77	July 31, 1980[9]
Cinema International Corp. (Paramount and Universal) South America, Africa, Middle East and Europe	56	July 31, 1980[10]

Sources: [1] Annual report for the year ending on the date indicated.
[2] Second quarter report for the date indicated.
[3] Company newsletter.
[4] *Boxoffice*; issues correspond with dates given above.
[5] Interview.
[6] *Variety*; issues correspond with dates given above.
[7] *Hollywood Reporter*; issue date given above.
[8] Letter to author.
[9] Form 10-K Report for the year ending on the date indicated.
[10] Form 10-K Report for Gulf + Western Industries.
[11] Estimate.

ducer-distributors know that at the retail end of the industry they have but a handful of best customers who together control a substantial share of first-run theaters. The establishment and financing of major chains, moreover, is predicated on the assumption that they will be able to rent a substantial share of the major first-run films from the big companies. Similarly, the studios and distributors assume as a basis for their own operations that they will be able to place their films in enough of the important houses so as to have adequate play-off. The congruence of interests, multiplied market-by-market to a national scale, demonstrates that the industry, from manufacturer to retailer, moves on the basis of decisions made in a dozen or so of the largest companies. Other firms that elect to do business on that level have to conform, or else they try to carve niches elsewhere in which they will be more secure.

Major theater groups and distributors do the most business with each other. In the five years up to 1978, General Cinema was the largest customer for each of the major distributors, with the exception of United Artists distribution company.[115] In fiscal 1978, for example, General Cinema contributed about $12 million in film rental to Columbia, or about 8.5% of the distributor's total domestic rentals. Probably in second and third places were United Artists Theatre Circuit and ABC Theatres (subsequently sold to Plitt), each contributing about $6 million in rentals.[116] Consequently, three chains provided, perhaps, 17% of Columbia's domestic theatrical revenue. Similarly, a blockbuster or two running in a significant number of a chain's theaters can have an explosive effect on an exhibition company's annual admission revenue as well as on concession stand receipts, which might amount to 20 cents for each dollar spent at the box office of a conventional theater. As the nation's largest circuit, General Cinema accounted for more than 8% of total theatrical admission in 1980, compared to slightly more than 3% in 1969.[117]

Concentration in the production and distribution end of the industry is somewhat greater than that in other communication fields. Table 5.26 reveals that for production, distribution and allied services, the four largest firms in 1977 accounted for almost 29% of all receipts, and the eight largest firms accounted for about 40%. In exhibition concentration is comparable to other media. The four largest companies had 18% of all receipts, and the eight largest had over 26%, but they had, respectively, only 8% and 11% of all establishments. In these cases, the concentration was actually slightly lower than in 1972. Among manufacturing fields, the four largest newspaper publishing companies accounted for 19% of the value of shipments, and the eight largest accounted for 31%. Figures for periodicals were 22% and 35%; radio and TV communications equip-

**Table 5.26: Concentration of Revenue in the Motion Picture Industry,
1972 and 1977
(in millions)**

	Production, Distribution and Services		Motion Picture Theaters	
	Receipts	Percent of Total	Receipts	Percent of Total
1977				
All firms	$5,411.7	100.0%	$2,605.5	100.0%
4 largest firms	1,540.3	28.5	460.8	17.7
8 largest firms	2,146.7	39.7	678.8	26.1
20 largest firms	2,803.6	51.8	982.9	37.7
50 largest firms	3,347.1	61.9	1,272.9	48.9
1972				
All firms	$2,920.4	100.0%	$1,833.0	100.0%
4 largest firms	852.4	29.2	350.4	19.1
8 largest firms	1,295.6	44.4	482.2	26.3
20 largest firms	1,628.9	55.8	639.1	34.9
50 largest firms	1,882.2	66.4	819.3	44.7

Source: U.S. Department of Commerce, Bureau of the Census, *Census of Service Industries, 1977 and 1972; Establishment and Firm Size*; SC77-S-1, May 1980.

ment, 20% and 33%; and photographic equipment and supplies, 72% and 86%.[118]

Another indicator of concentration is that in film production, distribution and allied services, 13 firms captured 47% of all 1977 revenue, as shown in Table 5.27. The top 30 firms constituted only 0.3% of all firms, yet they received 57% of all receipts. In the theatrical sector, 15 firms accounted for 34% of all receipts. The top 32 theater firms constituted only 0.5% of all firms, but they generated 43% of all receipts. Concentration in the film industry as a whole is significantly greater than in all service industries, in which the four largest firms accounted for only 1.7% of receipts. In advertising, the four largest captured 7.9% of all receipts, and in computer and data processing the comparable figure was 13%, according to the 1977 census.

Ownership of Individual Firms

Information about market concentration is significant in its own right to demonstrate trends toward oligopoly. However, an important aspect customarily overlooked is the narrow structure of private ownership of the

Table 5.27: Concentration of Firms by Annual Receipts, 1977
(in millions)

	Production, Distribution and Services			Motion Picture Theaters		
	Number of Firms	Receipts	% of Receipts	Number of Firms	Receipts	% of Receipts
All firms	10,163	$5,411.7	100.0%	6,198	$2,605.6	100.0%
Firms with annual receipts of:						
$50 million or more	13	2,530.6	46.8	N.R.	N.R.	N.R.
$20 million or more	30	3,075.3	56.8	15	895.2	34.4
$10 million or more	55	3,423.8	63.3	32	1,128.4	43.3

N.R.: Not reported.
Source: U.S. Department of Commerce, Bureau of the Census, *Census of Service Industries, 1977; Establishment and Firm Size*; SC77-S-1, May 1980.

companies that dominate the business. In firms whose stock is not available for public purchase, the proprietors might be a family, or several business associates, or just one person. Stock offerings to investors at large somewhat widen this circle of ownership. But in contrast to political democracy in which "one person, one vote" is the theoretical rule, "one share, one vote" is the principal in corporate governance. Even so, stock owners as a group have very little to do with operational control of a corporation, and their ritualistic power is exercised once a year when they vote for the single slate of directors that has been proposed by these same directors. Stockholders also are called upon to approve mergers, acquisitions or sales of significant assets and the selection of the corporation's auditors. However, stockholders usually follow the advice of the board of directors and vote the way they are advised.

Because the typical individual owner of a corporation has only a miniscule portion of all outstanding stock, a large minority holding of 15% or even less can convey enormous power through representation on the board of directors. Moreover, "Control of a small block of stock in a widely held company by a single or few like-minded financial institutions," according to one government report, "provides them with disproportionately large powers within the company."[119] Consequently, while the thousands of stock owners, each with a tiny percentage of shares, may be powerless to influence a corporation, a few large blocks of stock (not even the majority of shares) may dominate affairs and control the board of directors. Occasionally, this significant power may have to be shared with banks and investment houses that are lenders to the corporation, and these institutions may be represented on the board as well. The day-to-day running of the corporation is left to managers who are hired by the board. But the directors maintain overall control, establish broad business strategy and approve use of the corporation's assets, which means in terms of the film industry, that they approve how the firm's funds will be employed, by whom, to make or acquire what films.

There are no public studies disclosing ownership of stock specifically in the motion picture industry. However, the findings of government investigations of companies owning broadcasting properties are suggestive because several film companies are broadcast station licensees. An inquiry into the holdings of the 25 largest bank trust departments[120] revealed that as of mid-1972 the Bank of New York had voting rights to 6.6% of the common stock of Columbia Pictures and 4.2% of Twentieth Century-Fox, as well as 3.7% of Cox Broadcasting and 1.3% of Wometco, two companies that have coproduced a number of films with Fuqua Industries. Bankers Trust Company of New York voted 1.1% of Columbia, 1.6% of Wometco and 2% of Cox. Old Colony Trust of Boston held 2.1% of Columbia and 1.9% of Twentieth Century-Fox. The Chase Manhattan Bank held 2.4% of Fox's common stock and 7.4% of Fuqua Industries' stock, while Chemical Bank of New York held 1.5% of Columbia's stock. In sum, over 11% of Columbia's stock was voted by four bank trust departments, and 8.5% of Fox's stock was voted by three. Four banks voted 5.9% of Wometco's common stock and two banks voted 5.7% of Cox Broadcasting. Film companies without broadcasting properties escaped attention.

There is considerable range in the dispersion of stock from companies with interests in the film business, as Table 5.28 demonstrates, and the number of shareholders tends to increase with the diversification of the company. Hidden, however, are important concentrations of holdings that render dispersion figures somewhat irrelevant. Indeed, a concentration of holdings becomes all the more significant when the remainder of stock is widely held.

Although MCA had about 6300 stockholders at the beginning of 1981, the largest owners were Jules Stein (who died later that year) with 15.8% of the shares and Lew Wasserman with 8.1%. Both were members of the board of directors, and Wasserman also was chief executive officer of the company. Other members of the board were beneficial owners of an additional 1.7% of the shares. At the end of 1980, the two largest owners of common stock of Gulf & Western Industries (parent of Paramount Picture Corp.) were American Financial Corp., with almost 7.9%, and Charles Bluhdorn with about 5.2%. Bluhdorn is chairman of the board and chief executive officer of Gulf & Western. As a group, directors and senior management of the corporation owned 10.2% of the common shares as well as 37.6% of one series of preferred stock. The board of directors of Warner

Table 5.28: Number of Shareholders of Selected Companies with Interests in the Motion Picture Business

Company	Number of Shareholders	Date
Cablecom-General Inc.	468	November 30, 1980
Commonwealth Theatres Inc.	500	November 28, 1980
United Artists Theatre Circuit Inc.	739	August 1, 1980
First Artists Production Company Ltd.	1,292	June 30, 1980
Movielab Inc.	1,804	March 23, 1981
General Cinema Corp.	3,236	January 16, 1981
Technicolor Inc.	5,357	September 12, 1980
Filmways Inc.	5,400	February 29, 1980
MCA Inc.	6,300	January 31, 1981
Columbia Pictures Industries Inc.	7,100	June 28, 1980
Wometco Enterprises Inc.	7,200	March 6, 1981
Loews Corp.	8,565	March 4, 1980
Twentieth Century-Fox Film Corp.	10,800	December 29, 1979
Fuqua Industries	18,678	December 31, 1980
Warner Communications Inc.	16,000	March 15, 1981
Metro-Goldwyn-Mayer Film Co.	21,206	August 31, 1980
Avco Corp.	43,578	November 30, 1980
Gulf + Western Industries Inc.	53,878	July 31, 1980
Walt Disney Productions	62,000	September 30, 1980
Eastman Kodak Co.	234,009	December 28, 1980

Sources: Form 10-K reports of the various companies.

Communications owned about 4.4% of that corporation's common stock early in 1981, and the director with the largest portion was Steven Ross, also chief executive officer, with 1.2%. The 61.6 million outstanding shares of Warner common stock were spread among 16,000 owners, which meant that the typical stockholder had about 3850 shares, or 0.006% of the total.

Changes in Ownership

Samuel Arkoff, board chairman and president of American International Pictures, owned 34.7% of that corporation's common stock, making him its largest share owner when it was acquired by Filmways in July 1979. As a result of the merger, Arkoff obtained preferred and common stock of Filmways amounting to about 9% of voting power. At the end of 1980, however, he sold his holdings to three producers, Jerry Perenchio, Norman Lear and Bud Yorkin, who are the principals of Tandem Productions Inc. A substantial portion of these shares was sold in 1981 to Filmways' board chairman and president, Richard Bloch, and to board member Donald Pitt, giving them more than 12% of the voting power in the company. Early in 1982, however, control of Filmways passed to four major executives of Orion Pictures Corp., who were backed chiefly by investment bankers and venture capitalists. Home Box Office also contributed $10 million toward the $26 million that was involved in the purchase of Filmways.

Important changes in ownership have taken place at other motion picture companies, too. Beginning around December 1977, Chris-Craft Industries started buying Twentieth Century-Fox's common stock and by October 1980 it had accumulated about 21.3% of the outstanding shares. Although Chris-Craft management claimed it had acquired the stock for investment purposes only, Fox owners and management fought back, fearing that Chris-Craft sought to control Fox. An offering by Fox to buy back its stock was refused by Chris-Craft, and then Fox sued the company, hoping Chris-Craft would be required to dispose of its Fox stock. Meanwhile, toward the end of 1980, Tandem Productions also began buying Fox common stock, and by mid-1981 it had 7.3% of the shares. Fox tried to resist a possible takeover from Tandem as well, and at one point was formulating plans to go private, which would remove its stock from public exchanges. On another level, negotiations were taking place with Colorado oil baron Marvin Davis, who was interested in acquiring Fox. On June 12, 1981, Fox was merged with a company controlled by Davis and others, and at that point the film corporation became a private concern. The acquisition reportedly cost Davis and his associates about $700 million. Fox broadcasting properties were spun off into a new public company, United Television Inc., of which Chris-Craft was said to own about a third of the common stock.

Allen and Co. interests successfully defeated an attempt by Kirk Kerkorian to maintain, and perhaps enlarge, his ownership of Columbia Pictures Industries. Herbert Allen began acquiring Columbia stock in 1973, the year he and two other Allen associates were elected to the board of directors. Throughout the late 1970s, it was generally conceded that Allen interests were the chief governors of Columbia. However, in 1978 Kerkorian announced he already controlled 5.5% of Columbia's stock and that an investment company he owned would seek to buy an additional 20% of Columbia. In January 1979, the Department of Justice filed suit to block this acquisition on the grounds that it would diminish competition and lead to further concentration in the film industry, because Kerkorian and his investment company already owned 48% of the common stock of Metro-Goldwyn-Mayer. A federal judge dismissed the suit. Shortly before increasing his holdings to 25% of Columbia's stock, Kerkorian met with Allen interests to agree on the extent of his participation in the company.

Meanwhile, between April 1978 and the beginning of 1979, General Cinema Corp. acquired about 4.6% of Columbia's common stock, and sought management's blessing to increase this by an additional 20%. Antitrust implications undoubtedly were the basis for Columbia's cold reception of this move, and in August 1980 General Cinema made plans to dispose of its shares. General Cinema's ownership of Columbia stock was an interesting relationship because the theater chain was the distributor's chief customer. Moreover, the president of General Cinema was a director of the First National Bank of Boston (a prominent lender to the film industry), and one of the bank's officers served on the General Cinema board. In 1976, during the tenure of this interlock, Columbia negotiated a $113 million revolving credit agreement with a group of banking institutions, for which First National Bank of Boston was agent and one of the chief lenders.

Toward the end of 1979, arrangements between Kerkorian and Columbia became less satisfactory. Kerkorian wanted to increase his ownership of Columbia, but was rebuffed by management. He sued Columbia and its executives, alleging a range of misdeeds, and in turn was sued by Columbia to force him to dispose of its stock. In 1980, he proposed to merge Columbia into Metro-Goldwyn-Mayer, and Allen interests predictably resisted. This high-level corporate warfare was brought under control early in 1981 when Kerkorian agreed to sell his holdings to Columbia for about $137 million. The parties also dropped legal proceedings against each other, and Kerkorian agreed not to acquire any Columbia securities for a period of ten years.

Also during 1981, American Financial Corp. was reported to own 5.2% of Columbia's stock, and National Amusements Inc. (a prominent theater circuit) disclosed it owned more than 9%. But the capstone to these ownership changes occurred in 1982 when the Coca-Cola Co. agreed to acquire Columbia for more than $800 million. The attraction of Columbia was its film library and its position in the growing pay TV and home video markets.

Effective May 30, 1980, Metro-Goldwyn-Mayer Inc. was divided into two separate publicly held corporations—MGM Grand Hotels Inc. and Metro-Goldwyn-Mayer Film Co. Kirk Kerkorian, who was the principal stockholder of the predecessor company, also became the dominant owner of the new film corporation with almost 47% of its common stock. MGM's worldwide distribution system had been closed almost a decade earlier, when management and chief owners at that time disposed of most of the company's assets. With the general turnaround in the film business during the 1970s, MGM began to produce more pictures toward the end of the decade and anticipated continued production on that level into the

1980s. Domestic distribution of MGM films since 1973 had been handled by United Artists. In May 1981, however, Metro-Goldwyn-Mayer Film Co. purchased United Artists Corp. from Transamerica for an aggregate price of $380 million. MGM contemplated financing the transaction through a bank loan that would be repaid in part through equity financing. Kerkorian agreed to purchase about half of any shares of MGM common stock that the company would offer for this purpose.

Avco-Embassy Pictures had been a tiny subsidiary of Avco Corp., a company involved in armaments, space research, aircraft, consumer finance, insurance, farm machinery, medical products and real estate development. Early in 1982, Norman Lear and Jerry Perenchio completed their purchase of the film company, ending a long quest to acquire a motion picture corporation.

Publicly owned corporations in theatrical exhibition also reveal dominant clusters of control. Loews Corp's principal owners are the Tisch brothers, each of whom holds about 20% of the common stock. Similarly, United Artists Communications is controlled by the Naify brothers, who own almost 56% of the stock. Richard Smith, president of General Cinema, owns about 21% of that corporation's stock. Shares owned by other members of the family increase the amount to 25%. Members of the Wolfson family own approximately 37% of the common stock of Wometco Enterprises.

It is evident, therefore, that even though a corporation's stock may be held by thousands of owners, significant concentrations of power continue to exist, sometimes in the hands of the families that started the enterprises. In the film industry, the companies that matter are controlled by a very narrow slice of powerful owners, who occasionally share this dominance with major banks and other influential lenders.

Activities of Conglomerates in the Film Industry

Oligopolistic market structures and concentration of ownership are only parts of a pattern that includes cross-media holdings, diversification into spheres beyond communications and global operations. A cursory survey reveals an elaborate array of enlarging connections in which film companies are either parts of considerably larger concerns or conglomerates in their own right.

In April 1979, Allied Artists Industries filed for voluntary reorganization under federal bankruptcy statutes. The company was formed early in 1976 from a merger of Allied Artists Pictures Corp., Kalvex Inc. and PSP Inc. Its business consisted of motor home manufacture and distribution, importation of consumer products, cosmetic and drug distribution, and film financing, production, and distribution. Theatrical and television rentals provided about 30% of the company's revenue in fiscal 1978.

By contrast, about 96% of American International's fiscal 1978 revenue came from rentals. As described earlier, this firm was acquired in 1979 by Filmways, a company engaged in production and distribution of programming and feature-length films for television, the publication of hardcover and paperback books, and the manufacture of electronic equipment. (Filmways' insurance and data processing subsidiaries were to be sold in 1982.)

Since mid-1980, when Metro-Goldwyn-Mayer Inc. was divided into two separate companies, the film corporation has concentrated on the financing and production of entertainment for theatrical release and television. In addition to its film processing labs, MGM also now syndicates its motion pictures to television stations, and has formed a joint venture with CBS to market video cassettes and discs for the burgeoning home video market. In 1980, about 35% of MGM's revenue came from foreign markets, excluding Canada. As reported above, MGM acquired United Artists Corp., which not only will provide MGM with the most extensive global distribution organization, but in addition will give MGM access to a library of almost 1000 United Artists feature films, which can also be funnelled into its home video venture.

Among other motion picture companies, Paramount is a subsidiary of the massive conglomerate, Gulf + Western Industries. The Leisure Time Group, of which Paramount is part, provided about 15% of G + W's 1980 revenue. Aside from the financing, production and distribution of theatrical films and television programs, the Leisure Time Group also includes Famous Music Corp., the Simon and Schuster publishing house, a sports arena company and Famous Players Limited. The latter operates close to 400 screens in Canada, and has theaters in France as well. Other major divisions of Gulf + Western are engaged in manufacturing, natural resource development, consumer and agricultural products, auto replacement parts, apparel, building products, home furnishings and financial services.

Walt Disney Productions, associated in the public mind with children's films, drew less than 18% of its 1980 revenue from motion pictures and television. The bulk of revenue came from Walt Disney World ($433.4 million) and Disneyland ($207.1 million). Tokyo Disneyland was scheduled to open in 1983.

The major activities of Columbia Pictures Industries include production and global distribution of theatrical films, TV programs and made-for-TV features; the design, manufacture and sale of pinball machines; production of TV commercials; and the operation of five radio stations. In 1980, theatrical distribution provided about 49% of the company's total revenue, and television contributed another 28%. Overall, slightly more than a third of Columbia's revenue is derived from foreign countries. The company disposed of its recorded music operation in 1979.

MCA finances, produces and distributes theatrical films and television programming in the United States and abroad, and this activity provided 59% of the company's 1980 revenue. MCA also is engaged in recorded music and music publishing, book publishing, retail and mail order sales, recreation services, financial services, data processing and in the development of video discs. Early in 1981, MCA announced a long-term agreement under which Universal would distribute theatrical films in the United States and Canada for Associated Film Distribution, a British company that closed its own North American distribution system.

Warner Communications operates one of the world's three largest music businesses, and in 1980 about 39% of its total revenue came from that source. Filmed entertainment, including production of TV series, and the production and distribution of films for theaters and television, provided another third of Warner's revenue. Consumer electronics and toys generated another 25%; publishing and magazine distribution provided about 4%. Warner and American Express share ownership of Warner Amex Cable Communications and Warner Amex Satellite Entertainment Co. which distributes programming to cable systems. In 1978, Warner launched QUBE, the country's first operational interactive cable TV system.

In 1980, Twentieth Century-Fox's last year as a public company, it was engaged in financing, producing and distributing theatrical films and television programming; film processing; records and music publishing; manufacturing and distributing video cassettes; soft drink bottling; development of real estate, resorts and recreation areas; the operation of theater circuits in Australia and New Zealand; and the ownership of three television stations. Filmed entertainment yielded 67% of Fox's revenue, followed by the soft drink business, which provided 12%.

A company that also has moved aggressively into beverages is General Cinema, which operates the world's largest theater chain. Whereas the theater division contributed about 41% of General Cinema's 1980 revenue, its soft drink business provided 57%. The company is the licensee of a television station and four radio stations, as well. Another exhibitor, Wometco Enterprises, also is in the beverage and broadcasting businesses. Loews Corp. is widely diversified, with interests in tobacco products, financial services, hotels and watches, in addition to theater ownership. As of January 1981, Loews also owned approximately 6.5% of the outstanding common stock of American Broadcasting Cos. Inc. Commonwealth Theatres, although not extensively diversified, has expanded its operation through the acquisition of several circuits.

RECENT ANTITRUST ACTION

Antitrust activity, whether initiated on the federal level or by private parties, has been greater in the film industry than in any of the other media covered in this book. Basically, the objective of antitrust litigation is to eliminate business-inspired obstacles to commerce as well as to maintain and encourage competiton. In this way, antitrust action seeks through legal means to adjust the way enterprises operate within the capitalist economy, although it does not tamper with the underlying assumptions of private ownership.

Recent federal suits drew a "no contest" from Fox on block booking,[121] a consent order from Warner forbidding it to engage in four-wall deals* with exhibitors[122] and a consent decree from United Artists Theatre Circuit to divest itself of certain theatrical holdings in the New York metropolitan area.[123] A Department of Justice suit, which was dismissed in court, sought to prevent Kirk Kerkorian from acquiring a substantial interest in Columbia Pictures Industries.[124]

The *Paramount* case, decided by the Supreme Court in 1948, resulted in consent decrees entered into between 1948 and 1952 with RKO, Paramount, Columbia, Universal, United Artists, Warner, Twentieth Century-Fox and Loew's. Part of the relief required the integrated companies to divorce their exhibition interests. These circuits also were obliged to divest certain of their holdings, and prohibitions were placed on future acquisitions. However, there have been frequent modifications of these decrees as they pertain to exhibition. From 1954 up to 1980, the court responsible for monitoring and enforcing the *Paramount* judgments held some 500 hearings that involved acquisition of theaters by circuits operating under the *Paramount* decrees. In 1974, an order applicable to all the divorced circuits allowed them to acquire newly constructed theaters without permission from the court. In significant 1980 decisions, the court permitted Mann Theatre Corporation and Loews Theatres to acquire and operate theaters, except in a limited number of specific markets. The order further provided that after 10 years, Mann and Loews could acquire theaters

---

*Four-walling describes the rental by a distributor of a fully staffed theater for a short period of time, for exhibition of a particular film. The distributor often sets the admission price. The theater operator receives a fixed compensation from the distributor during the rental period, rather than the usual percentage of gross receipts. This approach is often used by a small distributor that otherwise has trouble getting films booked into movie theaters.

anywhere without prior court approval. A major feature of the Loews order now allows the company to produce and distribute films, as well as to exhibit them.[125]

The Department of Justice was the victor in a 1980 suit against a consortium of companies—Getty Oil Co., Columbia Pictures, MCA, Paramount and Twentieth Century-Fox—that formed Premiere, a service intended to distribute via satellite their theatrical feature films to pay television systems.[126] Existing networks—Home Box Office (Time Inc.), Showtime (Teleprompter and Viacom) and The Movie Channel (Warner Amex)—applauded that decision. For some time, the film companies had objected to HBO's dominance in pay TV, which they complained made it possible for HBO to continue paying insufficient fees for the licensing of theatrical films. To bypass that, the defendants created their own delivery system that was scheduled to begin operating in 1981. Their agreement obliged the production-distribution companies (1) to license to Premiere all English-language features exhibited theatrically after November 1, 1979, and (2) not to license these films to any other network service until nine months after they were made available to Premiere. Payment by Premiere for these films was to be determined according to a price formula established by the defendants. Getty was to provide a certain amount of cash as well as satellite distribution facilities.

The suit charged that the agreement violated the Sherman Act. The Department of Justice argued that program services such as HBO, Showtime and The Movie Channel would be unable to exhibit defendants' pictures until at least nine months after they were made available to Premiere. Moreover, the defendants were said to have agreed among themselves on the price Premiere would charge pay TV systems to use the program service. The suit contended that defendants had conspired to raise and fix prices of films, and to refuse to deal with competing program services.

Defendants argued that because HBO (with about 69% of subscribers) had monopoly and monopsony power, their companies faced a substantial barrier to entry. Launching Premiere, they asserted, was the only way they could gain a foothold in the pay TV market and reach the 8 million subscribers on a reasonable business basis.

On the last day of 1980, a federal judge granted a preliminary injunction prohibiting the inauguration of the Premiere network.[127] He ruled that there was a reasonable probability that a future trial would substantiate that the consortium violated the Sherman Act and that the agreement among defendants constituted price fixing and a group boycott. The judge's decision indicated that if Premiere went into operation, it could cause irreparable harm to "new and struggling companies," such as Showtime and The Movie Channel. Moreover, during the time needed for pretrial discovery and the full trial itself, according to the judge, these companies could be driven out of business by Premiere's operation.

The decision did not actually rule on the legality of Premiere, but it did result in an injunction on the assumption that a future trial would likely yield a decision against the defendants. In any case, during the early months of 1981, plans for the Premiere network were disbanded and the four film companies involved began to license their recent features to various pay TV programming networks.

This was not the first collision between HBO and major production-distribution companies. In 1979, Paramount Pictures, supported by Columbia, MCA, Metro-Goldwyn-Mayer and United Artists, petitioned the Federal Communications Commission to deny the transfer of the license for WSNS (channel 44) in Chicago to a subsidiary of Time Inc. The latter's plan was to enter the over-the-air pay TV business in that city, but the license transfer never materialized.

Although antitrust proceedings on the federal level have resulted in some important decisions, their significance pales when viewed in the context of the entire film industry's structure and behavior. Private suits, on the other hand, have been more outspoken, some projecting anti-competitive conduct to national levels, as a few citations demonstrate.

In *Syufy Enterprises* v. *Columbia Pictures Industries et al.,* the plaintiff alleged that several major distributors engaged in a "horizontal combination or conspiracy to fix prices and to institute blind bidding."[128] In mid-1981, Syufy also filed suit against another theater circuit, American Multi Cinema, charging that it conspired with six major film distributors to corner the film market in northern California.

In *United Artists Theatre Circuit Inc. et al.* v. *Twentieth Century-Fox Film Corporation, RKO-Stanley Warner Theatres Inc. and Mann Theatres Corporation of California,*[129] the plaintiff charged among other points that the defendants "have combined, conspired and agreed that Fox would not offer licenses to the New York plaintiffs for first-run feature length motion pictures distributed by Fox on a picture by picture, theater by theater basis solely on the merits and without discrimination, but rather that Fox would arbitrarily license such pictures to theaters operated by RKO, Mann and coconspirators in the New York Metropolitan Area." Similar conduct was alleged in the Milwaukee metropolitan area. UATC also charged that "Fox agreed to unconditionally guarantee repayment of the principal and interest on the indebtedness incurred by RKO to the [First National] Bank [of Boston] under [a] Credit Agreement" that allowed RKO to renovate and construct theaters. "Fox agreed to give RKO preferential license terms and conditions for Fox-distributed first-run feature length motion pictures exhibited at the RKO theaters to enable

RKO to repay the indebtedness to the Bank under the Credit Agreement and to limit Fox's exposure under its guarantee of such indebtedness." This case was settled out of court.

In *National Amusements Inc.* v. *Columbia Pictures Industries Inc. and ITC Entertainment,*[130] the plaintiff declared that "Columbia has combined, contracted and conspired . . . with the competitors of National in cities throughout the United States in which National owns and operates theaters, to restrain the trade of National and to limit and to exclude National in and from the right to compete in the licensing and exhibition of motion pictures."

In *Balmoral Cinema Inc.* v. *Allied Artists Pictures Corporation et al.,*[131] defendant distribution and exhibition companies were said to be part of a "national conspiracy" to restrain trade and competition in the film business. Members and employees of the Motion Picture Association of America and the law firm of Sargoy, Stein & Hanft were identified as coconspirators.

The issues raised, and the defendants identified, in the *Balmoral* case were so similar to those in other private suits around the nation that in April 1979 a Judicial Panel on Multi District Litigation consolidated eight such actions and assigned them to federal district court in Houston. Subsequently, the judge refused to add 10 or so other cases to those already consolidated, and denied a motion to make the case a class action suit on behalf of a broad group of exhibitors.

DISCUSSION

The film world is a business world and companies' similarity of interest is considerably more profound than mere market concentration data would indicate. The pinnacles of the various pyramids of concentration are linked to the country's centers of financial power, as even rudimentary data reveal. Within this context, it is somewhat myopic to debate ease of entry because entrance is only a ritualistic fig leaf confirming oligopolistic control. Access to a film camera can make one a director, and a bit of capital can make one a producer as well. But those resources yield about as much power to the individual as that enjoyed by the owner of a mimeograph machine when confronting Time Inc. or the Gannett newspaper chain. In broadcasting and cable, there are formal barriers to entry—the license and the franchise—which more and more are construed as perpetual rather than temporary grants. Neither exists in the film industry. Anyone with capital can rent a hall, install a screen, a projector, some seats, call it a theater, and request distributors to send bid invitation letters and announcements of availabilities. Although this is part of the American myth, realities demonstrate that the business does not operate like that, as suits throughout the industry's history have argued and current ones seek to prove.

Meanwhile, the emerging pattern of the 1980s shows new markets for films, such as pay TV, are extensions of older ones because they are shaped and fed by the same few companies that already dominate film and broadcasting. Although the precise extent to which the film and video fields are blending is debatable, a principal matter for attention is that major stakes in the new fields already have been claimed by already preeminent media giants, who now are left to scramble among themselves for maximum control. Not surprisingly, the new fields have been defined by, and absorbed completely into, the private system. Thus, they are not just additional outlets for the same, old products, but more importantly, extensions of the entire marketing structure that has given all communication a commodity status.

Market concentration and anti-competitive behavior are not unique to the motion picture business, although its history demonstrates how those conditions have characterized the industry. The difficulty exists in the inherent features of the private enterprise system, of which the film industry is only one part. After all, no economic law makes the competitive process automatically self-perpetuating, especially in industries of great capital requirements. If anything, there is a compelling propensity toward oligopoly and oligopsony. But even if extensive competition did exist, it would not resolve the more fundamental question of whether profit-motivated private ownership is the most suitable way of meeting people's needs. Failing to deal systematically with that basic issue means the problem is defined according to the narrow dichotomy between monopoly capitalism and competitive capitalism. In reality, the choice reduces itself, not to monopoly or competition, but to monopoly, shared monopoly, or oligopoly. When that happens, rationalizations and legitimations appear that either excuse monopoly or invent competition where it does not exist.

The job of antitrust laws and enforcement is to maintain and encourage competitive market structure and conduct, and this is supposed to insure that private enterprise performs in an acceptable manner. On this basis, the theory of antitrust is not an adversary of the institution of business; to the contrary, it seeks, against an evident tide, to make capitalism perform according to the principles of competition in an idealized world. Although symbolic progress toward that goal can be made sporadically, such action is a palliative at best, and a placebo at worst. The problem of concentration in the film industry cannot be separated from the entire economic system. Because the problem refuses to go away, and a general structural change in the entire economic system is not being contemplated in those places where decisions are made, relatively limited solutions are sought. Antitrust is one, of course; magic technology is another. Antitrust enforcement, even if vigorously pursued, cannot be expected to have more than limited impact, and certainly is not a cure.

However, the response need not—and should not—be thought of as government control of the industry within the present context of society. That becomes the red herring to justify maintaining things as they are. Other alternatives, among them democratic public trusts and worker control, need to be explored, as they have been in other countries. But a change of this magnitude could not be isolated in the film industry, for it really demands a complete remodeling of our economic system away from capitalism and its ideology, and an upheaval of the class structure associated with that system. Because this prospect has great political and cultural, as well as the obvious economic, implications, it is resisted on all fronts by owners and supporters of the present system. Whatever their opinions about the efficacy of the antitrust program, the dangers or benefits of concentration of ownership and market power, and the impact of trade practices, they take for granted the capitalist basis of the industry. Consequently, the bulk of debate is not about alternatives to capitalist ownership, nor even about how to change monopoly tendencies within capitalism, but about how to manage them while preserving the system as a whole. As this appears to be the acceptable arena for debate, discussions about media ownership necessarily will remain on the technical level, which is where the owners would undoubtedly like to keep them.

NOTES

1. Michael Conant, *Antitrust in the Motion Picture Industry* (Berkeley: University of California Press, 1960), p. 19.

2. Temporary National Economic Committee, *Investigation of Concentration of Economic Power;* Monograph 43, "The Motion Picture Industry—A Pattern of Control" (Washington: Government Printing Office, 1941), p. 6.

3. The concept of media imperialism has been discussed by several writers. See, for example, Herbert Schiller, *Mass Communications and American Empire* (New York: Augustus M. Kelley, 1969); Herbert Schiller, *Communication and Cultural Domination* (White Plains: M.E. Sharpe, Inc., 1976); Cees Hamelink (editor), *The Corporate Village* (Rome: International Documentation and Communication Centre, 1977); Armand Mattelart, *Multinationales et Systèmes de Communication* (Paris: Editions Anthropos, 1976).

4. Conant, p. 84.

5. *United States* v. *Paramount Pictures,* 334 U.S. 131, 142, 161.

6. *Motion-Picture Films (Compulsory Block Booking and Blind Selling),* hearings before the Committee on Interstate and Foreign Commerce, U.S. House of Representatives, 76th Congress, 3rd Session (Washington: Government Printing Office, 1940).

7. Temporary National Economic Committee, p. ix.

8. Ibid., p. 56.

9. *Motion Picture Distribution Trade Practices,* hearings before a subcommittee of the Select Committee on Small Business, U.S. Senate, 83rd Congress, 1st Session (Washington: Government Printing Office, 1953); and *Motion-Picture Distribution Trade Practices—1956,* hearings before a subcommittee of the Select Committee on Small Business, U.S. Senate, 84th Congress, 2nd Session (Washington: Government Printing Office, 1956).

10. *Problems of Independent Motion-Picture Exhibitors,* report of the Select Committee on Small Business, U.S. Senate, 83rd Congress, 1st Session, August 3, 1953 (Washington: Government Printing Office, 1953), p. 18.

11. *Motion-Picture Distribution Trade Practices–1956,* report of the Select Committee on Small Business, U.S. Senate, 84th Congress, 2nd Session, July 27, 1956 (Washington: Government Printing Office, 1956), p. 54.

12. Paramount Pictures Inc., et al. Consent Judgments and Decrees Investigation. Report of the Federal Trade Commission, February 25, 1965.

13. *Impact of Imports and Exports on Employment, Part 8,* hearings before the Subcommittee on the Impact of Imports and Exports on American Employment, Committee on Education and Labor, U.S. House of Representatives, 87th Congress, 1st and 2nd Sessions (Washington: Government Printing Office, 1962).

14. *Unemployment Problems in American Film Industry,* hearings before the General Subcommittee on Labor, Committee on Education and Labor, U.S. House of Representatives, 92nd Congress, 1st Session (Washington: Government Printing Office, 1972).

15. *Tax Reform Act of 1975,* hearings before the Committee on Finance, U.S. Senate, 94th Congress, 2nd Session (Washington: Government Printing Office, 1976).

16. *Communications–Pay Cable Television Industry,* hearings before the Subcommittee on Antitrust and Monopoly, Committee on the Judiciary, U.S. Senate, 94th Congress, 1st Session (Washington: Government Printing Office, 1975); and *Cable Television Regulation Oversight, Parts 1 and 2,* hearings before the Subcommittee on Communications, Committee on Interstate and Foreign Commerce, U.S. House of Representatives, 94th

Congress, 2nd Session (Washington: Government Printing Office, 1977).

17. For example, see *Overseas Information Programs of the United States, Part 2,* hearings before a subcommittee of the Committee on Foreign Relations, U.S. Senate, 83rd Congress, 1st Session (Washington: Government Printing Office, 1953).

18. *U.S. Informational Media Guaranty Program,* hearings before the Committee on Foreign Relations, U.S. Senate, 90th Congress, 1st Session (Washington: Government Printing Office, 1967). The Informational Media Guaranty Program was established in 1948 as part of the Economic Cooperation Administration. The program allowed the U.S. government to buy for dollars (at attractive rates) certain foreign currencies earned abroad by American private media businesses, provided that the information materials earning the money reflected the best elements of American life. Print and films were eligible under IMG's provisions. The total cost of the program, from its inception until early 1967, was $37 million. Of this amount, American film companies received close to $16 million.

19. *International Communications and Information,* hearings before the Subcommittee on International Operations, Committee on Foreign Relations, U.S. Senate, 95th Congress, 1st Session (Washington: Government Printing Office, 1977).

20. Federal Trade Commission, *Webb-Pomerene Associations: A 50-Year Review* (Washington: Government Printing Office, 1967), pp. 34, 59.

21. *International Aspects of Antitrust, 1967,* hearings before the Subcommittee on Antitrust and Monopoly, Committee on the Judiciary, U.S. Senate, 90th Congress, 1st Session (Washington: Government Printing Office, 1967).

22. Federal Trade Commission, *Webb-Pomerene Associations: Ten Years Later* (Washington: Government Printing Office, November 1978).

23. *Consent Decree Program of the Department of Justice,* report of the Antitrust Subcommittee (Subcommittee No. 5), Committee on the Judiciary, U.S. House of Representatives, 86th Congress, 1st Session (Washington: Government Printing Office, 1959).

24. *Economic Concentration, Parts 1 to 8,* hearings before the Subcommittee on Antitrust and Monopoly, Committee on the Judiciary, U.S. Senate, 88th Congress, 2nd Session to 91st Congress, 2nd Session (Washington: Government Printing Office, 1964-1970).

25. *Multinational Corporations,* hearings before the Subcommittee on International Trade, Committee on Finance, U.S. Senate, 93rd Congress, 1st Session (Washington: Government Printing Office, 1973).

26. *Investigation of Conglomerate Corporations, Parts 1 to 4,* hearings before the Antitrust Subcommittee (Subcommittee No. 5), Committee on the Judiciary, U.S. House of Representatives, 91st Congress (Washington:

Government Printing Office, 1970); and *Investigation of Conglomerate Corporations,* report by the staff of the Antitrust Subcommittee (Subcommittee No. 5), Committee on the Judiciary, U.S. House of Representatives, 92nd Congress, 1st Session (Washington: Government Printing Office, 1971).

27. Federal Trade Commission, Bureau of Competition, *Proceedings of the Symposium on Media Concentration,* December 14 and 15, 1978 (Washington: Government Printing Office, 1979).

28. *Media Concentration, Parts 1 and 2,* hearings before the Subcommittee on General Oversight and Minority Enterprise, Committee on Small Business, U.S. House of Representatives, 96th Congress, 2nd Session (Washington: Government Printing Office, 1980).

29. *Disclosure of Corporate Ownership,* prepared by the Subcommittee on Intergovernmental Relations and the Subcommittee on Budgeting, Management and Expenditures, Committee on Government Operations, U.S. Senate, 93rd Congress, 1st Session (Washington: Government Printing Office, 1973); *Corporate Ownership and Control,* prepared by the Subcommittee on Reports, Accounting and Management, Committee on Government Operations, U.S. Senate, 94th Congress, 2nd Session (G.P.O., 1976); *Institutional Investors' Common Stock,* prepared by the Subcommittee on Reports, Accounting and Management, Committee on Government Operations, U.S. Senate, 94th Congress, 2nd Session (G.P.O., 1976); *Interlocking Directorates Among the Major U.S. Corporations,* a staff study prepared by the Subcommittee on Reports, Accounting and Management, Committee on Governmental Affairs, U.S. Senate, 95th Congress, 2nd Session (G.P.O., 1978); *Voting Rights in Major Corporations,* a staff study prepared by the Subcommittee on Reports, Accounting and Management, Committee on Governmental Affairs, U.S. Senate, 95th Congress, 1st Session (G.P.O., 1978); *Structure of Corporate Concentration,* 2 volumes, a staff study, Committee on Governmental Affairs, 96th Congress, 2nd Session (G.P.O., 1980).

30. *Self-Policing of the Movie and Publishing Industry,* hearings before the Subcommittee on Postal Operations, Committee on Post Office and Civil Service, U.S. House of Representatives, 86th Congress, 2nd Session (Washington: Government Printing Office, 1960).

31. *Movie Ratings and the Independent Producer,* hearings before the Subcommittee on Special Small Business Problems, Committee on Small Business, U.S. House of Representatives, 95th Congress, 1st Session (Washington: Government Printing Office, 1977); and *Movie Ratings and the Independent Producer,* report of the Subcommittee on Special Small Business Problems, Committee on Small Business, U.S. House of Representatives, 95th Congress, 2nd Session (Washington: Government Printing Office, 1978).

32. Joseph P. Kennedy, ed., *The Story of the Films* (Chicago: A.W. Shaw Co., 1927), p. 6.

33. *Official Report of the Eighth National Foreign Trade Convention,* Cleveland, OH, May 4-7, 1921 (New York: National Foreign Trade Council, 1921), pp. 160, 165.

34. William Seabury, *The Public and the Motion Picture Industry* (New York: The MacMillan Company, 1926) and William Seabury, *Motion Picture Problems—The Cinema and the League of Nations* (New York: The Avondale Press, Inc., 1929).

35. Benjamin B. Hampton, *History of the American Film Industry* (New York: Dover Publications, Inc., 1970), previously published as *A History of the Movies* (New York: Covici, Friede, 1931).

36. Howard T. Lewis, *The Motion Picture Industry* (New York: Van Nostrand Co., 1933).

37. Frank Ricketson, Jr., *The Management of Motion Picture Theatres* (New York: McGraw-Hill Book Co., Inc., 1938).

38. Raymond Moley, *The Hays Office* (New York: The Bobbs-Merrill Co., 1945).

39. Mae D. Huettig, *Economic Control of the Motion Picture Industry* (Philadelphia: University of Pennsylvania Press, 1944).

40. Huettig, p. 143.

41. Ibid., pp. 149-150.

42. Conant, p. 220. See also Robert W. Crandall, "The Postwar Performance of the Motion-Picture Industry," *The Antitrust Bulletin,* 20:1, Spring 1975.

43. *Analysis and Conclusions of the Washington Task Force on the Motion Picture Industry* [1978], p. 15. According to the *Wall Street Journal* (June 9, 1978), the Washington Task Force consisted of John Larmett, an aide to Senator Gaylord Nelson; Frederic Schwartz Jr., an attorney; and Elias Savaba, director of the Motion Picture Information Service, which collects film industry data. In correspondence with me, Mr. Larmett said "It was not the intention of the Task Force to come up with anything new or startling but merely to put in a comprehensive analysis information that had been previously written and talked about before within the film industry."

44. David Waterman, *Economic Essays on the Theatrical Motion Picture Industry,* Ph.D. dissertation, Stanford University, 1978, p. 8.

45. Janet Wasko, *Movies and Money: Financing the American Film Industry* (Norwood, NJ, Ablex Publishing Corporation, in press).

46. Thomas H. Guback, *The International Film Industry* (Bloomington: Indiana University Press, 1969).

47. F.D. Klingender and Stuart Legg, *Money Behind the Screen* (London: Lawrence and Wishart, 1937).

48. Peter Bächlin, *Der Film als Ware* (Basel: Burg Verlag, 1947); also published with very slight changes as *Histoire Economique du Cinéma* (Paris: La Nouvelle Edition, 1947). See also Georg Schmidt, Werner Schmalenbach and Peter Bächlin, *The Film–Its Economic, Social and Artistic Problems* (London: The Falcon Press, 1948).

49. Henri Mercillon, *Cinéma et Monopoles* (Paris: Librarie Armand Colin, 1953).

50. Jean-Claude Batz, *A Propos de la Crise de l'Industrie du Cinéma* (Bruxelles: Université Libre de Bruxelles, 1963).

51. Claude Degand, *Le Cinéma, Cette Industrie* (Paris: Editions Techniques et Economiques, 1972).

52. René Bonnell, *Le Cinéma Exploité* (Paris: Editions du Seuil, 1978).

53. *Cinema and the State,* report of the Committee on Culture and Education, Lisbon symposium, June 14-16, 1978; Strasbourg, Council of Europe, 1979, p. xi.

54. Nicholas Garnham, *The Economics of the U.S. Motion Picture Industry,* Commission of the European Communities, 1980.

55. Philippe Pochet and Jean-Yves Pitoun, *Les Films Francais aux États-Unis,* Consulate of France, Los Angeles [1978], p. 2.

56. Political and Economic Planning, *The British Film Industry* (London: P.E.P., 1952), and *The British Film Industry 1958,* 24:424, June 1958.

57. John Spraos, *The Decline of the Cinema* (London: George Allen and Unwin Ltd., 1962).

58. Terence Kelly, *A Competitive Cinema* (London: Institute of Economic Affairs, 1966).

59. *Films, A Report on the Supply of Films for Exhibition in Cinemas,* The Monopolies Commission (London: Her Majesty's Stationery Office, 1966).

60. Association of Cinematograph, Television and Allied Technicians, *Nationalising the Film Industry* (London: ACTT, 1973).

61. *Future of the British Film Industry,* report of the Prime Minister's Working Party (London: Her Majesty's Stationery Office, 1976).

62. Georg Roeber and Gerhard Jacoby, *Handbuch der Filmwirtschaftlichen Medienbereiche* (Pullach bei München: Verlag Dokumentation, 1973).

63. Enrico Giannelli, *Economia Cinematografica* (Rome: Reanda Editore, 1956).

64. Pierre Berton, *Hollywood's Canada, The Americanization of our National Image* (Toronto: McClelland and Stewart Ltd., 1975).

65. Manjunath Pendakur, *Canadian Feature Film Industry: Monopoly and Competition,* Ph.D. dissertation, Simon Fraser University, 1979.

66. *Mutual Film Corp.* v. *Ohio,* 236 U.S. 230.

67. *Burstyn* v. *Wilson,* 343, U.S. 495.

68. For example, see Judith Adler Hennessee, "Gross Behavior: How to Get Your Percentage Back," *Action,* 2:4, January-February 1978.

69. Jack Valenti, president, Motion Picture Association of America, quoted in *Variety,* September 6, 1978.

70. Twentieth Century-Fox Film Corp., 1978 First Quarter Report and 1978 Second Quarter Report.

71. *Boxoffice,* May 5, 1980.

72. Walt Disney Productions, Third Quarter Report, June 30, 1980.

73. Presentation to the Seventh Annual Entertainment Seminar, March 17, 1981.

74. *Hollywood Reporter,* May 26, 1981.

75. *Boxoffice,* June 1981.

76. *Greenbrier Cinemas Inc.* v. *Attorney General of the United States et al.,* U.S. District Court for the Western District of Virginia, Charlottesville Division, Civil Action No. 77-0035 (C), *Motion for Reconsideration,* p. 2, April 13, 1981.

77. As one example, on September 30, 1975, Warner Bros. Distributing Corp. announced it was accepting bids no later than October 9, 1975 for the April 9, 1976 release in Washington, DC of *All the President's Men.* Naturally, this was a blind bid. Warner's suggested terms included a minimum of 12 weeks playtime, a guarantee of $175,000 payable no later than seven days prior to opening, an advance of $175,000 and rental terms of 90%/10% over house expenses versus 70% of the gross for the first three weeks, sliding to 40% for the last three weeks. Warner proposed a run in a maximum of four theaters, and therefore sought to have guaranteed at least $700,000 in rentals from Washington, DC alone.

78. *Superman II* (Warner) 1408 screens; *For Your Eyes Only* (United Artists) 1086 screens; *Stripes* (Columbia) 1077 screens; *Raiders of the Lost Ark* (Paramount) 1078 screens; *The Great Muppet Caper* (Universal) 680 screens; *Cannonball Run* (Twentieth Century-Fox) 1692 screens; *Clash of the Titans* (United Artists-MGM) 1140. *Hollywood Reporter,* June 30, 1981.

79. *Boxoffice,* June 1981.

80. *Hollywood Reporter,* June 11, 1981.

81. Jack Valenti, "The Challenge of Change," *Boxoffice,* March 1981.

82. *Variety,* December 6, 1978.

83. *Hollywood Reporter,* March 4, 1981.

84. *Variety,* May 17, 1978.

85. *Variety,* January 3, 1979.

86. *Hollywood Reporter,* May 15, 1980; *Variety,* January 14, 1981.

87. Aljean Harmetz, "Orion's Star Rises in Hollywood," *Warner World,* No. 2, 1978.

88. *Hollywood Reporter,* March 18, 1981.

89. Columbia Pictures Industries Inc., presentation to the New York Society of Security Analysts, February 14, 1978.

90. U.S. Department of Commerce, *U.S. Service Industries in World Markets,* December 1976, p. A-211.

91. U.S. Department of Commerce, *U.S. Industrial Outlook, 1981* (Washington: Government Printing Office, 1981), p. 531.

92. Bureau of Labor Statistics, *Employment and Earnings,* 25:10, October 1978.

93. Classification and Rating Administration, annual reports for years cited.

94. National Association of Theatre Owners, *1980 Encyclopedia of Exhibition,* and editions for previous years.

95. U.S. Department of Commerce, *U.S. Service Industries in World Markets,* December 1976, p. A-213.

96. Richard Albarino, *Variety,* January 8, 1975.

97. Metro-Goldwyn-Mayer Inc., preliminary prospectus, September 25, 1975.

98. American International Pictures used a table of production costs amortization based on the rate at which theatrical revenue is earned. The first 13 weeks of release contribute 49% of rentals, and the next 13 weeks, 26%. The rest of the first year yields another 13%. American International Pictures, Form 10-K Report for 1978.

99. U.S. Department of Commerce, Bureau of the Census, *1972 Census of Selected Service Industries, Motion Picture Industry* (Washington: Government Printing Office, 1975).

100. National Association of Theatre Owners, *1980 Encyclopedia of Exhibition.*

101. U.S. Department of Commerce, Bureau of the Census, *1972 Census . . .*

102. *Variety,* July 2, 1980.

103. Frank Rosenfelt, president, Metro-Goldwyn-Mayer, *The Hollywood Reporter,* January 8, 1979; and Jack Valenti, president, Motion Picture Association of America, *The Hollywood Reporter,* January 5, 1979.

104. *Variety,* February 15, 1978.

105. *Syufy Enterprises* v. *Columbia Pictures Industries Inc., et al.,* U.S. District Court for the District of Utah, Civil No. C-77-0181. *Supplemental Memorandum in Support of Motion for Preliminary Injunction,* p. 10.

106. *Syufy Enterprises* v. *Columbia Pictures . . . ,* p. 23.

107. *Syufy Enterprises* v. *Columbia Pictures Industries Inc., et al., Memorandum of Points and Authorities for Motion for Preliminary Injunction,* pp. 15, 20.

108. Several members of the Motion Picture Association of America filed suit in 1970 against ABC and CBS, charging the networks with monopoly and conspiracy to deprive plaintiffs of access to television markets. At that time, both networks were engaged in the production, distribution and exhibition (via television) of feature length motion pictures, and ABC also owned a circuit of motion pictures theaters. In 1972, the Department of Justice filed suits against ABC, CBS and NBC. The suits were refiled in 1974 after the original ones were dismissed without prejudice. The government suits charged that each of the networks had used and continued to use its control over access to network air time to restrain and to monopolize prime-time television entertainment programming. NBC agreed to a consent stipulation in 1976, but parts of it could not be put into effect until the other defendants approved, something which they declared they had no intention of doing. In 1978, a group of 20 independent film producers filed an antitrust suit against ABC, CBS and NBC alleging the networks and their owned and operated stations in New York City restrained trade and monopolized news and public affairs programming. The plaintiffs contended that the networks refused to purchase or broadcast independently produced news or public affairs programs.

109. Computations based upon data presented in *Broadcasting,* May 12, 1980.

110. See Thomas Guback and Dennis Dombkowski, "Television and Hollywood–Economic Relations in the 1970s," *Journal of Broadcasting,* Fall 1976, 20:4, and Thomas Guback, "Les Relations Cinéma-TV aux États-Unis Aujourd'hui," *Film Exchange,* No. 2, Spring 1978.

111. *Hollywood Reporter,* March 4, 1980.

112. Speech to Academy of Television Arts and Sciences, September 30, 1980.

113. *Hollywood Reporter,* July 2, 1981.

114. *Hollywood Reporter,* June 8, 1981.

115. Richard Smith, president and chief executive officer, General Cinema Corp., deposition, November 17, 1978; *Balmoral Cinema Inc.* v. *Allied Artists Pictures Corporation et al.,* U.S. District Court for the Western District of Tennessee, Civil No. 77-2101.

116. Norman Levy, president of distribution for Columbia Pictures, deposition, August 8, 1978; *Balmoral Cinema Inc.* v. *Allied Artists Pictures Corporation et al.* See also *The Hollywood Reporter,* January 4, 1979.

117. General Cinema Corp., presentation to New York [Society of Security] Analysts, October 29, 1980.

118. U.S. Department of Commerce, Bureau of the Census, *Concentration Ratios in Manufacturing, 1977 Census of Manufacturers* (Washington: Government Printing Office, 1981).

119. *Disclosure of Corporate Ownership,* prepared by the Subcommittee on Intergovernmental Relations and the Subcommittee on Budgeting, Management and Expenditures of the Committee on Government Operations, U.S. Senate, 93rd Congress, 1st Session (Washington: Government Printing Office, 1973), p. 9.

120. *Ibid.,* pp. 163-182.

121. *United States* v. *Twentieth Century-Fox Film Corporation,* U.S. District Court for the Southern District of New York, September 12, 1978. Fox was fined $25,000 and ordered to pay court costs of $18,171.67.

122. *United States* v. *Warner Bros. Pictures Inc.,* U.S. District Court for the Southern District of New York, Equity No. 87-273; consent order filed April 2, 1976.

123. *United States* v. *United Artists Theatre Circuit Inc.,* U.S. District Court for the Eastern District of New York, Civil No. 71-C-609; consent decree filed July 26, 1976.

124. *United States of America* v. *Tracinda Investment Corporation and Kirk Kerkorian,* U.S. District Court for the Central District of California, Civil Action No. 79-0174-AAH(SX), *Complaint,* January 15, 1979.

125. *United States of America* v. *Paramount Pictures Inc., et al.,* U.S. District Court for the Southern District of New York, Equity No. 87-273, *Memorandum Opinion,* August 28, 1980.

126. *United States of America* v. *Columbia Pictures Industries Inc., et al.,* U.S. District Court for the Southern District of New York, Civil Action No. 80-4438, *Complaint,* August 4, 1980.

127. *1980-1981 Trade Cases,* 63,698.

128. *Syufy Enterprises* v. *Columbia Pictures Industries Inc., et al., Memorandum of Points,* p. 29.

129. *United Artists Theatre Circuit Inc., et al.* v. *Twentieth Century-Fox Film Corporation, RKO-Stanley Warner Theatres Inc. and Mann Theatres Corporation of California,* U.S. District Court for the Southern District of New York, Civil No. 77-3489, *Complaint.*

130. *National Amusements Inc.* v. *Columbia Pictures Industries Inc. and ITC Entertainment, an ATV Company,* U.S. District Court for the District of Massachusetts, Civil No. 77-155-5, *Complaint.*

131. *Balmoral Cinema Inc.* v. *Allied Artists Pictures Corporation et al.,* U.S. District Court for the Western District of Tennessee, Civil No. 77-2101, *Complaint.*

Appendix 5.1

Revenue and Income of Selected Publicly Owned Companies in the Motion Picture Industry*
(in millions)

Table 5.1(A): Allied Artists Industries Inc.[1]

| Fiscal Year | Revenue | Net Income | Motion Pictures | |
			Revenue	Operating Income
1978	$63.7	$4.2	$19.8	$1.8
1977	53.2	(2.1)	12.5	(2.7)
1976	55.8	(3.4)	17.4	(2.5)
1975[2]	11.7	(1.1)	11.1	N.A.
1974	23.4	1.3	23.0	N.A.
1973	15.3	1.5	14.6	N.A.
1972	8.3	.1	7.9	N.A.
1971	2.7	(3.3)	2.5	N.A.
1970	6.8	.05	6.6	N.A.

N.A.: Not available.

[1] Filed bankruptcy proceedings in April 1979.

[2] 39 weeks.

---

* Throughout this appendix, amounts in parentheses indicate losses.

Table 5.2(A): Avco Corporation

Fiscal Year	Revenue	Income	Avco-Embassy Pictures Corp.	
			Revenue	Net Income
1980	$2,150.0	$118.6	N.R.	N.R.
1979	1,932.2	132.3	N.R.	N.R.
1978	1,727.6	122.7	N.R.	N.R.
1977	1,537.9	116.6	$19.0	$(4.3)
1976	1,345.4	91.3	22.0	(3.9)
1975	1,268.5	50.2	17.1	(5.9)
1974	1,224.4	(27.5)	34.0	(5.2)
1973	1,164.9	(14.8)	27.3	(8.1)
1972	1,032.5	39.8	22.2	(2.9)
1971	1,053.8	44.7	27.3	(2.1)
1970	1,235.7	29.2	55.1[1]	.9[1]

N.R.: Not reported publicly.

[1] Motion pictures and broadcasting.

Table 5.3(A): Cablecom-General Inc.

Fiscal Year	Revenue	Net Income	Motion Picture Theaters		CATV	
			Revenue	Operating Income	Revenue	Operating Income
1980	$46.8	$6.3	$11.7	$1.2	$30.9	$10.7
1979	37.4	5.0	10.9	1.1	22.7	7.6
1978	33.6	4.6	12.1	1.9	18.3	6.6
1977	29.2	4.0	11.4	1.5	15.3	3.8
1976	26.1	3.0	10.0	1.2	13.7	2.8
1975	23.8	2.7	9.2	.8	13.0	2.5
1974	22.2	1.1	8.4	.8	12.8	.3
1973	20.2	(4.4)	7.5	.4	12.1	(.3)
1972	19.0	(1.1)	8.0	1.0	10.4	(1.4)
1971	17.4	1.1	8.5	1.3	8.2	.1
1970	15.2	1.1	8.9	1.3	6.3	.6

Table 5.4(A): Columbia Pictures Industries, Inc.

Fiscal Year	Revenue	Net Income	Filmed Entertainment Revenue	Operating Income	Feature Films Theater Revenue	Feature Films TV Revenue	TV Programs Revenue	Records and Music Revenue	Operating Income	Broadcasting Revenue	Operating Income	Amusement Games Revenue	Operating Income
1980	$691.8	$44.9	$599.3	$59.5	$341.6	$42.4	$148.7	[1]	[1]	$18.3[3]	$3.1[3]	$74.2	$15.7
1979	544.9	39.0	458.0	59.0	263.1	37.1	103.2	$76.7	$ .4	10.8	3.1	67.8	16.5
1978	574.6	68.8	437.0	80.2	269.0	25.3	95.0	73.5	3.6	12.2	3.2	51.9	12.2
1977	390.5	34.6	298.3	30.8	153.5	24.8	79.8	42.1	1.4	17.9	5.4	32.2	7.3
1976	332.1	11.5	272.1	28.3	152.2	19.3	67.8	35.4	1.1	24.6	5.5		
1975	325.9	10.5	278.0	33.2	170.3	30.8	53.5	24.1	.9	23.8	4.2		
1974	250.1	(2.3)	211.7	24.9	111.3	28.8	51.9	16.3	(.5)	22.1	4.4		
1973	205.4	(50.0)	164.5	(61.5)	101.5	11.5	33.1	20.2	3.3	20.7	4.0		
1972	223.5	(3.4)	182.2		110.0	34.4	37.8	17.8		15.7	1.9		
1971	222.6	(28.8)	176.0		113.0	16.6	46.4	18.0		12.9	1.3		
1970	242.1	(10.9)	196.6		137.9	20.5	38.2	45.4[2]					

[1] In September 1979, Columbia closed the sale of its record operations.

[2] Includes records, music, broadcasting and other.

[3] Broadcasting and other.

Table 5.5(A): Commonwealth Theatres, Inc.

Fiscal Year	Revenue	Net Income	Theater Operation
1980	$73.2	$2.8	$69.9
1979	63.7	2.6	61.8
1978	50.0	1.9	48.3
1977	33.9	1.6	32.1
1976	30.1	1.4	28.2
1975	28.3	1.4	26.7
1974	24.4	1.0	22.8
1973	22.2	1.0	21.0
1972	20.4	.9	19.2
1971	20.2	1.0	18.4
1970	19.1	.9	18.1

Table 5.6(A): Filmways, Inc.[1]

Fiscal Year	Revenue	Net Income	Entertainment and Entertainment Services		Publishing	
			Revenue	Operating Income	Revenue	Operating Income
1980	$168.6	$1.6	$106.5	$14.5	$ 36.0	$(8.2)
1979	153.4	7.8	28.1	1.7	113.7	1.1
1978	140.6	3.5	33.6	4.3	100.6	2.9
1977	125.3	2.7	26.7	6.3	92.4	3.0
1976	100.9	2.2	21.6	4.9	74.0	2.5
1975[2]	50.3	1.0	14.0	2.2	33.6	1.5
1974[3]	70.8	1.5	22.9	4.2	42.8	.7
1973	54.8	1.1	16.4	2.9	34.0	.9
1972	54.2	(2.9)	19.8	.4	30.5	(2.6)

[1] Acquired American International Pictures in July 1979.

[2] Six months ended February 28, 1975.

[3] Year ended August 31, 1974.

Table 5.7(A): General Cinema Corporation

Fiscal Year	Revenue	Net Income	Theater Division		Beverages		TV Broadcasting and Other	
			Revenue	Operating Income	Revenue	Operating Income	Revenue	Operating Income
1980	$759.4	$29.9	$307.8	$27.5	$434.0	$42.3	$20.8	$4.1
1979	656.1	26.5	266.5	27.7	374.5	35.3	17.5	3.2
1978	594.9	24.2	266.4	25.9	315.2	38.7	13.3	3.1
1977	465.1	20.2	213.8	14.3	240.4	31.2	10.9	2.3
1976	365.3	17.1	168.4	13.4	188.9	23.4	8.0	1.9
1975	358.4	14.9	180.0	18.4	178.4	18.0		
1974	299.5	11.1	142.9	15.1	156.6	13.1		
1973	244.9	9.4	177.1	14.4	127.8	9.0		
1972	220.0	10.3	99.6	13.7	120.4	8.9		
1971	195.0	9.2	80.2	12.1	114.8	9.2		
1970	178.9	7.0	70.1	11.1	108.7	7.6		

Table 5.8(A): Gulf + Western Industries, Inc.

| Fiscal Year | Revenue | Net Income | Leisure Time Group[1] | | Theatrical Motion Pictures | Series and Films for TV | Theater Operation | Book Publishing |
			Revenue	Operating Income				
1980	$5,338.5	$255.3	$1,041.6	$100.1	$330	$224	$122	$127
1979	4,842.9	227.4	957.9	110.5	427	124	113	99
1978	4,419.1	180.5	802.0	84.1	287	97	103	86
1977	3,709.8	150.3	440.0	35.6	150	82	102	72
1976	3,442.2	190.1	427.0	44.9	152	65	103	71
1975	2,640.8	134.1	344.0	21.2	165	62	91	2
1974	2,321.2	101.9	275.0	25.5	103	63	78	
1973	1,971.9	89.2	277.0	38.7	120	50	66	
1972	1,723.1	69.4	291.0	31.2	142	43	65	
1971	1,620.6	55.6	279.0	20.1	139	44	64	
1970	1,671.4	44.8	241.0	2.0	101	54	55	

[1] Includes Paramount Pictures Corporation.

[2] 1976 was the first full year for which Gulf + Western had publishing operations; therefore no figures exist for this segment prior to 1976.

Table 5.9(A): MCA, Inc.

Fiscal Year	Revenue	Net Income	Filmed Entertainment[1]				Records and Music Publishing
			Revenue	Operating Income	Theaters	TV	
1980	$1,297.1	$137.6	$767.7	$133.9	$397.7	$285.1	$184.9
1979	1,266.1	178.7	781.5	174.3	305.1	410.9	164.0
1978	1,120.6	128.4	724.4	159.8	318.7	348.2	131.5
1977	877.6	95.1	561.4	107.4	222.8	289.4	99.8
1976	802.9	90.2	506.9	100.6	213.4	249.7	112.4
1975	811.5	95.5	509.9	124.0	289.1	189.6	137.9
1974	663.2	59.2	387.5	68.0	205.1	158.5	126.7
1973	437.4	27.1	227.7	20.2	87.5	119.9	86.8
1972	345.9	20.9	204.6	19.9	61.9	127.3	61.4
1971	333.7	16.7	194.6	15.1	57.8	124.2	45.8
1970	333.5	13.3	220.0	32.4	96.7	110.0	36.0

[1] Includes Studio Tours, Amphitheatre and other, as well as Universal.

Table 5.10(A): Metro-Goldwyn-Mayer, Inc.[1]

Fiscal Year	Revenue	Net Income	Filmed Entertainment[2] Revenue	Feature Films	TV Programs
1980	$181.2	$16.5	$138.4	$ 98.8	$39.6
1979	193.0	29.4	160.1	126.4	33.7
1978	401.4	49.3	155.0	110.7	43.8
1977	288.5	33.2	114.7	85.8	28.4
1976	266.6	35.6	123.3	77.2	27.8
1975	255.5	31.9	117.6	83.2	17.5
1974	234.4	26.8	145.8	111.1	20.7
1973	152.8	9.3	152.8	124.9	14.0
1972	148.2	10.7	148.2	120.4	13.7
1971	149.5	15.6	149.5[3]	136.1[2, 3]	13.4
1970	149.4	(13.6)	149.3[3]	130.8[3]	19.0

[1] Effective May 30, 1980, the operations of Metro-Goldwyn-Mayer, Inc. were divided into two separate publicly owned corporations: Metro-Goldwyn-Mayer Film Co. and MGM Grand Hotels, Inc.

[2] Includes revenue from film processing laboratory, prior to 1977.

[3] Presumably includes revenue from theater operation overseas.

Table 5.11(A): United Artists Theatre Circuit, Inc.

Fiscal Year	Revenue	Net Income	Theater Operation
1980	$227.1	$ 6.5	$223.5
1979	211.4	11.2	206.6
1978	181.8	6.3	178.1
1977	147.0	4.2	143.5
1976	120.3	4.1	116.5
1975	123.9	4.1	121.3
1974	106.5	4.1	104.6
1973	85.2	3.1	83.6
1972	80.2	2.6	79.1
1971	74.4	1.5	73.2
1970	76.9	2.4	75.2

Table 5.12(A): Transamerica Corporation

Fiscal Year	Revenue	Net Income	United Artists Corporation		Theatrical Revenue	TV Film Rentals	Records and Others
			Revenue	Operating Income			
1980	$4,384.1	$240.0	$424.8	$20.1	$296.1	$88.3	$ 23.2[2]
1979	4,044.6	238.8	468.9	26.6	376.3	57.0	24.3[2]
1978	3,526.5	208.3	416.8	28.8	288.1	76.0	25.4[2]
1977	3,210.0	169.1	474.1	26.6	318.5	59.7	92.7
1976	2,730.9	113.7	377.7	16.0	229.5	55.5	89.5
1975	2,404.7	73.8	319.7	11.5	187.4	29.6	98.7
1974	2,201.4	33.9	288.6	9.9	141.9	40.6[1]	102.0
1973	2,110.4	89.3	327.5	14.0	163.8	51.7	107.0
1972	1,936.6	88.1	317.2	10.8	152.7	50.6	111.6
1971	1,643.5	61.9	205.1	1.0	97.2	19.1	88.0
1970	1,483.9	42.6	211.0	(45.5)	118.0	18.4	74.6

[1] May include revenue from broadcasting station operation.
[2] Music publishing only.

Table 5.13(A): Twentieth Century-Fox Film Corporation

Fiscal Year	Revenue	Net Income	Filmed Entertainment		Feature Films	TV Programs	Theater Operation	Film Processing	Broad-casting	Records and Music Publishing
			Revenue	Operating Income						
1980	$865.2	$54.6	$581.9[1]	$55.2	N.R.	N.R.	$71.6	N.R.	$39.0	N.R.
1979	678.4	57.3	405.4	63.8	$316.4	$89.0	60.2	$17.9	34.7	$ 8.5
1978	625.9	58.4	408.0	91.1	346.6	61.4	52.1	21.1	31.8	13.8
1977	506.8	50.8	369.4	69.7	321.5	48.0	37.9	30.7	25.7	22.7
1976	355.0	10.7	254.8	17.1	217.2	37.7	34.3	29.7	22.6	9.9
1975	342.7	22.7	242.1	28.9	210.8	31.3	44.3	26.3	9.9	17.9
1974	280.1	11.0	186.7	12.9	159.7	27.0	43.1	23.9	7.0	16.1
1973	250.4	10.7	180.0	12.1	152.6	27.4	34.6	20.0	6.6	7.7
1972	198.7	7.8	144.7	8.1	118.8	25.9	25.4	20.2	5.8	2.1
1971	222.5	9.7	171.5	12.4	143.2	28.3	20.8	23.2	5.0	2.0
1970	246.5	(80.4)	195.0	(77.2)	159.3	35.7	19.2	24.1	5.1	2.1

N.R.: Not reported publicly.

[1] Includes production and distribution for theaters and television, processing of motion picture film, production of phonograph records and tapes, marketing of music, as well as the manufacture and sale of prerecorded video cassettes.

Table 5.14(A): Walt Disney Productions

| Fiscal Year | Revenue | Net Income | Motion Picture and Television Distribution | | Theaters | | TV | Records and Music | Publications | Educational Media |
			Revenue	Operating Income	Domestic	Foreign				
1980	$914.5	$135.2	$161.4	$48.7	$63.4	$78.3	$19.7	$23.4	$22.3	$32.5
1979	796.8	113.8	134.8	40.2	49.6	57.3	27.9	16.1	19.0	29.2
1978	741.1	98.4	152.1	54.1	69.0	57.9	25.2	17.2	15.0	24.8
1977	629.8	81.9	118.1	50.4	58.7	36.6	22.7	13.9	12.9	20.7
1976	583.9	74.6	119.1	57.9	60.5	39.8	18.8	12.2	11.1	17.7
1975	520.0	61.7	112.5	56.6	61.2	37.6	13.7	10.2	9.9	15.8
1974	429.9	48.5	90.4	45.8	48.6	29.9	11.9	15.2	8.6	12.5
1973	385.1	48.0	76.2	36.0	40.2	26.3	9.6	13.7	8.4	8.6
1972	329.4	40.3	70.8	35.7	35.5	26.2	9.1	10.8	5.0	7.5
1971	174.6	26.9	65.1	26.8	35.4	21.6	8.0	8.5	5.2	6.5
1970	167.1	21.8	63.3		33.9	22.0	7.4	7.0	4.0	5.4

Table 5.15(A): Warner Communications Inc.

Fiscal Year	Revenue	Net Income	Filmed Entertainment		Feature Films			Recorded Music and Music Publishing	Publishing	CATV
			Revenue	Operating Income	Theatrical Revenue	TV Revenue	TV Series			
1980	$2,059.4	$137.1	$668.9	$ 60.8	$369.6	$142.7	$156.6	$805.7	$72.0	[2]
1979	1,648.0	200.7	609.7	117.6	433.7	62.7	113.3	725.3	74.9	$81.3
1978	1,243.1	87.4	393.0	79.9	261.3	59.5	72.2	617.1	55.1	66.3
1977	1,143.8	66.9	353.0	58.0	253.6	39.6	60.0	532.4	52.2	55.7
1976	826.8	57.5	285.2	42.2	221.6	42.5	21.0	406.1	48.4	51.6
1975	669.8	46.6	255.9	41.7	202.3	27.3	26.3	313.8	62.0	38.1
1974	720.1	42.9	319.0	57.7	275.5	18.9	24.6	291.7	78.7	30.8
1973	549.6	43.1	209.5	31.1	152.7	24.9	31.9	236.0	76.7	27.5
1972	498.6	43.1	193.4	22.7	144.3	17.7	31.4	214.5	66.5	24.3
1971	377.1	34.2	124.3	14.8	86.3	20.2	17.8	170.9	61.2	20.7
1970	304.2	33.6	114.9	6.8	64.2		50.7[1]	115.8	48.6	15.8

[1] Includes revenue from distribution to television of feature films.

[2] In December 1979, Warner sold 50% of its cable television operations to American Express Company. Revenues of Warner Amex Cable are not reported publicly.

6

Television and Radio Broadcasting

by Christopher H. Sterling

INTRODUCTION

In the coming decade, the American broadcasting business will change more dramatically than at any time in its long past. The advent of various alternative and competing delivery technologies, especially after 1985, promises to change the structure and operations of radio and especially television. The chapter that follows must thus be viewed to some extent as a review of trends and ownership policy in the broadcasting industry before any impact made by these new technologies could be felt. Much of what is detailed here is likely to be swept away either by conscious policy decisions on the part of government and business, or simply in the aftermath of increasingly rapid technological change.

This chapter explores the two traditional controversies in the concentration of radio and television broadcasting: ownership of individual stations, and the more generalized dominance of the industry for more than half a century by centralized networks. Information is provided first on the development of concentration patterns followed by a review of government regulatory moves and industry countermeasures. The discussion should serve as an introductory primer to the issues of, trends in and literature about broadcast ownership concentration. It does not take sides or espouse specific points of view. As few trends or controversies in broadcasting are totally new, the approach here is historical.[1] An understanding of past trends and regulations is essential to an assessment of current problem areas and points of view.

Following a short overview of broadcasting's structural and financial history is a discussion of the rationale for regulation—the major areas cited over the years as requiring government regulatory action in order to control concentration trends in broadcasting. The bulk of the chapter then reviews available descriptive and research information on ownership of individual stations including entry into broadcasting, duopoly, various kinds of multiple ownership of stations, newspaper-broadcast cross-ownership, public broadcast station ownership, and the evidence on the effects of station ownership, as well as the issues raised by centralized networking such as affiliate relations, programming practices and sale of advertising time. The chapter concludes with a brief discussion and commentary.

As the subject matter dealt with here is complex and is substantially documented in recent literature, several topics are either not dealt with at all, or only in passing. These include the effects television advertising discounts may have on concentration in other industries,[2] most specific licensing or diversification of ownership case decisions and control of cable television (the latter covered in Chapter 4). Because broadcasting has been subject to far more regulation than other media in this book, this chapter must focus on these developments. In all, this is an overview of what we know now, what we still need to know and some of the policy options taken or being considered to deal with the problem of industry concentration.

DEVELOPMENT OF BROADCASTING

A brief background of highlights of the development of AM broadcasting, and (after World War II) of both FM and television is included here. Economic and structural matters, including allocation decisions, are emphasized for they are important to an understanding of the ownership trends and policies detailed later.

Radio to 1927: The Formative Years

For most of this initial period, radio combined a relatively new distribution technology with old content (vaudeville, talks, a little drama and less news). Initially seen as a fad or experimenter's toy, broadcasting after 1923 began to show signs of being a lasting business as the concepts of local stations, some kind of network interconnection and advertiser support all developed on parallel paths. Radio was operated as a secondary occupation at best—it was a sideline to another line of business. Electrical and radio manufacturers and dealers, who early in 1923 controlled nearly 40% of the country's 576 stations, operated broadcast outlets as a means of providing entertainment to attract listeners—and thus purchasers of receivers. Educational institutions (72 stations, or about 13% of the 1923 total) flirted with the exciting notion of radio as an extension of the classroom—but educational broadcasting was in decline long before the Depression as costs mounted and results appeared inconclusive. Newspapers and other publishers (69 stations, or 12%) built or bought radio stations out of fear (a new competitor for their audience), prestige (first into a new service), or community-mindedness (the duty of a local paper to boost services to the coverage area). Department stores (5%) sought sale of receivers, or just general advertising of their name by association with a station. Likewise, car and motorcycle dealers (3%), music and jewelry stores (2%) and hardware stores (1%) sought the "advertising" value of radio identification as well as some indirect sales.[3] All shared in common the operation of radio for some reason other than broadcasting itself—i.e., to "sell" an image, a service, or a name in what amounted to a direct forerunner of advertising as we know it now.

Radio advertising grew very slowly at first, due partially to strong official concern over such use of the new medium,[4] and partially to a genuine search by many in the industry for other means of support such as subsidies from the wealthy, donations from the public and the like.[5] By the late 1920s, advertising (then akin to what would today be termed "institutional advertising" with little mention of price or hard-sell techniques) was almost reluctantly accepted as the best approach to resolving the ever-increasing technical and programming costs of an increasingly organized and popular industry. As radio's audience grew, the interest of potential advertisers followed until the pattern typical today was already at work in the larger stations, i.e., programming was used to attract listeners who were then "sold" to advertisers. The need to appeal to advertiser demands became increasingly paramount in broadcast station operation.

One reason for radio's increasing audience was experimentation with temporary chains or networks of stations after 1923. Nearly all of these were special arrangements built around single events, until AT&T, using WEAF in New York and its national web of telephone wires, began regular operation of an interconnected network several hours a week, thus allowing nationally popular individuals and groups to be heard on hinterland stations otherwise unable to afford such entertainment. Thus almost from the start there was a basic operating dichotomy in broadcasting—local stations becoming increasingly dependent on national networks.[6]

The single biggest problem in this formative period was not easily resolved—the chaos on the airwaves brought about by the lack of regulation of spectrum assignments, power use and hours of operation of the ever-growing number of stations. Radio broadcasting was regulated during this period under the provisions of the Radio Act of 1912 which was designed to control point to point radio transmission, not broadcasting. Unable to get rapid Congressional action, Secretary of Commerce Herbert Hoover called four national radio conferences in 1922-1925 to deal with industry control and development inadequately channeled by an obsolete law.[7]

Legally binding regulation of broadcasting was needed as many stations "jumped" to different frequencies, power and hours of operation at will, creating chaos on the air and limiting development of the fad into a legitimate business. By 1925, Hoover had been joined by many listeners and even broadcasters in urging Congressional action.

Hegemony of Radio: 1928-1948

A series of seminal developments transformed the radio business in 1927-1928: the arrival of effective government regulation as the key to stability, development of permanent national networks, and acceptance of advertising as the prime support for station operation.[8] For the next two decades, the AM industry slowly developed many of the structures and processes still evident in broadcasting today, though without competition from either FM or television, which began commercial service only at the very end of this period.

With the Radio Act of 1927, Congress created the five-member Federal Radio Commission (FRC) which moved quickly to stabilize the industry. In 1928-1929, the FRC set up a system of AM radio station classification to reduce interference while providing the most widespread service possible.[9] Specific frequency assignments, hours of operation, and power limits were set up and enforced, and far fewer stations were permitted to broadcast at night (when radio waves travel farther, thus complicating interference problems). In an important series of licensing and renewal decisions over a five-year period, the FRC established important operational definitions for the 1927 act's controlling but otherwise undefined dictum that radio broadcasting must be regulated to best serve in the "public interest, convenience, or necessity."

The FRC gave way to the Federal Communications Commission (FCC) in mid-1934 as Congress pulled the regulation of all electrical communications together in a new seven-member body with wider regulatory responsibilities. The new commission continued to make important strides in technical and allocation affairs but increasingly turned its attention to the business and programming affairs of broadcasting stations, including concerns over network and other ownership patterns in radio.

Underlying these two decades of developing regulation was an FRC/FCC concern with local station service to local communities. "In the context of broadcasting, localism means three things: local ownership of broadcast facilities, a preference for smaller as opposed to larger service areas for each station, and actual program control and selection being exercised at the station level."[10] Allocation plans for radio and later television were based on this policy (which usually meant less overall choice of service, but did provide one or more locally based services instead), as was rising FCC criticism of centralized programming by networks. The alternative could have been six or seven regional or national services instead of the two or three local stations in many of today's smaller markets.

The other important structural addition to broadcasting was the rise to dominance of national networks. The Radio Corporation of America created NBC as a wholly owned subsidiary in 1926, and it was soon operating two parallel networks in competition with the Columbia Broadcasting System (CBS) and the weaker Mutual cooperative network, the latter serving mainly smaller stations in more rural areas. The American Broadcasting Company (ABC) appeared only at the very end of this period, its creation due to government action (see below).

By providing a national audience, networks attracted large advertising accounts, and were thus able to provide program variety and quality unavailable to any single station. The key to radio success was affiliation with one or more networks. In 1927 only 6% of stations were network affiliated, but a decade later this jumped to 46%. Nearly all stations (97%) were network affiliates in the peak year of 1947.[11] Competitive pressures bound stations to networks for up to five years, while networks were bound to their affiliates for but a year at a time. Large chunks of station time were assigned to networks by means of "option time" which effectively gave networks final say on what local stations programmed.

The central role played by national networks is shown by the fact that networks and their owned and operated stations took in fully half the industry income in 1937, and still accounted for 25% in the much larger industry of 1947, leaving the remaining hundreds of other stations to share the rest.[12] Naturally, larger stations in bigger markets (especially the 50,000-watt clear channel stations, 10 of which were network owned) made more money—but their profit margins were also substantially larger than those of the average station.

Regulation, networks, and advertising income contributed to an industry that grew fairly slowly (due to regulatory decisions and then Depression economy problems). By the early 1930s, the operation of stations became a full-time occupation and a degree of ownership centralization set in as the economic promise of radio became evident. Although in 1939 networks owned 4% and newspapers about 28% of all stations, their ownership was concentrated such that among the clear channel and higher-powered regional stations, networks and newspapers each had about a fourth and radio-electrical manufacturers about 13%, for a combined two-thirds of the total.[13]

Rise of the Modern Industry

The year 1948 is the dividing line between the essentially prewar AM business and the postwar rise of a more complex AM and FM radio and television industry. More specifically, 1948 saw formal establishment of the television networks—and the start of the four-year Freeze on television station applications, both developments demonstrating the rising clout of the new visual medium. Several quantitative measures of broadcast growth from 1950 to 1980 are provided in Table 6.1.

This table only touches on the development of growth patterns in all three media. For example, AM broadcasting grew strongly until the 1960s when a combination of few available frequencies and a determined FCC policy to deflect radio development into FM greatly slowed the pace. While the number of radio communities increased from under 600 in 1945 to over 2200 by the 1970s, many of the new AM outlets were supplementary stations in suburban and urban areas. While virtually all stations (except the 50kw operations) had more power, by the 1970s fully half of all AMs were on the air only in the daytime in an attempt to lessen evening interference patterns. Many others used less power at night and/or directional antennas to limit interference.

Under FCC regulatory care, FM radio initially expanded after World War II, but the limited number of FM receivers—and greater chance for economic gain in expanding AM and TV—turned the medium sour by 1950. Stations went off the air through the 1950s, dropping to just over 500 stations in 1957 before the upturn began again. The decline was speeded by the medium's lack of separate identity, as most FM programming was duplicated from AM stations. The saturation of AM in major markets, leaving FM the only way to build new stations, and the end of the initial building spree of television stations in the late 1950s helped respark interest in FM. Other factors which have paced its expansion for the past two decades include development of subsidiary communications authorizations (providing specialized services such as Muzak) as a means of income production after 1955, the ongoing high fidelity recording boom, combined with approval of FM stereo standards (1961), a series of FCC decisions which gradually forced FM to program separately from AM stations after the mid-1960s, cheaper and more readily available FM receivers, and thus larger audiences which brought a new flicker of advertiser interest. Only in 1976 did the FM industry break into the black financially, having finally caught up with its rapid expansion and large start-up costs. Advertisers who were happy with AM and did not see what FM could add finally moved significant portions of their radio budgets to FM.[14]

After the FCC Freeze Was Lifted

Television growth was limited to about 100 stations before the FCC's

Table 6.1: Indicators of Broadcasting's Economic Growth, 1950, 1960, 1970 and 1980

Comparative Factor	AM Radio				FM Radio				Television			
	1950	1960	1970	1980	1950	1960	1970	1980	1950	1960	1970	1980
Number commercial stations	2061	3431	4267	4532	733	688	2184	3216	97	515	677	831
Number educational stations	25	25	25	25	48	162	413	1050		44	185	282
Total number of stations	2086	3456	4292	4557	781	850	2597	4266	98	559	862	1113
% network affiliates	56%	33%	50%	68%	—	—	—	—	98%	96%	84%	82%
Number employed	52,000	51,700	65,000	70,580	—	1300	6100	(See under AM)	14,000	40,600	58,400	70,822
Total revenues (in millions)	$444.5	$597.7	$1077.4	$2,297.9[1]	$2.8	$9.4	$84.9	$782.7[1]	$105.9	$1268.6	$2808.2	$8807.7
Total pre-tax earnings (in millions)	$68.2	$45.9	$104.0	$157.1[1]	—	—	($11.1)	$58.4[1]	($9.2)	$244.1	$453.8	$1653.5
% total advertising exp.	11%	6%	7%	7%	—	—	—	—	3%	13%	18%	21%
% families with receivers	95%	96%	98%	99%	—	10%	74%	ca. 95%	9%	87%	95%	98%
FCC budget	$6.7	$10.5	$24.5	$72.5	(See under AM)	(See under AM)			(See under AM)	(See under AM)		
FCC employees	1285	1396	1537	2236	(See under AM)	(See under AM)			(See under AM)	(See under AM)		

[1] 1979 data.

N.B. This and other tables compile data from many sources, including FCC reports. Full citations are provided in the sources listed.

Sources: Christopher H. Sterling and Timothy R. Haight, *The Mass Media: Aspen Institute Guide to Communications Industry Trends* (New York: Praeger Special Studies, 1978) for all except FCC budget and employee data; Christopher H. Sterling and John M. Kittross, *Stay Tuned: A Concise History of American Broadcasting* (Belmont, CA: Wadsworth Publishing Co., 1978). All 1980 data from FCC except network affiliations (from networks), advertising expense (McCann-Erickson), and families with sets (A.C. Nielsen and Radio Advertising Bureau).

Freeze was lifted early in 1952 with its celebrated Sixth Report and Order on TV allocations.[15] That lengthy document, built on the localism doctrine, added the vast UHF spectrum to the already-operating VHF band of channels. Such a divided system would have been bad enough, but the FCC ignored engineering advice and intermixed the new UHF assignments with VHF channels in the same market, thus forcing direct competition of two very unequal services. The UHF problem plagued the commission, Congress and many hapless broadcasters through the 1950s. Following the FM pattern, television's "second service," after a short initial spurt of growth, went into a decade of decline, only turning the corner in 1965. In this case, the change in fortune was due both to a lack of additional VHF channels for major markets, and to Congressional action in 1962 which required UHF reception capability on receivers shipped in interstate commerce after 1964.[16] Thus, while only 10% of TV sets could receive UHF stations in 1963, well over half could do so just five years later and virtually all could by the 1980s.[17] Still, UHF stations generally did poorly economically when compared to VHFs, and networks shunned them as affiliates, forcing them into independent operation, which in television was a grey world of limited profit until the 1980s. UHF broke into the black economically on a national basis in 1975.

The national networks strengthened their dominance of the industry in the 1950s, but now their domain was television as radio networks lapsed into mere news and feature services. (Only ABC's split into four formatted networks in 1968 helped to reverse the decline in radio station affiliations by the 1970s.) Four networks, including Dumont which had not operated in radio, began TV service in the late 1940s, going national when the country was connected by coaxial cable and microwave in 1951. As in radio, advertising agencies dominated network programming in the 1950s until the race for ratings led to the quiz show and payola scandals of the late 1950s, and public pressure to "clean up television." Faced with these issues, plus a revitalized FCC, as well as rising costs of production and station time, networks took control of their own programming and time sales. Advertising turned from program sponsorship (paying all costs) to "participations," or buying time in television much as advertisers do in print media, with little control over editorial content. Thus the financial risks passed back to the networks and to "package agencies" which produced network series programs on old film lots in Hollywood.

That the networks clearly dominated television is evident in Table 6.2. The profit margins reflected in the table, summarizing vast seas of official FCC annual industry financial data, demonstrate (1) the greater profitability of television over radio, (2) the far greater return to VHF than to UHF stations, and (3) the dominant, though stable, role of networks and

Table 6.2: Broadcasting Industry Profits, Selected Years, 1955–1980

		Commercial Television Industry						
	Radio Industry Pretax Earnings as % of Revenues	Pretax Earnings as % of Revenues			% Industry Profit Accruing to		% Stations Reporting Profit	
Year		Total TV	Net- works	Net- work O&Os	Nets & O&Os	Other Stations	VHF	UHF
1955	10%	20%	N.A.	N.A.	45%	55%	63%	27%
1960	8	19	7%	42%	39	61	81	50
1965	10	23	8	44	36	64	87	66
1970	10	16	4	38	37	63	82	32
1972	11	17	9	31	37	63	86	44
1974	7	20	15	28	45	55	86	47
1976	9	24	14	35	36	64	91	67
1978	12	24	13	32	34	66	92	73
1980	N.A.	19	8	30	32	68	89	58

Note: O&Os = Network owned and operated stations.
N.A.: Not available.
Source: Sterling and Haight (1978), table 370-C (for radio), and 380-B, 380-C and 381-A (for television) through 1976. All data taken from annual FCC financial reports, which is the source for 1978-1980 data.

their owned and operated (O&O) stations. The latter have nearly always numbered but 15 stations (all VHF, concentrated in the top markets) which makes their proportion of total industry profit that much more startling. This apparent economic centralization has led to continued Congressional investigations of "monopoly" in television and to several FCC investigations of the networks.

One overriding trend of the past 30 years has been a clear delineation between broadcast industry "haves" and "have nots."[18] The former are the networks, larger AM stations and VHF television outlets. The latter are smaller AMs, most FM stations and all UHF operations. Most popular programming, and thus audience and advertising income, accrues to the "haves." The "have nots" in all cases entered the industry after the "haves" were well situated. They have struggled just to break even, often suffering years of declining numbers. As will be discussed later, much of this dichotomy is accentuated by ownership patterns and stems from the FCC's localism guidelines.

RATIONALE FOR REGULATION

Broadcasting is far more heavily regulated than any of the other media discussed in this book. Under the Communications Act of 1934, the FCC is charged with making effective use of spectrum space by means of allocation to broadcasting and other services. This is performed with "the public interest, convenience, or necessity" as the key, though undefined, guiding principle. In practice, this breaks down into several more specific factors explaining why the FCC regulates broadcasting, and why concern over concentration is a prime aspect of that regulation.

Spectrum Scarcity

The prime rationale for government's role in broadcasting has long been the technical limitation of usable spectrum space. Potential use of the spectrum depends on priorities and needs at any given time and on technical discoveries impinging on its efficient use. Spectrum which is serviceable for broadcasting is limited in amount as only certain areas have characteristics conducive to broadcasting, and other services compete for, and have been assigned, some of that same space. The result is insufficient space for all who might wish to broadcast, and thus only some can be allowed to do so if any are to be heard (as the confusion of the 1920s demonstrated). This in itself would not imply government regulation. But Congress specifically retained ownership of spectrum as a public resource, and thus services using a portion of the spectrum have to be licensed for given periods of time while specifically giving up any vested interest in any part of the spectrum. Such a system obviated the normal pricing mechanism as a means of market control, and required some choice among applicants wishing to broadcast. Under this approach, a broadcast license is thus a limited privilege—the right to make use of a specific frequency assignment for a specified period (usually three years until 1981 when Congress extended radio licenses to seven years and television licenses to five), subject to renewal if deemed in the public interest.

In reality, however, the number of broadcast stations is not really strictly limited—especially when compared to the far smaller number of daily newspapers in the U.S. The scarcity is government-mandated by allocation systems developed by pitting competing spectrum users and priorities against one another. The scarcity is really the result of compromise. And the compromises in allocation have created at least one type of station with plenty of frequencies and few takers: UHF television in many areas of the country (see discussion below), while cable technology has moved ahead to provide competition which may eliminate the need for more spectrum space. The problem, then, is a forced scarcity brought about by a doctrine of localism.

Localism

Though expressed in different ways over the years, the FCC and its predecessors have clearly held that the "best" broadcast station is locally owned and operated. Such ownership was deemed in the public interest as it would presumably be closer to local needs and concerns, and thus the station would more adequately reflect and project that community than some absentee-owned operation or central network. Such a policy strongly affected such basic decisions as AM station classes, e.g., a 1928 ruling for a few national "clear" channels but many more local signals; and television allocations, e.g., the 1952 Sixth Report and Order, wherein the need to provide as many local TV channels as possible led directly to the intermixture phenomenon of combining VHF and UHF stations in direct competition. Thus, a fairly consistent public social policy has been developed at as vast an economic cost as has been deemed politically acceptable. But "in practice, localism is futile because it is much more profitable for stations to affiliate with a network or provide syndicated material distributed by land-lines or satellite (thus giving up most of their practical control over programming) than to produce or select their own programs."[19] Further, because of localism, few markets have more than three television channels, which limits the formation of additional national networks with the potential benefit of greater diversity.

Public Interest

The FCC regulates broadcasting, beginning with the essential licensing process itself, "in the public interest, convenience, and necessity," the undefined standard on which the Communications Act of 1934 (and its 1927 predecessor) is built. Virtually all FCC decisions and court reviews of those decisions have been decided on varied interpretations of just what the public interest requirement was at any given time. As but one example, the FCC's 1965 "Policy Statement on Comparative Broadcast Hearings"[20] declared it in the public interest that seven factors be taken into account when two or more applicants for the same facility were being considered for a license: diversification of control of the media;[21] full-time participation in station operation by owners; proposed program service; past broadcast record; efficient use of frequency; character of the applicant; and "other factors."

In the 1943 *NBC* case, Justice Frankfurter specifically noted that the public interest requirement put on the FCC the "burden of determining the composition" of broadcast content as well as supervising it.[22] At the same time, Section 326 of the 1934 Act just as specifically bans the FCC from censorship of programming, going on to say that "no regulation or condition shall be promulgated or fixed by the Commission which shall interfere with the right of free speech by means of radio communication." The horns of this seeming dilemma are manifestly evident in the Fairness Doctrine—and are but one reason why the initial attempt in 1978 to rewrite the 1934 Communications Act included no mention of a vague public interest standard, but instead called for regulation only "to the extent marketplace forces are deficient." Subsequent 1979 and 1980 versions of the rewrite bills retained the public interest standard under considerable pressure from lobbying factions (both for industry and citizen groups), uneasy with a different approach.[23] In the meantime, the FCC has been developing an indirect approach to improve broadcast content.

Structure Affecting Content

Concerned with promoting diversity of content reaching a public with sundry interests, the FCC has followed an unwritten but fairly clear policy of seeking to modify the ownership of broadcasting facilities as a means of effecting changes in content. In the volumes of FCC hearings and reports on questions of ownership, a key and constant element is use of the term "diversity." It is repeatedly asserted that diversity of media control is in the public interest, not just because such diversity presumably prevents undue concentration of media editorial and economic clout, but because such ownership will be more likely to provide a broader variety of content choices to the public. While the economics of commercial broadcasting often mitigate against such a process, the fact remains that the FCC still follows a process of seeking *content* diversity through *ownership* diversity. Recent confirmation of this approach by both the FCC and its Appeals Court "watchdog" came early in 1979 when then FCC Chairman Ferris and Appeals Court Judge Bazelon specifically noted that the key to diversity in the industry was "structural" regulation of the media.[24] A major rationale for regular investigations of network operations by both Congress and the FCC is recognition of the fact that as networks provide programming for virtually all television stations—even the independents, most of whose reruns are syndicated off-network productions—some degree of control over their operations is essential if government-fostered "improvements" in the level of programming are to have any effect whatever. As will be seen below, however, even this rationale was being questioned in the early 1980s in the face of new technological innovation and developing competition.

Requirement to Regulate Monopoly

Both the 1927 (Section 13) and the 1934 (Section 313 as amended) acts specifically apply antitrust laws to the field of broadcasting, calling for revocation of any station license from an owner accused of monopolistic activities in the industry. If any such license is so revoked, the FCC is further directed to refuse any future construction permits or license applications from that party. Just as these laws constrain the FCC, the Sherman (1890) and Clayton (1910) Acts direct the Antitrust Division of the Department of Justice. As the two governmental agencies most concerned with monopoly in broadcasting, the FCC and Justice have "acted sometimes in tandem, sometimes at cross purposes, and sometimes independently,"[25] partially owing to their differing "triggering" concerns. Whereas the Justice Department looks for undue economic concentration, the FCC is interested in diversifying the public's sources of entertainment and information. In 1978, the Federal Trade Commission (FTC) joined the fray in its investigation of overall mass media ownership. In a two-day symposium held in Washington late that year, the FTC gathered and later published a collection of papers assessing concentration in print and broadcast media.[26] A policy option report subsequently circulated within the agency, but was never publicly released in the changing political climate after 1980 when FTC interest in media ownership appeared to decline.

The FCC has typically acted either with a policy oriented rule-making or an *ad hoc* decision on specific situations. The Department of Justice has more options: it can and has taken part in FCC rule-making or *ad hoc* decision-making procedures as an interested party, it can actively petition the FCC to undertake some specific action, or it can file an antitrust suit in the courts. Both agencies have been strongly affected in the past by political aims and pressures of the administration in power as well as by Congress. Both, but especially Justice, can and have acted behind the scenes to pressure business or the other agency to its will without specific action. Justice is somewhat limited in initiating actions by the legal tradition of primary jurisdiction, which basically says that those seeking redress must first seek action from the regulatory agency in question (here, the FCC) before proceeding directly to the courts.[27] Thus, in several of the discussions which follow, note that the Antitrust Division first sought action from the Commission, and only after that took more direct action.

Public Investment

While the broadcast industry's investment in tangible property and programming is tremendous, it pales beside that of expenditures by consumers on receivers, both for purchases and repairs. From time to time suggestions appear as to new technological means of providing more stations in the same spectrum space or other technical breakthroughs that could unlock the spectrum stranglehold on industry expansion. The difficulty is that spectrum assignments to broadcasting and other services are dictated mainly by the political and technical realities at the time the assignments were made, i.e., the late 1920s for AM radio, the mid 1940s for FM and VHF television, and the early 1950s for UHF television. Then millions of receivers are sold, effectively locking in spectrum allocations which may nonetheless become archaic by later technical standards. The FCC is assigned its role as protector of the public investment partly because the latter represents considerable political clout if disturbed, as it might be if millions of receivers were made obsolete by some major allocations change.

In 1980-1981 the FCC attempted to change AM radio to 9 kHz channels (from the long-existing 10 kHz standard) to reduce expected future interference from other countries while providing expansion space for new stations and owners. This effort failed in part because of industry and Commission concern about public investment in many new digital receivers which would be useless with the projected channel spacing change.[28] Similar inertia due to public receiver investment is evident in the television industry's debate over development of higher-definition picture and sound systems which would have to use wider channels than the long-standard 6 MHz for which all existing receivers are designed.[29]

ENTRY INTO BROADCASTING

With most media, the process of entry is constrained mainly by economic factors. But in broadcasting, economic, legal and technical requirements combine to create a complex and expensive process, more controlled by government regulation than is the case in any other medium. These basic factors break into two categories: licensee qualifications and public interest qualifications. The first have been consistently upheld over the years, but over the latter, generally more deciding factors, considerably more controversy exists.[30]

License Qualifications Issues

There are essentially three basic categories of qualification, all of which must be satisfied in order to hold a construction permit or license for a broadcast station. First, applicants, officers, and stockholders (all but 20% of the latter) must be U.S. citizens. In addition, other background factors concerning character and legal status must be detailed, including any past problems with the FCC or other legal authorities. Second, basic technical qualifications include availability of a frequency on which to either build or buy a station, antenna and studio location issues, maximum and minimum power and antenna height limitations, signal strength and service area, etc. Finally, financial qualifications center on the applicant's ability to build or buy a station and meet operating expenses for a minimum of three months (changed in August 1978 from the former one full year standard) without depending on income from the station.

One aspect of these basic qualifications, which in the early 1980s began to receive considerable attention, was the heretofore generally accepted notion of a licensee having to possess good "character."[31] Concern rose to a peak with the FCC's decision early in 1980 to lift three television licenses from RKO General, Inc. due to findings of misconduct on the part of its parent firm (General Tire) which rendered RKO unfit to be a licensee.[32] Subsequent FCC action called into doubt RKO's right to operate an additional 13 broadcast stations.[33] Variations in determining character qualification led in 1981 to a general Commission inquiry into the value and scope of the requirement.[34]

Public Interest Qualifications

As nearly all applicants for new, transferred, or renewal licenses meet the requirements noted above, considerable importance falls on the wider ranging "public interest" qualifications which vary considerably for radio and television and on which there is less common ground for agreement.

Included in this category are questions of ascertainment of community needs; past programming and advertising standards and/or future plans for content; integration of management and station operation; minority control; and concentration of ownership. Early in 1981, commercial radio broadcasting was substantially deregulated by the FCC, which lifted requirements for detailed ascertainment surveys, program logs, and guidelines on nonentertainment programming and amount of commercial matter carried.[35] Supportive legislation on radio appeared likely at about the same time. Television stations, however, are still held to stricter standards, rules or guidelines in all these areas.[36]

Build or Buy

An important trend has been the ever increasing prices paid for existing stations since the number of unused radio and television channels makes it difficult to place a new station on the air. As of mid-1980, there were no available VHF channels in the top 100 markets for commercial stations—

and only 59 remained in all other markets. There were 76 UHF channels available in the top 100 markets: once these are gone there will be no more new stations in major markets. Of the remaining 243 vacant UHF channels in smaller markets, many are not economically viable. The same holds true for radio, although lacking a specific table of allocations, it is difficult to find a channel for a new AM station that is both technically feasible and economically viable. FM radio, the fastest growing broadcast medium of the 1970s, was within a few hundred assignments of filling its current allotment table. This shrinking of opportunity has had two immediate effects.

First, the prices paid for broadcast stations have continued to rise. Boston's channel 5 changed hands in 1981 for $220 million—better than twice the previous record price for a television station.[37] Prices for AM and FM stations were also reaching new record highs, demonstrating continued demand for ownership of stations. In 1980 the average price for a radio station rose by 30% while TV station prices increased an average of 125%.[38]

The prices being paid, demand from new kinds of owners (such as minorities—see below), and FCC concern about broadcasting's diversity, all helped to lay groundwork for the other effect—attempts to increase availability of new facilities. In AM radio, for example, the FCC in May 1980 "broke down" the last of the clear channel AM stations, thus adding a potential 125 new stations on the air.[39] A year later, nearly 170 applications were on file for those new facilities. Over a two-year period, the Commission considered (and temporarily adopted) a 9 kHz AM channel spacing plan which would have made possible several hundred new stations, as well as allowing some daytime-only stations to take up full-time broadcasting. Late in 1981, under considerable industry pressure, the FCC backed down and reinstated the 10 kHz standard.[40] One method of AM band expansion was the 1979 World Administrative Radio Conference (WARC) approval boosting the upper end of the AM band, which may allow several hundred new stations late in the 1980s.[41] The Commission also had changes for FM under consideration, such as additions to the present three classes of FM station along with possible use of directional antennas to allow still more FMs on the air.[42]

For television, several expansion plans were being pursued. The FCC, at the behest of Congress, undertook a two-year investigation into ways to make UHF television more "comparable" to VHF in signal quality and audience coverage. Clearly the effort was aimed at increasing the economic viability of the UHF channels already technically available.[43] More controversial were various proposals to "drop in" (to the television allotment plan) more VHF channels than are presently called for, by short-spacing new allotments due to the greater ease of putting a new VHF station on the air. After years of proceedings, the FCC finally approved only four drop-ins. Under consideration, however, were still more so-called "limited facility stations."[44] Finally, and already of considerable interest both within and without the present broadcast industry, is the low-power television proceeding. Briefly, the Commission established a whole new class of video service—both VHF and UHF stations with but a few watts of power. Such operations would have very limited coverage (a radius of a few miles at best), but are seen by many as ideal to serve urban subgroups or rural regions too scattered to afford the cost of a full-power television station. The demand to create such a service, especially among groups and individuals totally new to broadcasting, was such that the FCC had to place a freeze on new applications when the total on hand quickly rose to nearly 6,000![45]

As another indication of the blurring of the distinctions between traditional broadcasting and other means of expanding ownership options and diversity, there are such newer services as cable and pay cable (see Chapter 7), multipoint distribution systems, home video and direct broadcast satellites (DBS), all under active development in the early 1980s. Some observers, including the FCC's Network Inquiry of 1978-1980, see this oncoming competition as the chief rationale to abandon much of the ownership control discussed below.

Minority Groups

A relatively recent wrinkle affecting entry, especially station transfer or assignment of any new channels created in radio and television, is the pressure to assign broadcast licenses to racial and other minority groups. Public policymakers have been aroused by the fact that fewer than 1% of all broadcast properties are under racial minority group control, although such minorities constitute about 20% of the population. The FCC held hearings on the topic early in 1977 and subsequently adopted an industry proposal to defer capital gains taxes (under Section 1071 of the 1954 Internal Revenue Code) for current station owners selling to businesses in which a racial or ethnic minority held majority interest. By mid-1981, after four years of the tax certificate policy, 24 certificates had been granted covering 29 radio and television stations. Eighteen of the certificates had covered sales to Black owners while the other six were for sales to Hispanic owners.[46] At the same time, the FCC adopted a "distress sale" policy, whereby licensees that had been designated for hearings due to some infraction of Commission rules, but for whom the hearing had not yet actually begun, could sell the facility at a "distress" price to a minority-controlled owner.[47] This was later defined to be no more than 75% of fair market value of the station as established by at least two outside sources. After four years of this policy, the Commission had approved 26 distress sales, 18 to Black purchasers, four to Hispanics, two to Asian-American groups, and two to American Indians. Combined, these methods are slow but effective. In addition, they enjoy widespread support. A major drawback has been to find minority groups with sufficient funds and this has led to campaigns by industry trade groups, at least one major group owner and the Small Business Administration to make funds available for minority groups seeking to purchase broadcast stations. The Commission was also under pressure from minority interests to set aside some specified proportion of new services like low power television or new radio channels (and even communication satellite transponders) exclusively for minority applicants.

STATION OWNERSHIP: SINGLE MARKETS

While considerable concern had been expressed over ownership of broadcast stations as early as the 1920s, specific regulatory concern came to a head in the late 1930s, based partially on New Deal programs which encouraged closer control of business and industry. Arising at about the same time, with investigations of one feeding on the others, were FCC worries over newspaper control of radio stations, network dominance of radio broadcasting (including network ownership of stations) and "duopoly."

Duopoly

FCC concern over ownership of more than one AM station in the same market intensified in the Genesee Radio Corporation case (1938) when the FCC noted:

> It is not in the public interest to grant the facilities for an additional broadcast station to interests already in control of the operation of a station of the same class in the same community, unless there is a compelling showing upon the whole case that public convenience, interest or necessity would be served thereby.[48]

A number of such combinations existed at the time. Seeking to avoid an AM situation in the new broadcast media, the FCC in 1940 promulgated a rule against duopoly in FM radio. TV was likewise limited in April 1941. Such a rule controlling AM was proposed in August 1941 but became final only in November 1943.[49] Then, in an unusual action for an agency which more commonly "grandfathers" existing situations when new rules are created, the FCC in April of 1944 issued a rule requiring divestiture of duopoly-controlled AM stations to meet the standard.[50] Divestiture of stations was required in over 40 markets, although the FCC paved the way for tax breaks as the sales were clearly involuntary.[51]

Newspaper/Broadcasting Cross-Ownership

One of the oldest and most controversial ownership concerns is cross-ownership of newspapers and broadcast facilities, especially when both are in the same market. The newspaper-owned station is one of the oldest patterns in broadcasting and was once of considerable importance in each of the broadcast services.

Trends[52]

One of the first stations on the air, WWJ in Detroit, was owned by a local daily newspaper. Initially, newspapers entered radio to increase circulation through mention on the air, for prestige and good will, and to protect themselves against a fad which might become a competitor in news delivery. In the 1930s, newspaper control of the industry grew substantially —from about 6% of all stations in 1930 to nearly a third of all stations a decade later. Clearly radio was no longer a fad, but was becoming an obvious competitive threat to newspapers. Control of one or more radio stations was seen as one way of protecting newspaper investments, both against radio and against other newspaper-radio combinations. Late in the decade combined newspaper-broadcasting chains controlled about 11% of both newspapers and broadcast stations. With the coming of FM and television, newspapers moved rapidly into the new services, holding a quarter of FM authorizations in 1941, thereby prompting FCC action.

Table 6.3 provides a summary of the cross-ownership situation since 1945. For AM radio, the pattern is a clear one of diminishing proportions of control in both relative and absolute terms. The FM pattern has shown a relative decline in cross-ownership since 1970. With television, however, newspaper ownership has been increasing after a small percentage decline in the early 1970s. Initial entry into FM and television paralleled newspaper company entry into AM in that print owners sought to protect both their newspaper and older (AM) radio interests. Initial television purchases were usually co-located with the newspaper (over 80% were local in 1955), but under regulatory pressures and competition from other buyers, the local proportion of cross-ownerships declined to 72% in 1960, and only 46% in 1974.[53] This proportion declined still further late in the decade as newspaper owners, under increasing FCC and court pressure over local

Table 6.3: Newspaper/Broadcasting Cross-Ownership, Selected Years, 1945–1979

Year	AM Radio			FM Radio			Television		
	Total Stations	Newspaper-Owned Number	Percent	Total Stations	Newspaper-Owned Number	Percent	Total Stations	Newspaper-Owned Number	Percent
1945	919	260	28.3%	46	17	37.0%	8	1	12.5%
1950	2086	472	22.6	733	273	37.2	98	41	41.8
1955	2669	465	17.4	552	170	30.8	411	149	36.3
1960	3456	429	12.4	688	145	21.1	515	175	34.0
1965	4044	383	9.5	1270	159	12.5	569	181	31.8
1970	4292	394	9.2	2184	245	11.2	677	189	27.9
1975	4432	321	7.2	2636	236	9.0	711	193	27.1
1977	4497	322	7.2	2837	238	8.4	728	209	28.7
1979	4526	319	7.0	3107	252	8.1	728	221	30.4

Note: As table does not distinguish between local and non-local cross-ownerships, local market concentration is somewhat overstated here.

Sources: Sterling and Haight, table 261-A for information through 1975; *Statistical Abstract 1979*, p. 587, table 983, for information on 1977 and 1979. All data as of January 1 through 1960; 1965 is actually October 31, 1964, while remaining years are actually December 1 of previous year (December 1, 1969 for 1970, etc.). Total columns and other data refer to stations actually on the air, and with the exception of about 25 AM educational stations, are restricted to commercial outlets only.

cross-ownership, began to discuss and in a few cases carry out plans to exchange stations, thus breaking up local combinations, while maintaining interests in both media.

One landmark switch came in late 1977 when the Washington Post Co. and the Detroit News Co. exchanged television stations.[54] With final Supreme Court action requiring divestiture in only a few small markets, the future ownership situation is likely to parallel the past—a continued slow decline in newspaper ownership of local stations due to the court-supported FCC ban on formation of any such new combinations.

Regulation: Long Search for an Answer

Until the past decade, the government's stance on newspaper ownership of broadcast stations has had little consistency. While cited in a few licensing decisions of the 1930s, and argued on occasion in Congress, the newspaper ownership issue came to a head only after the substantial increase in press control of radio in the 1930s more or less forced FCC action. In 1941 the FCC froze newspaper-owned construction of or application for FM stations and began what was to be a three-year investigation into the entire press-radio interconnection. Three years later the Commission closed the proceeding and continued on its *ad hoc* basis of case by case consideration of ownership diversification.

Many newspaper-owned licenses were routinely renewed in the 1940s and 1950s, though in a very few cases, ownership diversification or some questionable business practice of a particular newspaper appeared to play a part in an application denial.[55] In 1956 something of a landmark was struck when, on appeal, the U.S. Court of Appeals for the District of Columbia upheld the FCC's right to consider diversification as a deciding factor in the awarding of broadcast licenses.[56] In the 1960s the situation was somewhat fuzzy:

> As a comparative factor, newspaper ownership: 1) is a discrediting, not a disqualifying factor; 2) will be decisive only where all other comparative criteria have been equally met by all the applicants; 3) will depend for its importance upon the nature and extent of newspaper interests of the applicant; and 4) where a non-comparative proceeding is involved, there will be no hearing save where collateral public interest matters, such as suppression of competition, are material.[57]

The focus of action turned from the case by case approach of the FCC to the Justice Department, which began in 1968-1969 to both contest FCC license decisions and to file actual suits to dissolve some ownership combinations. Further, Justice urged on the FCC a policy of breaking up existing newspaper-broadcast combinations and not allowing new ones to form. The focus switched rapidly back to the FCC early in 1969 when it voted to deny renewal of the license for Boston's channel 5 (WHDH) to the *Herald-Traveler,* turning it over instead to an independent local owner with no other media ties.* While many other factors entered into the case, the clear cross-media aspects of the decision shocked the industry.[58]

One clear result of the breaking up of local cross-ownerships, however, was, ironically, a decline in media voices. In Boston, the *Herald-Traveler* closed up about a year after the loss of the station, blaming its demise on the loss of the broadcast operation, which had been underwriting the paper's losses. More than a decade later, as a result of further decisions on cross-ownership (see below), the nation's capitol was left with a single daily paper when the afternoon *Washington Star* ceased operations in mid-1981. It too tried to survive after the loss of the AM-FM-TV combination in the city which had pumped cash into the sagging daily.[59] While certainly not the sole factor in the papers' closings, loss of the broadcast subsidies was crucial.

Prior to the 1969 WHDH decision, diversification of control had been taken into account for new applicants, but not renewals. Action was initiated in Congress to somewhat nullify the precedent value of this FCC decision, and the Commission itself adopted a position statement reiterating the primacy of incumbent licensees. It was nullified on appeal.[60]

In 1970, still under pressure from Justice, the FCC issued a proposed rule to require divestiture within five years of either newspaper or broadcast stations in all local markets where cross-ownership existed.[61] Massive filings against the proposal came from industry trade groups, all protesting that no effective case had been made against newspaper ownership—and that in any case such ownership was on the decline. The FCC's ability to act on the issue was questioned in that the Commission had no clear Congressional mandate to take such drastic action. While the debate in the trade press and among researchers continued,[62] the FCC took no action in the 1971-1974 period. Once again, the Justice Department entered with formal opposition to renewals of cross-owned media in several different markets.

Finally, in January 1975, the FCC issued a second report and order in the cross-ownership proceeding, considerably toning down its original

---

*This station went on to become a model for proponents of local ownership. It produced more hours of local programming—much of it aired in prime time—than any major market station in the country. It was sold by the local owners in 1981 for $220 million to Metromedia, the largest television chain other than the three networks.

divestiture proposal to cover but 16 smaller markets where the only news-paper owned either the only radio or only television station in the same coverage area. Future local cross-ownerships were also barred. Other existing cross-ownerships were exempted until sold, in which case they would have to be broken up as well.[63] The new rules were appealed by Justice and many others, and the case was thus taken up by the Court of Appeals for the District of Columbia. A three-judge panel remanded the rules back to the FCC early in 1977 saying that full divestiture was required, given the arguments the FCC had used to limit future combinations while calling for only limited divestiture. Only if such combinations could be found specifically in the public interest did the court suggest any exceptions should be made.[64] The court-ordered expansion of the FCC decision could have affected some 153 broadcast/newspaper combinations involving nearly 300 stations.[65]

The Supreme Court in June 1978 upheld the FCC, agreeing to a ban on future cross-ownerships, as well as to limiting divestiture to the 16 markets the FCC originally selected. Amidst all the verbiage was the important finding that the FCC was fully within its rights in limiting future cross-ownerships as a means of promoting the public interest in diversified mass communications, that such action did not violate the First Amendment rights of those denied broadcast licenses.[66] Thus this longest-lasting of the ownership questions appears finally laid to rest. The FCC is mandated to disallow any further local cross-ownerships, and existing combinations must be broken up if sold. A likely trend appears to be continued swapping of local cross-owned facilities for those in other markets.

One to a Customer Policy

Of considerably greater controversy—and having far greater long-term effect on the industry—was a policy first issued by the Commission in March 1968.[67] This had the announced purpose of limiting station ownership to no more than one station of any kind per market. While not calling for divestiture (considering there were some 1600 combinations at the time, including 1200 AM-FM, 212 AM-FM-TV, 124 AM-TV and 42 FM-TV) the projected rule was to affect any future sale of station combinations, thus forcing them to be broken up and sold to different owners. Furthermore, no future combinations could be built or purchased. The only exception was that daytime AM station owners could have one other station in the same market. The Justice Department agreed with the approach —but called for breakup by divestiture of existing combinations at the time of their first renewal. At about the same time, Justice began a series of antitrust suits in selected markets where it felt combinations were in restraint of competition. Industry reaction, as might be expected, was strongly against the proposed rules.

In March 1970, the FCC moved to formalize, and adjust, its initial proposal. The basic rule as proposed two years earlier was adopted in an expansion of the old duopoly rule, but all existing combinations were "grandfathered" until or unless sold. Included in the new order was a projected ban on newspaper/broadcast station cross-ownership and controls on ownership of broadcast operations and CATV systems.[68] Newspaper publishers and the broadcast industry rallied against the new rules and many critical research studies were prepared and filed with the FCC. In February 1971, the rules were modified to allow AM-FM combinations and to allow for a case-by-case decision process on radio-television combinations involving UHF stations. Shortly thereafter, the industry research studies were filed with the Commission—and there things sat for some four years.

This policy has already had a notable effect on station sales as existing combinations are broken up into two and sometimes three ownerships where only one existed before. Thus, the trend to intramarket concentration, which had sharply increased in 1950 with the coming of FM and television stations under combined ownership with older AM services, should slowly decline as combined ownerships break up at the time of sale.

In mid-1979, FCC Commissioner Tyrone Brown asked his staff to prepare a Notice projecting expansion of the "one to a customer" policy to AM and FM combinations in the same market. When he left the Commission in 1981, the proposed rule change had not come forth—and in light of the political transition at the FCC in 1981 it appeared unlikely any such rule calling for divestiture would come about. Indeed, although AM-FM assignment and transfer proceedings had been conditioned for two years on this projected rulemaking, having an impact some 300 stations, the FCC in 1982 lifted the conditions as a sign that the rule was no longer being considered. Though AM-FM combinations had been left out of the policy originally because FM was generally losing money and AM support was felt to be necessary, by the 1980s the situation had strongly reversed itself—and AM stations wanted to hold onto their increasingly popular FM outlets to help support their less profitable AM facilities.

Likewise, the FCC had considered radio-UHF combinations on a case-by-case basis for a decade. In 1982, however, radio-UHF combinations were formally approved and ownership restrictions were eliminated. Thus, in the early 1980s, the so-called "one to a customer" rule really limits only the intact sale of VHF television and radio combinations from one owner to another.

STATION OWNERSHIP: MULTIPLE MARKETS

Considerably different issues are raised by concern over ownership concentration across local markets—so-called group or conglomerate ownership of broadcast facilities on a regional or national basis, often incorporating cross-ownership as well.

Trends

Ownership of broadcast stations in different markets by the same owner is nearly as old as broadcasting. Westinghouse, which placed KDKA on a regular schedule in November of 1920, soon had WBZ near Boston and WJZ outside of New York (1921), followed later by stations in Chicago, Hastings (NE) and Cleveland. Though the purpose of these stations initially had been to sell Westinghouse receivers, by the 1960s, the same groups of stations, now known as "Group W," had expanded to FM and television and were no longer directly related to manufacturing as Westinghouse no longer made radio or TV receivers.[69] In similar fashion, and for related reasons, RCA and General Electric, and then other firms, built or bought stations in several different markets. Over the years, as shown in Table 6.4, the proportion of such groups in AM radio began to increase, slowed in the 1950s by expansion into FM and television, but rising again by the 1960s.

The first multiple licensee in television was the Dumont Broadcasting Co. which was building the basis for a television network.[70] The other two groups active by 1948 were Paramount Pictures (which soon sold its stations) and NBC, also building toward a national network. By the end of the Freeze in 1952, CBS and ABC networks had joined the group owner ranks along with 15 non-network groups including Storer (which had also been in radio group control), RKO General, Avco, Cox Broadcasting, Scripps-Howard and others. The drop in proportion of group-owned stations by 1956 is due partially to a somewhat successful FCC policy of encouraging non-group applications. Active buying and selling of stations in the late 1950s and 1960s increased the group proportion of all commercial TV stations. Evident in Table 6.5 is the fact that groups sought to improve their station portfolios by concentrating on major market purchases, often "trading up" to get stations in larger markets. At least one such case, between a network and a non-network group owner, led to an important court case and undoing of the "trade" in question (see NBC-Westinghouse trade later in this chapter). The proportion of group-owned stations in the top 100 markets increased by nearly 50% between 1956 and 1966, then leveled off through 1976 as more independent UHF stations (in which few

Table 6.4: Group Ownership in Broadcasting, Selected Years, 1929–1982

Year	Total Number of Stations	Number of Group Owners	Number of Group-Owned Stations	Percent of Stations under Group Ownership
AM Radio				
1929	600	12	20	3.3%
1939	764	39	109	14.3
1951	2232	63	253	11.3
1960	3398	185	765	22.5
1967	4130	373	1297	31.4
Television				
1948	16	3	6	37.5%
1952	108	19	53	49.1
1956	441	60	173	39.2
1960	515	84	252	48.9
1966	585	111	324	55.4
1976	710	119	415	58.5
1982	774	158	563	72.7

Source: Sterling and Haight, tables 260-C and 280-A, updated from H. Howard, "Television Station Group Ownership ... 1982," a research study prepared for National Association of Broadcasters, 1982. Figures are approximations and include newspaper owners. Includes only commercial stations.

groups are interested or active) came on the air.

As broadcast groups approached their saturation in the number of stations they were allowed to control (see below), they often diversified into other fields, began to produce programming for their stations and in other ways acted as mini-networks.[71] The largest group owners (identified in Table 6.6 in terms of the number of television homes reached in a typical week) are the network owned-and-operated stations, which have maintained their lead over two decades. Among the other, non-network groups, changes have been minimal, with some of the changes representing name rather than ownership shifts. Note that in half the cases, the total number of stations owned is but five, all of which are VHF. Note also that the overall cumulative proportion of television households reached by these top 15 has increased over the period, demonstrating the effects of "trading up" for stations in the larger markets.

A third of the 120 groups active in the top 100 markets in 1975 had but two stations (the minimal definition of a group) while 25 groups had three stations, 27 had four, 14 had five, nine had six, and only four groups had the full complement of seven television stations.[72] The pace of group building appeared to pick up in recent years. In mid-1977 Park Broadcasting Inc. became the first group owner to have 21 stations, seven in each ser-

Table 6.5: Group Ownership in Television by Market Size, 1956, 1966, 1982

Year/Type of Station	Markets 1-10	Markets 1-50	Markets 51-100	Markets 1-100	Markets 101 and up	Total Stations
1956						
All TV stations	—	163	134	297	159	456
Group-owned stations	—	92	48	140	65	205
% Group-owned	—	56%	36%	47%	41%	45%
1966						
All TV stations	—	193	164	357	235	592
Group-owned stations	—	134	112	246	150	396
% Group-owned	—	69%	68%	69%	64%	67%
1982						
VHF: All TV stations	41	160	103	263	N.A.	524
Group-owned stations	40	144	82	226	N.A.	N.A.
% Group-owned	98%	90%	80%	86%	N.A.	N.A.
UHF: All TV stations	36	90	67	157	N.A.	250
Group-owned stations	25	64	42	106	N.A.	N.A.
% Group-owned	69%	71%	63%	68%	N.A.	N.A.
Total: All TV stations	77	250	170	420	N.A.	774
Group-owned stations	65	208	124	332	N.A.	N.A.
% Group-owned	84%	83%	73%	79%	N.A.	N.A.

N.A.: Not available.
Source: Sterling, *Broadcasting Trends* (1982), table 280-B (in press).

Table 6.6: Financial Indicators for Selected Leading Broadcasting Firms, 1980

Firm	Corporate Revenues 1980 (in millions)	Fortune "1000" Ranking		Broadcasting Top "100" Rank 1980	Contribution to Corporate Revenues	Broadcasting Stations Held	
		1980	1970			Radio	TV
General Electric	$24,959	10	4	1	N.A.	8	3
Westinghouse	8,514	34	17	4	4%	12	6
RCA	8,011	41	21	5	19	8	5
CBS	3,963	94	99[1]	13	41	14	5
ABC	2,256	168	159[1]	18	87	13	5
General Tire	2,215	171	106	19	N.A.	14	4
Times Mirror	1,857	194	256	21	7	0	7
Schering-Plough	1,740	209	406/563[2]	22	N.A.	12	0
Gannett	1,215	270	532	26	10	13	7
McGraw-Hill	1,000	300	251	30	5	0	4
Capital Cities	472	485	—	45	35	13	6
Metromedia	454	497	—	46	44	13	7
Cox	309	601	—	57	50	12	5
Taft	236	723	—	62	43	12	7
Storer	197	788	—	68	N.A.	1	7
Scripps-Howard	77	—	—	84	93	6	6

[1] Simulated ranking assigned by Fortune (firm was not considered an industrial company in 1970).
[2] Ranked as two separate firms in 1970.
N.A.: Not available.
Sources: Broadcasting (January 5, 1981), pp. 39-72 "The Top 100 Companies in Electronic Communications;" Fortune (May 4, 1981, June 15, 1981 and May 1970); Standard & Poor's Standard Corporation Records.

vice, the largest possible complement of stations. Several other groups have 19 stations and CBS briefly owned 20 in 1958.[73] Two major ownership changes were announced in 1978, with General Electric, owner of 17 stations, offering to purchase Cox Broadcasting, with 11 television and radio stations, for nearly $500 million. While approved by the FCC early in 1980, the partnership had already been broken off due to inflationary impact on stock prices, among other things. Combined Communications, owner of 19 stations, completed a merger in May 1979 with the Gannett chain of newspapers in a deal valued at $370 million.[74] In 1980, Westinghouse announced the biggest merger deal yet—a takeover of Teleprompter, then the largest owner of cable systems in the country. The better than $600 million deal received FCC approval in 1981.[75]

Broadcasting's Role in Various Companies

As shown in Table 6.6, broadcasting plays a varied role in different firms. Among the networks, ABC is both the smallest and the most dependent on broadcasting as a substantial part of total corporate revenue. Note the comparatively small portion of revenues contributed by broadcasting in such large manufacturing companies as Westinghouse, RCA, and McGraw-Hill. But a sense of size is best perceivable when one notes that GE's after-tax earning of $1.5 billion almost equaled the pretax earnings of the entire television business as reported by the FCC. GE's overall revenues are almost triple the broadcasting revenues of the television networks and all stations combined![76] On the other hand, General Tire's broadcasting subsidiary, RKO General, has already lost three major market television stations in an FCC decision (which was still on appeal in 1981) and could lose the remainder of its holdings if the FCC ruling is upheld. Significantly, some firms thought of as large by broadcasting standards, such as Metromedia, Cox, Taft and Storer, do not even rank in the *Fortune* 500. One reason is that they are not manufacturing firms. But even if they were, their revenues would not qualify them for a ranking. Finally, the table demonstrates as well that with the exception of CBS, Times Mirror, Gannett and Schering-Plough (the last two products of significant mergers), the firms listed are all relatively smaller in 1980 than in 1970—their ranks in *Fortune*'s listings having declined in relation to other firms.

Yet these are still large firms in most cases. Tables 6.7 and 6.8 provide one insight as to why—the largest group owners in both radio and television reach potentially sizable audiences. There is considerable stability in the television business: of 1980's top 15 group owners, 10 appear (two with some ownership change) on the top 15 list for 1959. Note that all 10 companies owned as many or more stations in 1980 as in 1959. As FCC rules limit ownership to no more than 5 VHF stations, seven of the top 15 groups (but none of the networks) had ventured into control of at least one UHF station—an indicator of the newer service's improving financial outlook. Indeed, Field is made up totally of UHF stations, a group of independents acquired from Kaiser. Finally, there has been comparatively little change in rank order on the list. Comparing Table 6.7 to the radio ownership situation shown in Table 6.8, it can be seen that nine of the top 15 owners are represented on both lists in 1980. Further, the numbers charted on the radio list imply that a large number of FM stations are held by groups (no unit can own more than seven AM or seven FM stations), demonstrating that radio's former "second service" is rising to equality with AM on several levels. Table 6.8, and to some extent Table 6.7, shows the limitation of trying to control ownership by number of stations held without the presence of a similar control for size of market served. For example, RCA's eight radio stations serve a larger market area than the greater number of stations held by seven other owners. Likewise, the four large RKO-General television stations have a larger potential viewership than the greater number of stations held by eight other owners.

Numerical Limits on Multiple Ownership[77]

As had happened with consideration of duopoly, the FCC started instituting limitations early on in the development of the new FM and television services, before these had a chance to form unsatisfactory ownership patterns similar to those which had existed for AM. The first numerical restriction on broadcast ownership came in 1940 when ownership was limited to three television stations and up to six FM stations. In 1944, as a compromise to an NBC petition for a limit of seven TV stations to any one owner, the FCC increased the TV limit to five stations. No limit was suggested for AM broadcasting but in rejection of CBS's attempt to acquire KQW in San Jose as its eighth owned and operated station, the FCC created a *de facto* limit of seven stations to be held by any one AM station owner.

The Commission first considered a cohesive policy of multiple broadcasting ownership limitation in 1948. The rules finally adopted in November 1953 applied numerical limits of seven AM, seven FM, and five television stations, dropping earlier consideration of such variables as minority control, number of people served, etc. This was the first actual rule affecting AM control. Two licensees with greater ownership interest (minority holdings in both cases) were given three years to dispose of those holdings. With further consideration of the problems of UHF television then becoming apparent, the Commission increased the limit on television

Table 6.7: Group Ownership in Television: The Top 15 Groups, 1959 and 1980

Ownership Unit	Rank 1980	Rank 1959	Number of Stations Owned 1980	Number of Stations Owned 1959	Net Weekly Circulation[3] (in millions) 1980	Net Weekly Circulation[3] (in millions) 1959	% of U.S. TV Households 1980	% of U.S. TV Households 1959
CBS	1	1	5	5	16.0	11.3	22%	22%
ABC	2	3	5	5	15.8	9.6	22	19
RCA (NBC)	3	2	5	5	15.2	10.8	21	21
Metromedia	4	7[1]	7	4	13.9	3.9	20	8
RKO-General	5	4	4	4	9.5	5.4	17	11
Westinghouse	6	5	6	5	9.0	4.7	11	9
WGN/Continental	6	6	3	2	8.6	4.5	13	9
Storer	8	8	7	5	7.0	3.3	10	6
Field	9	—	5	—	6.1	—	14	—
Capital Cities	10	9[2]	6	6	5.8	2.8	7	5
Taft	11	—	7	—	5.6	—	9	—
Gaylord	12	—	7	—	5.6	—	9	—
Cox	13	—	5	—	5.2	—	6	—
Scripps-Howard	14	11	6	3	4.1	1.9	5	4
Post-Newsweek	15	—	4	—	4.1	—	5	—

[1] As Metropolitan stations in 1959.
[2] As Triangle stations in 1959.
[3] Indicates how many millions of households are served by each group taking all markets they serve collectively.

Note: 1980 data restricted to top 100 markets only, but that does not appear to change the relative comparison with 1959 study which covered all markets.

Sources: 1959 data from Sterling and Haight, table 280-C; 1980 data from H. Howard, "Television Station Group Ownership: 1980", a research study prepared for National Association of Broadcasters, 1981, p. 6. Percent of U.S. Households (1980) added by author using *Population Book, 1980-81* (New York: Arbitron, 1980).

Table 6.8: The Top 15 Group Owners in Radio, 1980

Rank	Ownership Unit	Number of Stations Owned	Total Weekly Listeners
1.	CBS	14	7,208,000
2.	ABC	13	6,932,000
3.	Group W	12	5,843,000
4.	Metromedia	13	5,239,000
5.	Capital Cities	12	4,760,000
6.	RCA (NBC)	8	4,657,000
7.	RKO	11	4,258,000
8.	SJR	9	3,749,000
9.	Bonneville	11	3,326,000
10.	Cox	12	3,307,000
11.	Taft	12	2,786,000
12.	Gannett	11	2,636,000
13.	Inner City	6	2,514,000
14.	Plough	12	2,120,000
15.	GE	8	1,742,000
	Total	164	—

Note: Total audience measures are misleading in that repeat listeners are not accounted for, but the figures provide at least a sense of magnitude difference. Data includes AM and FM stations. Source counts simulcast AM-FM stations as single stations, and includes only those groups with five or more stations showing up in market rating books (which does not substantially impact above list).

Source: James H. Duncan, Jr., *American Radio: Fall 1980* (Kalamazoo, Michigan, 1981), p. A-28.

ownership to seven stations, no more than five of which could be VHF. This final (September 1954) adjustment of the rules was upheld in a 1956 Supreme Court decision.[78] These regulations have never once been waived, a rare thing in FCC ownership policy.

Only in the early 1980s was serious disagreement heard on these long-accepted rules. (Indeed, only in the late 1970s had any single group owner first held the 21 station maximum.) It had become increasingly apparent, as previously noted, that an arbitrary limit on number of stations was not an effective way of limiting single-owner access to a large portion of the nation's population. Combined with this was a feeling that ownership limits, if any, should be applied equally across broadcasting, cable, and newer media. The growing potential for competition to broadcasting resulted in fresh examination of old rules written in a far simpler time.[79]

Top 50 Market Policy[80]

Concern over the increasing concentration of television station owner-ship after the end of the TV Freeze in early 1952 led to the adoption of an ill-fated Commission policy late in 1964. The Commission announced a policy of requiring a hearing for any application for a second VHF station in the 50 largest markets. The hearing, an expensive proceeding for dealing with complaints of all kinds, could be avoided only with a "compelling af-firmative showing" that granting a second VHF station to the same owner would serve the public interest.[81] In 1965 a formal rule-making began—a move made partially to spark UHF development—with the policy calling for a hearing if an owner applied for more than *three* stations (with a max-imum of two VHF outlets) in the largest markets. Divestiture of existing combinations (for examples, see Table 6.7) was not planned.[82] The top 50 markets were chosen as the arena for policy in that they encompassed about 75% of all television homes. The industry responded with massive filings and research, which suggested few positive and many negative results from such a policy, and proposed other approaches.[83] In addition, during the comment and consideration period on this Docket (1965-1968), the Commission granted waivers without hearings in each of the eight cases where the new proposed rules would have called for a rejection of the application. By February 1968, the formal rule-making was closed without action and the policy was continued on an *ad hoc* case-by-case basis. Over the next decade, 19 waivers of the *ad hoc* policy were requested and all were granted.[84] Not once was the so-called policy upheld. In December 1979, the FCC formally dropped the non-operative policy.[85]

This was lip service in its most classic form: a policy suggested but never once upheld in an actual case decision. Not one hearing took place. In a detailed critique of the policy just prior to its deletion, one observer noted that not only had the FCC relied totally on industry economic data, per-forming no economic analysis of its own, but it had based most of its case decisions more on rhetoric than fact, and ignored a trend to greater con-centration among VHF station owners in the large markets. Economic arguments of efficiency were accepted over non-economic social concerns.[86] And little or no research was done other than by the group owners affected.

Regional Concentration Rule

From time to time, other approaches to limiting ownership have been considered by the Commission, but nearly all have suffered from being arbitrary, with little or no specific research data backing them up, and have thus died along the way with little fanfare. One example was the 1975 proposed rule to limit ownership to no more than four stations within any one state. No final action was ever taken on this idea.[87]

On the other hand, in 1977 the Commission did issue a rule to limit concentration of control in a small geographic area. The Regional Concentration of Control Rule "prohibits any acquisition of a broadcast station or any modification of a station's facilities that would result in the common ownership of three broadcast stations, of which two are within 100 miles of the third, and there is, or will be, primary service contour overlap of any two of the three stations."[88] AM/FM combinations are counted as but one station if their communities of license are within 15 miles of one another and/or fall in the same general urban region. Translator TV stations (which generally rebroadcast from a parent station and are used to fill holes in coverage patterns) are not considered a part of the rule, and as with other regulations, the FCC considers UHF television stations on a case-by-case basis, hoping thereby to encourage that service's development.[89] In the overall scheme of rules, this is a very technical and somewhat minor limitation, given its exceptions and definitions. Still, the attempt to limit concentration in a single area has not thus far been eviscerated, as was the case with the Top 50 Market policy.

Multiple Holdings by Financial Organizations[90]

The 1953 order which established overall numerical limits to multiple ownership included a provision whereby licensees with more than 50 stockholders could include financial institutions (banks, investment funds, and the like) owning up to 1% of the total stock without that ownership figuring in or even having to be reported as a part of station ownership. This "one percent rule" recognized the difference between investment in a station as a pure investment and participaton in order to have a say in station management. A decade later several cases came to light where financial groups, especially mutual funds, controlled far more than 1% in cases involving a large number of group owners, thus technically violating the group ownership limits. In June 1968, the limit was raised to 3% for mutual funds signing statements specifying their interest in investment rather than station control. Four years later the rate was raised to 5% for bank trusts, a limit extended to insurance firms and other investment organizations in mid-1976.[91]

There, despite several further petitions and filings for rule-making, the issue sat for some five years. Pressure was building in that period for the

Commission to set a standard, across-the-board, 10% "benchmark" for all the different kinds of financial institutions, with a stipulation that such owners would not vote their stock holdings or be otherwise active in affairs of firms in which they held minority holdings. But critics, reviewing the trend from 1% to 3% to 5% and the projected push up to 10%, noted the slow decline in validity of the rules. They observed that the changes seemed to come about when the FCC discovered financial firms holding more than the existing benchmark, and thus changed the rule, revising it to a looser standard. In 1981, it was expected the Commission would finally revise all previous decisions in this area in an omnibus rule-making, setting a standard 5% or perhaps 10% benchmark for all financial institution minority holdings.[92]

STATION OWNERSHIP: SPECIAL CASES

Three categories of multiple ownership raise special questions: 1) network owned and operated stations (O&Os); 2) multimedia conglomerate owners; and 3) public radio and television stations, the latter generally exempted thus far from any of the rules discussed above.

Network O&Os

Occupying a special place among group owners are the national broadcasting networks, both radio and television. While they are under the same controls as other group owners, network owned and operated (O&O) stations have garnered more critical comment over the years due to their major market locations, their economic performance, and the fact that they are the only segment of networks which are directly regulated by the FCC.

Both CBS and NBC began radio operation with owned and operated stations, and over the years expanded their radio holdings. By 1933 (and for the decade thereafter), NBC controlled 10 stations, seven built or purchased in the 1930-1933 period. In addition, NBC programmed five stations actually owned by Westinghouse, giving the network complete control of 15 AM outlets.[93] CBS controlled nine stations (one was leased) by 1936.[94] Mutual had no owned and operated stations until 1978.[95] Of these network operations (discounting the Westinghouse stations programmed by NBC), 10 were Class I-A Clear Channel operations with 50,000 watts.[96] Operating two networks, NBC had two stations each in New York, Chicago, Washington and San Francisco. FCC concern about that ownership and its perceived unfairness helped bring about the first major investigation of the role of networks in broadcasting, the Chain Broadcasting investigation of 1938-1941. One result of that investigation, and the

Supreme Court decision of 1943[97] which supported the FCC decisions on network radio, was the forced divestiture of the NBC Blue network and its stations, which became ABC in 1945.

The development of television network O&Os was more complicated. As shown in Table 6.9, only ABC managed to build all of its O&O stations before the Freeze (and all on channel 7, helping to build a common identity), though the cost of television programming kept the network itself quite weak until a merger partner was found to increase capital. After several other proposals were considered, ABC merged in 1951 with United Paramount Theaters (approved by the FCC early in 1953), but continued as the weakest of the three networks until its ratings success began in 1975. Only Dumont was weaker until it left the business in 1955—primarily because of a lack of four station markets where it could obtain sufficient affiliations to compete. CBS was backing its own system of color transmission and receivers and held back on television expansion for that reason; it thus ended up purchasing most of its stations, including several minority ownerships and two UHF stations, in the 1950s. NBC also experimented briefly with UHF ownership in the 1950s.

An important cause celebre for network O&O stations is represented by NBC's operations in Cleveland and Philadelphia. Following the normal group owner policy of attempting to "trade up," NBC pressured Westinghouse, another group owner, and an NBC affiliate in several markets, into "trading" its Philadelphia station for the NBC outlet in Cleveland plus several million dollars to sweeten the deal. Westinghouse was pressured by the threat of losing its all-important network affiliations. Though approved by the FCC in 1955, a year later the Justice Department brought suit in Philadelphia to undo the trade, charging parent RCA with antitrust violations by use of the network affiliation threat to force Westinghouse to give in. The case went to the Supreme Court which found against RCA,[98] but attempts by the network to modify the result dragged on for six more years. Not until 1965 was the trade actually undone. As important as the events and court case was the adverse publicity and Congressional attention directed to network station ownership and general operating tactics. Early in 1979, NBC announced it planned to expand its radio holdings by purchase of an additional three AM and three FM outlets, though specific target markets or stations were not named nor had action been taken by 1981 (earlier in the decade, NBC had tried to sell off its radio holdings entirely).[99]

At no time has the FCC seriously considered a policy of network O&O divestiture, though on several occasions the Commission has suggested that if the issue were being approached for the first time, it might well have been better to separate network operation from station ownership. The prime concern expressed by critics is the excessive economic clout the net-

Table 6.9: Network Ownership of Broadcast Stations, 1980[1]

Market Ranking and Number of TV Households	% of All U.S. Households	ABC-Owned Stations	CBS-Owned Stations	NBC-Owned Stations
1. New York 6,432,000	8.3%	WABC/7 (1948,C,R)	WCBS/2 (1941,C,R)	WNBC/4 (1941,C,R)
2. Los Angeles 4,181,600	5.4	KABC/7 (1949,C,R)	KNXT/2 (1951,P,R) *KTTV/11 (1948-51,P)*	KNBC/4 (1947,P)
3. Chicago 2,847,200	3.7	WLS/7 (1948,C,R)	WBBM/2 (1953,P,R)	WMAQ/5 (1948,C,R)
4. Philadelphia 2,358,400	3.1	—	WCAU/10 (1958,P,R)	*WRCV/3 (1955-65,P)*
5. San Francisco 1,917,800	2.5	KGO/7 (1949,C,R)	(R only)	(R only)
6. Boston 1,859,900	2.4	—	(R only)	—
7. Detroit 1,606,200	2.1	WXYZ/7 (1948,C,R)	—	—
8. Washington 1,400,400	1.8	(R only)	*WTOP/9 (1950-54,P)*	WRC/4 (1947,C,R)
9. Cleveland 1,328,800	1.7	—	—	WKYC/3 *(1948-55,C)* (1965,P)
12. Houston 1,151,400	1.5	(R only)	—	—
13. Minneapolis-St. Paul 1,009,500	1.3	—	*WCCO/4 (1952-54,P)*	—
14. St. Louis 1,000,800	1.3	—	KMOX/4 (1957,P,R)	—
22. Hartford-New Haven 676,100	.9	—	*WHCT/18 (1956-58,P)*	*WNBC/30 (1956-58,P)*
28. Milwaukee 660,700	.9	—	*WXIX/18 (1954-59,P)*	—
29. Buffalo 629,900	.8	—	—	*WBUF/17 (1955-58,P)*

[1] Listings show the television station call letters and channel number of first line, and in parentheses below, the year the station began operations for that network. The symbol C indicates the station was constructed by the network; P indicates purchased by the network from a previous owner; R indicates a combination AM-FM radio station owned by the network in that market. Those stations in italics are no longer network-owned. The end date, if any, indicates the year the network relinquished control of the station.

Source: Market data and rank data for 1980 from *Population Book, 1980-81* (New York: Arbitron, 1980), p. 52; station data from Sterling and Kittross (1978), p. 266.

works have with their own operations plus the stations—which, as Table 6.7 shows, have always been the three top groups in number of homes reached (and in per station profits as well). For a number of years, the networks argued that the O&Os were their prime source of income, as network operation otherwise lost money. Table 6.2 shows that network margins were indeed low for many years but that by the mid-1970s, the networks were making substantial profits even without their O&Os, which continued to garner substantial profits as well.

In the late 1970s, as investigations of network concentration mounted, one target was again the network O&O. The FCC's network investigation, begun in 1977, included this issue although the Justice Department's antitrust suits did not. One factor recently discussed is the limitation on effective competition from a potential fourth network, given the O&O base of the existing three in the major markets, and the difficulty any new network would face in being able to build a similar stable of stations in major markets both as an economic base and as a core around which to sign up affiliates among independent stations. Somewhat of a conflict of interest exists for networks which, on one hand, are concerned with network operations and their stations as outlets for that programming and advertising, and on the other hand with the stations as individual outlets in their markets and the latitude they should have in selecting other programming. The outlook, however, is for little or no change in status of network O&Os in the foreseeable future.

Media Conglomerates

Of somewhat more recent vintage as an ownership concern in broadcasting is the role of conglomerate firms. Loosely defined, these are business organizations with control of a wide variety of manufacturing and/or service divisions, which may include media interests. Often such conglomerates are also group owners of broadcast stations and may have one or more chains of newspapers or other media holdings.

It has been suggested that there are at least three kinds of conglomerate media owners:

- the media conglomerate with holdings in several different media but not much else;

- the concentric conglomerate with one or more major media industry holdings plus substantial revenues from non-media business or manufacturing industry; and

• the diversified conglomerate which includes media holdings in an otherwise patternless combination of many unrelated business and industry holdings.[100]

As shown in Table 6.6, these organizations differ significantly in size and depend to varying degrees on broadcasting as a contributor to corporate revenues. Some overall trends in conglomerate ownership can be summarized as follows:

1) All three networks are now conglomerates to some extent, paced by giant RCA. Acquisitions in the past two decades by CBS have led to its diversification, while ABC is still predominantly a broadcasting firm, though it has branched out heavily into publishing.

2) Though not shown on Table 6.6, almost without exception, broadcasting's contribution to corporate *earnings* is substantially higher than the contribution to revenues which is shown. Broadcast income is often used to subsidize other segments of a firm (note, for example the case of the afternoon newspapers discussed earlier), or to allow investment in other media—especially cable systems.

3) Thus far, conglomerates appear more likely to have broadcast rather than other media holdings, although this appears to be changing with respect to cable system ownership. A detailed analysis of media conglomerates as of early 1977 supports this. Of 10 firms controlling holdings in six or more different media industries, all but one had broadcasting properties; of eight firms with holdings in five media industries, five included broadcasting; of 13 firms with holdings in four different media industries, 10 included broadcast holdings; of 38 firms with holdings in three media, 31 had at least one radio or television station; and of 18 additional firms with holdings in two media industries, only one lacked broadcast stations.[101]

4) As is true for other group owners, conglomerates have generally shunned UHF television, preferring instead the more profitable VHF stations. Of the top 39 companies included in a 1978 survey, only nine stations held were UHF, compared to 112 VHF operations.[102]

5) Some of the changes in conglomerate makeup are due to regulatory initiatives as well as market forces. In releasing the results of a study purporting to show a decline in media cross-ownership in the 1968-1978 period, National Association of Broadcasters President Vincent Wasilewski said, "The increased number of stations on-the-air, and the Federal Communications Commission's policy on cross-ownership are the two major factors attributable to the decrease in concentration" reported for the top 50 markets.[103]

Some of the sales and transfers of the 1970s were prompted by what the sellers termed government pressure over such issues as cross-media controls. For example, Newhouse Broadcasting, part of the multi-media conglomerate built mainly on newspapers and magazines, late in 1978 announced plans to sell its five television stations (while holding on to five radio stations) to Times Mirror, giving the latter its full complement of seven television stations. Newhouse executives claimed they "were not happy" over the $82 million sale but did it to eliminate the pressures put on them by the FCC and other parties over their broadcast properties amidst their larger print holdings.[104]

Author Kevin Phillips suggests three major approaches to the control of such organizations:

- treating the media as semi-governmental bodies due to their key role as information conduits both to and from government;

- regulation of content; or

- using antitrust action to break the conglomerates into smaller media business units which would obviate the need for the first two somewhat more odious regulatory options.[105]

A good example of the problems that emerge in facing such approaches can be seen in the 1965-1967 attempted takeover of ABC by the ITT conglomerate. Several issues were raised as the FCC considered the merger (because title to ABC's O&O stations was involved): whether money would be funneled into or siphoned off from ABC; the effect on ABC news of all ITT's other (including extensive defense) interests; excessive concentration in communication (broadcasting, recordings, filmmaking and distribution/exhibition); and the effect on ABC of ITT's extensive overseas business (about 60% of its income at that time).

The Commission approved the merger in a 4-3 vote in December 1966.

Acting a few days before the order became final, the Justice Department petitioned the FCC to reconsider the whole affair. Despite Justice's argument concerning anti-competitive aspects of the case, the Commission again approved the merger in May 1967, feeling that ABC needed the greater financial security ITT backing would provide. It was felt that this move would enable the then weakest network to deal more effectively with RCA-owned NBC and highly diversified CBS. The Justice Department then appealed the decision to the Court of Appeals for the District of Columbia, not on antitrust grounds (where the Department felt its case was too speculative), but rather because the FCC had not adequately considered the public interest. Faced with further delays, and a change in stock values which would have cost ITT nearly $300 million more for the merger than when it had been proposed late in 1965, ITT withdrew its offer in January 1968.[106] Some of the same arguments had been raised in the two years of FCC consideration that preceded ABC's 1953 merger with United Paramount Theaters.

Prompted both by the ABC-ITT spectacle as well as by a perceived trend to more merger activity in general, the FCC initiated a broad investigation into conglomerate ownership of broadcast stations in 1969. That year, and again in 1971, the Commission sent out detailed survey questionnaires to elicit information on which firms really owned what. While the study group continued its work, no specific rule-makings resulted. Various hearings in both houses of Congress on conglomerate trends had one specific related result—the ownership limit suggested in the initial rewrite of the 1934 Communications Act. Only five radio or five television stations were to be allowed—a policy which would have required substantial industry divestiture.[107]

Public Broadcasting

Unlike commercial broadcasting, the noncommercial alternative service, Public Broadcasting, is essentially decentralized. As shown in Table 6.1, the number of noncommercial stations has always represented just a fraction of the number of commercial stations in any of the broadcast services. Prior to 1962, the noncommercial system was small, localized and struggled for funds with no federal input whatever. Supported mainly by state and local taxes, contributions from viewers and businesses, and the largesse of the Ford Foundation, educational broadcasting, as it was then known, had a miniscule audience and was more interested in instruction and adult education than anything else. Beginning in 1962, limited tax funds on the federal level began to support facilities construction for educational television. The really important landmark in educational broadcasting history came with the 1967 publication of the Carnegie Commission report, which led to the Public Broadcasting Act a few months later.

The act established the Corporation for Public Broadcasting (CPB) as a national nonprofit organization through which greatly increased Congressional funding for the public television and radio system would be funneled. The report and act of 1967 provided not merely a new name (public instead of educational) and increased funding, but afforded the basis for a broader conception of what public broadcasting should be, and the beginnings of a nationally centralized series of organizations to carry through the new concept. The Corporation, as funding agent, was forbidden to own facilities or control networking (a new concept in public television except for some Ford Foundation-supported experiments). In 1969, CPB formed the Public Broadcasting Service (PBS), and a year later followed up with National Public Radio (NPR) to operate network interconnection and programming for television and radio stations, respectively.

The greatly increased funding, the rapidly increasing number of new public stations coming on the air, and the changing political scene of the early 1970s led to some dramatic confrontations and a substantial shakeout in the public broadcasting establishment. Friction between CPB as money source and PBS as network and representative of the public TV stations flared up in the 1970-1974 period, exacerbated by pressure from the Nixon administration, which was critical of the seeming liberal bias of revitalized public affairs programming on PBS. The arguments all seemed to center on funding. For one thing, there was never enough (despite the greatly increased federal input). And, substantial disagreement existed on the degree to which the noncommercial system should be centralized around the new national "networks" as opposed to the localism which had characterized the system up to the mid-1960s, and to which many political figures seemed to want to return. The peak of the battle came in 1973 when President Nixon vetoed a proposed two-year funding package for public broadcasting, feeling the system was getting too centralized and "networky."

The subsequent departure of Nixon paralleled substantial changeover in personnel at CPB and PBS (NPR was largely able to avoid the cross-fire, operating as it did with fewer than 100 small stations). CPB and PBS worked out an uncomfortable compromise which removed CPB substantially from programming decisions while Congress finally agreed to the principle of five-year long-range funding legislation in 1975, revised and extended in 1978 and 1981. But through all this debate ran a basic and still existing question: Just what is the role of noncommercial public broadcasting in a basically commercial system? The complaints of insufficient funding are merely a result of this quandary about which there is little agreement.

History

While noncommercial stations are as old as broadcasting itself, dating back to the early 1920s, educational radio went into a decade-long decline after peaking around 1925. The pressure from commercial operators for frequencies, the lack of funding and the nonexistence of a clear idea of what public radio could or should do all led to a decline which left about 35 stations still operating at the end of World War II. In 1945, as a part of its allocation on the 88-108 MHz band for FM radio, the FCC adopted a long-discussed notion of reserving some of those frequencies for noncommercial educational facilities. This precedent underlay the very important 1952 decision to reserve some television channels in 1952 as the four-year Freeze was ended. These reservations on FM and television prevent direct facilities competition between well-funded commercial applicants and more limited educational institutions. The reservations also underlie *de facto* national policy administered by the FCC that setting aside such stations —and providing for them first with facilities and later with funding—is in the public interest.

Table 6.10 shows development of the four types of public television station owners. While public school systems were initially interested in public TV for classroom education, the costs of television and constricting enrollments have led to a decline in public school licensees. The core of public television from the beginning were the college and university licensees, most of which had experience with educational radio. A number of state tax-supported authorities built networks of public TV stations. But the most important and usually financially well-off stations have been those operated by community organizations especially set up (and often consisting of representatives of major cultural and educational organizations within a given area) to cooperatively operate the station. As might be expected, the community stations have been most interested in broad cultural/entertainment/public affairs programming, and have played the major role in producing prime-time programming for PBS. The other licensee groups have a stronger stake in instructional programming, and generally play a more passive role in the national system. Virtually all public television stations are a part of this overall system.

Not so with public radio. While there are more than 1000 noncommercial radio stations today (all but 25 of them on FM frequencies), and they fall into a similar ownership pattern as the four categories for television,

Table 6.10: Ownership of Public Television Stations, 1962, 1968, 1974 and 1980

Ownership Category	1962	1968	1974	1980
Colleges and universities				
Number	12	31	74	79
Percent of total	19%	21	30	27
Public school systems				
Number	19	22	20	18
Percent of total	31%	15	8	6
State/municipal authorities				
Number	13	52	84	115
Percent of total	21%	36	35	39
Community organizations				
Number	18	41	65	80
Percent of total	29%	28	27	27
Total transmitting stations	62	146	243	292

Sources: 1962, 1968, 1974: Sterling and Haight, table 281-A; 1980: National Association of Public Television Stations.

there is an additional dimension. Several hundred of the FM stations operated for decades with just 10 watts of power—providing training for personnel, but service to only a small area. In the late 1970s, the FCC required such stations either to increase power (to at least 100 watts) or move to an unprotected status on the commercial band (meaning they would have to give way for any full-time applicant for those facilities). Even in the early 1980s, these small stations and many hundreds of others, most with fewer than five employees, and often broadcasting for only a limited number of hours per week, made up the vast bulk of noncommercial radio stations. National Public Radio planners faced a difficult decision in trying to construct a national system. They could not adequately serve all the stations on the air, and thus had to choose only the largest and best funded as an initial core. Known as "CPB-Qualified" stations (meaning they met minimal criteria in staffing, programming, hours on air, and local financial support), only these stations are eligible for CPB funding grants, and activity within NPR including the right to carry its programming. The core is small—about 20% of the total noncommercial stations on the air —creating a small "have" and much larger "have not" category in noncommercial radio.

Through all of this development and confusion on goals, the FCC has generally held public radio and television exempt from the ownership rules discussed earlier. Specifically:

- There is no duopoly rule in public broadcasting. Thus, the same licensee controls two television channels (both noncommercial) in such communities as San Francisco, Pittsburgh, Milwaukee. Usually one of the stations is programmed as a general-appeal "public" station while the other schedules instructional material during school hours, often going off the air in the evening and on weekends. Some recent challenges to license renewals have contended that such part-time use of a television channel is a public disservice best met by another licensee holding the facility.[108]

- Public broadcasting is specifically excluded from the numerical multiple station limits, or the 7-7-7 rule.[109] Thus, several states have been able to build networks of television and/or radio licenses, holding as many as eight to 10 licenses rather than the seven-station limit applicable to commercial operations. A special Alabama state commission, for example, holds the licenses to an eight-station network (which it lost but was able to regain in a long FCC renewal procedure concerned with the role of Black employees on the air and in station employment).

Beginning in 1981, the FCC planned to reexamine all of these rule exemptions for noncommercial broadcasting, including such basic rules as allowing licenses in reserved bands to be held only by noncommercial groups or institutions. Some of this investigating is the result of long-standing concerns over the justification for the exemptions: a lack of diversity in viewpoint can occur in public as well as commercial broadcasting. But some is due to the rapidly changing financial support picture for public broadcasting as federal (and to a lesser extent, state) tax funds diminish and broader means are sought to support the system, up to and including advertising. The change in the financial role of the system speaks directly to ownership structure. All of this suggests that the ownership, let alone national structure of public broadcasting, is likely to undergo what may be substantial change in the next several years.

Low-Power Television Stations

After a lengthy rule-making and considerable controversy, the FCC early in 1982 issued a report and order formally establishing a system of low-power television (LPTV) stations—the first new use of the broadcast spectrum in some three decades. While far too involved to detail here, a fundamental decision concerning ownership of LPTV stations shed light on the FCC's likely direction on ownership questions generally. In its

LPTV *Report and Order,* the Commission adopted no ownership restrictions of any kind.[109a] Existing local radio and television stations were to be allowed to own an LPTV facility; networks could own LPTVs (though the original proposed rule-making had projected a ban here); there was to be no limit on either regional or national multiple ownership; and cross-ownership between low-power television and cable stations or newspapers was to be allowed. Even such heretofore fundamental broadcast rules as duopoly and one-to-a-market were not to apply to LPTV. To be sure, a major reason for this *laissez-faire* approach was the secondary nature of the new and untried service on which considerable disagreement existed as to its economic viability. But the fact remains that LPTV thus would be something of an experiment for a true marketplace environment, with ownership (and even trafficking in facilities reduced to a one-year holding period, as opposed to the normal [for other broadcast services] three) totally subject to business conditions and free of any regulatory restraint. Expected delays in processing due to the applications backlog, however, promised to delay assessment of the experiment's impact.

EVIDENCE ON THE EFFECTS OF STATION OWNERSHIP

Most of the research done on broadcast concentration issues has served to provide various descriptive measures of how extensive that ownership trend is—but comparatively little work has analyzed the effects of such concentration. Many FCC and court decisions on various ownership cases have spoken out about this dearth of reliable and valid information on what really is the most important policy-related question of all—just what effect on programming and advertising does ownership appear to have? In addition, if there are substantial differences, do owners of multiple broadcast stations do a "better" or "worse" job of serving the public interest? Or, on the other hand, if there are no discernable differences, is there really any point in making clearly arbitrary rules concerning ownership?

In 1974 the Rand Corporation published the best single integrated analysis of research literature to that date on the effects of concentrated ownership.[110] Massive problems with published studies were found in both methodology and in simply defining the criteria for determining "good" or "bad" broadcast station performance in the context of serving the public interest, convenience or necessity. The Rand researchers found that most studies dealt with economic effects of ownership, as these, while less important to the public in many ways, were clearly easier to quantify than content measures—especially when the problem of policy (let alone operational) definitions was raised. Assessing many studies of both economic and content variety, they concluded:

. . . The results of assessing the state of current knowledge about the effects of media ownership concentration can be expressed in the well-known Scotch verdict: "Not proved." . . . The form of media ownership generally seems to have a small impact on economic or content performance. . . . Most statistical studies simply show no significant differences among media ownership classes. Differences reported in certain studies have not been reproduced in other situations. And many of the prior studies seem flawed by inadequate data or by methodological problems, such as failure to control for other important variables.[111]

More specifically, the Rand researchers found:

- ". . . There is little evidence of a statistically significant relationship between cross-ownership and newspaper flat line advertising rate or the price of an hour of prime-time television. . . ."[112]

- ". . . Findings of no significant cross-ownership effects on individual station audience ratings. . . ."[113]

- ". . . Any effects of cross-ownership are not strong enough to distort an entire market's behavior in competing for national advertising."[114]

- "The question of cross-ownership's effects on local advertising rates at the individual station and newspaper level is the one most pertinent to the cross-ownership debate, but it remains unresolved on the basis of presently available research."[115]

- ". . . Group ownership does raise the average time sales, revenue, and income of television stations in a market. . . ." (but the study did not control for market competition, UHF-VHF status, market demographics, etc.).[116]

- ". . . Studies . . . do not provide evidence of any significant differences [in televised news and public affairs programming, or hours with excessive advertising] among group owners, cross-media owners, and other broadcast station owners. . . ."[117]

- "In none of these program types—news, public affairs, instructional or local programs generally—do the newspaper owners systematically outclass the non-newspaper licensees" when measuring quantity (not quality) of these programming types.[118]

- ". . . Network affiliation variables seem to be the most consistently significant. The group ownership variable is insignificant . . ." in assessing amounts of news, local programming, feature films, high and low brow entertainment, and public affairs programming.[119]

- "There is case evidence showing abuses by media owners with both concentrated and nonconcentrated holdings. But taken individually or collectively, the body of case evidence has not shown that group or cross-media owners influence their media outlets or otherwise behave differently from other media owners."[120]

These Rand results are important because, first, they represent the best unbiased and detailed assessment of all the literature, regardless of who supported it (and many of the studies, if not most of them, have received support from one or more interested parties in the regulatory proceedings discussed earlier). Second, they are quite consistent in their findings of little or no difference between concentrated and non-concentrated ownership across a number of variables in many different situations. Third, they clearly pinpoint the difference between broad statistical surveys and specific case studies; most of the regulatory proceedings are studded with the latter, which, while useful in adversary proceedings, are not clear indicators necessarily of industry-wide practice. Finally, very little has appeared in the eight years since the Rand overview to change any of the judgments summarized above.

A later study assessing the amount of news and public affairs programming by television stations in the top 75 markets concluded that ". . . Deficiencies in the communication flow . . . cannot then be blamed on the preponderance of group owners in the business structure. The local owner, like the group owner, is most likely to avoid that programming which is most likely to approximate a forum function . . . his allocations [of] air time do not differ from that of the group owner."[121] When controlled for VHF affiliates only, the results are the same.

Another analysis of FCC quantitative data on news and public affairs programming of 677 commercial TV stations in 1973 concluded that "multimedia-owned television stations perform at least as well, and sometimes significantly better, than all other stations. In particular, multimedia-owned stations are likely to provide significantly more news."[122] The authors also found, as have other studies, that network affiliated stations do better on similar program measures than independents, and VHFs do better than UHFs. As most group-owned stations are VHF affiliates, that factor may well be of more importance than any ownership difference. On the other hand, a detailed content analysis of newspaper and television news stories in cross-owned and independent operations "found that common ownership of a newspaper and a television station in the same city does tend to restrict the variety of news available to the public—and further, that the homogenizing effects of cross-ownership are most noticeable in smaller cities."[123]

Clearly, there is no strong research underpinning for breaking up various kinds of combined ownership situations. There are a number of negative case findings,[124] but overall studies (done mainly in the cross-ownership area) can generally be summed up as reporting "no significant difference" in either economic or quantity-of-programming effects. More basic is the problem that much of the needed research has yet to be done.[125]

THE ROLE OF NETWORKS

National networks exist to interconnect stations for common and simultaneous distribution of programs and advertising. The network acts as something of a broker between the local station (and its viewers or listeners), program producers and advertisers. From radio days to the present, basic issues of public policy concern about networks have remained, generally speaking, those of excessive domination of advertising, programming and local affiliate stations. These may be translated into four policy objectives which have guided government regulation:

1) to make available the highest quality programming, especially in news and public affairs;

2) to provide for diversity in the sources of those programs, and control over selection of programs by industry gatekeepers;

3) to minimize economic market power by any industry institution (or centralization of that power by a few groups); and

4) to encourage minority and specialized program content rather than wasteful duplication of the usual lowest common denominator broadcast content.[126] Clearly, these issues go beyond networks, but given the generally acknowledged dominant role of the networks over the past half century, most concerns have begun there.

Development of Network Regulation

Both the Radio Act of 1927 (Section 4h) and the Communications Act of 1934 (Section 303i) gave the FRC/FCC authority to make special regulations applicable to stations engaged in chain (or network) broadcasting. Few such regulations emerged until the FCC undertook the first detailed analysis of the role and impact of networks in the chain broadcasting investigation of 1938-1941. An initial report in 1940[127] and a final published report in May 1941[128] examined the rise of the radio networks, the predominance of NBC and CBS in radio, contractual arrangements between the networks and their affiliate stations, network option time and "clearance" policies, and the Commission's jurisdiction to consider and act upon such matters. The report's conclusion called for a limitation on the network's power to force affiliates to clear time for network programs; a shorter, one year affiliation contract period; limits on network control over station advertising rates; and an end to NBC's operation of two national networks.[129] As the FCC cannot directly regulate network companies, all regulations were couched in terms of station licensees—in other words, no station license would be granted to any station affiliated with a network that violated specified regulations. The 1941 report led directly to the network case of 1943,[130] and the eventual formation of what became the American Broadcasting Company.

The expansion of television in the 1950s led to various Congressional investigations, especially into the potential monopoly role of networks. Catalysts for the probes included the decline of the Dumont television network, the weakness of ABC as a distant third in television networking, the merger of ABC with Paramount Theaters Inc. in 1951 (approved by the FCC early in 1953), and the general problems of UHF, including the clear lack of network interest in affiliating with such stations. Frustration was widely expressed over the changes occurring in broadcasting and the dominant role of networks, which to many observers seemed to make allocations and other issues difficult to resolve.[131]

A second FCC investigation of networks was sparked by Congressional concerns, and occupied a special staff under Roscoe L. Barrow from 1955 to 1957. Its massive *Network Broadcasting* report focused on television networking, with detailed information on the measurement of network concentration and control, affiliation practices, option time, advertising rates, station compensation arrangements, "must buy" program practices, station ownership, etc.[132] Among the report's recommendations were a ban on option time, a curb on station ownership, separating networks from station representation, and a general loosening of network control over talent.[133]

While the FCC considered the recommendations of the network study, another staff began a detailed analysis of network programming methods, problems, and trends which had not been dealt with in the "Barrow" report. Reports from this investigation appeared in 1960, 1963, and finally in 1965.[134] At the same time, the quiz show and payola scandals rocked the industry and brought forth additional pressure on the FCC and on Congress to "clean up" television and to investigate still further the role of networks in program content. Partially as a result of these events, the FCC began to consider specific rules to limit network control of evening programming.

Network Regulation in the 1970s and Early 1980s

Eventually, the Prime Time Access Rule (PTAR) was unveiled in 1970 to take effect at the beginning of the Fall 1971 season. Networks were limited to three hours nightly of prime-time programming (effectively a half hour reduction in the existing pattern), and their role in ownership and distribution of independently produced programs was also reduced. The FCC hoped thereby to increase local program production at best, but to diversify program production sources at the very least.[135] The basic result was a glut of syndicated game shows (which cost about 40% of any other entertainment formats). On several subsequent occasions, the FCC modified PTAR to allow for various exemptions, but the basic rule remains in effect, despite court appeals.[136]

In April 1972, the Justice Department's Antitrust Division entered the fray with antitrust suits against all three national networks, aimed at further divorcing them from control, ownership and syndication rights to prime-time programming.[137] Apparently based on research activities going back to the early 1960s, but thought by others to be blatantly political given the then Nixon administration's views toward television,[138] the suits were dismissed late in 1974—and immediately reintroduced during the Ford administration. The networks were unable to get a summary dismissal of the refiled suits on political grounds,[139] and thus filings and counterfilings leading up to a potential trial continued through the 1970s. The suit against NBC was settled out of court late in 1976 and the CBS and ABC suits were similarly settled in 1980.[140] The resulting Consent Decrees limit network activity in some areas of programming and in their relationships with program producers and syndication.

The Office of Telecommunications Policy, under considerable political pressure from several quarters, conducted several years of investigation into network policy on expanding the number of reruns each season. No specific regulations came from the study.[141] In September 1976, Westinghouse Broadcasting brought a petition to the FCC calling for a major Commission investigation of the economic and programming domination of the television networks, charging that affiliate stations had become under-compensated pawns in the network race for supremacy.[142] Justice filed a supporting petition with the Commission, suggesting such a process would not interfere with the suits.[143] Only the networks opposed the study. Early in 1977, the FCC formally announced commencement of its third major study of the role of networks.[144] A political and funding hassle held up the study, but a staff was appointed and work began in mid-1978. Almost lost in the shuffle was the FCC's action lifting the radio network regulations of 1941 (based on the first FCC study of the networks), due to the totally changed role of radio in the 1970s.[145]

The third network study took place under the direction of economist Stanley M. Besen and Georgetown Law School dean Thomas G. Krattenmaker, who were given a substantially free hand to design their study and its supporting reports. In so doing, they broadened the study's mandate and in the process dramatically changed the course of some 40 years of FCC study on "the network problem." The new study looked at networks in the context of changing technology—the oncoming competition from cable, home video, microwave systems, various forms of pay television and the like. The broadcast business was no longer seen as a self-contained unit of limited competition, but rather as merely one form of input to home receivers.[146]

Network Domination of Affiliates

Central to the investigation of networks over the years has been the degree of freedom accorded to local station network affiliates. In television, the controlling factor has been the Commission's spectrum allocation decisions to provide local stations to as many communities as possible—thus creating about 70 of the top 100 markets with three commercial VHF channels, and only about 15 with more than three. There are many smaller markets with but one or two VHF channels. More than anything else, this has limited the number of networks to three, as affiliation with UHF channels is still avoided given the latter's smaller coverage area and limited appeal. Entry to network affiliation status is thus limited as there can be but one entry per network in a given market area, and except for markets with more than three VHF channels, a "bilateral oligopoly" exists where neither networks nor stations have much flexibility (changing affiliations, etc.) Markets with fewer than three VHF channels, the smaller markets, actually have the upper hand in network relations as one of the networks must take a secondary affiliation with but few of its programs being carried. Only in the largest markets, few in number but important economically because of the proportion of audience reached, do the networks have the upper hand by holding the threat to remove an affiliation by giving it to an independent VHF outlet.[147]

The length of affiliation contracts now generally runs for two years, though in fact they run until canceled by network or station, a fairly rare occurrence. With the staying power ABC demonstrated as the top-ranked network in prime-time popularity in the late 1970s, a number of traditional CBS and NBC affiliates switched over to ABC, giving that network true coverage parity with the others for the first time.

A prime factor behind the Westinghouse petition of 1966 was the level of affiliate compensation by the networks. As shown in Table 6.11 network income increased 575% between 1964 and 1976, while network payment to affiliates was up only 34%. This is reflected in the declining proportion of network revenue going to affiliates and the decline in network payments as a percent of station income. The networks retorted that the dramatically increased risks of program costs in a period of true three-network competition had to be covered in some fashion, and that stations did not share in the increased risk, so why should they share unduly in the "spoils" of success? But the Westinghouse figures clearly show a declining economic trend in network payments to individual affiliates over a 13-year period. To Group W, this suggested increased network economic power at the expense of local stations.

The FCC responded by setting up the third network inquiry—the results of which dismayed Westinghouse and other station owners when Besen, Krattenmaker, et al. concluded there was little public interest concern for the FCC in how profits were split up between networks, affiliates or programmers. Such splits had little immediate program diversity impact—and continued FCC concern with this matter merely demonstrated the uselessness of trying to regulate affiliation contract terms.[148]

Several factors enter into affiliate compensation. Where at one time there was a direct connection between station compensation and advertising sales rates, that is no longer the case—partially due to the end of program sponsorship on television. Instead, stations are compensated for network advertising only, not program time or public service announcements, on a contract basis; the contract details, on a station-by-station basis, are not made public, so that great differences may exist in what various stations are able to negotiate from the network. Furthermore, for all three networks, there is a basic 21 to 24 hour per week base for programs for which compensation is relatively low. Then, a higher rate of compensation is calculated for program time taken over that base. This naturally encourages higher levels of program "clearance" by the station.[149] An exam-

Table 6.11: Comparative Indexes of Network-Affiliate Economic Relations, 1964-1977
(Index: 1964 = 100)

Year	Consumer Price Index	Network Sales	Network Income	Index of Payment to Stations	Payments by Networks to Stations as % of Network Income	as % of Station Income	Station Income
1964	100	100	100	100	23.1%	19.8%	100
1965	102	109	99	107	24.0	19.6	109
1966	105	125	131	114	21.2	18.8	117
1967	108	130	93	115	20.6	18.7	101
1968	112	136	94	115	19.5	16.3	123
1969	118	150	154	118	18.6	15.4	130
1970	125	148	83	112	17.3	14.4	114
1971	131	143	89	107	17.4	13.9	94
1972	135	161	184	105	15.0	12.0	124
1973	143	180	307	109	14.2	11.3	132
1974	159	191	374	116	13.8	11.1	144
1975	174	206	346	120	13.4	10.7	161
1976	184	256	491	124	11.3	8.8	269
1977	196	310	675	134	10.0	8.7	280

Sources: 1964-1973: "Petition for Inquiry, Rule Making and Immediate Temporary Relief," filed before the Federal Communications Commission on September 3, 1976 by Westinghouse Broadcasting Company, Inc. Based on official FCC financial figures for the television industry.
1974-1977: Westinghouse Reply Comments (December 1, 1978), as reprinted in The Foreseeable Future of Television Networks (Los Angeles: UCLA School of Law, 1979), pp. 82-83.

ple of network clout came in 1969 when AT&T raised its interconnection charges, and that rise came out of compensation payments rather than overall network income.[150] Previous FCC action on compensation came with its rejection of a CBS plan in 1963 which called for a graduated increase in compensation depending on how many hours were taken ("cleared") from the network.[151]

A final matter of contention for many years has been the network practice of demanding options on large chunks of affiliate time—a right of first refusal to make use of such time. The chain broadcasting report of 1941 called for an end to this practice, saying it effectively removed the local station from responsibility for what it broadcast. But only in 1963, long after the Barrow report urged the same thing, did the Commission end the practice.

By the early 1980s, all of this control was in doubt. Spurred by strong deregulatory pressures combined with detailed economic analysis, the 1978-1980 network inquiry recommended eliminating virtually all existing FCC rules governing network/affiliate relations, suggesting such matters were better left to marketplace factors.[152] The FCC appeared likely to follow the recommendation, despite strong affiliate pressure to retain or strengthen the status quo.

Network Control of Advertising

An important factor underlying the FCC's undertaking yet another investigation of networks, as well as increasing FTC interest in network operation, is the radical change which has taken place in television network advertising in the past 15 years or so. Sponsored programs have given way to programming in which many different advertisers "participate," buying time in much the same way as space is purchased in print media. Another change is that the standard television commercial has shrunk in length from 60 to 30 seconds. Moreover, while the total number of commercial minutes has increased about 15%, the number of different commercials aired (due to the shorter length) has almost doubled, bringing on viewer and advertiser complaints about clutter and over-commercialization on television. This network TV advertising represents about 9% of total advertising expenditures in the country, and about 15% of the national advertising dollar.[153]

The prime cause for the decline of sponsorship and 60-second ads was the increasing cost of television. Given the fairly static amounts of time available, increased revenue grows only through increasing the rates charged. Advertisers, who sponsored and provided perhaps half the network programming in the 1950s, provided only 3% by 1968. As costs increased, advertisers preferred to spread their risk by placing messages in different programs rather than banking heavily on but one or a few.

The effects of this change in support have been widespread, and a cause for affiliate concern. For one thing, networks now compete directly with stations for national spot advertising income which was not the case when sponsorship was the rule. As a result of economies of scale and lower selling costs (a whole network of stations is sold rather than individual sales of separate stations), networks can and often have undercut local cost per thousand viewer rates, pulling national spot accounts to network coffers. This role has been strengthened as advertising agencies have gotten out of the programming business with the end of sponsorship, and now merely buy time. The higher resultant network income has not been passed on to the affiliate stations.

The effects of advertising rates on other businesses is also of concern, though too involved to detail here. Briefly, this issue concerns network volume discounts which encourage mergers of industries using television advertising extensively. The volume discounts not only save money, but research has shown that repeated ads sell better. When a special kind of programming (such as national sports, given a unique status under Congressional action in 1962) is combined with the network oligopoly, only a few can afford the advertising rates charged. Roger Noll points to the increasing concentration trend in the beer industry, stemming from the network advertising cost structure of sports telecast.[154] This is an extreme example of a concentration problem: limited entry into television advertising due to the high minimum fixed costs incurred limits effective use of the medium to large, usually consumer goods, firms. A substantial literature further explores these issues.[155]

Network Control of Programming and its Distribution

Of special concern to regulators is the control networks exercise over the form and structure of the TV programming industry. Prime-time viewing options for the majority of the national audience are provided by networks. Other viewing hours are also dominated by networks in that (1) affiliates use network programs about 65% of their total broadcast time, and (2) independent stations make heavy use of syndicated off-network material originally programmed by a network. Several trends are involved.

First, the decline of advertiser-supplied programming noted above was due mainly to cost factors—but also to the quiz show scandals of the late 1950s. That brought forth pressures for the networks to clean up their operation, and coincided with increased network concern for audience flow, requiring network control of which programs got on the air and when. At the same time, the impact of television on the film industry had created vast unused production facilities in Hollywood suitable for telefilm (series program) production. By the early 1960s, the program production company, or "package agency" (so named as it presents a finished program package to the network), was producing a majority of network programming, and today produces at least 80% of prime-time programming under contract to the networks. No longer are networks merely conduits for advertiser-supplied programming; now networks control the programs and sell participating time to advertisers.

Second, the number of network hours broadcast has increased at a steady rate over the past 15 years or so. Much of the increase has been from ABC's finally filling in its schedule to really compete with the offerings of CBS and NBC. Most of the increase has come in fringe time as prime was already fully occupied by the late 1950s. With imposition of the Prime Time Access Rule (PTAR) in September of 1971, the FCC limited network prime-time programming to three hours.

Spurred by this artificial protection, a sizable industry sprang up in the 1970s, catering to station needs for cheap syndicated programming— mostly game shows, but sparked here and there with some more expensive original local or regional programming as originally envisioned by the FCC. Spurred by the third network inquiry's recommendation that PTAR be scrapped, petitions and counterpetitions on that question flooded the FCC in 1981-1982. The network inquiry had concluded, in the first in-depth economic analysis of PTAR's impact, that the rule did not serve to increase program diversity, but merely provided substandard programming of network type. PTAR was seen by its critics as a key example of a paste-over rule which could not overcome the FCC-created limitation in television competition brought about by the 1952 allocation decision.

Third, while special *ad hoc* networks have often appeared in the past several seasons built around either single programs or multi-part dramatic serials, such operations face a difficult time because of network O&Os, which almost always take all network shows—and are thus effectively removed from the independent "network" market. The O&Os are important because of their large market locations (see Table 6.9) and thus hold a pivotal position when trying to reach sufficient audience to sell advertisers on such special hook-ups. But even reaching affiliates is made difficult by the fact that most clear 95% of network programs offered, which make up about 65% of their programming time. Only if an affiliate can be persuaded that a non-network offering is financially beneficial will the outside offering have a chance.

In the final analysis, that is the key question: networks succeed because, given the constraints of allocation, stations simply find it more profitable to affiliate than to go independent. As long as that is true, it is unlikely that market pressures will create substantial change in the dominating role of networks. Pressures for change will have to come from the outside.

One such source has been the independent production community in Hollywood, generally divided into the "majors," which are part of theatrical film firms, and the independents, which usually rent facilities for production from others. Although producers have been accused of being a rather tight group, there is in fact easy entry to the production circle. Pricing is affected by the ability of the networks to produce their own programming if costs become too high, and the combined program share of the top producers is under 60% of the total (and varies considerably from year to year). Moreover, the power of the producers is limited because they do not control first-run distribution, which is handled by the networks.[156]

Despite their lack of monopoly status, various package firms have tended to work most closely with one or two networks. In the 1970s, for example, CBS made heavier use of the independent firms than did the other networks. The packagers have felt constrained with only three markets for their product. But with the rise of more "independent network" operations and a slowly increasing market of stations for syndicated products (both off-network and first-run), the packagers are finding less reason to complain. The rerun issue remains, however, since the networks have increased their proportion of reruns per season simply because they cost only 25% of an original program. Increased emphasis on reruns means less work for the Hollywood craft unions, a factor which became a political issue in the early 1970s.[157] Further, network decisions on how long a series plays on a network are important to the potential syndication life of that series off-network, for with too few episodes, syndicators can't sell the material to local stations for typical "stripping" (running five days a week) for a minimum of several months at a time. Few series break even, let alone make money on network runs, as network payments do not usually cover the cost of production, so syndication is an important source of profits for producers. Network decisions on series length thus have a direct impact on the profits of program packagers.[158]

Policy Options on Network Power

Examining all of the issues, Willard Manning and Bruce Owen, in an article in *Public Policy,* conclude:

> . . . Network power is not based in the advertising and television program supply markets, which are nearly competitive. Instead the major sources of network dominance are the technological

economies of scale in simultaneous networking and the networks' bargaining position relative to stations in the largest television markets. However, the networks cannot realize all of the potential monopoly profits because they are locked into a dynamic non-cooperative rivalry, in terms of program quality, which is only partly offset by their ability to cooperate on the level of reruns. The policy options to reduce the remaining network power and to increase the diversity of program content and control tend to be ineffective or so radical that they are politically unfeasible.[159]

Summarizing the literature, the economists conclude that two types of option exist: behavioral approaches which serve to limit power in specific ways, but do little to change the underlying source of that power; and structural approaches which include antitrust and other approaches and are usually more effective over time.[160] Either category must be measured against gains and losses in freedom of expression generally, viewer welfare, the economic health of related industries (such as major advertisers), and the FCC's policy of localism. Theories expressed over the past 25 years or so to explain broadcast and specifically network behavior suggest that, given our present system of allocation and networks, similar common denominator programming will result. Therefore, economists have examined various kinds of "controlled monopolies" as effective ways to seek real change in both economic and programming concentration.

A commonly posed question concerns the likelihood of a fourth or even more commercial networks to compete with the three operating at present. For the reasons already noted above, especially the limited number of markets with more than three commercial VHF channels, a Rand study in 1973 concluded a permanent new network was extremely unlikely. No less than 17 specific options, many including combinations of television stations and cable systems, were considered and rejected for the same basic reason: the inability of any such new network, however based, to economically compete with the established system.[161] Revisiting the same question seven years later, a Rand researcher felt the chances of a new broadcast network were measurably improved due to (1) increasing number and status of UHF stations, and (2) rising per-household TV advertising expenditures, rising at a faster rate than fixed network operating costs.[162]

Spurred by the Rand findings and their own analyses, the third network inquiry researchers concluded in 1980 that more than anything else, the FCC's own rules and regulations stood in the way of additional networks and thus more program diversity. More specifically, they suggested "that the Commission should actively seek to remove existing regulatory barriers to entry by additional networks.''[163] They called for more outlets (in both broadcasting and competing services) to be available to viewers, guarding against local market monopoly by assuring access to cable channels, and regulating networks across technology in a more equal fashion than has thus far prevailed, where broadcasting is highly regulated while most competing services operate with few regulatory constraints.

A variety of other options have been considered by economic theorists and policy makers. As a rule, the theorists have concentrated more on the structural remedies, given their greater effectiveness, often purposely ignoring political/technical realities in their search for some new approach to the issues. An analysis by Owen,[164] for example, considers in detail such things as deintermixture (making UHF stations a more viable base for network expansion by limiting a given market to either *all* VHF or *all* UHF stations); divestiture of network O&O stations to even up chances for new network entrants; common carrier access to network facilities (though many critics fear this would throw television back to the hands of advertisers as in the 1950s, with little positive benefit for viewers); promotion of cable and pay television as competitors; geographic disintegration (limiting the number of affiliates for any network which would force either more national networks, or a series of regional networks, the latter somewhat paralleling German practice); and even outright nationalization. All of these have benefits but the drawbacks are often severe.

In one well-known economic model to which much attention has been devoted over the past quarter century, monopoly is given serious consideration as possibly better serving the public interest than the present oligopolistic network structure.[165] Theoretically, a monopolist might program a greater diversity of materials on two or three network channels (in an attempt to reach more of the total audience) than three competing network owners all trying to reach the same general audience. Since absolute monopoly is clearly a political impossibility, the suggestion of some kind of temporal (time-based) monopoly has been put forth. Here, one owner might control all network channels for a given part of the day (morning, afternoon, part of prime time, late evening, etc.) across the week, or for a whole given day in the week (firm A on Monday, firm B on Tuesday, etc.).

Something of an operating model of such an approach exists today in the way that Great Britain's commercial Independent Broadcasting Authority has divided the lucrative London market. One company telecasts the commercial channel during the week (Thames Television), while a separate firm provides service on Saturdays and Sundays (London Weekend). Thus there are two gatekeepers through which program access may be achieved rather than the more normal one (indeed, only one operates in the other IBA market areas). One important caveat to such an approach is that viewers would still have the same number of viewing options at any one time (three network choices) despite the actual number of temporal monopoly networks (seven if one a day, many more if the daypart approach is taken). But theoretically, at least, this could lead to greater segmentation of the market and hence to greater diversity of actual program types than now exists.

But, as exhaustively analyzed in the most recent FCC network inquiry, the most likely option for change is already underway in the marketplace—the continued development of a variety of competing services including cable, pay television in various forms, MDS, home video, and satellite-delivered video. While network television still clearly dominated viewer interest and advertiser dollars in the early 1980s, predictions beyond 1985 become fuzzy. But regulators in the 1980s are clearly not in the mood to control networks more stringently. On the contrary, the clear message from the FCC is that increasing market diversity may finally accomplish what four decades of regulatory focus has not—additional widely available national sources of video programming.

DISCUSSION

The beginning of this chapter suggested broadcasting would change more in the coming decade than in all its history thus far. This change, pushed by technology and assisted by a lower regulatory profile, will clearly have direct impact on the concerns analyzed here. As of this writing, the following generalizations seem reasonable:

1) Realizing the rising competition from alternative delivery systems is having increasing impact on radio and especially television broadcasting, the FCC and Congress will move fairly rapidly to dismantle much of the regulatory structure built up over the past five decades.

2) Moreover, regulation will be only sparingly applied to the "new media," to allow new entry and more outlets to serve the public.

3) Specifically, many if not most of the present restrictions on station ownership will be overturned, with the likely exception of some kind of regional concentration rule. But cross-ownership limits (newspaper-broadcasting, TV-cable, AM-FM, TV-radio, etc.) and rules existing or thought of, will nearly all be swept away in the deregulatory euphoria presently controlling the federal government. Further, the long-standard 7-7-7 rule is being strongly questioned for the first time, its basic rationale coming under close examination.

4) While some of this change will come from the FCC, considerable pressure will come from Congress, which in mid-1981 extended broadcast licenses (for the first time since 1934) to five years for television and seven

years for radio. This extended licensing alone has clear implications for ownership, making change by sale more the avenue for new ownership rather than the license renewal proceedings seized upon by activists in the early 1970s.

5) The Justice Department has given relatively clear signals that it will not question many of the media mergers which would have been at the least delayed in years past. The largest media merger in history was consummated in 1981 when Westinghouse took over Teleprompter (see Chapter 7). Further, the Federal Trade Commission's past interest in media concentration (see footnote 26) appeared to be dwindling as its role in federal antitrust proceedings was under Congressional and administration attack. Thus, two sources of pressure on the FCC in years past had considerably less impact in the early 1980s, leaving the Commission with wider latitude in its own analysis of what ownership restrictions to retain.

6) The broadcast industry, recognizing all of these changes, and chafing from what it long has perceived as an unfair regulatory burden, can be expected to mount considerable lobbying pressure on both Congress and the FCC to eliminate ownership restrictions presently on the books without creating new ones. Several network petitions to lift network operating limits held over from earlier network investigations were already under active consideration at the FCC in 1981 with others sure to follow—openly welcomed by a new FCC majority committed to major deregulation.

But as these major changes in past practice are considered, the basic question remains: Is the commercial broadcasting industry, more specifically television, monopolistic? Economist Roger Noll thinks not:

> Television is not among the most concentrated industries, such as automobiles, aluminum, tobacco, or copper. Nevertheless, in relatively few industries do three firms [in this case the networks and their O&O stations] account for over half the sales. The proportion of the market accounted for by the three largest firms is greater in television than in such industries as steel, farm machinery, and electric motors and generators, all of which are generally regarded as imperfectly competitive.[166]

Yet it has been said that commercial television is by some criteria the most concentrated of all mass media with the exception, perhaps, of pay cable distribution, though the trend to increased concentration appears to affect most media. Indeed, such a pattern of concentration even extends to the "support" industries manufacturing equipment for broadcasting.[167]

Ironically, concentration of power in broadcasting has its basis in the Federal Communication Commission's continuing doctrine of localism.

This chapter identified the close connection between localism as a policy and radio and television allocation as an outcome—and those allocations have decided the shape of the semi-competitive industry we have today. The concentrated ownership of stations is merely an accentuating overlay on this basic allocation; without the enforced scarcity of channels, ownership concentration would not be as likely. The operation of networks is quite clearly dictated by the large number of markets with three commercial VHF channels brought about by an allocation scheme whose first priority was to provide as much local service as possible—even if, as has proven to be the case, resultant programming all became very much alike. The division of the industry into economic haves and have-nots is a direct outgrowth of the FCC's attempts to broaden the number of stations in order to make localism work.[168]

In the end, much of the controversy analyzed in this chapter may become moot as competition from cable television, pay TV systems and home video (which places scheduling options in the hands of the viewer) continues to expand. FCC attempts to limit some of these competitors in order to preserve a localism-based system of broadcasting have been systematically thrown aside on court appeal.[169] More television users will get a broader variety of viewing options from cable systems using pay channels and satellite distribution than they ever could from traditional broadcasting. The television networks may well heed the lessons that should have been learned when television itself displaced the entrenched radio networks. An important policy question here is whether owners of the "old" business of broadcasting will become dominant in the "new" competing technologies, which have at least the *potential* to open up electronic communications to new communicators and types of content.[170]

NOTES

1. For a guide to the extensive existing literature on all aspects of radio and television, see S.W. Head with C.H. Sterling, *Broadcasting in America* (Boston: Houghton Mifflin, 1982, 4th ed.), "A Selective Guide to the Literature on Broadcasting." For an early official expression of concern about concentration in radio broadcasting and manufacturing, see *Report of the Federal Trade Commission on the Radio Industry* (Washington: Government Printing Office, 1924; reprinted by Arno Press, 1974). For fuller historical information on the broadcasting business, see E. Barnouw, *A History of Broadcasting in the United States* (New York: Oxford University Press, 1966-1970, three volumes); and C. Sterling and J. Kittross, *Stay Tuned: A Concise History of American Broadcasting* (Belmont, CA: Wadsworth Publishing, 1978).

2. See, for example, U.S. Senate, Committee on the Judiciary, *Possible Anticompetitive Effects of Sale of Network TV Advertising: Hearings . . .* 89th Cong., 2nd Sess. (two parts, 1966).

3. Department of Commerce figures as cited by W.P. Banning, *Commercial Broadcasting Pioneer: The WEAF Experiment 1922-1926* (Cambridge, MA: Harvard University Press, 1946), pp. 132-3.

4. Herbert Hoover's famous phrase, "I believe that the quickest way to kill broadcasting would be to use it for direct advertising," came in his comments to the Third National Radio Conference, as reprinted in *Recommendations for Regulation of Radio* (Washington: Government Printing Office, 1924), p. 4, reissued in J. Kittross, ed., *Documents in American Telecommunications Policy* (New York: Arno Press, 1977, vol. 1).

5. See, for example, G. Archer, *History of Radio to 1926* (New York: American Historical Society, 1938; reprinted by Arno Press, 1971), pp. 342-3.

6. Sterling and Kittross, *Stay Tuned,* pp. 68-69.

7. E. Sarno, Jr., "The National Radio Conferences," *Journal of Broadcasting* 13:189-202 (Spring 1969). The results of these conferences are reprinted in J. Kittross, ed., *Documents in American Telecommunications Policy.*

8. The classic discussion of this important turning point is found in J. Spalding, "1928: Radio Becomes a Mass Advertising Medium," *Journal of Broadcasting* 8:31-44 (Winter 1963-64).

9. See Sterling and Kittross, pp. 128-130; and W. Emery, *Broadcasting and Government: Responsibilities and Regulations* (East Lansing, MI: Michigan State University Press, 1971, 2nd ed.), especially chapter 7.

10. B. Owen, *Economics and Freedom of Expression: Media Structure and the First Amendment* (Cambridge, MA: Ballinger, 1975), p. 111.

11. C. Sterling and T. Haight, *The Mass Media: Aspen Institute Guide to Communication Industry Trends* (New York: Praeger, 1978); table 171-A provides a listing of radio network affiliates from 1927-77.

12. Ibid., table 303-C; Sterling and Kittross, p. 114; and *Broadcasting Yearbook 1951* (Washington, DC: Broadcasting Publications Inc., 1951), p. 12, table V.

13. Sterling and Kittross, p. 156.

14. Ibid., pp. 254-5, 322-3 and 379-81.

15. Federal Communications Commission (hereafter FCC), "Sixth Report and Order on Dockets 8736, 8975, 9175 and 8976 . . ." 41 FCC 148 (April 14, 1952).

16. See especially Sterling and Kittross, pp. 356-359, 381 and 417.

17. Sterling and Haight, table 680-A.

18. Sterling and Kittross, p. 452.

19. Owen, p. 112.

20. FCC, "Policy Statement on Comparative Broadcast Hearings," 1 FCC 2d 393 (also reprinted in F. Kahn, ed. *Documents of American Broadcasting* [Englewood Cliffs, NJ: Prentice-Hall, 1978, 3rd ed.], pp. 329-338).

21. For one analysis see J. Busterna, "Diversity of Ownership as a Criterion in FCC Licensing since 1965," *Journal of Broadcasting* 20:101-110 (Winter 1976).

22. *NBC* v. *United States* 319 US 190 (May 10, 1943).

23. For a cohesive analysis of the broadcast portions of the rewrite process, see E. Krasnow, et al., *The Politics of Broadcast Regulation* (New York: St. Martin's Press, 1982, 3rd ed.).

24. *Broadcasting* (February 5, 1979), p. 29. Both men were speaking at a UCLA-sponsored symposium on the future of the networks.

25. W. Baer, et al., *Concentration of Mass Media Ownership: Assessing the State of Current Knowledge* (Santa Monica, CA: Rand Corp. Publication R-1584-NSF, September 1974), p. 10.

26. Federal Trade Commission, Bureau of Competition, *Proceedings of the Symposium on Media Concentration* (Washington: Government Printing Office, December 1978), two volumes.

27. Owen, p. 139.

28. Decision reached August 4, 1981. (No official citation yet available.)

29. As but one example, see *Application of CBS Inc. for Authority to Construct an Experimental High Definition Television Satellite System in the 12 GHz Band,* FCC File No DBS-81-02 (July 16, 1981).

30. For general background, see Emery, *Broadcasting and Government: Responsibilities and Regulations* and D.H. Ginsburg, *Regulation of Broadcasting: Law and Policy Towards Radio/Television and Cable Communications* (St. Paul, MN: West Publishing, 1979), especially chapter 3.

31. Just before returning to the FCC as its General Counsel, Stephen Sharp authored an insightful analysis of the problem. See S. Sharp and D. Lively, "Can the Broadcaster in the Black Hat Ride Again? 'Good Character' Requirement for Broadcast Licensees," *Federal Communications Bar Journal* 32:173-203 (Spring 1980).

32. FCC "In Re RKO General Inc. (WNAC-TV)," Docket 18759, 78 FCC 2d 1 (June 4, 1980). While three stations were affected (WNAC in Boston, WOR in New York and KHJ in Los Angeles), the Boston case carries the major argument and is referenced in the brief decisions on the other two operations.

33. FCC, "In Re Applications of RKO General, Inc. for Renewals of Licenses for Stations . . .," Dockets 80-590 through 80-602. Memoran-

dum Opinion and Order released September 30, 1980.

34. FCC, "In the Matter of Policy Regarding Character Qualifications in Broadcast Licenses," Notice of Inquiry. Docket 81-500 (August 4, 1981).

35. FCC, "Deregulation of Radio," Report and Order in Docket 79-219, 84 FCC 2d 968 (January 14, 1981).

36. See, for example, W.K. Jones, *Cases and Materials on Electronic Mass Media: Radio, Television and Cable* (Mineola, NY: Foundation Press, 1979, 2nd ed.), pp. 12-16 ff, as well as chapters II and III.

37. "Metromedia-WCVB-TV Boston-$220 Million," *Broadcasting* (July 27, 1981), pp. 27-28.

38. *Broadcasting* (January 12, 1981), p. 34.

39. FCC, "In the Matter of Clear Channel Broadcasting in the AM Broadcast Band," Report and Order in Docket No. 20642, 78 FCC 2d 1345 (May 29, 1980).

40. See footnote 28.

41. FCC, "In the Matter of Implementation of the Final Acts of the World Administrative Radio Conference, Geneva 1979," First Notice of Inquiry in Docket 80-739 (November 25, 1980), see especially Appendix A, p. 31.

42. FCC, "In the Matter of Modification of FM Broadcast Station Rules to Increase the Availability of Commercial FM Broadcast Assignments," Notice of Proposed Rule Making in Docket 80-90 (February 28, 1980).

43. FCC, *Staff Report on Comparability for UHF Television: Final Report* (Washington: FCC, September 1980).

44. FCC, "In the Matter of Petition for Rule Making to Amend Television Table of Assignments to Add New VHF Stations in the Top 100 Markets and to Assure that the New Stations Maximize Diversity of Ownership, Control and Programming." Report and Order in Docket No. 20418 (September 9, 1980) added stations in four of the top 100 markets: Charleston, WV, Knoxville, TN, Salt Lake City, and Johnstown, PA. See also, for the "generic" VHF drop-in item of what became termed "Limited Facility Stations," "In re: Table of Television Channel Allotments," Notice of Proposed Rule Making in Docket 80-499 (September 18, 1980).

45. FCC, "Inquiry into the Future Role of Low-Power Television Broadcasting and Television Translators in the National Telecommunication System," Notice of Proposed Rule Making in Docket 78-252 (September 9, 1980). The later "freeze" on accepting any more applications (better than 5000 were already on hand) came on April 9, 1981.

46. FCC, "Statement of Policy on Minority Ownership of Broadcast

Facilities,'' 68 FCC 2d 979 (May 25, 1978).

47. Ibid.

48. *Genesee Radio Corporation* 51FCC 186 as quoted in R.R. Smith, "Duopoly and ETV," *NAEB Journal* (May-June 1966), p. 42.

49. See H.H. Howard, "Multiple Broadcast Ownership: Regulatory History," *Federal Communications Bar Journal* 27:1:1-70 (1974).

50. 11 FCC 12 (1945).

51. Ibid., and Baer et al., p. 17.

52. This discussion mainly from H. Sterling, "Newspaper Ownership of Broadcast Stations, 1920-68," *Journalism Quarterly* 46: 227-236, 254 (Summer 1969), as updated in Sterling and Haight, table 261-A.

53. R. Bunce, *Television in the Corporate Interest* (New York: Praeger Special Studies, 1976), p. 45, table 5.

54. *The New York Times* (December 13, 1977), p. 17; and *Broadcasting* (December 12, 1977), p. 19.

55. As in *Mansfield Journal Co.* v. *Federal Communications Commission,* 180 Fed 2d 28 (1948).

56. *McClatchy Broadcasting Co.* v. *Federal Communications Commission,* 299 Fed 2d 15 (1956).

57. D.W. Toohey, "Newspaper Ownership of Broadcast Facilities," *Federal Communications Bar Journal* 21:1:44-57 (1966), at p. 52.

58. For the background of this case, see R.R. Smith and P.T. Prince, "WHDH: The Unconscionable Delay," *Journal of Broadcasting* 18:85-96 (Winter 1974); a popular treatment is in S. Quinlan, *The Hundred Million Dollar Lunch* (Chicago: J. Philip O'Hara Inc., 1974).

59. The *Star* ceased publication on August 7, 1981. See Dale Russakoff, et al., "The Death of the Washington Star," *Washington Post* (August 16-18, 1981) which notes the role of the stations in the paper's survival for many years.

60. *Citizen's Communications Center et al.* v. *Federal Communications Commission* 477 F 2d 1201 (1970).

61. Howard, "Multiple Broadcast Ownership," p. 63.

62. W.S. Baer, et al., *Newspaper-Television Station Cross-Ownership: Options for Federal Action* (Santa Monica, CA: Rand Corp. R-1585-MF, September 1974).

63. FCC, "In the Matter of Amendment of Sections 73.34, 73.240 and 73.636 of the Commission's Rules Relating to Multiple Ownership of Standard, FM and Television Broadcast Stations," Second Report and Order in Docket 18110, 50 FCC 2d 1046 (January 28, 1975).

64. *National Citizens Committee for Broadcasting* v. *Federal Communications Commission et al.* 555 F. 2d 938 (1977).

65. *Broadcasting* (March 7, 1977), pp. 22-23.

66. *Federal Communications Commission* v. *National Citizens Committee for Broadcasting, et al.* 436 US 775 (1978).

67. What follows relies heavily on Howard, "Multiple Broadcast Ownership," pp. 57-63.

68. FCC, "In the Matter of Amendment of Sections 73.35, 73.240, and 73.636 of the Commission Rules Relating to Multiple Ownership of Standard, FM, and Television Broadcast Stations," First Report and Order in Docket 18110 22 FCC 2d 306 (March 25, 1970).

69. Sterling and Kittross, p. 61.

70. H.H. Howard, "The Contemporary Status of Television Group Ownership," *Journalism Quarterly* 53:399-405 (Autumn 1976), at p. 399.

71. Ibid., p. 401.

72. Ibid., p. 403, table 3. Although seven is the maximum, only five of these may be VHF stations. Few of the largest broadcasters have much interest at present in acquiring UHF facilities.

73. *Broadcasting* (June 27, 1977), p. 24.

74. *Broadcasting* (October 9, 1978), p. 21. Some stations had to be sold to meet FCC ownership limits, and to get the required FCC approval of the transfer of the Combined stations to Gannett ownership.

75. FCC, "In Re, Teleprompter Corporation . . . Applications for Transfer of Control in the Cable Television Relay Service," Memorandum Opinion and Order (July 30, 1981).

76. *Broadcasting* (January 5, 1981), p. 55.

77. Howard, "Multiple Broadcast Ownership;" pp. 8-18 provide the basis for what follows.

78. *United States* v. *Storer Broadcasting Corp.* 351 US 192 (1956).

79. FCC, Network Inquiry Special Staff. *New Television Networks: Entry, Jurisdiction, Ownership and Regulation* (Washington: Government Printing Office, 1980), Vol. I, pp. 437-440.

80. This discussion relies heavily on A. Coffey, "The 'Top 50 Market Policy:' Fifteen Years of Non-Policy," *Federal Communications Law Journal* 31:303-339 (Spring 1979).

81. FCC, Public Notice 3 RR 2d 909 (December 18, 1964).

82. Coffey p. 313 citing 5 RR 2d 1609 (1965).

83. A massive research study first issued in two volumes in 1966 was later commercially published in P.W. Cherington, et al., *Television Station Ownership: A Case Study of Federal Agency Regulation* (New York: Hastings House, 1971).

84. Coffey, pp. 314-317.

85. FCC, "In the Matter of Amendment of Section 73.636(a) of the Commission's Rules (Multiple Ownership of Television Stations)," Report and Order in Docket 78-101 44 FR 75421 (December 20, 1979).

86. Coffey, pp. 330-339.

87. M. Botein, *Legal Restrictions on Ownership of the Mass Media* (New York: Advanced Media Publishing Associates, 1977), p. 97.

88. *Regulatory Trends in the 1980s: More Owners—More Stations* (New York: Station Representatives Assoc., September 1980), p. 12.

89. T. Brown, "The Multiple Ownership Rules," informal internal FCC memo (May 22, 1979), p. 8, para 15.

90. Howard, "Multiple Broadcast Ownership;" pp. 14, 42-45 provide the basis for the following discussion.

91. FCC, "In the Matter of Amendment of Sections 73.35, 73.240, 73.636 and 76.501 of the Commission's Rules Relating to Multiple Ownership . . ." Report and Order in Docket 20520 (June 10, 1976).

92. Personal conversation with S. Bookshester, Policy and Rules Division, Broadcast Bureau, FCC, July 1981.

93. FCC, *Report on Chain Broadcasting* (Washington: Government Printing Office, 1941, reissued by Arno Press, 1974), p. 16.

94. Ibid., p. 23.

95. See *Broadcasting* (January 1, 1979), p. 60. Mutual got its first O&O with the purchase of WCFL in Chicago late in 1978.

96. FCC, *Report on Chain Broadcasting,* p. 67.

97. *National Broadcasting Co. Inc., et al.* v. *United States et al.* 319 U.S. 190 (1943).

98. *United States* v. *Radio Corporation of America* 358 U.S. 334 (1959).

99. *Broadcasting* (January 24, 1979), pp. 54-55.

100. Bunce, chapter 6.

101. Sterling and Haight, tables 201-A and 201-B citing 1977 data.

102. *Media Decisions* (October 1978), p. 64.

103. National Association of Broadcasters, News Release 146/80 (August 21, 1980).

104. *Broadcasting* (December 11, 1978), p. 29.

105. K. Phillips, "Busting the Media Trusts," *Harper's* (July 1977), pp. 23-34.

106. *Broadcasting* (January 8, 1968), pp. 34-36, 41-42.

107. H.R. 13015, Section 440, 95th Cong., 2nd Sess. (1978).

108. R.K. Avery, "Public Broadcasting and the Duopoly Rule," *Public Telecommunications Review* (Jan./Feb. 1977), pp. 29-37.

109. Ibid., p. 31.

109a. FCC, "In the Matter of An Inquiry Into the Future Role of Low-Power Television Broadcasting and Television Translators in the National Telecommunications System." Report and Order Terminating Proceeding in Docket 78-253 (March 4, 1982). See especially paragraphs 78-90.

110. Baer, et al., *Concentration of . . .,* especially chapters 4 and 5.

111. Ibid., p. 79.

112. Ibid., p. 92.

113. Ibid., p. 95.

114. Ibid., p. 100.

115. Ibid., p. 101.

116. Ibid., pp. 106-107.

117. Ibid., p. 127.

118. Ibid., p. 132.

119. Ibid., p. 133.

120. Ibid., p. 143.

121. Bunce, p. 34.

122. M. O. Wirth and J.A. Wollert, "Public Interest Program Performance of Multimedia-Owned TV Stations," *Journalism Quarterly* 53:223-230 (Summer 1976), at p. 230.

123. W.T. Gormley, Jr. "How Cross-Ownership Affects News-Gathering," *Columbia Journalism Review* (May/June 1977), pp. 38-46.

124. See especially S.R. Barnett, "Cross-Ownership of Mass Media in the Same City: A Report to the John and Mary R. Markle Foundation," (Santa Monica, CA: Rand Corp., September 1974); and P.M. Sandman, "Cross-Ownership on the Scales," *More* (October 1977), pp. 21-24.

125. See Baer, et al., *Concentration of . . .,* pp. 143-165. Considerably more official research attention has been paid to this issue in Canada. See *Ownership of Private Broadcasting: An Economic Analysis of Structure, Performance and Behavior—Report of the Ownership Study Group to the Canadian Radio-television and Telecommunications Commission* (Ottawa: CRTC, October 1978) as well as several of its background reports prepared under contract. See also S. McFadyen, et al., *Canadian Broadcasting: Market Structure and Economic Performance* (Montreal: Institute for Research on Public Policy, 1980; distribution in U.S. by Renous USA, Brookfield, VT), especially chapter 3.

126. W.G. Manning and B.M. Owen, "Television Rivalry and Network Power," *Public Policy* 24:33-57 (Winter 1976), at pp. 55-56.

127. "Report of the Committee Appointed by the Commission to Supervise the Investigation of Chain Broadcasting, Commission Order No. 37, Docket No. 5060," June 12, 1940 (Washington: FCC, 1940).

128. FCC, *Report on Chain Broadcasting,* p. 16.

129. Ibid., pp. 91-92.

130. Ibid., p. 67.

131. See, for example, the following reports all based on extensive hearings: all of these are U.S. Senate, Committee on Interstate and Foreign Commerce. R.F. Jones, "Investigation of Television Networks and the

UHF-VHF Problem,'' Committee Print, 84th Cong., 1st Sess. (1955). H.M. Plotkin, "Television Network Regulation and the UHF Problem," Committee Print, 84th Cong., 1st Sess. (1955). "The Television Inquiry: Television Network Practices," Committee Print No. 2, 85th Cong., 1st Sess. (1957).

132. U.S. House of Representatives, Committee on Interstate and Foreign Commerce, *Network Broadcasting,* Report . . . 85th Cong., 2d Sess., House Report 1297 (January 27, 1958).

133. *Broadcasting* (September 30, 1957), p. 31.

134. U.S. House of Representatives, Committee on Interstate and Foreign Commerce, *Television Network Program Procurement,* Report . . . 88th Cong., 1st Sess., House Report 281 (May 8, 1963). This includes "Responsibility for Broadcast Matter" (June 1960), as well as the title report of 1963. See also FCC, *Second Interim Report by the Office of Network Study: Television Network Program Procurement, Part II* (Washington: Government Printing Office, 1965).

135. *Broadcasting* (May 11, 1970), pp. 22-24, 26.

136. *The Wall Street Journal* (April 29, 1975), p. 22.

137. *Broadcasting* (April 17, 1972), pp. 8, 21.

138. *The New York Times* (December 11, 1974), p. 83.

139. *Washington Post* (April 23, 1976), p. D-9, and *Broadcasting* (March 6, 1978), p. 102.

140. See *Broadcasting* (August 25, 1980), p. 31.

141. Office of Telecommunications Policy (Executive Office of the President). *Analysis of the Causes and Effects of Increases in Same-Year Rerun Programming and Related Issues in Prime-Time Network Television* (Washington: OTP, March 1973).

142. Westinghouse Broadcasting Co., Inc., "Petition for Inquiry, Rule Making and Immediate Temporary Relief," filed before the FCC, September 3, 1976.

143. *The New York Times* (November 24, 1976), p. 43, and *The Wall Street Journal* (November 24, 1976), p. 40.

144. 42 *Federal Register* 4992 (January 26, 1977).

145. 40 RR 2d 80 (1977).

146. S.M. Besen and T.G. Krattenmaker, "Regulating Network Television: Dubious Premises and Doubtful Solutions," *Regulation* (May/June 1981), pp. 27-34.

147. Manning and Owen, p. 43.

148. FCC, Network Inquiry Special Staff. *New Television Networks . . .,* pp. 441-520.

149. R.G. Noll, "Television and Competition," unpublished paper prepared for the Federal Trade Commission Symposium on the Media,

December 1978, p. 11.

150. R.G. Noll, et al., *Economic Aspects of Television Regulation* (Washington: Brookings Institution, 1973), pp. 62-63.

151. 1 RR 2d 696 (1963).

152. "Recommendations of the Network Inquiry Special Staff to the Federal Communications Commission" (December 1980), p. 8.

153. Manning and Owen, p. 35.

154. Noll, "Television and Competition," p. 8.

155. See footnote 2, and also Noll, et al., *Economic Aspects,* p. 37, note 15; p. 62, notes 5-6.

156. B.M. Owen, et al., *Television Economics* (Lexington, MA: Lexington Books, 1974), p. 19.

157. OTP, 1973; see also D.B. McAlpine, *The Television Programming Industry* (New York: Tucker Anthony & R.L. Day, January 1975).

158. For a good text overview of the strategies involved in the rapidly changing world of television networks, syndication and station planning, see S.T. Eastman, et al., eds., *Broadcast Programming: Strategies for Winning Television and Radio Audiences* (Belmont, CA: Wadsworth, 1981).

159. Manning and Owen, pp. 34-35.

160. B.M. Owen, "Structural Approaches to the Problem of TV Network Economic Dominance," (Durham, NC: Duke University Graduate School of Business Administration, Center for the Study of Business Regulation Paper No. 27, 1978). Note: this paper is not paginated, so references are made to the text by means of the footnote numbers which appear throughout; in this case, text at notes 127-129.

161. R.E. Park, *New Television Networks* (Santa Monica, CA: Rand Corp. R-1408-MF, December 1973), especially pp. 27-30, which summarize the options and weigh them.

162. R.E. Park, *New Television Networks: An Update* (Santa Monica, CA: Rand Corp. Note N-1526-FCC, August 1980); also reprinted in FCC, Network Inquiry Special Staff, *New Television Networks . . .,* pp. 143-184.

163. "Recommendations of the Network Inquiry . . .," p. 14.

164. See Owen, "Structural Approaches . . ." generally.

165. Manning and Owen, pp. 43-53, review the models and their applications; see also the Owen paper, "Structural Approaches . . ." (footnote 160) and Noll, et al., *Economic Aspects . . .,* pp. 49-53.

166. Noll, "Television and Competition," p. 14.

167. Sterling and Haight, table 260-D summarizes Census data on three important related manufacturing industries.

168. For an excellent discussion of the limits and relatively few benefits

of localism, see Noll, et al., *Economic Aspects . . .*, pp. 108-120.

169. See Chapter 7, Cable and Pay Television.

170. See, for example, C. Christians, "Home Video Systems: A Revolution?" *Journal of Broadcasting* 17:223-234 (Spring 1973); and E. Sigel, et al., *Video Discs: The Technology, the Applications and the Future* (White Plains, NY: Knowledge Industry Publications, Inc., 1980).

7

Cable and Pay Television

by Christopher H. Sterling

The substantial change that will transform broadcasting in the next decade is due largely to the increasing scope and changing nature of cable television. Cable initially served to expand broadcast audiences, later became a curse to telecasters, and more recently has expanded considerably beyond the traditional network-station broadcast system. While the basic technique of cable is at least as old as broadcasting, development of modern full-service cable has been possible only since the 1975 inception of satellite-delivered programming to fill cable's expanding number of channels.

To clearly discern ownership patterns in the cable industry, we must first consider the local delivery process—the local cable systems numbering some 4500 in late 1981. Then we should examine the newer and developing program supply or network portion of cable—the several dozen satellite-supplied program services or networks.

CABLE TV SYSTEM OWNERSHIP

The literature on cable, after experiencing dramatic growth early in the 1970s and a comparative dearth later in the decade, is once again expanding, similar to cable itself. Aside from general treatments,[1] specialized materials exist in profusion on topics not covered here, such as cable and copyright, division of regulatory concern between federal, state and local governments, local origination and access rules, general franchising issues, pole attachments and the like.[2] But virtually anything written prior to 1979 is obsolete, for until that time the Federal Communications Commission's overriding concern had been to protect the primacy of broadcast television's localism by limiting the expansion of cable service. Cable's short development breaks into roughly three periods, divided primarily by changing federal regulatory initiatives.

Development of Cable Television

Early Years (to 1962)

Cable, or community antenna, television systems began in the late 1940s as a means of delivering television signals to areas unable to receive over-the-air TV channels, either because of distance from the transmitters, or because of interference by intervening hills or mountains. A master receiving antenna on a hilltop picked up the air signals, which were then transmitted by means of cables to homes in the area. Typically, there was a one-time installation charge and then a monthly subscription fee. Well into the 1950s, cable systems could be characterized as: 1) quite small, running to just a few hundred homes in most cases; 2) carrying perhaps three or four broadcast TV signals, usually the closest stations; 3) generally confined to mountainous areas with little or no regular TV reception; and 4) usually welcomed by broadcasters who knew the cable systems expanded their viewing audience. Ownership was typically a small local company often in some related primary line of business (such as selling receivers). Such "mom and pop" operations were often only marginally successful financially, though few records exist of the earliest years.[3]

Cable was but one of several industry responses to the limitations of localism-inspired television allocations (see Chapter 6). In the 1950s a proliferation of audience-extension facilities appeared: translator stations (which rebroadcast a weak signal on a higher UHF channel for immediate area reception), booster transmitters (which beefed up an incoming signal on the same channel), satellite stations (or "slave" stations which were merely secondary outlets for a station in a major community, though the satellite might be on a totally different channel) and cable. CATV was generally more expensive than the various broadcasting options, but it offered two important advantages: because it was a closed rather than broadcast delivery system, a charge could be made for the service, thus providing the key to support; and many channels could be carried at any one time. Still, cable grew very slowly for many years, as shown in Table 7.1, because it merely provided a different means of signal reception in rural, often sparsely populated, areas. Growth was strongest in Pennsylvania and many western states.

By the early 1960s, broadcasters began to have second thoughts about the role and effect of cable on over-the-air television. This was brought about by:

- Increasing use of microwave relay facilities by cable systems to bring in distant stations—thus providing competition for local telecasters and further dividing up the audience;

Table 7.1: Measures of Cable System Growth, Selected Years, 1955-1981

Year	Number of Systems	Number of Subscribers (in thousands)	% TV Homes with Cable	Average Subscribers Per System	System Size: % of Systems		Penetration by County Type			
					Under 5000 Homes	Over 10,000 Homes	A (most urban)	B	C	D (most rural)
1955	400	150	.5%	375	N.A.	N.A.	N.A.			
1960	640	650	1.4	1,016	N.A.	N.A.	N.A.			
1965	1,325	1,275	2.4	962	N.A.	N.A.	N.A.			
1970	2,490	4,500	7.6	1,807	92%	2%	2%	5%	17%	11%
1973	2,991	7,300	11.1	2,441	87	5	4	9	25	15
1975	3,506	9,800	14.3	2,795	84	7	5	11	27	17
1977	3,800	11,900	17.3	3,132	84	7	7	16	32	20
1979	4,150	14,100	19.0	3,398	82	9	8	17	35	22
1981[1]	4,637	19,800	27.3	4,270	77	11	N.A.			

[1] July 1.

N.A.: Not available.

Sources: 1955-1979 from Head and Sterling, *Broadcasting in America* (Houghton Mifflin Co., 1982), Unit 190; 1979 county penetration data from A.C. Nielsen Co.; 1981 based on *TV Digest* data for June 1, 1981.

- Inception of urban cable systems, such as that in San Diego begun in 1961 to import Los Angeles signals to a market already well served with local television; in New York in 1966 to improve reception among the tall buildings; and in Los Angeles in 1967;

- Rising concern by broadcasters and producers over lack of payments by cable operators for material that cable carried free; and

- A slow trend to consolidation of cable system ownership from hundreds of small local companies to larger multiple system operators (MSOs), indicating the potential for cable's economic future. Rather than expanding broadcast audiences, cable began to be viewed by broadcasters and advertisers as a system for dividing the audience into smaller segments across a greater number of television channels—usually to the financial detriment of local TV stations.

Though pressure from broadcasters began to build on Congress and the Federal Communications Commission, initially there was little or no regulation of cable on any level of government. In 1959, the FCC specifically declined to regulate cable, claiming it was neither broadcasting nor common carrier, and was thus outside of the scope of the Communications Act of 1934.[4] But this freewheeling period finally came to an end.

Search for a Regulatory Formula (1962-1972)

Pressures from broadcasters combined with FCC concern over possible economic harm to television stations by cable operations brought about initial FCC regulation of cable in 1962.[5] Using the regulation of microwave under its jurisdiction the Commission took over regulatory responsibility for cable systems using microwave to import distant signals and required all systems to carry any local stations in addition to distant signals. As an additional protection for local stations, any network service on a local station was not to be duplicated in an imported signal. In 1965 the FCC limited signal importation in the top 100 markets, required systems to carry local signals as well, and assumed regulatory control over common carriers providing cable service to local systems by means of microwave.[6] Just one year later, this federal regulation was expanded to cover all cable systems,[7] a decision upheld on review in a 1968 Supreme Court decision.[8] While the broadcast industry generally applauded this trend (and the clear statement by the FCC that cable was to be supplemental to broadcast television), they were frustrated by another 1968 Supreme Court decision that found cable systems were not infringing copyright by nonpayment for broadcast signals carried.[9] Despite such tight federal regulation, and increasing interest by some states (Connecticut had enacted the first state cable regulations in 1963),[10] the industry continued to expand.

One indication of cable's increasing importance in communications policy-making was the greatly increased rate of publication about cable in the late 1960s and early 1970s. In 1970-1971, for example, came the first of a continuing series of Rand Corporation studies on the applications, technology and regulation of cable.[11] It was followed late in 1971 by the report of the Alfred Sloan Foundation-funded commission on cable communications which conducted a number of detailed support studies to buttress its conclusion that cable should be allowed to develop in free competition with broadcasting.[12] It recommended retaining regulation to ensure development of the public service potential of cable (indeed, the report encouraged further establishment of state regulatory bodies), and requiring some kind of payment by cable operators for use of broadcast material. At the same time, behind the scenes, cable industry representatives, the National Association of Broadcasters and some of the copyright holders (film and video producers) met in Washington and hammered out a compromise agreement to govern the forthcoming "definitive" FCC rules on cable which were subsequently issued in February 1972.[13] They were detailed and extensive, calling for limited importation of signals to the top 100 markets, a provision for local origination of programming for large cable systems, a complex system of access and community channels, system size and capacity regulations, etc. with existing cable systems having about five years to comply. It appeared to many observers that with most issues resolved (copyright revision being the chief exception), cable could then develop under a known set of rules. The role of the federal government, at least, was clearly defined.

Deregulation (Since 1972)

The so-called definitive rules did not last long, however. In a decade marked initially by expanding state and local regulatory interest, and a worsening economy, the growth of cable systems began to slow down. Blue-sky predictions, voiced in the early years of the decade, became hollow. But in a series of FCC decisions and court rulings in this period, the FCC's carefully developed (but not evidence-supported) protectionist policy holding cable subordinate to broadcasting began to come apart.

Throughout this confusion and regulatory unraveling, cable developed significantly. Returning to Table 7.1, note that at the time of the "definitive rules" of 1972, cable was in only 10% of the nation's homes, whereas a decade later, cable penetration was approaching the 30% figure thought to be a critical mass by those interested in substantial advertising on cable. Cable systems became bigger—always paced, it seemed, by San Diego's Mission Cable system, largest in the country with over 200,000 homes as of early 1982. Still, the large majority of stations had but a few thousand subscribers. Major centers of growth were in suburban counties, the "not fully urbanized" "B" and "C" counties, followed closely by rural counties, and trailed by "A" counties, those that are expensive to cable, and are already well-served with over-the-air television.

Table 7.2 provides what little trend information exists on cable economics, based on somewhat scattered data gathered by the FCC. Based on cable ownership"entities"—the owners of more than one cable system (an MSO or multiple system operator) would count here as a single unit, for example—the more rapid growth toward the end of the decade is evident. Despite inflation, 1979 revenue and profit clearly outpaced 1977 and to a

Table 7.2: Economic Growth of Cable Television, 1975, 1977, 1979 and 1980

Indicator	1975	1977	1979	1980
Number of cable ownership entities	2,443	2,557	2,992	2,868
Average monthly subscriber rate	$6.21	$6.85	$7.37	$7.69
Industry totals (in millions):				
Operating revenue	$894.9	$1,205.9	$1,817.1	$2,238.0
In constant dollars[1]	714.8	864.4	1,119.6	1,251.0
Operating expense	567.4	716.9	1,126.6	1,439.0
Net income before taxes	26.9	133.7	199.3	168.1
In constant dollars[1]	21.5	95.8	123.3	94.0
Profit margin	3%	11%	11%	8%
Assets	$2,131.5	$2,450.0	$3,211.6	$4,443.4
Pay cable income (in millions):				
Revenue	N.A.	$85.9	$355.4	$574.8
In constant dollars[1]	N.A.	61.6	219.0	321.3
% of total cable revenue	N.A.	7%	20%	26%
Employment				
Full-time	24,000*	N.A.	33,000	39,300
Employment units with under 5 full-time	N.A.	N.A.	59%	58.2%
Minority	9%*	N.A.	12%	13%
Female	26%*	N.A.	44%	46%

* 1974 FCC estimates reported in Sterling and Haight (1978), table 490-A.

[1] Calculated using Price Deflator for Personal Consumption Expenditures. Based on 1972 = 100.

N.A.: Not available.

Source: FCC "Cable Television Industry Revenues Continued to Increase in 1979 . . ." News Release 05034 (December 29, 1980), pp. 1-2, table 1; and FCC, "Cable Television Employment Statistics," News Release 002269 (July 20, 1981), pp. 1-2.

far greater extent than was true from 1975 to 1977. The growth rate of cable industry assets, representing existing plant, accelerated substantially, paced to some degree by consumer demand for and connection with pay cable channels (note the sharply increased role pay cable played in overall cable revenue by 1979). Other trends include increased employment (and the generally small size of cable employment units, usually defined as individual systems), and the slowly increasing role of women and minorities brought about to some degree by FCC policies paralleling those for radio and television broadcasting.[14]

While early cable systems provided an average of five viewing channels, the industry soon standardized on 12 channels. Even in 1981, about 70% of the cable systems in the country offered no more than 12 channels of programming. After carrying all the local stations plus any defined by the FCC as "substantially viewed" in the local market, systems often had only a few remaining channels for discretionary programming. While most such "origination" early in the 1970s consisted of automated features (weather dials, news tickers, etc.), by the late 1970s two-thirds of all cable systems provided some kind of locally provided programs in addition to automation. Newer systems were built with greater system channel capacity, partially because of community franchise pressure for greater service in return for the franchise award, and partially in response to an ever-increasing number of cable programming services made available by satellite after 1975. With increased penetration of cable systems that programmed one or more channels locally, the National Cable Television Association, the chief trade organization in the field, began in 1980 to issue an annual directory of systems capable of and interested in carrying advertising. The 1981 edition was three times the size of the 1980 version, demonstrating the increased pace of cable growth—and its economic importance.[15]

Rationale for Deregulation

The move to deregulate cable communications received its impetus from a continuing series of policy papers following the pioneering Sloan Commission. Though some of its results, and indeed its very publication, got lost in the Watergate morass, the 1974 report of the Cabinet Committee on Cable Communications helped to nudge the FCC into softening some of the 1972 rules.[16] Assembled under the direction of Clay Whitehead, then director of the White House Office of Telecommunications Policy, the report advocated almost total deregulation of cable in the long run—but at the price of a "separations" policy discussed below. Just over a year later a generally conservative business research organization issued its analysis of cable and also called for a general loosening of government controls of cable.[17]

The most incisive of the analyses came in January 1976 when staff members of the House Subcommittee on Communications issued a review of cable development, current status and future options which criticized the FCC for siding with the broadcast industry to hold down cable development.[18] Both a 1977 publication made up during the Ford Administration, titled *Deregulation of Cable Television,*[19] and 1978-1980 drafts of a rewrite of the Communications Act moved in the same direction. Clearly, public policy on cable TV was being debated at the end of the decade by more divergent and broad-based groups than had been the case when the broadcasters and cable system operators tried to settle their differences in 1971. One reason for the change was the passage in 1976 (effective 1978) of the new copyright act,[20] which partly resolved a prime conflict between copyright holders and cable system owners. Now, under compulsory license, cable operators simply carry signals and pay a specified fee to the Copyright Tribunal, which handles processing for distribution to the copyright holders.[21]

Just as the U.S. Court of Appeals for the District of Columbia has been overruling the Federal Communications Commission in many important broadcasting cases, so it has been contravening FCC rule-making concerning cable. While earlier decisions nibbled away at FCC preemptive jurisdictional decisions on cable, a 1978 decision set aside the Commission's access requirements and channel capacity rules. The decisions on these FCC limitations on cable were upheld in final adjudication before the Supreme Court in early 1979.[22] The FCC itself, however, in a series of decisions, loosened controls on cable by easing distant signal importation rules, ending formal franchise considerations (leaving this step almost totally to local and state regulators) and generally delaying imposition of rules on older grandfathered systems.[23]

Changes in membership and leadership led to a considerable about-face at the Commission. In 1979, the FCC issued its "Report in the Matter of Inquiry into the Economic Relationship Between Television Broadcasting and Cable Television," a landmark research analysis which held most of the former commission policy positions to be invalid based on solid economic evidence.[24] The 300-page analysis "concluded that cable provided only a minor threat to broadcasters' profits and even less to their ability to perform in the public interest,"[25] generally defined as providing some kind of local news and public service programming. As a direct result of this assessment of economic data, the Commission in mid-1980 finally abolished both the syndicated exclusivity and distant signal importation rules, both key parts of the late 1960s' approach to holding cable down to protect television broadcasting.[26] The decision was upheld on appeal, suggesting the courts and the Commission were finally "in sync" on the regulatory approach to cable.[27] Within this latest and most research-based decision to deregulate cable lie some of the reasons for a changing view of cable versus broadcasting.

Impact on Broadcasting

The FCC had long been certain, though it had no research findings to back up its certainty, that cable expansion would harm television service to the public by taking away audience from stations—especially new operations, UHF stations and independent (non-network) outlets. The Commission couched its concern in terms of impact of cable on the localism doctrine (see Chapter 6). If broadcast station audiences were sufficiently cut ("sufficiently" never being adequately defined), the regulatory thinking was that cuts in advertising revenue would follow, to the eventual detriment of public service programming and other aspects of localism which usually lost money for the licensee anyway. The academic impact studies of the 1970s, done both before and during the FCC's economic inquiry, showed that cable's initial impact in this domino scheme was all but insignificant—often far less than 5%. Moreover, they indicated that in most cases in the years while cable penetration was increasing, so were broadcast station profits.[28] UHF stations continued to expand and by 1975 reported an overall national profitable status for the majority of outlets.[29] But based on these findings, an initially subtle change in the FCC's approach to the economic injury issue which had so long guided its cable regulation took on greater significance. Rather than protection of broadcasters on a presumed basis of competitive harm from expanding cable, the Commission now perceived a broader competitive situation where broadcasting would simply have to compete on its own without special protection.

Rising Video Competition

To a considerable degree, this new cable competition remains more predicted than real. Cable systems reached under a third of the nation's homes by the beginning of 1982 while broadcast television could be received in better than 98% of the households. But cable was expanding at an increasing pace in the 1980s while television, having reached saturation years before, stood still. Further, cable's broadband nature—and the resultant range of potential services—was also expanding. But even in urban areas already well served by cable, other competitors cropped up, including over-the-air pay television (STV and MDS, discussed later in this chapter), pay channels on cable systems, and satellite delivery of a wider variety of programming to all of these local outlets. In addition, the long anticipated development of various home video systems had finally begun to penetrate the market. Initially video tape and then increasingly video discs allowed total home control of when (the process of time-shifting) and what would be viewed. These pay and home video systems provided some new material—programming not available over the air—a benefit which naturally helped to increase demand.[30] Virtually none of these new competitors are regulated on any level of government, allowing full marketplace control over pace and direction of their expansion. The FCC's decision-making on cable increasingly took this oncoming competition into account. In speeches and decisions, Commissioners made clear their intention to let the marketplace decide what heretofore regulation had tried to control.

Administrative Deregulation

In part, this change was due to a general trend toward less governmental interference in commerce—a trend which was increasingly evident in FCC decisions after 1972. In part it was an ideological feeling, especially after 1980, that government was stifling business. But the primary factor was simply economic: the costs of government regulation were too high in an economy beset with inflationary pressures and other problems. Pressure on governmental agency budgets forced closer attention to priorities and at the FCC, close control of cable television simply did not stand up to scrutiny once the economic analysis studies showed the original basis for FCC concern was invalid. Economic motivation was evident in the changing status and size of the FCC's cable regulators. Beginning in August 1966 as a task force based in the FCC's Broadcast Bureau, the Commission eventually set up a Cable Television Bureau as an operating arm in January 1970. After growing to some 250 employees in 1975, the Bureau, due to the Court and Commission decisions vastly reducing its regulatory load, shrank to some 45 employees by late 1981 and was rumored to be about to once again lose full Bureau status.

Cable's Broadband Services

As cable service changed from extending of broadcast signals, to some local origination, to the new systems of the 1980s with dozens of channels of non-broadcast material, the conception of cable changed for both the Court and the Commission. The basis of the broadcast regulatory scheme into which cable had been fit involved scarcity of electromagnetic spectrum space (see Chapter 6). As it did not use spectrum, and thanks to technological improvements that allowed for an increasing number of channels, cable seemed almost the opposite of restricted service broadcasting. It held the promise of mass and specific services over the same cable. The channel abundance made many old regulations unnecessary and new regulation almost unthinkable. The same abundance spelled the end of most cable regulation by 1981. It cast into question virtually all of what remained—including limitations on ownership set up a decade before.

Entry

At the height of cable regulation in the early 1970s, a potential cable operator had to endure a welter of red tape on at least two, if not three, levels of government before any construction began. Over the last few years, the federal role (and in most cases states have played but a minor role) has disappeared, leaving most entry decisions to local levels of government.

Franchise

Every cable system needs a "license" to operate, coming in the form of a franchise from the local political entity (city or town council, mayor or whatever). The franchise is essentially a legal permission to do business in a given political area. It includes access to city or town streets and other utilities during construction, and the rules by which the system must operate when serving the public, e.g., services to be provided, rates charged, amount of return to the government for costs of administration of the franchise, complaint procedures and the duration of the franchise (usually about 15 years), etc. As a rule, older cable systems (those franchised prior to about 1975) have less demanding franchise requirements in terms of number of channels required, local programming provisions and the like, while newer franchises, especially in major markets, require high channel capacity (often more than 100 channels), interactive capacity if not actual use, extensive local production facilities and access channels, and strong rate controls. Indeed, the cost of competing for the franchise in the larger cities has been a major factor in the trend to ownership consolidation. Recent years have seen several cable firms competing for months and sometimes years (counting court appeals of "final" franchise decisions) at a cost of hundreds of thousands of dollars—all for naught if the franchise award is lost or at staggering expense of beginning operation if it is won.[31] If won, the security of 15 and sometimes more years is far greater than the five-year television license, at least on paper, for while the latter can be sought by a new owner at renewal time, in fact few change hands involuntarily.

Capital

Cable television has long been described as being head-end capital intensive," meaning simply that large amounts of money are needed at the beginning, both for franchise-winning and construction, before any income is derived from the system. The costs of building a cable system have vastly increased as cable's channel capacity has increased with new technology, as franchises call for a wider variety of cable services, and due to the past decade's inflation. Especially in urban areas which sometimes call for underground cables, the cost per mile can be in the millions. Even in suburban or rural areas, where cables are typically hung on already-existing utility poles, the cost of labor and pole rentals can be substantial. And, finally, the cost of capital (i.e., interest rates) has been at record highs for several years.[32] Thus, building sufficient reserves and obtaining capital is another key cause of cable ownership consolidation. Economies of scale are often important in cable—especially when many smaller communities can be wired by the same owner at the same time. As is explained later in this chapter, the need for income to repay the cost of construction has encouraged the rapid adoption of pay cable as an increasingly important factor of cable income and underlies the rising interest in advertising on cable channels.

Other Factors

A number of lesser factors can control entry into cable television. Perhaps most obvious is that most of the desirable franchises have either already been given out or are in advanced stages of decision. Observers have suggested that by the end of 1982 virtually all the country's cable-favorable cities and towns will have been awarded, though not necessarily constructed.[33] Thus, options for new entry into cable, given that franchises usually run about 15 years, are slim until nearly the turn of the century —and then only if the franchise changes hands. Many of the franchises awarded in the early years will be up for renewal in the 1980s. But there is insufficient experience with franchise renewal to date to make any reliable predictions.

One clear result of this rapid franchising process has been an old pattern from broadcasting renewed in cable—the near exclusion of minority groups from system ownership. While some have made accusations of incipient bias, the root cause of this inequality is the relative newness of minority ownership entities and their greater difficulty in obtaining the needed capital to compete for franchises, let alone construct systems. This relative lack of ownership status combined with demand for some kind of access has added fuel to the debate over leased access (see below).

Cross-Ownership with Other Media

The FCC's concern over ownership in cable systems focuses on three aspects: cross-ownership with other media, telephone company ownership and more general concerns about multiple system controls. The cross-ownership concerns break further into two levels: 1) the issue generally; but more seriously, 2) the concern over local market (or "co-located") cross-ownership.

Table 7.3 summarizes cross-ownership data since 1969. However, it does not account for differences between local cross-ownership and geographically separated cross-owners. Over the decade of the 1970s, broadcast stations held about a third of all cable systems, newspapers have generally increased their holdings (when combined with other publishers, print media holdings have better than doubled in relative terms while sharply increasing absolutely), program producers have owned about a fifth of all cable systems (see discussion of vertical integration below), and TV/cable equipment manufacturers have held a declining number of cable systems. Naturally, many cable systems, especially those owned in "mom and pop" fashion or in other entities without other media interests, are not included on the table.

Local TV Stations

FCC regulatory emphasis for local television stations has been totally with co-located (same market) combinations, specifically defined as any cable system operating within the Grade B coverage contour of the television station.[34] The question came up first in 1965 when the FCC considered, but rejected, a rule banning ownership of cable systems by television stations.[35] Five years later, the FCC reversed itself and banned local cross-ownerships of cable systems and TV stations (if the former was in any place within the B contour of the station) to "further the Commission's policy favoring diversity of control over local mass communications media.[36] Existing cross-ownerships were not allowed to stand (a break with usual FCC practice), but were ordered to divest. But over the years, many waivers to this divestiture order were granted and the deadline was pushed back.

Finally, in 1975, the FCC decided waivers would be brought into line with newspaper-broadcast cross-ownership policy (see Chapter 6) by requiring divestiture only in very concentrated markets. The Commission concluded: "While our concerns with economic competition and media

Table 7.3: Categories of Cable System Ownership, Selected Years, 1969-1981

Category of Owner[1]	1969 N[2]	1969 %[2]	1971 N[2]	1971 %[2]	1973 N[2]	1973 %[2]	1975 N[2]	1975 %[2]	1977 N[2]	1977 %[2]	1979 N[2]	1979 %[2]	1981 N[2]	1981 %[2]
Broadcasters	741	32%	766	30%	1048	35%	1090	32%	1179	30%	1371	33%	1776	38%
Newspapers	220	10	175	7	308	10	486	14	474	12	547	13	729	16
Publishers					221	7	247	7	501	13	463	11	545	12
TV program producers/distributors	N.A.		N.A.		604	20	772	23	772	20	736	18	967	21
Theater owners	N.A.		N.A.		130	4	296	9	301	8	166	4	144	3
Telephone companies	150	7	132	5	50	2	61	2	73	2	104	3	149	3
Community or subscriber control	N.A.		N.A.		75	3	88	3	106	3	99	2	96	1
TV manufacturers	N.A.		N.A.		320	11	630	19	422	11	282	7	97	2
Total systems	2300		2578		3032		3405		3911		4180		4637	

[1] Systems whose owner does business in more than one category are counted in each applicable category. Further, *any* degree of ownership interest is shown. Thus, columns are not additive. "Other" not shown (1981 = 777 systems).

[2] N = actual number of systems; % = percentage of all cable systems in that category.

N.A.: Not available.

Source: *TV Factbook*, published by Television Digest, Inc., annual issues.

diversity extend throughout a local television station's service area, the harshness of the divestiture remedy appears to us only warranted in those situations where there would otherwise be a virtual monopoly over local video expression."[37] Divestiture would now be required solely in those markets where the only television station in a market put out a coverage signal encompassing the entire cable service area.

By 1981, the situation was again somewhat confused. The FCC's 1975 decision had been appealed (as usual), but before a final court ruling could be made, the FCC had sought and received remand (or return) of the issue for further consideration. In 1980, the Commission proposed a return to the 1970 standard of divesting all existing co-located combinations, allowing some *ad hoc* waivers. Conflicting with this proposal were 1) a dramatic change in 1981 in the political makeup of the Commission's membership and direction, and 2) more specifically, a petition to entirely delete the section of the cable rules banning cross-ownership.[38] Faced with this question, among others, the Commission requested a detailed study of cable ownership problems and policy. One chapter of the report,[39] admittedly based on qualitative observation rather than solid quantifiable economic data, agreed with the earlier petition and called for dropping of the station-system cross-ownership ban.[40]

The recommendation to drop the prohibition was based primarily on expectation of an increasing amount of competition to both television stations and cable from such options as over-the-air subscription television (STV) and multipoint distribution services (MDS), as well as home video and potential direct broadcast satellite (DBS) operations. Further, the expansion in number of cable channels per system naturally suggests more program service from different sources will become available in each market, much of it non-broadcast in origin if not nature. At the same time, the FCC staff report dismissed several traditional concerns of cross-ownership. First, it said that the old argument that the broadcaster would hold down cable expansion or program offerings to protect the earlier television investment was offset by the reality that cable is too capital-intensive to allow this kind of treatment, and local franchises typically specify rate of system construction and offerings. Second, the concern that a combined owner would be able to limit editorial (or advertising) points of view and expression was balanced by the increasing channel capacity of cable systems and the resulting need to fill the channels provided. Moreover, other competing delivery systems should serve to limit any such control.

Still, the authors conclude after a detailed analysis of the issues, a limited ban along the lines of the 1975 proposal could be retained:

Such a limited rule could be justified on two grounds. First, if a subset of cross-ownership cases could be identified in which excessive market power is likely to be created [as in very small markets lacking much competitive video input], it might be more efficient to establish a rule than to rely on case-by-case action by the Justice Department. Second, the antitrust laws are not meant to promote the exercise of First Amendment rights; Justice Department action could not respond to concerns in this area.[41]

In the meantime, the existing ban (the Grade B contour standard) continues to stand, requiring divestiture of either stations or cable systems in mergers. The impact of this ban is exemplified by the largest merger to date—the Westinghouse-Teleprompter agreement of 1980, approved by the FCC in mid-1981. To get FCC approval, Westinghouse was given two years to divest Teleprompter cable systems within the Grade B contour of its television stations—affecting some 150,000 subscribers in 13 systems. The result is a combination of television stations and cable systems of considerable size, but along with other such combinations, these do not involve same-market combinations (see MSO section below).

Broadcast Networks

The initial kind of vertical integration in the cable industry considered by the FCC—network ownership—was banned in 1970 with a rule requiring divestiture of any broadcast network-owned cable system anywhere in the country.[42] The assumption behind the rule was that the networks' desire to maximize their own audiences would cause them to limit programming on cable, and that broadcast network control of systems might well hinder the development of new cable-based networking. CBS, as a result of the ruling, had to sell off its cable division, which became Viacom, now a major cable system owner and programmer.

With the expansion and changing nature of cable, the question of network ownership of cable systems was reconsidered. In its final report, the FCC network inquiry of 1978-1980 (see Chapter 6), recommended the ban be lifted.[43] So, too, did the staff report on cable ownership which noted that while

> . . . it is possible that independent suppliers . . . might be foreclosed from access to integrated cable systems . . . the theoretical case for foreclosure is weak; consumer demand, franchise authority power, and alternative transmission techniques all make it unlikely to occur. Furthermore, examples exist of integrated firms carrying rival pay channels on their affiliated systems.

Finally, as long as no firm controls a substantial share of all cable systems, the potential for foreclosure is very small; should a case of foreclosure arise, the antitrust laws are available for use in combating it.[44]

Clearly, broadcast networks have built up considerable interest in cable programming and this has spilled over to a rising interest in cable ownership. ABC filed supporting comments with the FCC to a petition calling for a total lifting of the ownership ban.[45] In 1981, CBS's petition for a limited ownership position in cable (90,000 subscribers or .05% of the total cable subscribership in the country, whichever is less) was granted by the FCC on CBS' showing of need for ownership to test programming and technical ideas.[46] In 1980, then-FCC Chairman Charles Ferris called for a lifting of the ban in light of the changed competitive situation in video distribution. Ferris' successor, Mark Fowler, and other Commissioners appeared inclined to agree.[47]

Other Media

There has never been an FCC ban on newspaper or other media ownership of cable systems, in striking contrast to the long rule-makings and many court cases on newspaper control of broadcast stations (see Chapter 6). In fact, the FCC has not even kept records of such ownerships since 1975,[48] the only consistent data being that gathered annually by *Television Digest* and summarized in Table 6.3. As noted earlier, publisher proportion of all cable systems has more than doubled during the 1970s.

To a considerable degree, newspaper ownership of cable systems came about for reasons similar to the print press' interest in broadcasting: protection of an older technology in the face of a new delivery system. It was also seen to provide entry into an additional means of news and feature delivery, to be an investment opportunity for increasingly profitable newspaper groups with strong earnings but little opportunity for additional newspaper purchases, and to serve as a means of circumventing FCC bans on broadcast ownership. As for major newspaper owners entering cable, much of the purchase or construction activity was not in markets congruent with their newspapers. The Hearst chain, The New York Times Co., the Tribune Co., Newhouse newspapers and the Times Mirror Co. are among the large cable owners with a newspaper base, the latter the seventh largest multiple system operator (see Table 7.5). The largest cable MSO is owned by Time Inc., perhaps the most successful magazine publisher in the country. All of these print firms see cable as a natural outlet for their content production, and a serious threat should any rule limiting their ownership role be put forth. One indication of the unlikelihood of federal limitations is the virtually complete absence of discussion on this topic in the otherwise broad-ranging FCC cable ownership staff report of 1981.[49] Nor has a ban on possible cable-radio cross-ownerships, co-located or otherwise, been seriously considered, primarily because the two media are seen as catering to different audiences and needs.

Some states, however, have stepped into the breach. Massachusetts, for example, prohibits a newspaper company from owning a local cable system. In Connecticut, state regulators ordered Times Mirror Co., owner of both the *Hartford Courant* and two cable systems in Hartford, to divest itself of the newspaper or the cable interests.

Cross-Ownership with Telephone

Considerably more controversial is the ownership of cable systems by telephone companies—especially the ubiquitous American Telephone and Telegraph Co. Since 1970, local telephone companies have been prohibited from owning or operating cable systems within their telephone service areas.[50] Waivers have been granted only on quite specific and controlled grounds, as will be seen shortly.

The Issues

The FCC staff report on cable ownership clearly sets the stage for cable-telephone policy problems:

> Telephone companies and cable systems both provide electronic information services over wire. Many services can be provided by either one. With adequate switching and consumer premises equipment a cable company can do just about anything a telephone company can. With some changes in telephone systems, telephone companies can do virtually anything that a cable company can. The potential for competition with the local telephone monopoly is central to arguments to ban cross-ownership of cable and telephone facilities and joint operation of these facilities.[51]

The second chief reason for the ban, other than protection of cable development from an established telephone industry, is the potential of cross-subsidization between the two businesses, one of them a rate-based common carrier and the other not. Summing up the disadvantages in allowing cross-ownership, the FCC staff concluded there were four main considerations:

First, cross-ownership may allow a telephone company partially to avoid rate-of-return regulation on its telephone service. It can do so by attributing costs to the regulated telephone division and revenues to an unregulated cable division.

Second, cable service can compete with telephone services in the areas of alarm systems, data transmission, meter reading and even plain old telephone service. Telephone companies may be able to forestall this facilities-based competition in two-way communications by owning the cable system. Cross-ownership or cooperative operations will also allow joint-monopoly profit maximization.

Third, the size of some telephone companies relative to cable companies could allow one or two telephone companies to gain a very large share of the national market in cable.

Fourth, telephone companies control substantial conduit and pole space. Unrestricted control over cable access can give the telephone company a powerful lever to gain control of the cable system, or to charge monopolistic rates for access. Rate or pole price regulation can limit exploitation of telephone company monopoly power unless cross-ownership is allowed.[52]

Looked at economically, there are, of course, potential benefits to allowing cross-ownership. There would be obvious savings in joint construction, operations and administrative costs. Cable might be introduced more rapidly in a telephone service area where the "home" phone firm had knowledge of demographic and market factors. Additionally, there could be substantial technological development factors which cross-ownership might hasten—especially, expanded use of fiber optics with its vastly increased capacity for many kinds of digital and analog communication.[53]

But weighing all of this and more, the FCC staff report finally concluded that the cross-ownership ban of 1970 should be continued, at least for the time being, because complete elimination of the ban "would substantially [en]danger the consumer by reducing competition in an already uncompetitive area."[54]

The Rural Waiver

The focal point for policy debate and trade group battle on the issues briefly noted above has been in the rural or "D" class counties. These are the areas most lacking in over-the-air broadcast service, and at the same time the most expensive to wire for cable due to dispersed low density population. Briefly stated, the rural issue considers who can best wire and serve these potential viewers—telephone companies or independent (non-telephone-owned) cable systems. The telephone argument notes the existing infrastructure and posits that only by building on that service can a cable system be economically constructed and operated, due to the economies noted above. The cable view is that independent operators can do the job just as well without the cross-ownership issue arising.

In fact, however, the argument boils down to "cherry-picking." In a number of cases thus far, an independent cable system seeks the franchise for a town or several towns, thus picking the most densely populated service areas and passing up the expensive-to-wire rural regions in between or beyond the towns. The telephone argument seizes on this and notes that by so doing, the cable companies effectively doom the rural areas to no service at all. Without the intervening towns as a part of a single system, no firm, not even an existing telephone operation, can afford the cost of wiring only the sparse rural counties. The telephone argument suggests the telephone cable cross-owned firm is more likely to wire both town and rural area due to its existing plant in both areas.

During the 1970s, the ban on co-located cross-ownership of telephone plant and cable systems was waived if a telephone company demonstrated that 1) cable service can exist only if provided by a telephone firm or 2) for some other good reason. But the waivers were not common and pressure for easing waivers—or an outright lifting of the cross-ownership ban in rural areas—built steadily. Late in 1980, the FCC issued a Notice of Proposed Rulemaking to drop the ban for rural regions in areas where there were no more than 30 homes per route mile.[55] An extensive set of comments was gathered on ways to clarify the definition of what was really "rural." By late 1981, in a final report, the Commission decided to adopt the definition long used by the Census Bureau to make absolutely clear "that the telephone company's entire cable television service area must be rural in order to qualify for the exemption" from the general cross-ownership ban.[56] The Commission found that the ban was preventing cable service to rural areas unable to support an independent cable operation—and that the existing process of waivers "appeared to be imposing costs which exceeded benefits."[57]

The debate over rural areas was seen by many in cable and telephony as but a rehearsal for a lifting of the ban on cross-ownership entirely. The issues led to heated debate and considerable emotionalism on the part of cable system operators fearful of telephone company takeover of the cable business, given the difference in financial size and clout of cable firms and most telephone companies. AT&T was long held to be disqualified from participation in cable activities due to the 1956 Consent Decree (by which AT&T agreed to stay out of "non-telephone" businesses).[58] But development of viewdata and related technologies, and the AT&T desire to experiment with electronic replacements for telephone directories, helped to spark renewed AT&T cable interest. In mid-1981 the 1956 Consent Decree was provisionally lifted, removing one barrier to AT&T cable activity.[59] But possible cable activity by telephone firms, especially AT&T, was intimately wrapped up in larger policy questions involving an AT&T unregulated separate subsidiary for "enhanced" (other than basic telephone) services (see Chapter 2).[60] For the cable business, telephone cross-ownership was the most salient ownership question of the early 1980s—of vastly more concern than other cross-ownership issues or questions about multiple system operators.

Multiple System Ownership

Another concern to cable owners is the increasing size and importance of multiple system operators (MSOs) which parallel the "group" owner in broadcasting, or the "chain" newspaper or theater owner. Simply defined, an MSO is any single ownership entity controlling more than one cable system.

Factors in Consolidation

A variety of interrelated factors underlie the trend to ever larger units of cable television system ownership. Some of the reasons are analogous to those in other media. But peculiar to cable television's up-front capital intensity is the impact of the franchise process. As one observer put it, "It's not the small MSO but the wealthy ones, like Warner Amex, that are scooping up the major markets. The leaders have the cash, the expertise and the clout that appeals to municipal decision makers."[61] A press report headline claimed "Cable TV Industry Growing Too Big For Small Investors",[62] as the days of venture capital rapidly passed in the face of the escalating costs of obtaining the remaining franchises. The large cities seeking cable franchisees have also been escalating their demands. They require detailed presentations. They propose specifications seeking multiple cables, connecting educational and government offices for "free" and low basic service charges for residential customers.

In 1980 alone, six firms vied for the Dallas franchise, at a cost to each of some $500,000 before any award was granted. Nine firms spent some $250,000 each for wealthy Connecticut suburbs of New York City.[63] In such contests, the losers are out their investment, while the winner becomes legally committed to spending millions more (often on the order of $100 million for an 80-100 channel major market system) on system construction. Small companies cannot raise the cash necessary to play in this game. And once a system is operating and subscriber revenue is coming in, today's cable system operators face sharply higher costs for programming to supplement once-staple off-air television stations. The risks are substantial and only large corporations can take them, firms with diversified holdings and extensive bank and investment corporation backing.

Additionally, there are efficiencies inherent in multiple system control. Large MSOs can reduce the cost of regional or national networking by use of their own systems in various markets. Such costs as construction, maintenance and overhead can be spread across many systems at a scale savings. Administrative costs and the increasingly important factors of market and program research can also be spread over many systems at a considerable savings. Likewise, the often substantial legal costs in the franchise process can be usefully spread over many similar franchising procedures. A pool of cable system subscribers provides an outlet for technical and programming experimentation—as exemplified by Warner's "Qube" systems in Columbus and Cincinnati, and the granting of a waiver to CBS on grounds of technical experimentation (see above).

To a far less quantifiable degree, the expansion of MSO size and scope represents fear, or at least precaution. Many of the MSOs have extensive older investments in broadcasting and/or print media which they feel are to some extent protected with extensive investment in cable ownership. A possibly extreme example came in 1980 when *The New York Times* paid more than $83 million for 55 small New Jersey cable franchises (or $1566 for each of the 53,000 subscribers at the time when the going rate was $600-$800 per subscriber) plus substantial committed construction costs for some of the systems' expansion.[64] But the major fear is of the telephone "colossus"—the potential for telephone company ownership of cable systems. The argument here is that large diversified entities, aside from the economic benefits noted already, can better withstand telephone firm competition for franchises—or outright bids for control of existing systems. To a degree, the construction pace of cable in the early 1980s is driven by concern of impending telephone entry and the ease with which small companies would be swallowed up should that occur.

Trends in MSO Development

Table 7.4 summarizes a hectic decade's development of MSO expansion, and shows a clear trend to greater consolidation. Control by the largest four MSOs has increased nearly 75% from 1969 to 1981 with a strong but less pronounced trend in the top eight companies. The pace of consolidation is somewhat slower in the top 25 and top 50 companies, but is still fairly clear with new heights of concentration evident in 1981 across all four groups of MSOs. But context is important here. Compared to many other businesses and industries, cable television is not considered by economists to be highly concentrated. The 1977 *Census of Manufacturers* notes substantially greater degrees of four-firm concentration in such industries as farm machinery, beer, aircraft, aluminum and cigarettes.[65] Further, concentration ratios as shown in Table 7.4 tend to overestimate market power in an industry as they do not account for possible entry by new competitors or changing technology—in this case, competing home video delivery systems.[66] In addition, the cable business is still sufficiently small so that one or two major consolidations, like the Westinghouse-Teleprompter merger, can substantially change the data from year to year as the variations in the table suggest.

Table 7.4: MSO Subscriber Concentration, Selected Years, 1969-1981

| Year | Percent of All Cable Subscribers Served by the Largest: | | | |
	4 Firms	8 Firms	25 Firms	50 Firms
1969	16.3%	26.7%	47.9%	61.1%
1971	21.7	31.6	53.7	67.3
1973	27.2	40.3	61.7	73.4
1975	26.4	38.1	58.5	69.8
1977	23.1	34.2	54.1	66.7
1979	24.0	36.5	58.4	71.5
1981	27.3	40.9	63.9	77.8

Source: Braunstein (1979), p. 14 for data through 1979; 1981 figures from *Television Digest*, NCTA Supplement, May 29, 1981, pp. 1-2, published by Television Digest, Inc.

Perhaps the most important contextual comparison is with other media. Cable system ownership is not anywhere near as concentrated as broadcast station ownership when compared on the basis of potential viewers. In 1980, for example, the largest MSO would have ranked 46th among television station groups, comparing the MSO's subscribers with the television group's "net weekly circulation" (see Chapter 6).[67] While the largest cable MSO can claim about 1.5 million subscribers, each of the network's owned and operated station groups (five stations) have a net weekly circulation of over 15 million. Concentration in film production is higher, while ownership concentration in the newspaper business is much lower on a national basis, though as with cable, most communities have but one outlet.

Table 7.5 shows the development over the past decade of the largest MSO firms. In 1981, Teleprompter, the traditional leader in cable system

Table 7.5: Largest Cable MSOs, by Basic Subscribers, Selected Years, 1970-1981 (in thousands)

Rank of Top 13 in 1981	Parent/MSO	1970	1973	1975	1977	1979	1981
1.	Time Inc./American Television and Communications Corp. (ATC)	112	350	474	585	905	1,752
2.	Westinghouse/Teleprompter Corp.	243	800	1,074	1,050	1,183	1,570
3.	Tele-Communications Inc.	142	387	526	557	673	1,362
4.	Cox Broadcasting/Cox Cable Communications	190	275	345	437	610	1,057
5.	Warner Communications & American Express Co./Warner Amex Cable	N.A.	450	513	554	630	837
6.	Storer Broadcasting/Storer Cable Communications	N.A.	100	135	179	285	802
7.	Times Mirror Co./Times Mirror Cable TV	N.A.	49	56	82	412[1]	650
8.	Newhouse Cable[2]	—	—	—	—	—	558
9.	Rogers UA Cablesystems[3]	N.A.	150	182	214	280	515
9.	Viacom Communications	150	254	306	324	400	515
11.	United Cable	—	—	—	—	—	444
12.	Sammons Communications	N.A.	221	253	286	340	441
13.	Continental Cablevision	—	—	—	—	—	429

[1] Includes Communication Properties Inc. acquisition.

[2] Newhouse Cable includes Vision Cable, MetroVision and NewChannels.

[3] Formerly UA-Columbia Cablevision.

N.A.: Not available.

Source: *Television Digest*, published by Television Digest, Inc., citing figures as of the spring of each year (generally March or April 1st), except for 1981, from *Broadcasting*, November 30, 1981, as of fall 1981.

ownership, was overtaken by Time Inc.-owned American Television and Communications (ATC) by a thin margin. Note the sharp increases evident for many of the firms in the two-year periods shown here. Most of this is due to consolidation through purchase of systems rather than internal growth by expansion of existing systems. Furthermore, essentially the same firms have been among the 10 largest.

Such numerical comparisons are misleading in one important fashion, however, especially when compared to broadcasting's "net weekly circulation" measure. In the case of cable, unlike a broadcast station's single channel, the potential audience is scattered across at least five or six channels on smaller systems, up to 12 on the majority of systems, and across 20 and more on the newer systems with much nonbroadcast material. Moreover, each of the systems in such ownership aglomerations in cable are operated under different franchise limitations, varied technical constraints (older systems have fewer channels, etc.), and different programming on varying numbers of channels. The statistics suggest greater sameness of input and audience "control" than, in fact, exists, except in overall economic terms.

A bit of background on the top MSOs says a good deal about trends in the cable industry. Number one-ranked ATC is a part (since 1978) of Time Inc.'s video division which includes pay television leader Home Box Office (see below) and three STV stations. Combined, the video portion of the print giant contributes over a third of its operating income.[68] Time Inc. is an excellent example of the integrated and diversified conglomerate providing muscle to cable system development. In 1981, long-time leader Teleprompter became a part of Westinghouse, the fourth largest electronics firm even without the cable acquisition, and has since been named Group W Cable.[69] Teleprompter's cable revenues accounted for more than half that company's total revenues prior to the merger. Teleprompter controls cable systems in the two largest markets in the country—Los Angeles and Manhattan (New York City).[70] Tele-Communications Inc. gets 80% of its income from cable—an unusual dependence on the medium amongst the top MSOs.[71] Cox Cable is part of the Cox family holdings that began as a newspaper chain in the 1920s, then entered broadcasting. In the first three months of 1981 Cox earned 47% of its income from cable to 44% from its broadcast stations, with cable revenue growing at nearly three times the rate of broadcasting revenue. Cox is presently wiring the Omaha and New Orleans markets, among others.[72] Warner-Amex Cable, the fifth largest MSO in 1981, came about through a joint venture between Warner Cable and American Express Co.

Storer Cable, like Cox, moved into cable from a broadcasting base. In 1979 cable provided only a quarter of total revenues. But Storer sold four of its five radio stations in 1979 to raise more capital for cable. This was part of a strategy to move out of broadcasting and further into cable, which may signal a trend for other broadcasters.[73] Times Mirror Co., the seventh largest MSO, continued its moves into broadcasting and cable, purchasing five TV stations from Newhouse in 1980, while expanding its cable holdings.[74] In 1981 UA-Columbia was purchased by Canadian-based Rogers Cablesystems—which made Rogers UA Cablesystems the ninth largest MSO—sparking a policy debate on foreign control of American cable systems. U.S. systems amounted to about 20% of the firm's total cable subscribers, with a goal of a 50-50 split between the two countries.[75] Viacom, the cable MSO spun off CBS by FCC order, and which shares ninth place with Rogers, owns cable systems and retains as well a half-ownership of the Showtime pay cable program distributor it founded. Its partner in Showtime is Teleprompter. Major Viacom systems include those in the San Francisco area and Nashville.[76] The 12th largest MSO, Sammons, is also the largest privately-held MSO firm. Though a subsidiary, Sammons owns four radio stations in addition to its generally smaller-market cable systems.[77]

Regulation

The FCC first expressed concern about multiple system ownership in 1968 when it announced a proposed 50-system limitation, making the assumption that each system would have at least 1000 subscribers. If other media interests were held (one TV station, two radio stations or two newspapers were suggested guidelines), then the ownership limit would be 25 systems. Or, looking at it another way, the Commission felt that no single entity should control more than about two million subscribers—a limit still not reached even by 1981. By proposing such limits in 1968, the Commission was clearly trying preemptive regulation before growth might force divestiture with some later rule-making.[78] No final action was ever taken on the proposal.

Certainly one reason for the lack of action was the slower-than-expected growth of cable, and recognition that large entities were increasingly necessary if large technically modern cable systems were to be successfully bid for and built. The House Subcommittee on Communications staff report of 1976 felt any action on MSOs was premature, though it felt both the FCC and the Justice Department should keep a watch on trends, collecting data on mergers and acquisitions in cable.[79] In one of the earliest official statements on the option, the House report provided backing to the "separations" approach to cable ownership (see the last section of this chapter).

The Commission returned to the multiple ownership in cable question in 1975, pushed partially by the seeming dichotomy between the limitations on group owners in broadcasting compared to the lack of any control in cable. But the FCC concluded once more that no limits were called for, though again agreeing that a kind of watchful waiting on industry developments was a good idea.[80] In late 1981, the FCC's staff report on cable ownership questions devoted a chapter to MSO concentration, and concluded:

> Since separate cable systems do not compete directly, MSO's have no direct effect on local markets. Workable competition there depends on the existence of alternative local transmission media. At the national level, MSO's compete for franchises and for programming. If a few MSO's were to gain control of most cable systems in the country, their share of total media outlets might be unacceptably high. . . . this point has not nearly been reached; concentration is low, other media are available, and there are many credible potential entrants into the cable business. Against this background, it seems likely that MSO growth (short of growth to a very high market share) is based on organizational efficiencies and hence is desirable.[81]

Other Ownership Concerns

There are three other issues which are raised from time to time on cable system ownership: foreign control of American cable systems, the role of financial entities and minority control of cable systems.

Foreign Control

Unlike the case with broadcasting, there has never been a ban on foreign ownership of cable systems in the U.S. The question has come up a number of times, most clearly in 1976 when the Commission dismissed as premature any rules to limit, let alone ban, alien control of U.S. cable.[82] Four years later, in response to a petition, the FCC again decided not to commence a rule-making as the major foreign ownership entities were Canadian, deemed not to be a social or political threat, and held less than 1% of the country's cable subscribers. Given the greater role and penetration of cable in Canada, their experience was deemed useful here. But the Commission noted it would continue to watch trends.[83]

The question came up shortly thereafter, however, this time in Congress. The spark in 1981 was the takeover of UA-Columbia, the ninth largest MSO, by Toronto-based Rogers Telecommunications, the largest

MSO in Canada. While a 1980 bill in the House had failed, H.R. 4225, introduced in July 1981, gained more backing as it was cloaked in terms of basic fairness. While no one really feared a Canadian takeover of American cable, the fact had long rankled some that while Canadians could own American systems, the reciprocal was not true—American ownership of Canadian cable was not allowed. The bill proposed to apply similar restrictions on Canadians in the U.S. as they applied on U.S. firms. Naturally, the Canadian-owned systems in the U.S. spoke out sharply against the proposal. There appeared to be general U.S. system owner backing for the bill, not only in light of Canadian-owned systems already in operation (in such areas as Portland, OR, Los Angeles, Minneapolis, Chicago, Atlanta and eastern Pennsylvania), but also because of active Canadian MSO franchise competition for more systems.[84] The issue appeared more political and competitive than due to any realistic concern over control of any substantial portion of American homes.

Financial Entity Control

With fewer rules on cable ownership than on broadcasting, the concerns about financial entity investment in cable are also somewhat less involved. But in considering cross-ownership between networks and systems, local stations and systems, and telephone companies and cable systems, the same concerns about minority investment holdings by banks, pension funds, foundations and the like arise as in broadcasting (see Chapter 6). The FCC applied to cable the same 5% limitation as applied in broadcasting rules. As with radio-television, the concern centered on the difference between investment for income purposes and investment with intention to have impact on cable system management and operational affairs, i.e., exercising the prerogatives of ownership. With the broad and scattered holdings of stock common in the larger MSOs and conglomerate parent firms, the concern about financial entities has an added element in that with 5% of the stock, an investment holding can be one of the larger blocks of stock held. While under current investigation by the FCC, the present limitation for TV station/cable system cross-ownership purposes is 5% for insurance firms, investment companies of various kinds, and banks under the condition that there is no attempt to control management or policies.[85]

Minority Ownership

In cable systems, as in broadcasting, there is a dearth of minority-owned entities. Of communities with cable service only six had minority ownership participation in 1977, not counting one cable radio system begun that year. The first minority-owned system had begun in Gary, Indiana in 1973.[86] Government policy to expand this minority role in cable parallels efforts in broadcasting, with the important difference that the FCC plays no licensing role in cable, and thus cannot initiate much in the way of incentive programs to encourage minority concerns. Growth has thus come slowly. In late 1981, Blacks controlled three operating systems (one in Columbus, OH being the largest market involved) with an additional three franchises won and in construction, for a total of six. Hispanics operated one system and had a franchise for another (in East Los Angeles), for a total of eight minority-controlled systems.[87] General thinking among media activists was that so-called equity participation or joint ventures involving minorities really do not provide anything meaningful to minority groups, but rather serve to provide a possible edge in the franchise stage.

BASIC AND PAY SERVICE DISTRIBUTION

Until 1975, a discussion of cable television ownership could have ended with the previous paragraph. But since then, and at an accelerating pace, a new expanded kind of cable television has developed, though even in 1981 it was at its very early stages of expansion. This broadband system, built on expanding channel capacity of cable systems (basically those with at least 20 channels), has given rise to a new program production industry, an expanded number and variety of distribution networks, and a substantial boost to expansion of basic cable.* To commit any description or analysis of such a nascent business to print is to stand on quicksand, for not only do details change from one day to the next, but also whole thrusts and directional shifts are born and die regularly and rapidly. This section must be viewed as but a snapshot of the structure and ownership of a newly emerging industry.

Just as basic cable systems already discussed somewhat parallel broadcast stations in their "local outlet" role, so do the newer systems of pay cable channels, subscription television (STV), and multipoint distribution systems (MDS), and the still tentative options like direct broadcast satellites (DBS). All of these are served by networks of program distribution. Considered first here are the newly developing outlets, followed by a discussion of the program distribution (and production) industry.

---

*"Basic" cable refers to the service provided to customers for the minimum monthly fee. It always includes carriage of all local broadcast signals. "Pay" cable refers to additional channels provided to customers willing to pay extra. It often includes movies and other premium programming.

Pay Cable Channels

Though not all the services discussed in this section are based on direct audience payment, it is important to note at the outset that pay or premium services have provided the economic and facilities base for the "basic" or free services.

Development

Although the idea of an electronic entertainment system delivering content directly to homes dates at least to an operating telephone-based system of the 1880s,[88] the notion was moribund in the early years of broadcasting development. A major debate in the 1950s over broadcast pay television (see below) sharpened the respective sides on the question and the idea died. The first pay cable experiment may have been the Bartlesville, Oklahoma project in 1957 which, under special FCC permission, operated for a time with a premium channel of movies. Predictably, it drew strong broadcaster and movie theater opposition.[89] Thus, pay cable when it finally began developing 15 years later was referred to as "old wine in new bottles," referring to the long gestation of the payment idea packaged in a new form.[90]

The real beginning of the modern pay cable business came November 8, 1972 when Home Box Office (HBO) began providing films to 365 subscribers on the Service Electric Cable TV system in Wilkes-Barre, PA. By the end of 1973, the firm served some 8000 subscribers on 14 systems in two states and had become a subsidiary of Time Inc.[91] From its inception HBO developed four principles which guided its operation and that of several competing firms which soon sprang up:

1) a monthly per-channel fee, rather than the technically complex per-program fee most operators had used experimentally earlier;

2) affiliation with the local cable operator rather than an outright lease of a channel;

3) a commitment to a combination of live sports, informative and instructive material as well as entertainment—mainly feature films; and

4) transmission of the programming from a central studio by use of common carrier microwave transmission facilities, rather than distribution by videotape.[92]

Over the next several months, other systems began operation: Theater-Vision in Sarasota, FL, Warner Communications' "Gridtronic" system in four communities in the mid-Atlantic area, two systems in California, and several others. By August 1973, less than a year after pay cable had begun operations, the operating systems served about 35,000 subscribers with primarily sports and film entertainment using a variety of distribution and payment systems.[93] By May 1974 there were some 45 pay cable operations serving about 67,000 subscribers—and Home Box Office had already emerged as the largest single pay cable distributor.[94]

The typical cable system might provide one of these premium channels, with the viewers required to pay an additional monthly fee over the regular subscriber charge. These early pay programming channels shared a number of features:

1) they depended mainly on theatrical films and some (usually local or regional) sporting events not shown on over-the-air television;

2) they operated only in a few evening hours—often providing but one film or sports event per evening, sometimes with a "short" or two as well;

3) they were provided either by the cable system operator, or a separate company would serve several systems, interconnecting or achieving delivery of the premium programming by means of microwave relay or video tape (physical delivery, meaning different systems showed different programs on different evenings); and

4) no advertising to break up program content, thus providing the second major appeal to potential subscribers in addition to otherwise unavailable programming.

The dramatic growth in pay cable after 1975, shown in Table 7.6, came after some important deregulatory moves and the switch to satellite delivery starting in that year. Several patterns developed within this overall trend. For one thing, newer systems with more channels tended to offer pay cable as an option from the start as a marketing strategy to get new basic cable subscribers. Some trade reports suggested that 90% of new system subscriptions included the pay channel offering. Beginning with a Louisiana system late in 1978, cable systems began to experiment with carrying more than one pay cable channel at a time—offering subscribers the chance to take one or more.[95] These multiple pay services were termed "tiers," and by 1979 larger capacity systems had begun to adopt the idea with the result that by mid-1981, nearly a quarter of all cable systems provided tiering of at least two pay cable channels, with far fewer beginning to move up to three and four tiers.[96] Further, the vast majority of cable systems provided at least one pay channel, with its extra-income potential helping to pace system expansion and reconstruction to increase channel capacity.

The single most important event which led to the rapid expansion of pay cable was HBO's decision to implement a communication satellite delivery system late in 1975, thus resolving the program delivery problem by replacing expensive microwave or mail interconnections. A year later, the FCC deregulated the size requirements for earth receive-only antennas and totally deregulated them shortly thereafter. This provided further incentive for expansion of pay cable channels on systems nationwide as the cost of "hooking up" dropped from $100,000 for a 10 meter "dish," down to as low as $5000 for a smaller dish in 1981. The pay cable figures in Table 7.6 show the impact of these business and government decisions: widespread availability of pay cable options. Table 7.7 provides a parallel statistical overview of pay cable penetration for the same years, showing how pay cable is now in more than half the cable homes in the country. Figuring that basic cable was in just over a quarter of the country's television homes

Table 7.6: Growth of Pay Television Systems, Selected Years, 1973-1981

| Year | Pay Cable | | STV Stations | MDS |
	Number of Systems	As % of Basic Cable Systems		
1973	10	0%	0	2
1975	75	2	0	6
1977	459	12	2	18
1979	1,498	36	6	44
1981	3,954[1]	90	20	54

[1] Includes systems providing one pay service, and additionally, the multi-tier approaches provided by some 800 systems in April 1981. See *Cablevision* (June 1, 1981), p. 137ff.

Note: Because of different methods of counting, and varied dates within years shown, the figures here are *not* strictly comparable—and should be considered close estimates.

Sources: Pay Cable data from Paul Kagan Associates, *Pay TV Census*, generally referring to mid-year in each case. STV data from Kagan's *Pay TV Newsletter* (July 31, 1981), p. 5. MDS information figured from "Census of MDS Pay TV" in *Multicast News* (May 11, 1981), pp. 2-3, showing for each year the number of systems in operation by the end of the year (except 1981 which is as of December 31, 1980).

in 1981 (see Table 7.1), then about 12%-13% of U.S. television homes received one or more channels of pay cable by that year.

One possible sign of future development began in 1977 when Columbus, Ohio became the site of an experiment in two-way or interactive pay cable. Selected as a test market for its representative demographics, the "Qube" system provided off-air channels, local origination material and a number of premium or pay channels. But Qube also provided an interactive option —its users could respond to questions or other options put on one of its 30 channels. The Qube system also experiments with pay-per-program charges, as opposed to the HBO model of pay-per-channel, regardless of how much viewing is done. In 1980, the experiment began to make money, and in 1981, it was provided on new Warner Cable systems in Cincinnati, Houston and Pittsburgh. Thus far, however, the very high construction costs for such an interactive system have kept other system operators from emulating the Warner example.

Regulation

Initial FCC regulation of pay cable came before any such systems existed, other than a few specially licensed experiments noted earlier. Although the FCC issued an order in 1969 calling for unlimited programming approaches on cable, under continuing broadcast industry pressure the Commission retreated to a 1970 rule severely limiting pay cable systems to the same kinds of content restrictions which had been placed on over-the-air pay television. The basis for the rules was the "anti-siphoning" principle intended to protect programming on free broadcast television from being purchased by the potentially greater buying power of a subscriber-supported system of broadcasting or cablecasting.[97] Although challenged on this decision, the Commission did not come to any final decision for nearly five years. In the meantime the restrictions stood, while the pay cable industry became more than just a potential medium.

A parallel set of rules, the "definitive" 1972 cable rules discussed previously, are thought by some to mark the real birth of pay cable, as they provided the important impetus to its growth. In the rules, the FCC encouraged local origination by cable systems to supplement signal importation, and allowed lease of extra cable channels to programmers other than the system operator, such outside firms including potential pay cable operations.[98] Late that same year, of course, HBO began its operations in Pennsylvania.

The year 1975 turned out to be a pivotal one for pay cable. On March 20th, the FCC finally issued its final pay cable rules, which had been in limbo since 1970. Continuing on its protectionist approach (to make cable

Table 7.7: Growth in Pay Television Penetration, Selected Years, 1973-1981

	Pay Cable			Subscription TV			Multipoint Distribution Systems		
Year	Subscriptions (in thousands)	% of Basic Cable	Average Rate	Subscriptions (in thousands)	% of Homes Passed	Average Rate	Subscriptions (in thousands)	% of Homes Passed	Average Rate
1973	35	N.A.	N.A.	N.A.	N.A.	N.A.	N.A.	N.A.	N.A.
1975	265	24%	$7.85	N.A.	N.A.	N.A.	N.A.	N.A.	N.A.
1977	1,174	23	7.81	5	4%	$14.98	65	21%	$10.39
1979	4,334	38	8.20	26	4	18.36	207	3	11.94
1981	11,320	52	8.80[1]	972	N.A.	19.38[1]	500	N.A.	15.08[1]

[1] Average rate data as of December 31, 1980.

N.A.: Not available.

Note: See text for definition of "homes passed" for STV and MDS.

Source: Compiled by the author based on 1973-1979 data from Paul Kagan, *The Pay TV Newsletter*, Census issues; 1981 subscriber information is as of June 30, 1981 as shown in *The Pay TV Newsletter* (July 15, 1981), p. 1. Data for earlier years also generally mid-year information, for slightly varying dates, though the same across services for any given year.

of all kinds clearly subsidiary to over-the-air broadcasting services), the Commission issued detailed and complicated rules limiting what films and sporting events could be carried on pay systems. The rules were designed to protect what "free" television was then presenting in order to prevent siphoning by pay cable systems. The rules were broader and stricter than necessary in the eyes of some observers and were appealed.[99] They were overturned by the U.S. Court of Appeals on March 25, 1977, the Supreme Court declined to review in October, and thus any and all rules limiting pay cable content were lifted.[100] In retrospect, then, the seeds for the complete freeing of pay cable from content controls were sown by the strict FCC rules of 1975.

Two important further regulatory developments came in 1978 and 1979, providing pay cable's final liberation. In April 1979 the U.S. Supreme Court upheld an Appeals Court ruling striking down the FCC mandatory access rules, thus freeing cable systems to provide their own premium channel programming as well as carry national or regional services. The Commission was again judged by the court to have exceeded its authority —and in this case to have violated the First Amendment, because with cable the spectrum limitations of over-the-air broadcasting do not exist.[100a] Combined with the 1977 decision overturning the pay cable content regulations, the Commission's controls on cable were substantially undermined. In a 1978 decision, the Appeals Court sustained FCC preemption of regulation of pay cable.[100b] Given the dearth of supported national regulations, the effect of the decision was to ensure that no state or local rules could be made to limit pay cable expansion while federal rule-making was unlikely unless enacted by Congress.

Ownership

As is evident in the discussion above, individual cable system operators own the channels over which pay programming is provided. "Ownership" in pay cable means ownership of the national distribution services which closely parallel networks in the broadcast sense, and are discussed more fully below. Pay cable channels and these national distributors do raise concerns of vertical integration, discussed later in this chapter.

Subscription Television Stations

Though by far the oldest pay television approach, subscription television, or over-the-air pay TV, is distinctly of secondary importance as a pay service. As noted in both Tables 7.6 and 7.7, STV is a very recent business with limited audience penetration, restricted mainly to the largest markets.

Development

STV was characterized for two decades up to 1968 by major controversy, several semi-successful experiments, constant FCC indecision and continuous anti-pay TV pressure from broadcasters and (usually) film theater owners. The controversy was dragged out by the competition of a number of approaches to the audience payment process.[101] At issue were several concerns, none of which were clearly resolved in the several experiments:

1) Whether pay TV would "siphon" programming away from "free" broadcast television. This fear arose out of the assumption that by directly charging viewers, station owners would have more money to bid for programming than would advertiser-supported stations. Thus, the argument went, viewers would soon be paying for what heretofore they had seen free of direct charge. These concerns were expressed most specifically over sports programming.

2) Motion picture interests, unless directly connected with the pay television scheme as they were in the 1957 pioneer Oklahoma experiment, saw pay television as but another serious threat to an already tottering motion picture industry where (in the 1950s) more theaters seemed to be closing on a weekly basis.

3) As would come up again with cable, there was concern from several fronts as to whether pay operations were sanctioned under the Communications Act of 1934. Further, critics asked what would happen to the public interest if pay television took over most or all TV service in a given area. Many arguments were expressed in terms of the pressure such TV payments might place on the poor.

When FCC and court review action finally opened the legal/regulatory way for subscription television in 1969-1970 (see below), there was no rush to place such operations on the air. "During the first five years after STV service was authorized (1970-74), only 15 applications were received by the Commission. Five of these were dismissed as unacceptable for filing for various reasons. Undoubtedly, the stringent rules limiting STV stations . . . in their use of movies and sports events was a major deterrent to the growth of subscription television."[102]

The first STV stations went on the air in 1977—one each in the New York and Los Angeles markets. The pace of application filing picked up in 1979 and more stations went on the air, all in major markets. The interest in STV, of course, was sparked to a considerable degree by the rapid development of pay cable. Considerable impetus came from program restriction deregulation in 1977-1978, due to lifting of pay cable restrictions and FCC recognition that the two different delivery systems were competitors in the same market.

But in 1981, considerable doubt existed as to whether STV had, in this "second birth" of activity, already reached its peak in the face of expanding cable systems—or conversely, whether the rising cost of cable construction would give STV yet another shot in the arm. A number of ownership changes and some vacated applications gave credence to the pessimistic view. Further, the number of new STV applications was reported to be down sharply.[103] A potential new element on the STV scene was possible final FCC approval of low-power TV stations which would be allowed to use STV features without need for further special permission—thus opening STV to virtually the whole country.

Regulation

STV is a broadcast service, and thus falls under most of the rules and regulations applied to television stations not providing pay material. The controversies noted above kept the FCC from approving regular pay TV operation over broadcast stations until adoption of rules late in 1968.[104] The accompanying report made clear the FCC's view that it was empowered to authorize such service—a view upheld on appeal in 1969-1970.[105] Fully concerned about possible inroads to commercial television, the Commission restricted STV only to markets with at least five television stations and then permitted only one STV station to operate per market. A minimal number of hours of free programming were required and quite detailed restrictions on types of films and sports suitable for STV were established. No set technical system of coding-decoding was required—though only those approved by the FCC could be used. Further, operators could only rent, not sell, decoding equipment to viewers to save the latter the cost of possible future technological changes.[106]

The program limitations were lifted in 1977 after the pay cable rules had been overturned by court review.[107] Less than six months later virtually all other program restrictions were also dropped.[108] The only remaining control is that STV stations must continue to air a minimum number of non-pay hours. The trend toward deregulation continued with Docket 21502 which, in a series of orders from 1979 through 1981, relaxed such restrictions as the one-to-a-market rule,[109] among other more technical limitations. Likely to be abolished in the future are rules limiting STV only to markets with four other non-pay stations. On the other hand, the FCC decided that cable systems did not have to carry the scrambled pay TV signals of local market STV stations which would otherwise have to be carried under the "must carry" regulations.[110]

Thus, paralleling events in cable television regulation, initially restrictive rulings designed to protect traditional television from STV competition have fallen due to both court review and changes in policy by the Commission. After nearly three decades of debate and five years of actual development, STV was opened to the marketplace test—and severe competition from pay cable, and to a lesser degree MDS and possibly DBS.

Ownership

The ownership limits on STV are the same as those for commercial television reviewed in Chapter 6, as STV service is based on over-the-air TV operations. The situation is a bit more complicated, however, as there are three forms of "ownership" in STV: the actual station licensee, the program service and the coding/decoding equipment or system used, with a considerable amount of vertical integration evident. Typically, the licensee takes direct responsibility for non-pay programming, which in recent years has trended toward specialized "narrowcasting," with a news, ethnic, or other special emphasis, in addition to the more usual independent station fare of off-network material. The pay programming is provided by a franchisee that leases the prime-time evening hours (and sometimes others) typically given over to subscription programming. While the technical equipment is independent of the program content, in fact, combinations or packages of programming, equipment and sometimes licensees are becoming common. The combinations listed in Table 7.8 should serve as examples of this setup.[111]

Table 7.8: Integration in Subscription Television

Licensee	Program Franchisee	Equipment
American Television and Communications Corp. (Time Inc.)	HBO/Cinemax	SSAVI I
National Subscription Television (Oak)·	ON-TV	Oak I
Wometco	Wometco Home Theatre	Blonder-Tongue
American Subscription Television/Clarion	SelecTVision	N.A.
American Subscription Television/Block	Choice Channel	N.A.

N.A.: Not available.
Sources: Compiled from data in Howard and Carroll, *Subscription Television: History, Current Status, and Economic Projections.*

Given the early stage of development in the STV business, such a comparative chart is merely indicative of the combinations capable of arising. There is thus far no regulatory limit—or even seriously expressed concern —about such combinations; and given the limited penetration of STV, there is not likely to be any. Further, there is considerable volatility in this field with ownership changes, partnerships made and unmade, and stock deals at all times. The listing above merely shows some of the combinations (in some cases through stock holdings, in other cases by contract) that existed in 1981.

Most of the STV operations now on the air, and the vast majority of those applications still pending, are for new stations entirely. Only a few are for conversions of existing independent (usually UHF) stations. The FCC views STV as one key means of promoting both conventional UHF stations and the potential low-power stations which may be authorized.[112]

While STV stations are held to the same cross-ownership limits applied to regular television stations, a number of STV licensees and/or program franchisees have extensive cable interests as well. To avoid the cross-ownership problem, these cable systems are held in markets different from those where the licensee holds or has applied for an STV station. Whether these holdings may lead to greater STV-cable similarity in programming and operation is difficult to predict at this stage.

Multipoint Distribution Service (MDS)

Least known of the three existing methods for distributing pay programming, and smallest in audience size, is the MDS business. This is a common carrier (not broadcast or cable) microwave service which operates at the high frequency of 2 GHz. An antenna on the subscriber's roof (often an apartment building or hotel in an urban area) receives the signal which is then processed through a "down converter" device to enable regular television sets to display the video signal. Like STV, an MDS operation can transmit only one channel at a time. Unlike STV, the MDS system owner must lease most available time to one or more programmers in accordance with common carrier tariffs filed with the FCC.

Development

The MDS service was created in 1962 as an "omnidirectional microwave transmission service to multiple fixed points," the intended purpose being transmission of business, government, educational and possibly individual data and information.[113] Nothing happened with the allocation because at 3.5 MHz, the MDS channel was too narrow to allow video transmission.

In 1970, in response to a petition from Varian Associates (a major equipment supplier for MDS), the FCC increased the channel width to the 6 MHz required for television program transmission (and reception on regular receivers).[114] Later rulings allowed two MDS channels in most of the top 50 markets, though at some risk of mutual interference. This action was taken as the FCC became fearful of spectrum limits on development of a new service, the parameters of which were as yet unclear.[115] While the same owner could apply for both channels in a given market, such action had to be taken sequentially: a second channel could be applied for only if the first was fully in use.[116]

This brief regulatory background opened up a potential new means of delivery for pay services into homes and apartments and a flood of applications came into the FCC after 1972.[117] As summarized in Tables 7.6 and 7.7, the number of MDS operations increased sharply after the first one aired in 1973. While the audience of such systems also increased, it represented but a small percentage of the audience served by pay cable (and, by 1981, by STV stations), and penetrated only a very small proportion of households capable of receiving MDS, that is, those within about 25 miles of the transmitter. Cities with substantial MDS service and well-established audiences include New York, Pittsburgh, Milwaukee, Denver and Washington, DC.[118]

Economic data on MDS is not widely available. Some operators have suggested that an MDS operation can break even with but 4000-8000 subscribers, due to its lower construction costs, while an STV station would need at least 50,000 viewers.[119] But MDS faces problems not common with STV, including great barriers to potential audience coverage due to the effect on transmissions of hills and valleys, and even tree foliage, on the high frequency direct-line-of-sight service. For this and other reasons, MDS is:

> widely viewed as an "interim" or bridge system. While MDS may continue to supply cable head ends or supply outlying areas of a cable system, once an area has been cabled, virtually no one expects MDS to ultimately prevail as a pay delivery system. The competition between MDS delivered pay services and STV may, in the short run, be much closer, depending from market to market on coverage area, and in many instances, who gets there first.[120]

The relatively small audience needed to break even, however, may prolong the bridge period. So, too, may a highly controversial spectrum reallocation between MDS and Instructional Television Fixed Services

(ITFS) proposed in 1980. As then FCC Chairman Charles Ferris explained:

> One development that the marketplace has identified is an apparent underutilization of the allocated spectrum by the educational community. ITFS is presently allocated 28 channels. In at least 25 of the top 50 metropolitan areas, 10 or more of the presently allocated ITFS channels are unassigned. And in each of these cities there are at least two mutually exclusive applications for an MDS channel.[121]

Allowing that log-jam of applications to be processed fairly rapidly would bring about a substantial increase in MDS systems and channels.

Ownership

There is no duopoly, multiple or cross-ownership restriction on MDS licensees. A single entity can control any number of MDS systems, including more than one channel in the same market area.[122] The largest group owner in MDS, Microband Corporation of America (a subsidiary of Tymshare, Inc.) holds no other media interests. Lack of cross-ownership interest is not the rule with other MDS operators, many of which are active in one or more cable systems (some of which are co-located, with MDS feeding the cable system as well as directly providing service to a limited urban area), or have interests in STV stations or programming. Given the lack of ownership rules and the common carrier tradition of separating licensee from a direct role in content, the few comparative hearings between competing applicants held thus far by the FCC have centered on which applicant proposes most efficient use of the spectrum; simply proposing leased access to pay TV programming is insufficient except in markets with no other pay service available.[123]

Indeed, most MDS licensees have their daytime hours free, as pay TV programming is generally fed only in evening and weekend hours. Tariffs for the "off" hours usually cater to business and institutional uses. For the evening hours, MDS systems are generally programmed by the major pay cable national distributors. Of the 54 MDS operations at the end of 1980, 23 were programmed by HBO and an additional 18 took material from Showtime.

New Services as Potential Threat to Broadcasting

Taken together, pay cable channels, STV stations and MDS operations are something of a parallel to local broadcast stations: they provide the outlet by which the viewer obtains commercial-free movies, sports events, special and cultural presentations. But there is one crucial and substantial difference when assessing competitive impact. Television receivers for off-air reception were in virtually all American homes in 1981. But cable penetration had not reached 30%, pay cable reached about 12% of the TV homes, while STV and MDS barely reached 2% of the audience. Home video devices (cassettes and discs) were in 2% to 3% of homes. Clearly, then, much of what we have discussed in this chapter is but *potential* competition for broadcasting, likely to be of substantial impact only in the late 1980s and beyond. And DBS systems will only just be starting to penetrate the TV audience after 1985—if such systems develop at all.

Policy on ownership must take such important differences in competitive impact into account—a total deregulation, for example, may make sense when there is real competition in most communities, but not make sense based only on potential competition not yet of great consequence. Already a structure is apparent however. Building on the ubiquitous broadcast model, the "new" technologies are rapidly filling in a network-local outlet design, sometimes advertiser-supported, sometimes viewer supported. The whole system is built on satellite distribution methods that should prove to be far more economical than terrestrial distribution methods for the foreseeable future.

Program Distribution Facilities

A combination of technological breakthroughs and lowered costs, deregulation and marketing expertise have led to radical expansion of viewer options within the past decade. Prior to late 1975, the only regular national networks were ABC, CBS and NBC. Just six years later, there were better than ten times as many networks, some of them programmed to specific audiences or interests. The technology that made this economically possible was the communications satellite.

Satellites

After a 15-year period of development for international communication applications, the first U.S. domestic communications satellite (domsat), Westar I, built by Western Union, was launched by NASA late in 1974. It was not the first domsat, as Canada had experimented with such technology for several years prior to the American launch. By 1977, several satellites had been built and launched for Western Union, RCA and Communications Satellite Corp. or Comsat (the latter's satellites on a leased basis for AT&T's exclusive use for several years). Late in 1980, the FCC granted permission for construction of as many as 25 "second generation" satellites, most of which were to be launched by 1986 to fill rising national demand for voice, data, audio and video communication links for government, business, education and entertainment television. The satellites operate and are regulated as common carriers. The controlling firms lease use of their transponders (currently 12 or 24 on each satellite, each transponder capable of carrying one television signal, or alternatively, more channels of voice or data transmission) to all corners for a rate specified by tariff.

The application of the domsat idea to television programming had long been considered—at least since the late 1960s when a proposal for public television networking was based on the satellite idea years before the first launch.[124] Use of satellite interconnection eliminated the need for expensive landline or microwave links to connect TV stations, though at the considerable cost of buying an earth station "dish", which in the early 1970s cost around $100,000. But once a signal was on the satellite, it could be instantly transmitted anywhere in the 50 states (including simultaneous transmission to both Alaska and Hawaii, heretofore subject to delayed transmission from the 48 states). Addition of new ground stations did not increase transmission costs at all, unlike the added landline costs for each new outlet prior to satellite use. Transmission thus became, for the first time, distance insensitive.

On April 10, 1975, Time Inc.'s Home Box Office announced it would convert its pay programming distribution from microwave (and the mails!) to the soon-to-be-launched RCA-owned Satcom I satellite. This was a rather bold and risky venture, in that virtually no cable systems had receiving dishes. Nonetheless, HBO implemented its plan at the end of September, utilizing two transponders to transmit two channels of programming for 12 hours per day.[125] Table 7.9 demonstrates that this pioneering effort led to more satellite space, an explosion of video services, and soon a rising number of earth stations.

From the beginning, however, the seemingly ideal satellite system has suffered from problems of access. At first, HBO and a few other pioneer programmers fought the chicken-and-egg problem: they provided the programming but the audience was miniscule due to the dearth of earth stations. As the number of earth stations then increased, demand for satellite space also grew, creating more demand for transponders than could be accommodated. Operating as common carriers under FCC regulations, the satellite carriers could only deal on a first-come/first-serve basis at set monthly lease fees based on their own costs. Early programmers soon found that their transponder lease was their most valuable asset. Indeed, some small programmers and independent producers sold out their trans-

**Table 7.9: Development of U.S. Satellite Distribution Facilities,
Selected Years, 1975-1981**

Year	Number of Available Domsats	Total Transponders Carried	Video Services			Earth Stations		
			Basic	Pay	Total	Radio	TV	Cable
1975	3	48	0	1	1	N.A.	N.A.	N.A.
1977	6	120	3	1	4	N.A.	N.A.	N.A.
1979	8	156	14	4	18	N.A.	150	1,579
1981	8	156	19	8	27	1,200	300	3,500

N.A.: Not available.
Note: In 1980-1981, only about a third of the transponders shown in the table were
    used for video transmission (the others were for voice, data, etc.), and many
    were for network news and other applications not directly aimed at end viewers.
Sources: Satellite and transponder data figured from *Cablevision* (June 1, 1981), p.
    393; services data figured from Table 7.10; data on earth stations as follows:
    radio figure from *TV/Radio Age* (May 18, 1981), p. 37; TV data for 1979 reflects
    only public stations while 1981 data includes PBS plus about 150 commer-
    cial TV stations as estimated by *Broadcasting* (August 10, 1981). Thus, about
    20% of commercial outlets had earth stations by mid-1981; cable data for
    1979 from *Satellite Communications* (May 1, 1979), projecting data for Octo-
    ber 1979, while 1981 figure is from *CableAge* (July 27, 1981), p. 13.

ponder space contracts for huge profits to new programmers who needed
access to the widening network of ground stations.[126]

Despite the 1980 FCC approval of more satellite launches, the problem
was one of incentive. Under the common carrier regulatory approach, the
satellite carrier could only charge a tariffed monthly fee based on costs and
a set profit or rate of return. Thus, the satellite carriers totally missed out
on the rising value of their transponders. They simply got their monthly
rate no matter who owned or bought the contract right to use the
transponder. The sale price of the long-term leases went not to the carrier
but to the contract holder. RCA, owning the valuable Satcom I to which
most cable system earth stations were aimed, was thus missing out on
millions in incentive profit.

In 1981, HBO again moved to the forefront by outright purchase of all
rights to six transponders on the forthcoming Hughes Satellite Corp.
Galaxy I satellite. Hughes had simply informed the FCC they did not propose to act as a common carrier, and would thus sell rights to transponders
outright for what the market would bear ($8 to $15 million each according
to press reports) rather than being limited to tariffed monthly fees. The
sales went ahead contingent on possible FCC action disallowing them.[127]
Hughes sold 18 transponders at full rate, and the final six at a lower pre-

emptible rate.* The preemption provision fulfilled two objectives: 1) it could service its main buyers should one of the 18 transponders stop functioning; and 2) public groups and smaller programmers could afford satellite access. The Hughes plan became highly controversial. First, it took place before any definitive FCC action. Second, it emphasized the advantage of sizable financial assets in laying claim to access to a satellite.[128] There is some feeling in the satellite business as well as the FCC that the addition of some 20 new satellites by 1986 will serve to dramatically lower transponder prices even if the FCC allows the sales to continue. By the end of 1984 there may be as many as 336 transponders in the heavily used C-band, with more in the higher frequency Ku-band.[129]

One of the reasons for the shortage and high prices in the 1980-1984 period, other than increasing demand from more program providers, is a severe limitation in ground facilities.

Ground Stations

The 1975 HBO decision to use Satcom I was a considerable gamble in that earth stations were then required to be at least nine meters in diameter, which cost some $100,000 to buy and install. Few cable systems could afford that level of outlay. HBO was counting on two developments: lower costs due to increased demand and subsequent mass production, and changes in FCC requirements to allow use of smaller and less expensive "dishes." At the end of 1976, the FCC did approve a half-size (4.5 meter) dish which allowed a dramatic cut in ground station price, thus putting the satellite interconnection within financial reach of most cable operators. Prices tumbled down to $30,000 and finally to between $5000 and $10,000.

But one reason the costs were cut so low is that the antenna could only be aimed to receive from one satellite at a time. RCA's Satcom I, as the first satellite specifically catering to cable programmers, became not only "cable I" to the trade, but could have been "cable only" for all practical purposes. Virtually all cable system ground stations were aimed at Satcom I, which meant that programmers who got transponder space on Westar or one of Comsat's Comstar series were at a severe disadvantage—most cable systems could not receive their signal without obtaining a second satellite dish. In some cases, major programmers offered to help finance additional antennas for systems that took their service. As prices dropped, it became easier to do this and many systems (especially those with greater channel

---

*Owners or lessees know that, in return for a discounted rate, they may be preempted by a full-rate payer whose transponder becomes inoperable.

capacity to fill) did so. But the industry continued to search for an inexpensive means of re-orienting ground stations to more easily pick up signals from several nearby satellites. With more satellites coming on line in the early 1980s, and more systems being promised and built with high channel capacity, the demand for movable ground stations, or multiple installations, increased.

In 1979, the FCC issued a final deregulatory order, removing all regulation and licensing requirements for small TV receive only (TVRO) earth stations, further lowering costs, though at some risk of increased microwave interference on the ground. This cut in red tape helped to increase the installation pace for smaller cable systems, making satellite-distributed pay and basic programming more widely available.[130]

System Channel Capacity

The development of these facilities and the programming channels that began to become available through the satellite system (see next section) created a capacity crisis for many older cable systems. Table 7.10 shows that new cable systems were being awarded franchises which specified a greater channel capacity. But in 1981, two-thirds of the systems still had 12 or fewer channels. When local "must carry" off-air signals are subtracted, along with a franchise-mandated local origination channel or two, many systems have very little capacity remaining for the burgeoning new services—thus creating a bottleneck on the ground that will not resolve itself as quickly as the satellite transponder or earth station problems. While virtually all new systems provide more than 20 channels (some have a capacity of 50-100 or more), the vast majority of systems will be of the small variety until they are upgraded or reconstructed during the 1980s. Subscriber demand for the touted new satellite-delivered services, as well as the

Table 7.10: Cable System Channel Capacity: 1969, 1975, 1979 and 1981

Capacity	1969	1975	1979	1981
Over 20 channels	1%	11%	27%	35%
13 to 20 channels		10	2	3
6 to 12 channels	68	71	67	57
Under 6 channels	25	7	4	3
Unspecified	6	—	—	—
(Number of systems)	2300	3405	4180	4637

Note: Totals may not add to 100% due to rounding of original numbers.
Sources: *TV Factbook* for 1970, 1976 and 1980; *TV Digest* for 1981. (For 1979-1981 the categories were changed to "20 and above," and "13 to 19.")

looming franchise renewal process, are twin pressures which should enlarge capacity for all but the smallest markets.

Pay Programmers

Table 7.11 traces the development of four of the oldest pay programmers, three of them available by 1975, though only HBO was satellite-distributed at that time. By 1981, all but TPS were on the satellite—one reason why the TPS share has dropped so substantially as its services were less in demand with near-universal ownership of ground stations. As Time Inc. owns both HBO and TPS, that corporation's share of the pay program markets is and has from the beginning been a substantial one—at least 60% in each of the years shown, peaking at close to 80% in 1977.

HBO

While HBO was initiated as an independent firm, Time Inc. purchased the small programmer in 1973, and since then has been a significant force in pay cable—indeed the pioneer on several fronts. HBO paid dearly for this role, losing millions in its first several years and only breaking into the black late in 1977.[131] The key to HBO's success, as already noted, was its 1975 decision to use satellite distribution:

> Rarely does a simple business decision by one company affect so many. . . . In deciding to gamble on the leasing of satellite channels, Time Inc. took the one catalytic step needed for the creation of a new national television network designed to provide pay TV programs. As a result, it has altered the business plans of cable-TV system operators, equipment manufacturers, communications common carriers, the performing arts, sports promoters, and private investors, to name just a few.[132]

HBO programming consisted primarily of motion pictures with a scattering of sports events and special events coverage, and presentations divided by film shorts, often produced by independents not before exposed to national television. To fill in various holes in its coverage (both geographically and in content), HBO has operated several additional services. Late in 1976, HBO purchased control of Telemation Program Services. TPS, called HBO Program Services since 1980, operated physically by supplementing satellite-distributed HBO with video cassettes delivered to cable systems lacking ground stations. In 1979, HBO initiated "Take 2", "providing a reduced schedule of all-family programming at a lower price

Table 7.11: Major Pay TV Program Distributors, 1975, 1977, 1979 and 1981

Year	Total Pay Subscribers[1] (in thousands)	HBO		Showtime		Warner[2]		TPS[3]		Others	
		Sub-scribers	Share of Total	Sub-scribers	Share of Total	Sub-scribers	Share of Total	Sub-scribers	Share of Total	Sub-scribers	Share of Total
1975	189	90	48%	—	—	8	4%	33	17%	58	31%
1977	1,244	718	58	50	4%	N.A.	N.A.	226	18	250	20
1979	4,801	2,889	60	720	15	143	3	303	6	746	16
1981	12,881	7,000	54	2,000	16	1,025	8	—	—	N.A.[4]	N.A.

[1] Counts subscribers to more than one service separately for each. Thus, total in 1981 includes more subscribers than there are households that subscribe to pay cable.

[2] Was Warner Star Channel until 1979, then renamed The Movie Channel.

[3] Telemation Program Services was a subsidiary of HBO (Time Inc.) which provided HBO service to systems lacking ground stations. TPS 1981 data are for March. Renamed HBO Program Services in 1980.

[4] Cannot be figured due to tiering of services.

Source: Compiled by the author based on data from Paul Kagan, *The Pay TV Newsletter*. All data as of June 30 of given years except 1975 (March 30). Total column includes pay cable, MDS and STV adding about half a million in 1979, a million in 1980 and 1.5 million in 1981 (see Unit 695).

than its regular service."[133] This was replaced in mid-1980 when HBO announced formation instead of Cinemax to carry movies 24 hours a day on two transponders as an addition to HBO, thus encouraging the "tiering" process. Cinemax carries about 25 films per month on a revolving schedule, repeating them 10 to 12 times at different times of the day in the course of a month. Cinemax is specifically designed to be tiered with HBO, offering different films and other content.

HBO is a subsidiary of Time Inc., as is the country's largest MSO, American Television and Communications Corp. (see Table 7.5). The vast majority of ATC subscribers to a pay channel are offered HBO and Cinemax, keeping pay revenues in the same parent firm. In addition, late in 1981, Time Inc. announced plans to purchase a half-interest (with an option to buy the other half) in the USA Network, a sports-oriented basic (advertiser-supported) service. Analysts noted that the $15 million dollar price paid for half-interest was heavily due to USA's transponder space which Time Inc. badly needed until its new Hughes transponders were in service.[134] With this purchase, Time Inc. controlled two pay services, one basic service, plus the largest MSO as a base on which to build more services.

Showtime

The second largest so-called "maxi" or "foundation" pay channel service began late in 1976 on some of the northern California cable systems operated by the ninth largest MSO, Viacom. As with HBO earlier, Showtime was distributed by tape or microwave until it began satellite delivery via Satcom I in March 1978, providing the first satellite pay channel competition to HBO. Later that year, Viacom sold half-ownership of the Showtime service to Teleprompter. Part of the sale involved some 280,000 Teleprompter systems which switched from carrying HBO to carrying Showtime, adding to the trend of MSO-controlled programming services carrying their own pay channel on their own systems (see Table 7.12). Programming on Showtime generally matches that of HBO, though initially little sports programming was included.[135]

The Movie Channel

Another MSO-controlled program service, the third general pay cable programmer in size, is Warner Amex's The Movie Channel, formerly Warner Star Channel. Like Showtime, it began as a service to Warner's own cable systems. The name change and expansion to offering the service to other systems, plus important changes in content, came in 1979. Though third in size, the Warner service has a number of advantages over the two older and larger pay channels: 1) Warner's role in the motion picture field; 2) the joint venture funding as the result of 50% ownership by American Express; 3) Warner Amex's pioneering role in developing interactive cable with its Qube system; and 4) Warner Amex's strong push for additional cable system franchises.[136] Programming on The Movie Channel is all feature films, 24 hours a day.

Premiere

The best indication of the competitive pressures between the film industry and pay television, the stakes involved in the battle and the regulatory dangers lurking in ownership combinations is the short and fierce saga of the Premiere venture (discussed also in Chapter 5). The film industry argument was that for years they had received insufficient income from pay cable showings of films, because HBO and Showtime had long controlled the market and could thus almost set the terms by which they would buy rights to show movies.

To try to gain some leverage, in April 1980, Columbia Pictures, MCA, Paramount and Twentieth Century-Fox, four major distributors, announced a joint venture with Getty Oil Co. to create Premiere as a film-industry-controlled pay program service. The crucial aspect of the new program cooperative was the plan to withhold from other firms (specifically HBO and its competitors) all of the film output of the four cooperating film companies for a period of nine months from original theatrical issue.[137] HBO and Showtime, which prior to the formation of Premiere had gotten nearly half their film output from the four film companies, charged this violated antitrust statutes. The Justice Department agreed and brought suit to stop the Premiere plan.[138] The preliminary injunction sought was granted on Decmber 31, 1980.[139]

The aftermath of the Premiere ruling was difficult to judge from the perspective of just a year later. The frustrated film firms gave in and folded Premiere, realizing the preliminary injunction bode ill for their case in the long run. HBO and Showtime had in the interim been forced to return to program levels of the 1975-1978 period due to lack of quality films to show. Experts agreed that although it failed to clear the legal barrier, Premiere would likely strengthen the position of the film companies resulting in more of a favorable return for their product from pay cable. Otherwise, they threatened that pay cable would be bypassed in favor of sales to broadcast networks and subsequent direct sales to the home video market.[140] Taking the broader view, the events of 1980 demonstrate yet another film industry frustration in dealing effectively with television, and now pay cable competition.

The Culture Trend

Premiere, though it received the most attention, was by no means the only competition to the reigning pay cable firms. As shown in Table 7.12, as of mid-1981 there were eight pay services competing for viewers, albeit five of them were quite new and clearly small beside the big four already discussed. Of the others, Home Theatre Network offers one G or PG-rated film each evening as a part-time service; Private Screenings goes to the other extreme, offering R-rated and "Hard-R" semi-porn films; Rainbow combines two nights a week of "culture" with five nights of "adult" films; and Galavision provides Spanish-language programming for cable systems and some STV stations and translators.

The emphasis of all these services is entertainment material of various kinds, in the tradition of broadcast television. Some observers feel there is already an entertainment overload (just so many films or sports events to supplement over-the-air-television). Inevitably, some services will likely not survive (and already a number of early ventures have failed for lack of satellite access or insufficient capital backing for both satellite fees and programming purchases). Yet many are looking to pay cable to provide alternative programming ventures. While only two small efforts were actually operational by mid-1981, the business was alive with the many plans for so-called cultural program services to begin in the early part of the decade.

After resisting cable for many years, the broadcast networks have joined in the fray. Three of the announced cultural efforts are being supported by broadcast networks.[141] In April 1981, ABC and Hearst started a performing and visual arts network called Alpha Repertory Television Service (ARTS), featuring several hours of dramatic productions and nightly performing arts. CBS Cable offered drama, concerts, ballet, modern dance and foreign films to cable systems (including presumably the 90,000 subscribers in cable systems that the FCC allowed the network to purchase in a waiver of the network-cable cross-ownership rule just to allow such experimentation). Desperately in search of support funds for over-the-air high-brow broadcasting, the Public Broadcasting Service ballyhooed its plans for what at first was dubbed the Public Subscriber Network and was later simply termed PBS Cable. This so-called "grand alliance" would tie together hundreds of the country's art museums and other cultural institutions in a cooperative to produce programming to be released first to a paying audience, and later to be shown free on PBS stations. In addition, several British video firms have announced interest in entering the U.S. market (along with Canadian firms) and these again raise rumbles of concern over foreign investment in American media. In one deal, the rights to programming were purchased from the British Broadcasting Corp. (BBC)

Table 7.12: Satellite-Fed Cable Network Distributors, Mid-1981

Service	Systems Carrying	Subscribers (in milllions)	Satellite/ Transponder		Date Sat. Service Began
Basic[1] (free)					
WTBS (superstation)	3,170	12,500	Sat I	6	12/76
Christian Broadcasting Network (CBN)	2,800	11,800	Sat I	8	4/77
Entertainment and Sports Programming Network (ESPN)	2,182	10,500	Sat I	7	9/79
Cable Satellite Public Affairs Network (C-SPAN)	1,150	8,100	Sat I	9	3/79
USA Network	1,425	8,000	Sat I	9	9/77
Black Entertainment Television (BET)	685	7,200	Sat I	9	1/80
Cable News Network (CNN)	1,270	7,000	Sat I	14	6/80
WGN (superstation)	1,735	6,000	Sat I	3	11/78
Nickelodeon	1,200	4,750	Sat I	1	4/79
People That Love (PTL)	319	3,850	Sat I	2	4/78
WOR (superstation)	859	3,700	Sat I	17	4/79
Modern Satellite Network	500	3,700	Sat I	22	1/79
Satellite Program Network (SPN)	252	2,800	West III	9	1/79
Spanish International Network (SIN)[2]	106	2,700	West III	8	9/79
Trinity Broadcasting Network	81	1,000	Com 2	9	5/78
Episcopal Television Network	53	1,000			6/81
Appalachian Community Service Network (ACSN)	150	900	Sat I	16	10/79
National Jewish Television	38	900	Sat I	16	—
North American Newstime	74	700	—		N.A.
Pay Services[3]					
Home Box Office (HBO)	2,500	6,000	Sat I	22/24	9/75
Showtime	1,100	2,000	Sat I	10/12	3/78
The Movie Channel	1,175	1,100	Sat I	5	1/80
Cinemax	350	500	Sat I	20/23	8/80
Home Theater Network	175	130	Sat I	21	9/78
Private Screenings[2]	5	84	West III	7	12/80
Rainbow	40	80	Com 2	7	—
GalaVision	88	77	Sat I	18	10/79

[1] Usually provided to subscribers as part of the basic monthly cable fee. Most are financed by advertising and/or small payments from cable operators.

[2] Subscriber totals include STV stations for both these services, and translators for SIN.

[3] Provided at additional cost above basic cable charge.

Table 7.12: (continued)

Sources: Subscriber counts as of June 30, 1981 from *Cablevision* (July 20, 1981), p. 24; start-up dates from *Panorama* (April 1981), pp. 54-55, 68-69; (June 1981), pp. 42-43. Satellite data from *Cablevision* (June 1, 1981), pp. 54-55. Abbreviations used here are: Sat I = RCA's Satcom I (also often referred to as Cable I); Com 2 = Comsat's Comstar D-2; West III = Western Union's Westar III. The numbers indicate transponder assignment; many are shared and thus duplications in number appear on the list.

by Rockefeller Center Television, a partnership with RCA, to be marketed as "Bluebird."

There is no uniformity in how these systems of culture will be supported. Some, like CBS, expect to be advertiser-supported. Others will charge viewers. Quite likely some combination of subscriber payment and either advertising or underwriting (likely meaning advertising between programs) will evolve. But whether the overall audience for this kind of programming is large enough to support one or two—let alone several more—such channels remains to be tested.

Meantime, we can start to draw several tentative conclusions as to ownership and control of these efforts. Not surprisingly, investment in the cultural services is coming largely from firms with existing investment in cable and broadcasting entertainment. ABC, CBS, Warner Amex, and the Post-Newsweek broadcast stations are examples. The degree of specialization in culture and how-to cable programming now being planned is attracting many media conglomerates with magazine interests. CBS researchers examined the 25 largest consumer periodicals and found that 14 of them were actively planning or considering cable program ventures. Many other magazines in the top 100 were also into cable program ventures.[142] Certainly one important reason why periodical publishers enter this new delivery market is the feeling that they have a particular content expertise and a base of subscribers and advertisers for the print product. Finally, a crucial problem for all these services—even before audience size and acceptance can be adequately tested—is access. This means access first to a satellite or other effective means of widespread delivery. But perhaps even more crucial, it means access to cable systems already faced with more program choices and viewer demands than they can handle. This will last until more systems are reconstructed to greater channel capacity. Most likely the established pay services of entertainment programs, with their strong audience acceptance, will continue to hold prime allegiance of cable operators with limited channel capacity. The many culture and other specialized services (most of the latter not detailed here) will have trouble getting clearance on all but the newer and higher capacity systems.[143]

Basic Programmers

Table 7.12 listed the 19 basic (i.e., usually provided free of extra charge to cable system subscribers) services available by satellite feed in mid-1981. Three are "superstations," four are news and public affairs oriented, and five have a religious emphasis. Many are only part time. Black Entertainment Television, for example, programs a few hours one evening per week, an example of share-time use of transponders. Most of these services developed after the pioneering pay services made the facilities available.

Superstations

Superstations are independent TV stations whose signals are transmitted by microwave or satellite to cable systems in many distant cities. The first superstation was Ted Turner's WTBS, an independent UHF station in Atlanta. In December 1976, just a year after HBO had begun satellite transmission, Turner arranged with Southern Satellite Systems (which he originally controlled) to carry his station on a Satcom I transponder, charging cable systems a few cents per subscriber per month to cover transmission costs. Turner expected added income to come from higher charges to advertisers who would be reaching a national market. As with most pioneers, it was a hard sell to advertisers who found this too new and different. In 1978, the FCC removed regulatory restraints on satellite carriers to allow other major market independent stations to be carried in similar fashion. Chicago's WGN and New York's WOR are also widely carried for their special film and sports coverage not found on network stations. To a considerable degree, cable provides for these stations an expanded version of cable's initial service of carrying broadcast signals.[144]

News and Public Affairs

Several of the basic services specialize in news and special events coverage. One of the oldest is C-SPAN, the industry-supported nonprofit service which fills only the daytime hours (unlike most other cable services which are either all day or concentrate on evening hours), primarily with coverage of the sessions of the U.S. House of Representatives, as well as speeches and other special events, most of which occur in Washington. C-SPAN has been described as an example of what cable can do best, i.e., provide the long-running and in-depth background to breaking news which over-the-air stations and networks do not have the time to provide.[145] C-SPAN is part of the industry's "conscience" money—using entertainment-based income to provide for those viewers who want in-depth live coverage of often dull but sometimes important events.

Better known, thanks to its flamboyant owner, is Ted Turner's Cable News Network, which began in 1980 with a 24-hour-a-day news and feature service based in Atlanta. CNN is advertiser supported. The Modern Satellite Network, headquartered in New York, is a distributor of industry- and business-sponsored films geared mainly to housewives during daytime hours. It features how-to shows, an increasing number of them from magazine publishers. ACSN is a consortium of some 45 colleges in the Appalachian region providing courses, continuing education and teleconferencing facilities seven days a week.[146]

Religion

One cable phenomenon is the increasing number of religious channels, of which Christian Broadcasting Network (CBN) is the most ambitious. Late in 1980 it went to a full round-the-clock schedule of a varied nature. Its goal is to be essentially a general network embracing a moral and somewhat conservative line, but within that arena providing news, entertainment and even an original daily soap opera. Support comes from telethons which raise funds covering 90% of the costs. PTL and Trinity operate in similar fashion but with a more pervasive religious overtone.[147] These cable networks are an outgrowth of both radio and television programs by conservative, usually evangelical preachers, but potentially capable of reaching a vastly larger audience by cable networking. That these services are of network status is evident in FCC action on a CBN request late in 1981 to provide it a waiver from commercial broadcast restrictions applied to networks. This was necessary because in hours per week, affiliates and number of states covered, the cable satellite-delivered services approached the formal FCC definition of network for regulatory purposes.[148]

DISCUSSION OF
OWNERSHIP ISSUES AND POLICY

To a considerable degree, the concern about cable system and related media ownership parallels the local vs. network issue in broadcasting, as described in Chapter 6. Indeed, the very expansion of these so-called "new technologies" or "new media" have sharpened the debate over ownership policy for all of what is now termed the video industry.

The Video Marketplace

No longer can policymakers or scholars consider questions of broadcasting, cable system, or any other delivery means separately from the others. Clearly, business and regulatory decisions on television broadcasting must increasingly take into account the *context* of increasing competition from cable systems, pay cable, STV and MDS. Indeed, discussion of ownership in cable must take into account cable systems and the rapidly growing multiple delivery of pay programming. To a considerable degree, the traditional basis for ownership controls—scarcity of the video resource—is fast becoming an historical artifact. There is a rising abundance of both outlets and program sources and distributors. Much of this abundance is, at this point, still at the potential stage. It is misleading to compare broadcasting, at nearly 100% household penetration, with cable (27% late in 1981), let alone with pay cable (about 12%) or STV, or MDS (perhaps 1%), or even home video (just a few percent) and DBS (still only in the planning stage). It is too easy to argue that what may be competitive reality in 1985 or 1990 is already present and should blindly dictate policy of the first-half of the 1980s. But the competition *is* coming and can no more be ignored in planning than it can be overstated. The principles can be pinned down even now.

Programming Role

With such a multiplicity of outlets even now in major markets and increasingly in smaller ones, simply determining who owns what, and in what kinds of patterns, becomes an important first step in any analysis of possible ownership policy options. The problem is well illustrated, first, when recognizing the national economic nature of programming:

> The particular economic nature of television programs may make equality of marginal cost and price unobtainable, whether sought through unfettered markets or government regulation. To this limited extent, competition is less successful as a means of organizing the video industry than it is for most others.[149]

As already noted in discussion of the earlier policy decisions in broadcasting, the long-held localism doctrine was economically undermined to the point of absurdity by the "public good" nature of expensive video programming. That is, once the program was made, it could be shown to any size audience at but a low marginal cost in distribution compared to the cost of production. The more people who could see the program, the less the cost per person—or per media unit carrying the program. Given this constant, there was no way local stations could produce their own program material in the face of competition from regional networks, or sharing arrangements, let alone national networks. Thus, to a considerably faster degree than took place with radio, television became and remained network dominated. The same pressures still apply with cable and related media discussed here. In fact, cable systems so divide up the total audience with increasing channel availability, that the network or at least syndication principle applies even more strongly in order for cable channels to be effectively filled.

The above quotation draws the connection between program economics and ownership trends and/or policy. To a considerable degree, economic demands will determine structure regardless of regulation. As networking dominates television broadcasting despite fairly strict ownership controls, so too does networking increasingly control a cable television industry which largely lacks any ownership limitations. Stated another way, the costs of program production make networking as a process (regardless of technology applied) an economic requirement for commercial success. Syndication is a close cousin to networking in this regard—both forms of production cost-sharing are important to broadcasting, cable systems, pay cable, STV and MDS to the degree that they will continue to dominate industry practice despite ownership controls (or lack of them), unless specifically regulated. This calls into question the whole argument which ties "ownership-control-to-create-or-maintain-diversity" to actual program output. Due to program costs, competition is not the most efficient (economically) or viable (in the political sense as defined by the public interest) means of getting a relatively diversified program output delivered to the home. Wide diversity of ownership and syndication/networking limitations (as were weakly attempted in broadcasting) merely creates multiple local copies of successful formats—along with a variety of means of syndication to share costs. At the opposite extreme, a long-held economic, though politically unpalatable, argument suggests that real monopoly in ownership of outlets might actually lead to greater choice of program inputs in a local area.[150] Recognition of the political unlikelihood of such an occurrence has forced a search for structural methods to achieve the same end (diversity) by different means (limits on degree of ownership concentration).

Classification

The complexity of the problem is demonstrated in the seemingly simple job of classifying different kinds of ownership units in either broadcasting or cable. As described by an FCC staff report:

Characterization of an activity as horizontal, vertical, or conglomerate . . . critically affects the policy issues the activity may raise. In turn, whether a given activity affects horizontal, vertical, or conglomerate structure depends, of course, on the definitions of the relevant markets under consideration. Therefore, classification is not always simple. For example, a broadcast station's ownership of a cable system in a different locality may be treated as horizontal (by viewing the two firms as competitors in a national video entertainment market) or vertical (since broadcast stations produce programming used by cable systems) or conglomerate (since cable service and broadcast service in different localities may be viewed as serving distinct product and/or geographic markets). To some extent, each of these views may be defensible; therefore it sometimes may be useful to analyze an activity under alternative characterizations to examine fully its possible effects on competition.[151]

In other words, once again one must view the situation in the previously mentioned context—and possibly the programming and/or geographical context of any ownership question examined. This discussion, however, must be limited to overall national trends. The "relevant market" phrase used in the comment above commonly appears in economic discussions of regulation. One useful definition suggests the relevant market "is an area within which the price of a service offered by different firms, such as video programming, *tends* toward equality. . . . The market concept has three dimensions: product characteristics, geography, and time."[152] The video programming referred to here clearly shares similar characteristics regardless of delivery source. Price varies (see, for example, Table 7.7) depending both on program content (e.g., "basic" or "pay"), or delivery source. Geography is a simple but certainly important point here, for there are significant policy differences concerning individual and cross-market ownerships, both in cable and allied media and broadcasting. Time is a trickier dimension and is often not considered. Basically, as a market develops, more suppliers and thus more alternatives will develop. Satellite-delivered signals are an example of the quick development possible when technology and economics combine with deregulation (see Table 7.8).

In the remainder of this section, the different classifications of ownership are briefly considered, along with some of the key policy questions raised by each.

Horizontal Integration

What It Is

"An activity is horizontal when it takes place within one relevant geographic and product market. Phenomena such as an arrangement between rivals or the merger of two firms operating in the same relevant market are horizontal."[153] The cable MSO or broadcast group owner is said to be horizontal. Cross-ownership is usually horizontal—broader control of outlets for similar material. Essentially then, horizontal control, for the purposes of this chapter, includes ownership of more than one cable system and/or STV station and/or MDS system. All are delivery outlets, and thus are on the "same level" of the production-delivery process; therefore, they are said to be matters of horizontal concern.

To date, horizontal integration is not considered a very serious problem in cable system, STV or MDS ownership, for the simple reason that the concentration ratios are well below commonly discussed economic "danger" levels. Current economic research reviews this question from different aspects, but one measure is that when the top four firms control between 45% and 59% of the total output of a business, or if the leading entity has better than 25% alone, then horizontal integration is sufficiently advanced to cause regulatory evaluation.[154] MSO levels have not yet approached either of these levels. STV stations are controlled horizontally by broadcast regulations which limit integration across units. While MDS can be and, to an extent, is integrated fairly closely horizontally, its common carrier status—and hence the lack of licensee control over programming—is generally taken as lowering what otherwise might be a high level of concern.

Other possible means of measuring horizontal integration—concentration ratios of assets or revenues, for example—are impossible to construct for more than four or five years due to lack of data, and because often the needed information is buried within a division of a larger firm.

From a policy point of view, at least four things directly affect the degree of horizontal integration: 1) The number of providers or outlets, and the number of these subject to sale; 2) the conditions controlling entry to the business; 3) the opportunity for "cheating" (charging slightly more or less than a generally agreed-upon amount for the same service); and 4) the existing merger guidelines of the Justice Department and the degree to which they are enforced.[155] Generally speaking, all these factors are reviewed for specific proposed mergers. The FCC, of course, reduces this to a concern with the number of facilities owned rather than an overall market context, even on a case by case basis. Yet as economists have pointed out again and again, it is the "share of production under common control, not how many facilities are employed . . . that determines the extent of monopoly power."[156] Thus the *size* of the market is important. Group ownership in STV, given the limited number of outlets presently operating, could well be of greater concern than MSO control of cable systems, despite the fact that the former is regulated and the latter is not.

The varied degree of government concern about or participation in horizontal activity is best exemplified by examining cable mergers over the past decade or so. The first big cable merger came in 1967 when Cypress was created by merger of Community Cablecasting and United Cablevision. In 1967 General Instrument and Jerrold combined. Three years later Teleprompter, then the fourth largest MSO, jumped to the top spot by acquiring H&B American. In none of these cases was there much government activity or concern. In the mid-1970s, however, the Justice Department either actively intervened or at least expressed concern, and thus helped to thwart a proposed 1972 merger between Cox and ATC (then the second and third ranked MSOs), the 1973 takeover by Viacom of Communications Properties and a proposed Cox-LVO merger. As cable expansion slowed in mid-decade, so too did merger activity. When the merger activity picked up again in 1977, Justice reverted to a low profile which has continued to date. Thus, neither the Time Inc. purchase of ATC, nor the Times-Mirror-Communications Properties, Inc. merger a year later, the proposed GE-Cox merger (which fell through for business reasons), nor the 1981 takeover of then number one-ranked MSO Teleprompter by Westinghouse, and the Rogers (Canadian) acquisition of number nine-ranked MSO UA-Columbia raised Justice Department concern.[157]

The lack of activity would seem to be due to two factors. First, it reflected changing political priorities in Washington. Second, it seemed to be a recognition that the more difficult and troublesome ownership problems lie in vertical and conglomerate integration.

Vertical Integration

Vertical integration also has a parallel in broadcasting: network ownership of broadcasting stations. Given the expansion of original basic and pay cable programming in the past five years, however, the trend to vertical integration raises more complicated concerns.

What It Is

"Vertical integration exists when an exchange that might have occurred by market transaction in a buyer/seller setting is handled administratively within a single 'firm.' "[158] In other words, a cable programmer might also own cable systems, as in fact is a common occurrence. Vertical integration can exist on a contractual basis without any actual ownership interest (such as an affiliation contract from a cable system to a cable programmer for one or more channels), or actual common ownership either by merger or subsidiary holding.

To some degree, vertical organization is better understood when one explores why such a relationship is established. Among other reasons advanced are: lower costs achieved by internal rather than marketplace negotiation; reduction in risk since the "bottom line" is within a single firm; price discrimination may be facilitated; and in some cases the effects of regulation may be avoided or reduced by ownership of unregulated subsidiaries by regulated companies.[159]

The reason for concern in vertical integration boils down to a matter of access:

> Such combinations may, in certain circumstances, have the effect of increasing barriers to entry in either the supplier's [programmers] or purchaser's [cable systems] market or foreclosing competitors of one firm from access to the market in which its partner operates.[160]

Pay Programming

One of the most oft-cited examples of such integration is the common ownership of cable systems and pay programming distribution firms. Table 7.13 shows the relationship between the three most important pay cable suppliers and co-owned MSOs. It demonstrates the dramatic relationship between ownership and pay service offered. Very few vertically owned systems were carrying the pay cable programs of a rival firm. However, this is likely to be a short-lived situation, at least in the dramatic terms shown in the table. The "multi-tier" phenomenon was, in 1980-1981, only at the very early stages of development. As multiple tiers become more common (a trend limited to some degree by system reconstruction to expand channel capacity), the obvious relationships now evident should become slowly less important as subscribers are provided rival programming. But even multiple tiers will only slowly change the *status quo,* because only the largest systems will offer two full pay services before

Table 7.13: Comparison of Pay TV Service Penetration on Affiliated and Unaffiliated MSOs, 1980

Pay Service	Percentage of Pay TV Customers Subscribing to:		
	ATC (Time Inc.)	Teleprompter	Warner Amex
Home Box Office (Time Inc.)	87%	3%	5%
Showtime (Viacom/Teleprompter)	3	75	—
The Movie Channel (Warner Amex)	1	2	79

Source: Calculated by Charles Oliver of CBS Inc., based on data in Paul Kagan Associates, *The Pay TV Census*, December 31, 1980.

offering one full and one supplemental pay service. Here the ownership by Time Inc. of HBO, Cinemax, and HBO Program Services becomes tactically clearer—to the degree possible, cable systems may offer multiple tiers yet still remain in the same corporate "family."

Without getting too deeply involved in the specifics, much of this effect is achieved by contract terms so that non-ownership vertical integration can have the same end effect on subscriber program choice and source as actual ownership.[161] Discount clauses in pay programmer contracts work against tiering of basic pay cable programmers by establishing discounts based on number of subscribers. Thus, a system operator is better off staying with one full (or "maxi") service and a supplemental (or "mini") service, than with two maxis. This can be strengthened by exclusivity clauses which often protect the pay distributor but do not equally protect the system. In other words, HBO or Showtime might not allow a cable system to contract for a competing maxi service without months of advance notice, and a possibly higher fee, while at the same time reserving to itself the right to sell its programming to any other outlet (say, an STV or MDS outlet) even in the same market without similar notice to its existing contract affiliate. There is no regulatory supervision on these contract provisions, though similar contracts in television broadcasting are under some regulatory constraint.[162] At this point, it is purely a matter of contractual negotiation.

Vertical integration increasingly moves in two directions. Program distributors can integrate "downstream" with cable system operators. But they can integrate "upstream" as well. This occurs when a program distributor gets actively into program production, either by ownership of an existing production company, or by contracting for original material. Time Inc., for example, has long operated Time-Life Films, and some films from this source have been used on HBO. It has also tried its hand at—and subsequently abandoned—theatrical or film production (see Chapter 5). In 1981, HBO announced it had signed for the first made-for-pay television motion picture—likely merely the first of many in the pay cable search for more material.[163] Likewise, the Teleprompter/Viacom ownership of Showtime has associations with such production facilities as Muzak, Filmation Associates and Viacom's connections with major television shows and series. Warner Amex naturally ties to Warner Communications and filmmaking, but also to David Wolper Productions and the material made at and/or for its Qube systems.

Cross-Subsidy

An important argument against ownership of cable systems by co-located telephone companies is the question of cross-subsidization by operations on different sides of the regulatory barrier. As noted previously, operation of a nonregulated business (e.g., cable, which for the purposes of the present discussion can be considered nonregulated other than by franchise) by a regulated common carrier can lead not only to support of one by the other, but more importantly to shifting of costs to the regulated side (and thus adding to the rate base), while profits are shifted to the unregulated side (thus not counting in the authorized rate of return levels for carriers). This is an extremely difficult practice to detect and is a key reason for generally not allowing co-located cross-ownerships of cable systems. More involved and not yet fully understood are parallel issues of telephone companies (or other common carriers) getting into information production as well as distribution.

Entry

Perhaps the most important negative aspect of vertical integration is its potential limiting effect on new entry. The argument is fairly simple. It takes a minimal level of assured delivery outlets (say, cable systems) to make economic production of programming viable. This can be achieved by either contract or ownership means. The producer who has this requisite minimal access to outlets has a miniature version of what the big film firms established in the 1930s for the same reason—ready-made production facilities, in-place distribution channels and widespread exhibition outlets: a closed system. The impact that such arrangements had on entry was a key factor in the eventual forced divestiture of pieces of these firms (see Chapter 5). In the cable or STV/MDS businesses, thus far at least, there is no comparable vertical closure of access to the business. There are relative giants (see Table 7.13 and compare to MSO size in Table 7.5 and pay distributor role in Table 7.11), as well as much smaller firms. But while a pattern seems tentatively clear, it is far too early in pay cable's development to determine whether the control of vertically integrated companies can even approach the film oligopolies of the 1930s.[164] As the 1980 final report of the Commission's Network Inquiry concluded:

> . . . we cannot discover justification for any Commission policy specifically directed at restricting the common ownership of networks and stations serving the newer television technologies, unless it is designed to deal with the special problem of integration by a rate-of-return monopolist [telephone company]. No reasonable prospect exists that vertical integration could be used as a strategy to foreclose actual or potential competitors at either the network or outlet level of the production process.[165]

To a considerable degree, the issue of conglomerate control involves situations where "non-competing, non-vertically related functions are undertaken" by a single firm.[166] These situations focus on potential price-cutting and reciprocal buying practices of conglomerates and possible trade-offs of "spheres of influence" among conglomerates. There is to date insufficient evidence of any concerted conglomerate activity in the cable industry or related businesses to allow even tentative discussion of trends, let alone policy questions. Evident in any discussion of horizontal, vertical or conglomerate ownership, however, is the need to develop a "trigger" measure of concentration. Such a trigger might bring on concerted policy analysis if concentration levels (measured by subscribers, assets, revenues or other means) reached announced levels. For nearly three decades the trigger in broadcast outlet control has been an arbitrary number of stations. There is common agreement that a less crude measure is needed, both for broadcast and newer means of delivery, which would allow analysis of trends across media. There is considerably less agreement on just what the trigger figure might be.

Access and Separations

If the primary reason for concern about ownership of any medium is access of different ideas to that medium, and thus to an audience, then access to cable television, STV, MDS and the pay distributors is of considerable import. At one extreme is common carrier status for some or all of these means of delivery—ownership of facilities totally divorced from any say in content. Access is controlled merely by ability to pay specified tariffs on a first-come, first-served basis. At the other extreme is total integration with one entity controlling delivery and all channels of content provided by that means of delivery.

Clearly such options have immediate impact on questions of ownership, for with the same entity controlling both facilities and content, broadcast-related and -originated concerns over ownership appear to have considerable validity. But as access or separations requirements are considered, ownership of facilities becomes less important, assuming a variety of program entities gain access to a potential audience. Adoption of a national, rigidly observed separations requirement, for example, would obviate most of the ownership concerns discussed thus far in this chapter. But that path appears unlikely, as development of the various options makes clear.

Mandated Access

In 1969, the FCC established a requirement that all cable systems with a minimum of 3500 subscribers were to provide at least one channel of locally originated material—acting, in effect, as local broadcasters on one channel.[167] Such a channel, or channels, remains under the control of the cable system operator, who makes decisions on what or whom is to be aired. Programming is often advertiser-supported, as on broadcast stations. These rules were appealed but upheld in the Supreme Court case known as *Midwest Video I*.[168] In 1974, rethinking the basic premise of the requirement, the FCC rescinded it.[169]

Two years earlier, the Commission's so-called definitive rules for cable included a controversial requirement for local access channels. Cable systems were to provide one channel each for local government, educational institutions and local public access use.[170] The system operator would not have any say over content on these channels. This requirement was also appealed (ironically by the same firm which appealed the local origination channels) and was overturned in *Midwest Video II*.[171] However, some states and a number of local franchise authorities continue to require some or all of these local access channels.

Local origination and access channels are thus not similar in content or control, though they both serve to increase the diversity and local emphasis of content on at least a few cable channels. Both, especially access channels, further serve to diversify control of content decisions. That neither requirement survived the 1970s added pressure in favor of cable and related media ownership controls, and encouraged some system operators with excess channel capacity to continue various local origination or access channels despite no longer being required to do so. But the cost of such channels and the economic benefits to be derived from carrying a nationally networked signal instead would appear to doom most such efforts in the near future.

Leased Access

Getting considerably closer to the notion of common carrier status is the leased access channel. Here:

> . . . the operator leases channel space to all comers at standard fees, in much the same way that satellite carriers lease transponder space. The lessee may use the channel for any type of programming that he may wish.[172]

The system operator sets rates and leases capacity. The operator, like the telephone companies, has nothing to say about content. While there is neither a consistent national policy concerning such channels, nor any solid data on the number or ways of setting up such operations, some patterns can be noted.

Of the basic satellite-delivered services (see Table 7.12), some, especially the religious programmers, lease channels full-time but do not charge viewers (or system operators) anything for the content, which is thus carried free. CBN, PTL and Trinity all are clear examples of leased channel use. In most other cases, the cable operator pays something for carrying the signal, though often providing the material on a "basic" or free basis for subscribers.

The pay programmers are not examples of the leased channel concept, for while they do pay for satellite transponders by lease or purchase, they charge cable system operators for their service, a charge passed on to subscribers in the form of a monthly fee. Though not yet well-developed, some observers project one or more advertiser-supported or underwritten channels of programming using the lease approach to gain access to systems and their subscribers.

Leased access, however, does not provide an important aspect of other access notions—provision of time for part-time communicators. The core notion of access is to allow a variety of points of view to be heard, and these are often one-issue comments or other onetime uses. Leased access is directed to full-time or at least long-term contract use of a major portion of hours on a channel. For entertainment or other format content, this makes business sense. But individual or group access to small units of time on an irregular schedule are not provided as was the intent of the original mandated access provisions of the FCC's rules.

From a policy point of view,

> . . . classifying leased access channels as common carrier channels and employing the existing legal structure to insure non-

discriminatory access and to restrict to the minimum any cable operator control over the content of the communications would . . . serve the . . . purposes of the Communications Act. Indeed, such classification would well serve the First Amendment purposes of guaranteeing wide-open, robust debate and information flow from diverse and antagonistic sources.[173]

However, cable system operators tend to believe that any kind of common carrier status would involve rate regulation, at least for those channels. This is anathema to the cable industry. In recent years, however, quite specific attention has been given to this notion. The fact is, there are numerous examples of industries classified as common carriage that do *not* have much or any rate regulation. The airline industry is one. The railroads—and increasingly trucking—are others.

Separations

More fundamental, but as yet only a proposal, is the "separations" approach to cable system ownership. Briefly stated, the idea is to separate ownership and control of the physical facilities of cable distribution from production of program material to be carried on those facilities. Entities could own one aspect of a given system or the other, but not both. The FCC's 1972 "definitive" rules raised this possibility for the future, contending that until cable grew to maturity, such a policy would only retard cable development.[174] Two years later, the Cabinet Committee on Cable Communications built its entire series of recommendations for cable around a separations principle, but again, only after cable reached a certain point (not made totally clear) of growth. The Committee's report indicated that other kinds of control of content and economics "would not be adequate to prevent anti-competitive behavior."[175] In 1976, the House Subcommittee staff report analyzed the issue, strongly recommending that Congressional action should formally require a separations policy no more than 10 years from such a law's enactment. Otherwise, the issue would be left to the FCC's discretion, which has only said it would re-examine the question at some unspecified time in the future, making it more difficult to demand divestiture at a later date.[176] If such a policy is put into effect, the various policy reports generally agree that cross-ownership of cable and other media would no longer need to be limited.[177] But for any separations policy to be made effective, some clear "trigger" event or date is needed in advance, such as 50% cable penetration in television households or a set future date.[178]

While separations would not reduce the nominal monopoly position of the system operator, it would limit its ability to exercise monopoly powers or to otherwise discriminate among different users. The cost or trade-off consistently raised by the cable industry, however, is the likelihood of considerably less program development under such a scheme. Further, cable systems will probably grow to smaller ultimate size, and at a slower rate. Whether these costs are a fair price to pay for increased ease of access is a fundamental policy problem with separations.[179] There is no impediment at the moment to either local or state-mandated separations policies, though no such steps have been taken thus far.

By the early 1980s, the likelihood of separations as a serious policy option was in decline. The development of satellite delivery and the plethora of services available because of the satellite option lessened concern about and demand for access to cable for different services aimed at specialized audiences. Continued announcement of new pay and basic services to come in the early 1980s suggested expansion in program options would continue. One possibility, however, is a separations policy for non-video services including security and other two-way options, where competition is not likely to be as widespread as with video. This is an area not widely studied as yet, but separations policy may make sense as system capacity increases sufficiently to allow cable system provision of non-video services.[180]

CONCLUSION

A basic problem with any review of cable ownership is that:

> Serious analysis of the effects of horizontal concentration and vertical integration has been virtually nonexistent, and these issues seem at the periphery of the concerns of the [Federal Communications] Commission. . . . [T]he attention given to the question of economic injury to broadcasters from cable expansion may have diverted resources from the consideration of questions which may be far more significant in the long run.[181]

There is generally insufficient data on which to base any serious analysis—and no attempt is being made to gather the needed information given the lack of policy concern to drive the gathering process. Something of a "chicken and the egg" problem thus ensues with too little data to raise policy concern, and too little policy concern to generate the data. Discussions are theoretical or appear based more on qualitative rather than quantitative concerns.

Projections of the future of the media discussed in this chapter abound—and most share a common feeling of almost unlimited expansion potential in both facilities and content offered. To note but a few of the most common assumptions:

- Cable penetration will continue to expand, likely reaching about 50% of the nation's homes by 1990. Pay cable options will be taken by an increasing proportion of cable subscribers, from about half in 1981 to nearly three-quarters late in the 1980s.

- Facilities serving this expansion will also increase. Cable systems are now being built to higher channel capacity standards, and older systems are being forced to rebuild by the number of available services and resulting subscriber demand. An entire second generation of domestic satellites will be placed in service in the mid-1980s, opening up vastly increased transponder availability for still more basic and pay services. The MDS service is likely to get additional channels allocated to its use, allowing greater growth of that common carrier service. STV will continue to be deregulated, leading to multiple STV outlets in major markets. The FCC may authorize one or more DBS services to begin operation by the mid-1980s, most likely on a pay or partial-pay basis.

- In addition to DBS delivery, whole new services are actively under development which may increase demand for basic cable. Videotext and teletext are the most discussed in 1981, but other two-way video and non-video services are already under experimental use.

With this expansion in options and audience penetration come other predictable structural outcomes:

- The need for capital to build increasingly expensive cable systems (or to rebuild older ones), STV outlets and other services will increasingly involve financial institutions in both lending and partial minority ownership roles in these media.

- The drive for capital and franchises (or franchise renewal to higher standards) will continue to force MSO concentration—and likely vertical integration as well. The economics of cable television and related media no longer allow entry by small firms, but increasingly demand the expertise and capital backing of large, often diversified entities. Smaller cable systems will increasingly be taken over by larger ones.

- Costs of video programming, and problems of dividing audience loyalty, will bring on a considerable shakedown among satellite-delivered program services and networks. Many part-time and/or limited-appeal services will depart from cable delivery in favor of home video cassette or video disc methods of delivery. Rising urban competition among cable, STV and MDS outlets will bring about a comparable shakeout in major cities, likely leading to spheres of influence for the services. STV may only survive in major urban areas, offering a less expensive construction option to cable. MDS and potential DBS are harder to adequately predict, but both are in any case likely to serve only a very small proportion of the television audience. In other words, after an initial expansion of both services and outlets, the number of both are likely to decline by the mid- to late 1980s.

If these predictions are borne out, a policy dilemma emerges. For reasons already detailed at the end of Chapter 6, government agencies are unlikely to pay much attention to media concentration trends in the 1980s. The FTC is removing itself from this subject, the Justice Department has made clear its looser reading of antitrust requirements, and the FCC is moving toward less rather than more ownership regulation. The dilemma grows from this lack of agency concern combined with the increasing economic concentration evident in cable and related media discussed here.

Patterns of concentration have appeared before in other media, as shown in previous chapters of this volume. It is not our purpose here to argue whether such a trend is "good" or "bad" (when, of course, it has elements of both at the very least)—but simply to note trends to date in a very new industry. Of all the media discussed in this book, further economic and structural research is most needed here. If even half the predictions made by industry observers come to pass, the importance of cable, pay cable, STV, MDS and related and newer media will be substantial indeed, as will the need to monitor their growth and operations. Policy is best initiated early if it is to have substantial impact in guiding media industry structure to serve the public interest.

NOTES

1. See, for example, Mary Louise Hollowell, ed. *The Cable/Broadband Communications Book, Volume 2, 1980-81* (Washington: Communications Press, 1980) for the best general current overview of cable and related media. An anthology of useful documents is *Current Developments in CATV 1981* (New York: Practising Law Institute, 1981), which

appears in revised versions irregularly. The most inclusive historical treatment of cable and its regulation up to 1972 is found in Don LeDuc, *Cable Television and the FCC: A Crisis in Media Control* (Philadelphia: Temple University Press, 1973).

2. See the bibliography in LeDuc, *Cable Television and the FCC: . . .* and Felix Chinn, *Cable Television: A Comprehensive Bibliography* (New York: Plenum, 1978) for citations on all of these subjects. Another recent overview which refers to important earlier studies is found in Stanley Besen and Robert Crandall, "The Regulation of Cable Television," *Law and Contemporary Problems* 44:77-124 (Winter 1981).

3. For the early history of cable, see Mary Alice Mayer Phillips, *CATV: A History of Community Antenna Television* (Evanston, IL: Northwestern University Press, 1972), and LeDuc, op. cit.

4. 26 FCC 403 (1959).

5. 32 FCC 459 (1962).

6. 38 FCC 683 (1965).

7. 2 FCC 2d 725 (1966).

8. *U.S.* v. *Southwestern Cable* 392 US 159 (1968).

9. *Fortnightly Corp.* v. *United Artists* 392 US 390 (1968).

10. U.S. Congress, House of Representatives, Committee on Interstate and Foreign Commerce, Subcommittee on Communications. *Cable Television: Promise v. Regulatory Performance* 94th Cong., 2nd Sess. (January 1976), p. 12. (Hereafter, "House Report.")

11. Most of these early Rand reports are detailed in LeDuc, op. cit.; the remainder can be found listed in Chinn, op. cit.

12. *On the Cable: The Television of Abundance: Report of the Sloan Commission on Cable Communications* (New York: McGraw-Hill, 1971).

13. 36 FCC 2d 143 (1972).

14. Part 76.311 of the Commission's rules (47 CFR) details the EEO requirements which directly track those for broadcast stations.

15. *Cable Advertising Directory* (Washington: NCTA, annual) was 81 pages long in 1980 and 425 pages in 1981, though some of the increase in length was due to increased detail in reporting in the latter year.

16. The Cabinet Committee on Cable Communications, *Cable: Report to the President* (Washington: GPO, 1974).

17. Research and Policy Committee of the Committee for Economic Development, *Broadcasting and Cable Television: Policies for Diversity and Change* (New York: CED, 1975).

18. See House Report.

19. Paul W. MacAvoy, ed. *Deregulation of Cable Television* (Washington: American Enterprise Institute for Public Policy Research, 1977), part of the series "Ford Administration Papers on Regulatory Reform."

20. Copyright Revision Act of 1976, P.L. 94-553 (also Title 17 of U.S. Code).

21. See "Defying Bureaucratic Gravity at the Copyright Royalty Tribunal," *Broadcasting* (June 1, 1981), pp. 62-66.

22. *FCC* v. *Midwest Video Corp.* 440 US 689 (1979). Often referred to as "Midwest Video II" to distinguish it from an earlier decision on a related matter.

23. See the discussion of this in Besen and Crandall, op. cit. and also Steven Rivkin, *A New Guide to Federal Cable Television Regulations* (Cambridge, MA: MIT Press, 1978) for the earlier decisions in the process.

24. 71 FCC 2d 632 (April 25, 1979).

25. Besen & Crandall, op. cit., p. 104.

26. FCC, "Report and Order in Dockets 20988 and 21284" 45 Federal Register 60186 (September 11, 1980).

27. *Malrite TV of New York* v. *FCC 652 F 2d 1140* (2nd Cir., June 16, 1981).

28. Besen & Crandall, op. cit., pp. 112ff reviews this briefly; see also 71 FCC 2d 632 at Sections III through V, pp. 673-713.

29. FCC data as cited in Christopher Sterling and Timothy Haight, *The Mass Media: Aspen Institute Guide to Communication Industry Trends* (New York: Praeger, 1978), table 380-C, p. 209.

30. For a broadcast industry view, see the CBS data on competition in the top 50 markets from cable, MDS and home video in "Enough Competition, Too Much Regulation," *Broadcasting* (August 10, 1981), p. 57.

31. Trade reports on the cost of franchise competition in Dallas etc. as reported in *Business Week* (December 8, 1980), pp. 62ff.

32. For information on bank and other investment loans to the cable business, see Tony Hoffman, "Availability of Funding to Industry Indicates Confidence of Lendors," *CableAge* (June 1, 1981), pp. 12-16.

33. For an example, see the investment report *Cable Television 1981* (New York: Donaldson, Lufkin & Jenrette, 1981), p. 15.

34. Kenneth Gordon, et al., *Staff Report on FCC Policy on Cable Ownership* (Washington: FCC Office of Plans and Policy, September 1981), Preliminary Draft, p. 54, note 10. (Hereafter "Gordon, et al.")

35. House Report, p. 93.

36. Ibid., p. 94.

37. 50 FCC 2d 1046 as reported in Rivkin, op. cit., p. 97.

38. Gordon, et al., p. 54.

39. Ibid.

40. Ibid., Chapter 4.

41. Ibid., p. 76.

42. FCC, "Second Report and Order in Docket No. 18397," 23 FCC 816 (July 1, 1970).

43. FCC, Network Inquiry Special Staff, *New Television Networks: Entry, Jurisdiction, Ownership and Regulation* (Washington: GPO, 1980), Vol. I, pp. 429-433. (Hereafter "NISS.")

44. Gordon, et al., p. 117.

45. *Broadcasting* (May 18, 1981).

46. *New York Times* (August 5, 1981), p. 6.

47. *Los Angeles Times* (December 9, 1980), p. IV-4.

48. *Editor and Publisher* (December 13, 1980), p. 12.

49. But see Gordon, et al., brief mention on p. 116.

50. FCC, "Final Report and Order in Docket 18509," 21 FCC 2d 307 (January 28, 1970).

51. Gordon, et al., p. 132.

52. Ibid., pp. 144-145 (footnotes omitted).

53. Ibid., pp. 135-143.

54. Ibid., p. 156. See pp. 156-157 for discussion of policy options for the future.

55. FCC, "Notice of Proposed Rulemaking in Docket 80-767" (December 19, 1980).

56. FCC, "Report and Order in CC Docket 80-767" (October 29, 1981), para. 36. The Census definition defines as rural all places or areas *outside* of (a) places of 2500 inhabitants or more, incorporated or unincorporated, and (b) other territory, incorporated or unincorporated, included in urbanized areas.

57. Ibid., para 1.

58. Gordon, et al., p. 152 (and footnote 46).

59. *Washington Post* (September 5, 1981), p. C-7.

60. For broad background, see General Accounting Office, *Regulating the Domestic Telecommunications Industry: FCC's Actions and Their Impact On Competitive Development* (Washington: GAO, September 1981). See also U.S. Congress, Senate, *Telecommunications Competition and Deregulation Act of 1981*. S. Rept. 97-170 on S. 898, 97th Cong., 1st Sess. (July 27, 1981). See also "A New Era for Bell—and Everyone Else," *Dun's Business Month* (September 1981), pp. 58-68.

61. Victoria Coits, "Media Concentration: Conglomerates Take Cable's Bait," *Cablevision* (December 15, 1980), p. 129.

62. *Los Angeles Times* (August 11, 1980), p. IV-1.

63. *Business Week* (December 8, 1980), p. 63.

64. *Editor and Publisher* (December 13, 1980), p. 12.

65. As reported in Gordon, et al., p. 82.

66. Ibid., p. 81.

67. Ibid., p. 85.

68. *CableAge* (June 29, 1981), p. 31.

69. *Broadcasting* (January 5, 1981), p. 72.

70. Ibid., p. 70.

71. *CableAge* (May 18, 1981), p. 66.

72. *CableAge* (June 1, 1981), p. 31.

73. *Broadcasting* (January 5, 1981), p. 68.

74. Ibid., p. 70.

75. *New York Times* (July 15, 1981), p. D-1.

76. *CableAge* (July 13, 1981), p. 28.

77. *Broadcasting/Cable Yearbook 1981* (Washington: Broadcasting Publications, 1981).

78. 33 FR 19028 (1968) as discussed in the House Report, pp. 91-92.

79. House Report, pp. 91-92.

80. 52 FCC 2d 170 (1975).

81. Gordon, et al., p. 99.

82. FCC, "Report and Order in Docket 20621," 59 FCC 2d 723 (1976).

83. FCC, "Memorandum Opinion and Order in RM 3528," 77 FCC 2d 73 (1980).

84. *Cablevision* (August 3, 1981), pp. 10-11; and *Broadcasting* (July 27, 1981), p. 99.

85. FCC, "Report and Order in Docket 20520," 59 FCC 2d 970 (June 10, 1976).

86. White House press release on minority ownership of broadcasting and cable television, January 31, 1978; and Marion Hayes Hull, "Economic Potential for Minorities—Obstacles and Opportunities," in Mary Louise Hollowell, ed., *The Cable/Broadband Communications Book 1977-78* (Washington: Communications Press, 1977), p. 80.

87. Personal conversation with National Black Media Coalition leader Pluria Marshall, Washington, September 11, 1981.

88. See discussion of the 19th century experiments by the Puskas brothers in Christopher H. Sterling and John M. Kittross, *Stay Tuned: A Concise History of American Broadcasting* (Belmont, CA: Wadsworth, 1978), p. 39.

89. Walter S. Baer and Carl Pilnick, "Pay Television at the Crossroads," (Santa Monica, CA: Rand Corp. P-5159, April 1974), p. 4.

90. John R. Barrington, "Pay Cable—An Old Idea Whose Time Has Come," In Hollowell, *The Cable/Broadband Communications Book 1977-78,* p. 119.

91. Technology & Economics Inc., *The Emergence of Pay Cable Television* (Cambridge, MA: T&E, 1980), Volume II, p. 50.

92. Barrington, op. cit., p. 122.

93. Baer and Pilnick, op. cit., pp. 10-11.

94. Sterling and Haight, op. cit., table 190-D, citing information from Paul Kagan.

95. Technology & Economics Inc., *The Emergence of Pay Cable Television,* p. 85.

96. *Cablevision* (August 31, 1981), p. 19.

97. 23 FCC 2d 825 (1970) as in House Report, pp. 62-63.

98. Richard Warren Rappaport, "The Emergence of Subscription Cable Television and its Role in Communications," *Federal Communications Bar Journal* 29:301-334 (1976), at 305.

99. House Report, pp. 64-68.

100. *Home Box Office* v. *FCC* 567 F2d 9 (1977).

100a. Midwest Video II (see note 22).

100b. *Brookhaven Cable TV Inc.* v. *Kelly* 573 F 2d 765 (1978).

101. See, for example, H.H. Howard and S.L. Carroll, *Subscription Television: History, Current Status, and Economic Projections* (Knoxville; University of Tennessee College of Communications, April 1980), pp. 6-32.

102. Ibid., p. 37.

103. "STV: A Passing Fancy or Permanent Industry?" *Cablevision* (February 23, 1981), p. 48.

104. FCC, "Fourth Report and Order in Docket 11279," 15 FCC 2d 466 (December 12, 1968).

105. *NATO* v. *FCC,* 420 F 2d 194 (1969); cert. den. 397 US 922 (1970).

106. Kristin Booth Glen, "Report on Subscription Television," in FCC, Network Inquiry Special Staff, *Preliminary Report on Prospects for Additional Networks* (Washington: FCC, January 1980), pp. 20-21.

107. FCC, "Report and Order in Docket 21311," 41 RR 2d 1491 (November 22, 1977).

108. FCC, "Report and Order on Docket 21311," 42 RR 2d 1207 (April 7, 1978).

109. FCC, "First Report and Order in Docket 21502," 46 RR 2d 460 (October 12, 1979).

110. FCC, "Memorandum Opinion and Order in RM-3223," 77 FCC 523 (April 24, 1980).

111. See *Broadcasting* (September 14, 1981), p. 77 for account of Oak Industries' purchase of NST from Chartwell, Inc.

112. Howard and Carroll, p. 44.

113. Kristin Booth Glen, "Report on Multi-Point Distribution Service," in FCC, Network Inquiry Special Staff, *Preliminary Report on Prospects for Additional Networks* (Washington: FCC, January 1980), pp. 2, 14.

114. 47 FCC 2d 957 (1970) as reported in Glen, op. cit., p. 15.

115. Glen, op. cit., p. 17.

116. Ibid., pp. 24-25.

117. Ibid., pp. 15, 25.

118. *Broadcasting* (October 13, 1980), p. 60.

119. Ibid.; see also Glen, op. cit., p. 104.

120. Glen, op. cit., p. 103 (notes omitted).

121. Speech of FCC Chairman Charles Ferris before the 1980 MDS Convention, Washington, DC, October 6, 1980, p. 5.

122. Glen, op. cit., p. 40.

123. Ibid., pp. 50-51.

124. See *Ford Foundation Activities in Noncommercial Broadcasting 1951-1976* (New York: the Foundation, 1976), p. 12 for short review of this proposal.

125. T&E, *The Emergence of Pay Cable Television,* p. 50.

126. "How Cable-TV Success Hinges on Satellites," *Business Week* (September 14, 1981), p. 89.

127. Ibid. FCC action was pending on Docket 79-252, the Competitive Common Carrier Proceeding, which proposed market rather than regulatory allocations.

128. M.J. Manning, "Satellite Transponder Sales: Clever Innovation or Illegal Ruse?" *Satellite Communications* (August 1981), p. 35.

129. Ibid., p. 37.

130. *Broadcasting* (October 22, 1979), p. 28; and "Commission Deregulates Receive-Only Terminals," *Satellite Communications* (December 1979), p. 18ff.

131. "HBO Landmarks" a chronological press release from HBO (no date), cites October 13, 1977 as the specific date.

132. Paul Kagan as quoted in HBO, *The Pay TV Guide: Editor's Pay-TV Handbook* (New York: Home Box Office/Time Inc., n.d.).

133. T&E, *The Emergence of Pay Cable Television,* p. 51.

134. *Wall Street Journal* (August 28, 1981), p. 8.

135. J.R. Barrington, "Pay TV: Now a Staple on the Cable Menu," in Hollowell, *The Cable/Broadband Communications Book, Volume 2, 1980-81,* p. 143.

136. T&E, *The Emergence of Pay Cable Television,* p. 59.

137. H. Polskin, "Inside Pay-Cable's Most Savage War," *Panorama* (March 1981); pp. 54ff is the best overview.

138. *U.S.* v. *Columbia Pictures, et al.* Civil Action No. 80-Civ 4438 (U.S. District Court for S. Dist. of New York), filed August 4, 1980.

139. *Broadcasting* (January 5, 1981), p. 31.

140. "Pay After Premiere," *Cablevision* (January 19, 1981), pp. 26ff.

141. For good overviews, see "Clash of Cultures," *Cablevision* (June 29, 1981), pp. 40ff; and "The Cable-TV Revolution: How it Affects the Arts," *New York Times* (July 5, 1981), p. II-1; and Martin Mayer, "Can Culture Channels Survive?" *American Film* (May 1981), pp. 14, 76.

142. Data from CBS Research, Washington, DC (Document 0099d, revised 8/18/81).

143. For a good discussion of this see "Traffic Jam on Cable's Ramp," *Cablevision* (August 31, 1981), pp. 32 ff.

144. "Superstation Breakthrough," *Broadcasting* (October 30, 1978), p. 25.

145. "C-SPAN: Carving Out a New Programming Niche," *Broadcasting* (November 3, 1980), p. 48.

146. "They're Free and Clear," *Panorama* (April 1981), pp. 54ff.

147. Ibid.

148. FCC, "Memorandum Opinion and Order on RM-3651" (October 1, 1981).

149. NISS, p. 328.

150. See the classic discussion in Peter O. Steiner, "Program Patterns and Preferences and the Workability of Competition in Radio Broadcasting," *The Quarterly Journal of Economics* (May 1952) LXVI:194-223.

151. NISS, p. 341 (citations omitted).

152. Gordon, et al., p. 18 (emphasis in original). See also NISS, pp. 333ff. for a variant view.

153. NISS, p. 339.

154. Scherer as quoted in NISS, p. 350.

155. NISS, pp. 352-357.

156. Ibid., p. 362.

157. Most of this paragraph is based heavily on Yale M. Braunstein, et al., "Recent Trends in Cable Television Related to the Prospects for New Television Networks," in FCC, Network Inquiry Special Staff, *Preliminary Report on Prospects for Additional Networks* (Washington: FCC, January 1980), pp.19ff.

158. Gordon, et al., p. 37.

159. Braunstein, op. cit., p. 24.

160. Ibid., p. 26.

161. This paragraph based on the discussion in Barry Litman and Susanna Eun, "The Emerging Oligopoly of Pay-TV in the USA," *Telecommunications Policy* (June 1981), pp. 121-135, especially 127-130.

162. See NISS, pp. 441-520.

163. *Broadcasting* (September 14, 1981), p. 62.

164. Litman and Eun, op. cit., pp. 125, 134-135.

165. NISS, p. 402.

166. Gordon, et al., p. 39.

167. FCC, "First Report and Order in Docket 18397," 20 FCC 2d 201 (1969).

168. *U.S.* v. *Midwest Video Corp.* 406 US 649 (1972). Or, "Midwest Video I."

169. FCC, "Report and Order re Program Origination by Cable Television Systems," 49 FCC 2d 1090 (1974).

170. See the detailed discussion of these in Rivkin, *A New Guide to Federal Cable Television Regulations.*

171. FCC v. Midwest Video II.

172. T&E, *The Emergence of Pay Cable Television,* Volume I, p. 21.

173. Paul J. Berman, "CATV Leased-Access Channels and the Federal Communications Commission: The Intractable Jurisdictional Question," (Cambridge, MA: Harvard Program on Information Resources Policy, June 1975), p. 68.

174. House Report, p. 89.

175. *Cable: Report to the President,* p. 30.

176. House Report, p. 91.

177. See, for example, *Cable: Report to the President,* pp. 30-33.

178. Bruce Owen, "Cable Television: The Framework of Regulation," in U.S. Congress, Senate, Committee on Governmental Affairs, Study on Federal Regulation: Appendix to Volume VI, Framework for Regulation. 95th Cong., 2d Sess. (December 1978), Committee Print, pp. 347-389, at 377.

179. For a comparison, see Owen, op. cit., and Gordon, et al., Chapter 7.

180. Gordon, et al., p. 131, note 33.

181. Besen & Crandall, "The Regulation of Cable Television," p. 121.

8

Who Owns the Media Companies?

by Benjamin M. Compaine

The preceding chapters identified the largest participants in each of the traditional media segments: newspapers, broadcasting, cable, magazines, books and film. They introduced the notion that competition for these media players may also be coming from less traditional sources, such as the common carrier telephone companies, banks, retailers, satellite carriers, microwave carriers, and others. In addition, they pointed out how some of the evolving hybrid technologies, such as text on the video screen or television programming transmitted directly by satellite to users, have given rise to a series of joint ventures, wherein traditional media companies combine their particular areas of expertise with those of nontraditional participants, e.g., AT&T, an experienced carrier of low-volume data joining with Knight-Ridder, a firm with skills in content creation.

This chapter presents a comprehensive listing of the leading media players, detailing which companies are major stakeholders in each media segment. It also identifies, within limits, the actual major owners of these companies—the stockholders.

MEDIA HOLDINGS OF LEADING MASS MEDIA ENTERPRISES

Table 8.1 lists those organizations whose names appeared in the tables charting the largest firms in each media segment for all the foregoing chapters. A review of those tables will show that the basis for determining these firms differs from segment to segment. In the case of book publishers it is revenue; in cable it is number of subscribers; for theater circuits it is number of theaters; for television broadcasters it is potential audience for its stations; and for newspaper and magazine publishers, it is circulation. Such measures appear to be most valid as benchmarks to indicate the degree of impact a given set of players has on the diversity of *content* that is available. Also, in some media segments it seemed appropriate to in-

451

Table 8.1: Leading Firms in One or More Media Segments, with Other Media Holdings, 1981

Company	News-papers	Broad-casting	Cable TV	Magazines	Books	Theatrical Film[1]
Leader in Four Media:						
Newhouse	+		+	+	+	
Leader in Three Media:						
CBS Inc.		+	0	+	+	0
Cox[2]	+	+	+			
Time Inc.	0	0	+	+	+	
Times Mirror Co.	+	0	+	0	+	
Leader in Two Media:						
Gannett	+	+				
Hearst	+	0		+	0	
McGraw-Hill				+	+	
New York Times Co.	+	0	0	+	0	
Reader's Digest Assn.				+	+	
E. W. Scripps[3]	+	+				
Storer Broadcasting		+	+			
Tribune Co.	+	+	0			
Warner Communications			+		0	+
Washington Post Co.	0	+		+	0	
Westinghouse		+	+			
Leader in One Medium:						
Allied Artists						+
American Broadcasting Cos.		+		0	0	
American Multi Cinema						+
Avco-Embassy Pictures[5]						+
Bonneville		+				
Capital Cities Communications	0	+		0		
Charter Co.				+		
Columbia Pictures Industries		0				+
Continental Cablevision			+			
Doubleday		0	0		+	
Dow Jones Co.	+		0	0	0	
Encyclopaedia Britannica					+	
Field Enterprises	0	+				
Gaylord Broadcasting Co.	0	+				
General Cinema			0			+
General Electric		+				
Grolier					+	
Gulf + Western					0	+
Harcourt Brace Jovanovich				0	+	
Inner City		+				
Knight-Ridder	+	0	0		0	
Macmillan					+	

Table 8.1: (continued)

Company	News-papers	Broad-casting	Cable TV	Magazines	Books	Theatrical Film[1]
Leader in One Medium: (continued)						
MCA Inc.				0	0	+
Meredith	0			+	0	
Metro-Goldwyn-Mayer						+
Metromedia		+				
Playboy Enterprises				+	0	
Plough		+				
Plitt Theatres						+
Prentice-Hall					+	
RCA		+				
RKO General[4]		+	0			
Rogers UA Cablesystems			+			
Sammons Communications			+			
San Juan Racing		+				
Scholastic Magazines				+	0	
Scott & Fetzer[6]					+	
SFN Cos.					+	
Taft Broadcasting		+				
Tele-Communications, Inc.	0		+			
Thomson Newspapers[7]	+					
Triangle Publishing				+		
Twentieth Century-Fox	0					+
United Artists Theatre Circuit						+
United Cable			+			
Viacom International	0		+			
Walt Disney Productions						+
Ziff Davis	0			+		

Key: + = Leading firm.
      0 = Area of other holdings.

[1] Production, distribution or exhibition.

[2] Includes interests of Cox family, including Cox Enterprises and 40% interest in Cox Communications.

[3] Includes Scripps-Howard Newspapers and Scripps Broadcasting.

[4] Parent is General Tire Co. In 1982 RKO lost the license for WNAC-TV in Boston.

[5] Avco-Embassy Pictures was sold in December 1981 to Embassy Communications, jointly owned by Norman Lear and Jerry Perenchio.

[6] Parent of World Book-Childcraft International.

[7] Controlling interest held by International Thomson Organisation, Ltd., which has other media interests.

Source: Compiled from lists in Chapters 2-7, with corrections where known through Dec. 31, 1981.

clude more firms than in others, so the film production/distribution list contained only the top nine, while in less concentrated segments, such as cable, the list was longer. For these and other reasons, Table 8.1 should not be viewed as the final authority on every aspect of media ownership. Nonetheless, it does provide a useful glimpse into the degree of conglomerate concentration across the media segments.

Sixty-four organizations are identified. Most are clearly recognizable as firms in the mass media business. Seven names, however, are of firms whose media interests represent a relatively small part of diverse holdings. These are (with their media interests): Westinghouse (cable and broadcasting), Charter Co. (magazines), General Electric (broadcasting), Gulf + Western (film production/distribution, books), Plough (broadcasting), General Tire (broadcasting) and Scott & Fetzer (books).

Perhaps one of the more useful findings of this book is that while there are many firms with major media holdings, few firms are predominant in more than one of the major media segments. Only one combination, the holdings of the Newhouse family, shows up as a lead player in four of the six media segments covered in this volume. Newhouse's positions in cable and book publishing are both of recent vintage: the company divested itself of its broadcast holdings in 1980 to deploy into cable and plunged into book publishing with its 1981 acquisition of Random House, purchased from RCA.

Four media conglomerates span as many as three segments. Of these, Time Inc. is perhaps the most successful; it is the leading book and magazine publisher in terms of revenue, and owns one of the largest cable systems in the country. Time Inc. has also been in the newspaper business, but closed down its major holding, *The Washington Star,* after failing to make it economically viable. The company has also been in and out of the theatrical film production business, and it is currently involved in financing films for its Home Box Office pay television service.

The Cox holdings actually reflect the role of the Cox family. Cox Enterprises is a privately owned firm that owns 19 daily newspapers. Cox Communications, which includes Cox Cable as a subsidiary, is a separate, publicly owned firm. However, as will be seen in Table 8.2, the Cox family owns 40% of the stock and therefore can be presumed to exercise control. Both CBS and Times Mirror Co. have media interests that span a broad range, but they are major players in only three of them.

Other well-known media companies, while perhaps considered to be lead players in a particular media segment, nonetheless are not significant participants in more than one or two segments. The Washington Post Co., for example, though most visible as a newspaper publisher, actually owned only two papers (albeit one a very influential one) in 1982 after selling off its Trenton, NJ paper. Its status as a major magazine publisher does not come from being a group owner, but from its ownership of a single, successful magazine, *Newsweek.* (Its 1980 start-up, *Inside Sports,* was sold in 1982.) Only as a broadcaster is the company a group owner.

Similarly, Gannett, though considered a giant in the newspaper segment and a leading player in the broadcasting sector, has no substantial involvement in other areas. Hearst, E.W. Scripps, Warner Communications, the New York Times Co., McGraw-Hill and Tribune Co. are among the media giants who have significant holdings in just two sectors.

In total, in 1981 48 of the 64 organizations could be considered substantial players in only one media segment. These include the major motion picture studios, some of the largest newspaper publishers and the owner of one of the three primary commercial television networks.

Table 8.1 does not tell the whole story of media ownership. It does not deal with the issues of cross-media ownership or one-newspaper cities, nor does it identify certain segments within the broad media categories that may be substantially concentrated (e.g., mass market paperback books). But it should help dispel the notion that a handful of gatekeepers has a tight grip on the channels of content production and/or distribution in the United States. To the extent that there is some overlap in function (for content providers, consumers, and, where appropriate, for advertisers), the traditional mass media business as a whole is controlled by a sizable cadre of rather diverse organizations.

WHO ARE THE PRINCIPAL STOCKHOLDERS
OF THE MEDIA COMPANIES?

Most of the media-owning companies are themselves owned by scattered and unseen investors. Control is often in the hands of stockholders who own far less than a majority of the stock. Several of the largest companies, however, are privately held, so that there are few public records identifying the owners.

Privately Owned Firms

Of the 16 firms that are leaders in two or more media segments, six are basically privately held. This includes Newhouse, which is not actually a single firm but a network of interlocking corporations ultimately owned by Advance Publications Inc., the company that publishes the *Staten Island*

*Advance.** It is generally assumed that this closely controlled corporation is owned directly or through trusts by the children and relatives of the late S.I. Newhouse.

Cox family holdings have already been shown to consist of a privately held newspaper company and control over a publicly held broadcasting/cable company. The Hearst Corp. is also closely held. Its interests include mining and ranch lands in addition to its more visible media parts. Little is known about its ownership structure, other than that its stock is probably scattered among the Hearst family. The Reader's Digest Association was founded by and for many years owned by De Witt and Lila Wallace. Presumably ownership is still in the family.

E.W. Scripps Co., like Cox, is privately held, but Scripps Broadcasting is a publicly held firm in which Scripps interests have a substantial share. The Tribune Co., although still private, has had its stock dispersed over several generations of McCormicks and Pattersons. Since the early 1970s it has been making public some of its financial results, such as revenues and profits. It has even published a glossy annual report for its stockholders. This has led to periodic speculation that the company intended to become publicly owned. There was talk that some stockholders wanted a "market" for their holdings, which otherwise were not very liquid. As of mid-1982, however, the company remained private.

Other privately held companies in Table 8.1 include Doubleday (which over the years has experienced some internal bickering among its relatively large number of owners, leading to some leaks regarding its financial results), and Field Enterprises, owned by the Field brothers. Sammons is the largest privately held cable system. Twentieth Century-Fox, which had long been a publicly held company, was 23% owned by Chris-Craft Industries and 7.3% controlled by Tandem Productions, neither of which pleased Fox management. But in 1981, a private company controlled by Marvin Davis, who made his money in oil, bought all Fox stock for about $700 million and made the company private. Fox's broadcasting properties, however, were spun off into a new, publicly owned company, United Television, Inc., of which Chris-Craft owns about 32%. Ziff Corp., the holding company for Ziff Davis, is closely held. William Ziff is the chief executive of the company that bears his name and control rests presumably with him.

---

*See N.R. Kleinfeld, "RCA Agrees to Sell Random House to Newhouse for $65-$70 million," *The New York Times,* February 2, 1980, p. A1; and "S.I. Newhouse and Sons: America's Most Profitable Publisher," *Business Week,* January 26, 1976, pp. 56-68.

Publicly Owned Corporations

Table 8.2 itemizes the individuals and institutions that are the major stockholders of selected publicly owned media companies. Holdings, especially those of institutions, change regularly, so that the figures on the table should not be accepted as absolute, except as of the date cited.

Nonetheless, three conclusions emerge from studying this table. First, ownership among the various media is widely dispersed. There is no evidence that a few individuals have meaningful control in several media companies. Some institutions, notably J.P. Morgan & Co., Inc. and The Capital Group, Inc. funds, do have substantial holdings in several of the largest media companies, but even these holdings are only in a handful of companies.

Second, many of the publicly owned companies are still controlled by the founders or their heirs. Often this is done through trusts for descendants of the founders. Such arrangements are evident among the Chandlers of the Times Mirror Co., the Grahams of The Washington Post Co., the Sulzbergers of The New York Times Co., Hugh Hefner of Playboy Enterprises, the Knight and Ridder family interests of Knight-Ridder Co., and the Bancroft family of Dow Jones & Co., Inc., to name a few.

Finally, Table 8.2 suggests and Table 8.3 confirms that, collectively, financial institutions own or control a substantial portion of the publicly held media companies, ranging from 44% in the newspaper segment to 33% of the film production and distribution companies.

The Role of Financial Institutions

A few words about financial institutions may be in order here, to better understand the nature of the control over the media they may or may not exert. Financial institutions include trust departments of banks, insurance companies, pension funds and mutual stock funds. They generally buy stocks and other securities for two reasons. In the case of banks, stocks are usually held for customers who have trust funds or similar accounts for which the bank has fiduciary responsibility. Thus, the shares in any given company are held for many individual customers, though they might be lumped into a single holding for the record. Depending on the arrangement with the bank, the individuals may or may not care about voting the stock held for them. For example, of the 2.3 million Westinghouse Electric shares managed by Capital Group, it owned none for itself and had voting authority for 1 million shares, or about 1.2%. This pattern is the rule rather than the exception.

Life insurance companies can invest some of their assets in common

Table 8.2: Largest Stockholders in Selected Publícly Owned Media
Companies, 1980–1981[1]

Company	Stockholders	Percent Ownership
American Broadcasting Cos.	The Capital Group, Inc.	7.1%
	Tisch family-Loew's Corp.	6.5
	Wells Fargo & Co.	4.6
	Pioneering Management	2.5
	Leonard Goldenson	1.4
CBS Inc.	Chase Manhattan Bank	8.9
	Bankers Trust Co.	8.2
	William Paley	5.6
	State Street Research	5.4
	Manufacturers Hanover Trust Co.	5.0
	Batterymarch Financial	4.5
	Prudential Insurance	4.2
	J.P. Morgan & Co., Inc.	2.4
	College Retirement Equities Fund (CREF)	2.1
Capital Cities Communications	Investment Corp. of America	3.2
	Morgan Guaranty Trust	3.2
Columbia Pictures Industries	Redstone family	7.1
Cox Communications[2]	Barbara Cox Anthony	13.6
	Anne Cox Chamber	13.4
	Dayton Trust	11.8
Dow Jones & Co., Inc.	Bancroft family, incl.	
	Jane B. Cook, Jessie B. Cox	59.3
	James H. Ottaway, Sr.	5.0
Gannett Co., Inc.	Gannett Foundation	11.4
	Linder family/American Financial Corp.	7.4
	Paul Miller	4.1
	CREF	2.3
General Cinema	Richard Smith and family	25.0
	Stoneman family	8.8[3]
Gulf + Western	American Financial Corp.	7.9
	Charles Bluhdorn	5.2
Knight-Ridder Newspapers	Knight family	29.5
	Ridder family	6.8
	The Capital Group, Inc.	6.6
	First National Bank of Akron	5.0
MCA, Inc.	Jules Stein estate	15.8
	Lew Wasserman	8.1

Table 8.2: (continued)

Company	Stockholders	Percent Ownership
McGraw-Hill, Inc.	McGraw family	20.0%
	J.P. Morgan & Co., Inc.	6.2
	Donaldson Lufkin & Jenrette	3.2
	CREF	2.4
Meredith Corp.	E.T. Meredith, III	19.2
	Iowa-Des Moines National Bank	13.6
	Mildred M. Bohen	11.0
	Barbara B. Pfeifer	8.4
	Frederick B. Henry	5.3
Metro-Goldwyn-Mayer Film Co.	Kirk Kerkorian	54.0
Metromedia	John W. Kluge	15.6
	Prudential	5.0
The New York Times Co.	Sulzberger family, trust	27.4 (A)[4]
	of Adolph S. Ochs	75.9 (B)
	Cowles Communications, Inc.	22.6 (A)
	Atalanta Corp.	9.3 (A)
Playboy Enterprises, Inc.	Hugh M. Hefner	70.5
Prentice-Hall, Inc.	U.S. Trust Co.	13.1
	FMR Corp.	2.3
	Oppenheimer Co.	2.1
RCA Corp.	Bankers Trust Co.	7.7
	J.P. Morgan & Co., Inc.	4.6
	CREF	4.4
	Merrill, Lynch	4.3
SFN Cos.	J.P. Morgan & Co., Inc.	6.3
	Northern Trust	4.4
	The Capital Group, Inc.	3.0
	U.S. Trust	2.6
Storer Broadcasting Co.	Detroit Trust (trustee)	4.9
	Peter Storer	3.3
Tele-Communications, Inc.	Kearns Tribune Co.	6.0-7.0
Time Inc.	Arthur Temple family	10.6
	The Capital Group, Inc.	6.0
	Henry Luce Foundation	5.7
	J.P. Morgan & Co., Inc.	3.2
	Fayez Sarofim	2.7
	Equitable Life	2.1
Times Mirror Co.	Chandler family	30.7
	J.P. Morgan & Co., Inc.	4.7

Table 8.2: (continued)

Company	Stockholders	Percent Ownership
Times Mirror Co. (continued)	The Capital Group, Inc.	4.0%
	Mellon Bank	2.8
	CREF	2.4
Tribune Co.[5]	R.R. McCormick Trust	19.9
	James P. Cowles	8.9
Twentieth Century-Fox	Marvin Davis interests	100.0
United Artists Theatre Circuit	Naify family	56.0
Warner Communications, Inc.	Putnam funds	6.5
	Fayez Sarofim	4.0
	Dreyfus funds	2.3
	Bankers Trust Co.	2.1
	Steven Ross	1.2
The Washington Post Co.	Katharine Graham	54.8 (A)[6]
		3.5 (B)
	Donald E. Graham	52.2 (A)
		19.9 (B)
	Berkshire Hathaway, Inc.	16.6 (B)[7]
	J.P. Morgan & Co., Inc.	11.8 (B)
	American Security Bank	7.6 (B)
	Eugene Meyer, III	7.3 (B)
Westinghouse Electric Co.	The Capital Group, Inc.	2.8
	J.P. Morgan & Co., Inc.	2.7

[1] Ownership data taken from various sources, as noted, for 1980 and 1981. The percent of stock does not necessarily equal voting control of the stock, as it may be held by a financial institution for many individuals. See explanation in text.

[2] Cox Enterprises, a separate corporation which includes 19 daily newspapers, is 98% owned by the Cox family.

[3] In 1982, General Cinema bought a sizable block of stock in Heublein Co., a distiller. In defense, Heublein started buying a substantial interest in General Cinema.

[4] Class A stock (A) elects 30% of the Board of Directors and has other limited voting rights. Class B stock (B) elects 70% of the Board and has unlimited voting rights. Both classes share equally in dividends and in liquidation. Atalanta Corp. purchased 78% of its 9.3% share of the stock for its clients, most of the remainder for company co-owner Martin T. Sosnoff.

[5] Tribune Co. is not a publicly owned firm, but some financial records are made public. The McCormick Trust stock is voted by Stanton Cook, chief executive officer, and R.M. Hunt.

Table 8.2: (continued)

[6] Class A stock (A) has unlimited voting rights. The shares listed include sole voting and sole investment power as well as shared voting and investment power. Class B stock (B) has limited voting rights and elects 30% of the Board of Directors. Both Katharine Graham and Donald Graham, as well as other holders of Class A stock, have rights to convert portions of it to Class B stock.

[7] Berkshire Hathaway is controlled by Warren E. Buffett. Buffett also owns the *Buffalo Evening News* in New York, through the Blue Chip Stamp Co. He also controlled .55% of Knight-Ridder, 8% of Affiliated Publications (publisher of *The Boston Globe*), 4% of Media General, Inc. (publisher of newspapers in Richmond, VA, Tampa, FL and Winston-Salem, NC), and almost 1% of Times Mirror Co. In 1982 he was elected to the Board of the Omaha WorldHerald Co., but as this is an employee-owned newspaper, he owns no stock in it. He is also a director of the Washington Post Co.

Sources: Proxy statements; FCC form 323; *Corporate Data Exchange Stock Ownership Directory, 1981*; *Editor & Publisher*; *The Wall Street Journal*.

stocks. These investments not only contribute assets that get applied to paying out death benefits to policyholders, but more important, they are also used to fund the annuities the insurance companies sell. Mutual funds invest in a portfolio of stocks, and they vote their shares in accordance with the best interests of the many stockholders in the mutual fund itself.

Pension funds, both public and private, invest in stocks and bonds to increase their assets so they can fund later payouts. Among the largest pension funds with holdings in the media businesses are: the College Retirement Equities Fund (CREF), the not-for-profit organization that manages most of the retirement funds for college and university faculty and staff; Ohio Public Employees Retirement System; the California Public Employees & Teachers Retirement System; and similar funds from cities and states around the country. Some corporations, such as General Electric Co., set up their own endowed pension trusts.

Some other institutions show up as stockholders in media (and, of course, other) industry groups. University and charitable foundation endowments are one category. Stanford University, for example, at one point owned .72% of Times Mirror Co. and .22% of Knight-Ridder. At least one church, the Corporation of Church of Jesus Christ, owns .76% of Times Mirror. Occasionally, government units may also invest in these companies when they have some excess cash they may not need for a while. The New York City Comptroller's Office at one time owned .63% of Time Inc.

In some cases, investors, often smaller pension funds, hire outside management firms to advise them on investments and handle the buying and

Table 8.3: Major Institutional Holders of Media Company Stocks[1]

Institution	Media Holdings	Percent Held
J.P. Morgan & Co., Inc.	SFN Cos.	6.3%
	McGraw-Hill, Inc.	6.2
	The Washington Post Co.	11.8 (B)[2]
	Times Mirror Co.	4.7
	RCA Corp.	4.6
	Time Inc.	3.2
	Westinghouse Electric Co.	2.7
	CBS Inc.	2.4
The Capital Group, Inc.	American Broadcasting Cos.	7.1
	Knight-Ridder Newspapers	6.6
	Time Inc.	6.0
	Times Mirror Co.	4.0
	SFN Cos.	3.0
	Westinghouse Electric Co.	2.8
College Retirement Equities Fund (CREF)	RCA Corp.	4.4
	Times Mirror Co.	2.4
	McGraw-Hill, Inc.	2.4
	Gannett Co., Inc.	2.3
	CBS Inc.	2.1
	American Broadcasting Cos.	1.5
	Dow Jones & Co., Inc.	1.5
Bankers Trust Co.	CBS Inc.	8.2
	RCA Corp.	7.7
	Warner Communications, Inc.	2.1
Prudential Insurance Co.	Metromedia	5.0
	CBS Inc.	4.2
	Knight-Ridder Newspapers	1.8
	American Broadcasting Cos.	1.6
	Gannett Co., Inc.	1.3
Manufacturers Hanover Trust Co.	CBS Inc.	5.0
	McGraw-Hill, Inc.	2.1
	Knight-Ridder Newspapers	2.0
	American Broadcasting Cos.	1.1
Donaldson Lufkin & Jenrette	McGraw-Hill, Inc.	3.1
	American Broadcasting Cos.	1.1
New York State Teachers Retirement	Knight-Ridder Newspapers	1.9
	McGraw-Hill, Inc.	1.8
	CBS Inc.	0.7

Table 8.3: (continued)

Institution	Media Holdings	Percent Held
Institutional Holdings as Percent of All Publicly Owned Media Companies:		
Broadcasting companies		35%
Newspaper companies		44
Book publishing companies		37
Magazine publishing companies		37
Film production & distribution companies		33

[1] Includes holdings voted by the institutions as well as holdings which are controlled by individuals, other institutions, or trusts.

[2] Class B common stock.

Sources: Proxy statements; FCC form 323; *Corporate Data Exchange Stock Ownership Directory, 1981*; Media General Financial Services, accessed via Dow Jones News/Retrieval.

selling of securities. The Capital Group, Inc., for example, is a holding company that includes Capital Guardian Trust Co., which is a trustee and investment manager of large institutional accounts. It is in this role that The Capital Group and J.P. Morgan & Co., for example, show up as major stockholders in at least six and eight, respectively, of the leading media companies.

What are the implications for control of the media by these financial institutions? If we are looking for evidence of direct control, the likelihood is slight. Investment managers choose to buy stock in a company because they have carefully evaluated the current management, its capability, the company's potential for growth, and its lines of business, among other factors. They invest because of what the company already *is* doing, not what they want it to do. Investment managers are not operating managers; they have no interest in dictating policy, editorial or otherwise, to the firms in which they own stock. If they do not like the directions being taken by companies in which they have investments, they will sell their stock rather than try to force management to adopt different policies.

The executives of some publicly owned companies will admit, however, that the institutional investors do have an indirect role in shaping their own policies. The executives, who often own stock themselves (acquired as options or otherwise), are concerned with the long-term price of their company's shares. This factor may be considered in deliberations on a wide variety of decisions, from how much money to allocate to editorial coverage to the level of dividends and the nature of expansion. It creates needs to fulfill short-term expectations for earnings and long-term requirements for viability and growth. However, it is unlikely that these executives are looking over their shoulders as they make basic editorial decisions. Institutional investors are most often looking for long-term growth. They are not overly concerned with the potentially controversial content of some successful movies or best-selling books, nor with the lack of intelligence evidenced in top-rated television shows, as long as these channels continue to produce revenues.

This decision-making process is at the heart of the private enterprise system and, like just about any other economic system that societies have tried, has its benefits and drawbacks. It is indeed hard to imagine an economic system in which conflicting pressures and influences are not present to some degree, although the source of these varies, depending on who is actually in control. But whether it is government, workers, or some other group, the controlling forces will expect the media to reflect their values, which may or may not be the "right" ones.

WHO THEN OWNS THE MEDIA?

The media industry overall has been shown to be widely controlled by a substantial number of firms. New technology has brought new members into the ranks. A list similar to that in Table 8.1 for the year 1920 would be much shorter and would likely include names that no longer exist, such as Munsey, Curtis or Pulitzer. Even a 1960 listing would not have been able to include firms such as Continental Cablevision or Tele-Communications, Inc. Thus, new technology has created its own democratic process in the world of media ownership and gateways to information.

Nor do these 64 companies exhaust the universe of firms with significant or influential media holdings. Bantam Books is a very visible publisher. Farrar, Straus and Giroux, an independent trade book publisher, plays a role in the stream of ideas far in excess of its relatively small size. Similarly, Ted Turner's innovative Cable News Network and his CNN II news headline service play increasingly important roles in the media mix. Magazine and newsletter publishers, many of these relatively small companies, play substantial roles in informing their readers and often influencing public and private policy. For example, a report in the *New England Journal of Medicine* may have an impact far beyond its limited circulation. The list could go on, naming smaller media groups and independent producers or carriers of content.

Tables 8.2 and 8.3, moreover, indicate that, far from cabalistic control by a small group of owners, the media companies themselves are held largely by their founding families together with a substantial number of institutional investors interested not in control but in long-term growth and intermediate term earnings. There is breadth in their holdings, in that most institutions seem to prefer to diversify by taking relatively small positions in a relatively large number of companies. The portion that is not directly controlled by institutions or by families of the founders is even further distributed among the public at large. CBS Inc., for example, though 62% of its shares are held by institutions (again, some of which is in trust for individuals), has nearly 31,000 stockholders. Westinghouse has 180,500 owners, while much smaller Metromedia, Inc. has 6300 stock owners.

Whether or not the quality or diversity of information in the United States is great enough is not a question that can be answered here. Each individual must set his or her own standard. To the question, "How few owners would be too few?" again the answer must be, "It depends." Clearly, however, within the broad boundaries established on the one hand by the First Amendment and on the other hand by economic structure that has evolved to implement it, the evidence of ownership patterns would appear to support the argument that the underlying structure of the system is able to encourage a robust exchange and competitive flow of ideas, entertainment, information and commerce throughout the media.

9

Conclusion: How Few Is Too Few?

by Benjamin .M. Compaine

The most salient conclusion that can be derived from the information presented in the previous chapters is that the traditional segments labeled the "mass media industry" do not exhibit many of the characteristics of classical economic concentration. With the exception of theatrical film distribution, the concentration levels of the four, eight, or 20 largest participants in the various industry segments are well below those found in industry in general. Nor have the percentages in the older media businesses changed very much over the past 40 years.

In the most conservative determination of oligopoly, proposed by Carl Kaysen and Donald Turner, the eight largest firms would have at least a third of sales and the 20 largest no more than 75%.[1] This is called a type II oligopoly. None of the print industries meets this standard. The cable system business in 1981, however, could be considered a type II oligopoly if the percentage of all wired households accounted for by the largest multiple system operators was the measure used. Broadcasters have long had limitations placed on their ownership of stations. Moreover, the percentage of industry profits accruing to the three major commercial networks has decreased from 45% in 1955 to 32% in 1980. Only the theatrical film production and distribution segment truly meets the Kaysen and Turner standard of oligopoly, with the eight largest distributors alone accounting for 91% of domestic receipts.

From an antitrust viewpoint, an industry must reach a type I oligopoly, at which time the eight largest firms have 50% of receipts and the 20 largest at least 75%, before the concentration allows firms to charge prices and make profits above competitive levels and to misallocate resources.

There are two weaknesses in using this approach to judge the degree of concentration in the mass communications industry. One defect is that this standard is based on a presumption of a national market. It fails to measure concentration at the local level, such as the case of a one-newspaper city or an exclusive cable franchise.

The second weakness is related and is perhaps more crucial to those most concerned with media concentration. This is that a narrow economic criterion ignores the question of the acceptable number of gatekeepers—those who control access to what becomes the content of the media. It is widely held that the mass media are powerful purveyors of opinion, culture and socialization. In this perspective, the concern is that diversity is constrained by a small group of unseen executives in corporations seeking only to maximize profits.

The key question is thus: How few is too few? Here, the traditional anti-trust view of concentration and the broader sociopolitical attitudes are at loggerheads. Presumably, the number of acceptable gatekeepers is some number greater than the number that would trigger antitrust action over economic concentration. A policy that judges concentration in the mass communications industry by a different antitrust standard than that used for other industries would require explicit recognition of the media business as unique.

NEED FOR NEW DEFINITIONS?

Just as we may have to recast the operational definition of concentration from that of the objective standards of antitrust law, so may relevant markets for the media have to be reformulated in recognition of the changing nature of the mass communications industry. It is myopic to be concerned with concentration in the television business, the newspaper business or any given segment if the true concern is with promoting diversity of conduits for information and knowledge. Less attention needs to be given to determining the threshold of concentration for each individual medium; instead, consideration of concentration should focus on the number of owners in the mass communications industry overall. From this perspective, the newsweekly magazines have direct competition from all newspapers, as well as local and national television news programs and all news radio stations. Motion picture distributors clearly compete with television producers, but also with book publishers and certain periodicals. Special interest magazines, already knocking heads in price with mass market paperback books, may increasingly find themselves covering the same topics and even competing for advertiser dollars with video disc recordings and programs distributed by cable operators.

One development that serves to illustrate the increased and real inter-media competitiveness is the effects of the extended newspaper strikes in New York, Philadelphia, St. Louis and other cities in recent years. Before radio, no newspapers meant no regular news or advertising sources. Now, even a city like New York can lose the services of its three major newspapers for three months (August to early November 1978) and notice barely a ripple. Advertisers turned to television, radio, local magazines and zoned editions of national magazines. Consumers made use of all-news radio stations, the national news magazines, and the extended newscasts on local television. Retailers reported little impact on sales. This is not to say that people did not miss the unique features that newspapers provide, but with the wide array of media available, information kept flowing. Even residents of smaller towns and cities would find many of the same options.

Other evidence illustrates how the traditional structural boundaries of the media industries are no longer as hard and fast as was once believed. As noted in Chapter 2, newspaper publishers and wire services are starting to distribute their content over telephone or cable-based systems to subscribers around the country. Chapter 6 explained how some local television stations are made available via satellite and cable to viewers a continent away, thereby upsetting traditional market boundary descriptions. New participants are continually entering the feature film business, able to bypass the theatrical film distribution network by marketing their output instead to television, pay television and offline via disc and cassette distributors. Certainly, intermedia competition is not absolute. But the overlap is sufficient to explain shifts in the roles of the traditional media.

Thus, it may be proposed that the relevant market must be redefined more broadly. First, the measure of diversity of ownership of the media could be the full range of all *content* providers, regardless of the process or format(s) used for distributing or displaying their product. A second measure is the sum of the alternative and often interchangeable conduits for distributing the content—i.e., over the air (including traditional broadcast radio and TV, multipoint distribution services, direct broadcast satellite), via terrestrial paths (telephone, cable, microwave), or physical distribution via private or public postal-type services (video cassettes, magazines, newspapers, etc.).

Television is More Than Broadcasting

Television and radio have faced far stricter content regulation than have the print media because of the presumed scarcity of the electromagnetic spectrum. Limits exist not only on how many outlets a single firm can own but indirectly on the content that can be broadcast. Even so, much of the population has access to far more television and radio than is generally appreciated. For example, more than 40% of households have access to at least five broadcast stations without the aid of cable. The 10 largest markets, which account for one-third of television households, have access to an average of nearly 10 UHF and VHF stations.[2] Though much of the programming on the independent stations consists of old movies, reruns and syndicated fare, this is a matter of economics, not scarcity.

(Radio stations are even more abundant. The 10 largest markets average nearly 43 stations each, while the 41st to 50th markets average nearly 21 stations each. Indeed, the factor limiting more radio stations is again not spectrum scarcity in many smaller cities, but economic considerations.)

In the 191st- to 200th-ranked markets (Jackson, Tennessee to Twin Falls, Idaho) there are one or two local television stations and between three and 11 radio stations (with a median of 5.5). But these smaller markets have a median of 54% of households wired for cable, more than twice the national average.[3]

The options for distribution of video programming are far greater in the 1980s than they were when the Communications Act of 1934 was designed. Table 9.1 shows evidence of the change. The number of channels in cable systems is increasing as older systems are upgraded. Sales of video cassette recorders in 1981 were over 1.2 million units, nearly 75% above 1980 sales. Also in 1981, Satellite Television Corp. (a subsidiary of Communications Satellite Corp.—Comsat), filed with the FCC for permission to establish a three- (and perhaps more) channel DBS television service. In 1982, Microband Corp. of America (a subsidiary of Tymshare, Inc.), sought FCC approval to set up a 15-channel MDS (microwave) television service in cities throughout the United States, in effect competing with cable and the proposed direct broadcast satellite service. Moreover, in response to its proposal to open up low-power VHF television across the country, the FCC was inundated with more than 5000 applications for licenses in 1981.

More Programmers and Choices

If, when, and which of these and other proposed or prototype television services actually become available is secondary to the point that technology has already expanded the choices available to media users and has provided opportunity for an expanded number of programmers. Even more important, perhaps, is the beginning of a vastly increased range of programming, as seen in Chapter 6. Special interest and targeted content is becoming possible for video, as the need to cater to the mass interest on a highly restricted number of traditional broadcast channels ceases to be critical.

Nor should we be surprised to find that much of the programming is being offered by familiar names, like Time Inc., CBS or Hearst. They and their competitors are, after all, in the content business. The magazine and

Table 9.1: Status of Video and Audio Outlets, 1981

Rank	Market	Cable % of Homes Passed	Cable Average Number of Channels	MDS Channels	Total UHF & VHF Channels	Video Cassette Players	Radio Stations
1.	New York City	28%	29	3	14	177,554	39
2.	Los Angeles	23	23	3	18	115,314	32
3.	Chicago	6	27	2	11	78,652	39
4.	Philadelphia	23	27	2	10	65,011	30
5.	San Francisco	59	23	2	12	52,861	28
6.	Boston	19	23	2	9	51,367	23
7.	Detroit	4	27	2	7	44,335	23
8.	Washington, D.C.	8	29	1	7	38,580	20
9.	Cleveland	32	20	3	5	36,465	21
10.	Dallas-Ft. Worth	1	35	2	6	33,465	20
15.	Seattle-Tacoma	41	23	2	7	26,857	26
20.	Denver	13	37	1	5	21,315	23
25.	Kansas City	30	30	1	6	19,183	19
30.	Nashville	3	16	1	5	16,839	17
40.	Orlando	44	18	2	5	13,855	12
50.	Dayton	51	30	1	4	11,936	12

Source: CBS Inc., used with permission. Video cassette players estimated, based on national penetration times television households in each market. Current to August 1981.

book businesses have long been hotbeds of competition. Now it appears that a similar opportunity is emerging for video. Religious broadcasters were among the first to take advantage of cable operators' needs for inexpensive programming. Christian Broadcasting Network is the most ambitious of these. A Spanish-language network, SIN, also provides Galavision, a Spanish-language pay service. Black Entertainment Television has been slowly expanding its hours of programming. Applied Communications proposed a network of 15 low-power VHF stations in the South featuring Afro-American programming. Children's television, long a sore point among critics of traditional TV programming, has been improved with Nickelodeon from Warner Amex, Calliope on USA Network, and a host of other ventures from ABC, Comsat, Scholastic Magazines and a joint venture of Taft Broadcasting and Tele-Communications, Inc. Ethnic, international, regional and educational video programming have also been advanced by a broad range of sources. Their plans focus on cable, low-power broadcasting, DBS, and video cassette and disc distribution. Not all of these will come to fruition, while others not yet conceived will become reality. But the impasse in video distribution appears to be on the verge of being broadened significantly.

"PROCESS" IS THE BOTTLENECK FOR CONTENT

There never seems to be a dearth of opinions from which to construct media content. The breadth of interests of Americans seems inexhaustible; a look at the list of nearly 10,000 consumer, professional, association and scholarly periodical titles is ready evidence of that. The limitation has generally been in avenues of distribution for the content. The greatest opportunities have been for those providers of content who have guaranteed access to a means of distribution. For those satisfied with a printed format, the U.S. Postal Service has provided a universal common carriage; hence the ubiquity of newsletters and periodicals.

Relying on other, private forms of physical delivery begins to restrict opportunities for dissemination. A magazine publisher that depends on newsstand sales must obtain the cooperation of one of a small number of national distributors. In most parts of the country, the actual delivery of periodicals (and mass market paperback books) is in the hands of a wholesaler who is often the exclusive agent in that area. To the extent that these distributors make decisions not to take on a new title, opportunity for this form of distribution is narrowed. It could also probably be demonstrated that a publisher of several periodicals or books has a better chance of getting a new title accepted for distribution than an independent publisher with no other products. The implications of this assertion can cut several ways in the discussion on the effects of media bigness.

Book publishing has also remained relatively diverse in its ownership structure because of access to a common carrier for both promotion and delivery. Many publishers use this avenue exclusively. Once a publisher decides to distribute through retail stores, again the channel narrows somewhat because of the limitations on the number of titles retail bookstores are able to carry—far fewer than the number of eligible titles that are offered.

The extent of the process bottleneck becomes far more pronounced when we look at the electromagnetic spectrum. Indeed, the oft-repeated rationale for the Communications Act of 1934 and its interpretation and extensions through the years has been the spectrum's bottleneck characteristics. This has resulted in far less access to radio and television broadcasting by those with something to say or an interest to promote. Despite the fairness doctrine, reasonable access, equal time for political candidates and "public interest, convenience and necessity" provisions, there has been no common carrier alternative to the television/radio formats.

The telephone and the switched telephone network, of course, have been the universal electromagnetic analogy to the Postal Service. But telephony's one-point-to-one-point structure has usually kept it in a different category from the mass communication processes that have been traditionally referred to as the "mass media." Thus, while broadcasting, telephony and physical delivery are really all terms that describe distribution mechanisms, only the former has ever been accorded the rubric of mass medium. This is no doubt due to the fact that it is the only one of these processes in which the distributor also enjoyed First Amendment rights as an information provider.

Bottlenecks in the "New" Media Picture

A number of developments are now requiring us to reexamine the nature and structure of the distribution end of the media. Having always had an excess of willing content providers, any additions to our supply of processes would presumably add to the diversity available to everyone.

The list of "new" media technologies includes cable, earth satellite, multipoint microwave distribution, fiber optics, viewdata, teletext, video cassettes and video discs. For the most part, these represent either restructuring of older technologies into new uses (such as computers and telecommunications into viewdata), or serve as alternatives for existing channels (such as satellites for terrestrial transmission). The advantage of the new over the old may be simple economics (as in satellite vs. terrestrial broadband), political (as the ability for cable operators to sell untariffed data transmission), social (as in the ability of teletext to provide captioning for the deaf), and, in most cases, combinations of these.

NATIONAL VS. LOCAL DIVERSITY

While the concentration ratios indicate that there is reasonable diversity of ownership of content and distribution on a national level, the situation becomes less clear-cut when focused on a particular geographic market. To wit:

Most cities or towns have a single ownership for the daily newspaper. The network-owned or affiliated television broadcast stations provide additional voices. In large cities, there may be dozens of radio stations, some with overlapping ownership with television broadcasters, but still rather diverse in ownership. The cable systems around the country, however, are local *de facto* monopolies. Though they might have 12, 54, or 108 channels, the franchisee has a monopoly on what goes out on most of these channels and at what cost to the user.

To the extent that cable is not a necessity, what the cable operator charges is not an important societal concern. Presumably, it must bear some relationship to marketplace demands and the high fixed capital cost in construction of the plant. Moreover, as the franchise does have a finite lifetime, it presumably is in the operator's long-term interest to respond to marketplace needs, despite such certain superficial monopoly-like characteristics. Indeed, it has been estimated by analysts that many of the newer big city cable systems now being bid on or installed will cost their operators so much money that they will have a nine or ten year pay-out. That means that the franchisee may not get to see a profit until the last third of its term. It therefore would be presumed to have a strong vested interest in first, charging a rate for basic service that maximizes households connected; and second, in serving its constituents sufficiently well so as to be in a strong position to get the franchise renewed.

Between 1973 and 1979, concentration of subscribers in the eight largest MSOs declined, from 40.3% to 36.5%. By 1981, the eight largest MSOs had inched back up to 39%. This trend reversal was due in part to the huge capital demands required to install systems in the large cities, and costs increased as well because of the demands of franchise boards for more elaborate and state-of-the-art systems for their cities. The older "mom and pop" operators found it difficult to compete in this climate. In addition, many of the older operators were enticed by the substantial sums being bid by the larger companies to acquire cable systems. During this period as well, many newspaper publishers, who had been sitting on the sidelines, decided they had better get a foothold in cable. The New York Times Co., The Boston Globe, Newhouse, and Dow Jones were among the new participants.

All these factors contributed to changing the ownership picture of MSOs. Many of the original participants continued their MSO status but now were in the hands of large parent corporations, such as Time Inc. and Westinghouse. Some of these same corporations initiated or purchased pay services as well, such as Time Inc.'s HBO.

TRENDS IN CONSUMPTION OF THE MASS MEDIA

The development of new media in the past has resulted in changing patterns of consumer and advertiser expenditures for media purchases, although the relative amount of money expended by both sources has remained remarkably constant over the years. This phenomenon has given rise to what Charles Scripps calls the "constancy hypothesis,"[4] which is verified in Tables 9.2 and 9.3.

Since 1933, the amount of money that consumers have spent on media, in the form of purchases of newspapers, magazines, books, television and radio set purchases and repairs, and on movie admissions, has remained level as a percentage of personal consumption expenditures. But the composition of those expenditures has shifted along with the introduction of new media. The proportion of expenditures on newspapers and magazines has remained constant since 1940 and was greater in 1979 than in 1929. The rise in 1933 may well be an aberration caused by Depression-related declines in purchases of radios.

Although audiovisual media account for a similar percentage of expenditures in 1979 as in 1929, the overall trend since 1945 has been upward. Within this category, however, a drastic switch has taken place, as relative expenditures for movie admissions have dropped dramatically in concert with the sizable increases spent on television and radio receivers. The most profound change came in the 1945 to 1950 period, as the end of the war and the introduction of television channeled funds away from movies and into the broadcast area. Another noticeable switch occurred in the 1960s, as color television produced a new wave of consumer investment. In the 1970s, movie admissions increased their share of expenditures as well, as spending for repairs of television and radio sets had been cut in half from their relative 1960 level.

Except for book publishers and theatrical filmmakers, advertisers provide all or most of the financial support for mass media businesses. As with consumer expenditures, advertising outlays have tended to remain at a constant proportion of the Gross National Product, staying near 2% of total goods and services. However, as seen in Table 9.3, the broadcast media have accounted for a slowly increasing share, as first radio and then television drew a considerably greater share from the older print media.

Table 9.2: Percentage of Consumer Spending on Print and Audiovisual Media, Selected Years, 1929-1979

Year	Media Expend. as % of Per. Consump. Exp.	Newspapers, Magazines, Sheet Music	Books & Maps	Total Print	Radio, TV Recv'rs, Records, Instruments	Radio & TV Repairs	Movie Admissions	Total AV Media[1]
1929	3.37%	20.65%	11.86%	32.51%	38.85%	1.00%	27.64%	67.49%
1933	2.76	33.20	12.04	45.24	15.45	1.11	38.19	54.75
1940	2.94	28.26	11.23	39.49	23.70	1.53	35.27	60.50
1945	2.82	28.66	15.44	44.10	10.22	2.61	43.07	55.90
1950	3.25	23.92	10.78	34.70	38.74	4.53	22.02	65.29
1955	2.94	25.10	11.64	36.74	38.53	6.97	17.81	63.31
1960	2.67	25.32	15.06	40.38	39.39	9.25	10.98	59.62
1965	3.00	22.23	15.98	38.21	46.61	8.00	7.19	61.80
1970	2.97	22.33	18.75	41.08	45.38	7.20	6.33	58.91
1975	3.05	23.77	13.68	37.45	48.16	4.46	9.93	62.55
1976	2.94	25.12	11.15	36.27	49.88	4.58	9.27	63.73
1977	3.06	24.14	11.93	36.07	48.66	4.27	11.00	63.93
1978	3.02	24.41	13.26	37.67	47.71	4.18	10.43	62.32
1979	2.89	23.77	13.68	37.45	48.16	4.46	9.93	62.55

[1] Total may not add to 100.00% due to rounding.
Source: U.S. Bureau of Economic Analysis, as published in the Statistical Abstract of the United States, annual and Historical Statistics of the United States, Colonial Times to 1970.

Table 9.3: Share of Advertising in Major Print and Broadcast Media, Selected Years, 1935-1980

Year	Advertising Expenditures (in millions)	As % of GNP	% from Broadcasting	% from Newspapers & Magazines
1935	$1,690	2.34%	6.7%	53.1%
1940	2,088	2.09	10.3	48.5
1945	2,875	1.36	14.7	44.7
1950	5,710	2.00	13.6	45.4
1955	9,194	2.30	17.1	37.9
1960	11,932	2.36	19.1	38.9
1965	15,250	2.22	22.5	36.6
1970	19,550	2.00	25.1	35.8
1975	28,230	1.86	25.6	35.1
1976	33,720	1.99	26.8	34.7
1977	38,120	2.02	26.9	34.9
1978	43,170	2.07	27.0	34.9
1979	49,520	2.09	27.2	35.4
1980	54,480	2.12	27.7	34.3
1981	61,320	2.10	27.5	34.2

[1] Preliminary.

Sources: 1935-1960—*Historical Statistics of the United States, Colonial Times to 1970.* Series T444-471; 1965-1981—*Advertising Age*, as prepared by McCann-Erickson, Inc., New York, for advertising; U.S. Bureau of Economic Analysis for GNP.

Implications

Given the fixed proportion of consumer and advertiser expenditures that appear to be devoted to the media over an extended period, regardless of the condition of the economy and the number of mass media outlets, it may be reasonably assumed that such relationships will continue to hold. This means that if consumers devote large portions of their implicit media budgets to expensive video cassette/disc players or monthly cable fees, they will have to cut back on other media expenditures, perhaps on magazines or books.

Similarly, as advertisers find new outlets for sponsorship, they will be spreading their budgets over more media, giving relatively less to the existing ones. For example, there are already some local merchants advertising on cable channels in some communities, with a likely cutback in the proportion of funds available for newspapers. A truly national cable audience may further scatter the mass audience of network television and also create identifiable market segments that could pull certain advertisers away from special interest magazines.

With this history and the implications for the future, it should not be surprising that owners of businesses in the mass communications industry would want to increase earnings by purchasing more properties or, even more to the point, become involved in the new media. This gives rise to the basic conflict of cross-media ownership and conglomeration that this book addresses. Can the existing media be expected or even obliged to ignore developing media? Is a financially healthy media industry—necessary if we want variety and quality*—at odds with those who see greater diversity and broader access fostered by small enterprises, locally owned and controlled?

The activity of existing media firms broadening their operations into new media areas is consistent with a marketing philosophy popularized by Theodore Levitt's concept of "marketing myopia." This demands that a firm carefully determine its field of operations. Is a newspaper publisher in the business of manufacturing and selling newspapers, or in the business of gathering and disseminating information? Given that choice, the latter would be the logical response. Thus, it would be natural to seek other ways of disseminating the vast quantities of information a newspaper staff can gather: news services, radio and television outlets are several. Similarly, an expertise in assembling and publishing specialized information makes it reasonable to assume that a book publisher would find a natural kinship with magazine publishing, or more recently, programming for video cassette, disc or cable distribution. Producers of theatrical films have found it a short and necessary jump into video programming.

In essence, the recognition of a mass communications industry, as opposed to simply a newspaper, broadcast, magazine, book or film industry lends itself to what has been termed conglomeration.

PUBLIC POLICY CONCERNS

The preceding discussion suggests at least five public policy issues that will require attention in the current decade. As of 1982 they were at different stages of public consciousness and resolution. None have right or wrong solutions.

1. What is the Appropriate Model of Content Regulation?

While all content is afforded equal First Amendment protection, distributors of that content fall into two regulatory categories. Content

---

*This is not to imply that a profitable industry necessarily provides the best quality at all times. Nonetheless, it is unlikely that a weakened industry would provide it.

distributed via print or over a common carrier has nearly absolute protection. Content distributed by broadcast, however, has more limited protection. Thus, a magazine publisher could, for example, repeatedly print articles giving a one-sided view of a particular issue. A radio or television broadcast station would risk loss of its license if it covered an issue with similar bias. Under the provisions, extensions and interpretations of the Communications Act of 1934, broadcasters have been faced with regulations regarding equal time for political candidates, fairness and balance in the treatment of controversial issues, personal attack limitations, etc. Print publishers have no such legal requirements (although the large majority of newspapers do make reasonable efforts to provide such balance and fairness as an *ethical* canon of their business). The difference between the print and broadcast standard of the First Amendment is best summarized in the *Tornillo* and *Red Lion** decisions of the Supreme Court.[5]

But now, with the burgeoning of video processes, the rationale for separate treatment of broadcast content may become obsolete. Moreover, decisions will have to be made on what content regulation is appropriate for cable-originated programming, as well as such hybrid services as over-the-air teletext or DBS.

Consider these possibilities:

- A pay television service distributed via cable transmits a speech by a presidential candidate. Another candidate asks for equal time and the programmer refuses.

- A cable system with two-way capability invites all the legitimate candidates for a local political office to use an hour of time to address viewers. At the end of each hour the cable operator asks viewers whether they wish to extend the program to include call-in questions for the candidate. As a result of varying levels of viewer interest, some candidates end up with more time on the air than others.

- A cable channel shows programs with nudity and/or profanity. Neither would be permitted on conventional broadcast television.

---

*The *Tornillo* decision affirmed the essential First Amendment restriction on government in any prior restraint on content for the print media. The *Red Lion* case, on the other hand, reaffirmed a somewhat different status for broadcast media in that the government did have the right to set certain content guidelines, such as fairness, equal time and right of reply.

- A city has a cable channel devoted exclusively to local government use. The mayor, who is running for re-election, also has a weekly program called "Ask the Mayor." Another mayoral candidate feels the incumbent is using the show for blatantly political purposes and demands equal time. The cable owner denies the request.

- A national cable network shows a documentary that takes an anti-smoking stand. Tobacco interests ask for time to present their case. The network refuses.

If any of these situations had arisen in conventional television broadcasting, a complaint would have been filed with the Federal Communications Commission. And it is very likely that the broadcaster would have been ordered to change his or her decision or remove the offending program from the air. Indeed, failure to do so would result in the broadcaster's license to operate being challenged and perhaps rescinded.

The Federal Election Campaign Act of 1971 made the equal-time provision of the Communications Act of 1934 applicable to cable. But enforcement is difficult. Cable systems have no federal license that can be revoked. And many of the older cable systems do not even have facilities to originate their own programming.

Over-the-air teletext is another area that has already been involved in litigation. Teletext is textual material coded and often transmitted in the vertical blanking interval—that portion of the 525 lines that make up the television picture that can be seen only as a black bar on a badly adjusted television set. With a decoder, users have access to screenfuls of text, as in Great Britain's Ceefax and Oracle services. But who owns the vertical blanking interval? The first attempt to answer this in the courts found that, based on copyright law, it was *not* necessarily owned by the licensee of the channel.[6] And, as in the cable example, what standard of fairness or equal time should be applied to content transmitted by this process?

These are only some of the questions raised in the content area. Their resolution has long-term significance for existing media owners and for the public. In 1981, several FCC commissioners, including the chairman, went on record favoring change. Commissioner Anne Jones said that to support the fairness doctrine based on scarcity was "to blink at reality."[7]

2. What Are the Limits of Cross-Media Ownership?

In 1981, an FCC staff report recommended the elimination of cable cross-ownership rules, except for those prohibiting cable and telephone company combinations.[8] The report concluded that the market for providing cable services was "workably competitive" because "no one firm has significant control over opportunities." The Justice Department, on the other hand, while agreeing with the FCC report that cross-ownership restrictions should be reviewed, warned against broadcast cable cross-ownership, stating that, "Common control of a broadcast station and cable system in the same locality may significantly impair competition in many local markets." Network ownership could also pose "serious anti-competitive problems."[9] In 1980, there were reported to be 31 television stations that held majority interests in cable systems in their broadcast territory.[10]

The cross-ownership question is muddied by the blurring definitions of business. Among the questions that need be considered:

- Is a newspaper defined by a manufacturing process that involves putting ink on paper and physically distributing that paper? Or, is a newspaper publisher one who distributes a package of content in whatever way is technologically and economically appropriate?*

- Should a local publisher be permitted to distribute information in any way that seems appropriate for the audience? If cable is that medium, then should the publisher be allowed access to it—either through reasonable expectation of access to one or more channels or by owning the system?

- Similarly, should a broadcaster be limited to over-the-air transmission if some other method becomes more feasible, especially since cable is beyond being held back by self-serving delaying tactics?

3. What is Vertical Integration?

It would appear useful to rethink the boundaries of industries. In the past we have relied on sometimes outdated standard industrial classifications. These run the risk of becoming ever less meaningful as the practical boundaries of the media blur into one another.

Newspaper publishers have long been vertically integrated. Many have interests in newsprint manufacturing. They all produce much of their own content, buying some from wire services and syndicates, which are often

---

*In many languages—German, French, Norwegian, etc.—the word for "newspaper" does not have as part of it the word for "paper": Zeitung, journal, avis, etc.

owned by newspaper publishers as well. Most daily papers own their own manufacturing facility, and they own the distribution network that gets the papers to the readers.

The broadcasting industry is far less vertically integrated due to regulation, and book and magazine publishers have little economic incentive for integration. But the cable business appears to be taking its cue from the film business. Initially merely distributors of the content of others, they have tried to extend their business to attract the 50% of nonsubscribers whose homes they pass by arranging for additional program content on their own. The long-term question is whether such combinations of program supply and distribution mechanism will lead to a restriction of programming or less than competitive pricing. Or, will the large number of channels that cable operators have to fill insure that even the largest integrated systems will have more than enough room for independent program providers?

There is ample precedent for separating content from process ownership. The television networks still have such restrictions. The courts ordered film distributors to divest ownership of theaters. The telephone industry has by its very nature been prohibited from providing content. That principle was reaffirmed in Senate and House bills that were making their way through Congress prior to the settlement of the antitrust case with AT&T in early 1982.

The importance of content to the cable industry is perhaps highlighted by a merger in 1981 that was treated quite matter-of-factly in the trade press. Tele-Communications, Inc., the large MSO, purchased two daily newspapers in Idaho.[11] At a time when newspaper publishers were running around trying to buy into cable, that was a distinct switch. But with the potential that some planners saw for combining newspaper-type content with cable distribution, the investment was logical. While the purchase could be viewed as a conglomerate merger, it might as readily—and probably more accurately—be viewed as a vertical merger.

4. Cable as Common Carrier?

The term common carrier is anathema to participants in the cable industry. It means to them loss of control, lower profits and far less glamour than the industry (and its financiers) sees for itself. The common carrier model does have certain appeal to some of those on the outside, however. It does minimize, if not eliminate, potential problems of access. It makes moot the question of how much vertical integration should be allowed; and it eliminates newspapers' fears that unless they can own the local cable system they may be locked out. Common carrier status for cable would make less troublesome the possible antitrust questions that arise as cable systems merge.

Still, it is likely that the benefits of cable would not have come as quickly (once the FCC burdens were lifted) if the industry had not perceived its growth in terms of its ability to be more than a conduit for transmission. And the proposals made to franchise authorities in the 1980s (some might say "extracted" from the cable industry) for state-of-the-art systems were clearly based on the financial returns that an unregulated system would allow.

There are those advocates, nonetheless, who look at cable as the missing broadband link equivalent to the Postal Service/telephone system for print and narrowband communication. By guaranteeing that a substantial portion of the 35, 54 or whatever number of channels in new systems is available to independent content providers, a major video access bottleneck could be reduced. At the same time, it should be recognized that a common carrier or leased access model does *not* necessarily have to bear the burden of rate of return regulation. It also appears that the telephone network will become increasingly important for the mass media, in that it is becoming a distributor for a portion of the media that heretofore has relied on physical delivery.

The trend, however, is towards some sort of conflict between cable and the highly regulated local telephone companies. Besides carrying video programming, the cable owners are already teaming up with newspaper publishers and data base services to provide home information services. Many of the same information services are carried over tariffed telephone lines. In lower Manhattan, cable is being used in 1982 for transmission of data among various offices of Citibank. Prior to cable, Citibank had used telephone lines.

At the same time, the local telephone companies, separated from AT&T, will be looking for new sources of business. Unlike the cable industry, the telephone already has almost universal penetration. The existing plant is reportedly able to be upgraded to carry a slow scan video signal. Over the years, the telephone companies may actually replace the twisted pair of copper wires that go into each home and business with a fiber optic cable, capable of full broadband carriage. Thus, over a period of time, the telephone industry may be expected to expand into high-speed data transmission to homes and smaller businesses, at the same time that the cable industry moves from video to more data transmission. The result may be two wires into the home or business, each with similar characteristics. But one, as it now stands, will be unfettered by regulation, while the other will come under common carrier rules and tariffed rates. The inequity in this situation may compel the state regulatory authorities to deter-

mine whether cable should be brought under its regulation—or the telephone companies deregulated.

5. The Standard for Bigness: Who Is the 800-Pound Gorilla?

In the classic image of the little fish being eaten by a bigger fish, which in
turn is swallowed by larger fish, what is "big" in the communications
ocean is relative. Computer makers look at IBM as the gorilla in their industry. But IBM is dwarfed by even a split AT&T.

In its argument for keeping AT&T out of the content supplying business, some executives in the newspaper industry referred to the giant telecommunications firm as an "800-pound gorilla," implying that it could
crush all the little animals in the jungle. In 1981 AT&T had revenues more
than three times those of the entire newspaper business. The publishers
were afraid that AT&T could use profits from its monopoly businesses to
subsidize any ventures in unregulated areas.

Ignoring for the moment whether that is any longer (or ever was) a valid
argument, the fact is it could readily be turned against the newspapers
themselves. Most newspapers have no direct daily competition in their
local communities. And most newspapers are part of groups of papers
under common ownership. More than one incident has been reported
where a small entity that tried to start a weekly newspaper or an all advertising "shopper" newspaper in the same market as the group-owned
"monopoly" daily suddenly found the established newspaper aggressively
cutting advertising rates and otherwise drawing on its corporate parent
during the competitive siege. From the perch of the small entrepreneur or
weekly publisher, even a modest chain of daily newspapers can look like an
800-pound gorilla. Thus, to the question, "Is big necessarily bad?" one
must add the more fundamental question, "What is big?"

We have learned in recent years that having only three large domestic
producers of automobiles does not mean that competition is limited to
those three. Foreign competition is very real and presumably it is in the
best interest of the U.S. to have an industry that can compete with the
Japanese giants. Similarly, we have seen how the seemingly overwhelming
size of IBM could not prevent successful competition from upstarts like
Digital Equipment Corp., Data General and even Apple Computer. Now,
competition from Japan, in the form of Fujitsu and the like, demonstrates
that size must be measured not on a national scale but in relation to a
world economy.

In the mass communications business, competition is not limited to the
traditional media segments. It is not even limited to intermedia competition. Instead, the traditional media players have begun to see the entry of
competition from new, heretofore unrelated participants:

- financial institutions, such as Citibank, interested in electronic home banking services and willing to provide associated information in a data base to help sell their home banking services;

- retailers, such as Sears, interested in in-home shopping transactions via electronic information services;

- computer time-sharing firms and service bureaus, such as CompuServe (a subsidiary of H&R Block Co.), that want to increase utilization of their computers and programs, especially in off-peak evening hours.

Each of these, and perhaps others, represents formidable industries and potential competition for significant segments of traditional media audiences.

FACTORS INVOLVED IN POLICY DETERMINATION

Policy, of course, is determined by more than lofty ideals of what is right or wrong, what is best for society, or what is technologically feasible. In the case of media concentration and ownership issues, policy combines at least four separate factors: the legal/political, economic, social and technological.

Legal/Political Factors

Those who have followed the attempts of successive Congresses in trying to rewrite the Communications Act of 1934 are well aware of the political booby traps in policymaking. Any time a part of a bill deregulated one piece of the pie, some new player came out of the woodwork to either claim injury or a piece of the pie himself. The broadcasters hoped to cripple the cable business, and everyone had something to say about what could or should be done to AT&T, not all of the suggestions reconcilable. Congress first had to abandon its hope of passing a comprehensive bill that addressed broadcast as well as telecommunications issues, then it had to tiptoe through the telecommunication mine field.

The process of changing FCC policy can be torturously slow, as the review of cable regulation in Chapter 7 demonstrates. Issues that may be on the FCC's agenda for the 1980s include balancing Microband Corp. of America's proposal for five MDS channels in the 50 largest cities with the reality that the spectrum space would have to be taken from instructional fixed service television allocation, which is available for education.

CBS Inc. has advanced the idea of high definition DBS television. This would make the television picture better than that provided by a 35mm movie. But to implement high definition would use considerably more bandwidth than traditional television. This would lessen the allocation available for those who wish to offer more DBS channels. But policymakers also have to deal with international issues addressed by the World Administrative Radio Conference for allocation of radio frequencies in space for nations, which is a political issue itself. These are just a few of the political factors involved.

Economic Factors

While it may be a pleasant fantasy to wish there could be two or three independent newspapers in every city or 15 radio stations in every town and village, the fact is that the economic infrastructure does not support such dreams. Indeed, the limitation on the number of radio stations in most parts of the country is not due to spectrum scarcity any more than the number of newspapers in a town is related to lack of printing presses. There is just not a large enough economic base to support more broadcasters or newspapers. The implications of this reality for public policymakers are just being recognized. A U.S. House of Representatives staff report noted:

> Since scarcity due to economic limitations does not provide a rationale for regulating other media, a strong argument can be maintained that such a rationale should not be a basis for broadcast regulation either.[12]

Similarly, it may be argued that the tendency toward mergers and acquisitions in cable is in large measure the result of the economic demands being made of cable systems, often by the same groups that decry media concentration. Someone must absorb the cost of wiring an entire city, the poorer areas along with the middle-class neighborhoods; and someone must provide the requisite neighborhood studios and programming funds for public access channels, while paying for the cable to link the city's educational facilities together as well as the government offices together and remitting a 5% franchise fee to the city in addition. Small firms cannot handle this. So the older cable systems with 12 channels, which must upgrade to meet the new specifications, are selling out to the media giants.

Other economic factors include the cost involved in new technology, the methods that are acceptable for financing a particular medium (i.e., by advertisers, users, government subsidy, etc.), or the cost of writing off undepreciated but often obsolete equipment (which is a problem facing state public utility commissions in allowing upgrading of local telephone company facilities). Digital switches and fiber optics would vastly improve the capability of the system and provide greater service to the user. But the existing equipment was being depreciated for periods of as long as 40 years. To write that off more quickly would mean increasing the rate base and would thus lead to higher telephone charges. The course of action is not clear-cut.

Social Factors

Social factors are related to political factors. In this case, the real question is, "How much diversity is enough?" And a corollary question is, "How is that determined?"

The fact is, once we abandon the antitrust standard for concentration, there is no acceptable guideline for what constitutes too few voices. It cannot be seriously proposed that the mass communications business must be so structured that any person or group can have unlimited access to whatever medium for whatever purpose for whatever period of time they so desire. Short of that impractical standard, what is acceptable and how can that be determined?

The issue of media control is particularly important to many critics and analysts because of the only partially supportable presumption of the media content's great influence on mass society. Those who control the media, goes the argument, establish the political agenda, dictate tastes and culture, sell the material goods and in general manipulate the masses. While there is certainly great power in the media, for two related reasons its strength may also be overemphasized.

First, so long as there are reasonably competing media sources as there are today, these can cancel each other out. Why is it we do not all eat Wheaties or believe everything that Mobil says in its advertisements? Second, there are media other than the "big" media that can be very effective, especially for reaching easily identified groups.

The use of media in the Iranian revolution is an historic case study.[13] In the typical coup d'etat, the rebel forces are supposed to take over the television and radio stations. The government meanwhile imposes censorship in the press. The Iranian revolution succeeded without the Ayatollah Khomeini overrunning a single broadcast facility. The Shah had control of all the media to the day he left. The revolutionary forces relied quite effectively on the "small" media. Khomeini used audio tapes to get his message to the mullahs, who in turn spread the word in the mosques. The Xerox machine, Everyman's printing press, was used to distribute his instructions. And the telephone was used to coordinate efforts between Teheran and exile headquarters in Paris.

Still, the perception no doubt persists that the mass media are all-powerful in the industrialized world, so this factor will be a dominant force in determining policy.

Technological Factors

Technological factors are addressed last to emphasize that they are only one of many interacting factors. With the rapid advancement in developments of integrated circuits, communications satellites and cable television, it sometimes seems that the communications world is technology driven. The preceding sections indicate that technology interacts with other forces. History seems to provide several lessons about the role of technology in change.

First, technology is rarely adapted for its own sake. It must fulfill some need. In the mid-1960s, the Bell System tried to introduce Picture-Phone® service. It did not catch on. During the same time period, the common wisdom in the educational establishment tried to implement computer-aided instruction throughout the land. It too failed miserably. In 1978, the government-owned telephone system in Great Britain, looking at its underutilized network, initiated an electronic data base service for the home market, dubbed Prestel. It expected to have 100,000 households subscribing by the end of 1980. It had fewer than 10,000.

Second, technology tends to cast a long shadow. Even in today's accelerated world, it takes nearly a decade to get a new piece of technology from discovery to commercial availability. That gives existing industry participants time to adjust. Even the ubiquitous telephone was not in place in 50% of U.S. households until 1946, 70 years after its invention.

Finally, there is an important difference between that which is technologically feasible and what is economically viable. Indeed, the technological graveyard is littered with better mousetraps that failed because they cost too much. What will the technology do, at what price and what will it replace are questions that must be resolved as part of the policymaking process.

MORE QUESTIONS

Besides the policy issues, there are questions for which this study provides no answers. Yet they are questions that need to be considered in the discussion of policy formation. A selection of such questions would include:

- Does increased diversity and access imply greater quality? What happened when the FCC took 30 minutes of prime-time programming from the three networks and forced this time on the individual stations? The prohibitive costs of single market productions have resulted in few quality shows and opened up the market to syndicators of low-cost game shows of little substance.

- Who should be the arbiter of what type of programming or content is most desirable for society? Much of the criticism of the networks centers on the supposedly mindless grade of the programming. However, when given a choice, the viewing public has "voted" by the way it turns the dial. Excellent programs, such as *60 Minutes* and *Roots,* have received viewer support. But many of the top-rated shows have outperformed presentations of supposedly higher intellectual content. By the same reasoning, newspaper publishers, even those with no direct local competition, must still offer a content that entices consumers to buy the product each day. Thus, publishers, like programmers, must show some response to the needs of the audience.

- How much control by any firm or group of firms must be manifest before we are threatened with perceivable restraints on true access to a broad spectrum of opinion and information? Most crucially, how can this be measured? On the one hand, there is a point at which some combinations may have to be limited. On the other hand, there can be no credence given to the argument advanced by some that every opinion or creative idea has a right to be heard through the mass media (although anyone with a few dollars can make up a picket sign or hand out leaflets at City Hall. Often, such viewpoints get aired by becoming news). Even not-for-profit university or other subsidized presses must employ some criteria of value to a specific market in determining which offerings to publish. Can concentration of ownership be measured by the total number of media properties? By the number of households reached by the media owned by a given firm? By the geographical concentration of the firm's properties?

- Besides the mass media companies themselves, who are the other participants in the mass communications industry that play important roles in determining the ultimate nature of the range of diversity available? Among those that might be considered:

1) State and federal regulators. Policies of pricing, access and degree of competition for telecommunications services, including telephone, satellite common carriers and, perhaps, cable will have a substantial impact on the traditional mass media. For example, the number of earth satellites, the frequencies assigned to them, the manner of tariffing, etc. will all affect the availability, capability and price of content transmission. One major unknown is the degree to which cable will maintain its largely unregulated status, particularly at the state level.

2) The Postal Service. The U.S. Postal Service is still the primary conduit for physical delivery. Magazine publishers have already had to incorporate a 500% increase in their second-class rate in less than a decade. The Postal Service continues to be the main carrier of publications, however, despite efforts to use private carriers. Many of the older media need a viable physical delivery infrastructure. Will the Postal Service be able to continue in that role?

3) Advertisers. Most of the mass media are totally or largely advertiser supported. Cable, which today derives its support primarily from subscribers, is expected to become an advertising outlet as its penetration increases. Yet, as previously mentioned, there is a limit to the number of media outlets that can expect to get a share of the advertising dollar. One reason for the demise of competing newspapers in many cities is the efficiency a single newspaper provides local merchants. Starting a new paper requires the support of advertisers, who do not necessarily see any benefit for themselves. New media will spread advertising dollars even thinner.

4) Gatekeepers. Few users of the media would consider themselves well-served by having unlimited access to all raw, unedited content. One of the values of the media is the role of editors in deciding what information should or should not be transmitted. Yet the role of the gatekeeper is a sensitive one. Although not scientifically rigorous in his data gathering, author Ben Stein added grist to the gatekeeper debate with his look at television programming. Stein concluded that a relative handful of scriptwriters and producers create the entertainment messages that are broadcast every day. He found that almost all of these people live in Los Angeles. "Television is not necessarily a mirror of anything besides what those few people think. The whole entertainment

component of television is dominated by men and women who have a unified idiosyncratic view of life."[14] In an empirical study of television and magazine news, sociologist Herbert Gans identified quite similar values to those Stein observed in entertainment programming. He also pointed out the socialization of journalists and their news organizations.[15] The implication of this work is that, short of basic social upheaval, trained journalists will make similar story decisions in large measure regardless of the media organization's ownership.

CONCLUSION

The most salient empirical conclusions that can be derived from this study are that media ownership does not presently appear to be substantially more concentrated than at other times in recent history and that the traditional media industries in general are far less concentrated than are other industries.

These findings are confirmed by a look at the concentration ratios of the largest firms in each of the traditionally discrete print media industries. In newspapers, periodicals and book publishing, the four largest firms accounted for a smaller proportion of the industry in 1977 than in 1947. At the levels of eight, 20 and 50 largest firms, the periodical business showed a lessening of concentration. Newspaper and book publishers were somewhat more concentrated, especially at the 20- and 50-firm level. But in neither case do we approach alarming levels, particularly compared to other industries such as tobacco, automobile and steel.

Stemming from its economic needs, the film production and distribution business has historically been relatively concentrated. Broadcasters have been limited in size by the FCC's 7-7-7 rule. Cable is the only video segment that has seen substantial change in its ownership structure in the past decade. It is a new industry and will no doubt have to seek an economic and capital equilibrium.

These findings are enhanced to the extent that we accept new market descriptions for the "media." Although the various media processes and formats are not all directly interchangeable, we cannot overlook the increasingly diverse types of media with which technology has been providing us over the years. Print is no longer the only rooster in the barnyard. And broadcasting is not its only companion. The new media processes working their way into the arena, such as MDS, DBS, viewdata, teletext, etc., involve some old players, but many new ones as well.

Table 8.1 is critical to this evaluation. In pulling together a compilation of who the leading players are, we see that there are few that dominate across traditional media lines, though they are quite logically often involved in more than one medium. Here again, let us recall that a firm that creates content would not want to be limited to a particular distribution mechanism to distribute the content.

Finally, Table 8.2 indicated that the media companies themselves are controlled either by their founders and their descendants, or by a rather diverse group of individual and institutional owners. There is little evidence of concentration at this level, although a few institutions show up as holders of presumably competing companies. We must keep in mind that much of the institutional holdings represent trusts or pension funds, whose shares are voted by many individuals. Their interest tends not to be in control of content but in the long-term economic performance of the company whose stock they own.

In the perspective of history, we would be hard pressed to find argument with the forceful proposal of former FCC Commissioner Lee Loevinger that, far from being faced with lessening diversity of media ownership, we are blessed with the greatest variety of any society at any time in history.

In 18th-century America, the populace of major cities in the United States had access to a few skimpy weekly newspapers. They were priced at levels placing them out of the reach of the ordinary citizen. A circulation of 3000 was impressive. The papers may each have been individually owned, but people still had access at best to just one or two local papers. In some cities, there began to appear public libraries with a few books. By 1900 the newspaper was flourishing, as were a few national magazines. Already there were chains and conglomerates, owned by Hearst, Munsey, Scripps and Pulitzer. Nonetheless, people had to get their information from a few daily newspapers (of questionable objectivity), a few magazines and books. Even with a wide range of ownership, it is not likely that individuals had the diversity of sources, from as great a variety of producers, as we have today.

We cannot take issue with the need to maintain a vigorous flow of varied ideas and information. It is important, however, to be able to separate occasional abuses of the right of the press and the freedom that goes along with private enterprise from an indictment of all media owners. Along with the right of freedom of individual action is the understanding that, in an imperfect world, there is the right to make mistakes and to take advantage of freedom.

The intent of this study has not been to propose a course of action that should be taken, if any, although some of the authors have provided some suggestions to that end in their chapters. As noted in Chapter 1, the primary objective of the book was to pull together the relevant data on the degree of concentration in each media segment, the leading participants and their market share, and, where possible, to report on the effects that ownership trends have had on content.

This final chapter, however, has attempted to indicate the complexity of the issue of concentration as well as the many variables that must enter into any policymaking decisions. First, we must decide on the critical definition of concentration. This involves not only the differentiation between the traditional antitrust standard and a broader social-economic-political concept, but an agreement on what the relevant market should be: each media segment or the mass communications industry. If, in fact, our concern is with diversity of media voices—that is the social-economic-political concept for defining concentration—then by the same reasoning we must support the broader mass communications industry, reinforced by the blurring of the boundaries among its traditional segments, as the proper designation of the market.

In deciding to accept or modify the rules under which the information business continues to develop, there are several trends that need be kept in mind.

One is that we live in an age of the $2.5 trillion economy. We must not be so idealistic as to believe that the small business entities of previous eras are as appropriate today. For any institution to provide competent and efficient service to a nation of more than 220 million people requires considerable resources. AT&T (whole or split up) may have awesome assets, but assets of sizable magnitude are necessary to keep a growing nation wired.

Second, we are also part of a world that is growing more economically competitive. The economic wherewithal of our western allies and Japan is certainly on a par with our own. Many third world nations, such as Singapore and South Korea, are anxious to exploit their labor strengths and our technology. U.S. information providers are facing stiff competition in world markets as a result. Artificially scaled-down institutions will not be able to win their share of the world market, especially when the governments of many of our competitors, including our close friends to the north, openly encourage business combinations that result in greater economic efficiency.

Finally, we must not burden the technology that is fueling much of the change in the media business with overly ambitions dreams of social change. Man has been notoriously unable to successfully predict the eventual social outcomes of new technology. Neither film nor the record player revolutionized the education process as Edison had so explicitly predicted. The telephone and telegraph did not spell the end of written communication, as the Postmaster General of the U.S. expected it would in 1873.

Given the vast array of separate entities with holdings in the mass communications industry, policymakers must avoid accepting at face value some assumed myths, such as that greater diversity yields higher quality. They must also discipline themselves not to impose their own values of what is good for society by encouraging the development of media with one kind of content over another.

In the tension that tends to exist between government and the press, Thomas Jefferson is often cited: "Were it left to me to decide whether we should have a government without newspapers or newspapers without government, I should not hesitate to prefer the latter." Jefferson continued to subscribe to this priority despite being viciously attacked by the press during his presidency. No one today is seriously proposing having to face the explicit choice Jefferson used to make his point.

The danger is not that any single action in the name of promoting wider press ownership will cause harm: individual actions, for cause, may be necessary, such as the *Associated Press* case in 1945. Yet at the same time, we should keep in mind the warning of Lord Develin:

> If freedom of the press perishes, it will not be by sudden death.
> . . . It will be a long time dying from a debilitating disease caused
> by a series of erosive measures, each of which, if examined singly,
> would have a good deal to be said for it.

* * * * * *

Who owns the media? Thousands of firms and organizations, large and small. They are controlled, directly and indirectly, by tens of thousands of stockholders, as well as by public opinion. The mass communications business is profitable—as it must be. It is an industry changing its boundaries from one defined by format (books, television, newspapers, etc.) to one defined by function—collecting and disseminating information.

Ultimately, it appears that public policy regarding the structure of the media industry will be based not on economic criteria but on some measure of social good as, indeed, was the First Amendment when originally conceived. But the media industry in this decade may be transformed by the array of systems now being assembled. The need to fill 50 cable channels, the ability of any user to have access to any computer data base via a telephone line, the possibility of aiming an antenna into the heavens and thereby having access to the programming of dozens of firms in this country and perhaps worldwide, may make today's concerns over concentration of media ownership obsolete. The old media firms will be joined by new firms and other industries to create a media marketplace which may be noted more for information overload and fragmentation than for concentration and scarcity. But we will save that debate for another time.

NOTES

1. Carl Kaysen and Donald F. Turner, *Antitrust Policy: An Economic and Legal Analysis* (Cambridge, MA: Harvard University Press, 1959), p. 27.

2. U.S. Congress, "Telecommunications in Transition: The Status of Competition in the Telecommunications Industry," Report by the Majority Staff of the Subcommittee on Telecommunications, Consumer Protection and Finance, U.S. House of Representatives, November 3, 1981, pp. 310-325. This report summarizes a wealth of data from contending players and neutral observers and provides some analysis. It covers common carriers, broadcasting, cable, print and content, along with basic views of market analysis.

3. Ibid.

4. Maxwell E. McCombs, "Mass Media in the Marketplace," *Journalism Monographs,* No. 24 (Lawrence, KS: Association for Education in Journalism, 1972), pp. 5-6.

5. *Miami Herald* v. *Tornillo* 418 U.S. 241 (1974); *Red Lion Broadcasting Co.* v. *F.C.C.* 395 U.S. 367 (1969). For the position of the cable industry, see "Cable Television, Government Regulation, and the First Amendment" (Washington, DC: National Cable Television Association, April 1981).

6. *WGN Continental Broadcasting Company and Albuquerque Cable Television, Inc.* v. *United Video, Inc.* 523 F. Supp. 403 (1981).

7. *Television Digest,* December 14, 1981, p. 5.

8. Kenneth Gordon, Jonathan D. Levy and Robert S. Preece, "FCC Policy on Cable Ownership: Staff Report," Federal Communications Commission, Office of Plans and Policy, November 1981.

9. "Justice Dept. Warns Against TV-Cable Cross Ownership," Dow Jones News/Retrieval, January 25, 1982.

10. "FCC Attacks Joint Ownership of Cable System and TV Station," Associated Press, June 25, 1981, from Nexis, Mead Data Central.

11. "Cable TV Firm Owns Newspaper Company," *Editor & Publisher,* September 12, 1981, p. 9.

12. House Telecommunications Report, p. 111.

13. Majid Tehranian, "Iran: Communication, Alienation, Revolution," *Intermedia,* March 1979, pp. 6-12.

14. Ben Stein, *The View From Sunset Boulevard* (New York: Basic Books, 1979), p. xiii.

15. Herbert J. Gans, *Deciding What's News: A Study of CBS Evening News, NBC Nightly News, Newsweek and Time* (New York: Vintage Books, 1979), pp. 279-299. See, however, Gans' review of Stein's book in *Nation,* March 10, 1979.

Bibliography

NEWSPAPERS

Books

Bleyer, Willard G. *Main Currents in the History of American Journalism.* Boston: Houghton Mifflin, 1927.

Commission on the Freedom of the Press. *A Free and Responsible Press.* Chicago: University of Chicago Press, 1948.

Compaine, Benjamin. *The Newspaper Industry in the 1980s: An Assessment of Economics and Technology.* White Plains, NY: Knowledge Industry Publications, Inc., 1979.

Davison, W. Phillips, and Frederick T.C. Yu. *Mass Communications Research: Major Issues and Future Directions.* New York: Praeger Publishers, 1974.

Emery, Edwin and Michael Emery. *The Press and America.* 4th ed. Englewood Cliffs, NJ: Prentice-Hall, 1978.

Gross, Gerald, ed. *The Responsibility of the Press.* New York: Simon & Schuster, A Clarion Book, 1966.

Mott, Frank Luther. *American Journalism.* 3rd ed. New York: Macmillan Co., 1962.

Owen, Bruce M. *Economics and Freedom of Expression.* Cambridge, MA: Ballinger Publishing Co., 1975.

Rivers, William L. and Wilbur Schramm. *Responsibility in Mass Communication.* rev. ed. New York: Harper & Row, 1969.

Tebbel, John. *The Compact History of the American Newspaper.* New York: Hawthorne Books, Inc., 1963.

Journals, Monographs and Other Serials

"The Big Money Hunts for Independent Newspapers." *Business Week,* February 21, 1977, pp. 58-62.

Bishop, Robert L. "The Rush to Chain Ownership." *Columbia Journalism Review,* November-December 1972, p. 14ff.

Borstell, Gerald H. "Ownership, Competition and Comment in 20 Small Dailies." *Journalism Quarterly* 33 (Spring 1956): 220-222.

"Canadian Panel Urges Action to Restrict Concentration of Newspaper Ownership." *The Wall Street Journal,* August 19, 1981, p. 19.

Carmody, Deirdre, and James P. Sterba. "Murdoch About to Take Over Post; Texas Papers Thrive on Violence." *The New York Times,* December 26, 1976, p. 49.

Clarke, Peter and Eric Fredin. "Newspapers, Television and Political Research." *Public Opinion Quarterly.* 42:143.

Dallos, Robert E. "Bidding Sends Prices Higher in Newspaper Acquisition Binge." *Los Angeles Times,* January 9, 1977, Sec. VI, p. 2.

Doogan, Mike. "Anchorage Daily News Files Suit to Break Joint Operating Accord With Rival Paper." *The Wall Street Journal,* February 14, 1977, p. 19.

Fawcett, Denby. "What Happens When a Chain Owner Arrives." *Columbia Journalism Review,* November-December 1972, pp. 29-30.

"53 Dailies in 1978 Purchases; 46 of Them Go Into Groups." *Editor & Publisher,* January 6, 1979, p. 47.

Friendly, Jonathan. "Publishers Seeks to Block Utility in Electronic Ad Test for Homes." *The New York Times,* December 4, 1980, p. D-21.

Gormley, William T. *The Effects of Newspaper-Television Cross-Ownership in News Homogeneity.* Chapel Hill, NC: Institute for Research in Social Science, University of North Carolina, 1976.

Hatfield, C. Donald. Letter to the Editor. *Columbia Journalism Review,* January-February 1973, pp. 65-66.

Hicks, Ronald G., and James S. Featherstone. "Duplication of Newspaper Content in Contrasting Ownership Situations." *Journalism Quarterly* 55 (Autumn 1978): 549-554.

Howard, Herbert H. "Cross-Media Ownership of Newspapers and TV Stations." *Journalism Quarterly* 51 (Winter 1974): 715-718.

Huenergard, H. Celeste. "Scripps Hoping for Quick Decision in Cincinnati Case." *Editor & Publisher,* February 6, 1979.

Interdependence of Computer and Communication Services and Facilities. (Computer I). Final Decision. 28 F.C.C.2d 11 (1966).

"Joint Ownership of Media Barred by Appeals Court." *The Wall Street Journal,* March 2, 1977, p. 4.

LeGates, John C. *Changes in the Information Industries—Their Strategic Implications.* Cambridge, MA: Harvard University, Program on Information Resources Policy, 1981.

Machalba, Daniel. "North Carolina Paper Strives to Ward off Bids by Press Empires." *The Wall Street Journal,* August 19, 1981, p. 18.

Nichols, Peter. "Check it with Bill." Review of Eric Veblen, *The Manchester Union Leader in New Hampshire Elections* (University Press of New England). *Columbia Journalism Review,* November-December 1975, p. 53.

Nixon, Raymond B. "Changes in Reader Attitudes Toward Daily Newspapers." *Journalism Quarterly* 31 (Autumn 1954): 421-433.

Nixon, Raymond B., and Tae-Youl Hahn. "Concentration of Press Ownership: Comparison of 32 Countries." *Journalism Quarterly* 38 (Spring 1978): 31ff.

Nixon, Raymond B., and Robert L. Jones. "The Content of Non-Competitive Vs. Competitive Newspapers." *Journalism Quarterly* 33 (Summer 1956): 299-314.

Rarick, Galen, and Barrie Hartman. "The Effects of Competition on One Daily Newspaper's Content." *Journalism Quarterly* 43 (Autumn 1966): 459-463.

Ray, Royal H. "Competition in the Newspaper Industry." *Journal of Marketing* 15 (April 1951): 444-456.

Rosse, James N. "Economic Limits of Press Responsibility." *Studies in Industry Economics,* No. 56. Stanford, CA: Department of Economics, Stanford University, 1975.

Rosse, James N., Bruce M. Owen and James Dertouzos. "Trends in the Daily Newspaper Industry 1923-1973." *Studies in Industry Economics,* No. 57. Stanford, CA: Department of Economics, Stanford University, 1975.

Schweitzer, John C., and Elaine Goldman. "Does Newspaper Competition Make A Difference to Readers?" *Journalism Quarterly* 52 (Winter 1975): 706-710.

Second Computer Inquiry (Computer II). Final Decision. 77 F.C.C.2d 384 (1980).

Stempel, Guido H. III. "Effects on Performance of a Cross-Media Monopoly." *Journalism Monographs* 29 (June 1973): 10-28.

Sterling, Christopher. "Trends in Daily Newspaper and Broadcasting Ownership, 1922-1970." *Journalism Quarterly* 52 (Summer 1975): 247-256.

Tate, Cassandra. "Gannett in Salem: Protecting the Franchise." *Columbia Journalism Review,* July-August, 1981, p. 52.

Urban, Christine D. *Factors Influencing Media Consumption: A Survey of the Literature.* Cambridge, MA: Harvard University: Program on Information Resources Policy, 1981.

Villard, Oswald Garrison. "The Chain Daily." *The Nation* 130 (1930): 595-597.

Wackman, Daniel et al. "Chain Newspaper Autonomy as Reflected in Presidential Campaign Endorsements." *Journalism Quarterly* 52 (Autumn 1975): 417-420.

Weaver, David H. and L.E. Mullins. "Content and Format Characteristics of Competing Daily Newspapers." *Journalism Quarterly* 52 (Summer 1975): 257-264.

"Yellow Pages and a Fearful Press." *The New York Times,* May 14, 1981.

Unpublished Papers

Dertouzos, James N. "Media Conglomerates: Chains, Groups and Cross Ownership." Discussion paper prepared for Federal Trade Commission Media Symposium. Washington, DC, December 1978.

Grotta, Gerald L. "Changes in the Ownership of Daily Newspapers and Selected Performance Characteristics, 1950-1968: An Investigation of Some Economic Implications of Concentration of Ownership." Ph.D. Dissertation, Southern Illinois University, 1970.

Keller, Kristine. "Quality of News in Group-Owned and Independent Papers: Independent Papers Have More," unpublished paper. Berkeley, CA: University of California, School of Journalism, 1978.

Langdon, John Henry. "An Intra Industry Approach to Measuring the Effects of Competition: The Newspaper Industry." Ph.D. Dissertation, Cornell University, 1969.

U.S. Federal Communications Commission. *Second Report and Order, Docket No. 18110: Multiple Ownership of Standard, FM and Television Broadcast Stations.* FCC 74-104, Mimeo 29942, January 29, 1975.

Reference Works

Editor & Publisher International Year Book. Annual, New York: Editor & Publisher, Inc.

U.S. Department of Commerce. *Statistical Abstract of the United States.* Annual.

BOOK PUBLISHING

Books

Altick, Richard D. *The English Common Reader: A Social History of the Mass Reading Public, 1800-1900.* Chicago & London: The University of Chicago Press, 1957.

Bound, Charles F. *A Banker Looks at Book Publishing.* New York: R.R. Bowker Co., 1950.

Burlingame, Roger. *Endless Frontiers: The Story of McGraw-Hill.* New York: McGraw-Hill Book Co., Inc., 1959.

Cheney, O.H. *Economic Survey of the Book Industry: 1930-1931.* New York: R.R. Bowker Co., 1960.

The College Market 1981-86. White Plains, NY: Knowledge Industry Publications, Inc., 1981.

Compaine, Benjamin. *The Book Industry in Transition: An Economic Study of Book Distribution and Marketing.* White Plains, NY: Knowledge Industry Publications, Inc., 1978.

Comparato, Frank E. *Books for the Millions.* Harrisburg, PA: The Stackpole Co., 1971.

Dessauer, John P., Paul D. Doebler and E. Wayne Norberg. *Book Industry Trends 1977.* Darien, CT: The Book Industry Study Group, Inc., 1977.

_____. *Book Industry Trends 1978.* Darien, CT: The Book Industry Study Group, Inc., 1977.

Duke, Judith S. *Children's Books and Magazines: A Market Study.* White Plains, NY: Knowledge Industry Publications, Inc., 1979.

Ehrlich, Arnold W., ed. *The Business of Publishing: A PW Anthology.* New York: R.R. Bowker Co., 1976.

The El-Hi Market 1982-87. White Plains, NY: Knowledge Industry Publications, Inc., 1981.

Foresman, Hugh A. *These Things I Remember.* Chicago: Scott, Foresman and Co., 1949.

Gross, Gerald, ed. *Publishers on Publishing.* New York: Grosset and Dunlap, Inc., 1961.

Irwin, John W. *Schoolbooks.* Columbus, OH: School and College Service, 1956.

Lawler, Thomas Bonaventure. *Seventy Years of Textbook Publishing: A History of Ginn and Company 1867-1937.* Boston: Ginn and Co., 1938.

Machlup, Fritz. *The Production and Distribution of Knowledge in the United States.* Princeton, NJ: Princeton University Press, 1962.

Madison, Charles A. *Book Publishing in America.* New York: McGraw-Hill Book Co., Inc., 1966.

Miller, William. *The Book Industry.* New York: Columbia University Press, 1949.

Oswald, John Clyde. *Printing in the Americas.* New York: Hacker Art Books, 1937; reprinted 1963.

Pratt, John Barnes. *A Century of Book Publishing: 1838-1938.* New York: A.S. Barnes and Co., 1938.

Tebbel, John. *A History of Book Publishing in the United States.* New York: R.R. Bowker Co., vol. 1, 1972; vol. 2, 1975; vol. 3, 1978.

Textbooks Are Indispensable. New York: American Textbook Publishers Institute, n.d. (ca. 1955-1956).

Textbooks In Education. New York: American Textbook Publishers Institute, 1949.

Yankelovich, Skelly, and White, Inc. *The 1978 Consumer Research Study on Reading and Book Purchasing.* Darien, CT: The Book Industry Study Group, Inc., 1978.

Periodicals

Book Production Industry (monthly); and predecessors, *Book Production* and *Book Industry.*

BP Report (weekly).

Educational Marketer (semi-monthly).

Publishers Weekly (weekly).

Unpublished Articles

Garvin, David A. "The Economics of Overproduction: A Critical Analysis of the 'Too Many Books' Debate." Unpublished paper. Harvard Business School, n.d.

____. "Mergers and Competition in Book Publishing." Unpublished paper. Harvard Business School, 1979.

Reference Works

Annual Survey of the Textbook Publishing Industry. Annual, New York: The American Textbook Publishers Institute.

The Bowker Annual of Library and Book Trade Information. Annual, New York: R.R. Bowker Co.

Industry Statistics. Annual, New York: Association of American Publishers.

Literary Market Place. Annual, New York: R.R. Bowker Co.

Government Publications

U.S. Department of Commerce. *Printing and Publishing.* Monthly.

____. *Survey of Current Business.* Monthly.

____. Bureau of the Census. *Annual Survey of Manufactures.* Annual except in census years.

____. Bureau of the Census. *Census of Manufactures.* Census years.

____. Bureau of the Census. *Historical Statistics of the United States: Colonial Times to 1970.* 1975.

____. Bureau of Economic Analysis. *The National Income and Product Accounts of the United States, 1929-1974: Statistical Tables.* 1976.

U.S. Department of Health, Education and Welfare. *Biennial Survey of Education in the United States.* Biennial.

U.S. Department of the Treasury. Internal Revenue Service. *Corporation Source Book of Statistics of Income.* Annual.

U.S. Office of the President. *Economic Report of the President.* Annual.

MAGAZINES

Books

Compaine, Benjamin M. *The Business of Consumer Magazines.* White Plains, NY: Knowledge Industry Publications, Inc., 1982.

Ford, James L.C. *Magazines for Millions.* Carbondale, IL: Southern Illinois University Press, 1969.

Mott, Frank Luther. *A History of American Magazines.* 5 vols. Cambridge, MA: Harvard University Press, 1968.

Peterson, Theodore. *Magazines in the Twentieth Century.* Urbana, IL: University of Illinois Press, 1964.

Servan-Schreiber, Jean-Jacques. *The Power to Inform.* New York: McGraw-Hill, 1974.

Tebbel, John W. *The American Magazine: A Compact History.* New York: Hawthorne Books, 1969.

Periodicals and Other Serials

Advertising Age (weekly).
Folio (monthly).
Marketing and Media Decisions (monthly).
Media Industry Newsletter (weekly).

Reference Works

Ayer Directory of Publications. Annual, Philadelphia: Ayer Press.

Bowker Annual of Library and Book Trade Information. Annual, New York: R.R. Bowker Co.

U.S. Department of Commerce. *U.S. Industrial Outlook.* Annual.

THEATRICAL FILM

Books and Reports

Association of Cinematograph, Television and Allied Technicians. *Nationalising the Film Industry*. London: Association of Cinematograph, Television and Allied Technicians, 1973.

_____. *Patterns of Discrimination Against Women in the Film and Television Industries*. London: Association of Cinematograph, Television and Allied Technicians, 1975.

Bächlin, Peter. *Der Film als Ware*. Basel: Burg Verlag, 1947.

Batz, Jean-Claude. *A Propos de la Crise de l'Industrie du Cinéma*. Bruxelles: Université Libre de Bruxelles, 1963.

Berton, Pierre. *Hollywood's Canada: The Americanization of Our National Image*. Toronto: McClelland and Stewart Ltd., 1975.

Bonnell, René. *Le Cinéma Exploité*. Paris: Editions du Seuil, 1978.

Conant, Michael. *Antitrust in the Motion Picture Industry*. Berkeley: University of California Press, 1960.

Degand, Claude. *Le Cinéma, Cette Industrie*. Paris: Editions Techniques et Economiques, 1972.

Gianelli, Enrico. *Economia Cinematografica*. Rome: Reanda Editore, 1956.

Guback, Thomas H. *The International Film Industry*. Bloomington: Indiana University Press, 1969.

Hampton, Benjamin B. *History of the American Film Industry*. New York: Dover Publications, Inc., 1970; previously published as *A History of the Movies,* New York: Covici, Friede, 1931.

Huettig, Mae D. *Economic Control of the Motion Picture Industry*. Philadelphia: University of Pennsylvania Press, 1944.

Kelly, Terence. *A Competitive Cinema*. London: Institute of Economic Affairs, 1966.

Kennedy, Joseph P., ed. *The Story of the Films*. Chicago: A.W. Shaw Co., 1927.

Klingender, F.D., and Stuart Legg. *Money Behind the Screen*. London: Lawrence and Wishart, 1937.

Lewis, Howard T. *The Motion Picture Industry*. New York: Van Nostrand Co., 1933.

Mercillon, Henri. *Cinéma et Monopoles*. Paris: Librarie Armand Colin, 1953.

Political and Economic Planning. *The British Film Industry*. London: Political and Economic Planning, Ltd., 1952.

Roeber, Georg, and Gerhard Jacoby. *Handbuch der Filmwirtschaftlichen Medienbereiche*. Munich: Verlag Dokumentation, 1973.

Schmidt, Georg; Werner Schmalenbach; and Peter Bächlin. *The Film—Its Economic, Social and Artistic Problems*. London: The Falcon Press, 1948.

Spraos, John. *The Decline of the Cinema*. London: George Allen and Unwin Ltd., 1962.

Journals, Monographs and Reference Works

The British Film Industry 1958. London: Political and Economic Planning, Ltd. 24 (June 1953).

Crandall, Robert W. "The Postwar Performance of the Motion Picture Industry." *The Antitrust Bulletin* 20 (Spring 1975).

Guback, Thomas. "Les Relations Cinéma-TV aux Etats-Unis Aujourd'hui." *Film Exchange* 2 (Spring 1978).

Guback, Thomas and Dennis Dombkowski. "Television and Hollywood— Economic Relations in the 1970s." *Journal of Broadcasting* 20 (Fall 1976).

National Association of Theatre Owners. *Encyclopedia of Exhibition,* various years.

Government Publications

Great Britain. The Monopolies Commission. *Films, A Report on the Supply of Films for Exhibition in Cinemas.* London: Her Majesty's Stationery Office, 1966.

Great Britain. Prime Minister. *Future of the British Film Industry.* Report of the Prime Minister's Working Party. London: Her Majesty's Stationery Office, 1976.

U.S. Commission on Civil Rights. *Behind the Scenes: Equal Employment Opportunity in the Motion Picture Industry.* Report prepared by the California Advisory Committee to the U.S. Commission on Civil Rights, 1978.

U.S. Congress. House. Committee on Education and Labor. *Impact of Imports and Exports on Employment, Part 8.* Hearings before the Subcommittee on the Impact of Imports and Exports on American Employment of the Committee on Education and Labor, 87th Cong., 1st and 2d sess., 1962.

_____. *Unemployment Problems in American Film Industry.* Hearings before the General Subcommittee on Labor of the Committee on Education and Labor, 92nd Cong., 1st sess., 1972.

U.S. Congress. House. Committee on Interstate and Foreign Commerce. *Cable Television Regulation Oversight, Parts 1 and 2.* Hearings before the Subcommittee on Communications of the Committee on Interstate and Foreign Commerce, 94th Cong., 2d sess., 1977.

U.S. Congress. House. Committee on the Judiciary. *Consent Decree Program of the Department of Justice.* Report of the Antitrust Subcommittee (Subcommittee No. 5) of the Committee on the Judiciary, 86th Cong., 1st sess., 1959.

_____. *Investigation of Conglomerate Corporations, Parts 1 to 4.* Hearings before the Antitrust Subcommittee (Subcommittee No. 5) of the Committee on the Judiciary, 91st Cong., 1970; and report by the staff of the Antitrust Subcommittee, 92d Cong., 1st sess., 1971.

U.S. Congress. House. Committee on Post Office and Civil Service. *Self-Policing of the Movie and Publishing Industry.* Hearings before the Subcommittee on Postal Operations of the Committee on Post Office and Civil Service. 86th Cong., 2d sess., 1960.

U.S. Congress. House. Committee on Small Business. *Movie Ratings and the Independent Producer.* Hearings before the Subcommittee on Special Small Business Problems of the Committee on Small Business, 95th Cong., 1st sess., 1977; and Report of the Subcommittee on Special Small Business Problems of the Committee on Small Business. 95th Cong., 2nd sess., 1978.

U.S. Congress. Senate. Committee on Finance. *Multinational Corporations.* Hearings before the Subcommittee on International Trade of the Committee on Finance, 93d Cong., 1st sess., 1973.

U.S. Congress. Senate. Committee on Foreign Relations. *International Communications and Information.* Hearings before the Subcommittee on International Operations of the Committee on Foreign Relations, 95th Cong., 1st sess., 1977.

____. *Overseas Information Programs of the United States, Part 2.* Hearings before a subcommittee of the Committee on Foreign Relations, 83d Cong., 1st sess., 1953.

____. *U.S. Informational Media Guaranty Program.* Hearings before the Committee on Foreign Relations, 90th Cong., 1st sess., 1967.

U.S. Congress. Senate. Committee on Government Operations. *Disclosure of Corporate Ownership.* Report by the Subcommittee on Inter-governmental Relations and the Subcommittee on Budgeting, Management and Expenditures of the Committee on Government Operations, 93d Cong., 1st sess., 1973.

U.S. Congress. Senate. Committee on the Judiciary. *Communications—Pay Cable Television Industry.* Hearings before the Subcommittee on Antitrust and Monopoly of the Committee on the Judiciary, 94th Cong., 1st sess., 1975.

____. *Economic Concentration, Parts 1 to 8.* Hearings before the Subcommittee on Antitrust and Monopoly of the Committee on the Judiciary, 88th Cong., 2d sess., to 91st Cong., 2d sess., 1964-1970.

U.S. Congress. Senate. Select Committee on Small Business. *Motion Picture Distribution Trade Practices.* Hearings before a subcommittee of the Select Committee on Small Business, 83d Cong., 1st sess., 1953; and 84th Cong., 2d sess., 1956.

____. *Motion Picture Distribution Trade Practices—1956.* Report of the Select Committee on Small Business, 84th Cong., 2nd sess., July 27, 1956.

____. *Problems of Independent Motion Picture Exhibitors.* Report of the Select Committee on Small Business, 83d Cong., 1st sess., August 3, 1953.

U.S. Department of Commerce. *U.S. Industrial Outlook,* various years.

____. *U.S. Service Industries in World Markets,* 1976.

U.S. Department of Commerce. Bureau of the Census. *1977 Census of Selected Service Industries: Motion Picture Industry.*

____. *Statistical Abstract of the United States,* various years.

U.S. Department of Commerce, Bureau of Labor Statistics. *Employment and Earnings* 25 (October 1978).

U.S. Federal Trade Commission. *Paramount Pictures, Inc. et al. Consent Judgments and Decrees Investigation.* Report, February 25, 1965.

____. *Webb-Pomerene Associations: A 50-Year Review.* 1967.

U.S. Temporary National Economic Committee. *Investigation of Concentration of Economic Power. Monograph 43, The Motion Picture Industry—A Pattern of Control.* 1941.

BROADCASTING

Books

Antitrust, the Media and the New Technology. New York: Practising Law Institute, Course Handbook 137, 1981.

Archer, G. *History of Radio to 1926.* New York: American Historical Society, 1938; reprinted by Arno Press, 1971.

Banning, W.P. *Commercial Broadcasting Pioneer: The WEAF Experiment 1922-1926.* Cambridge, MA: Harvard University Press, 1946.

Barnouw, E. *A History of Broadcasting in the United States.* New York: Oxford University Press, 1966-1970 (three volumes).

Botein, M. *Legal Restrictions on Ownership of the Mass Media.* New York: Advanced Media Publishing Associates, 1977.

Bunce, R. *Television in the Corporate Interest.* New York: Praeger Special Studies, 1976.

Cherington, P.W., et al. *Television Station Ownership: A Case Study of Federal Agency Regulation.* New York: Hastings House, 1971.

Eastman, S.T., et al., eds. *Broadcast Programming: Strategies for Winning Television and Radio Audiences.* Belmont, CA: Wadsworth, 1981.

Emery, W. *Broadcasting and Government: Responsibilities and Regulations.* East Lansing, MI: Michigan State University Press, 1971.

Ginsburg, D.H. *Regulation of Broadcasting: Law and Policy Towards Radio/Television and Cable Communications.* St. Paul, MN: West Publishing, 1979.

Head, S.W. and C.H. Sterling. *Broadcasting in America.* Boston: Houghton Mifflin, 1982.

Jones, W.K. *Cases and Materials on Electronic Mass Media: Radio, Television and Cable.* Mineola, NY: Foundation Press, 1979.

Kahn, F., ed. *Documents of American Broadcasting.* Englewood Cliffs, NJ: Prentice-Hall, 1978.

Kittross, J., ed. *Documents in American Telecommunications Policy.* New York: Arno Press, 1977 (two volumes).

Krasnow, E., et al. *The Politics of Broadcast Regulation.* New York: St. Martin's Press, 1982.

Levin, H.J. *Broadcast Regulation and Joint Ownership of Media.* New York: New York University Press, 1960.

_____. *Fact and Fancy in Television Regulation.* New York: Russell Sage, 1980.

McFadyen, S., et al. *Canadian Broadcasting: Market Structure and Economic Performance.* Montreal: Institute for Research on Public Policy, 1980.

Noll, G., et al. *Economic Aspects of Television Regulation.* Washington: Brookings Institution, 1973.

Owen, B. *Economics and Freedom of Expression: Media Structure and the First Amendment.* Cambridge, MA: Ballinger, 1975.

Quinlan, S. *The Hundred Million Dollar Lunch*. Chicago: J. Philip O'Hara Inc., 1974.

Sigel, E., et al. *Video Discs: The Technology, the Applications and the Future*. White Plains, NY: Knowledge Industry Publications, Inc., 1980.

Sterling, C. and T. Haight. *The Mass Media: Aspen Institute Guide to Communication Industry Trends*. New York: Praeger, 1978.

_____ and J. Kittross. *Stay Tuned: A Concise History of American Broadcasting*. Belmont, CA: Wadsworth Publishing, 1978.

Articles/Monographs

Avery, R.K. "Public Broadcasting and the Duopoly Rule." *Public Telecommunications Review* (Jan/Feb 1977), pp. 29-37.

Baer, W., et al. *Concentration of Mass Media Ownership: Assessing the State of Current Knowledge*. Santa Monica, CA: Rand Corp., R-1584-NSF (September 1974).

_____. *Newspaper-Television Station Cross-Ownership: Options for Federal Action*. Santa Monica, CA: Rand Corp., R-1585-MF (September 1974).

Barnett, R. "Cross-Ownership of Mass Media in the Same City: A Report to the John and Mary R. Markle Foundation." Santa Monica, CA: Rand Corp. (September 1974).

Besen, S.M. and T.G. Krattenmaker. "Regulating Network Television: Dubious Premises and Doubtful Solutions." *Regulation* (May/June 1981).

Busterna, J. "Diversity of Ownership as a Criterion in FCC Licensing Since 1965." *Journal of Broadcasting* 20 (Winter 1976): 101-110.

Christians, C. "Home Video Systems: A Revolution?" *Journal of Broadcasting* 17 (Spring 1973): 223-234.

Coffey, A. "The 'Top 50 Market Policy:' Fifteen Years of Non-Policy." *Federal Communications Law Journal* 31 (Spring 1979): 303-339.

Gormley, T., Jr. "How Cross-Ownership Affects News-Gathering." *Columbia Journalism Review* (May/June 1977).

Howard, H.H. "Multiple Broadcast Ownership: Regulatory History." *Federal Communications Bar Journal* 27 (1974): 1:1-70.

_____. "The Contemporary Status of Television Group Ownership." *Journalism Quarterly* 53 (Autumn 1976): 399-405.

Litman, Barry Russell. *The Vertical Structure of the Television Broadcasting Industry: The Coalescence of Power*. East Lansing: Michigan State University Graduate School of Business Administration, 1979.

Manning, W.G. and B.M. Owen. "Television Rivalry and Network Power." *Public Policy* 24 (Winter 1976): 33-57.

McAlpine, D.B. *The Television Programming Industry*. New York: Tucker Anthony & R.L. Day (January 1975).

Owen, B.M. "Structural Approaches to the Problem of TV Network Economic Dominance." Durham, NC: Duke University Graduate School of Business Administration, Center for the Study of Business Regulation, Paper No. 27 (1978).

Park, R.E. *New Television Networks.* Santa Monica, CA: Rand Corp., R-1408-MF (December 1973), pp. 27-30.

____. *New Television Networks: An Update.* Santa Monica, CA: Rand Corp., Note N-1526-FCC (August 1980).

Phillips, K. "Busting the Media Trusts." *Harper's* (July 1977), pp. 23-34.

Regulatory Trends in the 1980s: More Owners—More Stations. New York: Station Representatives Association, September 1980.

Sandman, P.M. "Cross-Ownership on the Scales." *More* (October 1977), pp. 21-24.

Sarno, E., Jr. "The National Radio Conferences." *Journal of Broadcasting* 13 (Spring 1969): 189-202.

Sharp, S. and D. Lively. "Can the Broadcaster in the Black Hat Ride Again? 'Good Character' Requirement for Broadcast Licensees." *Federal Communications Bar Journal* 32 (Spring 1980): 173-203.

Smith, R.R. "Duopoly and ETV." *NAEB Journal* (May-June 1966), p. 42.

____. and P.T. Prince. "WHDH: The Unconscionable Delay." *Journal of Broadcasting* 18 (Winter 1974): 85-96.

Spalding, J. "1928: Radio Becomes a Mass Advertising Medium." *Journal of Broadcasting.* 8 (Winter 1963-64): 31-44.

Sterling, C.H. "Newspaper Ownership of Broadcast Stations, 1920-68." *Journalism Quarterly* 46 (Summer 1969): 227-236, 254.

Toohey, D.W. "Newspaper Ownership of Broadcast Facilities." *Federal Communications Bar Journal* 21 (1966): 1:44-57.

Wirth, M.O. and J.A. Wollert. "Public Interest Program Performance of Multimedia-Owned TV Stations." *Journalism Quarterly* 53 (Summer 1976): 223-230.

Government Publications

Application of CBS Inc. for Authority to Construct an Experimental High Definition Television Satellite System in the 12 GHz Band. Federal Communications Commission File No. DBS-81-02, July 16, 1981.

[Canada] *Ownership of Private Broadcasting: An Economic Analysis of Structure, Performance and Behavior—Report of the Ownership Study Group to the Canadian Radio-television and Telecommunications Commission.* Ottawa: CRTC, October 1978.

Federal Communications Commission. *Report on Chain Broadcasting.* Washington: Government Printing Office, 1941, reissued by Arno Press, 1974.

____. Network Inquiry Special Staff. *New Television Networks: Entry, Jurisdiction, Ownership and Regulation.* Washington: Government Printing Office, 1980 (two volumes).

____. "Sixth Report and Order on Dockets 8736, 8975, 9175 and 8976." 41 FCC 148, April 14, 1952.

____. "Policy Statement on Comparative Broadcast Hearings." 1 FCC 2d 393 (1965).

____. *Second Interim Report by the Office of Network Study: Television Net-*

work Program Procurement, Part II. Washington: Government Printing Office, 1965.

_____. "In the Matter of Amendment of Sections 73.35, 73.240, and 73.636 of the Commission Rules Relating to Multiple Ownership of Standard, FM and Television Broadcast Stations." First Report and Order in Docket 18110, 22 FCC 2d 306, March 25, 1970.

_____. "In the Matter of Amendment of Sections 73.34, 73.240 and 73.636 of the Commission's Rules Relating to Multiple Ownership of Standard, FM and Television Broadcast Stations." Second Report and Order in Docket 18110, 50 FCC 2d 1046, January 28, 1975.

_____. "Statement of Policy on Minority Ownership of Broadcast Facilities." 68 FCC 2d 979, May 25, 1978.

_____. "In the Matter of Modification of FM Broadcast Station Rules to Increase the Availability of Commercial FM Broadcast Assignments." Notice of Proposed Rule Making in Docket 80-90, February 28, 1980.

_____. "In the Matter of Clear Channel Broadcasting in the AM Broadcast Band." Report and Order in Docket No. 20642, 78 FCC 2d 1345, May 29, 1980.

_____. "In Re RKO General Inc. (WNAC-TV)." Docket 18759, 78 FCC 2d 1, June 4, 1980.

_____. *Staff Report on Comparability for UHF Television: Final Report.* Washington: FCC, September 1980.

_____. "In the Matter of Petition for Rule Making to Amend Television Table of Assignments to Add New VHF Stations in the Top 100 Markets and to Assure that the New Stations Maximize Diversity of Ownership, Control and Programming." Report and Order in Docket No. 20418, September 9, 1980.

_____. "Inquiry into the Future Role of Low-Power Television Broadcasting and Television Translators in the National Telecommunication System." Notice of Proposed Rule Making in Docket 78-252, September 9, 1980.

_____. "In Re Applications of RKO General, Inc. for Renewals of Licenses for Stations . . ." Dockets 80-590 through 80-602. Memorandum Opinion and Order released September 30, 1980.

_____. "In the Matter of Implementation of the Final Acts of the World Administrative Radio Conference, Geneva 1979." First Notice of Inquiry in Docket 80-739, November 25, 1980.

_____. "Deregulation of Radio." Report and Order in Docket 79-219, 84 FCC 2d 968, January 14, 1981.

_____. "In the Matter of Policy Regarding Character Qualifications in Broadcast Licenses." Notice of Inquiry. Docket 81-500, August 4, 1981.

Federal Trade Commission. *Report of the Federal Trade Commission on the Radio Industry.* Washington: Government Printing Office, 1924; reprinted by Arno Press, 1974.

_____. Bureau of Competition. *Proceedings of the Symposium on Media Concentration.* Washington: Government Printing Office, December 1978 (two volumes).

Office of Telecommunications Policy. *Analysis of the Causes and Effects of In-*

creases in Same-Year Rerun Programming and Related Issues in Prime-Time Network Television. Washington: OTP, March 1973.

Third National Radio Conference. *Recommendations for Regulation of Radio.* Washington: Government Printing Office, 1924; reprinted by Arno Press, 1977.

U.S. House. Committee on Energy and Commerce. *Telecommunications in Transition: The Status of Competition in the Telecommunications Industry.* A Report by the Majority Staff of the Subcommittee on Telecommunications, Consumer Protection and Finance. 97th Cong., 1st sess., Committee Print 97-V, November 3, 1981.

_____. Committee on Interstate and Foreign Commerce. *Network Broadcasting. Report . . . .* 85th Cong., 2d Sess., House Report 1297, January 27, 1958.

_____. *Television Network Program Procurement. Report . . . .* 88th Cong., 1st Sess., House Report 281, May 8, 1963 (includes "Responsibility for Broadcast Matter," June 1960).

_____. Committee on Small Business. *Media Concentration: Hearings.* 96th Cong., 2d Sess., January/March 1980 (two parts).

U.S. Senate. Committee on the Judiciary. *Possible Anticompetitive Effects of Sale of Network TV Advertising: Hearings . . . .* 89th Cong., 2nd Sess., 1966 (two parts).

_____. Committee on Interstate and Foreign Commerce. "Investigation of Television Networks and the UHF-VHF Problem: Report." Committee Print, 84th Cong., 1st Sess., 1955.

_____. "Television Network Regulation and the UHF Problem: Report." Committee Print, 84th Cong., 1st Sess., 1955.

_____. "The Television Inquiry: Television Network Practices: Report." Committee Print No. 2, 85th Cong., 1st Sess., 1957.

U.S. Supreme Court. *National Broadcasting Co. Inc., et al.* v. *United States et al.* 319 U.S. 190 (1943).

_____. *United States* v. *Radio Corporation of America.* 358 U.S. 334 (1959).

_____. *Federal Communications Commission* v. *National Citizens Committee for Broadcasting, et al.* 436 U.S. 775 (1978).

CABLE

Books

Berman, Paul J. "CATV Leased-Access Channels and the Federal Communications Commission: The Intractable Jurisdictional Question." Cambridge, MA: Harvard Program on Information Technology and Public Policy, June 1975.

Cable Television 1981. New York: Donaldson, Lufkin & Jenrette, 1981.

Current Developments in CATV 1981. New York: Practising Law Institute, 1981.

Ford Foundation Activities in Noncommercial Broadcasting 1951-1976. New York: the Foundation, 1976.

HBO. *The Pay TV Guide: Editor's Pay-TV Handbook.* New York: Home Box

Office/Time Inc., n.d.

Hollowell, Mary Louise, ed. *The Cable/Broadband Communications Book, Volume 2, 1980-81.* Washington, DC: Communications Press, 1980.

____. *The Cable/Broadband Communications Book 1977-78.* Washington, DC: Communications Press, 1977.

____. *Cable Handbook 1975-76.* Washington, DC: Communications Press, 1975.

Howard, H.H. and S.L. Carroll. *Subscription Television: History, Current Status, and Economic Projections.* Knoxville: University of Tennessee College of Communications, April 1980.

LeDuc, Don. *Cable Television and the FCC: A Crisis in Media Control.* Philadelphia: Temple University Press, 1973.

On the Cable: The Television of Abundance: Report of the Sloan Commission on Cable Communications. New York: McGraw-Hill, 1971.

Phillips, Mary Alice Mayer. *CATV: A History of Community Antenna Television.* Evanston, IL: Northwestern University Press, 1972.

Research and Policy Committee of the Committee for Economic Development. *Broadcasting and Cable Television: Policies for Diversity and Change.* New York: CED, 1975.

Rivkin, Steven. *A New Guide to Federal Cable Television Regulations.* Cambridge, MA: MIT Press, 1978.

Sterling, Christopher H. and Timothy R. Haight. *The Mass Media: Aspen Institute Guide to Communication Industry Trends.* New York: Praeger, 1978.

____ and John M. Kittross. *Stay Tuned: A Concise History of American Publishing.* Belmont, CA: Wadsworth Publishing, 1978.

Technology & Economics Inc. *The Emergence of Pay Cable Television.* Cambridge, MA: T&E, 1980 (three volumes).

Articles

Baer, Walter S. and Carl Pilnick. "Pay Television at the Crossroads." Santa Monica, CA: Rand Corp. P-5159 (April 1974).

Besen, Stanley and Robert Crandall. "The Regulation of Cable Television." *Law and Contemporary Problems* 44 (Winter 1981): 77-124.

"Clash of Cultures." *Cablevision* (June 29, 1981), p. 40ff.

Coits, Victoria. "Media Concentration: Conglomerates Take Cable's Bait." *Cablevision* (December 15, 1980), p. 129ff.

"Enough Competition, Too Much Regulation." *Broadcasting* (August 10, 1981), p. 57.

Litman, Barry and Susanna Eun. "The Emerging Oligopoly of Pay-TV in the USA." *Telecommunications Policy* (June 1981), p. 121-135.

Manning, M.J. "Satellite Transponder Sales: Clever Innovation or Illegal Ruse?" *Satellite Communications* (August 1981), p. 35ff.

"Pay After Premiere." *Cablevision* (January 19, 1981), p. 26ff.

Polskin, H. "Inside Pay-Cable's Most Savage War." *Panorama* (March 1981), p. 54ff.

Rappaport, Richard Warren. "The Emergence of Subscription Cable Television

and Its Role in Communications." *Federal Communications Bar Journal* 29 (1976): 301-334.
"STV: A Passing Fancy or Permanent Industry?" *Cablevision* (February 23, 1981), p. 48.
"They're Free and Clear." *Panorama* (April 1981), p. 54ff.
"Traffic Jam on Cable's Ramp." *Cablevision* (August 31, 1981), p. 32ff.

Reference Works

Broadcasting/Cable Yearbook. Annual, Washington, DC: Broadcasting Publications.
Cable Advertising Directory. Annual, Washington, DC: National Cable Television Association.
Chin, Felix. *Cable Television: A Comprehensive Bibliography*. New York: IFI/Plenum, 1978.
Television Factbook. Annual, Washington, DC: Television Digest.

Government Publications

Braunstein, Yale M., et al. "Recent Trends in Cable Television Related to the Prospects for New Television Networks," in FCC, Network Inquiry Special Staff, *Preliminary Report on Prospects for Additional Networks*. Washington, DC: FCC, January 1980.
The Cabinet Committee on Cable Communications. *Cable: Report to the President*. Washington, DC: GPO, 1974.
Copyright Revision Act of 1976, P.L. 94-553 (also Title 17 of U.S. Code).
Federal Communications Commission. 71 FCC 2d 632, April 25, 1979.
____. "Report and Order in Dockets 20988 and 21284." 45 Federal Register 60186, September 11, 1980.
____. Network Inquiry Special Staff. *New Television Networks: Entry, Jurisdiction, Ownership and Regulation*. Washington, DC: GPO, 1980, Vol. I.
General Accounting Office. *Regulating the Domestic Telecommunications Industry: FCC's Actions and Their Impact on Competitive Development*. Washington, DC: GAO, September 1981.
Glen, Kristin Booth. "Report on Subscription Television." In FCC, Network Inquiry Special Staff. *Preliminary Report on Prospects for Additional Networks*. Washington, DC: FCC, January 1980.
____. "Report on Multi-Point Distribution Service." In FCC, Network Inquiry Special Staff. *Preliminary Report on Prospects for Additional Networks*. Washington, DC: FCC, January 1980.
Gordon, Kenneth, et al. *Staff Report on FCC Policy on Cable Ownership*. Washington, DC: FCC Office of Plans and Policy, September 1981, preliminary draft. (Note: the version cited here is the initial draft leading to the public, and somewhat revised version under the same title, of November 1981).
Owen, Bruce. "Cable Television: The Framework of Regulation." In U.S. Con-

gress, Senate, Committee on Governmental Affairs, *Study on Federal Regulation: Appendix to Volume VI, Framework for Regulation.* 95th Cong., 2d Sess., December 1978, Committee Print.

U.S. Congress. House. Committee on Interstate and Foreign Commerce. *Cable Television: Promise versus Regulatory Performance.* Report of the Subcommittee on Communications of the Committee on Interstate and Foreign Commerce, 94th Cong., 2d Sess., January 1976.

U.S. Supreme Court. *U.S.* v. *Southwestern Cable.* 392 U.S. 159 (1968).

_____. *Fortnightly Corp* v. *United Artists.* 392 U.S. 390 (1968).

_____. *FCC* v. *Midwest Video Corp.* 440 U.S. 689 (1979).

_____. *U.S.* v. *Midwest Video Corp.* 406 U.S. 649 (1972).

OTHER

Compaine, Benjamin M. *A New Framework for the Media Arena: Content, Process and Format.* Cambridge, MA: Program on Information Resources Policy, Harvard University, 1980.

_____. "Shifting Boundaries in the Information Marketplace." *Journal of Communication* 31:1 (Winter 1981).

Frech, H.E. and Linda Nielsen. "Competition, Concentration and Public Policy in the Media: A Survey of Research." Working Paper in Economics #154, University of California, Santa Barbara.

Gans, Herbert J. *Deciding What's News: A Study of CBS Evening News, NBC Nightly News, Newsweek and Time.* New York: Vintage Books, 1979.

Gordon, Kenneth, Jonathan D. Levy and Robert S. Preece. "FCC Policy on Cable Ownership: Staff Report." U.S. Federal Communications Commission. November 1981.

Kaysen, Carl and Donald F. Turner. *Antitrust Policy: An Economic and Legal Analysis.* Cambridge, MA: Harvard University Press, 1959.

McCombs, Maxwell E. "Mass Media in the Marketplace." *Journalism Monographs* No. 24.

McLaughlin, John. *Mapping the Information Business.* Cambridge, MA: Program on Information Resources Policy, Harvard University, 1981.

Stein, Ben. *The View From Sunset Boulevard.* New York: Basic Books, 1979.

Tehranian, Majid. "Iran: Communication, Alienation, Revolution." *Intermedia,* March 1979.

U.S. Congress. House. "Telecommunications in Transition: The Status of Competition in the Telecommunications Industry." Report by the Majority Staff of the Subcommittee on Telecommunications, Consumer Protection and Finance. November 3, 1981.

Index

About the Authors

Benjamin M. Compaine is executive director, media and allied arenas, at the Program on Information Resources Policy at Harvard University. His current work involves research on the policy implications of changing information technology. He is author of *The Business of Consumer Magazines, The Newspaper Industry in the 1980s: An Assessment of Economics and Technology* and *The Book Industry in Transition,* all published by Knowledge Industry Publications, Inc. Dr. Compaine has written many other studies and articles about mass communications and technology, including *A New Framework for the Media Arena: Content, Process and Format.* A graduate of Dickinson College, he holds an M.B.A. from Harvard and a Ph.D. in mass communications from Temple University.

Christopher H. Sterling directs the Center for Telecommunications Studies at the George Washington University in Washington, DC. For 12 years he was on the faculty of Temple University's School of Communications and Theater (1970-1982); he spent the last two of these on leave serving as Special Assistant to FCC Commissioner Anne P. Jones. He is the co-author of a number of books, including *Broadcasting in America* (1982, with Sydney Head), *The Mass Media: Aspen Institute Guide to Communications Industry Trends* (1978, with Timothy Haight), and *Stay Tuned: A Concise History of American Broadcasting* (1978, with John Kittross), among others. Author of numerous research and bibliographic articles, Sterling is editor of *Communications Booknotes,* a monthly publication he founded in 1969, and was editor of *Journal of Broadcasting* for four years. He has a Ph.D. from the University of Wisconsin.

Thomas Guback is research professor of communications at the University of Illinois at Urbana-Champaign, where he earned his Ph.D. He is the author of *The International Film Industry,* as well as numerous articles on the motion picture business. He also is a consultant on industry issues, communications policies, and other aspects of mass media.

J. Kendrick Noble, Jr. spent 1957-1966 with Noble & Noble Publishers, Inc. and became that company's executive vice president. Since 1966 he has been an analyst of media stocks and is presently vice president of Paine Webber Mitchell Hutchins, Inc. He holds an M.B.A. from New York University.